Chambers

primary thesaurus

Chambers
primary
thesaurus

Chambers

CHAMBERS

An imprint of Chambers Harrap Publishers Ltd
7 Hopetoun Crescent
Edinburgh, EH7 4AY

Previous edition published 2002
This edition published by Chambers Harrap Publishers Ltd 2008

A CIP catalogue record for this book is available from the British Library.

ISBN 978 0550 10320 8

Designed and typeset by Chambers Harrap Publishers Ltd, Edinburgh
Printed by L.E.G.O. Spa - Lavis (TN)

Contents

Contributors

Project Editor
Mary O'Neill

Editors
Pat Bulhosen
Lorna Gilmour

Editorial Assistance
Vicky Aldus

Data Management
Patrick Gaherty

Prepress
Nicolas Echallier

*The editors would like to acknowledge with thanks the
assistance and advice of the following:*

Briar Hill Lower School, Northampton
Chirnside Primary School, Chirnside, Scottish Borders
Hatherleigh Community Primary School, Hatherleigh, Devon
Ide First School, Ide, Exeter
St Patrick's Primary School, Coatbridge, Lanarkshire
Woodlands Junior School, Tonbridge, Kent

Preface

Chambers Primary Thesaurus has been specially compiled for use by primary school pupils aged 7–11, and this edition complements the renewed Primary Framework in England and Wales, the revised Key Stage 2 Curriculum in Northern Ireland and National Guidelines in Scotland. It has been designed with the benefit of advice from a number of primary school teachers, ensuring that the book provides all the words a pupil at this level needs.

Thousands of synonyms, or alternative words, provide a variety of vocabulary choices. These range from short and simple to slightly longer, more challenging words. This thesaurus also contains antonyms, or opposites, and these are clearly labelled. Those synonyms and antonyms that are particularly formal or informal are also separated from the rest and highlighted, to increase awareness of different levels of language and the need to use words in the appropriate context.

Examples have been chosen to properly distinguish different meanings of a word and relate to the synonyms for that sense. In many cases, these examples have been taken directly from our corpus of children's literature, a resource which has helped the editors to make informed decisions about the words a child is likely to meet in his or her reading. The synonyms provided are words that can be used in the given contexts, rather than terms that are just loosely connected to the entry word.

Hyponyms are included in highlighted boxes throughout the text, answering the question 'What kinds of ... are there?'. They provide useful and interesting lists of, for example, animals and buildings, and give children even more options for expressing their ideas. Particularly useful for younger thesaurus users is the series of larger panels throughout the book, each concentrating on a word that is often overused, such as *bad*, *happy*, *say*, etc. These panels guide the pupil in using more descriptive vocabulary to express various ideas.

Chambers Primary Thesaurus will help pupils to use words creatively and choose words that have impact.

> **www**
> For lots of free online resources that can be used in conjunction with the thesaurus, visit our website at
> www.chamberslearning.co.uk

Word panels in this book

There are some words that people use too much in their writing. On each of the pages below, you will find a large box about one of these words. These boxes give you many more words and phrases you could use instead.

How do I use my Primary Thesaurus?

A **thesaurus** is a book which gives you words that have a very similar meaning to the word you are looking up.

You can use it to find other words to use instead of one you are using too much. You can also use it to find a word that describes something more clearly.

Many people, such as writers, use a thesaurus often so that they can find better, more interesting words to use!

You may be writing a report about a book you have read, and realize that you have used the word good three times.

This is a **good** book. The plot is **good** and the characters are **good**.

The person reading your report may become bored if you keep repeating the same word, so to find another way to describe the book, you could look up the word good in the *Primary Thesaurus*.

❶ The alphabet down the side of the page shows you the letter that the words on that page begin with, so look for the pages where **Gg** is marked.

Ee

Ff

Gg

Hh

❷ The blue words at the top of the page show you which words appear in alphabetical order on that page, for example on page 140:

goal → gossip

Because the word good comes between these two words in alphabetical order, you know to look for it on that page.

❸ The words that you look up are in alphabetical order. These words are large and coloured blue so it is easy to find them.

good

The look-up word and the block of information below it is called a thesaurus **entry**.

❹

NOUN
VERB
ADJECTIVE

The word in capital letters tells you the **word class** the main word is.
This simply tells you the job a word does – whether it names a person or
thing (a **noun**), names an action (a **verb**), describes a person or thing (an
adjective), describes an action (an **adverb**) or shows you the connection
between two things (a **preposition**).
You have to check this label to see if the words in the group are doing
the same job as the word you want to replace.

❺

1 *That was a good story.*
satisfactory, pleasant, nice, pleasing,
enjoyable, wonderful, excellent,
marvellous
2 *She got a good mark in her test.*
excellent, wonderful, first-class, first-
rate, superior
3 *She is very good at her job.*
competent, skilled, expert, professional,
skilful, clever, talented, gifted, able,
capable
4 *It was good of you to help out.*
kind, considerate, thoughtful, generous

Numbers show you that there are different meanings of the look-up
word. There are different groups of words for the different meanings.
The phrase or sentence in blue is an **example** of how you might use
the main word. It tells you that the group of words that follow have the
same meaning.
So, if there is more than one meaning of the word, you can look at the
examples to decide which group of words has the meaning you want. The
first one here, *That was a good story*, matches the meaning of *good* you are
looking for when you want to talk about a good book that you have enjoyed.

⑥

1 *That was a good story.*
satisfactory, pleasant, nice, pleasing,
enjoyable, wonderful, excellent,
marvellous

The words that come after the examples are **synonyms** of the main
word. These are words that have a similar meaning to it, and that you
could use in its place.

Now that you have found these synonyms, you can use them to make your writing more interesting:

> This is a **wonderful** book. The plot is **enjoyable**, and the characters are **excellent**.

7 ◇ INFORMAL WORDS great, super, cool

The words that come after a white diamond ◇ sign are **informal** words and phrases. These are words and phrases that you can imagine yourself using when speaking to friends, but which you might not use when you are speaking to your teacher or writing a piece of school work! However, you could use informal words in a story, for example when a young character is speaking:

> 'That story was **great**, it was really **cool**,' said Meera enthusiastically.

8 **grateful** ADJECTIVE
I am grateful for your help.
thankful, appreciative
◆ FORMAL WORDS obliged, indebted

The thesaurus also gives you some **formal** words and phrases. These come after a blue diamond ◆ sign. These are words and phrases that you are not likely to use when speaking to friends, but which you might use when you are being very polite! You could use formal words in your writing, for example when an older or very polite character is speaking:

> 'Thank you for your help. I am **indebted** to you,' said the head teacher.

9 **5** *a good person*
moral, upright, honest, trustworthy, worthy, righteous
≠ OPPOSITES wicked, evil

The words that come after a 'does not equal' sign ≠ are **opposites** of the main word. These are also called **antonyms**. You can use these opposites to make comparisons and so make your writing interesting:

> In the story, Han is an **honest** and **trustworthy** person. He is not at all like Tony, who is very **wicked** at times.

⑩ What if the word you are looking for is part of a **phrase**? A phrase is a group of words that always appear together and have a single meaning, for example, in fact.
If you have used a phrase such as in fact more than once in your writing, it might be better to replace one with something else:

> I liked this book. **In fact**, it is the best book I have ever read. I wanted to read it again and again. **In fact**, I did.

Phrases like these come after a blue dot •, so all you need to do is look up the main word, and if the phrase is there you will spot it right away.

> **• in fact**
> *I like Art; in fact, it's my favourite subject.*
> actually, in actual fact, as a matter of fact, in reality, indeed

Once you have checked the example to make sure this is what you mean, you can use the words and phrases that follow to replace the phrase:

> I liked this book. **Actually**, it is the best book I have ever read. I wanted to read it again and again. **As a matter of fact**, I did.

⑪ Some entries have boxes that contain words which are not synonyms. Instead these give you the names of the different *types* of the main word.
Imagine again you are writing your book report, and you keep using the word **book** or **story**.

> This is a **book** I would tell other people to read. It is a good **story**.

If you look at the box at the entry for **book**, and the one at the entry for **story**, you will find the names of different kinds of book and story.

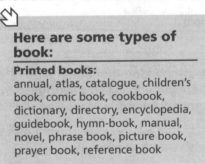

Here are some types of book:

Printed books:
annual, atlas, catalogue, children's book, comic book, cookbook, dictionary, directory, encyclopedia, guidebook, hymn-book, manual, novel, phrase book, picture book, prayer book, reference book

Here are some types of story:

adventure story, bedtime story, children's story, comedy, crime story, detective story, fable, fairy tale, fantasy, folk tale, ghost story, historical tale, horror story, legend, love story, mystery, myth, parable

You have to decide which type of book or story it is, and you could use these words instead.

This is a **novel** I would tell other people to read. It is a wonderful **ghost story**.

Perhaps you are writing a story yourself, and you want to describe a dog. The word **dog** does not tell you much about the kind of dog it is, or what it looks like.

Alice had a huge **dog** which growled fiercely.

You can look up **dog** in the Primary Thesaurus and find the names of different breeds of dog.

Here are some breeds of dog:

Afghan hound, Airedale, alsatian, basset-hound, beagle, Border collie, borzoi, boxer, bulldog, bull-mastiff, bull terrier, cairn terrier, chihuahua, chow, cocker spaniel, collie, corgi, dachshund, Dalmatian, Doberman pinscher, foxhound, fox terrier, German shepherd, golden retriever

You can choose one that will give the person reading your story a much clearer picture of the dog:

Alice had a huge **German shepherd** which growled fiercely.

⑫ Some words are used far too much. There are some special pages in this thesaurus where you can find out even more about these words, and the other words you can use instead.

If you look up a word that has one of these special pages, you are told where you can find the page:

> ⇒ For even more about this word, see
> the next page

Aa

abandon VERB
1 *He **abandoned** his family.*
desert, leave
◇ INFORMAL WORDS dump
2 ***abandon** the car at the side of the road*
strand, leave behind
◇ INFORMAL WORDS dump
3 *The police are going to **abandon** the search.*
give up, drop, stop
≠ OPPOSITES go on with, continue

abduct VERB
*The child was **abducted**.*
kidnap, snatch, seize, take away

ability NOUN
*You have the **ability** to pass the test.*
capability, competence, expertise, skill, talent, know-how
≠ OPPOSITES inability

able ADJECTIVE
*Are you **able** to come to the party?*
allowed, permitted, free, willing
≠ OPPOSITES unable

abnormal ADJECTIVE
*His behaviour was **abnormal**.*
strange, odd, unusual, peculiar
≠ OPPOSITES normal

abolish VERB
*a plan to **abolish** smoking in public places*
do away with, eliminate, stamp out, end, put an end to
≠ OPPOSITES keep, continue

about¹ ADVERB
1 *There are **about** twenty pupils in the class.*
around, approximately, roughly, in the region of, more or less
2 *The children were running **about** in the garden.*
to and fro, here and there, from place to place
• **about to**
*I'm **about to** go to school.*
on the point of, on the verge of, ready to

about² PREPOSITION
1 *a book **about** a wizard*
to do with, concerning, relating to, concerned with
2 *wandering **about** the streets*
round, around, throughout, all over

above PREPOSITION
*a light **above** the door*
over, higher than, on top of
≠ OPPOSITES below, under

abroad ADVERB
*We are going **abroad** on holiday.*
overseas, out of the country, to a foreign country

abrupt ADJECTIVE
1 *We made an **abrupt** departure.*
sudden, quick, rapid, swift, hasty, hurried
≠ OPPOSITES gradual, slow
2 *She has a very **abrupt** way of speaking.*
curt, brisk, snappy, gruff, rude, impolite, blunt, direct
≠ OPPOSITES polite

absence NOUN
1 *Jack's **absence** from school*
non-attendance, non-appearance, truancy
≠ OPPOSITES presence, attendance, appearance
2 *There is an **absence** of colour in this picture.*
lack, need, want
≠ OPPOSITES presence

Aa
Bb
Cc
Dd
Ee
Ff
Gg
Hh
Ii
Jj
Kk
Ll
Mm
Nn
Oo
Pp
Qq
Rr
Ss
Tt
Uu
Vv
Ww
Xx
Yy
Zz

deed, action, undertaking, exploit, feat

2 *His friendliness was just an act.*
pretence, sham, show, front

3 *a juggler's act*
turn, routine, performance

action NOUN
Her prompt action saved the child's life.
act, move, deed

active ADJECTIVE
Louise is a very active child.
lively, energetic

activity NOUN
The youth centre offers lots of activities.
hobby, pastime, interest

actor NOUN
a film actor
performer, player

actual ADJECTIVE
The story is about actual events.
real, true, genuine, factual

actually ADVERB
It actually snowed in June one year.
in fact, as a matter of fact, in truth, in reality, really, truly

adapt VERB
The building has been adapted for wheelchairs.
alter, change, modify, adjust, convert

add VERB
1 *You can add accessories to the computer.*
attach, join, combine, tack on
(≠) OPPOSITES take away, remove
2 *Add eight and eleven.*
count, count up, sum up, tot up, total
(≠) OPPOSITES subtract

• **add up to**
The bill adds up to £42.
amount, come to, total

additional ADJECTIVE

We have two additional class members.
extra, more, further, new, fresh

adequate ADJECTIVE
1 *The food they have is barely adequate.*
enough, sufficient
(≠) OPPOSITES insufficient
2 *Her singing is adequate for the choir.*
acceptable, satisfactory, passable, fair
(≠) OPPOSITES inadequate

adjust VERB
Turn this knob to adjust the volume.
change, adapt, alter, modify

admiration NOUN
I am full of admiration for my parents.
respect, approval, appreciation, affection
(≠) OPPOSITES contempt

admire VERB
1 *Are there any TV stars you admire?*
look up to, adore, worship, idolize
(≠) OPPOSITES despise
2 *I admire your honesty.*
respect, approve of, appreciate, value

admission NOUN
1 *Admission to the theme park is £5.*
entry, entrance
2 *an admission of guilt*
confession, declaration
(≠) OPPOSITES denial

admit VERB
He admits that he cheated in the test.
confess, own up, acknowledge, agree
(≠) OPPOSITES deny

adopt VERB
The couple adopted a baby.
take in, foster

adore VERB
1 *She adores her baby sister.*
love, cherish, dote on, think the world of
(≠) OPPOSITES hate

2 *Tommy adores his local team.*
worship, idolize

advance¹ NOUN
the advance of technology
progress, forward movement,
development, improvement
• **in advance**
Let me know in advance if you are coming.
beforehand, earlier, sooner, ahead
⊟ OPPOSITES later

advance¹ VERB
You are ready to advance to the next level.
proceed, go forward, move on, move forward, go ahead, progress

advantage NOUN
Fresh air is one of the advantages of living in the country.
benefit, good point
⊟ OPPOSITES disadvantage, drawback

adventure NOUN
I read about the explorer's adventures in the jungle.
exploit, venture, experience

advertise VERB
a poster advertising a new game
publicize, promote, push
◇ INFORMAL WORDS plug

advice NOUN
The teacher gave us advice about the test.
guidance, help, suggestions, recommendations, do's and don'ts

advise VERB
I advise you to tell the truth.
guide, suggest, recommend, urge
◆ FORMAL WORDS counsel

aeroplane
⇒ see aircraft

affair NOUN
the affair of the missing purse
business, concern, matter, question, issue, subject, episode

affect VERB
1 *The changes to school lessons will affect you.*
concern, involve, relate to, apply to
2 *Pictures of starving children affect us deeply.*
influence, sway, move, touch, upset

affectionate ADJECTIVE
an affectionate aunt
fond, devoted, doting, loving, tender, caring, warm-hearted
⊟ OPPOSITES cold

afford VERB
We can't afford a holiday.
have enough money for, be able to pay for, manage

afraid ADJECTIVE
I feel afraid in the dark.
frightened, scared, alarmed, terrified, fearful, anxious, nervous, timid
⊟ OPPOSITES brave, bold, confident

again ADVERB
Come and see us again.
once more, once again, another time

against PREPOSITION
1 *leaning against the wall*
close up to, touching, in contact with, on
2 *We will take action against bullying.*
opposed to, in opposition to, hostile to, resisting
⊟ OPPOSITES for

age NOUN
the age of the steam engine
era, day, days, time, period, years

aggressive ADJECTIVE
His aggressive behaviour caused problems at school.
quarrelsome, warlike, violent, hostile
⊟ OPPOSITES friendly

agile ADJECTIVE
The old lady is very agile for her age.
active, lively, nimble, flexible
⊟ OPPOSITES clumsy, stiff

Aa
Bb
Cc
Dd
Ee
Ff
Gg
Hh
Ii
Jj
Kk
Ll
Mm
Nn
Oo
Pp
Qq
Rr
Ss
Tt
Uu
Vv
Ww
Xx
Yy
Zz

Aa
Bb
Cc
Dd
Ee
Ff
Gg
Hh
Ii
Jj
Kk
Ll
Mm
Nn
Oo
Pp
Qq
Rr
Ss
Tt
Uu
Vv
Ww
Xx
Yy
Zz

agitated ADJECTIVE
He became agitated when the police arrived.
upset, disturbed, worked up, worried, troubled, alarmed, flustered, ruffled
≠ OPPOSITES calm

agony NOUN
He was in agony with toothache.
anguish, torment, torture, pain, suffering, distress

agree VERB
1 *I agree with you that cricket is boring.*
be in agreement, see eye to eye
≠ OPPOSITES disagree, differ
2 *She agreed to help out at the jumble sale.*
consent, promise

agreement NOUN
They finally reached an agreement.
settlement, deal, arrangement, understanding

ahead ADVERB
Go straight ahead at the traffic lights.
on, forwards, onwards

aid¹ NOUN
A passing motorist came to our aid when our car broke down.
help, assistance, support
≠ OPPOSITES hindrance

aid² VERB
A short holiday will aid your recovery.
help, assist, support, encourage
≠ OPPOSITES hinder

aim¹ NOUN
Her aim in life is to become a doctor.
ambition, hope, dream, desire, wish, plan, purpose, intention, objective, target, goal

aim² VERB
1 *The hunter aimed his gun at the deer.*
point, direct, target
2 *He is aiming to beat the world record.*
intend, mean, plan, strive, try, attempt, endeavour

aircraft NOUN

Here are some types of aircraft:
aeroplane, airship, amphibian, biplane, glider, helicopter, hot air balloon, jet, jumbo jet, microlight, rocket, seaplane
Parts of an aircraft:
cabin, engine, fuselage, hold, landing gear, propeller, rudder, wing

airy ADJECTIVE
a bright and airy classroom
roomy, spacious, open
≠ OPPOSITES airless, stuffy

alarm¹ NOUN
He jumped back in alarm.
fright, scare, fear, terror, panic, horror, shock, dismay, distress, anxiety
≠ OPPOSITES calmness

alarm² VERB
The sound of screaming alarmed us.
frighten, scare, startle, terrify, panic, dismay, distress, agitate
≠ OPPOSITES reassure, calm, soothe

alarming ADJECTIVE
The look on his face was quite alarming.
frightening, scary, startling, terrifying, threatening, disturbing, distressing, shocking, dreadful
≠ OPPOSITES reassuring

alert ADJECTIVE
Security guards have to be alert.
attentive, wide-awake, watchful, on the lookout, sharp-eyed, observant
≠ OPPOSITES slow, unprepared

alien NOUN
an alien from outer space
extraterrestrial

alike ADJECTIVE
The two sisters are alike.
similar, identical
≠ OPPOSITES dissimilar, different

alive ADJECTIVE
*We didn't know if he was still **alive**.*
living, live, surviving, breathing, existing, in existence
≠ OPPOSITES **dead, extinct**

all¹ ADJECTIVE
*He ate **all** the cake and the biscuits.*
each of, every one of, each and every one of, the whole of, every bit of
≠ OPPOSITES **no**

all² ADVERB
*I feel **all** sore.*
completely, entirely, wholly, fully, totally, utterly, altogether

allow VERB
*Will you **allow** us to stay up late?*
permit, let, authorize
≠ OPPOSITES **forbid, prevent**

all right ADJECTIVE
1 *The film was **all right**, I suppose.*
satisfactory, passable, acceptable, adequate, fair, average
≠ OPPOSITES **unacceptable, inadequate**
2 *Are you **all right**?*
well, healthy, unhurt, uninjured, unharmed

ally NOUN
*a close **ally** of the president*
friend, supporter, partner
≠ OPPOSITES **enemy**

almost ADVERB
1 *I have **almost** finished my homework.*
nearly, practically, virtually, just about, not quite
2 *I made **almost** ten pounds in the sale.*
close to, around, nearly

alone ADJECTIVE AND ADVERB
*The child was **alone** in the house.*
solitary, by yourself, by itself, on your own, unaccompanied, solo
≠ OPPOSITES **together, accompanied**

aloud ADVERB
*reading **aloud** in class*
out loud, loudly, audibly
≠ OPPOSITES **silently**

also ADVERB
*I **also** like swimming.*
too, as well, additionally, in addition, besides

alter VERB
*I'm having my dress **altered** to fit me.*
change, modify, adjust, adapt, convert, transform

alternative NOUN
*The menu includes a vegetarian **alternative**.*
option, choice, selection, replacement

altogether ADVERB
*I'm not **altogether** happy about the news.*
totally, completely, entirely, wholly, fully, utterly, absolutely, perfectly, thoroughly

always ADVERB
*I **always** have cereal for breakfast.*
every time, without exception, regularly, repeatedly, continually, constantly
≠ OPPOSITES **never**

amaze VERB
*He **amazed** us with his card tricks.*
surprise, startle, astonish, stun, stagger, shock

ambition NOUN
1 *His **ambition** is to be a racing driver.*
aim, goal, target, objective, intent, purpose, ideal, dream, hope, wish, desire
2 *To be successful you must have **ambition**.*
drive, push, determination, enthusiasm, commitment

amend VERB
*The list has been **amended** to include Paul.*

Aa
Bb
Cc
Dd
Ee
Ff
Gg
Hh
Ii
Jj
Kk
Ll
Mm
Nn
Oo
Pp
Qq
Rr
Ss
Tt
Uu
Vv
Ww
Xx
Yy
Zz

revise, correct, fix, repair, mend, remedy, change, alter, adjust, modify

among PREPOSITION

I like to be among my friends.
between, in the middle of, surrounded by

amount¹ NOUN

1 *a large amount of water*
quantity, volume, mass
2 *the final amount we raised for charity*
sum, total, sum total

amount² VERB

• **amount to**
The bill amounts to £20.
add up to, total, come to, make, equal, be equivalent to

amphibian NOUN

Here are some animals that are amphibians:
eel, frog, newt, salamander, toad

ample ADJECTIVE

an ample supply of food
considerable, substantial, generous, abundant, plentiful
≠ OPPOSITES insufficient, inadequate, meagre

amuse VERB

He amused us all with his jokes.
entertain, make laugh, cheer up, delight
◇ INFORMAL WORDS tickle
≠ OPPOSITES bore

amusement NOUN

Videos were provided for our amusement.
entertainment, fun, enjoyment, pleasure, delight
≠ OPPOSITES boredom

amusing ADJECTIVE

an amusing story

funny, humorous, hilarious, comical, enjoyable, entertaining
≠ OPPOSITES dull, boring

ancestor NOUN

My ancestors came from Italy.
forebear, forefather, predecessor
≠ OPPOSITES descendant

ancient ADJECTIVE

ancient monuments
old, aged, antique, prehistoric
≠ OPPOSITES recent, modern

anger¹ VERB

Their stupidity angered me.
annoy, irritate, offend, madden, enrage, infuriate
◇ INFORMAL WORDS wind up
≠ OPPOSITES calm

anger² NOUN

He shouted at the vandals in anger.
annoyance, irritation, displeasure, temper, rage, fury

angle NOUN

Consider the problem from a different angle.
point of view, position, viewpoint, perspective

angry ADJECTIVE

⇒ For even more about this word, see page 10
Cruelty to animals makes me angry.
annoyed, cross, irritated, displeased, mad, enraged, furious, raging
≠ OPPOSITES content, calm

animal NOUN

Some animals can be kept as pets.
creature, beast

Here are some types of animal:
Household pets:
cat, dog, gerbil, guinea pig, hamster, rabbit

Aa Bb Cc Dd Ee Ff Gg Hh Ii Jj Kk Ll Mm Nn Oo Pp Qq Rr Ss Tt Uu Vv Ww Xx Yy Zz

Wild animals:
aardvark, antelope, ape, armadillo, baboon, badger, bear, beaver, bison, buffalo, camel, chimpanzee, deer, elephant, elk, ermine, ferret, fox, gazelle, gibbon, giraffe, gorilla, hare, hedgehog, hippopotamus, hyena, kangaroo, koala, lemur, llama, mink, mole, mongoose, monkey, moose, mouse, orang-utan, otter, panda, platypus, polar bear, polecat, rabbit, racoon, rat, reindeer, rhinoceros, skunk, squirrel, wallaby, weasel, wolf, wombat, zebra
Farm animals:
bull, cow, goat, horse, pig, sheep
Sea animals:
dolphin, seal, sea lion, walrus, whale
Big cats:
cheetah, cougar, jaguar, leopard, lion, panther, puma, tiger
Baby animals:
calf, chick, cub, cygnet, duckling, fawn, fledgling, foal, gosling, kid, kitten, lamb, piglet, puppy
⇒ Also look up **amphibian**, **bird**, **butterfly**, **cat**, **dog**, **fish**, **horse**, **insect**, **reptile**, **snake**

announce VERB
*They have **announced** their engagement.*
declare, state, reveal, make known

announcement NOUN
*The head teacher is going to make an **announcement** at assembly.*
declaration, report, statement

announcer NOUN
*The **announcer** introduced the next programme.*
broadcaster, presenter, newsreader, compère

annoy VERB
*My little brother's constant questions **annoy** me.*
irritate, rile, needle, displease, anger, madden, exasperate, bother, pester, harass
⊜ OPPOSITES please

annoyance NOUN
1 *The delay was an **annoyance**.*
nuisance, pest, bother, trouble, bore
◇ INFORMAL WORDS bind, pain, headache
2 *The teacher showed her **annoyance**.*
irritation, displeasure, anger
⊜ OPPOSITES pleasure

annoyed ADJECTIVE
*Mum was **annoyed** about the mess.*
angry, cross, irritated
⊜ OPPOSITES pleased

answer[1] NOUN
1 *I didn't get an **answer** to my question.*
reply, response, reaction, retort
2 *I have the **answer** to your problem.*
solution, explanation

answer[2] VERB
*Grace **answered** the teacher's question.*
reply to, respond to
• answer back
*Don't **answer back** when your mother tells you off.*
talk back, retort, disagree, argue

anxious ADJECTIVE
*He was **anxious** that he might fail the test.*
worried, concerned, nervous, apprehensive, afraid, fearful, uneasy, in suspense, on tenterhooks, tense, disturbed, troubled
⊜ OPPOSITES calm

apart ADVERB
*He was standing **apart** from the group.*
separately, alone, on your own, by yourself, aside

apologize VERB
*She **apologized** for hurting her brother.*
say sorry, be sorry
◆ FORMAL WORDS express regret

appal VERB
*His rudeness **appalled** me.*

angry

If you want to talk or write about someone being **angry**, there are lots of interesting words and phrases you can use. You must be careful when you use them though, because some of them are very informal. This means that although you might use these words and phrases with your friends, you would not use them in school exercises.

If someone is a little bit angry, they might be
> **annoyed**
> **cross**
> **irritated**
> **displeased**

If someone is very angry, they might be
> **mad**
> **hopping mad**
> **enraged**
> **furious**
> **irate**
> **raging**
> **beside themselves with anger**

If someone is in an angry mood, you could say that they
> **are like a bear with a sore head**
> **got out of bed on the wrong side**

If someone loses their temper, you could say that they
> **fly into a rage**
> **see red**
> **throw a tantrum**
> **lose their head**
> **blow their top**
> **blow a fuse**
> **fly off the handle**
> **hit the roof**

If you make someone angry, you
> **make someone's blood boil**
> **drive someone mad**
> **drive someone up the wall**

If someone speaks angrily, they
let fly
rant and rave
rage
give someone a piece of their mind
give someone the rough side of their tongue

Over to you

Can you make this piece of writing more lively by using some of the words and phrases above?

Dad was **angry** with me yesterday. He **became angry** when I broke the window. He **spoke angrily**, and told me I **made him angry**. He was **in an angry mood** for a long time afterwards.

Which words and phrases sound informal?

horrify, shock, outrage, disgust, dismay
≠ OPPOSITES reassure, encourage

appalling ADJECTIVE
the **appalling** news about the crash
horrifying, horrific, shocking, awful, dreadful, frightful, terrible, horrible, horrid

apparent ADJECTIVE
1 Reshma's happiness was **apparent**.
visible, noticeable, distinct, clear, obvious, evident, unmistakable
2 Her **apparent** unfriendliness was really just shyness.
seeming, outward

appeal¹ NOUN
1 The charity made an **appeal** for funds.
request, plea
2 the **appeal** of holidays
attraction, interest, fascination, charm, attractiveness, beauty

appeal² VERB
1 The charity is **appealing** for donations.
request, call, apply, plead, beg

2 Bright colours **appeal** to children.
attract, draw, interest, fascinate, charm, please

appear VERB
1 Cracks **appeared** in the ceiling.
develop, come into sight, come into view, occur, come to light, emerge
≠ OPPOSITES disappear, vanish
2 Jane did not **appear** in school today.
turn up, attend, show up, arrive
3 She **appeared** to be dead.
seem, look
4 He has **appeared** in five Hollywood films.
act, perform, play, take part

appearance NOUN
He had a proud **appearance**.
look, image, manner, air

appetite NOUN
I lost my **appetite** when I was ill.
hunger, taste

applaud VERB
The crowd **applauded** the band at the end of the concert.

clap, cheer, congratulate
⊘ OPPOSITES criticize

application NOUN
an application for a job
request, appeal, claim

apply VERB
1 *I have applied for a passport.*
request, ask for, put in for, claim
2 *These rules apply to all of us.*
refer, relate, be relevant
3 *Apply sun cream before going out in the sun.*
put on, spread on, lay on, cover with, smear

appoint VERB
A new head teacher has been appointed.
choose, select, elect, employ, take on

appointment NOUN
I have an appointment with the doctor.
arrangement, engagement, date, meeting, interview

appreciate VERB
You don't appreciate good music.
enjoy, relish, prize, treasure, value, admire, respect, welcome, take kindly to
⊘ OPPOSITES despise

approach¹ VERB
1 *We are approaching the airport.*
move towards, draw near, near, gain on, catch up, reach, meet
2 *She approached the work with enthusiasm.*
begin, set about, undertake

approach² NOUN
1 *We could hear the approach of the train.*
advance, coming, arrival
2 *They walked up the approach to the house.*
access, road, drive, avenue, way in, passage, entrance
3 *Let's try a different approach to this problem.*
attitude, manner, style, method, means

appropriate ADJECTIVE
You must wear appropriate shoes in the gym.
suitable, well-chosen, apt, fitting, proper, right, correct
⊘ OPPOSITES inappropriate, unsuitable

approve VERB
The plans were approved by the school board.
agree to, consent to, allow, permit, pass, authorize, support, back, accept, adopt
• **approve of**
My mum doesn't approve of mobile phones.
admire, regard, appreciate, favour, accept, respect, value
⊘ OPPOSITES disapprove of, condemn

approximate ADJECTIVE
the approximate time of arrival
guessed, estimated, rough, inexact, loose, close, near
⊘ OPPOSITES exact

approximately ADVERB
There were approximately twelve boys in the gang.
roughly, around, about, more or less, loosely

apt ADJECTIVE
1 *an apt comment*
appropriate, fitting, suitable, proper, correct
◇ INFORMAL WORDS spot-on
⊘ OPPOSITES inapt
2 *The boys are apt to be noisy.*
liable, prone, likely

arch NOUN
a gateway shaped like an arch
archway, bend, curve, semicircle

area NOUN
1 *a run-down area of the city*
neighbourhood, district, region, zone
2 *an area of desert*
expanse, stretch, section, patch, portion

Aa
Bb
Cc
Dd
Ee
Ff
Gg
Hh
Ii
Jj
Kk
Ll
Mm
Nn
Oo
Pp
Qq
Rr
Ss
Tt
Uu
Vv
Ww
Xx
Yy
Zz

argue VERB
1 *The two boys are always arguing about football.*
quarrel, squabble, row, fight, feud, fall out, disagree, dispute
2 *She argued that it was my turn to wash up.*
reason, claim, suggest

argument NOUN
1 *They had an argument about films.*
quarrel, squabble, row, debate, discussion, dispute, disagreement, clash, feud
2 *There is a strong argument against closing the school.*
reasoning, reason, logic, claim, defence, case

armour NOUN

Here are some pieces of armour:
breastplate, chain mail, gauntlet, greave, helmet, shield, tabard, visor

arms NOUN
The soldiers laid down their arms.
weapons, firearms, guns, ammunition

army NOUN
He served in the army during the war.
armed forces, military, soldiers, troops

aroma NOUN
the aroma of fresh flowers
smell, scent, odour, perfume, fragrance

around[1] ADVERB
1 *We've just been driving around.*
everywhere, all over, in all directions, on all sides, here and there, to and fro
2 *Stick around till I'm ready.*
close, close by, near, nearby, at hand

around[2] PREPOSITION
1 *He had his arm around his daughter's shoulders.*
surrounding, round, encircling, enclosing

2 *There were around a dozen spectators.*
approximately, roughly, about, more or less

arrange VERB
1 *He arranges his CDs in alphabetical order.*
order, tidy, position, set out, lay out, group, class, classify, sort, file
(≠) OPPOSITES untidy, disorganize, muddle
2 *We have arranged a game of snooker.*
organize, prepare, fix, plan

arrangement NOUN
1 *We have changed the arrangement of the furniture.*
order, layout, grouping, structure, system, set-up, organization
2 *We have an arrangement to meet in town at the weekend.*
agreement, plan

arrest VERB
He was arrested for murder.
capture, catch, seize

arrive VERB
Our visitors arrived early.
appear, turn up, show up, enter
(≠) OPPOSITES depart, leave

arrogant ADJECTIVE
He upset people with his arrogant attitude.
boastful, proud, conceited, self-important, high and mighty
(≠) OPPOSITES humble

art NOUN
the art of conversation
skill, knack, technique, method

art and craft NOUN

Here are some arts and crafts:
Painting:
oil painting, watercolour

Aa Bb Cc Dd Ee Ff Gg Hh Ii Jj Kk Ll Mm Nn Oo Pp Qq Rr Ss Tt Uu Vv Ww Xx Yy Zz

Drawing:
animation, architecture, calligraphy, graphics, illustration, sketching
Photography:
film, video
Making objects:
ceramics, metalwork, modelling, mosaic, sculpture, stained glass, woodwork
Crafts with paper:
collage, origami
Crafts with fabric:
batik, silk-screen printing, spinning, tie-dye, weaving
Needlework:
crochet, embroidery, knitting, patchwork, tapestry

article NOUN
1 *I read an article on skateboarding.*
feature, report, story, composition, essay
2 *articles of clothing*
item, thing, object, piece

artificial ADJECTIVE
1 *His sympathy was artificial.*
false, fake, insincere, forced
≠ OPPOSITES genuine, true
2 *an artificial leg*
false, fake, synthetic, plastic, man-made
≠ OPPOSITES real, natural

artist NOUN

Here are some types of artist:

animator, architect, blacksmith, carpenter, cartoonist, craftsman, craftswoman, designer, draughtsman, draughtswoman, engraver, goldsmith, graphic artist, graphic designer, illustrator, jeweller, painter, photographer, potter, printer, sculptor, silversmith, weaver

artistic ADJECTIVE
Her cake decoration is very artistic.

ornamental, decorative, beautiful, stylish, tasteful, creative, imaginative
≠ OPPOSITES unimaginative

ashamed ADJECTIVE
He was ashamed of his bad behaviour.
sorry, guilty, embarrassed, blushing, red-faced
≠ OPPOSITES unashamed

ask VERB
1 *He asked for more ice cream.*
request, appeal, plead, beg
2 *I asked my sister about her boyfriend.*
inquire, query, question, quiz
3 *Danielle asked me to her party.*
invite

asleep ADJECTIVE
The baby is asleep in his cot.
sleeping, napping, snoozing, fast asleep, sound asleep, resting, unconscious, dozing

assault¹ NOUN
a serious assault
attack, mugging

assault² VERB
The gang assaulted a man in the street.
attack, strike, hit, beat up

assemble VERB
1 *The whole school assembled in the playground.*
gather, meet, join up, group, collect
≠ OPPOSITES scatter, disperse
2 *He is assembling a model aeroplane.*
construct, build, put together, piece together, make
≠ OPPOSITES dismantle

assembly NOUN
1 *a school assembly*
gathering, rally, meeting, convention, conference, congregation, council, group
2 *assembly of the different parts*
construction, building, manufacture

assign VERB
The teacher assigned the children tasks.

allocate, grant, distribute, set, specify

assignment NOUN
today's assignments in class
task, project, duty, responsibility, errand

assist VERB
Adam assisted his dad with the gardening.
aid, co-operate with, collaborate with, support
(≠) OPPOSITES hinder

assistance NOUN
Thank you for your assistance.
aid, co-operation, collaboration, backing, support, encouragement
(≠) OPPOSITES hindrance

assistant NOUN
The manager's assistant will stand in for him.
helper, supporter, colleague, partner, ally, associate

associate VERB
1 *I always associate Beth with horses.*
connect, link, identify
2 *Matthew has been associating with bad company.*
mingle, mix
◇ INFORMAL WORDS hang around, hang out

assorted ADJECTIVE
assorted biscuits
of different kinds, mixed, various, varied, miscellaneous

assortment NOUN
assortment of odd socks
jumble, mixture, variety, collection, selection

assume VERB
I assume you don't need this old book any more.
presume, accept, take for granted, expect, guess, suppose, imagine

assure VERB
The children will be safe, I assure you.
guarantee, promise, vow to, swear to, reassure

astonish VERB
I have some news that will astonish you.
startle, amaze, stun, dumbfound

astounding ADJECTIVE
astounding skill
amazing, breathtaking, overwhelming, stunning, surprising

astronaut NOUN

Here are some parts of an astronaut's equipment:
boots, gloves, helmet, jetpack, oxygen, spacesuit, visor

athletic ADJECTIVE
The team captain is strong and athletic.
fit, energetic, active, sporty, muscular, powerful
(≠) OPPOSITES puny

atmosphere NOUN
There was a happy atmosphere at the party.
feeling, mood, spirit, character, quality, flavour

atrocious ADJECTIVE
Your handwriting is atrocious.
dreadful, terrible, horrible, hideous, monstrous
(≠) OPPOSITES fine

attach VERB
Attach this address label to your suitcase.
stick, adhere, fasten, fix, secure, tie, bind, join, connect, link
(≠) OPPOSITES detach, unfasten

attack¹ NOUN
There has been an air attack on a military base.
invasion, raid, strike, charge, assault
(≠) OPPOSITES defence

Aa
Bb
Cc
Dd
Ee
Ff
Gg
Hh
Ii
Jj
Kk
Ll
Mm
Nn
Oo
Pp
Qq
Rr
Ss
Tt
Uu
Vv
Ww
Xx
Yy
Zz

Aa
Bb
Cc
Dd
Ee
Ff
Gg
Hh
Ii
Jj
Kk
Ll
Mm
Nn
Oo
Pp
Qq
Rr
Ss
Tt
Uu
Vv
Ww
Xx
Yy
Zz

attack² VERB
The castle was attacked by enemies.
invade, raid, strike, storm, charge, assault
(≠) OPPOSITES defend, protect

attempt¹ VERB
I will attempt to be there on time.
try, endeavour, seek, strive

attempt² NOUN
an attempt to break the world record
try, endeavour, effort, bid, struggle
◇ INFORMAL WORDS shot, go

attend VERB
Did John attend lessons today?
be present, go to, visit
• **attend to**
I will attend to the washing-up. deal with, see to, take care of, look after, manage, supervise

attention NOUN
1 *Give your homework full attention.*
concentration, consideration
2 *people needing medical attention*
treatment, care, service

attitude NOUN
Jamal has a very positive attitude.
feeling, mood, manner, point of view, opinion, view, outlook, approach

attract VERB
The show will attract thousands of visitors.
lure, entice, tempt, appeal to, interest, fascinate
(≠) OPPOSITES repel, disgust

attractive ADJECTIVE
1 *a very attractive model*
pretty, good-looking, handsome, beautiful, gorgeous, stunning, glamorous
2 *an attractive little town*
pleasant, pleasing, agreeable, appealing, charming, lovely

audience NOUN
The audience cheered when the band came on stage.
spectators, listeners, viewers, crowd, fans

authentic ADJECTIVE
authentic French food
genuine

author NOUN
the author of the Harry Potter books
writer, novelist, scriptwriter

automatic ADJECTIVE
an automatic reaction
unconscious, unthinking, natural, instinctive, spontaneous

available ADJECTIVE
1 *The band's new CD will be available. from Monday.*
ready, obtainable
(≠) OPPOSITES unavailable
2 *Pick up the nearest pencil available.*
to hand, at hand, on hand, within reach, handy, convenient

average ADJECTIVE
1 *How long do you spend on homework on an average day?*
normal, ordinary, standard, typical, usual, regular, common, run-of-the-mill
(≠) OPPOSITES extreme, exceptional, remarkable
2 *an average mark in the test*
medium, moderate, satisfactory, fair, middling, so-so, passable

avoid VERB
I try to avoid arguments.
dodge, duck, escape, elude, evade, get out of, steer clear of

awake ADJECTIVE
I lay awake worrying in the night.
wide awake, alert, conscious

award¹ NOUN
The gymnastics team won an award.
prize, trophy, medal, cup, shield

award² VERB
Chloe was awarded the top prize for her story.

give, present, grant, confer

aware ADJECTIVE
• **aware of**
People are aware of the dangers of smoking.
conscious of, familiar with, informed of
≠ OPPOSITES unaware of, oblivious to

awful ADJECTIVE
an awful journey through a snow storm
terrible, dreadful, unpleasant, nasty, horrible, hideous, shocking
≠ OPPOSITES wonderful, excellent

awkward ADJECTIVE
1 *Sophie's movements are too awkward for a dancer.*
clumsy, unskilful, ungraceful
≠ OPPOSITES graceful
2 *He made me feel awkward by not speaking to me.*
uncomfortable, ill at ease, uneasy, embarrassed
≠ OPPOSITES relaxed
3 *You're disagreeing with me just to be awkward.*
obstinate, stubborn, unhelpful, unpleasant
≠ OPPOSITES amenable, pleasant
4 *This present is an awkward shape to wrap.*
inconvenient, difficult, fiddly, troublesome, unmanageable, tricky
≠ OPPOSITES convenient, handy, easy

Aa
Bb
Cc
Dd
Ee
Ff
Gg
Hh
Ii
Jj
Kk
Ll
Mm
Nn
Oo
Pp
Qq
Rr
Ss
Tt
Uu
Vv
Ww
Xx
Yy
Zz

Bb

baby NOUN
*The **baby** is asleep in her cot.*
infant, new-born, child, toddler

babyish ADJECTIVE
*Her behaviour is very **babyish** for a nine-year-old.*
childish, immature, infantile, silly, foolish
≠ OPPOSITES mature

back¹ NOUN
*sitting at the **back** of the bus*
rear, end, tail, tail end, hindquarters
≠ OPPOSITES front

back² ADJECTIVE
*The dog stood up on its **back** legs.*
rear, end, tail, hind
≠ OPPOSITES front

back³ VERB
1 *Caroline **backed** the car carefully out of the drive.*
reverse, go backwards, back away
2 *The parents are **backing** the school's anti-bullying campaign.*
support, assist, side with, sponsor
≠ OPPOSITES oppose
• **back up**
*The boy denied breaking the window and his friend **backed** him **up**.*
confirm, second, support
≠ OPPOSITES contradict

backing NOUN
*We have the head teacher's **backing** for our fundraising scheme.*
support, encouragement, moral support, aid, assistance

bad ADJECTIVE
⇒ For even more about this word, see the next page
1 *There is a **bad** smell in this room.*
unpleasant, nasty, undesirable

≠ OPPOSITES good, pleasant
2 *Stealing is a very **bad** thing to do.*
evil, wicked, sinful, criminal, wrong
≠ OPPOSITES good
3 *Emma is grounded because she has been a **bad** girl today.*
naughty, mischievous, badly behaved, disobedient
≠ OPPOSITES well-behaved
4 *Her spelling is really **bad**.*
poor, inferior, unsatisfactory, useless
≠ OPPOSITES excellent
5 *Smoking is a **bad** habit.*
harmful, damaging, dangerous, unhealthy
≠ OPPOSITES good
6 *This apple is **bad**.*
rotten, mouldy, decayed, spoilt, sour, off
≠ OPPOSITES fresh
7 *There has been a **bad** accident.*
serious, grave, severe, terrible
≠ OPPOSITES mild, slight
8 *Have I called at a **bad** time?*
inconvenient, unfortunate, unsuitable
≠ OPPOSITES good

badly ADVERB
1 ***badly** injured*
seriously, severely, extremely, greatly, intensely, deeply
≠ OPPOSITES slightly
2 *He has behaved very **badly**.*
wickedly, shamefully, unfairly, naughtily
3 *He sings really **badly**.*
poorly, wrongly, incorrectly, imperfectly, unsatisfactorily, incompetently
≠ OPPOSITES well

bad-tempered ADJECTIVE
*Paul gets very **bad-tempered** when his team loses.*
irritable, cross, snappy, grumpy, grouchy
≠ OPPOSITES good-tempered

bad

Often when you are writing you want to use a word that means **bad**. You have to be careful not to use the word **bad** too often, or your writing will become boring. You could try out some of the following words instead.

You can describe many different things as
awful
dreadful
horrible
terrible
disagreeable
atrocious
nasty
unpleasant

bad behaviour, or someone who behaves badly
naughty
mischievous
ill-behaved
disobedient
unruly

a bad person
evil
wicked
cruel
mean

a bad piece of homework
poor
unsatisfactory
inferior
inadequate
unacceptable

a bad day
unpleasant
unenjoyable

something that is bad for you or the environment
harmful

damaging
unhealthy
destructive
ruinous

If you feel bad about something you have done, you could say you feel

ashamed
guilty
sorry
remorseful
embarrassed

a bad cold

serious
severe
grave

feel bad

ill
unwell
sick
poorly
under the weather

food that has gone bad

rotten
mouldy
decayed
sour
off

Over to you

Can you change the word **bad** in these sentences to make it more clear what you mean?

I had a **bad** day at school today. I got into trouble for being **bad** and talking in class.

Then the teacher told me my English homework was **bad**. At playtime I had an apple that was **bad**.

bag NOUN

Here are some types of bag:
backpack, carrier bag, case, handbag, holdall, rucksack, sack, satchel, shopping bag, shoulder-bag, suitcase

baggage NOUN
the passengers and their baggage
luggage, bags, belongings, suitcases, things
◇ INFORMAL WORDS gear, stuff

baggy ADJECTIVE
baggy trousers
loose, slack, roomy, saggy, droopy
(≠) OPPOSITES tight

bald ADJECTIVE
a bald man
bald-headed, hairless, bare
(≠) OPPOSITES hairy

ball NOUN
a ball of wool
sphere, globe

ballet NOUN

Here are some words used in ballet:
arabesque, ballerina, barre, jeté, pas, plié, pointe, position, pirouette
Clothes for ballet:
ballet shoes, jazz pants, leotard, pointe shoes, pumps, shorts, skirt, tights, tutu, unitard

ban VERB
Mobile phones are banned in school.
forbid, prohibit, bar, exclude
(≠) OPPOSITES allow, permit, authorize

band¹ NOUN
a rubber band
strip, belt, ribbon, tape, bandage, binding, tie, strap, cord

band² NOUN
1 *a rock band*
group, ensemble, orchestra
2 *a band of robbers*
troop, gang, crew, group

bang¹ NOUN
1 *She's had a bang on the head.*
blow, hit, knock, bump, crash, smack, thump
◇ INFORMAL WORDS wallop, whack
2 *We heard a loud bang.*
explosion, pop, boom, thud, thump, slam

bang² VERB
I banged my head on the cupboard door.
hit, bump, knock, strike, bash

banish VERB
After her outburst Stephanie was banished to her room.
dismiss, exile, expel, evict, ban, bar, exclude, shut out, remove, get rid of

bank NOUN
a grassy bank
slope, mound, ridge, side, edge, shore

banner NOUN
The crowd waved banners as the team paraded through the town.
flag, poster, placard, standard, colours, streamer

bar¹ NOUN
1 *a bar of chocolate*
slab, block, lump, chunk, wedge
2 *an iron bar*
rod, stick, shaft, pole, stake, rail, railing

bar² VERB
1 *Luke has been barred from the youth club for bad behaviour.*
exclude, ban, forbid, prohibit, prevent
2 *A policeman barred our way.*
obstruct, hinder, block

bare ADJECTIVE
Don't go outside in your bare feet.

Aa
Bb
Cc
Dd
Ee
Ff
Gg
Hh
Ii
Jj
Kk
Ll
Mm
Nn
Oo
Pp
Qq
Rr
Ss
Tt
Uu
Vv
Ww
Xx
Yy
Zz

naked, nude, unclothed, undressed, stripped, uncovered
(≠) OPPOSITES clothed

barely ADVERB
I had barely enough money for my bus fare.
hardly, scarcely, only just, just

bargain¹ NOUN
I'll make a bargain with you – I'll take you to the cinema if you tidy your room.
deal, agreement, pact, promise, understanding, arrangement, negotiation

bargain² VERB
We were bargaining over a T-shirt on the market stall.
negotiate, deal, trade, haggle

barge VERB
A boy barged into her.
bump, collide, hit

barren ADJECTIVE
barren waste land
dry, desert, empty, flat, treeless, waste, useless
(≠) OPPOSITES fertile, useful

barrier NOUN
I met him at the ticket barrier.
wall, fence, railing, barricade

base¹ NOUN
1 *the base of the statue*
bottom, foot, stand, rest, support, foundation
2 *an army base*
headquarters, centre, camp

base² VERB
1 *The company is based in Dublin.*
locate, establish, position
2 *The story is based on true events.*
found, build, construct

basic ADJECTIVE
the basic rules of the game
fundamental, essential, elementary, primary, central, general

basically ADVERB
This is basically a good idea but it needs careful planning.
fundamentally, essentially, at bottom, at heart

basin NOUN
Just stack all the dishes in the basin.
bowl, dish, sink

basis NOUN
What is the basis of your argument?
base, foundation

batch NOUN
a new batch of students
set, lot, bunch, collection, assortment, parcel, pack, amount, quantity

batter VERB
The village was badly battered by the storm.
beat, smash, thrash, damage, hurt, injure
◇ INFORMAL WORDS wallop

battle NOUN
a sea battle
war, combat, fight, attack

bay NOUN
swimming in the bay
gulf, inlet, cove

be VERB
1 *We will always be best friends.*
stay, remain, last, continue, survive
2 *The wedding will be in April.*
happen, occur, come about, take place, develop

beach NOUN
The children made a sandcastle at the beach.
seaside, seashore, sands, sand, shore, water's edge, coast

beam¹ NOUN
1 *a beam of light from a torch*
ray, shaft, glow
2 *There are wooden beams across the ceiling.*
plank, board, timber, rafter, bar

Aa
Bb
Cc
Dd
Ee
Ff
Gg
Hh
Ii
Jj
Kk
Ll
Mm
Nn
Oo
Pp
Qq
Rr
Ss
Tt
Uu
Vv
Ww
Xx
Yy
Zz

beam² VERB

Live coverage of the concert was beamed around the world.
broadcast, transmit

bear VERB

I can't bear the heat in the sun.
tolerate, stand, put up with, cope with, suffer, take

bearable ADJECTIVE

A cool breeze made the heat bearable.
tolerable, endurable, acceptable
⊘ OPPOSITES unbearable, intolerable, insufferable, unacceptable

bearings NOUN

I took a wrong turning and lost my bearings.
position, situation, location, whereabouts, way, direction, aim

beast NOUN

lions and other wild beasts
animal, creature

beat¹ VERB

1 *The old lady was badly beaten by the mugger.*
hit, thrash, batter, punch, strike, whip
2 *My heart was beating very fast after being chased home.*
pound, throb, thump, race, flutter
3 *Jasmeet beat his friend in the race.*
defeat, conquer, outdo
◇ INFORMAL WORDS hammer, thrash

beat² NOUN

1 *the quick beat of his heart*
pulse, stroke, throb, thump, thud, flutter
2 *dancing to the beat of the music*
rhythm, time

beautiful ADJECTIVE

1 *a beautiful princess*
attractive, pretty, lovely, good-looking, handsome, gorgeous, stunning
⊘ OPPOSITES ugly, hideous
2 *Megan painted a beautiful picture of a tiger.*
delightful, fine, charming, attractive
⊘ OPPOSITES unattractive

beauty NOUN

an actress who is admired for her beauty
attractiveness, prettiness, loveliness, good looks, handsomeness, glamour, grace, elegance
⊘ OPPOSITES ugliness, repulsiveness

become VERB

She became a doctor when she grew up.
develop into, change into, turn, grow, get

bed NOUN

1 *My new bed is very comfortable.*
couch, bunk, cot, mattress
2 *a bed of roses*
garden, border, patch, plot

before ADVERB

Have you been to France before?
previously, earlier, sooner, ahead, in front, in advance, formerly
⊘ OPPOSITES after, later

beg VERB

He begged me not to tell his parents he had played truant.
ask, request, plead

begin VERB

1 *The family began a new life in Australia.*
start, commence, set about, introduce
⊘ OPPOSITES finish
2 *The Second World War began in 1939.*
arise, emerge, appear, start, commence
⊘ OPPOSITES end

beginner NOUN

gentle ski slopes for beginners
starter, learner, trainee, student, recruit, novice
⊘ OPPOSITES expert

beginning NOUN

I missed the beginning of the film.

Aa
Bb
Cc
Dd
Ee
Ff
Gg
Hh
Ii
Jj
Kk
Ll
Mm
Nn
Oo
Pp
Qq
Rr
Ss
Tt
Uu
Vv
Ww
Xx
Yy
Zz

start, commencement, opening, introduction, starting point
⊉ OPPOSITES **end, finish**

Aa

Bb

behave VERB

*Kieran **behaved** very badly in class.*
act, react, perform

Cc

Dd

behaviour NOUN

*Jennifer got a prize for good **behaviour**.*
conduct, manners, actions, performance, ways, habits

Ee

Ff

behind PREPOSITION

*A dog was running **behind** the car.*
after, at the back of, following
⊉ OPPOSITES **in front of, before**

Gg

Hh

being NOUN

*a **being** from another planet*
creature, animal, beast, individual, thing

Ii

Jj

Kk

belief NOUN

*religious **beliefs***
faith, principle

Ll

Mm

believable ADJECTIVE

*Her excuse was not **believable**.*
credible, plausible, likely to be true, acceptable
⊉ OPPOSITES **unbelievable, implausible**

Nn

Oo

Pp

believe VERB

1 *I don't **believe** a word he says.*
accept, trust, count on, depend on, rely on
◇ INFORMAL WORDS **swallow**
⊉ OPPOSITES **disbelieve, doubt**
2 *I **believe** it may rain.*
think, consider, imagine, guess, reckon, suppose

Qq

Rr

Ss

Tt

Uu

Vv

belong VERB

*This book **belongs** in the children's section.*
fit, go with, be part of, link up with, tie up with, be connected with, relate to

Ww

Xx

Yy

belongings NOUN

*Remember to take all your **belongings** with you.*

Zz

possessions, property, goods, things
◇ INFORMAL WORDS **stuff, gear**

below PREPOSITION

*From the top we could see the river far **below** us.*
under, underneath, beneath
⊉ OPPOSITES **above**

bench NOUN

*sitting on a park **bench***
seat, form

bend¹ VERB

1 *The road **bends** sharply to the right.*
curve, turn, swerve, twist
⊉ OPPOSITES **straighten**
2 *She **bent** to pick up a magazine from the floor.*
stoop, lean
⊉ OPPOSITES **straighten**

bend² NOUN

*a sharp **bend** in the road*
curve, loop, turn, twist, bow

beneath PREPOSITION

*sitting **beneath** an umbrella for shade*
under, underneath, below, lower than

benefit¹ NOUN

*the **benefits** of having your own garden*
advantage, good, interest, help, aid, assistance, gain
⊉ OPPOSITES **disadvantage, harm, damage**

benefit² VERB

*The new law will **benefit** the elderly.*
help, aid, assist
⊉ OPPOSITES **hinder, harm**

bent ADJECTIVE

*a piece of **bent** wire*
angled, curved, arched, folded, doubled, twisted
⊉ OPPOSITES **straight**

beside PREPOSITION

*We sat **beside** the pool.*
alongside, next to, bordering, next door to, close to, near

besides¹ PREPOSITION

*There are other people **besides** you in the class.*
apart from, other than, in addition to, over and above

besides² ADVERB

*I don't feel like going out tonight. **Besides**, I don't have any money.*
also, as well, too, in addition, additionally
◆ FORMAL WORDS furthermore, moreover

best ADJECTIVE

*the **best** book I have ever read*
greatest, finest, highest, largest
⌦ OPPOSITES worst

bet¹ NOUN

*He placed a **bet** on the result of the Cup Final.*
wager, gamble
◇ INFORMAL WORDS flutter

bet² VERB

*He **bets** too much money on football results.*
gamble, wager, risk

betray VERB

1 *He **betrayed** his friend to the police.*
inform on, be disloyal to, double-cross, desert, abandon
⌦ OPPOSITES defend, protect
2 *The expression on her face **betrayed** her true feelings.*
disclose, give away, tell, expose, reveal, show
⌦ OPPOSITES hide

better ADJECTIVE

1 *This is a much **better** story than your last one.*
superior, greater, preferable
⌦ OPPOSITES inferior
2 *I had flu but I am much **better** now.*
improving, progressing, on the mend, fitter, healthier, stronger, recovered
⌦ OPPOSITES worse

between PREPOSITION

*We shared the sweets **between** us.*
among, amongst

beyond PREPOSITION

*the house just **beyond** the bus stop*
past, further than, apart from, away from, out of range of, out of reach of

bicycle
⇒ see **cycle**

bid NOUN

1 *He made a **bid** of £2000 for the painting.*
offer, sum, amount, price
2 *his latest **bid** to climb the mountain*
attempt, effort, try
◇ INFORMAL WORDS go

big ADJECTIVE

⇒ For even more about this word, see page 27
1 *a **big** car*
large, great, huge, enormous, immense, massive, gigantic
⌦ OPPOSITES small, little
2 *Going to high school is a **big** step.*
important, serious
⌦ OPPOSITES unimportant

bill NOUN

*Our last telephone **bill** was huge.*
statement, account, charges

bind VERB

*The prisoners' hands were **bound** together with rope.*
attach, fasten, secure, tie, strap

bird NOUN

Here are some types of bird:

Birds common in Britain:
blackbird, bluetit, bullfinch, chaffinch, crossbill, crow, cuckoo, dove, greenfinch, jackdaw, jay, linnet, magpie, martin, nightingale, nuthatch, pigeon, raven, robin, rook,

Aa
Bb
Cc
Dd
Ee
Ff
Gg
Hh
Ii
Jj
Kk
Ll
Mm
Nn
Oo
Pp
Qq
Rr
Ss
Tt
Uu
Vv
Ww
Xx
Yy
Zz

Aa
Bb
Cc
Dd
Ee
Ff
Gg
Hh
Ii
Jj
Kk
Ll
Mm
Nn
Oo
Pp
Qq
Rr
Ss
Tt
Uu
Vv
Ww
Xx
Yy
Zz

skylark, sparrow, starling, swallow, swift, thrush, tit, wagtail, woodpecker, wood pigeon, wren, yellowhammer
Water birds:
albatross, auk, coot, cormorant, crane, curlew, duck, flamingo, gannet, goose, grebe, heron, kingfisher, lapwing, mallard, moorhen, peewit, pelican, petrel, plover, puffin, seagull, snipe, stork, swan
Birds of prey:
buzzard, eagle, falcon, hawk, kestrel, owl, red kite, sparrowhawk, vulture
Birds that do not fly:
emu, kiwi, ostrich, penguin
Farm and game birds:
chicken, duck, goose, grouse, partridge, pheasant, quail, turkey
Birds from overseas:
bird of paradise, budgerigar, canary, cockatiel, cockatoo, kookaburra, lovebird, macaw, mockingbird, myna bird, parrot, peacock, toucan

bit NOUN
a bit of cheese
piece, scrap, slice, fragment, part, segment

bite¹ VERB
1 *He bit into an apple.*
chew, munch, gnaw, nibble, crunch
2 *The dog bit her hand.*
nip, pierce, wound, tear

bite² NOUN
1 *a dog bite*
nip, wound, pinch
2 *Would you like a bite to eat?*
snack, refreshment, mouthful, taste

bitter ADJECTIVE
1 *This grapefruit is very bitter.*
sour, sharp, acid, vinegary, unsweetened
⧧ OPPOSITES sweet
2 *He felt bitter about being fired.*
resentful, hostile
⧧ OPPOSITES contented

3 *a bitter wind*
severe, harsh, stinging, biting, freezing, raw
⧧ OPPOSITES mild

bizarre ADJECTIVE
a bizarre coincidence
strange, odd, curious, weird, extraordinary
⧧ OPPOSITES normal, usual, predictable

black ADJECTIVE
1 *black hair*
jet-black, coal-black, dark
2 *His hands were black after working on the car.*
filthy, dirty, soiled, grubby
⧧ OPPOSITES clean

blame VERB
The two drivers blamed each other for the accident.
accuse, charge, criticize, find fault with, condemn

blank¹ ADJECTIVE
1 *a blank page*
empty, unfilled, clean, white, plain, clear, bare, unmarked
2 *He gave me a blank look.*
expressionless, vacant

blank² NOUN
Fill in the blanks in these sentences.
space, gap, break

blanket NOUN
The baby was wrapped in a blanket.
cover, sheet, rug, throw

blare VERB
The music was blaring from loudspeakers.
boom, blast, roar, ring, peal, clang, hoot, toot, honk

blast NOUN
1 *A block of flats was destroyed in the blast.*
explosion, bang, crash, crack
2 *A blast of cold air blew through the tunnel.*
gust, gale, draught, storm

big

If you want to describe something **big**, you can spice up your writing by choosing words that create pictures in a reader's mind.

Think carefully about which word to choose. Be precise and choose the best word for the job.

You can describe most big things as
> **large**

If something is very big indeed, you can describe it as
> **huge**
> **giant**
> **enormous**

A big space or place could be
> **immense**
> **vast**
> **infinite**

To describe a big person or creature who looks very strong, you could use
> **bulky**
> **hefty**
> **hulking**

You could use these words to describe something very big, like a mountain or a building:
> **massive**
> **towering**
> **gigantic**
> **colossal**
> **tremendous**

If something is important, like a big decision, you could describe it as
> **important**
> **significant**
> **serious**

Over to you

Can you change the word **big** in the writing below to make it more interesting?

The **big** singer appeared on stage in front of a **big** audience. He was a **big** man with a **big** voice. He saw his **big** reflection in a **big** mirror as he walked across the stage. He worried about his **big** appetite but he had a weakness for **big** steaks and **big** piles of chips.

Can you think of any informal words for **big** that you might use when speaking to your friends?

blaze¹ NOUN
Firemen were called to the blaze.
fire, flames, bonfire, flare-up

blaze² VERB
Very soon the fire was blazing.
burn, flame, flare, flare up, explode, flash, gleam, shine, glow

bleak ADJECTIVE
1 *The future looked bleak.*
gloomy, grim, depressing, hopeless, discouraging, disheartening
≠ OPPOSITES bright, cheerful
2 *a bleak hillside*
cold, chilly, raw, unsheltered, windy, windswept, exposed

blend VERB
1 *Blend the sugar and margarine until creamy.*
mix, combine, merge, unite, mingle
≠ OPPOSITES separate
2 *These colours blend well together.*
go together, combine, fit, match

blessing NOUN
1 *a blessing in disguise*
benefit, advantage, gift, gain, help
≠ OPPOSITES curse
2 *The teacher gave the idea his blessing.*
approval, backing, support, consent, permission

blind ADJECTIVE
1 *a blind person*
sightless, unsighted, unseeing
≠ OPPOSITES sighted
2 *She was blind to her son's faults.*
ignorant of, unaware of, unconscious of, oblivious to
≠ OPPOSITES aware of, conscious of

bliss NOUN
Breakfast in bed – sheer bliss!
joy, happiness, paradise, heaven, ecstasy
≠ OPPOSITES misery

blob NOUN
a blob of jam
drop, bead, bubble, spot, lump, mass, ball

block¹ NOUN
1 *a block of wood*
piece, lump, mass, chunk, bar
2 *a road block*
obstacle, barrier, bar, jam, blockage, obstruction, hindrance

block² VERB
1 *The toilet is blocked.*
choke, clog, plug, dam up, close
2 *A lorry was blocking our way.*
bar, obstruct, hinder, stop, check

bloom VERB
The roses are blooming.
flower, blossom, open, bud, sprout, grow, develop
OPPOSITES fade, wither

blossom NOUN
The blossom has appeared on our cherry tree.
bloom, flower, bud

blotch NOUN
blotches of paint on his shirt
splash, splodge, patch, mark, stain

blow¹ VERB
I blew on my soup to cool it down.
breathe, pant, puff, fan
• **blow up**
1 *The bomb blew up.*
explode, go off, burst, blast, detonate
2 *Dad blew up the balloons for the party.*
inflate, pump up, swell, fill, fill out, puff up, expand

blow² NOUN
1 *She has suffered a blow to the head.*
punch, clip, clout, bash, slap, smack, bang, knock
◇ INFORMAL WORDS whack, wallop
2 *Failing the exam was a blow to Aidan.*
misfortune, setback, disappointment, upset, shock

blue NOUN

Here are some shades of blue:
azure, baby, cornflower, indigo, navy, powder, royal blue, sapphire, sky-blue, ultramarine

blunt ADJECTIVE
My pencil is blunt.
unsharpened, worn, rounded
OPPOSITES sharp, pointed

blurred ADJECTIVE
When I don't wear my glasses, everything looks blurred.
out of focus, fuzzy, unclear, vague, hazy, misty, foggy, cloudy, dim
OPPOSITES clear, distinct

blush VERB
Kerry blushed when Josh paid her a compliment.
flush, redden, colour, glow

board¹ NOUN
a wooden board
sheet, panel, plank, beam, timber, slat

board² VERB
We boarded the plane just before take-off.
get on, enter, catch

boast VERB
She is always boasting about how clever her daughter is.
brag, show off, claim, swagger

boastful ADJECTIVE
He is very boastful about his achievements.
arrogant, big-headed, cocky, proud, conceited, bragging
OPPOSITES modest, humble

boat NOUN

Here are some types of boat and ship:
barge, canal boat, canoe, catamaran, clipper, cruise ship, destroyer, dinghy, dredger, ferry, freighter, frigate, galleon, gondola, house boat, hovercraft, hydrofoil, lifeboat, liner, motor boat, paddle steamer, pedalo, rowing boat, schooner, speedboat, trawler, tug, yacht

bob VERB
bobbing about on the water
bounce, twitch, jerk, jolt, wobble

Aa **Bb** Cc Dd Ee Ff Gg Hh Ii Jj Kk Ll Mm Nn Oo Pp Qq Rr Ss Tt Uu Vv Ww Xx Yy Zz

body NOUN

*My hands are cold but my **body** is warm.*
trunk, torso, build, figure

bog NOUN

The rain had turned the pitch into a bog.
marsh, swamp, quicksands

boil VERB

*The kettle is **boiling**.*
simmer, stew, bubble, steam

boiling ADJECTIVE

*Let's open a window – it's **boiling** in here!*
baking, roasting, scorching, stifling
(≠) OPPOSITES chilly, cool, freezing

boisterous ADJECTIVE

*The children are getting too **boisterous**.*
loud, noisy, rowdy, rough, wild
(≠) OPPOSITES quiet, calm

bold ADJECTIVE

1 *a **bold** knight*
fearless, daring, brave, courageous, adventurous, confident
(≠) OPPOSITES cautious, timid, shy
2 *a **bold** pattern*
strong, bright, colourful, loud, showy, eye-catching

bolt VERB

*He **bolted** the door.*
fasten, secure, bar, lock

bond NOUN

*There is a strong **bond** between the two brothers.*
attachment, connection, relation, link

bone NOUN

Here are some names of human bones:

breastbone, collarbone, femur, fibula, hip-bone, pelvis, rib, shoulderblade, skull, tarsal, thigh-bone, tibia, vertebra

bonus NOUN

*My mum gets a Christmas **bonus** at work.*
extra, prize, reward, tip, gift, handout

book¹ NOUN

*Have you read the new Jacqueline Wilson **book**?*
hardback, paperback, volume, booklet

Here are some types of book:

Printed books:
annual, atlas, catalogue, children's book, comic book, cookbook, dictionary, directory, encyclopedia, guidebook, hymn-book, manual, novel, phrase book, picture book, prayer book, reference book, story book, textbook, thesaurus, treasury
Books for writing in:
album, diary, exercise book, jotter, journal, notebook, photograph album, scrapbook, sketchbook, workbook

book² VERB

*We have **booked** tickets for the concert.*
reserve, order, arrange, organize
(≠) OPPOSITES cancel

boost VERB

*Winning the prize **boosted** her confidence.*
increase, raise, improve, develop, help, aid, assist, encourage
(≠) OPPOSITES hinder

border NOUN

1 *We crossed the **border** between Scotland and England.*
boundary, frontier, bound, bounds, limit, borderline
2 *a lace **border***
trimming, frill, hem, edge

Aa
Bb
Cc
Dd
Ee
Ff
Gg
Hh
Ii
Jj
Kk
Ll
Mm
Nn
Oo
Pp
Qq
Rr
Ss
Tt
Uu
Vv
Ww
Xx
Yy
Zz

bore VERB
boring a hole
drill, mine, pierce

boring ADJECTIVE
I found that book boring.
dull, dreary, uninteresting, unexciting, uneventful
⧧ OPPOSITES interesting, exciting

borrow VERB
Can I borrow your ruler, please?
take, obtain, use
⧧ OPPOSITES lend

boss NOUN
He asked his boss for a pay rise.
employer, head, chief, director, manager, foreman, superintendent, supervisor

bother¹ VERB
Would it bother you if I opened the window?
disturb, annoy, irritate, trouble, worry, concern, upset, pester, nag
◇ INFORMAL WORDS hassle

bother² NOUN
I don't want to put you to any bother.
trouble, problem, difficulty, fuss, nuisance, annoyance, worry
◇ INFORMAL WORDS hassle

bottle up VERB
You shouldn't bottle up your feelings.
hold back, hide, conceal
⧧ OPPOSITES express, let go

bottom NOUN
at the bottom of the bed
foot, base, underside, underneath
⧧ OPPOSITES top

bounce VERB
Jessica bounced up and down on the trampoline.
spring, jump, leap, bound

bound¹ ADJECTIVE
1 *This plan is bound to succeed.*
sure, certain, destined, fated, doomed

2 *I felt bound to help her.*
obliged, forced, compelled, required, duty-bound

bound² VERB
A big dog came bounding towards us.
jump, leap, spring, bounce, hop, prance

boundary NOUN
This fence marks the boundary of the property.
border, limits, edge, margin, fringe, frontier, barrier, line, borderline

bouquet NOUN
a bouquet of flowers
bunch, posy, wreath, garland

bowl¹ NOUN
a bowl of soup
dish, basin, container, vessel

bowl² VERB
It's Jonathan's turn to bowl the ball.
throw, hurl, fling, pitch

box NOUN
a box of chocolates
container, carton, packet, pack, package, case, crate, chest, trunk

boy NOUN
This is a photo of my dad when he was a boy.
lad, youngster, kid, youth, son, fellow

brain NOUN
Use your brain!
head, mind, intelligence, wit, reason, sense, common sense, understanding
◇ INFORMAL WORDS brains

brainy ADJECTIVE
Am I brainy enough to pass the test?
clever, intelligent, bright, brilliant, smart
⧧ OPPOSITES stupid

branch NOUN
1 *The squirrel scampered along a branch of the tree.*
bough, limb, shoot

Aa
Bb
Cc
Dd
Ee
Ff
Gg
Hh
Ii
Jj
Kk
Ll
Mm
Nn
Oo
Pp
Qq
Rr
Ss
Tt
Uu
Vv
Ww
Xx
Yy
Zz

2 *the Glasgow **branch** of the company*
division, section, department, office,
part

brand NOUN
*This is the most popular **brand** of
trainers.*
make, type, brand-name, label

brave ADJECTIVE
*Owning up to breaking the window
was a very **brave** thing to do.*
courageous, fearless, bold, daring,
heroic
OPPOSITES cowardly, afraid, timid

bravery NOUN
*The boy was given an award for
bravery.*
courage, fearlessness, boldness, daring,
spirit
◇ INFORMAL WORDS guts
OPPOSITES cowardice, timidity

breadth NOUN
*Measure the length and **breadth** of the
room.*
width, broadness, wideness, thickness

break¹ VERB
1 *I **broke** my arm playing football.*
fracture, crack, snap
2 *Tom **broke** a glass.*
smash, shatter, splinter, ruin, destroy,
demolish, split, divide
OPPOSITES mend
3 *Paul is hoping to **break** the world
record.*
exceed, beat, better, outdo
• **break down**
*The bus **broke down**.*
fail, stop, seize up
◇ INFORMAL WORDS conk out
• **break up**
1 *School **broke up** for the summer.*
disband, finish, suspend
2 *Break up the word into parts.*
take apart, divide, separate, split up
3 *My sister is **breaking up** with her
boyfriend.*
split up, separate, part

break² NOUN
*We'll have a **break** from work.*
interval, pause, halt, lull, rest, time out
◇ INFORMAL WORDS let-up, breather

breakable ADJECTIVE
breakable objects made of glass
fragile, delicate, flimsy
OPPOSITES durable, sturdy,
unbreakable

break-in NOUN
*The police are investigating a **break-in**
at the factory.*
burglary, robbery, raid

breakthrough NOUN
*Scientists have made an important
breakthrough in cancer research.*
discovery, find, finding, invention,
progress, development, improvement

breathe VERB
*I had trouble **breathing** in the smoky
atmosphere.*
inhale, exhale, sigh, gasp, pant, puff

breathless ADJECTIVE
*She was **breathless** from climbing the
stairs.*
out of breath, gasping, panting
◇ INFORMAL WORDS puffed out

breathtaking ADJECTIVE
*the **breathtaking** beauty of the
countryside*
stunning, magnificent, overwhelming,
amazing, astonishing, awe-inspiring

breed¹ NOUN
*a rare **breed** of cat*
species, variety, family, sort, kind, type,
pedigree

breed² VERB
*The zoo hopes the giant pandas will
breed young.*
reproduce, rear, raise, bring up

breeze NOUN
*A pleasant **breeze** cooled us down.*
wind, gust, puff, breath, draught, air

bury VERB

The car was **buried** under snow.
cover, hide, engulf, submerge

bushy ADJECTIVE

bushy eyebrows
hairy, thick, dense, shaggy

business NOUN

1 I want to go into **business** when I leave school.
trade, commerce, industry, manufacturing, trading, buying, selling
2 My mum owns a dry-cleaning business.
company, firm, organization
3 What **business** are you in?
job, occupation, work, employment, trade, profession, line, career
4 I've got some **business** to attend to.
matter, issue, problem, question, subject, topic, point, affair

busy ADJECTIVE

1 I've been very **busy** tidying up my room.
occupied, engaged, employed, working, active
◇ INFORMAL WORDS busy as a bee, flat out
✑ OPPOSITES idle
2 a **busy** street
crowded, teeming, swarming, bustling, lively
✑ OPPOSITES quiet
3 Christmas is a very **busy** time in the shops.

hectic, eventful, strenuous, tiring
✑ OPPOSITES quiet, restful

butt VERB

The referee sent a player off for **butting** an opposing player.
hit, bump, knock, push, shove, ram
• **butt in**
He kept **butting in** on our conversation.
interrupt, cut in, intrude, meddle, interfere

butterfly NOUN

Here are some types of butterfly:

cabbage white, common blue, fritillary, orange-tip, painted lady, peacock, red admiral, swallowtail, tortoiseshell

buy VERB

I'm saving up to **buy** a CD player.
purchase, invest in, pay for, obtain, get
◆ FORMAL WORDS acquire
✑ OPPOSITES sell

buyer NOUN

We've found a **buyer** for our house.
purchaser, shopper, customer
✑ OPPOSITES seller

by PREPOSITION

the house **by** the lake
next to, beside, alongside, near

breezy ADJECTIVE

a **breezy** day
windy, blowy, fresh, airy, gusty, blustery
✑ OPPOSITES still

brief ADJECTIVE

1 a **brief** description
short, concise, compressed
✑ OPPOSITES long
2 a **brief** interruption
short-lived, momentary, passing, temporary, hasty, quick, swift, fast
✑ OPPOSITES lengthy

bright ADJECTIVE

1 a **bright** light
shining, flashing, glittering, sparkling, twinkling, glowing, brilliant, dazzling, glaring, blazing
✑ OPPOSITES dim
2 a **bright** and cheerful person
happy, cheerful, glad, joyful, merry, jolly, lively, vivacious
✑ OPPOSITES sad
3 The future looks **bright**.
promising, hopeful, encouraging, rosy, optimistic
✑ OPPOSITES gloomy, depressing
4 a very **bright** child
clever, smart, intelligent, brilliant, quick-witted, quick, sharp
◇ INFORMAL WORDS brainy
✑ OPPOSITES stupid
5 a **bright** colour
clear, brilliant, vivid, strong, bold
✑ OPPOSITES dull, dark
6 a **bright** day
fine, sunny, cloudless
✑ OPPOSITES dull

brilliant ADJECTIVE

1 a **brilliant** musician
gifted, talented, expert, skilful, exceptional, outstanding, superb
✑ OPPOSITES untalented
2 **brilliant** sunshine
sparkling, glittering, dazzling, glaring, blazing, vivid, bright, shining, glorious
✑ OPPOSITES dull, dim
3 a **brilliant** plan
clever, intelligent

◇ INFORMAL WORDS brainy
✑ OPPOSITES stupid

brim NOUN

My glass was full to the **brim**.
rim, top, limit, edge, margin, border

bring VERB

1 **Bring** a jacket in case it gets cold.
carry, fetch, take, deliver, transport
2 I'll **bring** the children later.
guide, conduct, lead, accompany, usher
◆ FORMAL WORDS escort
3 The new baby **brought** great joy to the family.
cause, produce, create
• **bring up**
She has **brought up** three children on her own.
rear, raise, foster, educate, teach, train

brink NOUN

on the **brink** of disaster
verge, edge, margin, fringe, border

brisk ADJECTIVE

a **brisk** walk
energetic, refreshing

broad ADJECTIVE

a **broad** avenue
wide, large, vast, roomy, spacious
✑ OPPOSITES narrow

broadcast¹ NOUN

listening to radio **broadcasts**
programme, show, transmission

broadcast² VERB

The concert will be **broadcast** next Friday.
air, show, transmit, televise

brochure NOUN

a holiday **brochure**
leaflet, booklet, pamphlet, catalogue

broken ADJECTIVE

The computer is **broken**.
out of order, damaged, faulty
◆ FORMAL WORDS defective
✑ OPPOSITES in working order, working

Aa
Bb
Cc
Dd
Ee
Ff
Gg
Hh
Ii
Jj
Kk
Ll
Mm
Nn
Oo
Pp
Qq
Rr
Ss
Tt
Uu
Vv
Ww
Xx
Yy
Zz

brown NOUN

Here are some shades of brown:
beige, bronze, chestnut, chocolate, fawn, sepia, tan, taupe, terracotta

bruise VERB
I bruised my knee walking into the coffee table.
hurt, injure, blacken, mark

brush VERB
1 *She brushed the floor.*
clean, sweep, polish, shine, flick
2 *Her hair brushed against his cheek.*
touch, contact, graze, stroke, rub, scrape
• **brush up**
I'm brushing up my Spanish for my holidays.
revise, improve, polish up, study, read up, swot

brutal ADJECTIVE
his brutal treatment of the dogs
cruel, heartless, harsh, rough, unfeeling, inhuman, vicious, insensitive
≠ OPPOSITES kindly

bubble VERB
The water is bubbling in the pan.
fizz, sparkle, froth, foam

bucket NOUN
a bucket of water
pail, can, scuttle

buckle¹ NOUN
a belt buckle
clasp, clip, catch, fastener

buckle² VERB
1 *Buckle your shoes.*
fasten, clasp, catch, hook, close, secure
2 *The trolley wheels had buckled.*
bend, warp, twist

bud NOUN
The buds are appearing on the trees.
shoot, sprout

budge VERB
The wardrobe was so heavy we couldn't budge it.
move, shift, dislodge, stir

budget VERB
We have budgeted for a holiday this year.
plan, estimate, allow, allocate

bug¹ NOUN
1 *a tummy bug*
virus, germ, infection, disease
2 *a computer bug*
fault, defect, flaw, error
◇ INFORMAL WORDS gremlin

bug² VERB
Their telephone was bugged.
tap, spy on, listen in on

build¹ VERB
We are building a garage.
construct, erect, raise, make, develop
≠ OPPOSITES destroy, demolish, knock down

build² NOUN
a man of muscular build
physique, shape, figure, form, body, frame

building NOUN
a beautiful Victorian building
construction, structure

Here are some types of building:
Buildings where people live:
barracks, block of flats, bungalow, cabin, castle, cottage, farmhouse, house, maisonette, mansion, palace, tower block, villa
Religious buildings:
abbey, cathedral, chapel, church, convent, gurdwara, kirk, mandir, monastery, mosque, pagoda, synagogue, temple

Buildings where people work:
factory, garage, office block, shop, store, warehouse
Other types of building:
barn, beach hut, café, cinema, college, fort, gallery, gymnasium, health centre, hospital, hotel, library, lighthouse, mill, museum, observatory, outhouse, pier, power station, prison, pub, restaurant, school, shed, skyscraper, sports centre, stable, summerhouse, theatre, university, windmill
⇒ Also look up **house**, **shop**

bulge¹ NOUN
The growing baby made a bulge in her tummy.
swelling, bump, lump

bulge² VERB
His eyes seemed to bulge in his head.
swell, puff out, stick out, expand, enlarge

bulk NOUN
We have done the bulk of the work.
majority, most

bulky ADJECTIVE
The box is too bulky to carry.
big, large, awkward, unwieldy, cumbersome

bully VERB
Nicholas was bullied at his new school because he had a different accent.
pick on, push around, intimidate, torment, terrorize

bump¹ NOUN
1 *The car hit the van with a bump.*
thump, thud, bang, blow, knock, smash, crash, jolt
2 *a bump on the head*
lump, swelling, bulge

bump² VERB
1 *I bumped my head on the door.*
hit, strike, knock, bang, crash
2 *The car was bumping along the dirt track.*

jolt, jerk, rattle, shake, bounce
• **bump into**
I bumped into Yusuf at the bowli alley.
meet, run into, come across

bumpy ADJECTIVE
1 *a bumpy road*
rough, lumpy, uneven
≠ OPPOSITES smooth, even
2 *a bumpy ride*
jerky, jolting, bouncy, choppy, rough

bunch NOUN
1 *a bunch of keys*
bundle, cluster, batch, lot, mass, number, collection
2 *a bunch of flowers*
bouquet, posy, spray
3 *a bunch of thugs*
gang, band, team

bundle NOUN
a bundle of magazines
pile, stack, heap, collection, set, bunch, batch

burden¹ NOUN
1 *The camel was carrying a heavy burden.*
cargo, load, weight
2 *She didn't want the burden of looking after her dog.*
trouble, stress, pressure, responsibi obligation, duty, strain, worry

burden² VERB
I don't want to burden you with problems.
bother, worry, saddle, weigh dov

burn VERB
1 *A fire was burning in the gra*
flame, blaze, flare, flash, glow, smoulder, smoke
2 *They burned the rubbish in garden.*
set fire to, set alight, light

burst VERB
The little girl burst her ball
puncture, tear, split, crack,

cabin NOUN
  1 *the captain's **cabin***
  berth, quarters, compartment, room
  2 *a log **cabin***
  hut, shack, lodge, chalet, cottage, shed,
  shelter

cable NOUN
  *an electric **cable***
  line, cord, wire, flex, lead

café NOUN
  *We had lunch in a small **café**.*
  coffee shop, tea room, coffee bar,
  cafeteria, snack-bar

cake¹ NOUN

Here are some types of cake:

Battenberg cake, birthday cake,
brownie, carrot cake, cheesecake,
chocolate cake, Christmas cake, coffee
cake, cream cake, cup cake, fairy
cake, fruit cake, gateau, ginger cake,
hot cross bun, muffin, sponge cake,
stollen, Victoria sponge, wedding cake

---

cake² VERB
  1 *Your boots are **caked** with mud.*
  coat, cover, plaster
  2 *The blood had begun to **cake** around
  the wound.*
  dry, harden, solidify, thicken

calculate VERB
  *Try to **calculate** how long this
  homework will take.*
  work out, figure out, estimate, count

call¹ NOUN
  *We had some **calls** to make on the way
  home.*
  visit, stop

call² VERB
  1 *He is **called** Joel.*
  name, title, entitle, christen, baptize
  2 *He **called** her name.*
  shout, yell, cry, exclaim
  3 *She **called** us all in for tea.*
  summon, invite, send for, order
  4 ***Call** me on my mobile.*
  telephone, phone, ring, ring up, contact
  • **call for**
  1 *This problem **calls for** drastic action.*
  demand, require, need, involve
  2 *My dad **called for** me at six o'clock.*
  fetch, collect, pick up
  • **call off**
  *I had to **call off** the party.*
  cancel, drop, abandon

calm ADJECTIVE
  1 *I tried to look **calm** even though I was
  nervous.*
  relaxed, cool, unemotional, untroubled,
  unflustered
  ◇ INFORMAL WORDS laid-back
  ⧧ OPPOSITES worried, anxious
  2 ***calm** weather*
  still, quiet, mild, peaceful, windless
  ⧧ OPPOSITES rough, wild, stormy

cancel VERB
  *We had to **cancel** our sports day
  because of the rain.*
  call off, abandon, drop

candidate NOUN
  *Which **candidate** will win the election?*
  applicant, contender, contestant,
  competitor

capable ADJECTIVE
  *She is a very **capable** teacher.*
  able, competent, efficient, experienced,
  skilful, gifted, talented
  ⧧ OPPOSITES incapable, incompetent,
  useless

cape NOUN
a long black cape
cloak, robe, shawl

capital NOUN
Write your name in capitals.
capital letter, block capital, block letter

capsize VERB
The canoe will capsize if you rock it too much.
overturn, turn over, keel over, upset

captivity NOUN
prisoners released from captivity
imprisonment, custody, detention, confinement
◆ FORMAL WORDS incarceration
⧧ OPPOSITES freedom

capture VERB
The police captured the criminals.
catch, seize, arrest, take, trap

car NOUN
We travel to school by car.
motor car, motor vehicle

care¹ NOUN
1 *We forgot our cares while we were on holiday.*
worry, concern, trouble, anxiety, stress, strain, pressure
2 *When the signal changes to green, cross the road with care.*
carefulness, caution, attention, consideration
⧧ OPPOSITES carelessness, thoughtlessness, neglect
3 *They left their cat in our care.*
keeping, protection, charge, guardianship, supervision

care² VERB
I don't care what happens next.
worry, mind, bother
• **care for**
1 *She cares for her elderly parents.*
look after, nurse, mind, watch over, attend to
2 *I don't care much for porridge.*

like, be fond of, be keen on, enjoy

career NOUN
a career in journalism
job, profession, trade, employment, occupation, calling

carefree ADJECTIVE
She has a very carefree attitude to life.
unworried, untroubled, unconcerned, happy-go-lucky, light-hearted, happy, easy-going
◇ INFORMAL WORDS laid back
⧧ OPPOSITES worried, anxious

careful ADJECTIVE
1 *Be careful when you are near traffic.*
cautious, wary, watchful, alert, attentive
⧧ OPPOSITES careless, thoughtless
2 *The teacher praised my careful work.*
thorough, detailed, accurate, precise
⧧ OPPOSITES careless

careless ADJECTIVE
1 *a careless remark*
thoughtless, unthinking, inconsiderate, uncaring
⧧ OPPOSITES thoughtful
2 *a careless mistake*
forgetful, irresponsible
3 *careless work*
inaccurate, messy, untidy, sloppy, slipshod, slap-dash
⧧ OPPOSITES careful, accurate

cargo NOUN
a ship carrying a cargo of bananas
load, freight, contents, goods

carnival NOUN
dancing in the streets at the carnival
festival, gala, fête, fair

carriage NOUN
a railway carriage
coach, wagon, car, vehicle

carry VERB
1 *Help me to carry the shopping into the house.*
take, bring, move, fetch, transfer, convey

Aa
Bb
Cc
Dd
Ee
Ff
Gg
Hh
Ii
Jj
Kk
Ll
Mm
Nn
Oo
Pp
Qq
Rr
Ss
Tt
Uu
Vv
Ww
Xx
Yy
Zz

2 *How many passengers can this bus carry?*
transport, take, convey

• carry on
1 *Carry on with your homework.*
continue, proceed, keep on
⧧ OPPOSITES stop, finish
2 *The noise carried on all night.*
last, keep on, persist

• carry out
We carried out the task successfully.
do, perform, fulfil, accomplish, achieve
◇ INFORMAL WORDS bring off

cartoon NOUN
1 *the new Disney cartoon*
animated film, animation
2 *a cartoon in the newspaper*
comic strip, sketch, drawing

carve VERB
1 *Who will carve the turkey?*
cut, slice, hack
2 *a figure carved out of wood*
chisel, sculpt, sculpture, shape, form

case¹ NOUN
1 *Let me carry your case.*
suitcase, bag, trunk
2 *a case of jewels*
container, crate, box, carton, chest

case² NOUN
1 *I'll let you off in this case but in future you must not be late.*
situation, event, occasion, circumstances, condition, position
2 *a severe case of appendicitis*
example, occurrence, instance
3 *a legal case*
trial, lawsuit

cash NOUN
I didn't have enough cash to pay my fare home.
money, banknotes, notes, coins, change

cast¹ NOUN
a film with a great cast
actors, players, performers

cast² VERB
1 *The children were casting stones into the river.*
throw, hurl, fling, toss
◇ INFORMAL WORDS sling
2 *a model of a dog cast in bronze*
mould, shape, form, model

castle NOUN
A grey stone castle stood on top of the hill.
stronghold, fort, fortress

Here are some parts of a castle:

arrow slit, battlements, drawbridge, dungeon, great hall, keep, kitchen, moat, parapet, portcullis, ramparts, stable, tower, well

casual ADJECTIVE
1 *casual clothes*
informal, comfortable, relaxed, leisure
⧧ OPPOSITES formal
2 *a casual attitude*
relaxed, unconcerned, indifferent, offhand
◇ INFORMAL WORDS couldn't-care-less, laid back
⧧ OPPOSITES enthusiastic
3 *casual work*
temporary, short-term, irregular, part-time
⧧ OPPOSITES permanent

cat NOUN

Here are some breeds of cat:

Abyssinian, Burmese, Himalayan, Manx, Persian, Siamese, tabby, tortoiseshell

catalogue NOUN
a catalogue of the museum's exhibits
list, brochure, directory, index, inventory, record

Aa
Bb
Cc
Dd
Ee
Ff
Gg
Hh
Ii
Jj
Kk
Ll
Mm
Nn
Oo
Pp
Qq
Rr
Ss
Tt
Uu
Vv
Ww
Xx
Yy
Zz

Aa
Bb
Cc
Dd
Ee
Ff
Gg
Hh
Ii
Jj
Kk
Ll
Mm
Nn
Oo
Pp
Qq
Rr
Ss
Tt
Uu
Vv
Ww
Xx
Yy
Zz

catastrophe NOUN

The earthquake was a catastrophe.
disaster, calamity, tragedy, blow, misfortune

catch¹ NOUN

1 *The window is fitted with a catch.*
fastener, clip, hook, clasp, latch, bolt
2 *The offer seems too good to be true – what's the catch?*
snag, disadvantage, drawback, hitch, obstacle, problem

catch² VERB

1 *Catch the rope and hang on to it!*
seize, grab, take hold of, grasp, grip, clutch
≠ OPPOSITES drop
2 *The police have caught the thieves.*
capture, trap, arrest
≠ OPPOSITES release, free
3 *We tried to catch a fish.*
capture, trap, snare, hook, net
≠ OPPOSITES release, free
4 *Did you catch what he said?*
hear, understand
≠ OPPOSITES miss
5 *The teacher caught the boys cheating.*
discover, find, find out, surprise
6 *I hardly ever catch colds.*
get, develop, go down with
• **catch up**
Try to catch up with the other runners.
draw level, gain on, overtake

catching ADJECTIVE

Is the disease catching?
infectious, contagious, transmittable

category NOUN

The entries are divided into four categories.
class, classification, group, grouping, sort, type, section, division, heading

cater VERB

Mum catered for twelve people at Christmas.
cook, provide, supply, serve

cattle NOUN

The farmer keeps cattle and sheep.
cows, bulls, oxen

cause¹ NOUN

1 *What was the cause of the argument?*
source, origin, beginning, root, basis
≠ OPPOSITES effect, result, consequence
2 *You have no cause to complain.*
reason, grounds, motive, justification
3 *The event raised money for a good cause.*
purpose, object, end, ideal, belief

cause² VERB

What caused the accident?
bring about, lead to, result in, produce, create, begin
≠ OPPOSITES stop, prevent

caution NOUN

Use caution when you cross the road.
care, carefulness, watchfulness, alertness, wariness
≠ OPPOSITES carelessness, recklessness

cautious ADJECTIVE

a cautious cyclist
careful, watchful, wary, alert, guarded, unadventurous
◇ INFORMAL WORDS cagey
≠ OPPOSITES reckless

cave NOUN

We went exploring caves at the seaside.
cavern, hole, pothole, hollow, cavity

cave in VERB

The roof of the shelter caved in.
collapse, give way, fall, slip

ceaseless ADJECTIVE

the ceaseless noise of the traffic
endless, never-ending, continuous, continual, perpetual, non-stop
≠ OPPOSITES occasional, irregular

celebrate VERB

1 *We're celebrating our grandfather's 80th birthday.*
commemorate, remember, observe, keep

2 *a concert to celebrate Mozart's life and work*
commemorate, remember, honour, praise

celebrated ADJECTIVE
the celebrated author
famous, well-known, renowned, distinguished, acclaimed
≠ OPPOSITES unknown, obscure

celebration NOUN
1 *the celebration of their first anniversary*
commemoration, observance
2 *This news calls for a celebration!*
merrymaking

☞

Here are some names of celebrations:
anniversary, Baisakhi, baptism, bar mitzvah, bat mitzvah, birthday, centenary, christening, Christmas, coming-of-age, confirmation, Diwali, Easter, Eid, feast, festival, fête, gala, graduation, Hanukkah, harvest festival, Hogmanay, Holi, homecoming, housewarming, Independence Day, jubilee, marriage, May Day, party, reception, retirement, reunion, thanksgiving, tribute, Vesak, wedding
⇒ Also look up **party**

celebrity NOUN
a nightclub where celebrities go
star, superstar, personality, name, big name, VIP
≠ OPPOSITES nobody

cemetery NOUN
the graves in the cemetery
burial-ground, graveyard, churchyard

central ADJECTIVE
1 *the central area of town*
middle, mid, inner, interior
≠ OPPOSITES outer

2 *the central part of the book's plot*
main, chief, key, principal, vital, essential, fundamental, important
≠ OPPOSITES minor

centre NOUN
1 *a bus to the city centre*
middle, mid-point, heart
≠ OPPOSITES edge
2 *Her family is the centre of her life.*
heart, core, focus

ceremony NOUN
a wedding ceremony
service, commemoration, celebration

certain ADJECTIVE
1 *I'm certain he's telling the truth.*
sure, positive, confident, convinced
≠ OPPOSITES uncertain, unsure, doubtful
2 *It's now certain that they will win.*
definite, undoubted, unquestionable, undeniable, plain, true
3 *It was certain to happen some time.*
bound, inevitable, unavoidable, fated
≠ OPPOSITES unlikely

certainly ADVERB
I will certainly come to the party.
of course, definitely, naturally, undoubtedly

certificate NOUN
a birth certificate
document, licence, authorization

chain NOUN
a chain of events
sequence, string, series, set

challenge VERB
1 *I challenged him to prove his claim.*
dare, defy
2 *pupils who try to challenge the authority of the teachers*
defy, confront, provoke, try

chance NOUN
1 *I came across this letter by chance.*
accident, coincidence, luck, fortune, fate, destiny, fluke

Aa
Bb
Cc
Dd
Ee
Ff
Gg
Hh
Ii
Jj
Kk
Ll
Mm
Nn
Oo
Pp
Qq
Rr
Ss
Tt
Uu
Vv
Ww
Xx
Yy
Zz

2 *There is a good* **chance** *that she will come.*
possibility, probability, likelihood
3 *I had no* **chance** *to warn him.*
opportunity, occasion, time

change[1] NOUN
a **change** *in the weather*
alteration, conversion, transformation, variation, shift, difference, break

change[2] VERB
1 *The witch* **changed** *the prince into a frog.*
alter, convert, transform
2 *His moods* **change** *very quickly.*
alter, vary, shift
3 *I'd like to* **change** *this book for another one.*
swap, exchange, trade, switch, substitute, replace

changeable ADJECTIVE
changeable weather
unsettled, uncertain, unpredictable, variable, shifting
(≠) OPPOSITES constant, reliable, predictable

chaos NOUN
The class was in complete **chaos**.
disorder, confusion, disorganization
(≠) OPPOSITES order

chapter NOUN
the first **chapter** *of the book*
part, section, division, stage, episode

character NOUN
1 *Jack is like his father in looks and his mother in* **character**.
personality, nature, temperament, quality, type
2 *an attempt to blacken his rival's* **character**
reputation, name
3 *Auntie Val is a bit of a* **character**.
eccentric, oddity, personality
◇ INFORMAL WORDS case
4 *the* **characters** *in a play*
person, individual, role, part

characteristic[1] NOUN
The house has several attractive **characteristics**.
feature, quality, point

characteristic[2] ADJECTIVE
the **characteristic** *features of the landscape*
typical, distinctive, individual, specific, special
(≠) OPPOSITES uncharacteristic, untypical

charge[1] NOUN
1 *There is no* **charge** *to get into the park.*
price, cost, fee, rate, payment
2 *a* **charge** *of burglary*
accusation, allegation
3 *My aunt left the dog in our* **charge** *for the afternoon.*
custody, keeping, safekeeping, guardianship

charge[2] VERB
1 *How much did they* **charge** *you for your ticket?*
ask, demand
◆ FORMAL WORDS debit
2 *He was* **charged** *with theft.*
accuse of, blame for
3 *The children* **charged** *into the classroom.*
rush, run
4 *The general ordered his men to* **charge** *the city.*
attack, storm, rush

charity NOUN
1 *She was too proud to accept* **charity**.
aid, assistance, gift, handout
2 *Show a bit of* **charity** *to people in trouble.*
kindness, generosity, compassion, humanity, goodness
(≠) OPPOSITES selfishness

charm[1] NOUN
1 *a seaside village with* **charm**
attraction, appeal, enchantment
2 *a lucky* **charm**
trinket, talisman, mascot

charm² VERB
She charms everyone she meets.
delight, please, enchant, attract
⊘ OPPOSITES repel

charming ADJECTIVE
a charming young man
delightful, enchanting, pleasant,
pleasing, lovely, appealing, sweet
⊘ OPPOSITES unattractive, repulsive

chart NOUN
a chart showing the layout of the school
diagram, table, graph, map, plan

charter VERB
1 *We chartered a bus for the trip.*
hire, rent
2 *The company has been chartered to build the new canal.*
authorize, license

chase VERB
The man chased the thief.
pursue, follow, hunt, track

chat¹ NOUN
We had a good long chat.
talk, conversation, gossip, heart-to-heart
◇ INFORMAL WORDS natter

chat² VERB
We were chatting about the party.
talk, gossip, chatter
◇ INFORMAL WORDS natter, rabbit

cheap ADJECTIVE
1 *a cheap hotel*
inexpensive, cut-price, dirt-cheap
⊘ OPPOSITES expensive, costly
2 *good quality products at a cheap price*
reasonable, bargain, reduced, budget,
economical, economy
3 *Those trousers are made of cheap material.*
inferior, second-rate, shoddy, tacky,
worthless
⊘ OPPOSITES good-quality, superior

cheat¹ NOUN
No one likes a cheat.
cheater, fraud, swindler, deceiver,
double-crosser
◇ INFORMAL WORDS con artist

cheat² VERB
1 *The old lady was cheated out of her money.*
defraud, swindle, double-cross, trick,
mislead, deceive
◇ INFORMAL WORDS con, fleece, diddle
2 *Don't even think about cheating in the game!*
not play fair

check¹ NOUN
a health check
examination, inspection, check-up,
investigation, test

check² VERB
Check your homework before you hand it in.
examine, inspect, look at, go through,
study, scrutinize

cheeky ADJECTIVE
Don't be cheeky to your parents.
impertinent, impudent, insolent,
disrespectful, forward
◇ INFORMAL WORDS saucy
⊘ OPPOSITES respectful, polite

cheer VERB
1 *The crowd cheered when the teams ran out.*
clap, applaud
⊘ OPPOSITES boo, jeer
2 *They were cheered by the good news.*
comfort, encourage
⊘ OPPOSITES discourage
• **cheer up**
We cheered up when the sun came out.
brighten up, take heart
◇ INFORMAL WORDS perk up

cheerful ADJECTIVE
Despite his problems, he is always cheerful.

Aa
Bb
Cc
Dd
Ee
Ff
Gg
Hh
Ii
Jj
Kk
Ll
Mm
Nn
Oo
Pp
Qq
Rr
Ss
Tt
Uu
Vv
Ww
Xx
Yy
Zz

happy, glad, carefree, light-hearted, cheery, jolly
≠ OPPOSITES sad, depressed

chess NOUN

Here are the names of the chess pieces:
bishop, king, knight, pawn, queen, rook

chew VERB
Always chew your food properly.
gnaw, munch, crunch
◇ INFORMAL WORDS chomp

chief[1] NOUN
1 *the chief of the tribe*
ruler, chieftain, lord, master, head, leader, governor
2 *the chief of police*
commander, captain, boss, director, manager, superintendent, superior, principal

chief[2] ADJECTIVE
1 *the chief doctor at the hospital*
leading, head, highest, supreme
≠ OPPOSITES lowest
2 *the chief cause of the problem*
main, major, key, central, principal, prime
≠ OPPOSITES minor

chiefly ADVERB
School work consists chiefly of reading and writing.
mainly, mostly, for the most part, primarily, principally

child NOUN
one adult and one child
youngster, baby, infant, toddler
♦ FORMAL WORDS minor, juvenile
◇ INFORMAL WORDS kid, nipper, tot

childhood NOUN
He spent his childhood in the country.
infancy, youth, boyhood, girlhood, schooldays

childish ADJECTIVE
His childish behaviour is very annoying.
babyish, boyish, girlish, immature
♦ FORMAL WORDS juvenile
≠ OPPOSITES mature, sensible

chill VERB
1 *Chill the fruit salad in the fridge.*
cool, ice
≠ OPPOSITES warm, heat
2 *His threats chilled us.*
frighten, terrify, dismay

chilly ADJECTIVE
1 *chilly weather*
cold, wintry, fresh
◇ INFORMAL WORDS nippy
≠ OPPOSITES warm
2 *We were put off by her chilly manner.*
cool, unfriendly, unsympathetic, unwelcoming, stony
≠ OPPOSITES friendly

chip NOUN
1 *chips in the paintwork*
notch, nick, scratch, dent
2 *wood chips*
fragment, scrap, flake, shaving

choice NOUN
1 *a really good choice of books*
selection, variety, assortment
2 *Have you made your choice for our class representative?*
selection, pick, decision
3 *I had no choice but to do as he said.*
option, alternative

choke VERB
1 *Someone tried to choke him.*
strangle
2 *The fumes from the boiler were choking her.*
suffocate, smother
3 *The thick smoke made us choke.*
cough, gasp
4 *leaves choking the gutters*
obstruct, clog, block, stop

choose VERB
1 *Choose a partner.*

pick, select, opt for, settle on, fix on, single out
2 *You can wear the casual school uniform if you **choose**.*
prefer, wish, want, desire, see fit

choosy ADJECTIVE
*a **choosy** cat that will only eat the best meat*
fussy, demanding, particular, selective, finicky
≠ OPPOSITES undemanding, easy-going

chop VERB
***Chop** the onion finely.*
cut, slice, hack, divide, split, dice

chubby ADJECTIVE
*I was quite **chubby** as a child.*
plump, podgy, tubby, round, stout, fleshy
≠ OPPOSITES slim, skinny

chuckle VERB
*children **chuckling** at the back of the class*
giggle, titter, snigger, chortle

chunk NOUN
*a **chunk** of cheese*
piece, lump, hunk, mass, wedge, block, slab

church NOUN
*My Gran goes to **church** every Sunday.*
chapel, house of God, cathedral, abbey, temple

cinema NOUN
*We're going to the **cinema**.*
pictures, picture-house, multiplex

circle NOUN
1 *a **circle** of stones*
ring, round, loop, hoop
2 ***circles** of pastry*
disc, sphere, globe, orb
3 *moving in a **circle***
cycle, turn, revolution
4 *my **circle** of friends*
group, crowd, set

circular[1] ADJECTIVE
*a **circular** piece of material*
round, ring-shaped, hoop-shaped, disc-shaped

circular[2] NOUN
*A **circular** has been sent out to parents.*
letter, announcement, notice, leaflet, pamphlet, advertisement

circulate VERB
1 *They plan to **circulate** the leaflets in schools.*
distribute, issue, pass round, publish
2 *He **circulated** rumours about his rival.*
spread, publicize

circumstances NOUN
1 *living in difficult **circumstances***
conditions, situation, state, position, lifestyle
2 *We don't know the **circumstances** of the case.*
details, facts

citizen NOUN
*the **citizens** of Exeter*
person, resident, inhabitant

civil ADJECTIVE
*He was always very **civil** to me.*
polite, well-mannered, well-bred
≠ OPPOSITES uncivil, rude

claim VERB
1 *He **claims** that he is innocent.*
state, assert, insist
◆ FORMAL WORDS hold
2 *She **claimed** the prize.*
take, collect, demand

clap VERB
1 *The audience **clapped** as he took a bow.*
applaud
2 *I **clapped** him on the back.*
slap, smack, pat, bang

clash NOUN
1 *the **clash** of the cymbals*
crash, bang, clatter, smash
2 *a **clash** between supporters of rival teams*

Aa
Bb
Cc
Dd
Ee
Ff
Gg
Hh
Ii
Jj
Kk
Ll
Mm
Nn
Oo
Pp
Qq
Rr
Ss
Tt
Uu
Vv
Ww
Xx
Yy
Zz

disagreement, argument, fight, conflict

clasp[1] NOUN

The clasp on my bag is broken.
fastener, catch, clip, buckle, hook

clasp[2] VERB

She clasped my hand as we crossed the road.
hold, grip, grasp, clutch, squeeze, press

class NOUN

1 *my class at school*
form, group, set
2 *a science class*
lesson, lecture, period, tutorial
3 *Frogs and toads belong to the same class of animals.*
category, group, type, sort, kind, set, section, division, grouping

classic ADJECTIVE

1 *a classic example of his genius*
typical, characteristic, standard, regular, usual
2 *one of the world's classic novels*
best, finest, first-rate, excellent
≠ OPPOSITES second-rate

classical ADJECTIVE

classical ballet
traditional, pure
≠ OPPOSITES modern

classify VERB

The books are classified by subject matter.
class, group, sort, arrange, grade, rank, catalogue, file

clean[1] ADJECTIVE

1 *clean clothes*
washed, laundered, spotless, unstained
≠ OPPOSITES dirty
2 *clean drinking water*
pure, fresh, purified, hygienic, sterilized

clean[2] VERB

I have to clean my bedroom.
wash, bath, rinse, wipe, sponge, scrub, mop, sweep, dust, freshen, disinfect, sterilize, clear
≠ OPPOSITES dirty

clear[1] ADJECTIVE

1 *I gave them clear instructions.*
plain, precise, unmistakable, unquestionable
≠ OPPOSITES unclear, vague, confusing
2 *It's clear that there has been a mistake.*
obvious, plain, apparent, evident
3 *You have good, clear writing.*
tidy, readable, legible
≠ OPPOSITES messy, illegible
4 *Are you clear about what to do?*
sure, certain, positive, definite
≠ OPPOSITES unsure, muddled
5 *a clear liquid*
see-through, transparent, unclouded, pure, colourless
≠ OPPOSITES cloudy
6 *a clear day*
cloudless, fine, bright, sunny
≠ OPPOSITES dull
7 *The road was clear.*
unblocked, passable, open, free, empty
≠ OPPOSITES blocked

clear[2] VERB

1 *Help me clear the weeds from the garden.*
remove, empty, get rid of, clean, tidy
2 *The janitor cleared the blocked drains.*
unblock, unclog, free
≠ OPPOSITES block
3 *The fog cleared.*
disappear, vanish, evaporate
≠ OPPOSITES appear
4 *He was cleared of the crime.*
◆ FORMAL WORDS acquit, absolve

• **clear up**
1 *Clear up the mess you've made.*
tidy, sort, rearrange, order
≠ OPPOSITES mess up
2 *We managed to clear up the confusion.*
solve, straighten out, explain, resolve

Aa Bb Cc Dd Ee Ff Gg Hh Ii Jj Kk Ll Mm Nn Oo Pp Qq Rr Ss Tt Uu Vv Ww Xx Yy Zz

clever ADJECTIVE

1 *a clever child*
intelligent, bright, smart, sensible, quick-witted, sharp, cunning
◇ INFORMAL WORDS brainy
≠ OPPOSITES foolish, stupid, senseless, ignorant
2 *a clever plan*
smart, sensible, cunning, ingenious
≠ OPPOSITES foolish, stupid, senseless
3 *He's very clever with his hands.*
able, capable, expert, gifted

client NOUN

the service we give to our clients
customer, user, buyer

climate NOUN

a country with a sunny climate
weather, temperature, environment

climax NOUN

the climax of the Olympic Games
height, high point, highlight

climb VERB

We climbed the hill.
ascend, go up, scale, mount

cling VERB

1 *The little boy clung to his mother.*
clasp, clutch, grasp, grip, embrace, hug
2 *His wet shirt was clinging to him.*
stick, adhere

clip VERB

He is clipping his toenails.
trim, cut, snip, shorten

cloak NOUN

She wore a long cloak over her dress.
cape, robe

clock NOUN

Here are some types of clock:

alarm clock, carriage clock, cuckoo clock, digital clock, grandfather clock

clog VERB

The drain was clogged up with leaves.
block, choke, jam
◇ INFORMAL WORDS bung up
≠ OPPOSITES unblock

close¹ VERB

1 *Close the gate behind you.*
shut, fasten, secure, lock, bar
≠ OPPOSITES open
2 *They closed the meeting with a speech.*
end, finish, complete, wind up
≠ OPPOSITES start

close² ADJECTIVE

1 *Our house is very close to the school.*
near, nearby, at hand, adjacent, neighbouring
≠ OPPOSITES far, distant
2 *close friends*
attached, devoted, loving, affectionate, intimate
≠ OPPOSITES unfriendly
3 *It's very close in here.*
heavy, muggy, airless, stuffy, stifling, suffocating
≠ OPPOSITES fresh, airy
4 *Pay close attention to what I say.*
careful, intense, concentrated

clothes NOUN

my best clothes
clothing, garments, wear, outfit, dress, costume, wardrobe
◇ INFORMAL WORDS gear, get-up

Here are some clothes:

Suits:
shalwar kameez, suit, trouser suit
Dresses:
dress, evening dress, kimono, pinafore, sari
Skirts:
kilt, mini skirt, sarong, skirt
Tops:
blouse, cardigan, crop top, fleece, hoodie, jersey, jumper, polo neck,

Aa
Bb
Cc
Dd
Ee
Ff
Gg
Hh
Ii
Jj
Kk
Ll
Mm
Nn
Oo
Pp
Qq
Rr
Ss
Tt
Uu
Vv
Ww
Xx
Yy
Zz

polo-shirt, pullover, shirt, sweater, sweatshirt, tank top, tee-shirt, T-shirt, tunic, turtleneck, twinset, waistcoat
Coats:
cagoule, cape, coat, duffel coat, jacket, parka, poncho, raincoat
Trousers:
Bermuda shorts, cargo pants, combat trousers, cords, denims, dungarees, flares, hipsters, hot pants, jeans, leggings, pedal-pushers, shorts, trousers
Shoes:
boots, clogs, flip-flops, sandals, shoes, slippers, walking boots, wellington boots
Sports clothes:
bathing costume, bikini, leotard, shorts, swimming costume, swimming trunks, swimsuit, tracksuit, wet suit
Clothes for sleeping in:
bed-jacket, bedsocks, nightdress, nightgown, nightshirt, pyjamas
Other kinds of clothes:
belt, bow tie, braces, burqa, earmuffs, gloves, hat, leg-warmers, mittens, niqab, scarf, shawl, socks, tie, tights, veil, yashmak

cloud¹ NOUN
a dark cloud on the horizon
haze, mist, fog

cloud² VERB
1 *The sky started to cloud over.*
dull, darken, mist, fog
⊘ OPPOSITES clear
2 *The snow clouded my vision.*
blur, dim

cloudy ADJECTIVE
1 *a cloudy day*
dull, overcast, hazy, misty, foggy, dark, sunless
⊘ OPPOSITES clear, bright, sunny, cloudless
2 *cloudy water*
milky, muddy
⊘ OPPOSITES clear

club NOUN
1 *a member of a club*
society, association, company, league, union, group, set, circle
2 *carrying a heavy club*
bat, stick, truncheon, cosh

clue NOUN
1 *The police are still searching for clues.*
evidence, lead, sign, indication, trace
2 *Can you give me a clue about how to solve this puzzle?*
hint, tip, suggestion, pointer, tip-off
3 *I haven't a clue what he's talking about.*
idea, notion, inkling

clump NOUN
a clump of grass
cluster, bundle, bunch, mass, tuft

clumsy ADJECTIVE
a clumsy girl who kept bumping into things
awkward, ungraceful, bungling, bumbling, blundering
◇ INFORMAL WORDS gawky
⊘ OPPOSITES careful, graceful

cluster NOUN
1 *a cluster of teenagers on the street corner*
bunch, group, crowd, gathering
2 *a cluster of houses at the foot of the valley*
bunch, clump, group, collection

clutch VERB
1 *a child clutching a teddy bear*
hold, clasp, grip, hang on to, grasp
2 *He clutched at the rope and held on tight.*
grab, seize, snatch, catch

clutter¹ NOUN
Tidy up the clutter in your room.
mess, litter, jumble, muddle, untidiness, disorder

clutter² VERB
a desk cluttered with rubbish
litter, scatter, mess up

coach NOUN
a football coach
trainer, instructor, tutor, teacher

coarse ADJECTIVE
a coarse surface
rough, unpolished, uneven, lumpy
⊯ OPPOSITES smooth, fine

coast NOUN
a drive down the coast
coastline, shore, beach, seaside

coat¹ NOUN
1 *The stoat's coat turns white in winter.*
fur, hair, fleece, pelt
2 *a coat of paint*
layer, coating, covering

coat² VERB
The biscuits are coated with chocolate.
cover, spread, smear, plaster, cake

coax VERB
We coaxed Yvonne to come to the cinema with us.
persuade, entice, tempt, wheedle

code NOUN
a code of conduct
rules, regulations, principles, custom, convention

coil¹ NOUN
coils of rope
curl, loop, ring, twist, spiral

coil² VERB
The snake coiled around his wrist.
wind, curl, loop, twist, twine, spiral

coincidence NOUN
By coincidence we went to the same school.
chance, accident, luck, fluke

coins NOUN
She gave the beggar some spare coins.
change, money, cash, small change, loose change, silver, copper

cold¹ ADJECTIVE
1 *a cold winter wind*
cool, chilly, raw, biting, bitter, wintry, frosty, icy, freezing
◇ INFORMAL WORDS nippy
⊯ OPPOSITES hot, warm
2 *a cold bedroom*
unheated, cool, chilled, chilly, freezing, frozen
3 *a cold look*
unfriendly, distant, standoffish, unsympathetic, unfeeling, indifferent
⊯ OPPOSITES friendly

cold² NOUN
I was numb from the cold.
coldness, chill, chilliness, coolness, iciness
⊯ OPPOSITES warmth

collaborate VERB
Pupils collaborated with teachers on the project.
work together, co-operate, join forces, team up

collapse VERB
1 *She collapsed with exhaustion.*
faint, pass out, fall down
2 *The building collapsed.*
fall, fall apart, give way, cave in, crumple

colleague NOUN
my father's colleagues at work
workmate, co-worker, team-mate, partner

collect VERB
We must collect some wood for the fire.
gather, obtain, hoard, save
⊯ OPPOSITES scatter

collection NOUN
1 *a strange collection of people*
crowd, group, gathering
2 *a collection of foreign coins*
hoard, mass, heap, pile

collide VERB
A car collided with a bus.
crash into, smash into, bump into

Aa
Bb
Cc
Dd
Ee
Ff
Gg
Hh
Ii
Jj
Kk
Ll
Mm
Nn
Oo
Pp
Qq
Rr
Ss
Tt
Uu
Vv
Ww
Xx
Yy
Zz

Aa
Bb
Cc
Dd
Ee
Ff
Gg
Hh
Ii
Jj
Kk
Ll
Mm
Nn
Oo
Pp
Qq
Rr
Ss
Tt
Uu
Vv
Ww
Xx
Yy
Zz

collision NOUN
a collision involving several vehicles
crash, bump, smash, accident
◇ INFORMAL WORDS pile-up

colossal ADJECTIVE
a colossal monument
huge, enormous, massive, gigantic, monstrous
≠ OPPOSITES tiny, minute

colour[1] NOUN
all the colours of the rainbow
hue, shade, tinge, tone, tint

Here are some colours:

amber, apricot, aquamarine, auburn, beige, black, blue, bottle-green, bronze, brown, burgundy, cerise, charcoal, cherry, chestnut, chocolate, copper, coral, cream, crimson, ebony, emerald, fawn, gold, green, grey, indigo, jade, jet, khaki, lavender, lemon, lilac, maroon, mauve, navy, ochre, orange, peach, pink, plum, purple, red, rose, rust, salmon-pink, scarlet, silver, tan, tangerine, turquoise, violet, white, yellow
⇒ Also look up **blue, brown, green, purple, red, yellow**

colour[2] VERB
You can colour the eggs with paints.
paint, dye, tint, stain, tinge

colourful ADJECTIVE
1 *colourful clothes*
multicoloured, bright, brilliant, vivid
≠ OPPOSITES colourless, drab
2 *a colourful story*
exciting, interesting, vivid, lively

colourless ADJECTIVE
a colourless liquid
clear, transparent

column NOUN
1 *a marble column*
pillar, post

2 *a column of figures*
list, line, row

comb VERB
Comb your hair.
untangle, tidy, neaten

combat NOUN
My grandfather was wounded in combat.
war, warfare, battle, fight

combine VERB
1 *Combine all the ingredients together.*
blend, mix, bind, fuse, bond
≠ OPPOSITES separate
2 *The two classes combined to work together.*
join, unite, co-operate
≠ OPPOSITES divide, separate

come VERB
1 *Come here at once.*
move towards, approach, draw near
≠ OPPOSITES go, leave
2 *Two teachers came into the room.*
reach, arrive, enter, appear
≠ OPPOSITES leave
• **come about**
How did this accident come about?
happen, occur, result, arise
• **come across**
1 *Did you come across my keys while you were tidying up?*
find, discover, notice
2 *I came across an old school friend in town.*
bump into, meet
• **come round**
She came round from the anaesthetic.
recover, wake up, come to

comfort[1] NOUN
1 *His words brought me no comfort at all.*
reassurance, encouragement, consolation, support, help, aid, ease
≠ OPPOSITES distress
2 *living in comfort*
ease, luxury, wellbeing
≠ OPPOSITES discomfort

comfort[2] VERB

Shereen's friend comforted her when she lost her cat.
console, cheer, reassure, encourage, strengthen

comfortable ADJECTIVE

a comfortable room
snug, cosy, relaxing, restful, pleasant, delightful
◇ INFORMAL WORDS comfy
⊯ OPPOSITES uncomfortable

comic ADJECTIVE

the comic antics of the clowns
funny, hilarious, comical, humorous, amusing, ridiculous, laughable
⊯ OPPOSITES tragic, serious

command NOUN

1 *The general gave the command to advance.*
order, direction, instruction
2 *He took command of the company.*
power, leadership, control, authority, rule, government, management

comment NOUN

1 *They make nasty comments behind his back.*
remark, statement
2 *The teacher wrote comments in the margin of my essay.*
note, explanation, criticism

commit VERB

1 *He has committed no crime.*
do, perform, carry out
2 *I don't want to commit myself to a definite date yet.*
promise, decide

commitment NOUN

The children made a commitment to try harder.
promise, pledge, vow, guarantee, assurance

common ADJECTIVE

1 *Tornadoes aren't very common in Britain.*
usual, frequent, commonplace
⊯ OPPOSITES uncommon, unusual, rare
2 *a common practice among teachers*
usual, routine, regular, frequent, widespread, general, standard, accepted, popular
⊯ OPPOSITES uncommon, unusual, rare
3 *He's just a common man with ordinary tastes.*
everyday, average, ordinary, plain, simple
4 *They share a common interest.*
shared, joint, mutual

commotion NOUN

a commotion out in the street
excitement, fuss, uproar, racket, rumpus, disturbance

communal ADJECTIVE

a communal hall
public, shared, joint, general, common
⊯ OPPOSITES private, personal

communicate VERB

We communicate several times a week.
talk, correspond, contact

communication NOUN

communication between teachers and parents
contact, correspondence, connection

Here are some forms of communication:

advertising, answering machine, blog, Braille, broadcasting, email, fax, intercom, Internet, leaflet, letter, loudspeaker, magazine, media, memo, mobile phone, Morse code, newspaper, note, pager, podcast, post, postcard, poster, press, radar, radio, semaphore, signing, smoke signal, SMS (short message service), speech, tannoy, telecommunications, telephone, teletext, television, text, text message, video, voicemail, walkie-talkie, webcast, website

Aa
Bb
Cc
Dd
Ee
Ff
Gg
Hh
Ii
Jj
Kk
Ll
Mm
Nn
Oo
Pp
Qq
Rr
Ss
Tt
Uu
Vv
Ww
Xx
Yy
Zz

Aa
Bb
Cc
Dd
Ee
Ff
Gg
Hh
Ii
Jj
Kk
Ll
Mm
Nn
Oo
Pp
Qq
Rr
Ss
Tt
Uu
Vv
Ww
Xx
Yy
Zz

community NOUN
people in this community
area, district, locality

compact ADJECTIVE
a compact dictionary
small, short, brief, concise
(≠) OPPOSITES large

companion NOUN
He introduced me to his companions.
friend, partner, associate, colleague

company NOUN
1 *a computer company*
firm, business, corporation, establishment, house, partnership
2 *We're having company tonight.*
guests, visitors, callers

compare VERB
1 *Compare the two pictures and note the differences.*
contrast, balance, weigh
2 *His music was compared to Bach's.*
liken
3 *My cooking can't compare with John's.*
match, equal, be as good as

compartment NOUN
a lunchbox with two compartments
section, division, area

compel VERB
We were compelled to do as he said.
force, make, oblige, pressurize, bully

compelling ADJECTIVE
a compelling argument
forceful, powerful, persuasive, convincing, irresistible
(≠) OPPOSITES weak, unconvincing

compensation NOUN
He received £3000 in compensation for the damage to his house.
repayment, refund, damages, payment
◆ FORMAL WORDS reimbursement

compete VERB
1 *Darren's mother is competing in the London Marathon.*
participate, take part, be a competitor
2 *They are competing for control of the company.*
fight, battle, struggle, contest

competition NOUN
a swimming competition
contest, match, game, event, race, championship, tournament

competitor NOUN
1 *The competitors are at the starting line.*
contestant, contender, entrant, candidate
2 *The company is doing twice as well as its main competitor.*
competition, opposition, opponent

complain VERB
We all complained when the trip was cancelled.
protest, grumble, moan, whine, groan, grouse
◇ INFORMAL WORDS gripe

complaint NOUN
1 *David's parents received complaints about his behaviour.*
protest, objection, grumble, moan, criticism, accusation
◇ INFORMAL WORDS gripe
2 *a chest complaint*
ailment, illness, sickness, disease, disorder, trouble

complete¹ ADJECTIVE
1 *a complete set of stickers*
full, entire, total, whole, intact
2 *My work isn't complete yet.*
finished, done, ended, concluded, over, accomplished
3 *I made a complete mess of my painting.*
utter, total, absolute, downright, out-and-out, thorough, perfect
(≠) OPPOSITES partial, incomplete

complete² VERB
We completed the exercise quickly.
finish, accomplish, perform, end, wind up, conclude

complex ADJECTIVE
a complex problem
complicated, elaborate, involved, difficult
≠ OPPOSITES simple, easy

complexion NOUN
a pale complexion
skin, colour, colouring

complicated ADJECTIVE
1 *a complicated pattern*
complex, elaborate, involved
≠ OPPOSITES simple
2 *a complicated puzzle*
complex, difficult, problematic, puzzling, perplexing
≠ OPPOSITES easy

complication NOUN
Complications developed after her operation.
difficulty, drawback, snag, obstacle, problem

compliment NOUN
She was showered with compliments after her performance.
praise, tribute, admiration, approval, congratulations, honour
≠ OPPOSITES insult, criticism

compose VERB
1 *What is this material composed of?*
make up, form
2 *I composed a letter to my penfriend.*
write, create, invent, make, form, construct
3 *She composed herself before going on stage.*
calm, settle, control, soothe, quiet

composition NOUN
a composition by Mozart
work, piece, study, exercise

comprehend VERB
Their reasons are difficult to comprehend.
understand, see, grasp, appreciate, fathom

compulsory ADJECTIVE
Wearing a bicycle helmet is compulsory.
required, obligatory
≠ OPPOSITES optional, voluntary

computer NOUN
the latest in computers
personal computer, PC, mainframe, desktop, laptop, microcomputer, minicomputer, notebook computer, processor, word processor

Here are some words used in computing:
Hardware:
CPU (central processing unit), disk drive, joystick, keyboard, microprocessor, modem, monitor, motherboard, mouse, mouse mat, printed circuit board, printer, scanner, screen, VDU (visual display unit)
Software:
compact disk, disk, floppy disk, hard disk, program
Memory:
CD-ROM (Compact Disc Read Only Memory), DVD-ROM (Digital Versatile Disc Read Only Memory), memory stick, RAM (Random Access Memory), ROM (Read Only Memory), storage, USB (Universal Serial Bus) flash drive
The Internet:
address, blog, bookmark, broadband, chatroom, cookie, cyberspace, data logging, download, firewall, homepage, hyperlink, hypertext, link, networking, online, podcast, pop-up, search engine, server, surf, webcam, webcast, web design, weblog, web page, website, wiki, World Wide Web
Email:
attachment, email address, emoticon, junk mail, link, spam
Other words used in computing:
backup, bit, boot, bug, byte, character, chip, clip art, conferencing, copy and paste, cursor, data, database, directory, DOS (disk

Aa
Bb
Cc
Dd
Ee
Ff
Gg
Hh
Ii
Jj
Kk
Ll
Mm
Nn
Oo
Pp
Qq
Rr
Ss
Tt
Uu
Vv
Ww
Xx
Yy
Zz

Aa
Bb
Cc
Dd
Ee
Ff
Gg
Hh
Ii
Jj
Kk
Ll
Mm
Nn
Oo
Pp
Qq
Rr
Ss
Tt
Uu
Vv
Ww
Xx
Yy
Zz

operating system), file, folder, format, function, grammar checker, graphics, icon, interface, kilobyte, macro, megabyte, menu, microchip, multimedia, network, silicon chip, spellchecker, spreadsheet, template, video game, virtual reality, virus, window, word processing, work station

conceal VERB
*I could not **conceal** my excitement.*
hide, disguise, mask, screen, veil, cloak, cover
≠ OPPOSITES reveal

concede VERB
*I have to **concede** that she was right.*
admit, confess, accept, acknowledge
≠ OPPOSITES deny

conceited ADJECTIVE
*She is **conceited** because she knows she is beautiful.*
vain, boastful, self-important, self-satisfied, smug, proud, arrogant
◇ INFORMAL WORDS bigheaded, stuck-up
≠ OPPOSITES modest, humble

concentrate VERB
*Try to **concentrate** on your work.*
pay attention, apply oneself, think, attend

concept NOUN
1 *a difficult **concept** to understand*
idea, notion, thought, theory
2 *his **concept** of himself as a musical genius*
idea, conception, image, picture

concern[1] NOUN
1 *a cause for **concern***
anxiety, worry, unease, distress, apprehension
≠ OPPOSITES joy
2 *I am grateful for your **concern**.*
consideration, attention, thoughtfulness, interest, involvement
≠ OPPOSITES indifference

3 *How he spends his money is not your **concern**.*
business, affair, problem

concern[2] VERB
1 *It **concerns** me that you are in trouble so often.*
worry, bother, trouble, disturb, upset, distress
2 *Don't interfere in things that don't **concern** you.*
involve, affect, relate to, refer to, matter to

concerned ADJECTIVE
1 ***concerned** parents*
anxious, worried, troubled, uneasy, unhappy, distressed, disturbed, bothered
≠ OPPOSITES unconcerned, indifferent
2 *All those **concerned** should stay behind after school.*
involved, affected, connected, related, interested

concerning PREPOSITION
*a letter **concerning** the new school uniform*
about, regarding, with regard to, as regards, with reference to, relating to, in the matter of

concise ADJECTIVE
*a **concise** description*
short, brief, compact
≠ OPPOSITES wordy

conclude VERB
1 *The head teacher **concluded** that he was innocent.*
judge, deduce, reckon, assume, suppose
2 *They **concluded** the meeting by three o'clock.*
end, close, finish, complete
≠ OPPOSITES start

concrete ADJECTIVE
***concrete** proof*
real, actual, definite, firm, substantial, factual, specific
≠ OPPOSITES vague

condemn VERB
He condemned the vandals who had damaged the statue.
disapprove, blame
◆ FORMAL WORDS disparage, castigate
◇ INFORMAL WORDS slam, slate
≠ OPPOSITES praise, approve

condense VERB
She condensed her essay into a single paragraph.
shorten, summarize, abridge
≠ OPPOSITES expand

condition NOUN
1 *the condition of the country*
state, circumstances, case, position, situation, predicament, plight
2 *a condition of the contract*
requirement, rule, terms, obligation, restriction
3 *a heart condition*
disorder, weakness, problem, complaint, disease
4 *He's out of condition.*
fitness, health, shape, form
5 *The house is in excellent condition for its age.*
state, shape, form

conditions NOUN
The family was living in terrible conditions.
situation, circumstances, state, surroundings, environment

conduct¹ NOUN
a gold star for good conduct
behaviour, attitude, manners, actions

conduct² VERB
1 *Who will conduct the art class?*
run, handle, manage, direct, control, organize, regulate
2 *The assistant conducted me to my seat.*
lead, guide, direct, accompany, usher, steer
◆ FORMAL WORDS escort
• **conduct yourself**
I hope you conduct yourself well in class.
behave, act

conference NOUN
a business conference
meeting, discussion, debate, consultation

confess VERB
He confessed that he had broken the window.
admit, own up, acknowledge, concede
◇ INFORMAL WORDS come clean
≠ OPPOSITES deny, conceal

confide VERB
She confided to her friends that she was scared.
admit, confess, tell, reveal, disclose
≠ OPPOSITES hide, suppress

confidence NOUN
1 *I do not have the confidence to sing in public.*
self-confidence, self-assurance, self-reliance, boldness, courage
2 *I have complete confidence in his judgement.*
faith, trust, reliance, dependence
≠ OPPOSITES distrust

confident ADJECTIVE
1 *She is a very confident performer.*
self-confident, self-assured, unselfconscious, bold, fearless, self-reliant
2 *I am confident that we can win the tournament.*
sure, certain, positive, convinced
≠ OPPOSITES doubtful

confidential ADJECTIVE
confidential information
secret, private, top-secret, restricted
≠ OPPOSITES public

confine VERB
1 *We confined ourselves to one sweet each.*
limit, restrict
2 *She was confined to her room.*
enclose, imprison, cage, shut up
≠ OPPOSITES free, release

Aa Bb Cc Dd Ee Ff Gg Hh Ii Jj Kk Ll Mm Nn Oo Pp Qq Rr Ss Tt Uu Vv Ww Xx Yy Zz

Aa
Bb
Cc
Dd
Ee
Ff
Gg
Hh
Ii
Jj
Kk
Ll
Mm
Nn
Oo
Pp
Qq
Rr
Ss
Tt
Uu
Vv
Ww
Xx
Yy
Zz

confirm VERB

1 *James confirmed that he would come to the party.*
verify, promise, guarantee
2 *The evidence confirmed her story.*
prove, back, support, reinforce, strengthen
≠ OPPOSITES disprove

confiscate VERB

The teacher confiscated their sweets.
take away, seize, take possession of, commandeer

conflict[1] NOUN

1 *There is conflict between the two gangs.*
disagreement, discord, dispute, opposition, hostility, friction, unrest
≠ OPPOSITES agreement
2 *a conflict between the two countries*
battle, war, combat, fight, feud, clash

conflict[2] VERB

His views conflict with mine.
clash, collide, disagree, contradict, oppose
≠ OPPOSITES agree

confront VERB

I confronted Noel about his rudeness.
challenge, oppose, face, defy

confuse VERB

1 *Does mathematics confuse you?*
puzzle, baffle, perplex, mystify, bewilder
≠ OPPOSITES enlighten, clarify
2 *Don't confuse the blue and the brown wires.*
muddle, mix up, mistake, jumble

congested ADJECTIVE

The roads are congested at rush hour.
crowded, jammed, blocked, packed, full, overcrowded, clogged
≠ OPPOSITES clear

congratulate VERB

I congratulated Ben on passing his exams.
praise, compliment, wish well
≠ OPPOSITES commiserate

congregate VERB

The children congregate by the school gates.
gather, come together, collect, assemble, crowd, mass
≠ OPPOSITES disperse

connect VERB

1 *We need to connect the printer to the computer.*
join, link, unite, fasten, attach
≠ OPPOSITES disconnect, cut off
2 *I always connect Florida with Disneyland.*
relate, associate

connection NOUN

I have no connection with that family.
link, association, relation, relationship

conquer VERB

He tried to conquer his fear of heights.
beat, get the better of, defeat, overcome, overpower, triumph over
≠ OPPOSITES surrender, give in

conscientious ADJECTIVE

a conscientious worker
hard-working, painstaking, thorough, particular, careful, responsible, dutiful
≠ OPPOSITES careless, irresponsible, unreliable

conscious ADJECTIVE

1 *The boy remained conscious despite the blow to his head.*
awake, wide awake
≠ OPPOSITES unconscious
2 *a conscious decision to get up earlier*
deliberate, intentional, calculated, premeditated

consent[1] NOUN

You must get your parents' consent to go on the school trip.
agreement, permission, approval, authorization
◇ INFORMAL WORDS go-ahead
≠ OPPOSITES disagreement, refusal, opposition

consent² VERB
• **consent to**
The teacher consented to my plan.
agree to, permit, allow, grant, approve
⊘ OPPOSITES refuse, oppose

consequence NOUN
Your carelessness could have had serious consequences.
result, outcome, end, effect
◆ FORMAL WORDS repercussion
⊘ OPPOSITES cause

conservation NOUN
the conservation of the rainforests
protection, preservation, maintenance, safeguarding
⊘ OPPOSITES destruction

consider VERB
1 *Consider what you want to do when you leave school.*
think about, ponder, reflect, contemplate, meditate, mull over, examine
◇ INFORMAL WORDS chew over
2 *He never considers my feelings at all.*
think about, remember, take into account
3 *I would consider it an honour to be her bridesmaid.*
regard, think, believe, judge, rate, count

considerable ADJECTIVE
1 *a considerable sum of money*
great, large, big, sizable, substantial, ample, plentiful
⊘ OPPOSITES small
2 *The new equipment has made a considerable difference.*
great, substantial, significant, marked, noticeable, noteworthy
⊘ OPPOSITES small, slight, insignificant, unremarkable

considerate ADJECTIVE
Try to be more considerate towards other people.
kind, thoughtful, caring, sensitive, tactful, discreet, unselfish

⊘ OPPOSITES inconsiderate, thoughtless, selfish

consistency NOUN
soup with the consistency of porridge
thickness, texture, density

consistent ADJECTIVE
a consistent player
steady, stable, regular, unchanging, uniform, constant
⊘ OPPOSITES irregular, erratic

consist of VERB
The meal consisted of bread, cheese and fruit.
be composed of, be made up of, contain, include

console VERB
Penny consoled her friend when she was upset.
comfort, soothe, calm, cheer, encourage
⊘ OPPOSITES upset

conspicuous ADJECTIVE
The bright pink house is very conspicuous.
noticeable, visible, obvious, apparent, marked, clear, evident, striking
⊘ OPPOSITES inconspicuous, concealed, hidden

constant ADJECTIVE
1 *constant interruptions*
continuous, continual, persistent, endless, never-ending, non-stop, unbroken
⊘ OPPOSITES variable, irregular, fitful, occasional
2 *a constant temperature*
steady, stable, unchanging, regular, uniform
⊘ OPPOSITES variable, changing, fluctuating

construct VERB
a house constructed in the 17th century
build, erect, raise, make, put together, form, create
⊘ OPPOSITES demolish, destroy

Aa
Bb
Cc
Dd
Ee
Ff
Gg
Hh
Ii
Jj
Kk
Ll
Mm
Nn
Oo
Pp
Qq
Rr
Ss
Tt
Uu
Vv
Ww
Xx
Yy
Zz

Aa
Bb
Cc
Dd
Ee
Ff
Gg
Hh
Ii
Jj
Kk
Ll
Mm
Nn
Oo
Pp
Qq
Rr
Ss
Tt
Uu
Vv
Ww
Xx
Yy
Zz

constructive ADJECTIVE
Constructive criticism can be helpful.
practical, positive, helpful, useful
≠ OPPOSITES destructive, negative, unhelpful

consult VERB
I will have to consult my parents before I say yes.
ask, refer to, question

consume VERB
My brother consumes too much junk food.
eat, drink, swallow, devour, gobble
◇ INFORMAL WORDS polish off

consumer NOUN
a group that protects consumers' rights
user, customer, buyer, purchaser, shopper

contact¹ NOUN
He's had no contact with his parents for weeks.
communication, correspondence

contact² VERB
Please contact your mother.
get in touch with, communicate with, notify, speak to, reach, approach, apply to

contain VERB
This leaflet contains all the information you need.
include, enclose, hold, comprise
≠ OPPOSITES exclude

contempt NOUN
I have nothing but contempt for bullies.
scorn, disrespect, dislike, loathing
≠ OPPOSITES admiration

content ADJECTIVE
The baby is very content in her cot.
satisfied, contented, pleased, happy
≠ OPPOSITES dissatisfied, troubled

contents NOUN
the contents of the dish
parts, elements, ingredients, content, items

contest NOUN
1 *a talent contest*
competition, game, match, tournament
2 *a contest for the leadership of the party*
fight, struggle, dispute

contestant NOUN
All contestants must answer six questions.
competitor, player, participant, entrant, candidate, contender

continual ADJECTIVE
continual interruptions
constant, frequent, repeated, regular, eternal
≠ OPPOSITES occasional, temporary

continue VERB
1 *We will continue with our lesson after lunch.*
resume, carry on, go on, proceed
≠ OPPOSITES stop
2 *They continued with their campaign until they achieved their goal.*
carry on, go on, persevere, stick at, persist
3 *The snow continued all day.*
persist, last, remain, stay
≠ OPPOSITES stop
4 *We can't continue for long without water.*
last, endure, survive

continuous ADJECTIVE
continuous noise from next door
unbroken, uninterrupted, non-stop, endless, constant, prolonged, continued
≠ OPPOSITES broken

contract¹ NOUN
a contract to play for Liverpool
agreement, commitment, deal, settlement, arrangement

contract² VERB
1 *Wood contracts when it gets cold.*
shrink, reduce, shorten, shrivel
≠ OPPOSITES expand, enlarge, lengthen
2 *Contract your muscles for three*

seconds, then relax them.
tighten, tense

contradict VERB
Ewan contradicts everything I say.
deny, challenge, oppose, dispute
≠ OPPOSITES agree, confirm

contrary ADJECTIVE
The result of the vote was contrary to all expectations.
opposite, reverse, conflicting, opposed
≠ OPPOSITES like

contrast NOUN
the contrast between him and his brother
difference, dissimilarity, distinction
≠ OPPOSITES similarity

contribute VERB
We contributed some money for our teacher's wedding present.
donate, give, provide, supply
◇ INFORMAL WORDS chip in
≠ OPPOSITES withhold

control¹ NOUN
The class will be under Mr Burns's control while their teacher is away.
charge, authority, command, government, rule, direction, management, supervision

control² VERB
1 *the man who controls the company*
lead, govern, rule, command, direct, manage, oversee, supervise, superintend, run
2 *The rocket is controlled by a computer.*
direct, manage, run, operate
3 *Try to control your temper better.*
hold back, restrain, contain, manage, handle

controversial ADJECTIVE
the controversial subject of the new motorway
disputed, debated, debatable, questionable, doubtful

controversy NOUN
the controversy about the closing of the school
disagreement, argument, dispute, quarrel, debate, discussion
≠ OPPOSITES agreement

convenient ADJECTIVE
1 *Our house is very convenient for the shops.*
handy, accessible, nearby, at hand, available
≠ OPPOSITES inconvenient
2 *a convenient gadget*
handy, useful, helpful
≠ OPPOSITES awkward
3 *I can call again at a more convenient time.*
suitable, appropriate

conventional ADJECTIVE
1 *conventional ideas about marriage*
traditional, formal, correct, proper, accepted, unoriginal, usual, customary
≠ OPPOSITES unconventional, unusual
2 *These batteries last twice as long as the conventional ones.*
standard, regular, normal, ordinary, usual, commonplace, common, run-of-the-mill

conversation NOUN
a long conversation on the phone
talk, chat, gossip, discussion, communication

convert VERB
1 *They are planning to convert the basement into a playroom.*
alter, change, turn, transform, adapt
2 *He's trying to convert me to his way of thinking.*
win over, convince, persuade

convey VERB
1 *The school bus conveys the children to school.*
carry, bear, bring, transport, fetch, move, deliver, transfer
2 *The teacher conveyed her disapproval with a look.*

Aa
Bb
Cc
Dd
Ee
Ff
Gg
Hh
Ii
Jj
Kk
Ll
Mm
Nn
Oo
Pp
Qq
Rr
Ss
Tt
Uu
Vv
Ww
Xx
Yy
Zz

Aa
Bb
Cc
Dd
Ee
Ff
Gg
Hh
Ii
Jj
Kk
Ll
Mm
Nn
Oo
Pp
Qq
Rr
Ss
Tt
Uu
Vv
Ww
Xx
Yy
Zz

communicate, tell, reveal, express, make known

convict¹ NOUN
an escaped convict
prisoner, inmate, criminal, offender

convict² VERB
He appeared in court and was convicted.
find guilty, condemn, sentence, judge

convince VERB
At first I didn't believe he was innocent, but you have convinced me.
assure, persuade, satisfy, reassure, win over, bring round

convincing ADJECTIVE
not a very convincing excuse
believable, likely, plausible, credible, persuasive
⊘ OPPOSITES unconvincing, unbelievable, implausible, not credible

cook VERB

Here are some ways of cooking food:
bake, barbecue, boil, braise, deep fry, grill, microwave, shallow fry, simmer, steam, stir-fry, toast

cool ADJECTIVE
1 *The weather has turned cool.*
chilly, fresh, breezy, cold
⊘ OPPOSITES warm, hot
2 *a cool drink*
cold, chilled, iced
⊘ OPPOSITES hot
3 *She always stays cool in a crisis.*
calm, unexcited, unemotional, relaxed
◇ INFORMAL WORDS laid back
⊘ OPPOSITES excited, angry
4 *We got a cool reception at the party.*
unfriendly, unwelcoming, cold, unenthusiastic, distant, standoffish
⊘ OPPOSITES friendly, welcoming

co-operate VERB
1 *The teachers and pupils co-operated in raising money for the school trip.*
work together, collaborate, join forces, combine
2 *He has promised to co-operate with the investigation.*
help, assist, aid, contribute, participate

cope VERB
I can't cope unless you help me.
manage, carry on, survive, get by, make do
• **cope with**
It's hard trying to cope with all this homework every night.
manage, handle, deal with, struggle with, grapple with, wrestle with

copy¹ NOUN
Is that the original painting or a copy?
duplicate, reproduction, replica, imitation, counterfeit, forgery, fake
⊘ OPPOSITES original

copy² VERB
1 *Copy these sums into your jotters.*
duplicate, reproduce
2 *Andrew made the other children laugh by copying the teachers.*
imitate, impersonate, mimic, ape

cord NOUN
a cord tied round the curtain
string, twine, rope, line, cable, flex

core NOUN
the core of the apple
heart, centre, middle

corner NOUN
1 *driving round the corner*
angle, joint, bend, turning
2 *a shady corner of the garden*
part, place, cranny, nook, recess, niche

correct¹ ADJECTIVE
1 *the correct answer*
right, accurate, precise, exact, true
⊘ OPPOSITES incorrect, wrong, inaccurate

2 *the correct way to behave*
proper, acceptable, appropriate

correct² VERB

The teacher corrected my mistakes.
put right, amend, right
◆ FORMAL WORDS rectify

correspond VERB

1 *Their answers don't correspond with ours.*
match, fit, agree, coincide, tally
2 *I corresponded with my penpal over a number of years.*
communicate, write

corrode VERB

Some acids corrode metal.
eat away, wear away, erode

corrupt ADJECTIVE

a corrupt politician
dishonest, crooked, untrustworthy
◇ INFORMAL WORDS shady
⊯ OPPOSITES honest, trustworthy

cost NOUN

the total cost of the trip
price, charge, expense, payment, rate, amount, figure, worth

costly ADJECTIVE

costly jewellery
expensive, dear, valuable, precious, priceless
◇ INFORMAL WORDS pricey

costume NOUN

Our parents made the costumes for the play.
outfit, dress, clothing, fancy dress

cosy ADJECTIVE

1 *I was very cosy under the blankets.*
snug, comfortable, warm
◇ INFORMAL WORDS comfy
⊯ OPPOSITES uncomfortable, cold
2 *a cosy little cottage*
snug, comfortable, homely, intimate, sheltered
◇ INFORMAL WORDS comfy
⊯ OPPOSITES uncomfortable

count VERB

1 *Count the number of words in your essay.*
add, total, tot up, calculate, reckon, number
2 *Your opinion doesn't count.*
be important, be significant, mean anything, carry weight
• **count on**
You can count on me to keep a secret.
depend on, rely on, trust, bank on, reckon on, expect

countless ADJECTIVE

He has changed the lives of countless people.
many, a great many, huge numbers of, innumerable

country NOUN

1 *a European country*
state, nation, kingdom, people
2 *a walk in the country*
countryside, outdoors, wilds
⊯ OPPOSITES town, city

countryside NOUN

the beauty of the countryside
country, outdoors, landscape, scenery

coupon NOUN

a coupon for a free hot dog
voucher, token, slip, ticket

courage NOUN

It took courage to admit you made a mistake.
bravery, fearlessness, nerve, daring, boldness, spirit, heroism
◇ INFORMAL WORDS guts
⊯ OPPOSITES cowardice, fear

courageous ADJECTIVE

a courageous fighter
brave, fearless, heroic, bold
⊯ OPPOSITES cowardly, afraid

course NOUN

1 *a computer course*
classes, lessons, lectures, studies

Aa Bb Cc Dd Ee Ff Gg Hh Ii Jj Kk Ll Mm Nn Oo Pp Qq Rr Ss Tt Uu Vv Ww Xx Yy Zz

Aa
Bb
Cc
Dd
Ee
Ff
Gg
Hh
Ii
Jj
Kk
Ll
Mm
Nn
Oo
Pp
Qq
Rr
Ss
Tt
Uu
Vv
Ww
Xx
Yy
Zz

2 *We continued on our course for another mile or so.*
way, path, track, road, route, trail, line, direction
3 *a course of action*
plan, schedule, programme, method

courteous ADJECTIVE
Be courteous to other people.
polite, well-mannered, considerate, respectful, gracious, obliging
⟨≠⟩ OPPOSITES rude

cover¹ NOUN
1 *Put a cover over it to keep it clean.*
coating, covering, layer, top, lid, screen
2 *the cover of the book*
front, jacket, wrapper, case
3 *We had no cover from the thunderstorm.*
shelter, refuge, protection, shield, guard, defence

cover² VERB
1 *She covered her face with a veil.*
hide, conceal, obscure, screen, mask
⟨≠⟩ OPPOSITES uncover
2 *His boots were covered with mud.*
coat, spread, plaster, cake
3 *I covered myself with a sheet.*
wrap, clothe, dress
4 *The gardener covered the young plants.*
shelter, protect, shield, guard
⟨≠⟩ OPPOSITES expose
5 *Our history lessons cover the Second World War.*
deal with, consider, examine, investigate, involve, include, contain
⟨≠⟩ OPPOSITES exclude, ignore, leave out, overlook

covering NOUN
a light covering of snow
layer, coat, coating, blanket, film, skin, crust

cowardly ADJECTIVE
He was too cowardly to own up.
fearful, scared, spineless, weak
◇ INFORMAL WORDS chicken, yellow, soft
⟨≠⟩ OPPOSITES brave, courageous, bold

cower VERB
The abandoned dog cowered in the corner.
crouch, cringe, shrink, flinch

crack¹ NOUN
1 *a crack in the mug*
break, fracture, line, flaw, chip
2 *I watched him through a crack in the door.*
split, gap, chink, crevice
3 *We heard a crack of thunder.*
explosion, burst, crash, clap
4 *a crack on the head*
blow, smack, slap
◇ INFORMAL WORDS whack

crack² VERB
The ice cracked when I stood on it.
split, fracture, break, snap

crafty ADJECTIVE
a crafty plan
sly, cunning, scheming, sharp

cram VERB
1 *He crammed his gym kit into his bag.*
stuff, jam, ram, force, press, squeeze
2 *Don't cram your mouth with food.*
stuff, overfill, pack

cramped ADJECTIVE
1 *a family of five living in a cramped flat*
crowded, packed, overcrowded, jam-packed
⟨≠⟩ OPPOSITES spacious
2 *I always feel cramped sitting in the back seat.*
uncomfortable, squashed, squeezed

crash¹ NOUN
1 *a car crash*
accident, collision, bump, smash, pile-up, wreck
2 *The plates fell to the ground with a crash.*
smash, clash, clatter, racket

crash² VERB
1 *The bike crashed into the wall.*

smash, hit, collide, knock, bump, bang
2 *The statue crashed to the ground.*
fall, topple, plunge, collapse, pitch
3 *The computer has crashed.*
fail, break down, cut out

crawl VERB
The baby crawled under the table.
creep, edge, slither, wriggle

craze NOUN
the skateboarding craze
fashion, trend, obsession, novelty,
passion, enthusiasm

crazy ADJECTIVE
1 *a crazy person*
mad, insane, daft, unbalanced, crazed
◇ INFORMAL WORDS off your head
(≠) OPPOSITES sane
2 *a crazy idea*
silly, foolish, idiotic, senseless, unwise,
ridiculous, outrageous, wild
(≠) OPPOSITES sensible
3 *crazy about computer games*
enthusiastic, passionate, mad, wild

crease¹ NOUN
There are creases in this poster.
fold, line, wrinkle, crinkle, ridge, groove

crease² VERB
Try not to crease your skirt.
wrinkle, crumple, rumple, crinkle

create VERB
1 *He has created a model of a dinosaur.*
invent, make, form, design, compose,
set up
(≠) OPPOSITES destroy
2 *The new road could create problems.*
cause, produce, bring about

creative ADJECTIVE
*Stephanie is creative and hopes to go to
art college.*
artistic, inventive, imaginative, original
(≠) OPPOSITES unimaginative

creator NOUN
the creator of The Simpsons
maker, inventor, designer, author

creature NOUN
1 *every creature on the planet*
animal, beast, bird, fish, organism,
being
2 *You are the nastiest creature I've ever
met.*
individual, person, man, woman

credit NOUN
*The whole class should share the credit
for the splendid concert.*
praise, glory, honour, recognition,
acknowledgement, thanks, fame
(≠) OPPOSITES shame

creep VERB
1 *I crept quietly upstairs.*
steal, tiptoe, sneak, slink, edge
2 *He felt something slimy creeping over
his hand.*
crawl, slither, worm, wriggle, squirm

creepy ADJECTIVE
a creepy old house
eerie, spooky, threatening, frightening,
scary, unpleasant, disturbing

crest NOUN
1 *the crest of the hill*
top, peak, head, ridge, crown
2 *a crest of feathers*
mane, plume, tuft, comb
3 *the family crest*
emblem, badge, symbol, insignia, device

crew NOUN
*I don't like you going around with that
crew.*
gang, group, band, bunch, set, mob

cricket NOUN

Here are some words used in cricket:

bail, ball, bat, batsman, boundary,
bowl, bowler, catch, century, crease,
duck, field, fielder, four, googly, in,
innings, LBW (leg before wicket),
maiden, out, over, pitch, run, six,

Aa
Bb
Cc
Dd
Ee
Ff
Gg
Hh
Ii
Jj
Kk
Ll
Mm
Nn
Oo
Pp
Qq
Rr
Ss
Tt
Uu
Vv
Ww
Xx
Yy
Zz

slip, spin, square, stump, test match, umpire, wicket, wicketkeeper

Aa
Bb
Cc
Dd
Ee
Ff
Gg
Hh
Ii
Jj
Kk
Ll
Mm
Nn
Oo
Pp
Qq
Rr
Ss
Tt
Uu
Vv
Ww
Xx
Yy
Zz

crime NOUN
1 *Murder is a very serious crime.*
offence, wrong
2 *He turned to a life of crime.*
wrongdoing, law-breaking, vice, villainy, wickedness

criminal NOUN
a convicted criminal
law-breaker, crook, offender, wrongdoer, culprit

cringe VERB
I cringed when he started to shout.
shrink, flinch, wince, cower, draw back

crisis NOUN
the refugee crisis
emergency, catastrophe, disaster, calamity

crisp ADJECTIVE
a crisp biscuit
crispy, crunchy, brittle, firm, hard, crumbly
⊭ OPPOSITES soggy, limp

critical ADJECTIVE
1 *at the critical moment*
crucial, vital, essential, all-important, urgent
⊭ OPPOSITES unimportant
2 *The doctors say he is in a critical condition.*
serious, grave, dangerous, perilous
3 *He's always making critical remarks about her appearance.*
uncomplimentary, disapproving
⊭ OPPOSITES complimentary, appreciative

criticism NOUN
Unfair criticism can be damaging to children's confidence.
condemnation, disapproval, fault-finding, blame
⊭ OPPOSITES praise

criticize VERB
The teacher criticized me for being lazy.
find fault with, condemn, blame, denounce
⊭ OPPOSITES praise

crooked ADJECTIVE
1 *a crooked nose*
bent, warped, misshapen, deformed, twisted, lopsided
⊭ OPPOSITES straight
2 *The picture is crooked.*
lopsided, uneven, tilted, slanting, angled
⊭ OPPOSITES straight
3 *He was accused of crooked business practices.*
dishonest, corrupt, illegal, unlawful, deceitful, fraudulent, shifty, underhand
◇ INFORMAL WORDS bent, shady
⊭ OPPOSITES honest

crop¹ NOUN
this year's potato crop
harvest, yield, produce, growth

crop² VERB
Jim's hair was cropped when he went into the army.
cut, shorten, shear, trim, snip, clip
• **crop up**
Let me know if any problems crop up.
occur, happen, appear, arise

cross ADJECTIVE
Children often get cross when they are tired.
irritable, annoyed, bad-tempered, grumpy, grouchy, snappy
⊭ OPPOSITES pleasant

crouch VERB
The boys crouched out of sight in the long grass.
squat, stoop, bend, hunch, duck

crowd¹ NOUN
1 *a crowd of demonstrators*
pack, group, bunch, company, mob, rabble

2 *He kicked the ball into the crowd.*
spectators, audience

crowd² VERB

1 *People crowded round the film star.*
gather, swarm, flock, surge, press
2 *Hundreds of people were crowded into the hall.*
cram, pack, bundle, herd, pile, squeeze

crowded ADJECTIVE

a crowded room
packed, full, overcrowded, busy, teeming
⊘ OPPOSITES empty, deserted, quiet

crucial ADJECTIVE

1 *a crucial point in the match*
central, important, critical
⊘ OPPOSITES unimportant, trivial
2 *crucial repair work*
urgent, vital, essential, important
⊘ OPPOSITES unimportant, trivial

crude ADJECTIVE

1 *crude materials*
raw, unprocessed, unrefined, rough, coarse
⊘ OPPOSITES refined
2 *a crude hut*
rough, primitive
3 *a crude remark*
rude, dirty, vulgar, coarse, indecent, obscene, gross
⊘ OPPOSITES polite, decent

cruel ADJECTIVE

1 *It would be cruel to invite all the children except him.*
unkind, spiteful, heartless, unfeeling, hard-hearted
⊘ OPPOSITES kind
2 *the cruel treatment of the prisoners*
ruthless, harsh, severe, vicious, savage, bloodthirsty, brutal, inhuman
⊘ OPPOSITES kind
3 *a cruel blow across the face*
vicious, cutting, painful, fierce, savage, severe

crumble VERB

1 *The ancient castle was crumbling.*
break up, decay, collapse
2 *Crumble the biscuits with a rolling pin.*
break up, crush, pound, grind, powder

crush VERB

1 *Crush one clove of garlic.*
squash, squeeze, press, break, pound, grind, crumble
2 *You have crushed your dress.*
crumple, wrinkle

cry¹ NOUN

a cry for help
shout, call, yell, scream, shriek

cry² VERB

⇒ For even more about this word, see the next page
1 *The little girl was crying because she was lost.*
weep, sob, wail, bawl, whimper, snivel, blubber
◇ INFORMAL WORDS cry your eyes out
2 *The stranded climbers cried for help.*
shout, call, exclaim, yell, scream, shriek

cuddle VERB

The little girl cuddled her teddy bear.
hug, clasp, hold, snuggle

culprit NOUN

Someone has stolen my phone and I will find the culprit.
guilty person, offender, wrongdoer, law-breaker, criminal

culture NOUN

people from different cultures
civilization, society, way of life, tradition

cunning ADJECTIVE

a cunning criminal
crafty, sly, tricky, sharp, ingenious, skilful

cure¹ NOUN

a cure for the illness
remedy, healing, treatment, medicine, therapy

cure² VERB

an operation to cure my knee injury
heal, remedy, correct, repair, mend

Aa
Bb
Cc
Dd
Ee
Ff
Gg
Hh
Ii
Jj
Kk
Ll
Mm
Nn
Oo
Pp
Qq
Rr
Ss
Tt
Uu
Vv
Ww
Xx
Yy
Zz

cry

The word **cry** tells you very little about the action. If you use a word or phrase that tells you more about the way a person cries, it is much more interesting for your reader.

If someone suddenly starts crying, you could say that they

burst into tears

If someone is crying quietly, you might say that they

weep
whimper
whine

If someone is crying loudly, you can say that they

bawl
cry their eyes out
howl
sob
wail

There are other words for **cry** that give away how you feel about the person crying.

If you use these next words, it means that the person crying is annoying you, or you feel contempt for them. It might sound a little cruel if you use these words!

blubber
snivel
turn on the waterworks

Over to you

Can you put some of these words to use? Try to replace the word **cry** in these sentences.

1 I heard my brother cry quietly on the stairs.

2 There was an awful noise as the people all cried.

3 She is always crying and it gets on my nerves.

Which of the words would not sound right in the sentences?

curious ADJECTIVE

1 *The neighbours are very **curious** about what we're up to.*
inquisitive, questioning, inquiring, interested
◇ INFORMAL WORDS nosey
≠ OPPOSITES uninterested
2 *a **curious** sight*
odd, queer, funny, strange, peculiar, extraordinary, unusual
≠ OPPOSITES ordinary, usual, normal

curl VERB

*His hair **curls** over his forehead.*
curve, loop, twist, wind, twine, coil
≠ OPPOSITES uncurl

current ADJECTIVE

1 *the **current** prime minister*
present, existing
2 *the **current** music scene*
contemporary, present-day, modern, up-to-date, up-to-the-minute, trendy
≠ OPPOSITES obsolete, old-fashioned
3 *current opinions about education*
popular, widespread, common, general, accepted

curse NOUN

*He let out a **curse** when he hit his thumb with the hammer.*
swear word, oath, obscenity

curve VERB

*A path **curves** round the hillside.*
bend, arch, turn, wind, twist

custom NOUN

*It's a local **custom** to gather in the square at New Year.*
tradition, habit, routine, practice, way

customary ADJECTIVE

*sitting at his **customary** table*
usual, normal, familiar, regular, established

customer NOUN

*The shop was full of **customers**.*
client, consumer, shopper, buyer, purchaser, regular

cut¹ NOUN

*Jamie had a deep **cut** in his finger.*
wound, nick, gash, slit, slash

cut² VERB

1 *I want to **cut** my hair.*
trim, crop, clip, snip, shave
2 *I **cut** my foot on a piece of broken glass.*
wound, pierce, nick, gash, slit, slash
3 *Cut the potatoes into small pieces.*
chop, dice, mince, divide, carve, slice
4 *The school canteen is going to **cut** its prices.*
reduce, decrease, lower

cutting NOUN

*a **cutting** from a magazine*
clipping, extract, piece

cycle NOUN

Here are some types of cycle:

bicycle, BMX bike, moped, motorcycle, mountain bike, penny farthing, racing bike, scooter, tandem, tricycle, unicycle

Aa
Bb
Cc
Dd
Ee
Ff
Gg
Hh
Ii
Jj
Kk
Ll
Mm
Nn
Oo
Pp
Qq
Rr
Ss
Tt
Uu
Vv
Ww
Xx
Yy
Zz

Dd

Aa
Bb
Cc
Dd
Ee
Ff
Gg
Hh
Ii
Jj
Kk
Ll
Mm
Nn
Oo
Pp
Qq
Rr
Ss
Tt
Uu
Vv
Ww
Xx
Yy
Zz

daft ADJECTIVE
a daft idea
silly, foolish, stupid
⊘ OPPOSITES sensible, wise

daily ADJECTIVE
their daily walk to school
regular, routine, common, everyday
⊘ OPPOSITES occasional, rare

dainty ADJECTIVE
Your sister is a dainty little girl.
delicate, elegant, fine, graceful, neat, charming
⊘ OPPOSITES clumsy, awkward

dam NOUN
A dam has been built across the river.
barrier, blockage, obstruction

damage¹ NOUN
The floods caused a lot of damage.
harm, destruction, suffering, injury, hurt, loss

damage² VERB
Our house was damaged in the explosion.
harm, injure, hurt, spoil, ruin, wreck, weaken
⊘ OPPOSITES mend, repair, fix

damp ADJECTIVE
a damp cloth
moist, wet, soggy, clammy, humid, muggy, drizzly, misty
⊘ OPPOSITES dry, arid

dampness NOUN
dampness in the air
moisture, clamminess, dankness, humidity, wet, dew, drizzle, fog, mist, vapour
⊘ OPPOSITES dryness

dance NOUN

Here are some styles of dance:

ballet, ballroom dance, barn dance, belly dance, breakdance, cancan, cha-cha, Charleston, conga, country dance, disco, flamenco, foxtrot, hip hop, hornpipe, jazz dance, jig, jive, limbo, line dance, mambo, mazurka, minuet, morris dance, paso doble, polka, quickstep, reel, rumba, salsa, samba, swing dance, tango, tap, twist, waltz

danger NOUN
1 *The climber's life was in danger.*
insecurity, precariousness, vulnerability
⊘ OPPOSITES safety, security
2 *the dangers of smoking*
risk, threat, peril, hazard, menace

dangerous ADJECTIVE
1 *a dangerous journey through the jungle*
unsafe, insecure, risky, perilous, threatening, hazardous, precarious, menacing
⊘ OPPOSITES safe, secure
2 *a dangerous illness*
critical, severe, serious, grave, nasty, alarming
⊘ OPPOSITES harmless

dangle VERB
The acrobat was dangling from a rope.
hang, droop, swing, sway, flap, trail

dare VERB
1 *I wouldn't dare ask him his age.*
risk, brave, gamble
2 *Her friends dared her to jump.*
challenge, defy, goad, provoke, taunt

daring ADJECTIVE

a daring explorer
bold, adventurous, fearless, brave,
reckless, rash, impulsive
✒ OPPOSITES cautious, timid, afraid

dark ADJECTIVE

a dark room
unlit, black, dim, shadowy, cloudy, dingy
✒ OPPOSITES light

dash¹ NOUN

1 *We made a dash for the bus.*
run, sprint, dart, bolt, rush, spurt, race
2 *lemonade with a dash of lime*
drop, pinch, touch, flavour, hint, bit, little

dash² VERB

1 *I must dash or I'll be late.*
rush, hurry, race, sprint, run, dart, bolt,
tear
2 *The waves dashed the boat against
the rocks.*
smash, strike, lash, pound, throw, crash,
hurl, fling

data NOUN

We store all our data on computer.
information, documents, facts, statistics,
figures, details

date NOUN

1 *a later date*
time, age, period, era, stage, day, year
2 *We made a date to meet next Friday.*
appointment, engagement, meeting

dawdle VERB

*Matt was dawdling along behind his
friends.*
delay, loiter, hang about, dally, trail,
potter, dilly-dally
✒ OPPOSITES hurry

dawn NOUN

1 *We got up at dawn.*
sunrise, daybreak, morning, daylight
✒ OPPOSITES dusk
2 *the dawn of a new age*
beginning, start, birth
✒ OPPOSITES end

day NOUN

1 *Mum goes to work during the day.*
daytime, daylight
✒ OPPOSITES night
2 *in the days of King Henry VIII*
age, period, time, date, era

dazed ADJECTIVE

*The blow to the head left him feeling
dazed.*
stunned, stupefied, shocked,
bewildered, confused, baffled,
dumbfounded

dazzle VERB

He dazzled the crowd with his skill.
impress, amaze, astonish, overwhelm
✒ OPPOSITES bore

dead ADJECTIVE

1 *dead on arrival at hospital*
lifeless, departed, late, gone
◆ FORMAL WORDS deceased
✒ OPPOSITES alive
2 *My fingers went dead with the
cold.*
numb, insensitive, cold
3 *I was dead on my feet after running
the marathon.*
exhausted, tired, worn out, dead-beat
✒ OPPOSITES refreshed

deaden VERB

a device to deaden the noise
reduce, dampen, mute, muffle, lessen,
suppress, stifle, smother
✒ OPPOSITES heighten

deadly ADJECTIVE

deadly poison
lethal, fatal, dangerous, murderous,
mortal
✒ OPPOSITES harmless

deafening ADJECTIVE

*The noise from the low-flying planes
was deafening.*
piercing, ear-splitting, booming,
resounding, thunderous, roaring
✒ OPPOSITES quiet

Aa
Bb
Cc
Dd
Ee
Ff
Gg
Hh
Ii
Jj
Kk
Ll
Mm
Nn
Oo
Pp
Qq
Rr
Ss
Tt
Uu
Vv
Ww
Xx
Yy
Zz

deal¹ NOUN

1 *a great **deal** of trouble*
quantity, amount, extent, degree, portion, share
2 *a better **deal***
agreement, contract, understanding, pact, bargain, buy

deal² VERB

1 *I will **deal** the cards.*
distribute, share, dole out, divide, give
2 ***dealing** in antiques*
trade, negotiate, bargain, treat

• **deal with**
1 *You have to learn to **deal with** your own problems.*
attend to, see to, manage, handle, cope with
2 *This book **deals with** birds of prey.*
treat, consider, concern

dear ADJECTIVE

1 *my **dear** friend*
loved, beloved, treasured, valued, precious, favourite, intimate, close
≠ OPPOSITES disliked, hated
2 *A taxi would be too **dear** – let's take the bus.*
expensive, high-priced, costly, overpriced
◇ INFORMAL WORDS pricey
≠ OPPOSITES cheap

death NOUN

*my grandfather's **death***
end, finish, loss, departure, fatality, passing
≠ OPPOSITES life, birth

debate¹ NOUN

*a **debate** on capital punishment*
discussion, argument, controversy, consideration, dispute

debate² VERB

1 *Every week the class **debates** an issue.*
dispute, argue, discuss
2 *I am **debating** whether to go swimming or not.*
consider, ponder, reflect, wonder, mull over

decay VERB

*Plants **decay** to form compost.*
rot, go bad, decompose, spoil, perish

deceitful ADJECTIVE

*You cannot trust someone who is **deceitful**.*
dishonest, deceiving, false, insincere, untrustworthy, two-faced, underhand, sneaky, hypocritical
≠ OPPOSITES honest, open

deceive VERB

*He had **deceived** the police about where he was going.*
mislead, cheat, betray, fool, take in, trick, hoax, double-cross
◇ INFORMAL WORDS con, take for a ride

decent ADJECTIVE

1 *I got a **decent** mark for my project.*
adequate, acceptable, satisfactory, reasonable, sufficient
2 *His behaviour is just not **decent**.*
respectable, proper, fitting, suitable, modest, appropriate, presentable, nice
≠ OPPOSITES indecent

decide VERB

*I have **decided** to join the youth club.*
choose, reach a decision, make your mind up, settle, opt

decision NOUN

*the final **decision***
result, conclusion, outcome, verdict, finding, settlement, judgement, ruling

decisive ADJECTIVE

1 *There is **decisive** evidence against the accused.*
conclusive, definite, absolute, final
≠ OPPOSITES inconclusive
2 *My mum is usually very **decisive**.*
determined, decided, positive, firm, forceful, strong-minded, resolute, strong-willed
≠ OPPOSITES indecisive, hesitant
3 *a **decisive** moment in history*

significant, critical, crucial, influential, momentous, fateful
⊈ OPPOSITES insignificant

declare VERB
The man declared his innocence.
state, claim, maintain, confess, confirm, swear, assert

decline¹ NOUN
the decline in support for the plan
decrease, fall, downturn, deterioration, lessening
⊈ OPPOSITES increase, improvement, rise

decline² VERB
1 *Her health is declining rapidly.*
worsen, decrease, dwindle, lessen, fall, sink
2 *I had to decline his invitation to the cinema.*
refuse, reject, turn down, deny

decorate VERB
1 *I like to decorate the Christmas tree.*
ornament, adorn, beautify, trim, deck, trick out
2 *We decorated the bedroom.*
paint, paper
◇ INFORMAL WORDS do up

decrease¹ NOUN
a decrease in prices
reduction, lessening, decline, dwindling, loss, cutback
⊈ OPPOSITES increase

decrease² VERB
Crime has decreased in this area.
lessen, lower, dwindle, reduce, cut down, drop, shrink, slim
⊈ OPPOSITES increase

dedicate VERB
He has dedicated his whole life to his work.
devote, commit, give over to, present, offer, sacrifice, surrender

dedicated ADJECTIVE
a dedicated United fan

devoted, committed, enthusiastic, single-minded, whole-hearted
⊈ OPPOSITES uncommitted

deed NOUN
the daring deeds of the knights of old
action, act, exploit, feat, achievement, performance

deep ADJECTIVE
1 *a deep gorge*
bottomless, fathomless, yawning
⊈ OPPOSITES shallow
2 *a deep sleep*
intense, serious, earnest, extreme
⊈ OPPOSITES light
3 *a deep voice*
low, booming, resonant
⊈ OPPOSITES high

defeat¹ NOUN
a 2-0 defeat at home
loss, conquest, beating
◇ INFORMAL WORDS thrashing
⊈ OPPOSITES win, victory

defeat² VERB
The army was defeated in the battle.
conquer, beat, overpower, overthrow
◆ FORMAL WORDS vanquish
◇ INFORMAL WORDS thrash

defect NOUN
There are defects in this program.
fault, mistake, error, imperfection, flaw, failing, inadequacy, blemish, shortcoming

defective ADJECTIVE
A defective railway track caused the accident.
faulty, imperfect, out of order, flawed, broken
⊈ OPPOSITES in order, operative

defence NOUN
1 *Some people carry a weapon for defence.*
protection, resistance, security, cover, safeguard, guard, shield, immunity
⊈ OPPOSITES attack
2 *evidence in his defence*

Aa
Bb
Cc
Dd
Ee
Ff
Gg
Hh
Ii
Jj
Kk
Ll
Mm
Nn
Oo
Pp
Qq
Rr
Ss
Tt
Uu
Vv
Ww
Xx
Yy
Zz

justification, explanation, excuse, argument, plea, pleading, alibi, case
≠ OPPOSITES accusation

defenceless ADJECTIVE
attacking a defenceless old lady
vulnerable, helpless, powerless, unprotected

defend VERB
1 *defending the borders*
protect, guard, safeguard, shelter, secure, shield, screen, cover
≠ OPPOSITES attack
2 *the lawyer defending the accused*
support, stand up for, stand by, argue for, speak up for, justify, plead
≠ OPPOSITES accuse

defiant ADJECTIVE
The boy gave his teacher a defiant stare.
challenging, aggressive, rebellious, disobedient, bold, insolent

deficiency NOUN
a deficiency of vitamin C
shortage, lack, inadequacy, scarcity, insufficiency, absence

definite ADJECTIVE
1 *a definite job offer*
certain, settled, sure, positive, fixed, decided, determined, assured, guaranteed
≠ OPPOSITES indefinite
2 *His answer was a definite 'no'.*
clear, clear-cut, exact, precise, specific, explicit, obvious, marked
≠ OPPOSITES vague

definitely ADVERB
I will definitely see you on Monday.
positively, surely, unquestionably, absolutely, certainly, categorically, undeniably, clearly, doubtless

definition NOUN
a dictionary definition
explanation, description, interpretation, clarification

defy VERB
She defied her teacher by not doing her homework.
disobey, challenge, confront, resist, dare, brave, face, repel, disregard, scorn
≠ OPPOSITES obey

degree NOUN
I agree with you to a certain degree.
extent, amount, stage, step, level, intensity, standard

delay¹ NOUN
a flight delay
postponement, hold-up, setback, pause, wait

delay² VERB
1 *I was delayed because the bus broke down.*
hold up, obstruct, check, hold back, set back, hinder, stop, halt
≠ OPPOSITES accelerate
2 *The wedding was delayed because the bride broke her leg.*
put off, postpone, suspend, hold over, stall
≠ OPPOSITES bring forward

delete VERB
I deleted the file by mistake.
erase, cross out, cross off, remove, strike
≠ OPPOSITES add, restore

deliberate ADJECTIVE
1 *a deliberate mistake*
intentional, planned, calculated, prearranged, premeditated, conscious
≠ OPPOSITES unintentional, accidental
2 *He has a very deliberate way of speaking.*
careful, unhurried, thoughtful, methodical, cautious, slow
≠ OPPOSITES hasty

delicate ADJECTIVE
1 *delicate lace*
fine, fragile, dainty, exquisite, flimsy, elegant, graceful
≠ OPPOSITES coarse, clumsy

Aa
Bb
Cc
Dd
Ee
Ff
Gg
Hh
Ii
Jj
Kk
Ll
Mm
Nn
Oo
Pp
Qq
Rr
Ss
Tt
Uu
Vv
Ww
Xx
Yy
Zz

2 *a delicate child*
frail, weak
≠ OPPOSITES healthy, robust

delicious ADJECTIVE
The food was delicious.
appetizing, tasty, scrumptious, mouth-watering

delight¹ NOUN
squeals of delight
bliss, happiness, joy, pleasure, ecstasy, enjoyment, rapture
≠ OPPOSITES disgust, displeasure

delight² VERB
The show delighted the audience.
please, charm, thrill
≠ OPPOSITES displease, disappoint

delighted ADJECTIVE
I was delighted to hear your news.
thrilled, happy, pleased, overjoyed, charmed, ecstatic
≠ OPPOSITES disappointed, dismayed

delightful ADJECTIVE
a delightful story
charming, enjoyable, pleasant, attractive, pleasing, entertaining, fascinating
≠ OPPOSITES nasty, unpleasant

deliver VERB
The postman delivered this parcel.
bring, convey, send, give, carry, supply

delivery NOUN
the delivery of letters and parcels
conveyance, transfer

demand¹ NOUN
1 *a demand for payment*
request, question, claim, order, inquiry, desire
2 *There is not much demand for bikes around here.*
need, necessity, call

demand² VERB
I demand to speak to the manager.
ask, request, call for, insist on

demanding ADJECTIVE
a demanding job as a nurse
hard, difficult, challenging, tough, exhausting, wearing, back-breaking, trying
≠ OPPOSITES easy, undemanding

demolish VERB
The old cinema has been demolished.
destroy, knock down, pull down, flatten, bulldoze, tear down
≠ OPPOSITES build, build up, construct, erect

demonstrate VERB
1 *This incident demonstrates the efficiency of the police.*
show, display, prove, indicate
2 *The first-aid instructor demonstrated the kiss of life.*
explain, describe, teach

demonstration NOUN
1 *a demonstration of how a computer works*
presentation, display, exhibition, explanation, description, test, trial
2 *an anti-war demonstration*
protest, march, rally, picket, sit-in, parade

dense ADJECTIVE
1 *a dense forest*
compact, thick, close, heavy, solid, packed, crowded
≠ OPPOSITES thin
2 *You were really dense not to realize he was joking.*
stupid, dull, slow, slow-witted
◇ INFORMAL WORDS thick, dumb
≠ OPPOSITES quick-witted, clever

dent¹ NOUN
There is a dent in the car door.
hollow, depression, dip, crater, dimple, pit

dent² VERB
A car reversed into ours and dented it.
depress, bend, push in, buckle, crumple, damage

Aa Bb Cc **Dd** Ee Ff Gg Hh Ii Jj Kk Ll Mm Nn Oo Pp Qq Rr Ss Tt Uu Vv Ww Xx Yy Zz

deny VERB

1 *Steven denied that he had lied.*
contradict, oppose, disagree, disprove
(≠) OPPOSITES admit
2 *Injury denied him the chance to play for Scotland.*
refuse, turn down, reject, withhold
(≠) OPPOSITES allow

depart VERB

1 *We depart for Paris on Sunday.*
leave, set off, set out
(≠) OPPOSITES arrive, return
2 *They departed without saying goodbye.*
withdraw, exit, make off
(≠) OPPOSITES arrive

department NOUN

the sportswear department
division, branch, section, office, unit

dependable ADJECTIVE

a very dependable friend
reliable, trustworthy, steady, trusty, responsible, faithful
(≠) OPPOSITES unreliable

depend on VERB

1 *You can depend on Ahmed to lend a hand.*
rely upon, count on, bank on, trust in, lean on, expect
2 *How well you do in your test depends on how hard you work.*
hinge on, rest on, revolve around, hang on

deposit NOUN

1 *We put down a deposit on a house.*
down payment, part payment, instalment, security, stake
2 *muddy deposits that formed the rocks*
sediment, accumulation, dregs

depressed ADJECTIVE

I felt depressed when I failed my exam.
dejected, down, low, downhearted, despondent, melancholy, sad, unhappy, discouraged
◇ INFORMAL WORDS fed up
(≠) OPPOSITES cheerful

depressing ADJECTIVE

I find that dreary music depressing.
dismal, bleak, gloomy, saddening, disheartening, sad, melancholy, sombre, discouraging, hopeless
(≠) OPPOSITES cheerful, encouraging

depression NOUN

The man went into a deep depression when he lost his job.
dejection, despair, despondency, melancholy, sadness, gloominess, glumness, hopelessness
◇ INFORMAL WORDS dumps, blues
(≠) OPPOSITES cheerfulness

deprived ADJECTIVE

children from a deprived background
poor, needy, underprivileged, disadvantaged, lacking
◆ FORMAL WORDS impoverished
(≠) OPPOSITES prosperous, rich, well-off, affluent

deputy NOUN

the deputy head teacher
representative, agent, substitute, second-in-command, surrogate, subordinate, assistant

derelict ADJECTIVE

a derelict warehouse
abandoned, neglected, deserted, desolate, dilapidated, ruined

derive VERB

They derive a lot of pleasure from their grandchildren.
gain, obtain, get, draw, extract, receive
◆ FORMAL WORDS acquire

derogatory ADJECTIVE

She made derogatory remarks about his singing.
insulting, offensive, uncomplimentary
◆ FORMAL WORDS disparaging
(≠) OPPOSITES complimentary, admiring, approving, appreciative

descend VERB

1 *descending from 30,000 feet*

Aa
Bb
Cc
Dd
Ee
Ff
Gg
Hh
Ii
Jj
Kk
Ll
Mm
Nn
Oo
Pp
Qq
Rr
Ss
Tt
Uu
Vv
Ww
Xx
Yy
Zz

drop, go down, fall, plummet, plunge, tumble, swoop, sink
⊠ OPPOSITES ascend, rise
2 *She is descended from French kings.*
originate, proceed, spring, stem

descendants NOUN
descendants of the original settlers
offspring, children, successors

descent NOUN
1 *a steep descent*
fall, drop, plunge, dip
⊠ OPPOSITES ascent, rise
2 *He is of Irish descent.*
ancestry, parentage, heredity, extraction, origin

describe VERB
Describe how you felt when you won the prize.
express, outline, explain, relate, report, portray, depict, illustrate, specify, draw

description NOUN
a good description of what he looks like
portrayal, representation, account, depiction, sketch, presentation, report, outline, explanation

descriptive ADJECTIVE
descriptive writing
expressive, graphic, vivid, colourful
⊠ OPPOSITES dull, bland, inexpressive, flat

desert VERB
He deserted his family several years ago.
abandon, leave, strand, give up, jilt, quit
⊠ OPPOSITES stand by, support

deserted ADJECTIVE
deserted streets
empty, abandoned, forsaken, desolate
⊠ OPPOSITES busy, crowded, bustling

deserve VERB
You deserve to win the cup.
be worthy of, be entitled to, merit

deserved ADJECTIVE
The award is richly deserved.
merited, earned, well-earned, rightful, just
⊠ OPPOSITES undeserved

design¹ NOUN
1 *I like the design of this uniform.*
style, shape, form, structure
2 *a design for a bicycle*
blueprint, plan, outline, sketch, draft, drawing, model
3 *a striped design*
pattern, arrangement

design² VERB
The bride designed her own dress.
create, outline, draw up

designer NOUN
a fashion designer
creator, maker, inventor, stylist

desirable ADJECTIVE
a desirable place to live
advantageous, worthwhile, advisable, appropriate, preferable, sensible, pleasing
⊠ OPPOSITES undesirable

desire¹ NOUN
a desire for lots of money
want, longing, wish, need, yearning, craving, hankering, appetite

desire² VERB
You may not get all the things you desire.
want, wish for, long for, need, crave, hunger for, yearn for, fancy, hanker after

desolate ADJECTIVE
1 *a desolate landscape*
deserted, uninhabited, abandoned, bare, bleak, gloomy, dismal, dreary, lonely, depressing
2 *I felt desolate when my friends moved away.*
depressed, despondent, melancholy, miserable, lonely, gloomy, disheartened, downcast
⊠ OPPOSITES cheerful

Aa
Bb
Cc
Dd
Ee
Ff
Gg
Hh
Ii
Jj
Kk
Ll
Mm
Nn
Oo
Pp
Qq
Rr
Ss
Tt
Uu
Vv
Ww
Xx
Yy
Zz

despair[1] NOUN
*I comforted the girl in her **despair**.*
despondency, gloom, hopelessness, desperation, misery
(≠) OPPOSITES cheerfulness

despair[2] VERB
*War makes me **despair**.*
lose heart, lose hope, give up, give in
(≠) OPPOSITES hope

despatch
⇒ see **dispatch**

desperate ADJECTIVE
1 *in **desperate** need*
hopeless, wretched, despondent
(≠) OPPOSITES hopeful
2 *a **desperate** situation*
difficult, critical, serious, severe, extreme, urgent, dangerous
3 *a **desperate** act*
reckless, rash, impetuous, daring, dangerous, risky, wild, violent, frantic
(≠) OPPOSITES cautious

despise VERB
*I **despise** people who drop litter in the street.*
detest, loathe, dislike, scorn, look down on, condemn
(≠) OPPOSITES admire

despite PREPOSITION
*The girl went into town **despite** her parents' wishes.*
in spite of, regardless of, in the face of, against, defying

destination NOUN
*We reached our **destination** safely.*
journey's end, terminus, station, stop

destined ADJECTIVE
1 *The band was **destined** to be a success.*
fated, doomed, certain, meant, intended, designed, appointed
2 *goods **destined** for the United States*
bound, directed, headed, heading

destiny NOUN
*We wondered what our **destiny** was to be.*
fate, doom, fortune, karma, lot

destroy VERB
1 *The boy **destroyed** his sister's sandcastle.*
demolish, ruin, devastate, shatter, wreck, smash
(≠) OPPOSITES build up
2 *The injury **destroyed** his career in football.*
ruin, wreck, undo, waste, smash, crush, finish
(≠) OPPOSITES create

destruction NOUN
1 *the **destruction** of the city*
ruin, devastation, shattering, crushing, wreckage, demolition
2 *the **destruction** of thousands of rare species*
extermination, extinction, slaughter, massacre, end
(≠) OPPOSITES creation

destructive ADJECTIVE
***destructive** storms*
devastating, damaging, disastrous, harmful, hurtful
(≠) OPPOSITES creative

detach VERB
***Detach** the coupon at the bottom of the page.*
cut off, pull off, tear off, disconnect, unfasten, undo, remove, separate
(≠) OPPOSITES attach, fix, connect, do up, fasten

detail NOUN
*correct in every **detail***
particular, factor, element, aspect, feature, point, ingredient, count, respect, fact

detailed ADJECTIVE
*a **detailed** description of the robber*
full, thorough, exact, specific, particular, elaborate, complex, complicated

detain VERB
*I was **detained** by a last-minute phone call.*

delay, hold up, hinder, slow, stop

detect VERB
*The device **detects** smoke in the atmosphere.*
notice, note, observe, recognize, distinguish, identify, sight, spot, spy

deter VERB
*CCTV cameras help to **deter** crime.*
discourage, put off, restrain, hinder, frighten, prevent, prohibit, stop
⊘ OPPOSITES encourage

deteriorate VERB
*The patient's condition **deteriorated**.*
worsen, decline, fail, fall off, lapse, slide, relapse, slip
◇ INFORMAL WORDS go downhill
⊘ OPPOSITES improve

determination NOUN
*He finished the marathon by sheer **determination**.*
will-power, perseverance, persistence, purpose, single-mindedness, will, insistence, dedication, drive
⊘ OPPOSITES irresolution

determined ADJECTIVE
*a **determined** attitude*
firm, strong-willed, single-minded, persevering, persistent, strong-minded, insistent, intent
⊘ OPPOSITES wavering

detest VERB
*I absolutely **detest** sewing.*
hate, loathe, dislike, despise
⊘ OPPOSITES adore, love

devastating ADJECTIVE
1 *devastating storms*
destructive, disastrous
2 *a **devastating** argument*
effective, overwhelming, stunning

develop VERB
1 *A caterpillar **develops** into a butterfly or moth.*
evolve, mature, progress, advance, expand, flourish, prosper, branch out

2 *The company has **developed** a new computer system.*
create, invent, begin, generate
3 *A problem has **developed**.*
result, come about, grow, arise, follow, happen

development NOUN
1 *the **development** of a network of stores*
growth, progress, improvement, advance, expansion, spread, maturity, refinement
2 *There has been an important new **development** in this case.*
occurrence, happening, event, change, outcome, result, phenomenon

device NOUN
*a **device** for peeling apples*
tool, implement, appliance, gadget, apparatus, utensil, instrument, machine

devious ADJECTIVE
1 *a **devious** plan*
underhand, deceitful, dishonest, scheming, insincere, calculating, cunning, sly, misleading
2 *a **devious** route*
indirect, rambling, roundabout, wandering, winding
⊘ OPPOSITES straightforward

devise VERB
*I have **devised** a plan to earn some money.*
invent, design, conceive, formulate, imagine, construct, form

devote VERB
*She **devotes** her time to working with children.*
dedicate, commit, give oneself, set aside, reserve, apply

devoted ADJECTIVE
*a **devoted** fan of the band*
dedicated, committed, loyal, faithful, loving, true, constant
⊘ OPPOSITES indifferent, disloyal

Aa
Bb
Cc
Dd
Ee
Ff
Gg
Hh
Ii
Jj
Kk
Ll
Mm
Nn
Oo
Pp
Qq
Rr
Ss
Tt
Uu
Vv
Ww
Xx
Yy
Zz

Aa
Bb
Cc
Dd
Ee
Ff
Gg
Hh
Ii
Jj
Kk
Ll
Mm
Nn
Oo
Pp
Qq
Rr
Ss
Tt
Uu
Vv
Ww
Xx
Yy
Zz

devotion NOUN

*his **devotion** to his friends*
affection, fondness, attachment, loyalty, faithfulness
⊉ OPPOSITES betrayal, disregard

devour VERB

*They **devoured** everything on the table.*
consume, guzzle, gulp, gorge, gobble
◇ INFORMAL WORDS polish off, wolf down

devout ADJECTIVE

*a **devout** Muslim*
godly, religious, saintly, holy, orthodox

diagnose VERB

*Her illness was **diagnosed** as measles.*
identify, determine, recognize, pinpoint, analyse

diagnosis NOUN

*The doctor will make a **diagnosis** after he has examined the patient.*
identification, verdict, explanation, conclusion, interpretation, analysis, opinion

diagram NOUN

*Draw a **diagram** of the machine.*
drawing, plan, sketch, illustration, picture

dial VERB

*For more information **dial** this number.*
phone, ring, call

dialogue NOUN

*the **dialogue** between the characters*
conversation, communication, talk, exchange, discussion, debate

dictate VERB

*I won't let him **dictate** what I must do.*
command, order, direct, instruct, rule

die VERB

*He **died** in a car crash.*
perish, pass away, breathe your last
⊉ OPPOSITES live

• **die away**
*The sound of their voices **died away**.*
dwindle, fade, sink, peter out, disappear, vanish, subside

• **die down**
*The teacher waited for the talking to **die down**.*
decrease, dwindle, fade, quieten, subside

• **die out**
*Many breeds of animal will **die out**.*
disappear, vanish, become extinct

diet NOUN

*a healthy **diet***
food, nutrition, nourishment, provisions, rations

differ VERB

1 *Her views **differ** from mine.*
vary, contradict, contrast
2 *We **differ** on the subject of exercise.*
disagree, argue, be at odds with, clash, quarrel, fall out
⊉ OPPOSITES agree

difference NOUN

1 *There is no **difference** between them.*
dissimilarity, discrepancy, diversity, variation, variety, distinctness, distinction, contrast
2 *The two sides have now settled their **differences**.*
disagreement, clash, dispute, controversy
⊉ OPPOSITES agreement

different ADJECTIVE

1 *My experience is very **different** from yours.*
dissimilar, unlike, contrasting, at odds, clashing, opposed
⊉ OPPOSITES similar
2 ***different** colours*
varied, various, assorted, miscellaneous, many, numerous, several, other
⊉ OPPOSITES same

difficult ADJECTIVE

1 *a **difficult** journey*
hard, laborious, demanding, strenuous, arduous, tough
⊉ OPPOSITES easy
2 *a **difficult** problem*
complex, complicated, intricate, involved,

problematical, tricky, thorny, baffling
≢ OPPOSITES straightforward
3 a *difficult* child
unmanageable, troublesome, trying, demanding, unco-operative, stubborn, obstinate, awkward
≢ OPPOSITES manageable

difficulty NOUN
1 the *difficulty* of the exam
complexity, complicatedness, trickiness
≢ OPPOSITES easiness
2 We encountered many *difficulties* on our trip.
problem, obstacle, hindrance, hurdle, complication
3 having money *difficulties*
predicament, dilemma, distress, hardship, trouble
◆ FORMAL WORDS quandary
◇ INFORMAL WORDS fix, mess, jam, spot

dig VERB
1 Workmen are *digging* a hole in the road.
excavate, burrow, mine, quarry, scoop, tunnel, pierce
2 She keeps *digging* me in the ribs.
poke, prod, jab, nudge

dignified ADJECTIVE
keeping a *dignified* silence
stately, solemn, noble, formal, distinguished, honourable
≢ OPPOSITES undignified, lowly

dignity NOUN
The freed prisoner spoke with *dignity*.
honour, nobility, self-respect, poise, respectability

dilapidated ADJECTIVE
a *dilapidated* old house
run-down, broken-down, derelict, ramshackle, in ruins

dilemma NOUN
I am in a *dilemma* over which topic to choose.
conflict, predicament, problem, difficulty, puzzle
◆ FORMAL WORDS quandary

diligent ADJECTIVE
a *diligent* worker
conscientious, hard-working, industrious, tireless
≢ OPPOSITES lazy, negligent

dilute VERB
Dilute the lemon squash with water.
water down, thin, thin out, weaken, decrease, lessen, reduce

dim ADJECTIVE
1 a *dim* light
soft, weak, feeble, dull, dusky, cloudy, shadowy, gloomy, dark
≢ OPPOSITES bright
2 a *dim* outline
indistinct, blurred, hazy, obscure, misty, unclear, foggy, fuzzy, vague, faint
≢ OPPOSITES distinct

dimensions PLURAL NOUN
the *dimensions* of the room
extent, size, measurement, measure, scope, capacity, scale, range, importance, greatness

din NOUN
a terrible *din* from upstairs
noise, row, racket, clatter, uproar, commotion, crash, outcry, shout, babble
≢ OPPOSITES silence, quiet, calm

dine VERB
We dined at eight.
eat, feast, sup, feed

dingy ADJECTIVE
dingy grey curtains
dark, drab, dull, dim, shabby, soiled, dirty, dreary, gloomy, seedy
≢ OPPOSITES bright, clean

dinosaur NOUN

Here are some types of dinosaur:

allosaurus, apatosaurus, brachiosaurus, brontosaurus, diplodocus, gigantosaurus,

Aa
Bb
Cc
Dd
Ee
Ff
Gg
Hh
Ii
Jj
Kk
Ll
Mm
Nn
Oo
Pp
Qq
Rr
Ss
Tt
Uu
Vv
Ww
Xx
Yy
Zz

pterodactyl, stegosaurus, triceratops, tyrannosaurus rex, velociraptor

dip[1] VERB

1 *He likes to dip his biscuit in his tea.*
plunge, duck, bathe, submerge
◇ INFORMAL WORDS dunk
2 *The sun dipped below the horizon.*
descend, drop, fall, sink, lower

dip[2] NOUN

1 *a dip in the road*
hollow, hole, fall, slope, lowering
2 *We're going for a quick dip.*
bathe, swim, soaking, ducking, drenching

direct[1] ADJECTIVE

1 *a direct route*
straight, through, uninterrupted
2 *a direct way of speaking*
straightforward, outspoken, blunt, frank, sincere, honest

direct[2] VERB

1 *Can you direct me to the stadium?*
guide, lead, conduct, point
2 *The police officer directed us to stay where we were.*
instruct, command, order, charge
3 *The chairman directs the company.*
control, manage, run, lead, govern, regulate, supervise

direction NOUN

The museum is in the opposite direction.
route, way, line, road

directions NOUN

Follow the directions on the packaging.
instructions, guidelines, orders, briefing, guidance, recommendations

director NOUN

the managing director of the company
manager, head, boss, chief, controller, governor, leader, organizer, supervisor

dirt NOUN

1 *covered in dirt*
filth, grime, muck
2 *digging in the dirt*
earth, soil, clay, dust, mud

dirty ADJECTIVE

dirty old jeans
filthy, grimy, grubby, mucky, soiled, unwashed, muddy, polluted, scruffy
≠ OPPOSITES clean

disability NOUN

a physical disability
handicap, inability, incapacity

disabled ADJECTIVE

a parking permit for disabled people
handicapped, incapacitated, paralysed
≠ OPPOSITES able-bodied

disadvantage NOUN

Poor eyesight is a disadvantage for many sports.
drawback, handicap, hindrance, inconvenience, snag, nuisance
≠ OPPOSITES advantage, benefit

disagree VERB

1 *We disagreed about who would win the match.*
quarrel, argue, fall out, fight, squabble, dispute
≠ OPPOSITES agree
2 *The two answers disagree.*
conflict, clash, contradict, differ
≠ OPPOSITES correspond

disagreeable ADJECTIVE

1 *a disagreeable smell*
disgusting, offensive, repulsive, obnoxious, nasty
≠ OPPOSITES agreeable
2 *a disagreeable old man*
bad-tempered, difficult, rude, irritable, cross
≠ OPPOSITES pleasant

disagreement NOUN

We had a disagreement over who should drive.

Aa
Bb
Cc
Dd
Ee
Ff
Gg
Hh
Ii
Jj
Kk
Ll
Mm
Nn
Oo
Pp
Qq
Rr
Ss
Tt
Uu
Vv
Ww
Xx
Yy
Zz

dispute, argument, quarrel, clash, falling-out, squabble
≠ OPPOSITES agreement

disappear VERB
1 *Spots will disappear gradually.*
vanish, fade, evaporate, dissolve
≠ OPPOSITES appear
2 *They disappeared as soon as the police arrived.*
go, flee, fly, escape, hide

disappointed ADJECTIVE
We were disappointed when the concert was cancelled.
let down, dissatisfied, discouraged, down-hearted, disheartened, saddened, depressed
≠ OPPOSITES pleased, satisfied

disappointment NOUN
1 *The girl couldn't hide her disappointment at losing.*
frustration, dissatisfaction, displeasure, discouragement, regret
≠ OPPOSITES pleasure, satisfaction, delight
2 *The match was a disappointment.*
failure, let-down, comedown, blow, misfortune, disaster
≠ OPPOSITES success

disapprove of VERB
My mother strongly disapproves of smoking.
condemn, take exception to, object to, dislike, reject, deplore
≠ OPPOSITES approve of

disaster NOUN
1 *Many people were killed in the disaster.*
calamity, catastrophe, misfortune, tragedy, blow, accident, act of God
2 *The party was a complete disaster.*
failure, fiasco, farce
◇ INFORMAL WORDS flop
≠ OPPOSITES success

disastrous ADJECTIVE
a disastrous event
calamitous, catastrophic, devastating, tragic, dreadful, dire, terrible, ill-fated, miserable
≠ OPPOSITES successful

discard VERB
She discarded the books she didn't want.
reject, abandon, dispose of, get rid of, dispense with, cast aside, drop, scrap
◇ INFORMAL WORDS ditch, dump

discomfort NOUN
Her headaches cause her a lot of discomfort.
pain, aches, uneasiness, trouble, distress, hardship, irritation, annoyance
≠ OPPOSITES comfort, ease

disconnect VERB
Disconnect the computer from the electricity supply.
unplug, cut off, detach, separate, unhook
≠ OPPOSITES connect, attach, plug in, hook up

discount NOUN
Employees of the firm get a staff discount.
reduction, allowance, cut, concession

discourage VERB
1 *Andrew felt discouraged by his exam results.*
dishearten, depress, demoralize, dismay, disappoint
2 *A large dog will discourage burglars.*
put off, hinder, deter, dissuade, prevent
≠ OPPOSITES encourage

discover VERB
1 *The explorers discovered a hidden valley.*
find, uncover, dig up, reveal, locate
≠ OPPOSITES miss
2 *The police are determined to discover the truth.*
find out, learn, recognize, see, spot, detect
≠ OPPOSITES conceal, cover up

Aa
Bb
Cc
Dd
Ee
Ff
Gg
Hh
Ii
Jj
Kk
Ll
Mm
Nn
Oo
Pp
Qq
Rr
Ss
Tt
Uu
Vv
Ww
Xx
Yy
Zz

Aa
Bb
Cc
Dd
Ee
Ff
Gg
Hh
Ii
Jj
Kk
Ll
Mm
Nn
Oo
Pp
Qq
Rr
Ss
Tt
Uu
Vv
Ww
Xx
Yy
Zz

discovery NOUN
a new scientific discovery
breakthrough, find, invention

discreet ADJECTIVE
I am very discreet and can keep a secret.
tactful, careful, cautious, delicate, reserved
(≠) OPPOSITES tactless, indiscreet

discrimination NOUN
racial discrimination
bias, prejudice, intolerance, unfairness, bigotry, favouritism

discuss VERB
We discussed where to go on holiday.
debate, talk about, argue, consider, examine

discussion NOUN
a political discussion
debate, conference, argument, conversation, consultation, consideration

disease NOUN
heart disease
illness, sickness, complaint, disorder, ailment, condition, affliction, infection
(≠) OPPOSITES health

disgrace NOUN
His crimes have brought disgrace to his family.
shame, dishonour, humiliation, discredit, scandal
(≠) OPPOSITES honour, esteem

disguise¹ NOUN
The prince travelled in disguise.
concealment, camouflage, cover, costume

disguise² VERB
1 *He was disguised as a beggar.*
conceal, cover, mask, hide, dress up
(≠) OPPOSITES reveal, expose
2 *They tried to disguise the truth.*
misrepresent, conceal, fake, fudge

disgust¹ NOUN
They walked out of the cinema in disgust.
revulsion, distaste, nausea, repulsion, loathing, detestation, hatred

disgust² VERB
His behaviour disgusted me.
offend, displease, nauseate, revolt, sicken, repel, outrage, put off
(≠) OPPOSITES delight, please

disgusting ADJECTIVE
disgusting habits
nasty, revolting, sickening, nauseating, offensive, objectionable, repugnant, repellent, unappetizing
(≠) OPPOSITES delightful, pleasant

dish NOUN
1 *a pile of dirty dishes*
plate, bowl, platter
2 *an Italian dish*
meal, food, recipe

dishonest ADJECTIVE
He had been dishonest about where he got the money.
untruthful, deceitful, false, lying, deceptive, cheating, crooked, shady, corrupt, disreputable
(≠) OPPOSITES honest, trustworthy

disintegrate VERB
The old paper disintegrated when I picked it up.
break up, decompose, fall apart, crumble, rot, separate, splinter

dislike VERB
He dislikes my friends.
hate, object to, disapprove of, despise
(≠) OPPOSITES like, favour

dismal ADJECTIVE
dismal weather
dreary, gloomy, depressing, bleak, dull, drab, melancholy, sorrowful
(≠) OPPOSITES cheerful, bright

dismantle VERB
The wardrobe can be dismantled so that it can be moved.

demolish, take apart, disassemble, strip
≠ OPPOSITES assemble, put together

dismay NOUN
*I read with **dismay** about the disaster.*
alarm, distress, apprehension, dread,
fear, discouragement, disappointment
≠ OPPOSITES encouragement,
reassurance

dismiss VERB
1 *She was **dismissed** from her job.*
sack, make redundant, lay off, fire
≠ OPPOSITES appoint
2 ***Dismiss** that idea from your mind.*
discount, disregard, reject, banish
≠ OPPOSITES retain, accept

disobey VERB
*She was punished for **disobeying** the
teacher.*
defy, rebel against, resist, disregard
≠ OPPOSITES obey, heed

disorder NOUN
1 *The room was in a state of complete
disorder.*
confusion, chaos, muddle, mess,
untidiness, shambles, disorganization
≠ OPPOSITES neatness, order
2 *The hooligans were charged with
public **disorder**.*
disturbance, riot, confusion,
commotion, uproar, brawl, fight,
quarrel
≠ OPPOSITES law and order, peace
3 *a stomach **disorder***
illness, complaint, sickness, condition

dispatch VERB
*Your order was **dispatched** on Monday.*
send, transmit, forward
≠ OPPOSITES receive

disperse VERB
1 *The crowd **dispersed** at the end of the
game.*
scatter, spread, break up, separate
≠ OPPOSITES gather
2 *The police **dispersed** the protesters.*
scatter, break up, dismiss, separate
≠ OPPOSITES gather

display¹ NOUN
*a **display** of paintings*
show, exhibition, demonstration,
presentation, parade

display² VERB
1 *The shop **displays** its goods in the
window.*
show, present, demonstrate, exhibit
≠ OPPOSITES conceal
2 *They **displayed** pride in their
daughter's achievements.*
betray, show, expose
≠ OPPOSITES disguise

dispose of VERB
***Dispose of** your litter in the bin.*
throw away, get rid of, discard, scrap
◇ INFORMAL WORDS dump
≠ OPPOSITES keep

dispute¹ NOUN
*a **dispute** between the two countries*
argument, debate, disagreement,
quarrel, feud, squabble
≠ OPPOSITES agreement

dispute² VERB
*I am not **disputing** that I made a mistake.*
argue about, question, challenge,
doubt, call into question
≠ OPPOSITES agree, confirm

disregard VERB
*You **disregarded** all my warnings.*
ignore, overlook, neglect, pass over
≠ OPPOSITES pay attention to

disrespectful ADJECTIVE
*his **disrespectful** behaviour towards the
teacher*
rude, impolite, impertinent, insolent,
cheeky
≠ OPPOSITES respectful, polite

disrupt VERB
*Some hecklers **disrupted** the meeting.*
disturb, interrupt, confuse, unsettle, upset

dissolve VERB
*The sugar **dissolved** in the hot tea.*
melt, disintegrate, soften

Aa
Bb
Cc
Dd
Ee
Ff
Gg
Hh
Ii
Jj
Kk
Ll
Mm
Nn
Oo
Pp
Qq
Rr
Ss
Tt
Uu
Vv
Ww
Xx
Yy
Zz

Aa
Bb
Cc
Dd
Ee
Ff
Gg
Hh
Ii
Jj
Kk
Ll
Mm
Nn
Oo
Pp
Qq
Rr
Ss
Tt
Uu
Vv
Ww
Xx
Yy
Zz

dissuade VERB
I tried to dissuade him from driving home in the snow.
deter, discourage, put off
≠ OPPOSITES persuade

distance NOUN
the distance between our house and the school
space, interval, gap, extent, range, reach, length, width
≠ OPPOSITES closeness

distant ADJECTIVE
1 *distant stars*
far, faraway, out-of-the-way, remote
≠ OPPOSITES close
2 *He is a little distant with strangers.*
cool, reserved, standoffish, formal, cold, unfriendly
≠ OPPOSITES approachable

distinct ADJECTIVE
1 *two distinct languages*
separate, different, individual
2 *a distinct lack of enthusiasm*
clear, plain, evident, obvious, apparent, marked, definite, noticeable, recognizable
≠ OPPOSITES indistinct, vague

distinction NOUN
1 *the distinction between right and wrong*
difference, discrimination, separation, contrast
2 *a writer of distinction*
worth, importance, excellence, greatness, fame, celebrity, reputation, superiority
≠ OPPOSITES unimportance

distinctive ADJECTIVE
the distinctive smell of her perfume
characteristic, individual, different, unique, special, original, extraordinary
≠ OPPOSITES ordinary, common

distinguish VERB
1 *I can't distinguish one twin from the other.*
tell apart, tell the difference between, differentiate

2 *It was difficult to distinguish his features in the dark.*
identify, make out, recognize, see

distort VERB
1 *Anger distorted his features.*
deform, bend, misshape, twist, warp
2 *The report distorted the facts.*
falsify, slant, twist

distract VERB
Sam is easily distracted from his homework.
divert, sidetrack, disturb

distress[1] NOUN
The boy's disappearance had caused his parents distress.
grief, misery, sorrow, suffering, sadness, worry, anxiety, pain, agony
≠ OPPOSITES contentment

distress[2] VERB
I didn't mean to distress you.
upset, disturb, trouble, sadden, worry, torment, harass, bother
≠ OPPOSITES comfort

distribute VERB
1 *The food was distributed equally among us.*
allocate, dish out, share, deal, divide
2 *We distributed leaflets round the houses.*
deliver, hand out, spread, circulate
≠ OPPOSITES collect

district NOUN
We have just moved to this district.
region, area, neighbourhood, community

distrust VERB
The teacher distrusted the boy as he had lied before.
mistrust, doubt, disbelieve, suspect, question
≠ OPPOSITES trust

disturb VERB
1 *The children disturbed their father's nap.*
disrupt, interrupt, distract

2 *I was disturbed by the reports on the famine.*
upset, distress, worry, trouble, annoy, bother
≠ OPPOSITES reassure
3 *Please don't disturb my jigsaw puzzle.*
disarrange, confuse, jumble, upset
◇ INFORMAL WORDS mess up
≠ OPPOSITES order

dive VERB
The boy dived into the pool.
plunge, plummet, jump, leap

diverse ADJECTIVE
a diverse CD collection
various, varied, varying, different, assorted, miscellaneous
≠ OPPOSITES similar, identical

divert VERB
Traffic has been diverted to avoid the accident.
redirect, reroute, switch

divide VERB
1 *Divide the orange into segments.*
split, separate, part, cut, break up
≠ OPPOSITES join
2 *Divide the money equally among all the children.*
distribute, share, deal out
≠ OPPOSITES collect

division NOUN
1 *the division of cells*
separation, detaching, parting, splitting
≠ OPPOSITES union
2 *a division in the group*
split, disagreement, feud
3 *the sales division*
section, part, department, branch
≠ OPPOSITES whole

dizzy ADJECTIVE
It was so hot that I began to feel dizzy.
giddy, faint, light-headed, shaky
◇ INFORMAL WORDS woozy

do VERB
1 *Have you done your homework?*

perform, carry out, complete, conclude, end, finish
2 *I didn't know what to do when I lost my purse.*
behave, act
3 *I'll do the washing-up.*
deal with, manage, look after, fix, prepare, organize, arrange, produce, see to
4 *A sandwich will do fine, thanks.*
suffice, satisfy
• do away with
I think we should do away with school uniform.
get rid of, dispose of, abolish, discontinue, remove, destroy, discard
• do up
1 *Do up your laces.*
fasten, tie, lace
2 *My bedroom has been done up.*
renovate, decorate, modernize, repair

dock VERB
The ship docked at Southampton.
anchor, moor, drop anchor, land, tie up

document NOUN
Copy the document onto your memory stick.
paper, certificate, record, report, form

dodge VERB
I dodged the snowball that the boy threw.
avoid, swerve, side-step

dog NOUN

Here are some breeds of dog:

Afghan hound, Airedale, alsatian, basset-hound, beagle, Border collie, borzoi, boxer, bulldog, bull-mastiff, bull terrier, cairn terrier, chihuahua, chow, cocker spaniel, collie, corgi, dachshund, Dalmatian, Doberman pinscher, foxhound, fox terrier, German shepherd, golden retriever, Great Dane, greyhound, husky,

Aa
Bb
Cc
Dd
Ee
Ff
Gg
Hh
Ii
Jj
Kk
Ll
Mm
Nn
Oo
Pp
Qq
Rr
Ss
Tt
Uu
Vv
Ww
Xx
Yy
Zz

Irish wolfhound, Jack Russell, King Charles spaniel, Labrador, Old English sheepdog, Pekinese, pit bull terrier, pointer, poodle, pug, red setter, Rottweiler, Scottish terrier, setter, sheepdog, shih tzu, springer spaniel, St Bernard, terrier, West Highland terrier, whippet, wolfhound, Yorkshire terrier

domestic ADJECTIVE

1 *domestic chores*
home, family, household, homely
2 *domestic animals*
house-trained, tame, pet

dominant ADJECTIVE

1 *a dominant leader*
controlling, governing, ruling, powerful, influential
2 *the dominant feature of the picture*
principal, main, outstanding, chief, important

dominate VERB

This band has dominated the charts this year.
lead, control, rule, direct

donate VERB

He regularly donates money to charity.
give, contribute, present
≠ OPPOSITES receive

donation NOUN

Please make a donation to the school fund.
gift, present, offering, contribution

done ADJECTIVE

1 *The job's done.*
finished, over, completed, ended, settled
2 *The turkey is done.*
cooked, ready, roasted

donor NOUN

a blood donor
giver, contributor, provider
≠ OPPOSITES beneficiary

doomed ADJECTIVE

Their plan was doomed from the start.
condemned, damned, fated, ill-fated, cursed

dot NOUN

Join the dots to make a picture.
point, spot, speck, mark, fleck, pin-point

double¹ ADJECTIVE

double doors
dual, twofold, twice, duplicate, twin, paired, doubled, coupled
≠ OPPOSITES single, half

double² NOUN

You are the double of your father.
twin, duplicate, copy, clone, replica, lookalike, spitting image, image

doubt¹ NOUN

1 *I have doubts about his trustworthiness.*
distrust, suspicion, mistrust, reservation, apprehension, hesitation
≠ OPPOSITES trust, faith
2 *There is no doubt about what we have to do.*
uncertainty, indecision, confusion
≠ OPPOSITES certainty, belief

doubt² VERB

1 *I doubt his reasons for coming.*
distrust, mistrust, query, question, suspect, fear
≠ OPPOSITES believe, trust
2 *I don't doubt that he has ability.*
be uncertain, be dubious, hesitate

doubtful ADJECTIVE

1 *I am doubtful about his ability.*
uncertain, unsure, undecided, suspicious
≠ OPPOSITES certain, decided
2 *a poem of doubtful origin*
unclear, vague, obscure, debatable, dubious, questionable
≠ OPPOSITES definite, settled

doze VERB

The cat dozed by the fire.
snooze, sleep

• doze off

I dozed off at my desk today.
fall asleep
◇ INFORMAL WORDS nod off, drop off

drab ADJECTIVE

She was wearing a drab grey dress.
dull, dingy, dreary, dismal, gloomy, grey, shabby
⊯ OPPOSITES bright, cheerful

draft[1] NOUN

a rough draft of a story
outline, sketch, plan, rough

draft[2] VERB

I have drafted a letter.
draw up, outline, write, sketch, plan, design, compose

drag VERB

1 *I dragged the box into the other room.*
draw, pull, haul, lug, tug, trail, tow
2 *Time drags when you are bored.*
go slowly, creep, crawl

drain[1] NOUN

The workmen are digging up the drains.
sewer, pipe, ditch, outlet, trench, channel

drain[2] VERB

1 *I drained the water from the pasta.*
empty, remove, strain, dry, milk, bleed
⊯ OPPOSITES fill
2 *The water drained out of the sink.*
discharge, trickle, flow out, leak, ooze
3 *The hot sun drained my energy.*
exhaust, consume, sap, use up

drama NOUN

Her life is full of drama.
excitement, crisis, turmoil

dramatic ADJECTIVE

Last night's episode was very dramatic.
exciting, striking, stirring, thrilling, impressive

drastic ADJECTIVE

a drastic change
extreme, radical, strong, forceful, severe, harsh, desperate
⊯ OPPOSITES moderate, cautious

draught NOUN

There is a draught from the window.
current, flow, puff

draw VERB

1 *The circus drew a huge crowd.*
attract, entice, bring in
⊯ OPPOSITES repel
2 *a caravan drawn by two horses*
pull, drag, haul, tow, tug
⊯ OPPOSITES push
3 *She drew a picture of a tiger.*
sketch, trace, design
4 *The teams drew.*
tie, be equal, be even
• draw up
A car drew up outside.
pull up, stop, halt

drawback NOUN

The main drawback of the house is that it has no garage.
disadvantage, snag, hitch, obstacle, hindrance, flaw, fault, catch
⊯ OPPOSITES advantage, benefit

dreadful ADJECTIVE

I got a dreadful fright.
awful, terrible, frightful, horrible, dire, shocking, ghastly, tragic, hideous, tremendous
⊯ OPPOSITES wonderful, comforting

dream[1] NOUN

1 *I had a strange dream last night.*
vision, nightmare
2 *my dream of being a footballer*
aim, hope, wish, goal, ambition, aspiration

dream[2] VERB

He dreams of becoming a rock star.
imagine, fancy, fantasize, daydream
• dream up
Who could dream up a story like that?

Aa
Bb
Cc
Dd
Ee
Ff
Gg
Hh
Ii
Jj
Kk
Ll
Mm
Nn
Oo
Pp
Qq
Rr
Ss
Tt
Uu
Vv
Ww
Xx
Yy
Zz

think up, invent, imagine, devise, conceive

dreary ADJECTIVE
a **dreary** life
boring, uneventful, dull, colourless, lifeless, gloomy, drab, dismal, bleak
⊘ OPPOSITES interesting

dress VERB
1 She **dressed** her baby in dungarees.
clothe, put on, wear
⊘ OPPOSITES strip, undress
2 The doctor **dressed** the cut in my finger.
bandage, tend, treat
3 I helped to **dress** the Christmas tree.
decorate, trim, adorn

drift¹ NOUN
1 a snow **drift**
mound, pile, bank, mass, heap
2 Do you catch my **drift**?
meaning, intention, significance, aim

drift² VERB
1 A raft **drifted** past.
float, wander, waft, stray, coast
2 The snow **drifted** against the garage.
gather, pile up, drive

drill VERB
He **drilled** a hole in the wall.
bore, pierce, penetrate, puncture

drink¹ NOUN
a **cool** drink
liquid, beverage, refreshment

👉
Here are some types of drink:
Hot drinks:
cappuccino, cocoa, coffee, herbal tea, hot chocolate, mocha, tea
Cold drinks:
barley water, cola, fizzy drink, fruit juice, lemonade, milk, milkshake, smoothie, squash, water
Alcoholic drinks:
beer, brandy, cocktail, gin, liqueur, rum, sherry, vodka, whisky, wine

drink² VERB
I'm just **drinking** my tea.
swallow, sip, drain, gulp, sup

drip¹ NOUN
a **drip** of blood on the carpet
drop, trickle, dribble, leak

drip² VERB
Water is **dripping** from the tap.
drop, dribble, trickle, plop, drizzle, splash, sprinkle

drive¹ NOUN
1 a long **drive** in the country
excursion, outing, journey, ride, spin, trip
2 You need **drive** and enthusiasm to win.
energy, ambition, initiative, vigour, motivation, determination
◇ INFORMAL WORDS get-up-and-go
3 the **drive** to succeed
urge, instinct, impulse, need, desire

drive² VERB
1 My brother can **drive** a car.
steer, control
2 an engine **driven** by steam
motor, propel, control, operate, run, power
3 His nasty remark **drove** her to cry.
force, press, push, oblige

drop¹ VERB
1 I **dropped** into a chair, exhausted.
fall, sink, plunge, plummet, tumble, lower
⊘ OPPOSITES rise
2 The temperature has **dropped** since yesterday.
lower, fall, sink, plunge, plummet, diminish
⊘ OPPOSITES rise
3 Let's just **drop** the plan.
abandon, give up, leave, discontinue, quit
◆ FORMAL WORDS cease
• **drop off**
1 Can you please **drop** me **off** at the supermarket?

Aa Bb Cc Dd Ee Ff Gg Hh Ii Jj Kk Ll Mm Nn Oo Pp Qq Rr Ss Tt Uu Vv Ww Xx Yy Zz

deliver, set down, leave
≠ OPPOSITES pick up
2 *I **dropped off** while watching television.*
nod off, doze
◇ INFORMAL WORDS snooze, have forty winks
≠ OPPOSITES wake up
• drop out
*Mike had to **drop out** of the race.*
back out, abandon, cry off, withdraw, leave, quit

drop² NOUN
1 *a **drop** of water*
drip, bubble, spot, blob
2 *Add a **drop** of cream.*
dash, pinch, spot, sip, trace, dab
3 *a **drop** in the number of school pupils*
fall, falling-off, lowering, decrease, reduction, slump, plunge
4 *a steep **drop** to the sea*
descent, slope

drown VERB
*The band **drowned** the singer's voice.*
overwhelm, overpower, overcome

drowsy ADJECTIVE
*The sunshine made me feel **drowsy**.*
sleepy, tired, dreamy, dozy
≠ OPPOSITES alert, awake

drug NOUN
*My gran needs **drugs** for her arthritis.*
medication, medicine, remedy, potion

dry¹ ADJECTIVE
*The land is too **dry** to grow crops.*
arid, parched, dehydrated, barren
≠ OPPOSITES wet

dry² VERB
*The hot sun has **dried** the earth.*
parch, scorch, dehydrate, shrivel, wither
≠ OPPOSITES soak

dubious ADJECTIVE
1 *I was a bit **dubious** about his story.*
doubtful, uncertain, undecided, unsure, suspicious, hesitant
≠ OPPOSITES certain

2 *He is a rather **dubious** character.*
questionable, unreliable, suspect
◇ INFORMAL WORDS fishy, shady
≠ OPPOSITES trustworthy

duck VERB
*He **ducked** to avoid hitting his head.*
crouch, stoop, bob, bend

due ADJECTIVE
1 *The payment is **due**.*
owed, owing, payable, unpaid, outstanding, in arrears
≠ OPPOSITES paid
2 *You must give praise where it is **due**.*
rightful, fitting, appropriate, proper, deserved, justified, suitable
≠ OPPOSITES inappropriate
3 *The train is **due** in five minutes.*
expected, scheduled

dull ADJECTIVE
1 *a **dull** morning*
dark, gloomy, drab, grey, cloudy, dim, overcast
≠ OPPOSITES bright
2 *I found the video very **dull**.*
boring, uninteresting, unexciting, dreary, unimaginative
≠ OPPOSITES interesting, exciting

dumb ADJECTIVE
*I was struck **dumb** with shock.*
silent, soundless, speechless

dumbfounded ADJECTIVE
*Her parents were **dumbfounded** at the news of her engagement.*
astonished, amazed, overwhelmed, speechless, taken aback, overcome, flabbergasted, floored

dummy ADJECTIVE
*The desk has a **dummy** door.*
false, fake, artificial, bogus
≠ OPPOSITES real, genuine

dump¹ NOUN
1 *We took the rubbish to the **dump**.*
rubbish tip, junkyard, rubbish heap, tip
2 *Our flat was a **dump** when we first moved in.*

Aa
Bb
Cc
Dd
Ee
Ff
Gg
Hh
Ii
Jj
Kk
Ll
Mm
Nn
Oo
Pp
Qq
Rr
Ss
Tt
Uu
Vv
Ww
Xx
Yy
Zz

slum, eyesore, mess
◇ INFORMAL WORDS hole, pigsty

dump² VERB

1 *We dumped our old newspapers at the recycling point.*
get rid of, scrap, throw away, dispose of, tip
◇ INFORMAL WORDS ditch
2 *He dumped his jacket on the floor.*
drop, throw down, let fall
◇ INFORMAL WORDS chuck

dusk NOUN

Be home before dusk.
twilight, sunset, nightfall, evening, sundown, dark, gloom, shadows, shade
≠ OPPOSITES dawn

dutiful ADJECTIVE

He's a very dutiful son.
devoted, obedient, respectful
≠ OPPOSITES disobedient, disrespectful

duty NOUN

1 *We all had duties to carry out.*
obligation, responsibility, assignment, role, task, job, business, function, work
2 *a sense of duty to your family*
obedience, respect, loyalty

dying ADJECTIVE

1 *his dying wish*
passing, last, final
≠ OPPOSITES reviving
2 *a dying breed*
disappearing, perishing, failing, fading, vanishing
• **be dying for**
I am dying for a cold drink.
long for, pine for, yearn for, desire

dynamic ADJECTIVE

a dynamic young film-maker
forceful, powerful, energetic, vigorous, go-ahead, spirited, vital, lively, active
≠ OPPOSITES inactive

Aa
Bb
Cc
Dd
Ee
Ff
Gg
Hh
Ii
Jj
Kk
Ll
Mm
Nn
Oo
Pp
Qq
Rr
Ss
Tt
Uu
Vv
Ww
Xx
Yy
Zz

Ee

eager ADJECTIVE

I am eager to go out on my new bike.
keen, enthusiastic, desperate
≠ OPPOSITES unenthusiastic

early¹ ADJECTIVE

1 *the early stages of the illness*
undeveloped
≠ OPPOSITES late
2 *early retirement*
premature, forward, advanced
≠ OPPOSITES late
3 *early history*
primitive, ancient, primeval
≠ OPPOSITES recent

early² ADVERB

If we leave now, we'll get there early.
ahead of time, in good time,
beforehand, in advance
≠ OPPOSITES late

earn VERB

1 *She earns a good salary.*
receive, obtain, make, get, bring in,
gain, draw
≠ OPPOSITES spend, lose
2 *Teachers have to earn their pupils'
respect.*
deserve, warrant, win, rate

earnest ADJECTIVE

1 *an earnest promise*
firm, serious, sincere, solemn, grave,
heartfelt
≠ OPPOSITES flippant
2 *an earnest student*
devoted, conscientious, keen, eager,
enthusiastic

earth NOUN

1 *all over the Earth*
world, planet, globe
2 *Plant the seeds in the earth.*
land, ground, soil

ease¹ NOUN

1 *She won the race with ease.*
effortlessness
≠ OPPOSITES difficulty
2 *They are living a life of ease.*
comfort, leisure, luxury, relaxation, rest
≠ OPPOSITES discomfort

ease² VERB

1 *This medicine will ease your pain.*
lessen, lighten, relieve, comfort, calm,
soothe, relax
≠ OPPOSITES worsen, intensify
2 *The wind is beginning to ease.*
lessen, lighten, relent
≠ OPPOSITES worsen, intensify
3 *He eased the door open.*
inch, slide, slip

easy ADJECTIVE

1 *an easy task*
effortless, simple, uncomplicated,
straightforward, manageable
≠ OPPOSITES difficult, complex
2 *The computer is easy to use.*
simple, straightforward, foolproof
3 *an easy life*
comfortable, peaceful, restful, leisurely,
contented, untroubled

easy-going ADJECTIVE

*She is easy-going and never loses her
temper.*
relaxed, tolerant, happy-go-lucky,
carefree, calm, even-tempered
◇ INFORMAL WORDS laid-back
≠ OPPOSITES strict, intolerant, critical

eat VERB

⇒ For even more about this word, see
the next page
1 *I eat an apple every day.*
consume, swallow, devour, chew,
munch
◇ INFORMAL WORDS scoff

eat

There are lots of different words that you can use in your writing instead of **eat**. These words will make your writing much more interesting, and really help you to build up a vivid picture of the situation you are describing.

When someone eats greedily or quickly, you can use these informal words:

tuck in(to)
gulp down
bolt down
wolf down
scoff
knock back
polish off
gobble

If someone is eating noisily, you can say they

crunch
munch
slurp

You can use these words to describe how someone is chewing:

munch
gnaw

If someone is not very hungry or is eating just a little at a time, you can say they

peck
pick
nibble

In more formal situations, you might say that people

dine
breakfast
lunch

2 *Let's go out to eat.*
feed, dine

eccentric ADJECTIVE

*an **eccentric** millionaire who lives in a windmill*
odd, peculiar, unconventional, strange, quirky, weird
◇ INFORMAL WORDS freaky, way-out
⧣ OPPOSITES conventional, orthodox, normal

echo VERB

1 *voices **echoing** in the empty room*
resound, repeat, ring
2 *She **echoed** what he had said.*
imitate, copy
3 *The poem's last line **echoes** its first one.*
reproduce, mirror, resemble

ecstasy NOUN

*The music filled me with **ecstasy**.*
delight, bliss, joy, happiness
⧣ OPPOSITES misery, torment

edge¹ NOUN

1 *the **edge** of the table*
border, rim, brim, fringe
2 *the **edge** of the water*
border, boundary, limit, threshold, brink, margin, side, verge

edge² VERB

*He **edged** closer to the front.*
creep, inch, ease, sidle

edible ADJECTIVE

*Some seaweeds are **edible**.*
eatable, safe to eat, harmless, wholesome
⧣ OPPOSITES inedible

edit VERB

***Edit** your essay to fix any mistakes in spelling, grammar and punctuation.*
correct, revise, rewrite, reorder, rearrange, check, rephrase

educate VERB

*She was **educated** at a private school.*
teach, train, tutor

educated ADJECTIVE

*Although he is intelligent, he is not **educated**.*
knowledgeable, informed, learned, cultured
⧣ OPPOSITES uneducated

education NOUN

*You'll receive a good **education** at this school.*
teaching, training, schooling, tuition, tutoring, coaching, guidance, instruction

eerie ADJECTIVE

an eerie old house
weird, strange, uncanny, frightening, scary, spine-chilling
◇ INFORMAL WORDS spooky, creepy

effect NOUN

1 *The shock had an effect on Anna's health.*
outcome, result, conclusion, consequence, upshot
2 *My warnings had little effect on the children.*
power, force, impact, impression, influence

effective ADJECTIVE

1 *an effective manager*
efficient, adequate, capable, useful
⧧ OPPOSITES ineffective, useless
2 *an effective road safety advertisement*
forceful, powerful, persuasive, convincing, telling

efficient ADJECTIVE

an efficient head teacher
effective, competent, skilful, capable, able, well-organized, businesslike
⧧ OPPOSITES inefficient, incompetent

effort NOUN

1 *Getting fit requires a lot of effort.*
exertion, strain, struggle, trouble, energy
2 *The teacher said my painting was a good effort.*
attempt, try
◇ INFORMAL WORDS go, shot, stab

Egypt NOUN

Here are some words connected with ancient Egypt:

canopic jar, hieroglyph, mummy, Nile, papyrus, pharaoh, pyramid, scarab beetle, shabti, sphinx, temple

eject VERB

The troublemakers were ejected from the hall.
throw out, drive out, turn out, expel, remove
◇ INFORMAL WORDS kick out

elaborate ADJECTIVE

1 *elaborate plans*
detailed, careful, thorough, exact, precise
2 *an elaborate design*
complex, complicated, involved, ornamental, fancy, decorated, showy
⧧ OPPOSITES simple, plain

elbow VERB

He elbowed me out of the way.
jostle, nudge, push, shove, bump, knock

elderly ADJECTIVE

elderly people like my gran
aging, aged, old
⧧ OPPOSITES young, youthful

elect VERB

Jamal was elected class representative.
choose, pick, opt for, select, vote for, appoint

elegant ADJECTIVE

an elegant fashion model
stylish, fashionable, smart, refined, tasteful, fine, exquisite, graceful
⧧ OPPOSITES inelegant, unrefined, unfashionable

element NOUN

1 *the various elements that make up a good novel*
factor, component, ingredient, part, piece, fragment, feature
⧧ OPPOSITES whole
2 *There is an element of fun in the lessons.*
trace, hint

elementary ADJECTIVE

1 *elementary music lessons*
basic, introductory
⧧ OPPOSITES advanced

Aa
Bb
Cc
Dd
Ee
Ff
Gg
Hh
Ii
Jj
Kk
Ll
Mm
Nn
Oo
Pp
Qq
Rr
Ss
Tt
Uu
Vv
Ww
Xx
Yy
Zz

2 *We'll deal with the **elementary** problems first.*
simple, clear, easy, straightforward, uncomplicated

eligible ADJECTIVE
*To be **eligible** for this competition, you have to be under 16.*
qualified, fit, appropriate, suitable, acceptable
⊠ OPPOSITES ineligible

eliminate VERB
1 *We will **eliminate** bullying from our school.*
remove, get rid of, cut out, dispose of, do away with, stamp out
⊠ OPPOSITES include, accept
2 *I was **eliminated** from the competition in the second round.*
remove, exclude, expel, drop, omit, reject, knock out, take out
⊠ OPPOSITES include, accept

embark VERB
*We **embarked** the ferry at Hull.*
board, go aboard
⊠ OPPOSITES disembark
• **embark on**
*We are about to **embark on** a big adventure.*
begin, start, set about, enter
⊠ OPPOSITES complete, finish

embarrass VERB
*Don't **embarrass** me in front of my friends.*
show up, humiliate, shame

embarrassment NOUN
*Martine blushed with **embarrassment**.*
humiliation, shame, shyness, self-consciousness, awkwardness

emblem NOUN
*The thistle is the **emblem** of Scotland.*
symbol, sign, token, logo, crest, mark, badge

embrace VERB
*The two sisters **embraced** each other.*
hug, clasp, cuddle, hold, squeeze

emerge VERB
*Several new problems have **emerged** since we last spoke.*
arise, rise, surface, appear, develop, crop up, turn up

emergency NOUN
*A mobile phone can be useful in an **emergency**.*
crisis, danger, difficulty, predicament

emigrate VERB
*My uncle **emigrated** to Australia.*
migrate, move, move abroad

emotion NOUN
*I was overcome with **emotion**.*
feeling, passion, sensation, sentiment, excitement

emotional ADJECTIVE
1 *I always get very **emotional** at Christmas.*
feeling, sensitive, responsive, tender, warm, moved, sentimental
⊠ OPPOSITES unemotional, cold, detached, calm
2 *He is prone to **emotional** outbursts.*
passionate, excitable, hot-blooded, heated, temperamental, fiery
⊠ OPPOSITES unemotional, cold, detached, calm
3 *an **emotional** scene in the film*
moving, thrilling, touching, stirring, heart-warming, exciting

emphasis NOUN
1 *Too much **emphasis** is given to exam results.*
significance, importance, priority, attention, urgency
2 *The **emphasis** is on the first beat of every bar.*
stress, accent, force, power, intensity, strength

emphasize VERB
1 *The belt **emphasizes** her small waist.*
stress, highlight, feature, spotlight, play up, draw attention to
⊠ OPPOSITES play down, understate

Aa
Bb
Cc
Dd
Ee
Ff
Gg
Hh
Ii
Jj
Kk
Ll
Mm
Nn
Oo
Pp
Qq
Rr
Ss
Tt
Uu
Vv
Ww
Xx
Yy
Zz

2 *I can't emphasize enough how important this is.*
stress, dwell on, insist on, press home
⊘ OPPOSITES play down, understate

employ VERB
The new company will employ one hundred people.
engage, hire, take on, recruit, enlist

employment NOUN
He is in search of employment.
job, work, occupation, situation
⊘ OPPOSITES unemployment

empty¹ ADJECTIVE
1 *an empty house*
unoccupied, uninhabited, deserted, unfilled, desolate
⊘ OPPOSITES full
2 *an empty page in my exercise book*
blank, clear, bare

empty² VERB
She emptied her bag onto the table.
drain, exhaust, clear, pour out, unload
⊘ OPPOSITES fill, fill up

enable VERB
1 *This bus pass will enable you to travel free.*
qualify, authorize, allow, permit, license
⊘ OPPOSITES prevent
2 *software which enables you to download music*
allow, equip, prepare

enchanting ADJECTIVE
an enchanting smile
charming, fascinating, attractive, appealing, delightful, bewitching
⊘ OPPOSITES repellent, disgusting

enclose VERB
1 *The dogs are enclosed in a compound.*
confine, hold, shut in, pen, hem in
2 *The garden is enclosed by a ten-foot wall.*
surround, fence, hedge
3 *I have enclosed a photograph with this letter.*

incorporate, include, insert

encounter VERB
We are going to encounter problems later on.
meet, come across, run into, run across, experience, face

encourage VERB
1 *My teacher encouraged me to carry on.*
stimulate, spur, rally, inspire, incite, egg on, urge
⊘ OPPOSITES discourage, dissuade
2 *I tried to encourage the sad little girl.*
cheer, comfort, console
⊘ OPPOSITES discourage, depress

encouraging ADJECTIVE
1 *He gave me an encouraging smile.*
reassuring, stimulating, uplifting, cheering, cheerful, comforting
⊘ OPPOSITES discouraging, depressing
2 *We got off to an encouraging start.*
promising, hopeful, reassuring, bright, rosy, satisfactory
⊘ OPPOSITES discouraging, depressing

end¹ NOUN
1 *the end of the class*
finish, conclusion, close, completion
⊘ OPPOSITES beginning, start
2 *the ends of the earth*
edge, limit, boundary, extremity
3 *a cigarette end*
tip, butt, stub
4 *a scarf knitted from ends of wool*
remainder, left-over, remnant, scrap, fragment
5 *He went out with one end in mind.*
aim, object, objective, purpose, intention, goal
6 *the end we are aiming for*
result, outcome, consequence, upshot
7 *He met his end in battle.*
death, destruction, downfall, doom, ruin
⊘ OPPOSITES birth

end² VERB
1 *He ended the lesson with a joke.*

Aa Bb Cc Dd Ee Ff Gg Hh Ii Jj Kk Ll Mm Nn Oo Pp Qq Rr Ss Tt Uu Vv Ww Xx Yy Zz

finish, close, complete, conclude, wind up
≠ OPPOSITES **begin, start**
2 *the injury that* **ended** *his career*
destroy, ruin, finish, stop

endanger VERB
Their foolishness **endangered** *all our lives.*
risk, put at risk, threaten, jeopardize
≠ OPPOSITES **protect, safeguard**

ending NOUN
The film had a happy **ending.**
end, close, finish, climax, finale
≠ OPPOSITES **beginning, start**

endless ADJECTIVE
1 *the* **endless** *universe*
infinite, boundless, unlimited
≠ OPPOSITES **finite, limited**
2 **endless** *patience*
everlasting, ceaseless, constant, continual, continuous, undying, eternal
≠ OPPOSITES **temporary, short-lived**

endure VERB
1 *The hostages* **endured** *great hardship.*
go through, experience, suffer, undergo
2 *I don't think I can* **endure** *any more of his company.*
bear, stand, take, put up with, tolerate, cope with, face, stomach
3 *a memory that will* **endure** *for ever*
last, remain, live, survive, stay, persist

enemy NOUN
1 *From that moment on, we were sworn* **enemies.**
opponent, foe, rival
≠ OPPOSITES **friend, ally**
2 *They will face their old* **enemies** *in the final.*
opponent, rival, the opposition, competitor, opposer, other side

energetic ADJECTIVE
1 *an* **energetic** *exercise routine*
lively, vigorous, active, brisk, strenuous
≠ OPPOSITES **inactive, idle**
2 *an* **energetic** *discussion*
active, lively, spirited, strong, forceful, powerful

energy NOUN
1 *I don't have the* **energy** *to play football today.*
strength, power, vigour, stamina
≠ OPPOSITES **lethargy, listlessness, sluggishness**
2 *My gran has amazing* **energy** *for an 80-year-old.*
liveliness, vigour, drive, life, spirit, vitality, zest
◇ INFORMAL WORDS get-up-and-go
3 *He spoke with great* **energy** *about his plans for the future.*
zest, zeal, fire, force, forcefulness, intensity, spirit, vigour

enforce VERB
More should be done to **enforce** *these laws.*
apply, insist on, carry out, impose, reinforce

engaged ADJECTIVE
1 *I'm afraid the headmaster is* **engaged** *in a meeting at the moment.*
occupied, busy, absorbed, preoccupied, involved, employed, tied up
2 *I kept getting an* **engaged** *tone when I called.*
busy, unavailable

engagement NOUN
I'd love to come, but I have a prior **engagement.**
appointment, meeting, date, arrangement

engrave VERB
Her name is **engraved** *on the trophy.*
inscribe, cut, carve, chisel

enjoy VERB
1 *I really* **enjoy** *a good comedy film.*
take pleasure in, delight in, appreciate, like
≠ OPPOSITES **dislike, hate**
2 **Enjoy** *yourself at the party.*
have a good time, have fun

enjoyable ADJECTIVE
a most **enjoyable** *evening*

Aa
Bb
Cc
Dd
Ee
Ff
Gg
Hh
Ii
Jj
Kk
Ll
Mm
Nn
Oo
Pp
Qq
Rr
Ss
Tt
Uu
Vv
Ww
Xx
Yy
Zz

pleasant, delightful, pleasing, entertaining, amusing, good
◇ INFORMAL WORDS fun
⊯ OPPOSITES disagreeable, unpleasant

enlarge VERB

1 *They can enlarge the photograph for a small cost.*
increase, expand, extend, stretch, blow up, widen, broaden
⊯ OPPOSITES shrink, diminish
2 *Weight training causes the muscles to enlarge.*
increase, expand, grow, extend, swell, stretch, develop, widen, broaden
⊯ OPPOSITES shrink, diminish
3 *Try to enlarge your vocabulary.*
increase, expand, add to, extend, multiply, develop, widen

enormous ADJECTIVE

an enormous St Bernard dog
huge, immense, vast, gigantic, massive, colossal, monstrous
⊯ OPPOSITES small, tiny

enough[1] ADJECTIVE

Do you have enough money for your fare?
sufficient, adequate, ample, plenty, abundant

enough[2] ADVERB

1 *I failed the exam because I didn't work enough.*
sufficiently, adequately, satisfactorily, amply
2 *I like dogs well enough but I wouldn't want one as a pet.*
passably, reasonably, moderately, fairly

enquire VERB

I am enquiring about the bicycle for sale.
ask, question, quiz, query, investigate, look into, probe, examine, inspect, scrutinize, search, explore

enquiry NOUN

He is helping the police with their enquiries.
question, query, investigation, hearing, examination, inspection, scrutiny, study, survey, search, probe, exploration

enrol VERB

1 *I enrolled in the Brownies.*
register, sign on, sign up, join up
2 *We will enrol you in the class next term.*
register, sign up, recruit, engage

ensure VERB

1 *Please ensure that your lunchboxes have your names on them.*
certify, make sure, guarantee
2 *We must work together to ensure our planet's future.*
protect, guard, safeguard, secure

enter VERB

1 *Please knock before you enter.*
come in, go in, arrive
⊯ OPPOSITES depart, go out
2 *The teacher entered my name on the list.*
record, log, note, register, take down, inscribe
⊯ OPPOSITES delete, cross out
3 *children who enter secondary school next year*
join, enrol, enlist, sign up, commence, start, begin
4 *We are entering a new phase in our work.*
set about, commence, start, begin

enterprise NOUN

1 *He used his money to start a new enterprise.*
business, company, firm, establishment, concern
2 *a dangerous enterprise*
undertaking, venture, project, plan, effort, operation, endeavour
3 *They showed a lot of enterprise.*
initiative, resourcefulness, drive, adventurousness, push, enthusiasm, spirit
◇ INFORMAL WORDS get-up-and-go

entertain VERB

1 *He entertained the children with magic tricks.*

amuse, please, delight
≠ OPPOSITES bore
2 *My mum is a great cook and loves entertaining.*
receive, have guests

entertaining ADJECTIVE
He is a very entertaining companion.
amusing, delightful, interesting, pleasant, pleasing, humorous, witty
◇ INFORMAL WORDS fun
≠ OPPOSITES boring, dull

entertainment NOUN
What do you do for entertainment around here?
amusement, enjoyment, play, pastime, fun, pleasure

Here are some types of entertainment:

Entertainment on a screen:
cinema, DVD, television, video, video game
Entertainment in a theatre:
concert, musical, opera, pantomime, play, recital
Entertainments you join in:
ceilidh, dance, disco, karaoke, magic show, Punch-and-Judy show, puppet show
Entertainments with animals:
circus, gymkhana, rodeo, safari park, zoo
Entertainments with lights:
fireworks, laser light show
Outdoor entertainments:
carnival, festival, fête, pageant

---

enthusiast NOUN
a railway enthusiast
admirer, fan, supporter, follower, fanatic, lover, devotee
◇ INFORMAL WORDS buff, freak, fiend

enthusiastic ADJECTIVE
He is an enthusiastic supporter of the team.
keen, eager, passionate, warm, whole-hearted, vigorous, spirited, earnest, devoted
≠ OPPOSITES unenthusiastic

entire ADJECTIVE
She is the best singer in the entire school.
complete, whole, total

entirely ADVERB
1 *You are entirely correct.*
completely, wholly, totally, fully, utterly, absolutely, thoroughly, altogether, perfectly
≠ OPPOSITES partially
2 *Looking after your pet is entirely your responsibility.*
solely, exclusively

entitle VERB
This ticket entitles you to unlimited travel.
authorize, qualify, allow, permit, license

entrance[1] NOUN
the rear entrance
opening, way in, door, doorway, gate
≠ OPPOSITES exit

entrance[2] VERB
Her performance entranced the audience.
charm, enchant, bewitch, spellbind, fascinate
≠ OPPOSITES repel, disgust

entry NOUN
1 *We were refused entry because we were too young.*
entrance, admittance, admission, access
2 *He made an entry in his diary.*
record, item, note, memo, statement
3 *a late entry in the race*
entrant, competitor, contestant, candidate, participant, player

envious ADJECTIVE
envious of his success
jealous, resentful, green with envy, grudging

Aa
Bb
Cc
Dd
Ee
Ff
Gg
Hh
Ii
Jj
Kk
Ll
Mm
Nn
Oo
Pp
Qq
Rr
Ss
Tt
Uu
Vv
Ww
Xx
Yy
Zz

environment NOUN

1 *products that are harmful to the environment*
surroundings, natural world, nature, world

2 *What kind of environment did these children grow up in?*
surroundings, conditions, circumstances, atmosphere, situation, background, setting

envy[1] NOUN

feelings of envy towards those who are better off
jealousy, resentfulness, resentment, dissatisfaction, bitterness

envy[2] VERB

I envy your ability to make friends.
resent, begrudge, grudge, crave

episode NOUN

1 *the next episode in the story*
instalment, part, chapter, passage, section, scene

2 *a sad episode in her life*
incident, event, occurrence, happening, occasion, circumstance, experience

equal ADJECTIVE

equal pay
identical, the same, alike, like, equivalent, corresponding, comparable
⊘ OPPOSITES different

equality NOUN

equality of treatment for all people
uniformity, evenness, equivalence, balance, proportion, sameness

equip VERB

1 *The gym is very well equipped.*
provide, fit out, supply, kit out, stock

2 *a course designed to equip students to find work after they leave school*
prepare, get ready, enable

equipment NOUN

gym equipment
apparatus, supplies, tackle, tools, things, accessories
◇ INFORMAL WORDS gear, stuff

equivalent ADJECTIVE

£200 or the equivalent amount in dollars
equal, same, similar, corresponding, alike, comparable
⊘ OPPOSITES unlike, different

era NOUN

in the Victorian era
age, period, date, day, days, time, stage

erase VERB

1 *The teacher erased the writing from the board.*
rub out, delete, remove

2 *He tried to erase the sad memories from his mind.*
blot out, cancel, get rid of

erect[1] ADJECTIVE

She stands very erect.
upright, straight, vertical, upstanding

erect[2] VERB

We erected our tent near the river.
build, construct, put up, raise, pitch

erode VERB

1 *The weather erodes the rocks over time.*
wear away, eat away, wear down, grind down, disintegrate

2 *The beach is eroding at the rate of one metre every year.*
wear away, disintegrate, deteriorate, crumble

errand NOUN

Kevin has gone on an errand for his grandmother.
message, task, job, duty

error NOUN

1 *There are several errors in your work.*
mistake, inaccuracy, miscalculation, misunderstanding, omission, flaw, fault

2 *His error has cost us the match.*
mistake, slip, slip-up, blunder, lapse

Aa
Bb
Cc
Dd
Ee
Ff
Gg
Hh
Ii
Jj
Kk
Ll
Mm
Nn
Oo
Pp
Qq
Rr
Ss
Tt
Uu
Vv
Ww
Xx
Yy
Zz

erupt VERB

*The volcano is likely to **erupt** any day now.*
break out, explode, burst, gush, spout, flare up

escape VERB

1 *A dangerous criminal has **escaped** from prison.*
get away, break free, run away, bolt, flee, fly, break loose, break out
2 *She narrowly **escaped** injury.*
avoid, dodge, evade, miss

escort¹ NOUN

*her **escort** for the evening*
companion, partner, attendant

escort² VERB

1 *Will you please **escort** me on my way home?*
accompany, partner, guard, protect
2 *He **escorted** me to my seat.*
accompany, guide, lead, usher, conduct

especially ADVERB

1 *I'm **especially** interested in the 19th century.*
chiefly, mainly, principally, above all
2 *She is **especially** clever for her age.*
particularly, specially, notably, exceptionally, unusually, very

essay NOUN

*an **essay** for the school magazine*
composition, paper, article, piece

essential ADJECTIVE

*It is **essential** that you hand in your homework on time.*
crucial, necessary, vital, required, needed, important
⊘ OPPOSITES inessential, unimportant

establish VERB

1 *the man who **established** the Scout movement*
set up, found, start, form, create, organize, introduce
⊘ OPPOSITES close down
2 *The head teacher is trying to **establish***
who is to blame.
prove, demonstrate

establishment NOUN

1 *the **establishment** of a school bus system*
formation, setting up, founding, creation
2 *a hairdressing **establishment***
business, company, firm, organization

estate NOUN

1 *The earl left his **estate** to his son.*
possessions, belongings, property, goods, lands
2 *a housing **estate***
area, development, site, zone

estimate¹ NOUN

1 *an **estimate** of the cost of the repairs*
assessment, valuation, guess
2 *my **estimate** of his character*
opinion, judgement, assessment, estimation

estimate² VERB

1 *I **estimate** that this exercise should take an hour.*
consider, assess, believe, guess, judge, think
2 *She tried to **estimate** how much money she had.*
calculate, assess, number, count, value

evacuate VERB

1 *The pupils were **evacuated** from the school as a safety measure.*
remove, clear, move out, withdraw
2 *We had to **evacuate** the city because a hurricane was on the way.*
leave, depart, withdraw, quit, retire from, clear out, abandon, desert

evade VERB

*You mustn't **evade** your responsibilities.*
avoid, escape, dodge, shirk, steer clear of, shun, duck
⊘ OPPOSITES confront, face

even ADJECTIVE

1 *an **even** surface*
flat, level, smooth

Aa
Bb
Cc
Dd
Ee
Ff
Gg
Hh
Ii
Jj
Kk
Ll
Mm
Nn
Oo
Pp
Qq
Rr
Ss
Tt
Uu
Vv
Ww
Xx
Yy
Zz

Aa

Bb

Cc

Dd

Ee

Ff

Gg

Hh

Ii

Jj

Kk

Ll

Mm

Nn

Oo

Pp

Qq

Rr

Ss

Tt

Uu

Vv

Ww

Xx

Yy

Zz

≠ OPPOSITES uneven, bumpy
2 *an even pace*
steady, unvarying, constant, regular
3 *The scores are even.*
equal, balanced, matching, fifty-fifty, level, side by side, neck and neck
≠ OPPOSITES unequal
4 *All the pieces should be of an even length.*
equal, matching, same, similar, like
≠ OPPOSITES unequal

evening NOUN
We are going to the cinema this evening.
nightfall, dusk, twilight, sunset, sundown

event NOUN
1 *events in history*
happening, occurrence, incident, occasion, affair, circumstance, episode
2 *a sporting event*
game, match, competition, contest, engagement

eventual ADJECTIVE
the eventual outcome of the war
final, ultimate, resulting, future, later

eventually ADVERB
Along this road, you will eventually come to the theme park.
finally, at last, in the end, at length, sooner or later

even up VERB
Even up the numbers on each side.
make equal, equalize, balance out

everlasting ADJECTIVE
everlasting joy
never-ending, endless, infinite, constant, permanent
≠ OPPOSITES temporary, short-lived

everyday ADJECTIVE
1 *Holidays give us a chance to escape from everyday life.*
ordinary, common, commonplace, familiar, run-of-the-mill, regular, usual, normal, daily

≠ OPPOSITES unusual, special
2 *Include some exercise in your everyday routine.*
day-to-day, regular, routine, usual, normal, daily

evidence NOUN
There is no evidence of his guilt.
proof, confirmation, grounds

evident ADJECTIVE
Their pride in their children was evident.
clear, obvious, apparent, plain, visible, conspicuous, noticeable, unmistakable

evidently ADVERB
1 *He was evidently the ringleader of the gang.*
obviously, clearly, plainly, undoubtedly, doubtless, doubtlessly
2 *Evidently his dog ate his homework.*
apparently, seemingly

evil¹ ADJECTIVE
1 *an evil crime*
wicked, wrong, sinful, bad, immoral, vicious, vile
2 *an evil influence on him*
harmful, destructive, deadly, hurtful

evil² NOUN
Goodness is better than evil.
wickedness, wrongdoing, wrong, badness, sin, sinfulness, vice, corruption

exact ADJECTIVE
1 *an exact description*
accurate, precise, correct, right, true, detailed, specific, strict, factual
≠ OPPOSITES inexact, imprecise
2 *She's very exact in her work.*
careful, particular, methodical, orderly, painstaking

exactly ADVERB
He told me exactly how to get there.
precisely, accurately, correctly, specifically, carefully, strictly
≠ OPPOSITES inaccurately, roughly

exaggerate VERB
I don't want to exaggerate the importance of this visit.
overstate, overdo, overemphasize

examination NOUN
1 *a medical examination*
check, inspection, analysis, investigation, observation, scan, check-up
2 *a French examination*
test, exam, quiz
3 *The court recalled the witnesses for further examination.*
questioning, cross-examination, cross-questioning, trial, interrogation

examine VERB
1 *Scientists are carefully examining the evidence.*
check, inspect, investigate, study, survey, analyse, explore, review
2 *The students were examined on science.*
test, quiz, question
3 *Dozens of witnesses have been examined in the course of the trial.*
question, cross-examine, cross-question, interrogate
◇ INFORMAL WORDS grill

example NOUN
Can you give me an example of an adjective?
instance, case, illustration, sample, specimen
2 *a perfect example of how to write a good essay*
pattern, model, ideal, standard, lesson

exasperate VERB
His rudeness exasperates me.
anger, infuriate, annoy, irritate, madden, provoke, get on your nerves, enrage
≠ OPPOSITES pacify, relax, settle

exceed VERB
You have exceeded all our expectations.
surpass, outdo, beat, better, pass, outshine

excel VERB
She excels at athletics.
be excellent, succeed, shine, stand out

excellent ADJECTIVE
That's an excellent idea.
great, superior, first-class, first-rate, outstanding, good, superb, fine, wonderful
◇ INFORMAL WORDS top-notch
≠ OPPOSITES inferior, second-rate

except PREPOSITION
The whole family was there except Dad.
apart from, but, excepting, other than, omitting, not counting, leaving out, excluding, except for, besides

exception NOUN
There are no exceptions to this rule.
special case, oddity, abnormality, irregularity, peculiarity, inconsistency

exceptional ADJECTIVE
1 *This case is exceptional.*
unusual, special, abnormal, strange, odd, irregular, extraordinary, peculiar, rare
≠ OPPOSITES normal, usual, regular
2 *He is an exceptional guitarist.*
marvellous, outstanding, remarkable, notable, noteworthy, superior

excerpt NOUN
an excerpt from the new Harry Potter book
extract, passage, portion, section, selection, quote, quotation, part

excess NOUN
1 *We have an excess of food.*
surplus, overabundance, overflow, surfeit
2 *Trim the pastry and keep the excess for decoration.*
remainder, surplus, left-over

excessive ADJECTIVE
excessive force
unnecessary, extreme, undue, uncalled-for, unneeded, unreasonable

Aa
Bb
Cc
Dd
Ee
Ff
Gg
Hh
Ii
Jj
Kk
Ll
Mm
Nn
Oo
Pp
Qq
Rr
Ss
Tt
Uu
Vv
Ww
Xx
Yy
Zz

♦ FORMAL WORDS superfluous
◇ INFORMAL WORDS steep
≠ OPPOSITES insufficient, inadequate

exchange VERB

I'd like to exchange this shirt for a bigger size.
change, trade, swap, switch, replace, substitute

excited ADJECTIVE

The band appeared before a very excited crowd.
thrilled, enthusiastic, eager, worked up, restless, frantic, frenzied, wild
◇ INFORMAL WORDS high
≠ OPPOSITES calm, cool

exciting ADJECTIVE

an exciting story
thrilling, stirring, rousing, moving, enthralling, sensational, interesting
≠ OPPOSITES dull, unexciting

exclaim VERB

'It's snowing!' she exclaimed.
cry, cry out, declare, call, yell, shout

exclude VERB

1 *Try to exclude sugar from your diet.*
leave out, omit, eliminate
≠ OPPOSITES include
2 *We can't exclude the possibility that he is still alive.*
rule out, ignore, eliminate
3 *Matthew was excluded from school for bullying.*
keep out, expel, ban, bar, shut out, prohibit, forbid
≠ OPPOSITES admit, let in

exclusive ADJECTIVE

a very exclusive club
select, classy, choice, elegant, fashionable
◇ INFORMAL WORDS posh

excuse¹ NOUN

There is no excuse for rudeness.
justification, explanation, grounds, defence, reason, pretext

excuse² VERB

You can't excuse such bad behaviour.
forgive, pardon, overlook, tolerate, ignore
≠ OPPOSITES criticize, condemn

execute VERB

He was executed for treason.
put to death, kill

exercise¹ NOUN

1 *Regular exercise keeps you healthy.*
activity, work-out
2 *piano exercises*
practice, training, drill, task, lesson, work

exercise² VERB

1 *It's important to exercise regularly.*
train, drill, work out, keep fit
2 *You must exercise some patience.*
use, apply, exert, practise

exhaust VERB

1 *You will exhaust yourself if you don't rest.*
tire, tire out, weary, fatigue, strain, overwork, wear out
≠ OPPOSITES refresh
2 *We have exhausted our supply of food.*
use up, consume, empty, drain, finish
≠ OPPOSITES renew, replenish

exhausting ADJECTIVE

an exhausting task
tiring, strenuous, hard, difficult, backbreaking, draining, punishing, arduous
≠ OPPOSITES refreshing, invigorating

exhibit VERB

1 *He will exhibit his paintings in the gallery.*
show, display, present
2 *They exhibited pride in their achievements.*
show, demonstrate, reveal, express, indicate
≠ OPPOSITES conceal

Aa Bb Cc Dd Ee Ff Gg Hh Ii Jj Kk Ll Mm Nn Oo Pp Qq Rr Ss Tt Uu Vv Ww Xx Yy Zz

exhibition NOUN
an art exhibition
show, display, demonstration, exhibit, presentation, fair

exist VERB
1 *Dinosaurs no longer exist.*
be, live
2 *It's not easy to exist on my wages.*
live, survive, continue

exit NOUN
1 *The singer left the theatre by a side exit.*
way out, door, doorway, gate
≠ OPPOSITES entrance, way in
2 *We made a quick exit after the game.*
departure, going, retreat, withdrawal, leave-taking
≠ OPPOSITES entrance, arrival

exotic ADJECTIVE
holidays in exotic locations
unusual, different, unfamiliar, extraordinary, curious, strange, fascinating
≠ OPPOSITES ordinary, bland

expand VERB
The company is expanding into other markets.
increase, grow, extend, enlarge, develop, spread, branch out

expect VERB
1 *I'm expecting a letter from you.*
await, look forward to, hope for, look for, anticipate
2 *I expect you to do the washing-up.*
want, require, wish, insist on, demand, rely on, count on
3 *I expect you're right.*
suppose, assume, believe, think, presume, imagine, reckon, guess, trust

expedition NOUN
an expedition through the rainforest
journey, excursion, trip, voyage, tour, exploration, trek, safari, mission

expel VERB
She was expelled from school for bad behaviour.
throw out, drive out, banish, ban, bar, exclude

expense NOUN
household expenses
cost, spending, payment, charge

expensive ADJECTIVE
a very expensive gift
dear, high-priced, costly, extravagant, lavish
◇ INFORMAL WORDS steep, pricey
≠ OPPOSITES cheap, inexpensive

experience NOUN
1 *I have some experience of babysitting.*
knowledge, familiarity, practice, understanding
◇ INFORMAL WORDS know-how
≠ OPPOSITES inexperience
2 *I had a strange experience on my way to school.*
event, incident, episode, happening, occurrence, adventure

experienced ADJECTIVE
an experienced teacher
knowledgeable, practised, capable, competent, expert, accomplished, adept, skilled
≠ OPPOSITES inexperienced, unskilled

experiment¹ NOUN
a scientific experiment
test, trial, investigation, research, examination, attempt

experiment² VERB
experimenting in science
test, try, investigate, examine, research

expert¹ NOUN
a computer expert
specialist, authority, professional
◇ INFORMAL WORDS dab hand

expert² ADJECTIVE
an expert knitter

Aa
Bb
Cc
Dd
Ee
Ff
Gg
Hh
Ii
Jj
Kk
Ll
Mm
Nn
Oo
Pp
Qq
Rr
Ss
Tt
Uu
Vv
Ww
Xx
Yy
Zz

skilled, skilful, knowledgeable, experienced, able, practised, professional
(≠) OPPOSITES amateurish

explain VERB
1 *Can you* **explain** *the meaning of this word?*
make clear, interpret, clarify, define, simplify, resolve, solve, spell out
(≠) OPPOSITES obscure
2 *The instructor will* **explain** *how to work the machine.*
describe, illustrate, demonstrate, teach

explode VERB
1 *The firework* **exploded**.
blow up, burst, go off, detonate, discharge, erupt
2 *The police have* **exploded** *the bomb safely.*
blow up, set off, detonate, discharge

explore VERB
1 **exploring** *the island*
travel, tour, search, scout, survey
2 *We must* **explore** *the possibilities for the plan.*
examine, investigate, inspect, research, probe, analyse

explosion NOUN
The gun went off with a loud **explosion**.
bang, blast, burst, discharge, clap, crack, report

expose VERB
The newspaper **exposed** *the businessman as a fraudster.*
reveal, show, exhibit, display, uncover, bring to light
(≠) OPPOSITES conceal, cover up

express VERB
1 *The girl* **expressed** *her point very clearly.*
state, voice, say, speak, communicate, put across, convey
2 *The teacher* **expressed** *her disapproval by frowning at us.*
show, exhibit, reveal, indicate, convey

expression NOUN
1 *a puzzled* **expression**
look, air, appearance
2 *a slang* **expression**
phrase, turn of phrase, saying, set phrase

exquisite ADJECTIVE
an **exquisite** *evening dress*
beautiful, attractive, charming, elegant, delightful, lovely, pleasing
(≠) OPPOSITES ugly, unsightly

extend VERB
1 *The grounds of the house* **extend** *for three acres.*
spread, stretch, reach, continue
2 *His stay has been* **extended** *for another six months.*
increase, enlarge, expand, lengthen, widen, draw out, prolong, spin out
(≠) OPPOSITES shorten, cut, reduce

extension NOUN
an **extension** *built onto the house*
addition, supplement, annexe

extent NOUN
1 *the* **extent** *of the universe*
size, dimensions, expanse, area, breadth, spread, stretch, volume, width, measure
2 *the* **extent** *of his knowledge*
limit, bounds, lengths, range, reach, scope

exterior NOUN
the **exterior** *of the building*
outside, surface, covering, coating, face, shell
(≠) OPPOSITES inside, interior

external ADJECTIVE
external *walls*
outer, surface, outside, exterior, outward, outermost
(≠) OPPOSITES internal

extinct ADJECTIVE
1 *Dinosaurs became* **extinct** *billions of years ago.*
dead, gone, ended, vanished, lost

≠ OPPOSITES living
2 *an extinct volcano*
inactive, extinguished, quenched, out

extinguish VERB

The firefighters extinguished the flames.
put out, blow out, snuff out, stifle, smother, quench

extra ADJECTIVE

1 *an extra room*
additional, added, more, further, other
2 *I have some extra paper that I don't need.*
spare, excess, unused, unneeded, leftover, reserve

extract¹ NOUN

an extract from the book
passage, selection, clip, cutting, quotation

extract² VERB

The dentist is going to extract one of my teeth.
remove, take out, draw out
≠ OPPOSITES insert, put in

extraordinary ADJECTIVE

1 *an extraordinary talent for impersonating people*
remarkable, notable, noteworthy, outstanding, special, amazing, wonderful, marvellous, fantastic
≠ OPPOSITES ordinary, unremarkable
2 *an extraordinary experience*
unusual, remarkable, rare, strange, peculiar, surprising
≠ OPPOSITES ordinary, unremarkable

extravagant ADJECTIVE

They have an extravagant lifestyle.
wasteful, spendthrift, lavish

extreme ADJECTIVE

1 *I can't stand extreme heat.*
great, intense, maximum, acute, exceptional, greatest, highest
≠ OPPOSITES mild
2 *his extreme views*
radical, intense, out-and-out, unreasonable, excessive
3 *the extreme corners of the universe*
farthest, far-off, faraway, distant, outermost, remotest, utmost

Aa
Bb
Cc
Dd
Ee
Ff
Gg
Hh
Ii
Jj
Kk
Ll
Mm
Nn
Oo
Pp
Qq
Rr
Ss
Tt
Uu
Vv
Ww
Xx
Yy
Zz

Ff

fable NOUN

1 the **fable** about the tortoise and the hare
story, tale, myth, legend
2 Is the Loch Ness monster just a **fable**?
fiction, yarn, myth, tall story, old wives' tale

fabric NOUN

a cotton **fabric**
material, cloth, textile, stuff

Here are some types of fabric:

corduroy, cotton, denim, felt, flannel, fleece, gingham, linen, nylon, organza, satin, silk, taffeta, velvet, wool

fabulous ADJECTIVE

1 We had a **fabulous** holiday.
wonderful, marvellous, fantastic, superb, amazing, unbelievable, incredible
2 The unicorn is a **fabulous** beast.
mythical, legendary, fabled, fantastic, fictitious, invented, imaginary
⟥ OPPOSITES real

face¹ NOUN

1 a pretty **face**
features, countenance
2 He's making **faces** at me.
grimace, frown, scowl, pout
• **face to face**
He ran round the corner and came **face to face** with a police officer.
opposite, facing, eye to eye, in confrontation

face² VERB

1 The garden **faces** south.
look, be opposite, front, overlook

2 They **faced** danger with great courage.
deal with, confront, face up to, cope with, tackle, brave, meet, experience
• **face up to**
1 You must **face up to** your responsibilities.
accept, come to terms with, acknowledge, recognize, cope with, deal with
2 She just can't **face up to** him at all.
stand up to, confront, defy, oppose

facilities NOUN

The school has excellent **facilities**.
services, resources, equipment, amenities
◇ INFORMAL WORDS mod cons

fact NOUN

1 **facts** and figures
information, detail, particular, point, item, circumstance
2 **fact** and fiction
reality, truth
◆ FORMAL WORDS actuality
⟥ OPPOSITES fiction
• **in fact**
I like Art; **in fact**, it's my favourite subject.
actually, in actual fact, as a matter of fact, in reality, indeed

fade VERB

1 The picture has **faded** in the strong sunlight.
discolour, bleach, pale, whiten, dim, dull, wash out
2 After a few years, the band's popularity **faded**.
fall, dwindle, disappear, vanish
3 The plants **faded** and died.
weaken, dwindle, droop, wilt, wither, shrivel, perish

fail VERB

1 Our plan has **failed**.

be unsuccessful, go wrong, misfire, miss, fall through, come to grief
◇ INFORMAL WORDS flop
≠ OPPOSITES succeed, prosper
2 *His business failed.*
go bankrupt, collapse, go under, founder
◇ INFORMAL WORDS fold, go bust, flop
≠ OPPOSITES succeed, prosper
3 *Her health is beginning to fail.*
weaken, break down, decline, fall, dwindle, fade, wane
4 *Don't fail to hand in your essay on time.*
omit, neglect, forget

failing NOUN

Untidiness is one of my failings.
fault, weakness, defect, imperfection, flaw, blemish, shortcoming
≠ OPPOSITES strength, advantage

failure NOUN

1 *The play was a failure.*
disappointment, fiasco
◇ INFORMAL WORDS flop, wash-out
≠ OPPOSITES success
2 *the failure of the business*
downfall, decline, ruin, crash, collapse, breakdown

faint¹ ADJECTIVE

1 *a faint sound*
slight, weak, feeble, soft, low, hushed, muffled, subdued
≠ OPPOSITES strong, clear
2 *a faint light*
dim, weak, soft, low, feeble
≠ OPPOSITES strong, clear
3 *a faint outline*
dim, faded, hazy, indistinct, vague
≠ OPPOSITES strong, clear
4 *It was so hot that I felt faint.*
dizzy, giddy, light-headed, weak
◇ INFORMAL WORDS woozy

faint² VERB

The woman fainted with shock.
pass out, black out, swoon, collapse, keel over, drop
◇ INFORMAL WORDS flake out

fair¹ ADJECTIVE

1 *Teachers must be fair with their pupils.*
just, impartial, objective, unbiased, unprejudiced
≠ OPPOSITES unfair, prejudiced
2 *fair rules in the game*
lawful, legitimate, honest, trustworthy, upright, honourable
3 *Is she fair or dark?*
blond(e), light, fair-haired, fair-headed
≠ OPPOSITES dark
4 *fair weather*
fine, dry, sunny, bright, clear, cloudless
≠ OPPOSITES cloudy, dull
5 *He is only a fair guitarist.*
average, moderate, not bad, all right, satisfactory, adequate, reasonable, passable
◇ INFORMAL WORDS OK, so-so
≠ OPPOSITES excellent, outstanding

fair² NOUN

I won a cuddly toy at the fair.
show, exhibition, market, bazaar, fête, festival, carnival, gala

faith NOUN

1 *I have no faith in his abilities.*
belief, trust, reliance, dependence, conviction, confidence, assurance
≠ OPPOSITES mistrust
2 *people of many faiths*
religion, belief, persuasion, church

faithful ADJECTIVE

1 *a faithful friend*
loyal, devoted, trusty, reliable, dependable, true
≠ OPPOSITES disloyal
2 *a faithful account of what happened*
accurate, precise, exact, strict, close, true, truthful
≠ OPPOSITES inaccurate

fake¹ ADJECTIVE

1 *a fake fur coat*
imitation, false, pseudo, sham, artificial, mock, reproduction
≠ OPPOSITES genuine, real
2 *a fake passport*

Aa
Bb
Cc
Dd
Ee
Ff
Gg
Hh
Ii
Jj
Kk
Ll
Mm
Nn
Oo
Pp
Qq
Rr
Ss
Tt
Uu
Vv
Ww
Xx
Yy
Zz

forged, false, bogus, counterfeit
◇ INFORMAL WORDS phoney
⊞ OPPOSITES genuine, real

fake² NOUN

*This diamond necklace is a **fake**.*
forgery, copy, reproduction, replica,
imitation, sham

fake³ VERB

1 *He **faked** his father's signature.*
forge, copy, imitate
2 *She **faked** illness to get out of sitting
the test.*
pretend, feign, put on

fall¹ VERB

1 *She **fell** to the ground.*
tumble, stumble, trip, topple, keel over,
collapse, slump, crash
2 *Huge flakes of snow **fell** from the sky.*
drop, descend, come down
⊞ OPPOSITES rise, go up
3 *I **fell** into the pond.*
plunge, slide, sink, dive
4 *The crime rate is **falling**.*
decrease, lessen, decline, diminish,
dwindle, fall off
⊞ OPPOSITES increase

• **fall asleep**
*Jasmeet **fell asleep** in the car on the
way home.*
drop off, doze off, nod off

• **fall in**
1 *Our bedroom ceiling **fell in**.*
collapse, cave in, come down, give way,
sink
2 *I'm happy to **fall in** with your plans.*
go along with, agree with, accept, co-
operate with

• **fall out**
*Katie has **fallen out** with her best
friend.*
quarrel, argue, bicker, fight, disagree,
differ
⊞ OPPOSITES agree

• **fall through**
*Our holiday plans **fell through**.*
fail, come to nothing, collapse
⊞ OPPOSITES come off, succeed

fall² NOUN

1 *a **fall** from her horse*
tumble, drop, dive, plunge
2 *a **fall** in food prices*
decrease, reduction, lessening, drop,
dwindling, slump

false ADJECTIVE

1 *false information*
wrong, incorrect, untrue, mistaken,
inaccurate, invalid, inexact
⊞ OPPOSITES true, right
2 *false eyelashes*
fake, unreal, artificial, synthetic,
imitation, mock
⊞ OPPOSITES real, natural
3 *a false name*
fake, forged, feigned, pretended, sham,
bogus, fictitious
⊞ OPPOSITES real, genuine

fame NOUN

***Fame** and money do not bring
happiness.*
celebrity, stardom, glory, honour,
reputation, name

familiar ADJECTIVE

1 *a **familiar** sight*
common, everyday, routine, ordinary,
well-known
⊞ OPPOSITES unfamiliar, strange
2 *Don't get too **familiar** with your
customers.*
friendly, close, informal, free, free-and-
easy, relaxed
⊞ OPPOSITES formal, reserved
3 *Are you **familiar** with Roald Dahl's
books?*
acquainted, aware, knowledgeable
⊞ OPPOSITES unfamiliar, ignorant

family NOUN

*her close **family***
relatives, relations, kinsmen, people,
folk

Here are some names of family members:

aunt, brother, cousin, daughter, father, foster-child, foster-parent, godchild, godfather, godmother, grandchild, grandfather, grandmother, grandparent, guardian, half-brother, half-sister, husband, mother, nephew, niece, parent, sister, son, spouse, stepfather, stepmother, uncle, wife

famine NOUN

aid for victims of **famine** *in Africa*
starvation, hunger, want
⊘ OPPOSITES plenty

famous ADJECTIVE

a **famous** *pop star*
well-known, famed, celebrated, noted, great, legendary, notable, prominent
⊘ OPPOSITES unheard-of, unknown, obscure

fan¹ NOUN

A **fan** *cooled the room down.*
ventilator, air-conditioner, blower

fan² NOUN

a rock-music **fan**
enthusiast, admirer, supporter, follower, lover
◇ INFORMAL WORDS freak, fiend

fanatic NOUN

1 *a keep-fit* **fanatic**
enthusiast, addict, maniac
◇ INFORMAL WORDS freak, fiend
2 *a religious* **fanatic**
bigot, extremist

fanatical ADJECTIVE

1 *a* **fanatical** *football supporter*
overenthusiastic, passionate, obsessive, single-minded
⊘ OPPOSITES moderate, unenthusiastic
2 **fanatical** *beliefs*
extreme, bigoted
⊘ OPPOSITES moderate

fancy¹ ADJECTIVE

a **fancy** *costume*
elaborate, decorated, ornamented, extravagant
⊘ OPPOSITES plain

fancy² VERB

1 *Do you* **fancy** *a pizza?*
desire, wish for, long for, yearn for, crave
2 *I think he* **fancies** *you.*
like, take a liking to, take to, go for, prefer, favour
⊘ OPPOSITES dislike
3 *He* **fancied** *himself as a singer.*
believe, think, conceive, imagine, dream of, picture
4 *I* **fancy** *it won't be as easy as it looks.*
think, imagine, believe, suppose, reckon, guess

fantastic ADJECTIVE

1 *a* **fantastic** *holiday*
wonderful, marvellous, sensational, superb, excellent, first-rate, tremendous, terrific, great
⊘ OPPOSITES ordinary
2 **fantastic** *creatures*
strange, weird, odd, outlandish
⊘ OPPOSITES real, real-life

fantasy NOUN

1 *She has a* **fantasy** *of becoming a famous singer.*
dream, daydream, vision
2 *He escaped into a world of* **fantasy**.
imagination, dream, daydream, vision, unreality
⊘ OPPOSITES reality

far¹ ADJECTIVE

1 *a house on the* **far** *side of the park*
further, opposite, other
⊘ OPPOSITES near, close
2 *travelling to* **far** *countries*
distant, far-off, faraway, remote, out-of-the-way
⊘ OPPOSITES near, close

far² ADVERB

1 *They live* **far** *away.*

Aa
Bb
Cc
Dd
Ee
Ff
Gg
Hh
Ii
Jj
Kk
Ll
Mm
Nn
Oo
Pp
Qq
Rr
Ss
Tt
Uu
Vv
Ww
Xx
Yy
Zz

Aa
Bb
Cc
Dd
Ee
Ff
Gg
Hh
Ii
Jj
Kk
Ll
Mm
Nn
Oo
Pp
Qq
Rr
Ss
Tt
Uu
Vv
Ww
Xx
Yy
Zz

a long way, a good way, miles
⊞ OPPOSITES near, close
2 *This album is far better than their last one.*
much, greatly, considerably, extremely
◇ INFORMAL WORDS miles
⊞ OPPOSITES slightly

fare NOUN
Children pay half fare on the bus.
charge, cost, price, fee

far-fetched ADJECTIVE
His excuse for being late was a little far-fetched.
unlikely, improbable, incredible, unbelievable, fantastic, unrealistic

farm NOUN

Here are some things you might see on a farm:

barn, chicken coop, haystack, milk churn, milking shed, pen, pig sty, scarecrow, stables, stalls, straw, trough

Farm animals:
bull, calf, cat, chicken, cow, donkey, duck, foal, goat, goose, horse, lamb, pig, piglet, sheep, sheepdog, turkey

Farm equipment:
bailer, combine harvester, cultivator, harrow, mower, plough, seed drill, sprayer, tractor, trailer

fascinate VERB
Wildlife programmes fascinate me.
absorb, engross, intrigue, delight, charm
⊞ OPPOSITES bore

fashion NOUN
1 *the latest fashion*
trend, vogue, style, fad, craze
2 *If you hear the fire alarm, walk out in an orderly fashion.*
way, manner, method, style
3 *Which fashion of furniture do you prefer?*
style, shape, form, type, sort, kind

fashionable ADJECTIVE
fashionable clothes
stylish, trendy, popular, current, latest, up-to-the-minute, contemporary, modern, up-to-date
◇ INFORMAL WORDS cool, hot, in
⊞ OPPOSITES unfashionable

fast¹ ADJECTIVE
⇒ For even more about this word, see the next page
a fast pace
quick, swift, rapid, brisk, speedy, hasty, hurried
⊞ OPPOSITES slow, unhurried

fast² ADVERB
We got out of there fast.
quickly, swiftly, rapidly, speedily, like a flash, like a shot, hastily, hurriedly
⊞ OPPOSITES slowly, gradually

fast³ VERB
You must fast for twelve hours before the operation.
go hungry, diet, starve

fasten VERB
1 *Fasten your seat belts.*
secure, close, shut, lock, bolt
2 *Fasten the two pieces together.*
attach, fix, seal, tie, bind, link, connect, join, unite
⊞ OPPOSITES unfasten, untie
3 *He fastened his coat.*
do up, button, lace, buckle
⊞ OPPOSITES unfasten, untie

fat ADJECTIVE
⇒ For even more about this word, see page 115
If you don't walk your dog, it will get fat.
overweight, plump, obese, tubby, stout, round, chubby, podgy
⊞ OPPOSITES thin, slim

fatal ADJECTIVE
1 *a fatal illness*
deadly, lethal, mortal, incurable, terminal, final

fast

If you want to use a different word from **fast**, you could describe someone or the action they do as

quick
swift
rapid
brisk

You could describe something such as a fast car using more informal words:

speedy
nippy

If something happens fast and it is over quickly, you could say it is

brief
fleeting

You could use these words create better pictures of someone or something moving, walking, talking or eating fast:

briskly
rapidly
speedily
swiftly
at high speed

You could use these informal phrases to describe the way someone does something:

like a flash
like a shot
like the wind

If someone is doing something fast because they are in a rush, they might do it

hastily
hurriedly
rashly
recklessly

Over to you

Can you use some of the words above to replace **fast** in the writing below?

I was late, so I ate my lunch **fast**. I **fast** explained to my mother where I was going, then walked **fast** down the garden path. Once I was round the corner, I started to run **fast** …

2 *a fatal mistake*
disastrous, destructive, calamitous, catastrophic

fate NOUN
1 *It was fate that brought us together.*
destiny, providence, chance, fortune
2 *What will be the fate of this war?*
outcome, destiny, end, future
3 *He met a terrible fate at the hands of his enemies.*
end, death, ruin, destruction, doom

fault NOUN
1 *I like her despite her faults.*
defect, flaw, blemish, shortcoming, weakness, failing
2 *There is a fault in the letter.*
error, mistake, blunder, slip-up, slip, lapse, inaccuracy
3 *It's your fault that we missed the train.*
responsibility

faulty ADJECTIVE
Faulty goods can be returned.
imperfect, flawed, blemished, damaged, out of order, broken
≠ OPPOSITES faultless, in working order

favour¹ NOUN
He did me a favour by looking after my cat.
kindness, service, good turn

favour² VERB
Which candidate do you favour?
prefer, choose, opt for, like, approve of, support, back
≠ OPPOSITES dislike

favourite¹ ADJECTIVE
I wore my favourite dress.
preferred, best-loved, dearest, beloved, chosen
≠ OPPOSITES hated

favourite² NOUN
1 *Which book is your favourite?*
preference, choice, pick
≠ OPPOSITES pet hate
2 *He's always been his mother's favourite.*
darling, pet, blue-eyed boy, blue-eyed girl, teacher's pet, the apple of your eye, idol

fear¹ NOUN
1 *The boy was trembling with fear.*
fright, alarm, terror, horror, panic, dread
≠ OPPOSITES courage, bravery
2 *There is growing fear for his safety.*
worry, anxiety, concern, distress, uneasiness, apprehension, dread
≠ OPPOSITES confidence

fear² VERB
1 *Many people fear spiders.*
be afraid of, take fright at, shrink from, dread, shudder at
2 *I fear we are too late.*
be afraid, worry, suspect, anticipate, expect the worst

fearful ADJECTIVE
1 *fearful of the outcome*
afraid, frightened, scared, alarmed, nervous, anxious, uneasy, panicky

fat

There are other words for **fat** that give away how you feel about something.

If the person or thing you are describing looks pretty or cute, you might say they are

chubby
plump

If you use these next words, it means you think the person or thing does not look very nice. It might sound a little cruel if you use these words!

podgy
tubby

If you want to describe a fat person but not show your opinion, you might describe them as

overweight
stout

Over to you

Which words could you use instead of **fat** in these sentences?

1 The fat baby looked cute when she laughed.

2 They fed the dog too much, and it got too **fat** to run.

3 The doctor told my uncle he was a little bit **fat**.

Which of the words would not sound right in the sentences?

⧧ OPPOSITES brave, courageous, fearless
2 a *fearful* storm
terrible, dreadful, awful, frightful, shocking, appalling, horrible
⧧ OPPOSITES wonderful, delightful

feat NOUN
a *daring* **feat**
deed, exploit, act, accomplishment, achievement

feature¹ NOUN
1 one of the most appealing **features** of the place
aspect, point, attribute, quality, property, trait, characteristic
2 a magazine **feature** on computer games
article, column, report, story, piece, item

feature² VERB
1 a programme **featuring** British rugby

Aa
Bb
Cc
Dd
Ee
Ff
Gg
Hh
Ii
Jj
Kk
Ll
Mm
Nn
Oo
Pp
Qq
Rr
Ss
Tt
Uu
Vv
Ww
Xx
Yy
Zz

highlight, show, present, promote, emphasize, spotlight, play up
2 *The actor has **featured** in several films.*
appear, participate, act, perform, star

fee NOUN
*The membership **fee** is £20.*
charge, bill, account, payment, subscription

feeble ADJECTIVE
1 *a **feeble** voice*
weak, faint, exhausted, powerless
⚡ OPPOSITES strong, powerful
2 *a **feeble** patient*
frail, weak, delicate, puny, sickly, powerless, helpless
3 *a **feeble** excuse*
lame, inadequate, poor, thin, flimsy

feed VERB
*We have enough food to **feed** everyone.*
provide for, nourish, cater for, supply
• **feed on**
*My pet snake **feeds on** mice.*
eat, live on, exist on

feel¹ VERB
1 *Do you **feel** any pain when you move?*
experience, go through, suffer, endure
2 *I **felt** his forehead and it was very hot.*
touch, finger, handle, hold
3 *Your hair **feels** soft.*
seem, appear
4 *I **feel** I have not worked hard enough.*
think, believe, consider, reckon, judge
5 *I **felt** there was a bad atmosphere in the room.*
sense, have a feeling, be aware of, notice, observe
6 *I **feel** like a curry.*
fancy, want, desire

feel² NOUN
1 *the **feel** of silk*
touch, texture, surface, finish
2 *The house has a cosy **feel**.*
quality, sense, impression, feeling

feeling NOUN
1 *I have a **feeling** he's lying to me.*
sense, sensation, instinct, hunch, suspicion, inkling, impression
2 *What are your **feelings** on this subject?*
opinion, impression, idea, notion, view, point of view
3 *She doesn't like to show her **feelings**.*
emotion, passion, sentiment, sentimentality, sensitivity
4 *He has no **feeling** for other people.*
sympathy, compassion, understanding, pity, concern, affection, fondness

fellow NOUN
*a young **fellow***
person, man, boy, individual, character
◇ INFORMAL WORDS chap, bloke, guy

female ADJECTIVE
*a **female** doctor*
feminine, she-
⚡ OPPOSITES male

feminine ADJECTIVE
*her **feminine** charms*
female, womanly, ladylike, gentle
⚡ OPPOSITES masculine

fence NOUN
*There was a **fence** round the field.*
barrier, railing, paling, wall, hedge, barricade

ferocious ADJECTIVE
*a **ferocious** attack*
fierce, vicious, savage, wild, brutal, cruel, bloodthirsty, violent
⚡ OPPOSITES gentle, mild, tame

ferry VERB
*The parents take turns to **ferry** the children to school.*
take, transport, convey, carry, drive, run, move

fertile ADJECTIVE
fertile land
fruitful, abundant, plentiful, rich, lush, luxuriant
⚡ OPPOSITES infertile, barren, sterile

festival NOUN
1 *We went to a music festival in Italy.*
celebration, gala, fête, carnival, fiesta, entertainment, festivities
2 *the religious festival of Easter*
holy day, celebration, anniversary, holiday, feast

festive ADJECTIVE
The village had a festive atmosphere with its bunting.
cheerful, merry, celebratory, holiday, carnival, happy, joyful, jolly
≠ OPPOSITES gloomy, cheerless

fetch VERB
1 *He went to the kitchen to fetch a jug.*
get, collect, bring, carry
2 *My gran fetched me from school.*
get, collect, bring, transport, deliver
◆ FORMAL WORDS escort

fetching ADJECTIVE
You look very fetching with your hair like that.
attractive, pretty, sweet, cute, charming, enchanting

few¹ ADJECTIVE
There are few buses out here on a Sunday.
not many, scarce, rare, uncommon, infrequent, inadequate, insufficient
≠ OPPOSITES many, plenty of

few² PRONOUN
Few would argue with that decision.
not many, hardly any, one or two, a couple, a handful, a small number
≠ OPPOSITES many

fiddle VERB
1 *She was fiddling with her necklace.*
play, toy, trifle, fidget
2 *Don't fiddle with that DVD player.*
tinker, tamper, mess around, meddle, interfere
3 *He has been fiddling the company's accounts.*
cheat, swindle
◇ INFORMAL WORDS cook the books

fidget VERB
1 *Sit still and don't fidget.*
move about, squirm, wriggle, shuffle, twitch, jerk, jump
2 *He was fidgeting with his keys.*
play around, fiddle, mess about, fuss

field NOUN
1 *a field of corn*
meadow, grassland, pasture, paddock
2 *a football field*
ground, playing-field, pitch, green
3 *an expert in the field of ecology*
area, territory, speciality, line

fierce ADJECTIVE
1 *a fierce lion*
savage, ferocious, vicious, cruel, brutal, aggressive
≠ OPPOSITES gentle, kind, calm
2 *a fierce desire to be famous*
intense, keen, strong, powerful

fiery ADJECTIVE
1 *a fiery sun*
burning, flaming, blazing, red-hot, glowing, hot
≠ OPPOSITES cold
2 *a fiery temperament*
passionate, excitable, impetuous, hot-headed, fierce, violent
≠ OPPOSITES impassive

fight¹ NOUN
1 *The two boys got into a fight in the playground.*
battle, bout, combat, brawl, scrap, scuffle, tussle
2 *the fight against crime*
battle, war, struggle
3 *They had a fight over whose turn it was to do the washing-up.*
quarrel, row, argument, dispute

fight² VERB
1 *The two men were fighting in the street.*
battle, wrestle, brawl, scrap, scuffle, tussle, grapple, struggle
2 *My grandfather was away fighting in the war.*

Aa
Bb
Cc
Dd
Ee
Ff
Gg
Hh
Ii
Jj
Kk
Ll
Mm
Nn
Oo
Pp
Qq
Rr
Ss
Tt
Uu
Vv
Ww
Xx
Yy
Zz

do battle, war, combat, battle
3 *The brothers seem to fight continuously.*
quarrel, argue, dispute, squabble, bicker, wrangle
4 *The locals fought the plan to build a motorway.*
oppose, resist, withstand, defy, stand up to

figure¹ NOUN

1 *Write the amount in figures.*
number, numeral, digit
2 *The total figure will be much higher.*
amount, sum
3 *She has a very slim figure.*
shape, form, outline, body, frame, build, physique
4 *public figures such as the Prime Minister*
personality, character, person, celebrity

figure² VERB

The wizard character figures in all her stories.
appear, feature, crop up
• **figure out**
I'm trying to figure out how to assemble this kit.
work out, calculate, reckon, puzzle out, understand, see, make out

file¹ NOUN

1 *a file of letters*
folder, binder, case
2 *your medical files*
record, information, documents, data

file² VERB

1 *He files his CDs alphabetically.*
arrange, classify, order, store
2 *I want to file an official complaint.*
register, record, note, enter
3 *The troops filed past.*
march, troop, parade

file³ VERB

File the rough edges.
smooth, rub, rub down, scrape, polish

fill VERB

I filled my trolley with groceries.

pack, stock, supply, crowd, cram, stuff
≠ OPPOSITES empty, unload
• **fill in**
1 *I filled in the application form.*
complete, fill out, answer
2 *A supply teacher will fill in for our usual teacher while she is ill.*
stand in, substitute, replace, cover

film¹ NOUN

1 *an action film*
motion picture, picture, video, DVD, feature film, short, documentary
◇ INFORMAL WORDS movie
2 *a thin film of dust*
layer, covering, dusting, coat, coating

Here are some types of film:

action, animation, cartoon, comedy, crime, horror, romance, science fiction, thriller, western

film² VERB

The concert was filmed for television.
photograph, shoot, video, videotape

filth NOUN

1 *The streets are covered with filth.*
dirt, grime, muck, refuse, rubbish, garbage, trash, slime
2 *The filth of the city is a disgrace.*
uncleanness, pollution, contamination, foulness, sordidness, squalor
≠ OPPOSITES cleanness, cleanliness, purity

filthy ADJECTIVE

1 *The boy's hands were filthy.*
dirty, soiled, unwashed, grimy, grubby, mucky, unclean
≠ OPPOSITES clean, spotless
2 *a filthy trick to play on someone*
vile, dirty, foul, sordid, squalid, low, mean

final ADJECTIVE

the final moments of the match
last, latest, closing, concluding,

finishing, end, last-minute
⊘ OPPOSITES **first, opening**

finally ADVERB

1 *We finally reached London at midnight.*
lastly, eventually, at last, in the end
2 *I'd like to finally stop biting my nails.*
for good, once and for all, for ever, definitely

finances NOUN

We'll have to look at our finances before we go on holiday.
money, cash, funds, resources, bank account, budget, income

find VERB

1 *I found my bangle under my bed.*
discover, locate, track down, come across, chance on, stumble on, spot
2 *When we arrived, we found that the others had gone home.*
discover, notice, observe, perceive, realize, learn
3 *He found happiness at last when he moved to France.*
achieve, attain, win, reach, gain, obtain, get
4 *I find long division difficult.*
consider, think, judge

• **find out**
I found out where Ewan lives.
learn, discover, detect, perceive, realize
◆ FORMAL WORDS **ascertain**

fine¹ ADJECTIVE

1 *a fine young man*
attractive, beautiful, handsome, lovely, nice
2 *This is a fine book.*
excellent, outstanding, exceptional, superior, splendid, brilliant, good
3 *dressed in fine clothes*
splendid, exquisite, magnificent, elegant, lovely
4 *a fine fabric*
thin, slender, sheer, gauzy, flimsy, delicate, dainty
⊘ OPPOSITES **thick, coarse**
5 *That all seems fine to me.*

all right, satisfactory, acceptable
◇ INFORMAL WORDS **OK**
6 *fine weather*
bright, sunny, clear, cloudless, dry, fair

fine² NOUN

a parking fine
penalty, punishment, damages

finish¹ VERB

1 *We finished the meeting with a song.*
end, stop, close, wind up, round off
◆ FORMAL WORDS **cease**
⊘ OPPOSITES **begin, start**
2 *I've finished my homework.*
do, complete, accomplish, achieve, fulfil, deal with
⊘ OPPOSITES **begin, start**
3 *Hari finished the milk.*
use up, eat, drink, drain, empty

finish² NOUN

The race had a very close finish.
end, completion, close, ending
⊘ OPPOSITES **beginning, start**

fire¹ NOUN

a blazing fire
flames, blaze, bonfire

fire² VERB

1 *They fired a rocket into the sky.*
shoot, launch, set off, let off, explode
2 *The shop assistant was fired for taking money from the till.*
sack, dismiss, discharge

firm¹ ADJECTIVE

1 *a firm mattress*
hard, solid, stiff, rigid, inflexible
⊘ OPPOSITES **soft, spongy**
2 *a firm foundation*
secure, steady, stable, sturdy, strong
⊘ OPPOSITES **unsteady, loose**
3 *firm control*
strict, unshakable, determined
⊘ OPPOSITES **hesitant**
4 *firm friends*
dependable, true
5 *a firm belief in his innocence*
sure, convinced, definite, settled, committed

Aa
Bb
Cc
Dd
Ee
Ff
Gg
Hh
Ii
Jj
Kk
Ll
Mm
Nn
Oo
Pp
Qq
Rr
Ss
Tt
Uu
Vv
Ww
Xx
Yy
Zz

firm² NOUN

an insurance firm
company, corporation, business, organization, association, partnership

first¹ ADJECTIVE

1 *a first course in computing*
elementary, introductory, preliminary, primary, basic, fundamental
2 *the first inhabitants of America*
earliest, original, primitive, oldest
⊯ OPPOSITES last, final
3 *Scotland's first minister*
chief, main, key, principal, head, leading, ruling, highest

first² ADVERB

Which of you was here first?
to begin with, to start with, initially, at the outset, beforehand, originally

fish NOUN

Here are some types of fish:

carp, catfish, cod, dogfish, dory, eel, flounder, goldfish, guppy, haddock, hake, halibut, herring, hoki, kipper, ling, mackerel, minnow, pike, pilchard, piranha, plaice, pollock, salmon, sardine, shark, skate, sole, stickleback, stingray, swordfish, trout, tuna
Shellfish:
clam, cockle, crab, crayfish, king prawn, lobster, mussel, oyster, prawn, scallop, shrimp, whelk

fit¹ ADJECTIVE

1 *She's not fit to be a teacher.*
suitable, capable, competent, qualified, worthy
⊯ OPPOSITES unsuitable
2 *This is not a fit time to discuss the matter.*
appropriate, suitable, apt, fitting, correct, right, proper
⊯ OPPOSITES unsuitable, inappropriate
3 *She keeps fit by swimming every day.*
healthy, well, in good form, in good shape, sturdy, strong
⊯ OPPOSITES unfit

fit² VERB

1 *He fits the description of the man the police are looking for.*
match, correspond to, follow, agree with, tally with, suit, go with
2 *I fitted the key into the lock.*
place, arrange, position

fit³ NOUN

I had a fit of the giggles.
attack, outbreak, bout, spell, burst, surge, outburst

fitting ADJECTIVE

It was only right and fitting that Gita got the award.
proper, apt, appropriate, suitable, correct, right, deserved
⊯ OPPOSITES unsuitable, improper

fix¹ VERB

1 *My dad fixed the broken TV.*
mend, repair, correct, adjust
⊯ OPPOSITES damage
2 *Let's fix a date for the picnic.*
arrange, set, specify, agree on, decide, determine, settle, resolve, finalize
3 *fixing a shelf to the wall*
fasten, secure, tie, attach, join, connect, link, stick
⊯ OPPOSITES move, shift

fix² NOUN

He's got into a bit of a fix with money.
mess, dilemma, predicament, plight, difficulty
◇ INFORMAL WORDS hole

fizzy ADJECTIVE

fizzy drinks
bubbly, sparkling, gassy, bubbling, frothy, foaming

flabby ADJECTIVE

flabby arms
slack, fat, fleshy, soft, floppy, sagging, loose
⊯ OPPOSITES firm, strong

Aa Bb Cc Dd Ee Ff Gg Hh Ii Jj Kk Ll Mm Nn Oo Pp Qq Rr Ss Tt Uu Vv Ww Xx Yy Zz

flag VERB
Halfway through the race I started to flag.
weaken, sink, fade, fail, slow, tire, weary, droop
⇎ OPPOSITES revive

flap VERB
1 *The washing was flapping about in the breeze.*
flutter, wave, swing, swish
2 *The bird began to flap its wings.*
beat, flutter, vibrate, shake, thrash

flare up VERB
Violence has flared up in the city overnight.
break out, erupt, blow up

flash¹ NOUN
a flash of light
beam, ray, shaft, spark, blaze, flare, burst, gleam, glint

flash² VERB
His glasses flashed in the sun.
shine, beam, flare, blaze, glare, gleam, glint

flat¹ ADJECTIVE
1 *a flat surface*
level, plane, even, smooth, horizontal
⇎ OPPOSITES bumpy, sloping, angled
2 *a flat voice*
boring, dull, monotonous, tedious, uninteresting, unexciting, lifeless
3 *a flat refusal*
absolute, utter, total, positive, point-blank, direct, straight, plain

flat² NOUN
We live in a top-floor flat.
apartment, penthouse, tenement, rooms, suite, bedsit, bedsitter

flatter VERB
He tries to win over his teachers by flattering them.
praise, compliment, play up to, curry favour with
◇ INFORMAL WORDS sweet-talk, butter up
⇎ OPPOSITES criticize

flavour NOUN
1 *a strong flavour*
taste, tang, relish, zest
2 *The film has the flavour of an old cowboy movie.*
quality, property, character, style, feel, atmosphere

flaw NOUN
1 *There is a flaw in this vase.*
imperfection, fault, blemish, spot, mark, speck, crack, split
2 *Vanity is the main flaw in his character.*
weakness, shortcoming, failing
3 *There are several flaws in this report.*
error, mistake, lapse, slip

fleck NOUN
flecks of dust
dot, spot, mark, speck, speckle, streak

flee VERB
The burglars fled before the police arrived.
run away, bolt, fly, take flight, make off, escape, get away
◇ INFORMAL WORDS take off
⇎ OPPOSITES stay

flexible ADJECTIVE
1 *A gymnast has to be very flexible.*
supple, lithe, double-jointed, stretchy
⇎ OPPOSITES inflexible, rigid
2 *a flexible hose*
pliable, bendable, bendy, elastic, springy
⇎ OPPOSITES inflexible, rigid
3 *flexible working hours*
adaptable, adjustable, open
⇎ OPPOSITES inflexible, fixed

flick VERB
He flicked me on the arm.
hit, strike, rap, tap, touch
• **flick through**
She was flicking through a magazine.
flip through, thumb through, leaf through, glance at, skim, scan

Aa
Bb
Cc
Dd
Ee
Ff
Gg
Hh
Ii
Jj
Kk
Ll
Mm
Nn
Oo
Pp
Qq
Rr
Ss
Tt
Uu
Vv
Ww
Xx
Yy
Zz

flicker¹ VERB

1 *A candle flickered in the window.*
twinkle, sparkle, glimmer, shimmer
2 *Her eyelids flickered and then opened.*
flutter, quiver, waver

flicker² NOUN

There was a flicker of annoyance in his eyes.
flash, gleam, glint, twinkle, glimmer, spark, trace

flight NOUN

a transatlantic flight
journey, trip, voyage

flimsy ADJECTIVE

a piece of flimsy material
thin, fine, light, slight, fragile, delicate
≠ OPPOSITES sturdy, durable

flinch VERB

1 *She flinched when she shut her finger in the car door.*
wince, cringe, cower, quail, shrink, draw back
2 *He has never flinched from doing his duty.*
shy away, duck, shirk, flee

fling VERB

He flung a cushion at me.
throw, hurl, toss, sling, launch, let fly, heave
◇ INFORMAL WORDS chuck

flip VERB

He flipped a coin in the air.
spin, flick, twirl, twist, turn, toss

float VERB

1 *a paper bag floating in the air*
glide, drift, waft, hover, hang
2 *a paper boat floating down the river*
drift, glide, sail, swim, bob
≠ OPPOSITES sink

flock¹ NOUN

a flock of seagulls
group, herd, pack, crowd, mass, bunch, gathering

flock² VERB

1 *people flocking to the sales*
swarm, crowd, herd, troop, mass
2 *The fans flocked round the film star.*
crowd, mass, bunch, cluster, huddle, group, gather, collect

flood¹ NOUN

Our carpets were ruined in the flood.
flow, tide, stream, rush, spate, outpouring, overflow
≠ OPPOSITES drought

flood² VERB

The river burst its banks, flooding the surrounding farmland.
swamp, soak, drench, fill, overflow

floor NOUN

1 *a wooden floor*
flooring, ground, base
2 *We live on the third floor.*
storey, level, stage, landing

flop¹ VERB

1 *hair flopping over her face*
droop, hang, dangle, drop, fall, tumble
2 *The play flopped.*
fail, fall flat, founder, fold

flop² NOUN

His last album was a flop.
failure, non-starter, disaster
◇ INFORMAL WORDS wash-out

flow¹ VERB

1 *The river flows by the house.*
run, rush, stream, sweep, move, ripple, drift, swirl
2 *The water flowed over the edge of the bath.*
spill, well, gush, run, pour, cascade, flood, overflow, surge

flow² NOUN

1 *the flow of the river to the sea*
current, tide, drift, stream, flood, spate
2 *a steady flow of questions*
stream, flood

Aa Bb Cc Dd Ee **Ff** Gg Hh Ii Jj Kk Ll Mm Nn Oo Pp Qq Rr Ss Tt Uu Vv Ww Xx Yy Zz

flower NOUN
wild flowers
bloom, blossom, bud

Here are some names of flowers:
aster, azalea, begonia, bluebell, carnation, chrysanthemum, cornflower, crocus, daffodil, dahlia, daisy, forget-me-not, foxglove, freesia, fuchsia, gardenia, geranium, gladiolus, hollyhock, hyacinth, iris, lily, lily-of-the-valley, lupin, marigold, nasturtium, orchid, pansy, petunia, phlox, poinsettia, poppy, primrose, primula, rose, snapdragon, snowdrop, sunflower, sweet pea, sweet william, tulip, violet, wallflower
Parts of a flower:
leaf, petal, pollen, seed, stalk, stem
⇒ Also look up **plant**

fluffy ADJECTIVE
fluffy pink slippers
soft, furry, fuzzy, downy, feathery, fleecy, woolly

fluid NOUN
the fluids in the body
liquid

flush VERB
She flushed when she was presented with flowers.
blush, go red, redden, glow

flutter VERB
1 *The streamers were fluttering in the breeze.*
flap, wave, ripple, flicker, toss
2 *The moth fluttered its wings.*
flap, wave, beat, shake, vibrate
3 *His eyelids fluttered as he slept.*
quiver, tremble, shiver, twitch

fly VERB
1 *A bird flew overhead.*
soar, glide, float, hover, flit
2 *The eagle flew into the air.*
take off, rise, soar
3 *Lindsay flew down the road.*
rush, race, sprint, dash, tear, hurry, speed, shoot, dart, zoom

foam¹ NOUN
the foam on top of the water
bubbles, froth, lather, suds

foam² VERB
The bubble bath made the water foam.
froth, lather, bubble, fizz

focus VERB
1 *I'm focusing on my schoolwork this year.*
concentrate, centre, spotlight
2 *He focused his gaze on the floor.*
aim, direct, fix

foggy ADJECTIVE
a foggy day
misty, hazy, smoggy, cloudy, grey
≠ OPPOSITES clear

foil VERB
The police arrived and foiled the burglars.
stop, defeat, thwart, frustrate, check, obstruct, block

fold¹ VERB
Fold the paper in half.
bend, double, tuck, pleat, crease

fold² NOUN
the folds of her skirt
crease, layer, overlap, tuck, pleat, line, wrinkle, furrow

follow VERB
1 *Tuesday follows Monday.*
come after, succeed, come next
≠ OPPOSITES precede, come before
2 *We followed him to see where he went.*
go after, track, trail, shadow, tail
3 *Follow the instructions to install the CD-ROM.*
carry out, obey, observe, practise
≠ OPPOSITES disobey

Aa
Bb
Cc
Dd
Ee
Ff
Gg
Hh
Ii
Jj
Kk
Ll
Mm
Nn
Oo
Pp
Qq
Rr
Ss
Tt
Uu
Vv
Ww
Xx
Yy
Zz

Aa
Bb
Cc
Dd
Ee
Ff
Gg
Hh
Ii
Jj
Kk
Ll
Mm
Nn
Oo
Pp
Qq
Rr
Ss
Tt
Uu
Vv
Ww
Xx
Yy
Zz

4 *I couldn't **follow** the plot of that film.*
understand, grasp
◆ FORMAL WORDS comprehend
◇ INFORMAL WORDS get

follower NOUN
1 *His **followers** agree with everything he says.*
supporter, attendant, helper, companion, backer, admirer, fan
◇ INFORMAL WORDS sidekick, hanger-on
⊨ OPPOSITES leader, opponent
2 *the great philosopher and his **followers***
pupil, disciple, imitator, believer

fond ADJECTIVE
*I'm very **fond** of chocolate ice cream.*
keen on, partial to, attached to, addicted to, hooked on

food NOUN
1 *Try to eat more organic **food**.*
nourishment, nutrition, diet
◇ INFORMAL WORDS eats, grub, nosh
2 *Our **food** is getting low.*
stores, rations, supplies
3 *I like the **food** at this restaurant.*
fare, cooking, cuisine, menu
◇ INFORMAL WORDS eats, grub, nosh

Here are some ways of preparing food:
baste, beat, blend, chop, cream, crush, cut, dice, grate, liquidize, marinate, mash, mince, mix, peel, slice, stew, whip

fool¹ NOUN
*I was a **fool** to trust him.*
idiot, blockhead, dunce, dimwit, simpleton, halfwit
◇ INFORMAL WORDS chump, dope

fool² VERB
*I was **fooled** into giving him money.*
deceive, take in, dupe, trick, hoax, con, cheat, swindle
• **fool about**

*Stop **fooling about** and do your homework.*
play about
◇ INFORMAL WORDS mess about, mess around, horse around, lark about

foolish ADJECTIVE
1 *You were very **foolish** to believe her.*
stupid, unwise, idiotic, unintelligent, silly, daft
⊨ OPPOSITES wise, sensible
2 *I've never heard such a **foolish** idea in my life.*
stupid, daft, unwise, ill-advised, half-baked, hare-brained, half-witted, absurd, ridiculous, nonsensical
⊨ OPPOSITES wise, sensible

football NOUN

Here are some words used in football:
assistant referee, bench, booking, corner, defender, dugout, extra time, foul, free kick, goal, goalkeeper, handball, hat trick, header, linesman, manager, midfielder, nutmeg, offside, onside, own goal, penalty, penalty shoot-out, pitch, referee, score, striker, substitute, sweeper, throw-in, winger

forbid VERB
*Access to this room is **forbidden** to pupils.*
ban, prohibit, refuse, deny, veto
⊨ OPPOSITES allow, permit, approve

force¹ NOUN
1 *They used **force** to get what they wanted.*
violence, influence, pressure, aggression
2 *the **force** of his personality*
power, strength, intensity, energy, vigour, drive
⊨ OPPOSITES weakness
3 *the armed **forces***
army, troop, body, regiment, squadron, battalion, division, unit

force² VERB
*We were **forced** to leave.*
make, oblige, pressurize, drive, push
◇ INFORMAL WORDS lean on

forecast¹ NOUN
*the weather **forecast***
prediction, expectation, outlook, guess

forecast² VERB
*trying to **forecast** the result of the match*
predict, prophesy, foretell, foresee,
anticipate, estimate

foreign ADJECTIVE
1 *foreign visitors*
alien, immigrant, imported,
international, overseas
⧧ OPPOSITES native
2 *travelling to foreign lands*
exotic, faraway, distant, remote,
strange, unfamiliar
⧧ OPPOSITES native

forge VERB
*Someone has **forged** my signature.*
fake, counterfeit, falsify, copy, imitate

foresee VERB
*We do not **forsee** any big problems.*
expect, predict, forecast, foretell,
anticipate

forgery NOUN
*This painting is a **forgery**.*
fake, copy, replica, reproduction,
imitation, phoney, fraud
⧧ OPPOSITES original

forget VERB
*I **forgot** my duties as a prefect.*
neglect, omit, fail, let slip, overlook,
ignore
⧧ OPPOSITES remember

forgetful ADJECTIVE
*My Granny is very **forgetful**.*
absent-minded, dreamy, vague

forgive VERB
*Can you **forgive** me for forgetting your
birthday?*

excuse, pardon, let off, overlook
⧧ OPPOSITES punish

form¹ VERB
1 *a horse **formed** out of clay*
make, shape, mould, model, fashion,
produce, create, build, construct
2 *They began to **form** their plans.*
arrange, make, construct, devise, put
together, organize
3 *a nest **formed** from twigs and moss*
make up, comprise, compose
4 *ice **forming** on the surface of the
water*
grow, appear, take shape, develop

form² NOUN
1 *a cake in the **form** of a castle*
shape, appearance, model, pattern,
design
2 *She has a slender **form**.*
shape, outline, silhouette, figure, build
3 *a novel in the **form** of a diary*
structure, format, arrangement,
organization, system
4 *a **form** of punishment*
type, kind, sort, order, variety
5 *in the sixth **form***
class, year, grade
6 *He is in good **form** today.*
health, fitness, condition, spirits
7 *Fill in the application **form**.*
document, paper, sheet, questionnaire

formal ADJECTIVE
*The wedding was a **formal** occasion.*
official, ceremonial, solemn,
conventional, regular

former ADJECTIVE
*his **former** girlfriend*
past, ex-, one-time, sometime, old,
earlier, prior, previous
⧧ OPPOSITES current, present, future,
following

fortunate ADJECTIVE
1 *It was **fortunate** that I kept the
receipt.*
lucky, convenient, advantageous,
favourable

Aa
Bb
Cc
Dd
Ee
Ff
Gg
Hh
Ii
Jj
Kk
Ll
Mm
Nn
Oo
Pp
Qq
Rr
Ss
Tt
Uu
Vv
Ww
Xx
Yy
Zz

⊉ OPPOSITES unlucky, unfortunate
2 *We should help those less **fortunate** than ourselves.*
lucky, happy, successful, well-off
⊉ OPPOSITES unlucky, unfortunate

fortune NOUN

1 *He won a **fortune** on the lottery.*
riches, wealth
◇ INFORMAL WORDS mint
2 *She left her entire **fortune** to her cats.*
wealth, riches, treasure, income, means, property, possessions
3 *By good **fortune** we bumped into each other at the station.*
luck, chance, accident, fate, destiny

forward¹ ADJECTIVE

1 *a **forward** movement*
onward, leading
⊉ OPPOSITES backward
2 *moving into a **forward** position*
front, first, head, fore, foremost, leading
⊉ OPPOSITES backward
3 *That child is becoming too **forward**.*
cheeky, pushy, bold, impudent, impertinent, familiar
⊉ OPPOSITES shy, modest

forward² ADVERB

*Go straight **forward** at the crossroads.*
on, forwards, ahead, onward

foster VERB

*They have **fostered** three children.*
take care of, raise, bring up, care for, support
⊉ OPPOSITES neglect

foul¹ ADJECTIVE

1 *a **foul** odour*
stinking, smelly, rotten, offensive, repulsive, revolting, disgusting
⊉ OPPOSITES pleasant
2 *foul language*
obscene, smutty, indecent, coarse, vulgar, gross
3 *foul weather*
bad, unpleasant, rainy, wet, stormy, rough
⊉ OPPOSITES fine

foul² VERB

*You shouldn't let your dog **foul** the pavement.*
dirty, soil, stain, taint, pollute, contaminate

found VERB

*The charity was **founded** in 2005.*
start, originate, create, set up, establish, organize

foundation NOUN

*The rumour has no **foundation**.*
base, basis, grounds

fountain NOUN

*I threw a coin in the **fountain**.*
spring, spray, jet, spout, well, reservoir

fracture¹ NOUN

*a hip **fracture***
break, crack, split

fracture² VERB

*He **fractured** his wrist playing football.*
break, crack, split, splinter, chip
⊉ OPPOSITES join

fragile ADJECTIVE

1 *a **fragile** crystal glass*
breakable, delicate, flimsy, dainty, fine, insubstantial
⊉ OPPOSITES robust, tough
2 *He is in very **fragile** health.*
frail, delicate, weak, feeble
⊉ OPPOSITES robust, tough

fragment NOUN

*a **fragment** of glass*
piece, bit, particle, scrap, shred, chip, splinter, sliver

fragrant ADJECTIVE

fragrant flowers
sweet-smelling, perfumed, scented, sweet

frail ADJECTIVE

1 *a **frail** old lady*
feeble, delicate, puny, weak, infirm
⊉ OPPOSITES tough, strong
2 *the dragonfly's **frail** wings*

delicate, brittle, breakable, fragile, flimsy, insubstantial, slight
≠ OPPOSITES **tough, strong**

frame NOUN

1 *built on a steel frame*
structure, framework, skeleton, casing, construction, bodywork
2 *a picture frame*
border, mounting, mount, setting, surround, edge

frank ADJECTIVE

He's always been frank about how he feels.
honest, blunt, sincere, open, direct, straight, straightforward, outspoken
≠ OPPOSITES **insincere**

frankly ADVERB

1 *Frankly, I couldn't care less.*
to be honest, to be frank, in truth
2 *She spoke frankly about what was troubling her.*
honestly, bluntly, openly, freely, plainly, directly, sincerely
≠ OPPOSITES **insincerely**

frantic ADJECTIVE

The woman was frantic with worry about her child.
desperate, beside yourself, mad, wild, raving, frenzied
≠ OPPOSITES **calm, composed**

fraud NOUN

1 *The businessman was charged with fraud.*
deception, deceit, cheating, swindling
2 *The healer turned out to be a fraud.*
fake, hoaxer, cheat, swindler, con man
◇ INFORMAL WORDS **phoney**

freak NOUN

She's a bit of a health freak.
fanatic, enthusiast, addict, fan
◇ INFORMAL WORDS **buff, fiend, nut**

free¹ ADJECTIVE

1 *The hostages were free at last.*
at liberty, at large, loose, unrestrained, liberated

≠ OPPOSITES **imprisoned, confined, restricted**
2 *Is this seat free?*
available, spare, unoccupied, vacant, empty
≠ OPPOSITES **busy, occupied**
3 *If you buy one hamburger, the second is free.*
without charge, free of charge, on the house

free² VERB

The prisoners were freed.
release, let go, discharge, loose, turn loose, set free, liberate
≠ OPPOSITES **imprison, confine**

freedom NOUN

You have the freedom to do as you wish.
power, scope, privilege, free rein, free hand, opportunity
≠ OPPOSITES **restriction**

freeze VERB

1 *The lake freezes every winter.*
ice over, ice up, solidify, harden, stiffen
2 *I used half of the meat and froze the other half.*
deep-freeze, ice, refrigerate

freezing ADJECTIVE

a freezing winter wind
icy, frosty, wintry, raw, bitter, biting, cutting, cold, chilly
≠ OPPOSITES **hot, warm**

frequent ADJECTIVE

1 *frequent complaints about the noise*
constant, numerous, countless, continual, persistent, repeated, regular
≠ OPPOSITES **infrequent, occasional**
2 *a frequent problem with this make of car*
common, commonplace, everyday, familiar, usual, customary

fresh ADJECTIVE

1 *fresh supplies*
additional, supplementary, extra, more, further, other

Aa
Bb
Cc
Dd
Ee
Ff
Gg
Hh
Ii
Jj
Kk
Ll
Mm
Nn
Oo
Pp
Qq
Rr
Ss
Tt
Uu
Vv
Ww
Xx
Yy
Zz

2 *a fresh approach*
new, novel, original, different,
unconventional
⊜ OPPOSITES old, hackneyed
3 *a fresh breeze*
cool, refreshing, brisk, crisp, keen
4 *fresh fruit*
raw, natural, unprocessed
⊜ OPPOSITES dried, processed
5 *I felt nice and fresh after a shower.*
refreshed, revived, restored, energetic,
vigorous, lively
⊜ OPPOSITES tired, stale

fret VERB
She's fretting about her missing cat.
worry, agonize, brood, pine

friend NOUN
Louise and Harriet are best friends.
companion, comrade, ally, partner,
associate, acquaintance
◇ INFORMAL WORDS mate, pal, chum,
buddy, crony
⊜ OPPOSITES enemy, opponent

friendly ADJECTIVE
Tariq is always friendly and pleasant.
kind, kindly, helpful, sociable, outgoing,
approachable, welcoming
◇ INFORMAL WORDS pally, chummy
⊜ OPPOSITES hostile, unsociable

friendship NOUN
Sean and Mark have a close friendship.
closeness, attachment, affection,
fondness, love, goodwill, friendliness

fright NOUN
1 *The girl screamed in fright.*
shock, alarm, dismay, dread,
apprehension, fear, terror, horror, panic
2 *You gave me such a fright!*
shock, scare, start

frighten VERB
Spiders frighten me.
scare, alarm, terrify, horrify, appal,
shock
◇ INFORMAL WORDS scare stiff
⊜ OPPOSITES reassure, calm

frightened ADJECTIVE
⇒ For even more about this word, see
the next page
I feel frightened in the dark.
scared, alarmed, afraid, fearful,
terrified, petrified
◇ INFORMAL WORDS scared stiff, scared
out of your wits

frightening ADJECTIVE
*Their trek through the jungle was a
frightening experience.*
scary, alarming, terrifying, hair-raising,
spine-chilling

frightful ADJECTIVE
1 *The animals were kept in frightful
conditions.*
awful, dreadful, terrible, appalling,
shocking, grim, ghastly, hideous, horrible
2 *The cats were making a frightful noise.*
unpleasant, disagreeable, awful,
dreadful, fearful, terrible, hideous,
horrible, horrid
⊜ OPPOSITES pleasant, agreeable

frilly ADJECTIVE
curtains with a frilly edge
ruffled, crimped, gathered, frilled, lacy
⊜ OPPOSITES plain

fringe NOUN
1 *on the fringes of the city*
margin, outskirts, edge, limits,
borderline
2 *a leather jacket with fringes*
border, edging, trimming, tassel, frill

frisky ADJECTIVE
a frisky puppy
lively, spirited, high-spirited, playful,
bouncy
⊜ OPPOSITES quiet, calm

front[1] NOUN
1 *the front of the building*
outside, face, exterior, facing
⊜ OPPOSITES back, rear
2 *the front of the queue*
head, top, start, lead
⊜ OPPOSITES back, rear

frightened

You can show how **frightened** someone is by choosing the correct words.

These words are arranged from being quite frightened to being very frightened!

uneasy → **alarmed** → **afraid** → **terrified** → **petrified**

If you are a little bit frightened, you might feel
uneasy
anxious
apprehensive

If you are more frightened than that, you might feel
afraid
fearful
scared
alarmed
shocked

If you are very frightened, you might feel
horrified
terrified
terror-stricken
petrified

Informal phrases for being frightened are
scared out of your wits
scared stiff

Things you might do when you are frightened are
panic
tremble
shudder

Informal phrases for things you might do:
shake like a leaf
have your heart in your mouth
freak out

Something that frightens you might
strike fear into your heart

make your blood run cold
scare the living daylights out of you
make your hair stand on end
make you jump out of your skin

To create a frightening atmosphere in scary story, you could say it is

spooky
eerie
grim

Over to you

Try using these words and phrases, just as this writer has done.

The humming started quietly – but then it grew louder as the sky darkened around him. He started to **tremble** then **shudder** as they started falling on him – not one, but thousands. He was **shocked** by the noise and could not move. It **struck fear into his heart** when he realized that his phone was dead …

Here are some ideas to get you started!

- You are stuck in a lift.

- Your brakes fail as you cycle down a steep hill.

- You are swimming near shore when a shark appears.

Aa
Bb
Cc
Dd
Ee
Ff
Gg
Hh
Ii
Jj
Kk
Ll
Mm
Nn
Oo
Pp
Qq
Rr
Ss
Tt
Uu
Vv
Ww
Xx
Yy
Zz

front² ADJECTIVE
the **front** row of the audience
foremost, fore, first, leading, head
(≠) OPPOSITES back, rear, last

frontier NOUN
Soldiers guard the **frontier** between the countries.
border, boundary, borderline, limit, edge, bounds, verge

frosty ADJECTIVE
1 a **frosty** morning
cold, icy, frozen, freezing, wintry, chilly
2 a **frosty** smile
unfriendly, unwelcoming, cool, standoffish, stiff, discouraging
(≠) OPPOSITES warm

froth NOUN
He blew the **froth** off his coffee.
foam, bubbles, lather, suds

frown¹ NOUN
a **frown** of displeasure
scowl, glower, glare

frown² VERB
The teacher **frowned** at his noisy pupils.
scowl, glower, glare

fruit NOUN

Varieties of fruit include:

apple, apricot, avocado, banana, cherry, damson, date, fig, grape, greengage, guava, kiwi fruit, lychee, mango, melon, nectarine, papaya, passion fruit, peach, pear, pineapple, plum, pomegranate, sharon fruit, star fruit

Berries:
blackberry, blackcurrant, blueberry, cranberry, gooseberry, raspberry, redcurrant, strawberry

Citrus fruit:
clementine, grapefruit, kumquat, lemon, lime, mandarin, minneola, orange, satsuma, tangerine

fruitful ADJECTIVE

1 *a lush and fruitful land*
fertile, rich, productive
≠ OPPOSITES barren
2 *a fruitful meeting*
successful, productive, rewarding, profitable, advantageous, worthwhile, useful
≠ OPPOSITES fruitless

fruitless ADJECTIVE

a fruitless search for survivors
unsuccessful, useless, pointless, vain, hopeless
≠ OPPOSITES fruitful, successful, profitable

frustrate VERB

1 *His hopes of playing for England were frustrated.*
thwart, block, check, defeat, foil
≠ OPPOSITES further, promote
2 *He was frustrated by his failure.*
discourage, disappoint, dishearten, depress
≠ OPPOSITES encourage

fulfil VERB

1 *I am sure he will fulfil most of his ambitions.*
achieve, complete, finish, accomplish, perform, carry out
≠ OPPOSITES fail
2 *This software package will fulfil all your needs.*
meet, satisfy, fill, answer

full ADJECTIVE

1 *full of people*
filled, loaded, packed, crowded, crammed, stuffed, jammed
≠ OPPOSITES empty, deserted
2 *the full range of colours*
whole, entire, total, complete
≠ OPPOSITES partial, incomplete
3 *a full report*
thorough, all-inclusive, broad
4 *a full supply of food*
ample, generous, abundant, plentiful
5 *a full sound*
rich, loud, deep, clear, distinct
≠ OPPOSITES thin
6 *at full speed*
maximum, top, highest, greatest, utmost

fully ADVERB

I have fully recovered from my illness.
completely, totally, utterly, wholly, entirely, thoroughly, altogether, quite
≠ OPPOSITES partly

fun NOUN

We had such fun at Disney World.
pleasure, enjoyment, amusement, entertainment, play, sport, merrymaking
• **make fun of**
We all made fun of my dad for wearing a silly shirt.
laugh at, jeer at, ridicule, mock, taunt, tease, rib

function¹ NOUN

1 *His main function is to direct the guests to their seats.*
job, role, duty, responsibility, task, occupation, business, purpose
2 *a formal function*
reception, party, gathering, affair, dinner
◇ INFORMAL WORDS do

function² VERB

The trains are now functioning properly again.
work, operate, run, go, act, perform

Aa
Bb
Cc
Dd
Ee
Ff
Gg
Hh
Ii
Jj
Kk
Ll
Mm
Nn
Oo
Pp
Qq
Rr
Ss
Tt
Uu
Vv
Ww
Xx
Yy
Zz

Aa
Bb
Cc
Dd
Ee
Ff
Gg
Hh
Ii
Jj
Kk
Ll
Mm
Nn
Oo
Pp
Qq
Rr
Ss
Tt
Uu
Vv
Ww
Xx
Yy
Zz

fundamental ADJECTIVE
1 *fundamental lessons in music*
basic, first, elementary
2 *a fundamental requirement*
main, important, central, principal,
prime, key, essential, necessary, crucial

funds NOUN
*We are trying to raising funds to buy a
school minibus.*
money, finance, backing, capital,
savings, wealth, cash

funny ADJECTIVE
1 *a funny joke*
amusing, humorous, entertaining,
comic, comical, hilarious, witty,
laughable
≠ OPPOSITES serious, solemn, sad
2 *There's something funny about this
whole business.*
odd, strange, peculiar, curious,
weird, unusual, mysterious, puzzling,
suspicious
≠ OPPOSITES normal, ordinary, usual

furious ADJECTIVE
The teacher was furious with us.
angry, mad, infuriated, raging, fuming
≠ OPPOSITES calm, pleased

furniture NOUN

Here are some types of furniture:

armchair, bed, bookcase, chair,
chest, chest of drawers, coffee table,
cupboard, desk, dresser, dressing
table, hat stand, shelves, sideboard,
sofa, stool, table, wardrobe

further ADJECTIVE
further investigation
more, additional, extra, fresh, new,
other

fury NOUN
1 *His fury was frightening.*
anger, rage, frenzy, madness, passion

≠ OPPOSITES calm, peacefulness
2 *the fury of the storm*
violence, fierceness, ferocity
≠ OPPOSITES calm

fuss¹ NOUN
1 *She didn't complain because she
didn't want to cause a fuss.*
row, commotion, squabble, stir, upset,
agitation
≠ OPPOSITES calm
2 *They want a quiet wedding without
any fuss.*
bother, trouble, inconvenience,
nuisance, excitement, bustle, worry,
confusion
◇ INFORMAL WORDS hassle, flap
≠ OPPOSITES calm

fuss² VERB
Please don't fuss over me.
worry, fret, take pains, bother
◇ INFORMAL WORDS flap

fussy ADJECTIVE
1 *She is very fussy about what she eats.*
particular, difficult, hard to please,
choosy, picky
2 *a fussy pattern*
fancy, elaborate, ornate
≠ OPPOSITES plain

futile ADJECTIVE
a futile attempt to pass the test
useless, pointless, vain, wasted,
unsuccessful, unprofitable,
unproductive
≠ OPPOSITES profitable, useful

future NOUN
His future looks very bright.
prospects, outlook, expectations
≠ OPPOSITES past

fuzzy ADJECTIVE
1 *fuzzy hair*
frizzy, fluffy, furry, woolly, fleecy
2 *a fuzzy outline*
unclear, blurred, unfocused, vague,
faint, hazy, shadowy
≠ OPPOSITES clear, distinct

Gg

gadget NOUN
*a useful **gadget** for the kitchen*
tool, device, invention, novelty

gain VERB
*Sally has **gained** confidence this term.*
obtain, build up, increase in, win
◆ FORMAL WORDS acquire
⊜ OPPOSITES lose

gallant ADJECTIVE
*a **gallant** knight*
noble, dashing, heroic, brave,
courageous, fearless, bold, daring
⊜ OPPOSITES cowardly

gamble VERB
*He **gambles** on the horse-racing.*
bet, wager, try your luck, play, chance,
take a chance, risk, back
◇ INFORMAL WORDS have a flutter

game NOUN
1 *Which **games** do you enjoy?*
recreation, sport, pastime,
entertainment, amusement
2 *a **game** of football*
match, competition, contest, event,
meeting

Here are some types of game:

Indoor games:
battleships, cards, chess, dominoes,
draughts, hangman, happy
families, I-spy, Jack Straws, ludo,
Monopoly®, noughts and crosses,
old maid, patience, Scrabble®,
snakes and ladders, snap, solitaire,
tiddlywinks
Playground games:
British bulldog, conkers, French
skipping, hide-and-seek, hopscotch,
it, jacks, marbles, oranges and
lemons, skipping, stuck in the mud,
tag, tig
Party games:
blind man's bluff, charades, Chinese
whispers, forfeits, musical bumps,
musical chairs, musical statues,
pass the parcel, pin the tail on the
donkey, postman's knock, sardines,
Simon says

gang NOUN
1 *a **gang** of teenagers*
group, band, ring, pack, mob, crowd,
party
◇ INFORMAL WORDS posse
2 *a **gang** of builders*
team, crew, squad, group

gap NOUN
1 *She had a **gap** between her two front
teeth.*
space, blank, hole, opening, crack
2 *a **gap** in the conversation*
interruption, break, pause, lull,
interval

gape VERB
*He lay in bed, **gaping** at the TV.*
stare, gaze, goggle
◇ INFORMAL WORDS gawp, gawk

gaping ADJECTIVE
*a **gaping** hole in the wall*
wide, broad, vast, yawning,
cavernous
⊜ OPPOSITES tiny

garbled ADJECTIVE
*a **garbled** message on the answering
machine*
confused, muddled, jumbled,
scrambled, mixed up

Aa
Bb
Cc
Dd
Ee
Ff
Gg
Hh
Ii
Jj
Kk
Ll
Mm
Nn
Oo
Pp
Qq
Rr
Ss
Tt
Uu
Vv
Ww
Xx
Yy
Zz

garden NOUN

Here are some things you might see in a garden:

bird table, compost bin, decking, fence, flower bed, flower pot, fork, garden furniture, greenhouse, hedge, hoe, hosepipe, lawn, lawnmower, patio, rake, shears, shed, shovel, spade, swing, vegetable patch, washing line, watering can

Garden visitors:
bee, beetle, blackbird, butterfly, cat, fly, fox, frog, greenfly, hedgehog, ladybird, moth, newt, robin, slug, snail, thrush, toad, wasp, worm

gash NOUN
There was a deep gash in his leg.
cut, wound, slash, slit, tear, split

gasp VERB
gasping for breath
pant, puff, blow, breathe, wheeze, choke, gulp

gate NOUN
Close the garden gate.
gateway, barrier, opening, entrance, exit, access

gather VERB
1 *The crowd gathered for the concert.*
meet, assemble, come together, collect, rally, round up, group
⊘ OPPOSITES scatter
2 *Gather all your books together.*
assemble, collect, group, hoard, heap, pile up
⊘ OPPOSITES scatter
3 *I gather they're getting married.*
understand, learn, hear

gathering NOUN
a gathering of anti-war protesters
assembly, meeting, round-up, rally, get-together, party, group, company, mass, crowd

gauge VERB
tests to gauge what students have learnt
estimate, judge, value, rate, figure, calculate, count, measure, weigh

gaunt ADJECTIVE
She looked gaunt after her illness.
haggard, hollow-eyed, bony, thin, skinny, scraggy, scrawny
◆ FORMAL WORDS emaciated
⊘ OPPOSITES plump

gaze VERB
gazing out of the window
stare, watch, view, look, gape, wonder

gear NOUN
1 *lifting gear*
equipment, kit, tackle, apparatus, tools, instruments
2 *Pack your gear in your bag.*
belongings, possessions, things
◇ INFORMAL WORDS stuff
3 *That shop sells some cool gear.*
clothes, clothing, garments, dress
◇ INFORMAL WORDS togs, get-up

gem NOUN
Gems sparkled in the queen's crown.
gemstone, jewel, precious stone, stone, treasure

Here are some types of gem:

amethyst, crystal, diamond, emerald, garnet, jade, opal, pearl, ruby, sapphire, topaz, turquoise

general ADJECTIVE
1 *There was a general feeling of disappointment in the class.*
broad, sweeping, total, across-the-board, widespread, overall
⊘ OPPOSITES particular, limited
2 *I can only give you a general idea of what happened.*
vague, indefinite, imprecise, inexact, approximate, unspecific
⊘ OPPOSITES specific

3 *the general way of doing things*
usual, regular, normal, typical, ordinary, everyday, customary, conventional, common, public
⊘ OPPOSITES rare

generally ADVERB
I generally prefer comedy films.
usually, normally, as a rule, by and large, on the whole, mostly, mainly, chiefly

generate VERB
The film has generated a lot of interest.
produce, create, whip up, arouse, cause, bring about, give rise to
⊘ OPPOSITES prevent

generous ADJECTIVE
1 *a generous person*
kind, charitable, unselfish, good, big-hearted
⊘ OPPOSITES selfish, mean
2 *a generous allowance*
large, substantial, ample, full, plentiful, overflowing, lavish, liberal
⊘ OPPOSITES meagre, miserly

genial ADJECTIVE
a genial group of friends
friendly, kindly, kind, warm, good-natured, easy-going, agreeable, pleasant, sociable
⊘ OPPOSITES cold, unfriendly

genius NOUN
1 *She is a genius at maths.*
expert, master, intellectual, mastermind, prodigy
◇ INFORMAL WORDS egghead, whizz
2 *Einstein's genius*
intelligence, intellect, brilliance, brightness, ability
◇ INFORMAL WORDS brains

gentle ADJECTIVE
1 *a gentle person*
kind, kindly, tender, soft-hearted, compassionate, sympathetic, mild, placid, calm, tranquil
⊘ OPPOSITES unkind, rough, harsh, wild
2 *a gentle slope*

gradual, easy, moderate, slight
3 *a gentle breeze*
light, soothing, peaceful, soft, slight

genuine ADJECTIVE
She smiled with genuine happiness.
real, actual, natural, pure, authentic, true, honest, sincere
⊘ OPPOSITES artificial, false, insincere

gesture NOUN
The teacher made an encouraging gesture to the boy.
sign, signal, movement, motion, act, action, wave, indication

get VERB
⇒ For even more about this word, see the next page
1 *I got a new jacket.*
obtain, buy, purchase, come by, gain
◆ FORMAL WORDS acquire
⊘ OPPOSITES lose
2 *Did you get a good mark in the test?*
receive, earn, win, achieve, gain
3 *It's getting dark.*
become, turn, go, grow
4 *I got Kerry to help me with my project.*
persuade, coax, urge, influence, sway
5 *We got home at midnight.*
reach, arrive, come
⊘ OPPOSITES leave, depart
6 *Let's get a bite to eat.*
fetch, collect, pick up, take, catch, grab
7 *I got chickenpox when I was six.*
catch, pick up, develop, come down with
• **get on**
How are you getting on at school?
cope, manage, get along, succeed
• **get out of**
I'm trying to get out of doing the washing-up.
avoid, escape, dodge, shirk
• **get over**
I'm just getting over a bad cold.
recover from, shake off, survive
• **get round**
I can get round my dad easily.
persuade, win over, talk round, coax

Aa
Bb
Cc
Dd
Ee
Ff
Gg
Hh
Ii
Jj
Kk
Ll
Mm
Nn
Oo
Pp
Qq
Rr
Ss
Tt
Uu
Vv
Ww
Xx
Yy
Zz

get

If you use the word **get** in your writing all the time, it is boring for the reader. There are many other words you could use instead.

get a job, letter or prize

> **receive**
> **obtain**
> **gain**
> **earn**
> **win**
> **achieve**

get something for yourself

> **fetch**
> **collect**
> **take**
> **catch**
> **capture**
> **seize**
> **grab**

get someone to do something

> **coax**
> **persuade**
> **urge**
> **influence**

get an illness

> **catch**
> **pick up**
> **develop**
> **come down with**

Over to you

The word **get** is used in a lot of different phrases. There are examples of these on the left.

Then look at the sentences on the right, which use other words and phrases instead. Can you write them again yourself, using some of the other choices?

get across	Liverpool's coach tried to impress upon his team the importance of accurate passing.
	Other choices: communicate to convey to
get away from	The Easter holidays are a great time to leave England and enjoy a warmer climate.
	Other choices: escape depart from
get on	Many pop stars have succeeded in life – and become millionaires!
	Other choices: prospered fared well
get over	Footballers usually recover from bad injuries.
	Other choices: shake off survive
get round	My brother was good at winning over my mum when he wanted to stay out late.
	Other choices: persuading coaxing

Aa
Bb
Cc
Dd
Ee
Ff
Gg
Hh
Ii
Jj
Kk
Ll
Mm
Nn
Oo
Pp
Qq
Rr
Ss
Tt
Uu
Vv
Ww
Xx
Yy
Zz

• **get up**
Get up out of your seat.
stand up, rise, arise

ghastly ADJECTIVE
What ghastly weather!
awful, dreadful, frightful, terrible, gruesome, hideous, horrible, horrid, shocking, appalling
(≠) OPPOSITES delightful, attractive

ghost NOUN
He thought he had seen a ghost.
phantom, spirit, spectre, ghoul
◇ INFORMAL WORDS spook

ghostly ADJECTIVE
We saw a ghostly shape.
supernatural, unearthly, ghostlike, phantom, eerie, creepy
◇ INFORMAL WORDS spooky

giant ADJECTIVE
a giant pizza
gigantic, mammoth, king-size, huge, enormous, immense, vast, large

giddy ADJECTIVE
I felt giddy when I stood up too quickly.
dizzy, faint, light-headed, unsteady, reeling

gift NOUN
1 *birthday gifts*
present
2 *The company made a gift to the charity.*
donation, contribution
3 *He has a real gift for football.*
talent, genius, flair, knack, aptitude

gifted ADJECTIVE
a gifted singer
talented, skilful, expert, skilled, able, capable, clever, intelligent, bright, brilliant

gigantic ADJECTIVE
a gigantic St Bernard dog
huge, enormous, immense, vast, giant, mammoth
(≠) OPPOSITES tiny

giggle VERB
*We couldn't stop **giggling** all afternoon.*
chuckle, chortle, laugh, titter, snigger

gimmick NOUN
*The free gift is just an advertising **gimmick**.*
trick, stunt, dodge, device, scheme

girl NOUN
*Nasreen made friends with the new **girl** in the class.*
lass, young woman

give VERB
1 *The head teacher is **giving** prizes at the ceremony.*
present, award, offer, hand over, deliver
⊘ OPPOSITES take, accept, receive
2 *Please **give** some money to our fund.*
donate, contribute, grant, provide
3 *The bench **gave** under their weight.*
sink, bend, give way, break, collapse, fall

• **give away**
*I would never **give away** a secret.*
reveal, let slip, leak, let out, betray

• **give in**
*Eventually her parents **gave in** and let her go into town with her friends.*
surrender, yield, give way, give up
⊘ OPPOSITES hold out

• **give up**
*My dad has **given up** his job.*
stop, quit, resign, abandon
◆ FORMAL WORDS cease
⊘ OPPOSITES start, take up

glad ADJECTIVE
1 *I am **glad** to hear you were not injured.*
pleased, delighted, contented, happy
⊘ OPPOSITES sad, unhappy
2 *I would be **glad** to help.*
willing, eager, keen, ready, inclined
⊘ OPPOSITES unwilling, reluctant

glamorous ADJECTIVE
*a **glamorous** film star*
beautiful, gorgeous, attractive, elegant, stylish, exciting, dazzling
⊘ OPPOSITES plain, drab, boring

glance VERB
1 *I **glanced** at my watch.*
peep, peek, glimpse
2 *Mum **glanced** through the pages of the magazine.*
scan, skim, leaf, flip, browse

glare VERB
*The teacher **glared** at the naughty children.*
scowl, frown, glower, stare
◇ INFORMAL WORDS look daggers

gleam VERB
*The bike was **gleaming** after I cleaned it.*
shine, sparkle, glitter, glint, shimmer, glimmer, glow

glide VERB
*skaters **gliding** across the ice*
skim, drift, slide, float, sail, coast

glimmer VERB
*There was a light **glimmering** in the window.*
shimmer, glisten, glitter, sparkle, twinkle, blink, flicker, gleam, shine

glimpse NOUN
*We caught a **glimpse** of the castle through the trees.*
peep, peek, glance, sight, sighting, view

glint VERB
*The sea was **glinting** in the sunshine.*
sparkle, glitter, twinkle, flash, gleam, shine, reflect, glimmer

glisten VERB
*The grass **glistened** with dew.*
gleam, glint, glitter, sparkle, twinkle, glimmer, shimmer

glitter VERB
*A diamond ring **glittered** on her finger.*
sparkle, twinkle, shimmer, glimmer, glisten, glint, gleam, flash, shine

gloom NOUN
1 *He was overcome by a feeling of **gloom**.*

Aa
Bb
Cc
Dd
Ee
Ff
Gg
Hh
Ii
Jj
Kk
Ll
Mm
Nn
Oo
Pp
Qq
Rr
Ss
Tt
Uu
Vv
Ww
Xx
Yy
Zz

depression, low spirits, sadness, unhappiness, melancholy, misery, desolation, despair
(≠) OPPOSITES **cheerfulness, happiness**
2 *We could see nothing through the gloom.*
dark, darkness, shade, shadow, dusk, twilight, dimness, obscurity, dullness
(≠) OPPOSITES **brightness**

gloomy ADJECTIVE

1 *We all felt gloomy after watching the news.*
depressed, down, low, down-hearted, sad, miserable, glum, pessimistic, dismal, depressed
(≠) OPPOSITES **cheerful, optimistic**
2 *a spell of gloomy weather*
dark, shadowy, dim, obscure, overcast, dull, dreary
(≠) OPPOSITES **bright**

glorious ADJECTIVE

1 *a glorious victory*
distinguished, famous, great, noble, splendid, magnificent, grand, triumphant
(≠) OPPOSITES **shameful**
2 *a glorious summer day*
fine, bright, shining, brilliant, dazzling, beautiful, gorgeous, superb, wonderful, marvellous

glossy ADJECTIVE

glossy black hair
shiny, sleek, silky, smooth, glassy, polished, bright, shining, brilliant
(≠) OPPOSITES **matt**

glow¹ NOUN

the glow from the lamp
light, gleam, shine, brightness, brilliance

glow² VERB

A fire glowed in the grate.
shine, gleam, burn

glue¹ NOUN

The children were making pictures with paper and glue.
adhesive, gum, paste

glue² VERB

I glued the handle back onto the mug.
stick, fix, gum, paste, seal, bond, cement

gnaw VERB

Mice had gnawed a hole in the bag.
bite, nibble, munch, chew

go¹ NOUN

Can I have a go on your scooter?
attempt, try, turn
◇ INFORMAL WORDS **shot, bash, stab**

go² VERB

1 *a car going along the motorway*
move, pass, advance, progress, proceed, continue
2 *We might go to France on holiday.*
travel
3 *What time do you have to go?*
leave, start, depart, set out
(≠) OPPOSITES **arrive**
4 *The engine was still going.*
operate, function, work, run, act, perform
(≠) OPPOSITES **break down, fail**
5 *Eat your soup or it will go cold.*
become, turn, grow
6 *Does the fruit go in the fridge?*
belong, fit, be kept
• **go away**
The people have all gone away.
leave, depart, disappear, vanish
• **go back**
I will go back to where I came from.
return, retreat, withdraw
• **go by**
1 *Time goes by quickly.*
pass, lapse, roll on
2 *We must go by the rules.*
observe, follow
• **go in**
You can go in to the house.
enter
• **go in for**
I'm going in for the chess tournament.
enter, take part in, participate in, take up, undertake, practise, pursue, follow
• **go off**
1 *A bomb went off.*
explode, blow up, detonate

Aa
Bb
Cc
Dd
Ee
Ff
Gg
Hh
Ii
Jj
Kk
Ll
Mm
Nn
Oo
Pp
Qq
Rr
Ss
Tt
Uu
Vv
Ww
Xx
Yy
Zz

Aa
Bb
Cc
Dd
Ee
Ff
Gg
Hh
Ii
Jj
Kk
Ll
Mm
Nn
Oo
Pp
Qq
Rr
Ss
Tt
Uu
Vv
Ww
Xx
Yy
Zz

2 *The milk has gone off.*
turn, sour, go bad, rot

• **go on**
1 *Go on with your work.*
continue, carry on, proceed, persist, stay, last
2 *What's going on?*
happen, occur, take place

• **go out**
I saw Tom go out in a hurry.
exit, leave, withdraw, depart

• **go over**
Go over your writing again when you finish.
examine, study, check, inspect, scan

• **go to**
I want to go to the shops with Mum.
make for, head for

• **go with**
That bag does not go with her jacket.
match, blend, suit, fit
(≠) OPPOSITES clash

goal NOUN
Our goal is to raise £1000.
target, aim, intention, purpose, ambition

gobble VERB
He gobbled all the food.
bolt, guzzle, gorge on, cram in, stuff in, devour, gulp down
◇ INFORMAL WORDS scarf, scoff

good¹ ADJECTIVE
⇒ For even more about this word, see the next page
1 *That was a good story.*
satisfactory, pleasant, nice, pleasing, enjoyable, wonderful, excellent, marvellous
◇ INFORMAL WORDS great, super, cool
(≠) OPPOSITES bad
2 *She got a good mark in her test.*
excellent, wonderful, first-class, first-rate, superior
(≠) OPPOSITES bad, poor
3 *She is very good at her job.*
competent, skilled, expert, professional, skilful, clever, talented, gifted, able, capable

(≠) OPPOSITES incompetent
4 *It was good of you to help out.*
kind, considerate, thoughtful, generous
(≠) OPPOSITES unkind, inconsiderate
5 *a good person*
moral, upright, honest, trustworthy, worthy, righteous
(≠) OPPOSITES wicked, evil
6 *You've been a good boy today.*
well-behaved, obedient, well-mannered
(≠) OPPOSITES naughty, disobedient
7 *Have a good look.*
thorough, complete, whole, substantial, considerable

good² NOUN
1 *the good and the bad in everyone*
goodness, right, virtue, morality
2 *I'm telling you this for your own good.*
welfare, wellbeing, interest, sake, behalf, benefit

• **no good**
These crayons are no good.
good for nothing, no use, useless, hopeless, pointless

good-looking ADJECTIVE
a good-looking young man
handsome, attractive, nice-looking, gorgeous, lovely, beautiful
◇ INFORMAL WORDS dishy, fit
(≠) OPPOSITES ugly, unattractive

goods NOUN
They sell their goods at the market.
merchandise, wares, stock, produce

gorgeous ADJECTIVE
1 *gorgeous weather*
magnificent, splendid, glorious, superb
(≠) OPPOSITES dull
2 *a gorgeous fashion model*
glamorous, attractive, beautiful, handsome, good-looking
(≠) OPPOSITES plain

gossip¹ NOUN
1 *Don't listen to silly gossip.*
rumour, scandal, hearsay, chitchat, tittle-tattle, report

good

Often when you are writing you want to use a word that means **good**. You have to be careful not to use the word **good** too often, or your writing will become boring. You could try out some of the following words instead.

You can describe many different things as
excellent
superb
wonderful
pleasant
nice
lovely

There are also many informal words for good:
great
cool
smashing
super

a good piece of work
satisfactory
first-class
first-rate

someone who is a good friend
true
dependable
kind
considerate
reliable
thoughtful
generous

a good person
honest
virtuous
trustworthy
moral
upright

Aa
Bb
Cc
Dd
Ee
Ff
Gg
Hh
Ii
Jj
Kk
Ll
Mm
Nn
Oo
Pp
Qq
Rr
Ss
Tt
Uu
Vv
Ww
Xx
Yy
Zz

a good time
> **enjoyable**
> **pleasing**

feel good
> **happy**
> **cheerful**
> **content**

a good time to visit
> **convenient**
> **suitable**
> **fitting**
> **appropriate**

someone who is good at something
> **competent**
> **able**
> **capable**
> **clever**
> **talented**
> **accomplished**
> **gifted**
> **expert**
> **skilled**
> **skilful**

good weather
> **fine**
> **sunny**

someone whose behaviour is good
> **well-behaved**
> **well-mannered**
> **polite**
> **obedient**
> **as good as gold**

have a good look
> **thorough**
> **complete**
> **whole**

Over to you

Some of these words have been used to write about a writer! Which other words could you use?

Roald Dahl was a **gifted** writer and an **accomplished** storyteller. His **wonderful** books have been translated into many languages. He was **talented** in other ways too – he won first prize for growing an orchid!

2 *Our neighbour is a terrible **gossip**.*
chatterbox, busybody, tell-tale, scandalmonger, whisperer
◇ INFORMAL WORDS nosey parker

gossip[2] VERB
gossiping on the phone for an hour
chat, chatter, gabble, tell tales
◇ INFORMAL WORDS natter

govern VERB
governing most of Europe
rule, reign, direct, manage, supervise, oversee, lead, head, command, guide

gown NOUN
an elegant evening gown
robe, dress, frock, dressing-gown, costume

grab VERB
He grabbed the money out of my hand.
seize, snatch, take, pluck, catch hold of, grasp, clutch, grip, catch
◇ INFORMAL WORDS nab

graceful ADJECTIVE
a graceful ballet dancer
nimble, agile, elegant, fine, natural, beautiful, charming
≠ OPPOSITES graceless, awkward, clumsy

gracious ADJECTIVE
She was very gracious towards her guests.
elegant, polite, considerate, sweet, obliging, kind, compassionate, kindly, generous

grade[1] NOUN
the top grade in the test
rank, status, place, position, level, quality, standard, class, category

grade[2] VERB
The children are graded according to ability.
sort, arrange, categorize, order, group, class, rate, rank, classify, evaluate

gradual ADJECTIVE
a gradual improvement
slow, unhurried, moderate, steady, continuous, progressive
≠ OPPOSITES sudden

gradually ADVERB
The cat moved gradually along the ledge.
little by little, bit by bit, inch by inch, step by step, slowly, gently, cautiously, steadily, progressively

grain NOUN
1 *a grain of sand*
bit, piece, speck, particle, fragment, scrap, crumb, jot, mite, trace
2 *flour made from the whole grain*
seed, corn, cereals

grand ADJECTIVE
the grand staircase

splendid, magnificent, glorious, superb, fine, impressive, striking, large, noble
⊘ OPPOSITES humble, common, poor

grant VERB
They were granted their freedom.
give, award, donate, present, assign, allot, allocate, provide, supply

grasp¹ NOUN
You have a good grasp of grammar.
understanding, familiarity, knowledge
◆ FORMAL WORDS comprehension

grasp² VERB
1 *He grasped the rope in both hands.*
hold, clasp, grip, grab, clutch, seize, snatch, catch
2 *She couldn't quite grasp the idea.*
understand, follow, see, realize
◆ FORMAL WORDS comprehend
◇ INFORMAL WORDS get

grate VERB
1 *Grate two carrots.*
shred, grind, mince, rub, scrape
2 *Her shrill voice grates on me.*
jar, set your teeth on edge, annoy, irritate, get on your nerves

grateful ADJECTIVE
I am grateful for your help.
thankful, appreciative
◆ FORMAL WORDS obliged, indebted
⊘ OPPOSITES ungrateful

grave ADJECTIVE
1 *a grave mistake*
important, significant, serious, critical, vital, crucial, dangerous
⊘ OPPOSITES trivial, slight
2 *We were in grave danger.*
acute, severe, serious
3 *When Dad read the letter, he looked grave.*
solemn, serious, thoughtful, grim
⊘ OPPOSITES cheerful

graze VERB
I grazed my elbow when I fell.
scratch, scrape, skin, cut

great ADJECTIVE
1 *the great hall*
large, big, huge, enormous, massive, gigantic, immense, vast, impressive
⊘ OPPOSITES small
2 *Handle this package with great care.*
considerable, extreme, excessive
⊘ OPPOSITES slight
3 *a great actor*
famous, distinguished, notable, remarkable, outstanding, fine
⊘ OPPOSITES unknown
4 *a great discovery*
important, significant, serious, major, principal, primary, main, chief, leading
⊘ OPPOSITES unimportant, insignificant
5 *That's great news!*
excellent, superb, wonderful, marvellous, tremendous, terrific, fantastic, fabulous
◇ INFORMAL WORDS cool, wicked

Greece NOUN

Here are some words connected with ancient Greece:

agora, athlete, citizen, column, democracy, frieze, gymnasium, hoplite, Olympic games, parthenon, philosophy, sculpture, slave, temple, theatre, toga, tragedy, trireme, wooden horse

greed NOUN
1 *He ate all the ice cream out of greed.*
gluttony, selfishness
2 *In his greed, the king kept all his riches.*
craving, avarice

greedily ADVERB
I looked greedily at the cakes.
hungrily, eagerly

greedy ADJECTIVE
1 *You are so greedy, eating all the sweets!*
gluttonous

Aa
Bb
Cc
Dd
Ee
Ff
Gg
Hh
Ii
Jj
Kk
Ll
Mm
Nn
Oo
Pp
Qq
Rr
Ss
Tt
Uu
Vv
Ww
Xx
Yy
Zz

2 *He has always been greedy for money and power.*
eager, grasping, selfish, avaricious

green NOUN

Here are some shades of green:
aquamarine, bottle-green, emerald, jade, khaki, lime, pea-green, pine, sea-green

greet VERB
The bride and groom greeted each guest as they arrived.
welcome, receive, meet, acknowledge, address
≠ OPPOSITES ignore

grief NOUN
She was overcome with grief at her husband's funeral.
sorrow, sadness, unhappiness, distress, misery, heartbreak, heartache
≠ OPPOSITES happiness, delight

grieve VERB
They are grieving for their dead friend.
sorrow, mourn, cry, weep
≠ OPPOSITES rejoice

grim ADJECTIVE
1 *The battlefield was a grim sight.*
unpleasant, horrible, horrid, ghastly, gruesome, grisly, frightening, terrible, shocking
≠ OPPOSITES pleasant
2 *The head teacher was wearing a grim expression.*
stern, severe, harsh, surly, sullen
≠ OPPOSITES jolly

grimy ADJECTIVE
grimy hands
dirty, mucky, grubby, soiled, filthy, sooty, dusty, smudgy
≠ OPPOSITES clean, spotless

grind VERB
1 *Grind the coffee beans.*
crush, pound, pulverize, powder, mill, grate
2 *He is grinding the kitchen knives.*
sand, file, smooth, polish, sharpen

grip VERB
1 *The child gripped his mother's hand.*
hold, grasp, clasp, clutch, seize, grab, catch
2 *We were totally gripped by the film.*
engross, enthral, absorb, fascinate, thrill

grit NOUN
I've got a piece of grit in my eye.
dust, sand, gravel, shingle

groan VERB
She groaned when it was time to get up.
moan, sigh, cry, whine, wail, complain, object, protest
≠ OPPOSITES cheer

grope VERB
She groped for the light switch in the darkness.
feel, fumble, scrabble, flounder, search, probe

gross ADJECTIVE
1 *gross stupidity*
obvious, plain, sheer, utter, serious, blatant, glaring, outright, shameful, shocking
2 *Don't be so gross!*
offensive, rude, coarse, crude, vulgar, tasteless, improper, indecent

grotesque ADJECTIVE
grotesque monsters
bizarre, odd, weird, unnatural, freakish, monstrous, hideous, ugly, deformed, distorted
≠ OPPOSITES normal, graceful

ground NOUN
1 *I dropped a sweet on the ground.*
earth, soil, land, clay, dirt, dust, dry land
2 *a football ground*
field, pitch, stadium, arena, park

Aa
Bb
Cc
Dd
Ee
Ff
Gg
Hh
Ii
Jj
Kk
Ll
Mm
Nn
Oo
Pp
Qq
Rr
Ss
Tt
Uu
Vv
Ww
Xx
Yy
Zz

Aa
Bb
Cc
Dd
Ee
Ff
Gg
Hh
Ii
Jj
Kk
Ll
Mm
Nn
Oo
Pp
Qq
Rr
Ss
Tt
Uu
Vv
Ww
Xx
Yy
Zz

grounds NOUN
*You have no **grounds** for complaint.*
reason, motive, cause, justification, foundation, excuse, basis

group NOUN
1 *a **group** of teenagers*
band, gang, pack, team, crew, troop, squad
2 *Our chess **group** meets every week.*
society, association, gathering
3 *Sort the blocks into **groups**.*
set, collection, bunch, clump, cluster, batch, lot

grow VERB
1 *You've **grown** two centimetres.*
get taller, get bigger, increase in height, stretch
⊟ OPPOSITES shrink
2 *The number of people in our club is **growing**.*
increase, rise, expand, enlarge, swell
⊟ OPPOSITES decrease, shrink
3 *The roses are **growing** in the garden.*
bud, flower, shoot, sprout, spread, extend, develop, thrive
⊟ OPPOSITES wilt
4 *He **grows** tomatoes in his greenhouse.*
cultivate, farm, produce, breed, raise
5 *They are **growing** older.*
become, turn

growl VERB
*The dog **growled** at me.*
snarl, grumble

grown-up ADJECTIVE
*They have two **grown-up** children.*
adult, mature, full-grown
⊟ OPPOSITES young, immature

growth NOUN
1 *the **growth** in population*
increase, rise, enlargement, expansion, spread, development
⊟ OPPOSITES decrease, failure
2 *a **growth** on the skin*
tumour, lump, swelling, outgrowth

grubby ADJECTIVE
*a **grubby** old raincoat*
dirty, soiled, unwashed, mucky, grimy, filthy, scruffy
⊟ OPPOSITES clean, spotless

grudge NOUN
*He bears a **grudge** against anyone who upsets him.*
ill-will, dislike, grievance, hard feelings, resentment, bitterness, spite, hate
⊟ OPPOSITES favour, goodwill

gruesome ADJECTIVE
*a **gruesome** story about a vampire*
horrible, disgusting, repulsive, hideous, grisly, grim, ghastly, awful, terrible, horrific
⊟ OPPOSITES pleasant

grumble VERB
*Stop **grumbling** about tidying your room!*
complain, moan, whine, bleat, mutter
◇ INFORMAL WORDS gripe

grumpy ADJECTIVE
*Beth is always **grumpy** first thing in the morning.*
bad-tempered, cross, irritable, surly, sullen, sulky, grouchy
⊟ OPPOSITES contented, happy

guarantee VERB
*I **guarantee** you will enjoy this film.*
assure, promise, pledge, swear, warrant

guard[1] VERB
1 ***Guard** your belongings carefully.*
protect, watch, mind
2 *A sentry **guarded** the castle entrance.*
safeguard, shield, cover, defend, police, patrol

guard[2] NOUN
*an armed **guard***
sentry, patrol, watchman, lookout, protector, minder, defender, warder

guardian NOUN
*We are the **guardians** of this land.*
keeper, protector, defender, warden,

guard, warder, steward, custodian

guess¹ NOUN

My guess is that there are 200 jelly beans in this jar.
estimate, judgement, prediction, idea, feeling

guess² VERB

1 *Guess how much I weigh.*
estimate, judge, gauge, work out, predict, speculate
2 *I guess you were right all along.*
suppose, reckon, assume, suspect, imagine, believe

guest NOUN

1 *We're having guests for the weekend.*
visitor, caller
2 *hotel guests*
lodger, resident

guide¹ NOUN

1 *Joe's working as a tour guide.*
leader, courier, usher, escort, attendant, companion, adviser
2 *a guide to the Lake District*
manual, handbook, guidebook, directory

guide² VERB

He guided me to the tourist office.
direct, lead, conduct, usher, accompany
◆ FORMAL WORDS escort

guilt NOUN

1 *He confessed his guilt.*
responsibility, blame

≠ OPPOSITES innocence
2 *a feeling of guilt*
shame, disgrace, dishonour, regret, remorse, conscience
≠ OPPOSITES shamelessness

guilty ADJECTIVE

1 *He was found guilty of many bad crimes.*
responsible, to blame, blameworthy, at fault
≠ OPPOSITES innocent, guiltless, blameless
2 *I feel guilty about not inviting Lindsay.*
ashamed, shamefaced, sorry, regretful, remorseful, conscience-stricken
≠ OPPOSITES shameless

gulp VERB

She gulped her tea.
swallow, bolt, gobble, guzzle, devour
◇ INFORMAL WORDS knock back, wolf
≠ OPPOSITES sip, nibble

gush VERB

oil gushing from the well
flow, run, pour, stream, cascade, flood, spurt, spout, jet

guts NOUN

It took guts to admit you were wrong.
courage, bravery, nerve

guy NOUN

the guy in the black T-shirt
man, chap, fellow, boy, person

Aa
Bb
Cc
Dd
Ee
Ff
Gg
Hh
Ii
Jj
Kk
Ll
Mm
Nn
Oo
Pp
Qq
Rr
Ss
Tt
Uu
Vv
Ww
Xx
Yy
Zz

Hh

Aa
Bb
Cc
Dd
Ee
Ff
Gg
Hh
Ii
Jj
Kk
Ll
Mm
Nn
Oo
Pp
Qq
Rr
Ss
Tt
Uu
Vv
Ww
Xx
Yy
Zz

habit NOUN

*I've got into the **habit** of recycling paper.*
custom, usage, practice, routine, rule, way, manner

hack VERB

*They **hacked** their way through the dense forest.*
cut, chop, hew, gash, slash

haggle VERB

*The woman **haggled** with the market trader over the price of a pot.*
bargain, negotiate, wrangle, squabble, bicker, quarrel, dispute

hair NOUN

Here are some hairstyles:

bob, bun, bunches, braids, corn rows, crew cut, curly, dreadlocks, long, Mohican, pigtail, pony tail, quiff, straight, wavy
Hair colours:
auburn, black, blonde, brown, chestnut, ginger, grey, mouse, red, strawberry blonde, white

hair-raising ADJECTIVE

*a **hair-raising** ride*
frightening, scary, terrifying, horrifying, shocking, alarming, thrilling

hairy ADJECTIVE

hairy arms
shaggy, bushy, fuzzy, furry, woolly, bearded
⊯ OPPOSITES bald, clean-shaven

half-hearted ADJECTIVE

*a **half-hearted** agreement to join in*
cool, weak, feeble, uninterested, indifferent

⊯ OPPOSITES whole-hearted, enthusiastic

hall NOUN

1 *All the rooms lead off the **hall**.*
hallway, corridor, passage, passageway, entrance hall, reception hall, foyer, vestibule, lobby
2 *We stood at the back of the **hall**.*
concert hall, chamber, assembly room

halt VERB

1 *You must **halt** at the red traffic light.*
stop, draw up, pull up, pause, wait, rest
⊯ OPPOSITES start, pull away
2 *Production has been **halted** at the factory.*
break off, quit, end
◆ FORMAL WORDS cease
⊯ OPPOSITES start, continue

hammer VERB

*Someone was **hammering** on the door.*
bang, knock, pound, drum, beat, hit, strike, bash, batter

hamper VERB

*Our progress was **hampered** by the thick fog.*
hinder, slow down, hold up, prevent, restrict
⊯ OPPOSITES aid, help

hand¹ NOUN

*Can you give me a **hand** with my homework?*
help, aid, assistance, support, participation

hand² VERB

*Lauren **handed** me a note.*
give, pass, offer, present, deliver
• **hand down**
*This necklace has been **handed down** through the generations.*
pass on, transfer, give

handicap[1] NOUN

Not having a computer is a bit of a handicap.
obstacle, block, barrier, hindrance, drawback, disadvantage, restriction, limitation
≠ OPPOSITES advantage

handicap[2] VERB

The search was handicapped by severe weather.
hinder, disadvantage, hold back, hamper, burden, restrict, limit
≠ OPPOSITES help, assist

handle[1] NOUN

He turned the door handle.
grip, handgrip, knob

handle[2] VERB

1 *Don't handle the fruit.*
touch, finger, feel, pick up, hold, grasp
2 *The teacher handled the problem carefully.*
tackle, treat, deal with, manage, cope with, control

handsome ADJECTIVE

1 *a handsome young man*
good-looking, attractive, fair, nice-looking, gorgeous, elegant
◇ INFORMAL WORDS dishy
≠ OPPOSITES ugly, unattractive
2 *a handsome sum*
generous, liberal, large, considerable
≠ OPPOSITES mean

handy ADJECTIVE

1 *Our house is handy for the shops.*
convenient, near, accessible, nearby, available, to hand, ready, at hand
≠ OPPOSITES inconvenient, inaccessible
2 *a handy tool*
convenient, practical, useful, helpful
≠ OPPOSITES inconvenient, awkward

hang VERB

1 *hanging from a branch*
suspend, dangle, swing
2 *long hair hanging down over his eyes*
drape, drop, flop, droop, sag, trail

3 *We hung the mirror above the fireplace.*
fasten, attach, fix, stick
• **hang about**
Don't hang about after the concert has finished.
hang around, linger, loiter, dawdle, waste time
• **hang on**
Hang on with us till it's time for your bus.
wait, hold on, remain, hold out, continue, carry on
• **hang onto**
The boy hung onto the rope with both hands.
grip, grasp, hold fast

haphazard ADJECTIVE

Their working methods seem totally haphazard.
random, chance, casual, hit-or-miss, disorganized, disorderly, careless, slapdash
≠ OPPOSITES methodical, orderly

happen VERB

What has happened while I've been away?
occur, take place, arise, crop up, develop, come about, turn out

happening NOUN

a news report on the happenings in New York
occurrence, event, incident, episode, adventure, experience, affair

happiness NOUN

The newly-weds' happiness showed in their faces.
joy, joyfulness, gladness, cheerfulness, contentment, pleasure, delight, ecstasy
≠ OPPOSITES unhappiness, sadness

happy ADJECTIVE

⇒ For even more about this word, see the next page
1 *We were happy to be home.*
joyful, merry, cheerful, glad, pleased, delighted, thrilled, satisfied, content, contented

Aa
Bb
Cc
Dd
Ee
Ff
Gg
Hh
Ii
Jj
Kk
Ll
Mm
Nn
Oo
Pp
Qq
Rr
Ss
Tt
Uu
Vv
Ww
Xx
Yy
Zz

happy

You can show how **happy** someone is by choosing the correct word.

These words are arranged from being quite happy to being extremely happy about something!

> **glad** → **pleased** → **delighted** → **joyful** →
> **overjoyed** → **elated** → **thrilled** → **ecstatic**

Someone who is in a happy mood could also be

> **jolly**
> **merry**
> **cheerful**

These words help readers to picture a character who has happy feelings:

> **satisfied**
> **content**
> **untroubled**
> **unconcerned**
> **light-hearted**
> **in a good mood**

These phrases that show a person is very happy:

> **walking on air**
> **thrilled to bits**
> **over the moon**
> **in high spirits**
> **tickled pink**

Over to you

Read the paragraph below. Can you replace the word **happy** with another word or phrase?

The lost soldiers were **happy** when they stumbled upon the clear pool. They drank until they were **happy** and were then **happy** to sit on the rocks and wait for someone to find them. Someone did …

≠ OPPOSITES unhappy, sad, discontented
2 a *happy* coincidence
lucky, fortunate, appropriate, apt, fitting
≠ OPPOSITES unfortunate, inappropriate

harass VERB
*The singer was being **harassed** by journalists.*
pester, plague, torment, exasperate, annoy, irritate, bother, disturb
◇ INFORMAL WORDS hassle

harbour VERB
*They have been **harbouring** a criminal.*
hide, conceal, protect, shelter

hard¹ ADJECTIVE
1 a *hard* seat
solid, firm, tough, strong, dense, stiff, rigid, inflexible
≠ OPPOSITES soft, yielding
2 *I found the exam quite **hard**.*
difficult, complicated, involved, baffling, puzzling, perplexing
≠ OPPOSITES easy, simple
3 *hard* work
strenuous, tiring, exhausting, backbreaking
4 *He is very **hard** on his employees.*
harsh, severe, strict, cruel, ruthless, unpleasant
≠ OPPOSITES kind, pleasant

hard² ADVERB
*She works very **hard**.*
steadily, strenuously, earnestly, keenly, intently, strongly, intensely, energetically, vigorously

harden VERB
1 *The cement will **harden** as it dries.*
set, freeze, bake, stiffen
≠ OPPOSITES soften
2 *He **hardened** his heart against the children's cries.*
strengthen, reinforce, toughen
≠ OPPOSITES weaken, soften

hardly ADVERB
*I am **hardly** ever late.*
barely, scarcely, just, only just, not quite

hardship NOUN
*The family suffered **hardship** during the war.*
misfortune, trouble, difficulty, distress, suffering, want, need, poverty, misery
≠ OPPOSITES ease, comfort

hardy ADJECTIVE
*My uncle is a **hardy** outdoor type.*
strong, tough, sturdy, robust, vigorous
≠ OPPOSITES weak

harm¹ NOUN
*I didn't mean you any **harm**.*
damage, loss, injury, hurt, misfortune, wrong
≠ OPPOSITES benefit

harm² VERB
*You might **harm** your eyesight if you sit too close to the TV.*
damage, spoil, ruin, hurt, injure, wound, misuse
≠ OPPOSITES benefit, improve

harmful ADJECTIVE
*Frost is **harmful** to plants.*
damaging, unhealthy, dangerous, poisonous, toxic, destructive
≠ OPPOSITES harmless, safe

harmless ADJECTIVE
1 a *harmless* substance
safe, non-toxic
2 a *harmless* prank
inoffensive, gentle, innocent
≠ OPPOSITES harmful, dangerous, destructive

harmony NOUN
*living in **harmony***
agreement, compatibility, peace, goodwill, sympathy, understanding, friendliness, co-operation, balance
≠ OPPOSITES conflict

harsh ADJECTIVE
1 a *harsh* punishment

Aa
Bb
Cc
Dd
Ee
Ff
Gg
Hh
Ii
Jj
Kk
Ll
Mm
Nn
Oo
Pp
Qq
Rr
Ss
Tt
Uu
Vv
Ww
Xx
Yy
Zz

severe, strict, unfeeling, cruel, hard, bleak, grim
(≠) OPPOSITES lenient
2 *a harsh sound*
rough, coarse, croaking, grating, raucous, sharp, shrill, unpleasant
(≠) OPPOSITES soft
3 *harsh colours*
bright, dazzling, glaring, gaudy
(≠) OPPOSITES subdued

harvest NOUN
a good harvest of grapes
crop, yield, produce

hasty ADJECTIVE
My answer was perhaps a bit too hasty.
hurried, rushed, impatient, rash, reckless, thoughtless, hot-headed, fast, quick, swift
(≠) OPPOSITES slow, careful

hat NOUN

Here are some types of hat:
balaklava, baseball cap, beanie, beret, bobble hat, bowler hat, cap, fedora, fez, helmet, sombrero, sou'wester, straw boater, sunhat, trilby

hatch VERB
The boys hatched a plot to trick their teacher.
devise, originate, think up, dream up, plot, scheme, plan

hate¹ VERB
⇒ For even more about this word, see the next page
Tina hates dogs.
detest, loathe, despise, dislike
(≠) OPPOSITES like, love

hate² NOUN
Sewing is one of my pet hates.
hatred, dislike, loathing
(≠) OPPOSITES liking, love

hatred NOUN
They didn't hide their hatred of each other.
hate, dislike, loathing, ill-will, hostility
(≠) OPPOSITES liking, love

haughty ADJECTIVE
With a haughty toss of her head, she flounced out of the room.
high and mighty, superior, snobbish, arrogant, proud, conceited
◇ INFORMAL WORDS snooty, stuck-up
(≠) OPPOSITES humble, modest

haul VERB
She hauled her suitcase upstairs.
pull, heave, tug, draw, tow, drag
(≠) OPPOSITES push

have VERB
1 *We have a new car.*
own, possess, get, obtain, gain, receive, accept, keep, hold
(≠) OPPOSITES lack
2 *I had a good time at the party.*
feel, experience, enjoy
3 *My grandfather had a heart attack.*
suffer, undergo, endure, put up with, experience
4 *Our house has three bedrooms.*
contain, include, consist of
5 *My aunt is going to have a baby.*
give birth to, bear
• **have to**
You have to return your library books today.
must, ought to, should, be obliged to, be required to

haven NOUN
the safe haven of their home
shelter, refuge, sanctuary, asylum, retreat

havoc NOUN
Hooligans created havoc in the city centre.
chaos, confusion, disorder, damage, destruction, ruin

hate

It is very easy to say that someone **hates** something, but you can choose a different word that will describe how someone truly feels.

If you don't really hate something, but you do not like it:
dislike

If you dislike something very much indeed:
abhor
despise
detest
loathe

Over to you

Replace the word **hate** in the sentences below with more precise or powerful verbs.

Arachnophobia!

She loved Autumn but hated evenings when, out of the corner of her eye, she caught the movement of the creatures she hated most of all – spiders. She really hated them!

hazard NOUN
a health hazard
risk, danger, threat, death trap, accident, chance
⊭ OPPOSITES safety

hazardous ADJECTIVE
a hazardous journey
risky, dangerous, unsafe, insecure, chancy, difficult, tricky, precarious
⊭ OPPOSITES safe, secure

hazy ADJECTIVE
1 *a hazy morning*
misty, foggy, smoky, clouded, cloudy, fuzzy, blurred, dim, faint, unclear
⊭ OPPOSITES clear, bright
2 *I have only a hazy memory of what happened.*
dim, faint, unclear, indistinct, vague, indefinite, uncertain

⊭ OPPOSITES clear, definite

head¹ NOUN
1 *I added up the numbers in my head.*
brain, mind, mentality, intellect, intelligence, understanding, thought
◇ INFORMAL WORDS brains
2 *the head of the queue*
front, lead, top, peak, summit, crown, tip, apex, height, climax
⊭ OPPOSITES base, foot, end
3 *the head of the maths department*
leader, chief, captain, commander, boss, director, manager, superintendent, principal

head² ADJECTIVE
the head teacher
leading, first, chief, main, principal, top

Aa
Bb
Cc
Dd
Ee
Ff
Gg
Hh
Ii
Jj
Kk
Ll
Mm
Nn
Oo
Pp
Qq
Rr
Ss
Tt
Uu
Vv
Ww
Xx
Yy
Zz

head³ VERB

1 *We need someone to **head** the group.*
lead, rule, govern, command, direct,
manage, run, supervise, control
2 *I was **heading** for the gym.*
move, go, travel

heading NOUN

*Give your story a **heading**.*
title, name, headline, caption

headquarters NOUN

*The company's **headquarters** is in Leeds.*
HQ, base, head office

heal VERB

*My blister has almost **healed** now.*
cure, remedy, mend, restore, treat,
soothe

health NOUN

*Eating fruit is good for your **health**.*
fitness, condition, state, healthiness,
good condition, wellbeing, welfare,
strength, vigour
⊘ OPPOSITES illness

healthy ADJECTIVE

1 *a **healthy** child*
well, fit, in condition, in good shape,
sturdy, robust, sound, strong, vigorous,
thriving
◇ INFORMAL WORDS fit as a fiddle
⊘ OPPOSITES ill, sick
2 *healthy food*
wholesome, nutritious, nourishing

heap¹ NOUN

*a **heap** of DVDs*
pile, stack, mound, lot, mass, collection

heap² VERB

*clothes **heaped** up on the floor*
pile, stack, mound, build, collect, gather

hear VERB

1 *I can **hear** him calling.*
listen, catch, pick up, overhear
2 *I **hear** she's going to Australia.*
understand, gather, learn, find out,
discover

heart NOUN

*the **heart** of the matter*
centre, middle, core, essence

heartbreaking ADJECTIVE

*The pictures of starving children were
heartbreaking.*
distressing, sad, tragic, heart-rending,
pitiful, agonizing
⊘ OPPOSITES heartwarming, heartening

heartbroken ADJECTIVE

*Yasmin was **heartbroken** when her cat
died.*
broken-hearted, sad, miserable,
downcast, disappointed, crushed
⊘ OPPOSITES delighted, elated

heartless ADJECTIVE

*It is **heartless** to treat animals badly.*
unfeeling, uncaring, cold, hard, hard-
hearted, unkind, cruel, inhuman,
brutal
⊘ OPPOSITES kind, considerate,
sympathetic

hearty ADJECTIVE

1 *a **hearty** welcome*
enthusiastic, whole-hearted, heartfelt,
sincere, genuine, warm, friendly
⊘ OPPOSITES half-hearted, cool,
cold
2 *a **hearty** laugh*
warm, jovial, cheerful, boisterous,
energetic, vigorous
⊘ OPPOSITES half-hearted
3 *a **hearty** breakfast*
large, sizable, substantial, filling,
generous

heat NOUN

*the **heat** of the day*
hotness, warmth, closeness, high
temperature
⊘ OPPOSITES cold, coldness

heated ADJECTIVE

*a **heated** debate*
angry, furious, bitter, fierce, intense
⊘ OPPOSITES calm

heave VERB
*The men **heaved** the piano up a flight of stairs.*
pull, haul, drag, tug, raise, lift, hitch, hoist

heavy ADJECTIVE
1 *a **heavy** load*
weighty, massive, large, bulky, solid, dense
(≠) OPPOSITES light
2 *heavy work*
hard, difficult, tough, strenuous, demanding, harsh, severe
(≠) OPPOSITES easy
3 *That film was a bit **heavy**.*
intense, serious, dull, tedious

hectic ADJECTIVE
*a **hectic** day at the office*
busy, frantic, chaotic, excited
(≠) OPPOSITES leisurely

heed VERB
*If you are wise, you will **heed** my warning.*
listen, pay attention, mind, note, observe, follow, obey
(≠) OPPOSITES ignore, disregard

height NOUN
*The nurse will check your **height** and weight.*
highness, tallness, stature
(≠) OPPOSITES depth

help¹ VERB
1 *Can you **help** me to carry my bags, please?*
aid, assist, lend a hand, be of use, co-operate, back, stand by, support
(≠) OPPOSITES hinder
2 *Shouting won't **help** the situation.*
improve, relieve, ease
(≠) OPPOSITES worsen

help² NOUN
*If you have any problems, ask for **help**.*
aid, assistance, support, advice, guidance, service, use, benefit
(≠) OPPOSITES hindrance

helpful ADJECTIVE
1 *helpful advice*
useful, practical, worthwhile, valuable, beneficial, advantageous
(≠) OPPOSITES useless, futile
2 *a **helpful** person*
co-operative, obliging, caring, considerate, kind, sympathetic, supportive

helping NOUN
*a second **helping** of dessert*
serving, portion, share, amount, plateful, piece

helpless ADJECTIVE
*a **helpless** baby*
weak, feeble, powerless, dependent, unprotected, defenceless, incapable
(≠) OPPOSITES strong, independent, competent

hem in VERB
*The singer was **hemmed in** by a crowd of fans.*
surround, enclose, box in, confine, restrict

herb NOUN

Here are some types of herb:
basil, bay, chives, coriander, dill, marjoram, mint, oregano, parsley, rosemary, sage, tarragon, thyme
⇒ Also look up **spice**

hero NOUN
*a footballing **hero***
idol, celebrity, star, superstar

heroic ADJECTIVE
heroic deeds
brave, courageous, fearless, bold, daring, adventurous, noble
(≠) OPPOSITES cowardly, timid

hesitate VERB
*He **hesitated** for a second before agreeing.*

Aa
Bb
Cc
Dd
Ee
Ff
Gg
Hh
Ii
Jj
Kk
Ll
Mm
Nn
Oo
Pp
Qq
Rr
Ss
Tt
Uu
Vv
Ww
Xx
Yy
Zz

pause, delay, wait, think twice, be uncertain, dither
≠ OPPOSITES decide

hide VERB
1 *hiding the key*
conceal, cover, screen, bury
≠ OPPOSITES show, display
2 *hiding the truth*
conceal, screen, mask, disguise, withhold, keep dark
≠ OPPOSITES reveal, show
3 *He hid behind some rocks.*
take cover, shelter, lie low

hideous ADJECTIVE
a hideous Hallowe'en mask
ugly, repulsive, grotesque, monstrous, ghastly, frightful, terrible, disgusting, revolting, horrible
≠ OPPOSITES beautiful, attractive

hiding NOUN
The boy was given a good hiding.
beating, whipping, spanking, thrashing, walloping

high ADJECTIVE
1 *a high cliff*
tall, lofty, towering
≠ OPPOSITES low, short
2 *a high wind*
great, strong, intense, extreme
≠ OPPOSITES light, gentle
3 *a high official*
important, influential, powerful, distinguished, chief, leading, senior
4 *a high voice*
high-pitched, sharp, shrill, piercing, soprano, treble
≠ OPPOSITES deep
5 *a high price*
expensive, dear, costly, excessive
≠ OPPOSITES cheap, inexpensive

highlight NOUN
Our visit to a theme park was the highlight of the holiday.
high point, high spot, peak, best

highly ADVERB
1 *highly intelligent*
very, considerably, decidedly, extremely, immensely, tremendously, exceptionally, extraordinarily
2 *His book was highly praised.*
greatly, enthusiastically, warmly, well

hike NOUN
We went for a hike in the country.
ramble, walk, trek, tramp, march

hilarious ADJECTIVE
a hilarious joke
funny, amusing, comical, hysterical
≠ OPPOSITES serious, grave

hill NOUN
a steep hill
slope, incline, ramp, drop

hinder VERB
We were hindered by not having a map.
hamper, handicap, hold up, delay, slow down, hold back, check, curb
≠ OPPOSITES help, aid, assist

hindrance NOUN
The rain was a hindrance to the rescue operation.
obstruction, handicap, obstacle, stumbling block, barrier, restriction
≠ OPPOSITES help, aid, assistance

hint[1] NOUN
some hints to help you with your homework
tip, advice, suggestion, help, clue, tip-off

hint[2] VERB
He hinted that he had a secret plan.
suggest, tip off, indicate, imply, mention

hire VERB
1 *We hired a car on holiday.*
rent, let, lease, book, reserve
2 *Andrew was hired as a paper boy.*
employ, take on, sign up, appoint
≠ OPPOSITES dismiss, fire

historic ADJECTIVE
a historic event

Aa Bb Cc Dd Ee Ff Gg Hh Ii Jj Kk Ll Mm Nn Oo Pp Qq Rr Ss Tt Uu Vv Ww Xx Yy Zz

momentous, important, significant, notable, remarkable, extraordinary, famous
⊒ OPPOSITES unimportant, insignificant, unknown

historical ADJECTIVE
a historical figure
real, actual, factual, documented, recorded, past
⊒ OPPOSITES legendary, fictional

history NOUN
characters from history
past, olden days, days of old

hit¹ VERB
1 *The boy hit his sister with a tennis racket.*
strike, knock, tap, smack, slap, whack, bash, thump, punch
◇ INFORMAL WORDS belt
2 *She hit her head against the door.*
bump, bang, crash, smash, damage, harm

hit² NOUN
Their last single was a huge hit.
success, triumph
◇ INFORMAL WORDS smash
⊒ OPPOSITES failure

hoard¹ NOUN
I keep my hoard of magazines in my desk.
collection, heap, pile, fund, supply, reserve, store
◇ INFORMAL WORDS stash

hoard² VERB
My sister hoards make-up.
collect, gather, save, put by, store, keep
◇ INFORMAL WORDS stash
⊒ OPPOSITES use, spend

hoarse ADJECTIVE
After the concert I was hoarse from screaming.
husky, croaky, throaty, gruff, growling, rough, harsh, grating
⊒ OPPOSITES clear, smooth

hoax NOUN
The phone call was a hoax.
trick, prank, practical joke, joke, fraud, deception, bluff, swindle, con

hobby NOUN
Danielle's hobby is swimming.
pastime, recreation, activity, relaxation, pursuit, occupation

Here are some types of hobby:
birdwatching, chess, cinema, climbing, collecting, computer games, cooking, cycling, dancing, fishing, gardening, horse riding, jigsaws, kite flying, knitting, martial arts, origami, photography, rambling, reading, sewing, skateboarding, skating, sports, stamp collecting, swimming, watching TV

hoist VERB
The removal men hoisted the piano up the stairs.
lift, raise, erect, jack up, heave

hold VERB
1 *Hold my hand when we cross the road.*
grip, grasp, clutch, clasp, keep, retain
⊒ OPPOSITES drop, let go
2 *The meeting was held in the town hall.*
conduct, carry on, continue, call
3 *The bus holds 50 passengers.*
bear, support, carry, contain
4 *The police are holding him for questioning.*
imprison, stop, arrest, restrain, keep
⊒ OPPOSITES release, free
• **hold up**
We were held up in traffic.
delay, slow, hinder

hole NOUN
1 *There's a hole in the pipe.*
opening, puncture, tear, split, outlet, slot, break, crack, fault, flaw

Aa Bb Cc Dd Ee Ff Gg Hh Ii Jj Kk Ll Mm Nn Oo Pp Qq Rr Ss Tt Uu Vv Ww Xx Yy Zz

2 *I dug a hole in the ground.*
dent, depression, hollow, pit, cave

holiday NOUN
I am on holiday from school for a week.
leave, time off, day off, break, rest,
half-term, bank holiday

Here are some things you might see on holiday:
aeroplane, beach, bucket and spade,
bus, campsite, caravan, coach, hotel,
ice cream, mountains, parasol,
passport, phrasebook, snow, suitcase,
sun cream, sunhat, sunshine, tent,
train

hollow¹ ADJECTIVE
1 *a hollow Easter egg*
empty, vacant, unfilled
≠ OPPOSITES solid
2 *hollow cheeks*
sunken, deep, concave
≠ OPPOSITES convex
3 *a hollow promise*
false, insincere, meaningless, empty,
vain, worthless
≠ OPPOSITES real

hollow² NOUN
a hollow in the ground
hole, pit, cavity, crater

holy ADJECTIVE
a holy man
religious, good, pure, sacred

home NOUN
She has a very comfortable home.
house, residence, base
◆ FORMAL WORDS dwelling

homely ADJECTIVE
The flat is comfortable and homely.
homelike, homey, comfortable, cosy,
snug, informal, simple,
unsophisticated
≠ OPPOSITES grand, formal

honest ADJECTIVE
1 *an honest answer*
truthful, sincere, frank, direct, straight,
straightforward, simple, open
≠ OPPOSITES dishonest
2 *an honest citizen*
moral, honourable, reputable,
respectable, reliable, trustworthy,
genuine
≠ OPPOSITES dishonourable

honour¹ NOUN
1 *He was defending the honour of his family.*
reputation, good name, respect, dignity,
self-respect, pride, morality, decency
≠ OPPOSITES dishonour, disgrace
2 *a statue erected in honour of the princess*
praise, admiration, worship, adoration

honour² VERB
a ceremony to honour the heroes
praise, celebrate, commemorate,
remember, admire, respect
≠ OPPOSITES dishonour, disgrace

honourable ADJECTIVE
1 *Owning up would be the honourable thing to do.*
noble, moral, fair, right, proper, decent,
respectable, honest, trustworthy, sincere
≠ OPPOSITES dishonourable, dishonest
2 *our honourable guests*
great, distinguished, respected, worthy,
reputable
≠ OPPOSITES dishonourable, unworthy

hop VERB
She hopped about on one leg.
jump, leap, skip, dance, prance

hope¹ NOUN
1 *We have not given up hope of finding survivors.*
hopefulness, optimism, expectation,
anticipation, prospect, belief, faith
≠ OPPOSITES pessimism, despair
2 *all her hopes and dreams*
wish, desire, longing, dream, ambition
≠ OPPOSITES fear

hope² VERB
I hope you have a good holiday.
wish, desire, long, expect, look forward, anticipate, foresee
⊘ OPPOSITES despair, lose heart

hopeful ADJECTIVE
1 *We are hopeful of a good result.*
optimistic, confident, assured, cheerful
⊘ OPPOSITES pessimistic, despairing
2 *a hopeful sign*
encouraging, reassuring, favourable, promising, bright
⊘ OPPOSITES discouraging

hopeless ADJECTIVE
1 *She felt hopeless about the future.*
despairing, downhearted, negative, pessimistic
⊘ OPPOSITES hopeful, optimistic
2 *a hopeless failure*
worthless, poor, helpless, lost

horde NOUN
Hordes of supporters headed towards the stadium.
band, gang, pack, herd, flock, swarm, crowd, mob

horizon NOUN
lots of boats on the horizon
skyline, vista, prospect

horrible ADJECTIVE
She was wearing a horrible orange sweater.
unpleasant, nasty, horrid, revolting, repulsive, hideous, awful, dreadful, frightful, terrible
⊘ OPPOSITES pleasant, agreeable, lovely, attractive

horrific ADJECTIVE
a horrific accident
horrifying, shocking, appalling, awful, dreadful, ghastly, gruesome, terrifying, frightening, scary

horrify VERB
His carelessness horrified me.
shock, disgust, sicken, dismay, alarm, scare, frighten, terrify
⊘ OPPOSITES please, delight

horror NOUN
1 *She screamed in horror.*
shock, disgust, revulsion, loathing, fright, fear, terror, panic, dread
⊘ OPPOSITES approval, delight
2 *the horrors of war*
ghastliness, awfulness, frightfulness, hideousness

horse NOUN

Here are some types of horse and pony:
Arab, Dartmoor, Exmoor, Falabella, Lipizzaner, New Forest, Palomino, Shetland, Shire, Suffolk Punch
Parts of a horse:
fetlock, forelock, haunch, hoof, mane, withers
Ways a horse can move:
canter, gallop, trot, walk
Equipment used for horse riding:
bit, bridle, crop, reins, riding helmet, saddle, spurs, stirrups

hospitable ADJECTIVE
Our new neighbours have been very hospitable.
friendly, welcoming, kind, gracious, generous, liberal
⊘ OPPOSITES unfriendly, hostile

hospital NOUN

Here are some things you might see in a hospital:
accident and emergency department, ambulance, bed, cleaner, clinic, doctor, matron, nurse, operating theatre, outpatients, patients, pharmacy, porter, shop, stethoscope, surgeon, thermometer, waiting room, ward, X-ray room

Aa Bb Cc Dd Ee Ff Gg Hh Ii Jj Kk Ll Mm Nn Oo Pp Qq Rr Ss Tt Uu Vv Ww Xx Yy Zz

hostile ADJECTIVE
hostile nations
warlike, unsympathetic, unfriendly, opposed, warring
⊕ OPPOSITES friendly, welcoming

hot ADJECTIVE
1 *a hot climate*
warm, burning, scorching, roasting, baking, boiling, sizzling, sweltering, sultry, tropical
⊕ OPPOSITES cold, cool
2 *a hot curry*
spicy, peppery, sharp, strong
⊕ OPPOSITES mild, bland

house NOUN
rows of neat little houses
building, residence, home
◆ FORMAL WORDS dwelling

Here are some types of house:

bungalow, chalet, cottage, croft, detached, farmhouse, hall, homestead, hut, igloo, lodge, log cabin, manor, manse, mansion, parsonage, ranch house, semi-detached, shack, shanty, terraced, town house, tree house, vicarage, villa

hover VERB
1 *a hawk hovering above*
hang, poise, float, drift, fly, flutter, flap
2 *He hovered by the telephone, waiting for a call.*
pause, linger, hang about, hesitate

however CONJUNCTION
I love most fruit. However, I don't like avocados.
nevertheless, nonetheless, still, yet, even so

hubbub NOUN
the loud hubbub of the swimming pool
noise, racket, din
⊕ OPPOSITES peace, quiet

huddle VERB
The campers huddled round a campfire.
cluster, meet, gather, crowd, press, cuddle, snuggle, nestle
⊕ OPPOSITES disperse, scatter

huff NOUN
Tina walked out in a huff.
sulks, mood, bad mood, anger, rage, passion

hug VERB
The little girl hugged her mother tightly.
cuddle, squeeze, hold, clasp, grip, cling to

huge ADJECTIVE
a huge elephant
immense, vast, enormous, massive, giant, gigantic
⊕ OPPOSITES tiny

hum VERB
I could hear the bees humming in the garden.
buzz, whirr, purr, drone, sing, murmur, mumble, throb, pulse, vibrate

human ADJECTIVE
He's quite human once you get to know him.
kind, considerate, understanding, compassionate
⊕ OPPOSITES inhuman

humble ADJECTIVE
1 *She is very humble despite being so talented.*
modest, meek, polite, respectful
⊕ OPPOSITES proud, conceited
2 *their humble home*
ordinary, plain, simple, modest, lowly, common, commonplace, unimportant
⊕ OPPOSITES important, grand

humid ADJECTIVE
The weather in Florida was hot and humid.
damp, moist, clammy, sticky, muggy, steamy
⊕ OPPOSITES dry

Aa Bb Cc Dd Ee Ff Gg **Hh** Ii Jj Kk Ll Mm Nn Oo Pp Qq Rr Ss Tt Uu Vv Ww Xx Yy Zz

humiliate VERB
*It was wrong to **humiliate** the boy in front of his friends.*
embarrass, crush, break, deflate, shame, disgrace, degrade, humble
≠ OPPOSITES dignify

humorous ADJECTIVE
*a **humorous** story*
funny, amusing, comic, entertaining, witty, comical, absurd, hilarious
≠ OPPOSITES serious, humourless

humour¹ NOUN
*She has a good sense of **humour**.*
wit, jokes, satire, comedy, farce, fun

humour² VERB
*I agreed just to **humour** him.*
go along with, indulge, pamper, please

hunch¹ NOUN
*I have a **hunch** that everything will be all right.*
feeling, impression, idea, guess, suspicion, intuition

hunch² VERB
*He **hunched** his shoulders against the cold wind.*
hump, bend, curve, arch, stoop, crouch, squat, huddle

hunger NOUN
*My stomach ached with **hunger**.*
hungriness, emptiness, starvation, famine, appetite

hungry ADJECTIVE
*I always feel **hungry** after swimming.*
starving, empty, hollow, famished, ravenous
◇ INFORMAL WORDS peckish
≠ OPPOSITES satisfied, full

hunt¹ VERB
1 *police **hunting** the thief*
chase, pursue, hound, stalk, track, trail
2 *She is **hunting** for her umbrella.*
seek, look for, search, rummage

hunt² NOUN
*the **hunt** for the clues*
chase, pursuit, search, investigation

hurdle NOUN
*The biggest **hurdle** is finding something I want to write about.*
barrier, obstacle, obstruction, hindrance, problem, snag, difficulty, complication

hurl VERB
*Groups of boys **hurled** stones at each other.*
throw, toss, fling, sling, propel, fire, launch

hurry¹ VERB
***Hurry** home before it gets dark.*
rush, dash, fly, get a move on, quicken, speed up
≠ OPPOSITES slow down, dawdle

hurry² NOUN
*I'm in a **hurry** to catch the school bus.*
rush, quickness, haste
≠ OPPOSITES calm

hurt VERB
1 *My leg **hurts**.*
ache, throb, sting
2 *I would never **hurt** an animal.*
injure, wound, mistreat, bruise, cut, burn, torture
3 *It **hurts** me when he behaves like that.*
upset, sadden, distress, offend

hurtful ADJECTIVE
***hurtful** remarks*
upsetting, vicious, cruel, mean, unkind, nasty, malicious, spiteful, cutting
≠ OPPOSITES kind

hurtle VERB
*A car came **hurtling** towards me.*
dash, tear, race, fly, shoot, speed, rush, charge, plunge, crash

hush VERB
*The teacher tried to **hush** the children.*
quieten, silence, still, settle, compose, calm, soothe

Aa
Bb
Cc
Dd
Ee
Ff
Gg
Hh
Ii
Jj
Kk
Ll
Mm
Nn
Oo
Pp
Qq
Rr
Ss
Tt
Uu
Vv
Ww
Xx
Yy
Zz

OPPOSITES disturb, rouse
• **hush up**
*The politicians **hushed up** the scandal.*
keep dark, conceal, cover up, stifle, gag
≠ OPPOSITES publicize, expose

husky ADJECTIVE

*My voice is **husky** because I have a sore throat.*
hoarse, croaky, croaking, throaty, rough, harsh

hut NOUN

*a wooden **hut** in the garden*
cabin, shack, booth, shed, shelter, den

hygienic ADJECTIVE

*Hospitals must be kept **hygienic**.*
disinfected, sterile, germ-free, clean, pure, healthy, wholesome
≠ OPPOSITES unhygienic

hysterical ADJECTIVE

1 *hysterical sobbing*
frantic, frenzied, uncontrollable, mad, raving, crazed
≠ OPPOSITES calm, composed, self-possessed
2 *That film was **hysterical**.*
hilarious, uproarious, side-splitting

Aa
Bb
Cc
Dd
Ee
Ff
Gg
Hh
Ii
Jj
Kk
Ll
Mm
Nn
Oo
Pp
Qq
Rr
Ss
Tt
Uu
Vv
Ww
Xx
Yy
Zz

icy ADJECTIVE
1 *an icy wind*
cold, ice-cold, freezing, frozen, raw,
bitter, biting, chilly
⊘ OPPOSITES hot
2 *icy roads*
slippery, frosty, frozen
3 *an icy silence*
unfriendly, hostile, cold, stony, distant
⊘ OPPOSITES friendly, warm

idea NOUN
1 *Do you have any idea what will
happen next?*
thought, notion, theory, guess, belief,
opinion, view, viewpoint, judgement
2 *This leaflet will give you an idea of
our organization's aims.*
impression, vision, image,
understanding, clue
3 *That's a good idea.*
suggestion, brainwave, proposal,
proposition, recommendation, plan,
scheme
4 *The general idea was to help the
homeless people.*
aim, intention, purpose, reason, point,
object

ideal ADJECTIVE
*Sunday is the ideal time for a quiet
drive.*
perfect, dream, best, supreme, highest,
model

identical ADJECTIVE
Their outfits were almost identical.
same, twin, duplicate, like, alike,
corresponding, matching
⊘ OPPOSITES different

identify VERB
1 *Would you be able to identify the
thief?*
pick out, recognize, know, single out,

make out, name, place
2 *You can identify your luggage with
these name tags.*
recognize, distinguish, make out,
notice, label, tag, place
• **identify with**
*Women tend to identify with the
heroine of the film.*
relate to, associate yourself with,
respond to, sympathize with, feel for

idiotic ADJECTIVE
an idiotic idea
foolish, stupid, silly, absurd, senseless,
daft, insane, crazy
⊘ OPPOSITES sensible, sane

idle ADJECTIVE
1 *machines lying idle*
unused, inactive, inoperative,
unoccupied
⊘ OPPOSITES active
2 *an idle layabout*
lazy, work-shy, shiftless
⊘ OPPOSITES busy, hard-working

idol NOUN
1 *worshipping idols made of gold*
image, icon, god
2 *pictures of my pop idols*
hero, heroine, icon, favourite, pin-up

idolize VERB
Abdul idolizes his older brother.
worship, hero-worship, admire, adore,
love, dote on
⊘ OPPOSITES despise

ignorant ADJECTIVE
1 *I was totally ignorant about classical
music.*
uneducated, inexperienced, stupid,
clueless, uninformed
⊘ OPPOSITES educated, knowledgeable,
clever, wise
2 *He was ignorant of the real situation.*

Aa

Bb

Cc

Dd

Ee

Ff

Gg

Hh

Ii

Jj

Kk

Ll

Mm

Nn

Oo

Pp

Qq

Rr

Ss

Tt

Uu

Vv

Ww

Xx

Yy

Zz

unaware, uninformed, unconscious, oblivious
⊯ OPPOSITES knowledgeable, aware

ignore VERB
1 *He **ignored** his parents' advice.*
disregard, take no notice of, shut your eyes to, pass over, neglect, reject
⊯ OPPOSITES notice, observe
2 *I said hello, but she completely **ignored** me.*
take no notice of, snub, cold-shoulder, overlook
⊯ OPPOSITES notice, observe

ill ADJECTIVE
1 *He was still **ill** when I went to see him.*
sick, poorly, unwell, infirm, off-colour, unhealthy
◆ FORMAL WORDS indisposed
◇ INFORMAL WORDS out of sorts, under the weather, laid up
⊯ OPPOSITES well
2 *an **ill** omen*
bad, evil, unpromising, sinister, threatening, unlucky, unfortunate
⊯ OPPOSITES good, favourable, fortunate
3 *Luckily he suffered no **ill** effects from the accident.*
harmful, damaging, unfortunate
⊯ OPPOSITES good, favourable, fortunate
4 *I bear you no **ill** will.*
unfriendly, hostile, bad, unkind
⊯ OPPOSITES good, favourable

illegal ADJECTIVE
*It's **illegal** to fish here.*
unlawful, criminal, wrongful, forbidden, prohibited, banned, unauthorized
⊯ OPPOSITES legal, lawful

illegible ADJECTIVE
*His handwriting is **illegible**.*
unreadable, scrawled, obscure, indistinct
⊯ OPPOSITES legible

illness NOUN
*He has a serious **illness**.*

sickness, disease, disorder, complaint, ill health

illusion NOUN
*I thought I saw something moving, but it was just an **illusion**.*
hallucination, fantasy, fancy
⊯ OPPOSITES reality, truth

illustrate VERB
1 *His actions **illustrate** his uncaring attitude.*
show, exhibit, demonstrate
2 *She **illustrated** her lecture with a slide show.*
explain, interpret

illustration NOUN
1 *a book with lots of colourful **illustrations***
picture, photograph, drawing, sketch
2 *Give me an **illustration** of what you mean.*
example, specimen, instance, case, demonstration, explanation

image NOUN
1 *He had an **image** of himself as a famous footballer.*
idea, notion, impression, vision
2 *images of the saints*
representation, likeness, picture, portrait, figure, statue

imaginary ADJECTIVE
*her **imaginary** friend*
imagined, pretend, make-believe, unreal, non-existent, fictional, made-up, invented, fictitious
⊯ OPPOSITES real

imagination NOUN
*She has a vivid **imagination**.*
creativity, inventiveness, originality, vision
⊯ OPPOSITES unimaginativeness, reality

imaginative ADJECTIVE
*His stories are very **imaginative**.*
creative, inventive, original, inspired, ingenious, clever
⊯ OPPOSITES unimaginative

imagine VERB

1 *Imagine what it would be like to go to the moon.*
picture, fantasize, pretend, make believe
2 *I imagine there will be a school disco in December.*
think, believe, suppose, guess, assume, take it

imitate VERB

1 *Sean is good at imitating his teacher.*
mimic, do an impression of, copy, impersonate
◇ INFORMAL WORDS take off, send up
2 *Many other writers have imitated his style.*
copy, follow, reproduce, duplicate, repeat, mirror

imitation¹ NOUN

This painting is not an original, it's an imitation.
copy, duplicate, reproduction, replica, fake, forgery

imitation² ADJECTIVE

imitation leather
artificial, synthetic, man-made, fake, mock, reproduction
◇ INFORMAL WORDS phoney
≠ OPPOSITES genuine, real

immature ADJECTIVE

1 *The teenagers were behaving in a silly immature way.*
childish, babyish
≠ OPPOSITES mature
2 *The immature plants can easily be killed by frost.*
young, undeveloped
≠ OPPOSITES mature

immediate ADJECTIVE

1 *an immediate response*
instant, direct, prompt, swift
≠ OPPOSITES delayed
2 *our immediate neighbours*
nearest, next, near, close
≠ OPPOSITES distant

immediately ADVERB

We need to leave immediately.
at once, now, straight away, right away, instantly, without delay, promptly
≠ OPPOSITES eventually, never

immense ADJECTIVE

an immense building
huge, vast, great, enormous, massive, giant, gigantic
≠ OPPOSITES tiny

immerse VERB

Immerse the tomatoes in boiling water.
plunge, submerge, sink, duck, dip, bathe

immobilize VERB

1 *His car was immobilized by the snow.*
stop, halt, fix
≠ OPPOSITES mobilize
2 *She was immobilized with pain.*
paralyse, cripple, disable
≠ OPPOSITES mobilize

immoral ADJECTIVE

They were shocked by his immoral behaviour.
wicked, wrong, bad, sinful, evil, corrupt
≠ OPPOSITES moral, right, good

immortal ADJECTIVE

1 *The gods were believed to be immortal.*
undying, eternal, everlasting, deathless
≠ OPPOSITES mortal
2 *the immortal legend of King Arthur*
timeless, eternal, everlasting, lasting, enduring

impact NOUN

1 *The new rules will have an impact on all of us.*
effect, consequences, impression, influence
2 *We were flung forward by the impact of the crash.*
collision, contact, force, crash, smash, jolt, knock, shock

Aa
Bb
Cc
Dd
Ee
Ff
Gg
Hh
Ii
Jj
Kk
Ll
Mm
Nn
Oo
Pp
Qq
Rr
Ss
Tt
Uu
Vv
Ww
Xx
Yy
Zz

impatient ADJECTIVE

1 *He became very **impatient** when he was kept waiting.*
irritable, cross, restless, edgy, snappy, bad-tempered
(≠) OPPOSITES patient
2 *We are all **impatient** to see the new puppy.*
eager, keen, anxious, longing

imperfect ADJECTIVE

*These items are cheap because they are **imperfect**.*
faulty, flawed, damaged, broken, incomplete
(≠) OPPOSITES perfect

impersonate VERB

*Sean is good at **impersonating** his teacher.*
imitate, mimic, do an impression of
◇ INFORMAL WORDS take off

impertinent ADJECTIVE

*The boy was punished for being **impertinent** to his teacher.*
rude, impolite, insolent, impudent, cheeky, bold
(≠) OPPOSITES polite, respectful

implement NOUN

*kitchen **implements***
tool, instrument, utensil, gadget, device, apparatus, appliance

imply VERB

1 *He **implied** that I was lying.*
hint, suggest, indicate
(≠) OPPOSITES state
2 *I didn't object, but that doesn't **imply** that I was happy about the decision.*
mean, point to, indicate

important ADJECTIVE

1 *an **important** difference*
significant, meaningful, noteworthy, major, substantial
(≠) OPPOSITES unimportant, insignificant, trivial
2 ***important** information*
vital, relevant, urgent, essential, valuable

(≠) OPPOSITES unimportant, insignificant, trivial
3 *an **important** person*
leading, high-level, high-ranking, influential, powerful, outstanding, noted

impose VERB

1 *New school rules have been **imposed**.*
introduce, enforce, set, fix, establish, apply
2 *James **imposed** on our conversation.*
intrude, butt in, force yourself

imposing ADJECTIVE

*a very **imposing** building*
impressive, striking, grand
(≠) OPPOSITES modest

impossible ADJECTIVE

*an **impossible** task*
unachievable, hopeless, unworkable, unobtainable, unreasonable, unthinkable
(≠) OPPOSITES possible

impress VERB

*His work really **impressed** me.*
excite, move, touch, affect, influence, inspire

impression NOUN

1 *I get the **impression** he doesn't want to come.*
idea, feeling, sense, notion, suspicion, hunch
2 *She does brilliant **impressions** of actresses.*
impersonation, imitation
◇ INFORMAL WORDS take-off, send-up
3 *He is keen to make a good **impression** on his teacher.*
impact, effect, influence

impressive ADJECTIVE

*His football skills are very **impressive**.*
striking, grand, powerful, effective, exciting
(≠) OPPOSITES unimpressive, uninspiring

imprison VERB

*He was **imprisoned** for his part in a bank robbery.*

jail, send to prison, detain, lock up, confine
◇ INFORMAL WORDS send down, put
away, cage
⚠ OPPOSITES release, free

improper ADJECTIVE

1 *improper use of school equipment*
wrong, incorrect, irregular, unsuitable,
inappropriate, out of place
⚠ OPPOSITES proper, appropriate
2 *improper behaviour*
rude, vulgar, indecent
⚠ OPPOSITES decent

improve VERB

1 *You must improve your manners.*
correct, better, mend, amend, reform
2 *Your handwriting is improving.*
get better, pick up, develop, advance,
progress
◇ INFORMAL WORDS look up
⚠ OPPOSITES worsen, deteriorate
3 *After some rest, the patient started to
improve.*
get better, recover, rally
◇ INFORMAL WORDS perk up
⚠ OPPOSITES worsen, deteriorate

impudent ADJECTIVE

*The teacher gave the impudent girl a
punishment exercise.*
cheeky, impertinent, saucy, bold,
forward, insolent, rude
⚠ OPPOSITES polite, respectful

impulse NOUN

She had a sudden impulse to slap him.
urge, wish, desire, inclination, whim,
notion

inability NOUN

*His failure was due to his inability as a
businessman.*
incapability, powerlessness, impotence,
inadequacy, weakness
⚠ OPPOSITES ability

inaccurate ADJECTIVE

an inaccurate account of events
incorrect, wrong, mistaken, imprecise,
inexact, unreliable, untrue
⚠ OPPOSITES accurate, correct

inadequate ADJECTIVE

1 *an inadequate supply of food*
insufficient, short, deficient, scanty,
sparse, meagre
⚠ OPPOSITES adequate, plentiful
2 *She felt inadequate as a teacher.*
incompetent, incapable, unfit,
unqualified, ineffective, deficient,
unsatisfactory
⚠ OPPOSITES satisfactory

inappropriate ADJECTIVE

1 *Dangly earrings are inappropriate for
school.*
unsuitable, out of place, improper,
unbecoming, unfitting
⚠ OPPOSITES appropriate, suitable
2 *He apologized for his inappropriate
remarks.*
improper, unsuitable, untimely, tactless,
unseemly
⚠ OPPOSITES appropriate, suitable

incapable ADJECTIVE

1 *He is completely incapable as a player.*
incompetent, unable, unfit, unsuited,
unqualified, inadequate, ineffective
⚠ OPPOSITES capable
2 *The accident left her an incapable
invalid.*
powerless, helpless, weak, feeble
⚠ OPPOSITES capable

incentive NOUN

*Sapna's parents promised her a mobile
phone as an incentive to work hard for
her exams.*
encouragement, enticement, reward,
reason, motive, motivation
⚠ OPPOSITES discouragement

incident NOUN

*a serious incident where two people
were killed*
event, occurrence, happening, episode,
affair, occasion

inclined ADJECTIVE

1 *She is inclined to be late with her
homework.*
liable, likely, apt

Aa
Bb
Cc
Dd
Ee
Ff
Gg
Hh
Ii
Jj
Kk
Ll
Mm
Nn
Oo
Pp
Qq
Rr
Ss
Tt
Uu
Vv
Ww
Xx
Yy
Zz

2 *We can go for a walk, if you feel inclined.*
willing, disposed

include VERB
1 *This album includes all the band's hit singles.*
contain, comprise, cover, take in, involve
≠ OPPOSITES exclude, omit
2 *Remember to include your travel expenses in your budget.*
add, allow for, take into account
≠ OPPOSITES exclude, omit

income NOUN
You cannot spend more than your income.
earnings, pay, salary, wages, proceeds, gains, profits, takings
≠ OPPOSITES expenses

incomplete ADJECTIVE
The workmen had done an incomplete job.
unfinished, lacking, partial, imperfect
≠ OPPOSITES complete

inconsiderate ADJECTIVE
1 *It was inconsiderate of you to use up all the milk.*
selfish, uncaring, self-centred, thoughtless, unthinking, careless
≠ OPPOSITES considerate
2 *an inconsiderate remark*
insensitive, tactless, rude, thoughtless, unthinking
≠ OPPOSITES considerate

inconsistent ADJECTIVE
1 *He is inconsistent in his treatment of the children.*
changeable, variable, irregular, unpredictable, inconstant
≠ OPPOSITES consistent
2 *a fact that is inconsistent with their story*
conflicting, at odds, incompatible, contradictory

inconvenient ADJECTIVE
Have I called at an inconvenient time?

awkward, unsuitable, difficult, annoying, troublesome
≠ OPPOSITES convenient

increase VERB
1 *Practice will increase your confidence in playing the piano.*
raise, boost, add to, strengthen, heighten, build up, develop
≠ OPPOSITES decrease, reduce
2 *Membership of the youth club has increased over the last year.*
grow, build up, expand, spread, swell, rise, mount, develop
≠ OPPOSITES decrease, reduce

incredible ADJECTIVE
1 *It's incredible that a young child could write this music.*
amazing, extraordinary, astonishing, astounding
2 *His story was too incredible to take seriously.*
unbelievable, improbable, far-fetched, absurd, impossible, unthinkable, unimaginable
≠ OPPOSITES credible, believable

indecent ADJECTIVE
an indecent remark
vulgar, improper, immodest, impure, indelicate, offensive, coarse, crude
≠ OPPOSITES decent, modest

indeed ADVERB
1 *Your painting is very good indeed.*
really, certainly, positively, truly, undoubtedly, to be sure, without doubt
2 *He admitted that he had indeed taken the money.*
in fact, actually

indefinite ADJECTIVE
an indefinite period of time
unknown, uncertain, undefined, unspecified, unlimited, vague, indistinct, unclear, inexact
≠ OPPOSITES definite, limited, clear

independent ADJECTIVE
1 *She's a very independent person.*

Aa
Bb
Cc
Dd
Ee
Ff
Gg
Hh
Ii
Jj
Kk
Ll
Mm
Nn
Oo
Pp
Qq
Rr
Ss
Tt
Uu
Vv
Ww
Xx
Yy
Zz

self-sufficient, free, liberated, self-supporting, self-reliant, unaided
2 *Two independent books have been published on the subject.*
separate, individual, unconnected, unrelated

indicate VERB

1 *The thermometer indicates that he has a temperature.*
show, record, reveal, display, mark
2 *His reply indicates that he disapproves.*
mean, express, suggest, imply

indication NOUN

Her expression is an indication of her true feelings.
sign, mark, evidence, signal, suggestion, hint, clue

indifferent ADJECTIVE

1 *He was indifferent to their sadness.*
unconcerned, uninterested, unmoved, uncaring, unsympathetic, detached, uninvolved
≠ OPPOSITES interested, caring
2 *The meal was indifferent.*
mediocre, average, middling, passable, moderate, fair, ordinary
≠ OPPOSITES excellent

indignant ADJECTIVE

I felt quite indignant when she accused me of lying.
angry, annoyed, furious, infuriated, outraged
≠ OPPOSITES pleased, delighted

indirect ADJECTIVE

an indirect route
roundabout, wandering, rambling, winding, zigzag
≠ OPPOSITES direct

indispensable ADJECTIVE

an indispensable kitchen tool
essential, vital, basic, crucial, required, needed, necessary
◇ INFORMAL WORDS requisite
≠ OPPOSITES unnecessary

indistinct ADJECTIVE

1 *an indistinct shape*
unclear, blurred, fuzzy, misty, hazy, obscure, dim, vague, indefinite
≠ OPPOSITES distinct, clear
2 *an indistinct sound*
dim, faint, confused
≠ OPPOSITES distinct, clear

individual¹ NOUN

a very strange individual
person, being, creature, soul, character, fellow

individual² ADJECTIVE

1 *She has a very individual style of singing.*
distinctive, characteristic, unique, special, personal, distinct, specific, particular
2 *an individual portion*
separate, single, personal, own
≠ OPPOSITES collective, shared, general

indulgent ADJECTIVE

They are too indulgent with their children.
easy-going, tolerant, lenient, permissive, generous, liberal, kind
≠ OPPOSITES strict, harsh

industry NOUN

the steel industry
business, trade, commerce, manufacturing, production

ineffective ADJECTIVE

1 *an ineffective system*
useless, worthless, unproductive, unsuccessful, inadequate
≠ OPPOSITES effective
2 *an ineffective leader*
inadequate, inefficient, useless, worthless, powerless, weak, incompetent
≠ OPPOSITES effective

inefficient ADJECTIVE

1 *He was lazy and inefficient at work.*
incompetent, inexpert, slipshod, sloppy, careless

Aa
Bb
Cc
Dd
Ee
Ff
Gg
Hh
Ii
Jj
Kk
Ll
Mm
Nn
Oo
Pp
Qq
Rr
Ss
Tt
Uu
Vv
Ww
Xx
Yy
Zz

≠ OPPOSITES efficient
2 an *inefficient* use of resources
wasteful, uneconomic, careless
≠ OPPOSITES efficient

inevitable ADJECTIVE
It is *inevitable* that there will be
disagreements in a group.
unavoidable, inescapable, certain, sure,
destined, fated
≠ OPPOSITES avoidable, uncertain

inexpensive ADJECTIVE
They offer good service at an
inexpensive rate.
cheap, low-priced, reasonable, modest,
bargain, budget, low-cost, economical
≠ OPPOSITES expensive, dear

inexperienced ADJECTIVE
an *inexperienced* junior doctor
new, inexpert, untrained, unskilled,
amateur, apprentice
≠ OPPOSITES experienced

infant NOUN
an *infant* in his mother's arms
baby, toddler, child, kid
≠ OPPOSITES adult

infect VERB
Bacteria in the pipes can *infect* the
water.
contaminate, pollute, poison

inferior ADJECTIVE
1 an *inferior* position
lower, lesser, minor, secondary, junior,
second-class, low, humble
≠ OPPOSITES superior, senior
2 *inferior* work
bad, substandard, second-rate,
mediocre, poor, unsatisfactory,
shoddy
≠ OPPOSITES excellent

infinite ADJECTIVE
1 She has *infinite* patience.
limitless, unlimited, endless, never-
ending, vast, immense, enormous
≠ OPPOSITES limited
2 an *infinite* number

countless, limitless, unlimited,
uncountable
≠ OPPOSITES limited

inflate VERB
Inflate your water wings.
blow up, pump up, blow out, puff out,
swell, expand, enlarge
≠ OPPOSITES deflate

inflict VERB
1 I wouldn't *inflict* my little brother on
you.
impose, enforce
2 He *inflicted* a fatal wound on his
opponent.
deal, deliver

influence¹ NOUN
1 Your friend has too much *influence*
over you.
rule, hold, control, pressure
2 his *influence* on my work
effect, direction, guidance, impact
3 He used his *influence* to get his son
a job.
power, authority, weight, importance
◇ INFORMAL WORDS pull

influence² VERB
1 She is trying to *influence* him to
change his decision.
control, dominate, direct, guide, move
2 What you eat *influences* your health.
affect, have an effect, control, change,
alter, modify

influential ADJECTIVE
1 an *influential* figure in politics
important, controlling, leading,
inspiring, powerful, strong, significant,
guiding
≠ OPPOSITES unimportant
2 an *influential* argument
persuasive, convincing, inspiring,
moving, powerful, effective, guiding
≠ OPPOSITES ineffective

inform VERB
You must *inform* us if you change your
address.
tell, advise, notify, let someone know

• inform on
One of the gang members informed on the others.
betray
◇ INFORMAL WORDS shop, tell on, squeal, blab, grass

informal ADJECTIVE
an informal atmosphere
relaxed, casual, easy, free, natural
≠ OPPOSITES formal

information NOUN
1 *You can find lots of useful information on the Internet.*
facts, data, advice, instruction, knowledge
2 *Is there any further information on the rail strike?*
news, report, bulletin, message, word, notice

infuriate VERB
His rudeness infuriates me.
anger, enrage, madden, provoke, annoy, irritate
≠ OPPOSITES calm, soothe

ingenious ADJECTIVE
an ingenious plan
clever, shrewd, cunning, crafty, imaginative, creative, inventive, original
≠ OPPOSITES unimaginative

ingredient NOUN
There is a list of ingredients on the packet.
element, component, part

inhabit VERB
the students who inhabit the area
live in, occupy, populate, stay in
◆ FORMAL WORDS reside in, dwell in

inhabitant NOUN
The original inhabitants of New Zealand were the Maoris.
resident, citizen, native, dweller, occupier, occupant

inherit VERB
She inherited the house from her parents.
be left, succeed to, come into, receive

inhuman ADJECTIVE
Their treatment of the prisoners was inhuman.
cruel, barbaric, vicious, savage, sadistic, cold-blooded, brutal, inhumane
≠ OPPOSITES human, humane

initial ADJECTIVE
Their initial suspicion turned to trust.
first, beginning, opening, original, early
≠ OPPOSITES final, last

initially ADVERB
Initially I thought I wasn't going to like skiing.
at first, at the beginning, to begin with, to start with, originally, first, firstly, first of all
≠ OPPOSITES finally, in the end

initiative NOUN
She showed great initiative in dealing with the problem.
energy, drive, ambition, inventiveness, originality
◇ INFORMAL WORDS get-up-and-go

injure VERB
1 *He was badly injured in a car crash.*
hurt, harm, damage, wound, disable, cripple, lame
2 *Avoid doing anything which might injure your health.*
harm, damage, spoil, ruin
3 *She felt injured when her friends ignored her.*
hurt, wound, ill-treat, abuse, offend, wrong, upset
◇ INFORMAL WORDS put out

injury NOUN
1 *a head injury*
wound, cut, fracture
2 *Luckily we both escaped serious injury.*
harm, hurt, ill, damage

innocent ADJECTIVE
1 *They have sent an innocent man to jail.*

Aa
Bb
Cc
Dd
Ee
Ff
Gg
Hh
Ii
Jj
Kk
Ll
Mm
Nn
Oo
Pp
Qq
Rr
Ss
Tt
Uu
Vv
Ww
Xx
Yy
Zz

Aa
Bb
Cc
Dd
Ee
Ff
Gg
Hh
Ii
Jj
Kk
Ll
Mm
Nn
Oo
Pp
Qq
Rr
Ss
Tt
Uu
Vv
Ww
Xx
Yy
Zz

guiltless, blameless, honest, virtuous, righteous
⊯ OPPOSITES guilty
2 *gossip which ruined an innocent woman's reputation*
virtuous, stainless, spotless, immaculate, pure
3 *an innocent question*
inoffensive, harmless, innocuous
4 *She was too innocent to understand what was going on.*
naïve, green, inexperienced, simple, unsophisticated, childlike, trusting
⊯ OPPOSITES experienced, worldly

inquire
⇒ see **enquire**

inquiry
⇒ see **enquiry**

inquisitive ADJECTIVE
My neighbour is too inquisitive.
curious, questioning, prying, snooping, interfering
◇ INFORMAL WORDS nosey

insane ADJECTIVE
1 *The poor man must be insane.*
mad, crazy, mentally ill, disturbed
⊯ OPPOSITES sane
2 *That was an insane thing to do.*
foolish, stupid, senseless, impractical
⊯ OPPOSITES sensible, wise

insect NOUN

Here are some types of insect:

Flying insects:
bluebottle, butterfly, cranefly, daddy-long-legs, dragonfly, firefly, fly, gnat, horsefly, lacewing, ladybird, locust, midge, mosquito, moth
Stinging insects:
bee, hornet, wasp
Garden pests:
aphid, blackfly, greenfly
Crawling or jumping insects:
ant, beetle, cicada, cockroach, cricket, earwig, flea, glowworm, grasshopper, louse, praying mantis, scorpion, stick insect, termite, weevil, woodlouse, woodworm

insecure ADJECTIVE
1 *I felt insecure on my first day at school.*
nervous, anxious, worried, uncertain, unsure, afraid
⊯ OPPOSITES confident
2 *in an insecure position*
unsafe, dangerous, hazardous, unprotected, defenceless, exposed, vulnerable
⊯ OPPOSITES secure, safe
3 *The platform has become insecure.*
unsteady, unsafe, dangerous, shaky, loose
⊯ OPPOSITES secure, safe

insensitive ADJECTIVE
1 *He was quite insensitive about other people's feelings.*
unfeeling, indifferent, unaffected, unmoved, uncaring, unconcerned, thoughtless, tactless
⊯ OPPOSITES sensitive
2 *She is insensitive to criticism.*
unaffected, hardened, thick-skinned, immune, indifferent, unmoved
⊯ OPPOSITES sensitive

insert VERB
Insert a coin in the slot.
put, place, put in, stick in, push in, implant, set

inside NOUN
A coconut is white on the inside.
interior, contents, middle, centre, heart, core
⊯ OPPOSITES outside

insignificant ADJECTIVE
an insignificant problem
unimportant, meaningless, minor, trivial, small, tiny
⊯ OPPOSITES significant, important

insincere ADJECTIVE
1 *I suspect his concern for others is insincere.*
false, untrue, pretended, hypocritical
◇ INFORMAL WORDS phoney
⊯ OPPOSITES sincere, genuine
2 *She's a shallow and insincere person.*
deceitful, hypocritical, two-faced, lying, untruthful, dishonest
◇ INFORMAL WORDS phoney
⊯ OPPOSITES sincere, genuine

insist VERB
1 *I insist that you let me pay.*
demand, require, urge
2 *She insisted that she had seen a ghost.*
swear, repeat, vow, persist, maintain

insolent ADJECTIVE
Don't be insolent to your parents.
cheeky, rude, insulting, impertinent, impudent, bold, forward
⊯ OPPOSITES polite, respectful

inspect VERB
The school nurse inspected my nails.
check, look over, examine, search, investigate, study, scan, survey

inspire VERB
The cookery programmes have inspired me to learn to cook.
encourage, influence, stir, arouse, prompt, motivate, provoke

install VERB
They are going to install the satellite dish on the roof.
fix, fit, lay, put, place, position, locate, situate, set up

instant¹ ADJECTIVE
an instant response
immediate, quick, fast, rapid, swift, unhesitating
⊯ OPPOSITES slow

instant² NOUN
It all happened in an instant.
moment, flash, split second, second, minute

◇ INFORMAL WORDS tick

instinct NOUN
1 *My instinct told me there was something wrong.*
intuition, sixth sense, feeling, hunch
2 *My first instinct was to hide.*
urge, impulse

instinctive ADJECTIVE
an instinctive reaction
natural, automatic, intuitive, impulsive, involuntary, spontaneous, immediate, unthinking
⊯ OPPOSITES conscious, voluntary, deliberate

instruct VERB
1 *The children have been instructed in road safety.*
teach, educate, tutor, coach, train
2 *The police instructed us to remain where we were.*
order, command, direct, tell, advise

instruction NOUN
Follow the instructions.
direction, recommendation, advice, guidance, information, order, command

instrument NOUN
an instrument for opening tins
tool, implement, utensil, appliance, gadget, device, apparatus

insufficient ADJECTIVE
We have insufficient food supplies.
inadequate, short, lacking, scarce
⊯ OPPOSITES sufficient, adequate

insult¹ NOUN
It's an insult to call me that name.
offence, abuse, rudeness, insolence, libel, slander, outrage
⊯ OPPOSITES compliment, praise

insult² VERB
He insulted me by calling me a liar.
offend, abuse, call names, libel, slander, outrage
⊯ OPPOSITES compliment, praise

Aa Bb Cc Dd Ee Ff Gg Hh Ii Jj Kk Ll Mm Nn Oo Pp Qq Rr Ss Tt Uu Vv Ww Xx Yy Zz

Aa
Bb
Cc
Dd
Ee
Ff
Gg
Hh
Ii
Jj
Kk
Ll
Mm
Nn
Oo
Pp
Qq
Rr
Ss
Tt
Uu
Vv
Ww
Xx
Yy
Zz

intact ADJECTIVE
I managed to get home with the cake still intact.
undamaged, unbroken, all in one piece, whole, complete, entire, perfect
≠ OPPOSITES broken, incomplete, damaged

integrity NOUN
I don't doubt his integrity.
honesty, purity, morality, principle, honour, virtue, goodness
≠ OPPOSITES dishonesty

intellectual ADJECTIVE
Even as a boy, he was very intellectual.
intelligent, studious, thoughtful, mental, highbrow, cultural
≠ OPPOSITES lowbrow

intelligence NOUN
a woman of high intelligence
cleverness, understanding, intellect, reason, wit, wits, brainpower
◇ INFORMAL WORDS brain, brains
≠ OPPOSITES stupidity, foolishness

intelligent ADJECTIVE
1 *Dolphins are very intelligent creatures.*
clever, bright, smart, quick, alert, quick-witted, sharp, thinking
◇ INFORMAL WORDS brainy
≠ OPPOSITES unintelligent, stupid
2 *That wasn't a very intelligent thing to do.*
clever, bright, smart, rational, sensible
≠ OPPOSITES stupid, foolish

intend VERB
I didn't intend to hurt you.
mean, aim, propose, plan, scheme, plot

intense ADJECTIVE
1 *intense pain*
great, strong, powerful, fierce, harsh, severe, sharp, violent
≠ OPPOSITES mild, weak
2 *an intense longing*
great, deep, powerful, keen, eager, earnest, passionate, energetic, violent
≠ OPPOSITES mild, weak

intent ADJECTIVE
1 *She was intent on solving the puzzle.*
absorbed, concentrating, preoccupied, engrossed, wrapped up, occupied
≠ OPPOSITES absent-minded
2 *The teacher looked at the intent faces of her pupils.*
attentive, eager, earnest, alert

intention NOUN
It's my intention to go to the library after school.
aim, purpose, target, goal, idea, plan

intentional ADJECTIVE
If I upset you, it was not intentional.
deliberate, conscious, planned, calculated, intended, meant
≠ OPPOSITES unintentional, accidental

interest¹ NOUN
1 *It's of no interest to me what happens next.*
importance, significance, note, concern
2 *The children watched the animals with great interest.*
attention, notice, curiosity, involvement, care, concern
3 *James has a lot of interests.*
hobby, activity, pursuit, pastime, amusement

interest² VERB
I think this book will interest you.
fascinate, involve, attract, appeal to, absorb, engross, intrigue
≠ OPPOSITES bore

interested ADJECTIVE
I spoke to Cassie about the Brownies but she wasn't interested.
curious, attentive, absorbed, engrossed, fascinated, enthusiastic, keen, attracted
≠ OPPOSITES uninterested

interesting ADJECTIVE
1 *an interesting story*
absorbing, entertaining, engrossing, fascinating, intriguing, gripping

OPPOSITES uninteresting, boring
2 *an interesting person*
attractive, appealing, entertaining, engaging, fascinating, intriguing, curious, unusual
OPPOSITES uninteresting, boring

interfere VERB
She's always interfering in our business.
meddle, intrude, pry, intervene
◇ INFORMAL WORDS poke your nose in, butt in
• **interfere with**
His broken ankle interfered with his holiday plans.
hinder, hamper, obstruct, block, clash
OPPOSITES assist

interior NOUN
the interior of the building
inside, centre, middle, core, heart, depths
OPPOSITES exterior, outside

internal ADJECTIVE
internal walls
inside, inner, interior, inward
OPPOSITES external

international ADJECTIVE
an international agreement on human rights
global, worldwide, cosmopolitan, universal
OPPOSITES national, local

Internet
⇒ see **computer**

interpret VERB
1 *I interpreted his silence as disappointment.*
understand, explain, take
2 *It's hard to interpret the film's message.*
explain, clarify, throw light on, define, make sense of, understand

interrogate VERB
The robbers were interrogated by the police.
question, quiz, examine, cross-examine

◇ INFORMAL WORDS grill, give the third degree

interrupt VERB
1 *It's rude to interrupt when people are talking.*
intrude, butt in, break in
◇ INFORMAL WORDS barge in
2 *They interrupted the programme with a newsflash.*
disrupt, disturb, hold up, stop, halt, suspend, discontinue

interval NOUN
1 *We bought ice cream at the interval.*
break, interlude, intermission, rest, pause
2 *the interval between applying for a passport and receiving it*
delay, rest, pause, wait, gap
3 *a long interval when nothing happened*
period, spell, time

intervene VERB
A teacher intervened to stop the fight.
step in, interfere, intrude

interview VERB
The police have interviewed several witnesses.
question, examine, interrogate

intimate ADJECTIVE
1 *an intimate atmosphere*
friendly, informal, cosy, warm, relaxed
OPPOSITES unfriendly, cold
2 *intimate friends*
close, familiar, affectionate, dear, near, confidential
OPPOSITES unfriendly, cold, distant
3 *all the intimate details*
secret, private, personal, confidential

intrepid ADJECTIVE
an intrepid explorer
fearless, bold, daring, brave, courageous, heroic
OPPOSITES cowardly, timid

intricate ADJECTIVE
1 *an intricate design*

Aa Bb Cc Dd Ee Ff Gg Hh Ii Jj Kk Ll Mm Nn Oo Pp Qq Rr Ss Tt Uu Vv Ww Xx Yy Zz

fancy, elaborate, complicated, complex, involved
≠ OPPOSITES simple, plain
2 an *intricate* problem
difficult, complicated, complex, involved, tangled, perplexing
≠ OPPOSITES simple, straightforward

intriguing ADJECTIVE

an *intriguing* woman
fascinating, attractive, charming, captivating

introduce VERB

1 The school has *introduced* a new anti-bullying policy.
begin, start, commence, establish, found, launch, open, bring in
2 I'd like to *introduce* you to my sister.
present
3 My uncle *introduced* me to folk music.
acquaint, familiarize, initiate

introduction NOUN

1 the *introduction* of a new law
start, beginning, commencement, establishment, launch
≠ OPPOSITES removal, withdrawal
2 the *introduction* to the book
foreword, lead-in, opening
≠ OPPOSITES conclusion

intrude VERB

I don't like to *intrude* when you're so busy.
interrupt, butt in, meddle, interfere, trespass
≠ OPPOSITES withdraw, stand back

intruder NOUN

An *intruder* broke into our house.
trespasser, prowler, burglar, raider, invader

invade VERB

They planned to *invade* the neighbouring village.
attack, burst in on, descend on, raid, seize, occupy
≠ OPPOSITES withdraw

invalid ADJECTIVE

1 an *invalid* ticket
unacceptable, unusable, out-of-date
2 an *invalid* argument
false, unsound, illogical, irrational, wrong, incorrect
≠ OPPOSITES valid

invaluable ADJECTIVE

Her advice was *invaluable*.
valuable, priceless, precious, useful
≠ OPPOSITES worthless, cheap

invasion NOUN

the *invasion* by foreign troops
attack, offensive, raid, occupation
≠ OPPOSITES withdrawal

invent VERB

1 Alexander Graham Bell *invented* the telephone.
create, produce, discover, devise, contrive
2 You'll have to *invent* a better excuse than that.
make up, think up, improvise, imagine, dream up
◇ INFORMAL WORDS cook up

invention NOUN

1 her latest *invention*
creation, design, discovery, development, device, gadget
2 His story was an *invention*.
lie, falsehood, fiction, tall story, fantasy
≠ OPPOSITES truth

investigate VERB

scientists *investigating* the cause of the disease
examine, inquire into, look into, study, inspect, analyse, go into, probe, explore

investigation NOUN

an *investigation* into the cause of the explosion
examination, inquiry, study, research, survey, inspection, analysis, probe, exploration

invisible ADJECTIVE
The castle was almost invisible in the fog.
unseen, out of sight, hidden, concealed, disguised, inconspicuous
⊅ OPPOSITES visible

invitation NOUN
1 *a wedding invitation*
request, call, summons
2 *Leaving your window open is just an invitation to burglars.*
temptation, encouragement, provocation, challenge

invite VERB
1 *I've been invited to Anila's birthday party.*
ask, call, summon, request
2 *Don't invite trouble by going into places like that.*
encourage, draw, attract, tempt

involve VERB
1 *Moving abroad would involve some careful thought.*
require, mean, imply
2 *The school would like to involve the parents in this project.*
include, bring in
⊅ OPPOSITES exclude
3 *This discussion doesn't involve you.*
concern, include, affect
⊅ OPPOSITES exclude

involved ADJECTIVE
1 *A note will be sent to the parents of the pupils involved in the bullying.*
concerned, mixed up, caught up, participating
⊅ OPPOSITES uninvolved
2 *The explanation was too involved to be easily understood.*
complicated, complex, intricate, elaborate, confusing
⊅ OPPOSITES simple

involvement NOUN
1 *his involvement in the scandal*
connection, association, participation, responsibility

2 *I've always felt an involvement with this school.*
interest, concern, connection

irate ADJECTIVE
irate motorists shouting at each other
angry, annoyed, irritated, indignant, mad, furious, infuriated
◇ INFORMAL WORDS worked up
⊅ OPPOSITES calm, composed

irrational ADJECTIVE
His behaviour has been completely irrational.
unreasonable, illogical, absurd, crazy, wild, foolish, silly, senseless, unwise
⊅ OPPOSITES rational, reasonable

irregular ADJECTIVE
at irregular intervals
variable, occasional, intermittent, random, haphazard, unsystematic
⊅ OPPOSITES regular

irrelevant ADJECTIVE
The cost of the gift is irrelevant.
beside the point, unrelated, unconnected, unimportant
⊅ OPPOSITES relevant

irresistible ADJECTIVE
1 *I had an irresistible urge to laugh.*
overwhelming, overpowering, uncontrollable, compelling, urgent
2 *Many men find her irresistible.*
tempting, seductive, enchanting, charming, fascinating
⊅ OPPOSITES repellent

irresponsible ADJECTIVE
1 *It is irresponsible to let a dog off its lead on a busy street.*
thoughtless, careless, rash, reckless
⊅ OPPOSITES responsible
2 *He is too irresponsible to be left in charge.*
careless, unreliable, untrustworthy, thoughtless, reckless, wild, carefree
⊅ OPPOSITES responsible, cautious

irritable ADJECTIVE
The child was tired and irritable.

Aa
Bb
Cc
Dd
Ee
Ff
Gg
Hh
Ii
Jj
Kk
Ll
Mm
Nn
Oo
Pp
Qq
Rr
Ss
Tt
Uu
Vv
Ww
Xx
Yy
Zz

cross, bad-tempered, crabby, short-tempered, snappy, peevish
(≠) OPPOSITES good-tempered, cheerful

irritate VERB
*Her pushiness really **irritates** me.*
annoy, get on your nerves, bother, provoke, anger, enrage, infuriate
(≠) OPPOSITES please

isolated ADJECTIVE
1 *an **isolated** community*
remote, out-of-the-way, deserted, cut off, lonely
(≠) OPPOSITES populous
2 *She felt **isolated** and left out.*
lonely, solitary, detached, cut off
3 *an **isolated** occurrence*
single, unique, special, exceptional, unusual, abnormal
(≠) OPPOSITES typical

issue¹ NOUN
1 *a political **issue***
matter, affair, concern, problem, point, subject, topic, question
2 *a special **issue** of stamps*
publication, release, distribution, supply, delivery, circulation
3 *last week's **issue** of the magazine*
copy, number, instalment, edition, printing

issue² VERB
*The prime minister has **issued** a statement.*
give out, publish, release, deliver, circulate, broadcast, announce, put out

item NOUN
1 *the **items** in the shop window*
object, article, thing, piece
2 *the next **item** to be discussed*
point, detail, particular, feature, consideration, matter
3 *an **item** in the local paper*
article, piece, report, story, account, paragraph

Jj

jab VERB
He jabbed me in the ribs.
poke, prod, dig, nudge, stab, elbow,
tap, thrust

jagged ADJECTIVE
a jagged piece of glass
uneven, irregular, rough, ragged,
ridged
⊘ OPPOSITES even, smooth

jail¹ NOUN
She was put in jail for life.
prison, custody, imprisonment,
confinement, detention

jail² VERB
He was jailed for theft.
imprison, send to prison, lock up,
confine, detain
◇ INFORMAL WORDS put away, send
down, cage

jam¹ NOUN
1 *a jam caused by an overturned lorry*
traffic jam, bottleneck, gridlock,
obstruction
2 *I'm in a bit of a jam.*
predicament, difficulty, plight, fix

jam² VERB
1 *twenty people jammed into a lift*
cram, pack, wedge, squash, squeeze,
press, crush, crowd, ram, stuff
2 *Cars jammed the road.*
block, clog, obstruct

jangle VERB
The keys jangled in the lock.
clank, clash, clink, clang, clatter, jingle,
chime, rattle

jar¹ NOUN
a glass jar
pot, container, vessel, vase, jug
◆ FORMAL WORDS receptacle

jar² VERB
1 *She jarred her spine when she fell
downstairs.*
jolt, jerk, rattle, shake
2 *Her harsh voice jarred on my ears.*
grate, rasp, grind

jealous ADJECTIVE
1 *She was always jealous of her
sister.*
envious, grudging, resentful
◇ INFORMAL WORDS green, green-
eyed
⊘ OPPOSITES contented, satisfied
2 *a jealous big brother*
protective, possessive

jeer VERB
The crowd all jeered the band.
boo, mock, scoff at, taunt, ridicule,
sneer at, make fun of, heckle

jerk VERB
*She jerked the dog's lead to tell it to
stop.*
jolt, tug, twitch, jar, jog, yank, wrench,
pull, throw

jewel NOUN
precious jewels
gem, precious stone, gemstone
◇ INFORMAL WORDS rock

jewellery NOUN

> ## Here are some types of jewellery:
> bracelet, brooch, cufflink, earring,
> necklace, ring, tiara, watch

jingle NOUN
the jingle of bells
clink, tinkle, ring, chime, jangle, chink

job NOUN
1 *What job would you like when you grow up?*
occupation
2 *The teacher gave the class jobs to do.*
task, assignment

Here are some different jobs:

actor, artist, astronaut, babysitter, baker, bank manager, beautician, builder, butcher, carer, carpenter, charity worker, childminder, cleaner, clerk, computer programmer, customer service adviser, dentist, DJ, doctor, electrician, fire fighter, fisherman, fishmonger, flight attendant, footballer, gardener, hairdresser, journalist, librarian, manager, mechanic, musician, nurse, nursery nurse, painter and decorator, pilot, plasterer, plumber, police officer, postman, publisher, sailor, scientist, shop assistant, singer, soldier, tailor, teacher, train driver, volunteer, web designer, writer, zookeeper

jog VERB
1 *He jogged my arm and I spilt my drink.*
jolt, jar, bump, jostle, jerk, joggle, nudge, poke, shake, prod, push, rock
2 *Perhaps this photograph will jog your memory.*
prompt, remind, refresh, stir, arouse
3 *My dad jogs to work every morning.*
run, trot

join VERB
1 *Join the two pieces of string together.*
unite, connect, combine, attach, link, fasten, merge, tie, add
(≠) OPPOSITES divide, separate
2 *This is where the village joins the next village.*
border on, verge on, touch, meet
3 *I have joined the chess club.*

enlist with, enrol with, enter, sign up with, team with
(≠) OPPOSITES leave

joint ADJECTIVE
a joint effort
combined, joined, shared, united, collective, common, mutual, co-operative

joke¹ NOUN
1 *My brother is good at telling jokes.*
gag, jest, quip, wisecrack
2 *The boys played a joke on Paul.*
trick, jape, prank

joke² VERB
I was only joking when I said I was angry.
jest, clown, fool, kid, tease

jolly ADJECTIVE
We had a jolly time at the party.
merry, cheerful, happy
(≠) OPPOSITES sad

jolt VERB
1 *Don't jolt my arm when I'm writing.*
jar, jerk, jog, bump, jostle, knock, shake, push
2 *I was jolted by the news.*
upset, startle, shock, surprise, stun, disturb

jot down VERB
I jotted down her name and address.
write down, take down, note, record, scribble

journal NOUN
1 *a medical journal*
newspaper, magazine, paper, publication, weekly, monthly
2 *I wrote about the day in my journal.*
diary, log, register, record

journalist NOUN
a sports journalist
reporter, news-writer, correspondent, editor, columnist, feature-writer

journey NOUN
*a **journey** to the Himalayas*
voyage, trip, travels, expedition, trek, tour, outing

joy NOUN
*The new baby brought **joy** to the family.*
happiness, gladness, cheerfulness, delight, pleasure, ecstasy, elation
≠ OPPOSITES despair, grief

joyful ADJECTIVE
*a **joyful** occasion*
happy, cheerful, delighted, merry, glad
≠ OPPOSITES sorrowful

judge VERB
*You will have to **judge** if it is safe to cross.*
decide, assess, estimate, evaluate

judgement NOUN
1 *The judge gave his **judgement**.*
verdict, sentence, ruling, decision, conclusion, result
2 *Their actions showed good **judgement**.*
understanding, wisdom, common sense, sense, intelligence, reason

juice NOUN
*orange **juice***
liquid, fluid, extract

jumble¹ VERB
*The necklaces and bangles were all **jumbled**.*
confuse, disorganize, mix, mix up, muddle, shuffle, tangle
≠ OPPOSITES order

jumble² NOUN
*a **jumble** of clothes*
disorder, confusion, mess, chaos, mix-up, muddle, clutter, mixture

jump VERB
1 *We **jumped** over the fence.*
leap, spring, bound, bounce, skip, hop, prance
2 *I **jumped** when the balloon burst.*
start, jerk, jump out of your skin, wince

junction NOUN
*the **junction** of the two roads*
joint, join, connection, union, intersection, linking, meeting-point, crossroads

junior ADJECTIVE
*a **junior** doctor*
younger, minor, lesser, lower
≠ OPPOSITES senior

junk NOUN
*Your room is full of **junk**.*
clutter, rubbish, trash, garbage, waste, scrap, odds and ends

just ADJECTIVE
*a **just** punishment*
deserved, well-deserved, appropriate, suitable, due, proper, reasonable, rightful, lawful, legitimate
≠ OPPOSITES undeserved, unfair

justice NOUN
*There is no **justice** in the way we were treated.*
fairness, justness, honesty, right, rightfulness, reasonableness, objectivity
≠ OPPOSITES injustice, unfairness

justify VERB
*She tried to **justify** her bad behaviour.*
defend, excuse, forgive, explain, pardon

jut out VERB
*He **jutted out** his chin.*
project, protrude, stick out, poke out, extend

Aa
Bb
Cc
Dd
Ee
Ff
Gg
Hh
Ii
Jj
Kk
Ll
Mm
Nn
Oo
Pp
Qq
Rr
Ss
Tt
Uu
Vv
Ww
Xx
Yy
Zz

Kk

keen ADJECTIVE

1 *a keen gardener*
eager, enthusiastic, earnest, devoted
2 *keen eyesight*
sharp, piercing, penetrating, acute
⊘ OPPOSITES dull

keep VERB

1 *I always keep some sweets.*
retain, hold, preserve, hold on to, hang on to, store, possess, collect
2 *Keep walking to the end of the road.*
carry on, keep on, continue, persist in, remain
3 *The farmer keeps pigs and chickens.*
look after, tend, care for, be responsible for, feed, manage
4 *Don't let me keep you from your work.*
detain, delay, hinder, hold up, obstruct, block, restrain, keep back, withhold
5 *You must keep the rules of the game.*
observe, respect, obey, fulfil, recognize, hold with, maintain, perform, mark
• **keep up**
Keep up the good work.
continue, maintain, persevere with, preserve

key NOUN

the key to the mystery
clue, pointer, explanation, sign, answer, solution

kick VERB

The boy kicked the ball.
boot, hit, strike

kid¹ NOUN

two adults and two kids
child, youngster, youth, infant
◆ FORMAL WORDS juvenile

kid² VERB

I was just kidding.
tease, joke, fool, pretend, trick, jest
◇ INFORMAL WORDS pull someone's leg

kidnap VERB

Rich people worry that their children may be kidnapped.
abduct, capture, seize, snatch, steal

kill VERB

She killed two people.
murder, put to death, assassinate, massacre, slaughter, execute
◆ FORMAL WORDS slay
◇ INFORMAL WORDS do away with

kind¹ ADJECTIVE

I like Laura because she is kind.
kind-hearted, good-natured, generous, giving, thoughtful, warm, warm-hearted, considerate, sympathetic, understanding
⊘ OPPOSITES cruel, inconsiderate

kind² NOUN

An apple is a kind of fruit.
sort, type, class, category, set, variety, style, brand, breed

kindly ADJECTIVE

a kindly old gentleman
kind, compassionate, good-natured, helpful, warm, generous, pleasant, sympathetic, gentle, patient
⊘ OPPOSITES cruel

kit NOUN

I've forgotten my gym kit.
equipment, gear, apparatus, tackle, outfit, set

knack NOUN

He has a knack of making people feel better.
flair, skill, talent, genius, gift, trick, ability
◇ INFORMAL WORDS hang

knock VERB
She knocked hard on the door.
hit, strike, thump, pound, slap, smack

knot VERB
He knotted the pieces of rope together.
tie, secure, entangle, tangle, knit,
weave

know VERB
1 *I don't know what to do.*
understand, be aware, see
2 *I know Sanjay very well.*
be acquainted with, be familiar with
3 *Do you know who I am?*
recognize, identify

knowledge NOUN
1 *He has a good knowledge of history.*
understanding, grasp, awareness,
consciousness, familiarity
2 *a quiz that will test your*
knowledge
wisdom, intelligence, education,
learning
≠ OPPOSITES ignorance

knowledgeable ADJECTIVE
She is very knowledgeable about motor
cars.
educated, learned, well-informed,
intelligent
≠ OPPOSITES ignorant

Aa
Bb
Cc
Dd
Ee
Ff
Gg
Hh
Ii
Jj
Kk
Ll
Mm
Nn
Oo
Pp
Qq
Rr
Ss
Tt
Uu
Vv
Ww
Xx
Yy
Zz

Ll

label¹ NOUN
There is no size on the label.
tag, ticket, mark, marker, sticker

label² VERB
Label all your school things with your name.
tag, mark, stamp

labour¹ NOUN
1 *hard labour*
work, task, job, toil, effort, exertion
◇ INFORMAL WORDS slog, sweat
(≠) OPPOSITES ease, leisure
2 *The company had to hire new labour.*
workers, employees, workforce, labourers
(≠) OPPOSITES management

labour² VERB
We laboured all night to finish the job.
work, toil, slave, strive, struggle
◇ INFORMAL WORDS sweat
(≠) OPPOSITES laze

lack¹ NOUN
They died through lack of food.
need, want, scarcity, shortage, insufficiency, absence, deprivation
(≠) OPPOSITES abundance

lack² VERB
The group lacks a leader.
need, want, require, miss

lag VERB
They walked on ahead with the children lagging behind.
dawdle, loiter, hang back, linger, straggle, trail, idle
(≠) OPPOSITES hurry, lead

lake NOUN
We went swimming in the lake.
lagoon, reservoir, loch

lame ADJECTIVE
1 *The old man was lame in one leg.*
crippled, disabled, handicapped, limping, hobbling
2 *a lame excuse*
weak, feeble, flimsy, inadequate, unsatisfactory, poor
(≠) OPPOSITES convincing

land¹ NOUN
1 *The land is rich around here.*
dirt, earth, soil
2 *They bought a plot of land.*
property, grounds, estate, country, countryside, farmland
3 *a foreign land*
country, nation, region, territory, province

land² VERB
1 *The plane landed smoothly on the runway.*
alight, touch down, come to rest, arrive
2 *Everyone's exercise books landed on my desk.*
arrive, wind up, end up, turn up

landscape NOUN
We stood on the hillside and admired the landscape.
scene, scenery, view, outlook, prospect

language NOUN
1 *I would like to learn a foreign language.*
speech, tongue, dialect
2 *Can you explain that to me in simple language?*
wording, style, phrasing, expression

lap¹ VERB
The cat lapped up the milk.
drink, lick, sip, sup

lap² NOUN
They ran four laps around the track.

circuit, course, round, circle, loop

lapse NOUN

1 *a lapse of concentration*
error, slip, mistake, failing, fault, omission
2 *Classes resumed after a lapse of a few weeks.*
break, gap, interval, lull, interruption, pause

large ADJECTIVE

1 *a large man*
big, huge, immense, massive, vast, great, giant, gigantic, enormous
(≠) OPPOSITES small, tiny
2 *a large house*
roomy, spacious, grand
(≠) OPPOSITES modest
3 *a large supply*
full, generous, plentiful
(≠) OPPOSITES meagre

largely ADVERB

They have largely ignored our complaints.
mainly, mostly, chiefly, generally, principally, by and large

last¹ ADJECTIVE

the last day of term
final, ultimate, closing, latest, concluding
(≠) OPPOSITES first

last² ADVERB

I came in last in the race.
finally, behind, after
(≠) OPPOSITES first, firstly
• **at last**
We arrived home at last.
eventually, finally, in the end, in due course, at length

last³ VERB

1 *The film lasted for two hours.*
continue, carry on, keep on, endure, remain, persist, stay
(≠) OPPOSITES stop, fade
2 *Animals can't last long without water.*
survive, hold out, live

late ADJECTIVE

1 *I was late for school.*
overdue, behind, slow, delayed
(≠) OPPOSITES early, punctual
2 *a late change of plan*
last-minute

later ADVERB

Later, we went to the cinema.
next, afterwards, after
(≠) OPPOSITES earlier

laugh VERB

⇒ For even more about this word, see the next page
The children laughed at the cartoons.
chuckle, giggle, snigger, titter, chortle

laughter NOUN

The audience roared with laughter.
laughing, giggling, chuckling, chortling, tittering, amusement

launch VERB

1 *They have successfully launched a rocket into space.*
send off, set in motion, propel, fire, float, discharge
2 *The school launched an appeal to raise funds.*
begin, commence, start, open, introduce

lavatory NOUN

You should always wash your hands after going to the lavatory.
toilet, bathroom, cloakroom, washroom
◇ INFORMAL WORDS loo, ladies', gents'

lavish ADJECTIVE

lavish praise
abundant, plentiful, unlimited

law NOUN

1 *a law against trespassing*
rule, act, order, regulation, command
2 *the laws of physics*
principle, standard, formula, code

lay VERB

1 *She laid her books on the desk.*
put, place, deposit, set, set down, leave, settle, plant

Aa
Bb
Cc
Dd
Ee
Ff
Gg
Hh
Ii
Jj
Kk
Ll
Mm
Nn
Oo
Pp
Qq
Rr
Ss
Tt
Uu
Vv
Ww
Xx
Yy
Zz

laugh

The word **laugh** tells you very little about the action. If you use a word or phrase that tells you more about the way a person laughs, it is much more interesting for your reader.

If someone laughs in quiet way, they might
> **chuckle**

If someone is laughing loudly or in an enthusiastic way, they might
> **chortle**
> **guffaw**
> **roar with laughter**

There are other words for **laugh** that tell you more about what the person is feeling or thinking.

If someone laughs in a silly way, you might say that they
> **giggle**

If someone laughs in a nervous way, you might say that they
> **titter**

If someone laughs in an unkind or unpleasant way, you might say that they
> **cackle**
> **snigger**

Over to you

Can you put some of these words to use? Try to replace the word **laugh** in these sentences.

1 Danny laughed quietly to himself when he remembered the joke.

2 The comedian was so funny he made the audience laugh.

3 I was very embarrassed and started to laugh.

4 The witch laughed as she cast her evil spell.

Which of the words would not sound right in the sentences?

2 *I laid the table for dinner.*
arrange, set out, prepare, position, present

layer NOUN
a thin layer of snow
cover, coating, coat, covering, film, blanket, sheet

laze VERB
He lazed in the garden all afternoon.
sit around, lie around, idle, lounge, loaf, loll

lazy ADJECTIVE
She was too lazy to walk to the shops.
idle, slack, inactive, lethargic

lead VERB
1 *An usher led us to our seats.*
guide, conduct, escort, steer, pilot, usher
⊘ OPPOSITES follow
2 *the woman who leads the country*
command, rule, govern, head, direct, supervise
3 *The evidence leads me to believe that he is guilty.*
cause, influence, persuade, incline
4 *They lead a quiet life in the country.*
live, pass, spend

leader NOUN
the leader of the council
head, chief, director, ruler, principal, commander, captain, boss, ringleader
⊘ OPPOSITES follower

league NOUN
1 *The league is dedicated to preserving wildlife.*
association, union, band, partnership, fellowship
2 *As a singer, he is not in the same league as you.*
class, category, level, group

leak¹ NOUN
a leak in the pipe
crack, hole, opening, puncture, chink

leak² VERB
1 *The water was leaking out of the tank.*
seep, drip, ooze, escape, spill, trickle
2 *Somebody leaked the information to the newspapers.*
reveal, give away, tell, let slip, make known, make public, pass on

lean¹ VERB
1 *The flagpole is leaning to the left.*
slant, slope, tilt, bend
2 *He was leaning against the wall.*
rest, recline, prop

lean² ADJECTIVE
a lean athlete
slim, slender, thin, skinny
⊘ OPPOSITES fat

leap VERB
He leapt over the wall.
jump, bound, spring, skip, hop, bounce

learn VERB
1 *I want to learn French.*
grasp, understand, master, pick up
◆ FORMAL WORDS acquire
2 *The actors learned their lines.*
memorize, learn by heart, commit to memory

learner NOUN
foreign learners of English
beginner, student, trainee, pupil, scholar, apprentice

leave¹ VERB
1 *If we leave now we can be home by noon.*
go, go away, depart, set out, take off, exit, withdraw, disappear
⊘ OPPOSITES arrive
2 *She left school at 16.*
give up, drop, pull out, quit, retire
◆ FORMAL WORDS cease
3 *He left his family and moved overseas.*
abandon, desert
4 *His mother left him all her money in her will.*
entrust, bequeath, will, hand down, leave behind, give over

Aa Bb Cc Dd Ee Ff Gg Hh Ii Jj Kk Ll Mm Nn Oo Pp Qq Rr Ss Tt Uu Vv Ww Xx Yy Zz

(≠) OPPOSITES **receive**
• **leave out**
*I was **left out** of the netball team.*
omit, exclude, miss out, overlook, pass over, count out, reject, ignore

leave² NOUN
*He is taking a few days' **leave**.*
holiday, time off, vacation

lecture¹ NOUN
1 *We went to a **lecture** on art.*
talk, lesson, speech, address
♦ FORMAL WORDS discourse
2 *Her mother gave her a **lecture** about tidying her room.*
scolding, reprimand
◊ INFORMAL WORDS telling-off, talking-to

lecture² VERB
*A police officer **lectured** us all on road safety.*
talk to, speak to, teach, address

legacy NOUN
*My grandfather left me a small **legacy**.*
inheritance, gift, bequest, heritage, endowment, estate, heirloom

legal ADJECTIVE
*the **legal** speed limit*
lawful, legitimate, permissible, allowed, authorized, valid, proper
(≠) OPPOSITES illegal

legendary ADJECTIVE
legendary monsters
mythical, fabulous, storybook, fictitious

legible ADJECTIVE
*Make sure your handwriting is **legible**.*
readable, clear, neat, distinct
(≠) OPPOSITES illegible

leisure NOUN
*He has been too busy for **leisure** recently.*
relaxation, rest, time off, spare time, recreation
(≠) OPPOSITES work

lend VERB
*Can you **lend** me a pound, please?*
loan
♦ FORMAL WORDS advance
(≠) OPPOSITES borrow

length NOUN
*a short **length** of time*
period, space, stretch

lengthen VERB
1 *My trousers need to be **lengthened**.*
extend, stretch
♦ FORMAL WORDS elongate
(≠) OPPOSITES shorten
2 *plans to **lengthen** the school day*
prolong, extend, increase
(≠) OPPOSITES reduce, shorten

lengthy ADJECTIVE
*After a **lengthy** wait, I was called into the head teacher's office.*
long, prolonged, extended, overlong
(≠) OPPOSITES brief

lenient ADJECTIVE
*The boy hoped his teacher would be **lenient** with him.*
gentle, forgiving, kind, tolerant
(≠) OPPOSITES strict, severe

lessen VERB
1 *The nurse will give you something to **lessen** the pain.*
reduce, decrease, lower, moderate, ease
(≠) OPPOSITES increase
2 *She felt her energy **lessen** as she kept running.*
decrease, diminish, dwindle, weaken
(≠) OPPOSITES increase

lesson NOUN
*a piano **lesson***
class, period, instruction, lecture, teaching, coaching

let VERB
1 *Her parents won't **let** her go to the party.*
permit, allow, give permission, agree to, authorize

⊭ OPPOSITES **forbid**
2 *They sometimes let out the scout hall for local events.*
hire, rent, lease
• **let down**
I needed help and was let down by my friends.
disappoint, fail, abandon, desert
• **let off**
I was let off by my brother for taking his sweets.
excuse, pardon, forgive

lethal ADJECTIVE
a lethal dose of poison
fatal, deadly, deathly, mortal, dangerous
⊭ OPPOSITES **harmless, safe**

letter NOUN
1 *I'm writing a letter to my pen pal.*
note, message, line
◆ FORMAL WORDS **communication**
2 *a capital letter*
character, symbol, sign

level¹ ADJECTIVE
1 *a level surface*
flat, even, smooth, horizontal
⊭ OPPOSITES **uneven**
2 *The teams were level at half-time.*
even, equal, neck and neck
⊭ OPPOSITES **unequal**

level² NOUN
1 *above sea level*
height
◆ FORMAL WORDS **altitude**
2 *I am moving to the next level of reading book.*
stage, class, grade, degree, standard, position, rank

level³ VERB
1 *Bulldozers were brought in to level the building.*
demolish, knock down, pull down, tear down, destroy
2 *We need to level the ground before we can start to build on it.*
flatten, even out, smooth

liable ADJECTIVE
1 *He is liable to be bad-tempered when he's tired.*
likely, apt, inclined, prone
2 *You will be liable for any damage you cause.*
responsible, answerable, accountable

liberty NOUN
Eventually the prisoners were given their liberty.
freedom, release
⊭ OPPOSITES **imprisonment**

licence NOUN
a driving licence
permit, warrant, certificate, authorization

license VERB
He is licensed to teach music in schools.
permit, allow, authorize, certify
⊭ OPPOSITES **ban, prohibit**

lie¹ NOUN
His story about finding the money was a lie.
untruth, falsehood, invention
◇ INFORMAL WORDS **fib, whopper**
⊭ OPPOSITES **truth**

lie² VERB
She lied about where she had been.
tell a lie, tell an untruth
◇ INFORMAL WORDS **fib**

lie³ VERB
1 *The cat was lying in front of the fire.*
rest, lounge, laze
◆ FORMAL WORDS **recline**
2 *The village lies at the foot of the hill.*
be positioned, be located, be situated

life NOUN
1 *He spent part of his life in Germany.*
existence, being
2 *Although she was old, she was still full of life.*
liveliness, energy, vitality, vigour, zest, spirit, sparkle

Aa Bb Cc Dd Ee Ff Gg Hh Ii Jj Kk **Ll** Mm Nn Oo Pp Qq Rr Ss Tt Uu Vv Ww Xx Yy Zz

Aa
Bb
Cc
Dd
Ee
Ff
Gg
Hh
Ii
Jj
Kk
Ll
Mm
Nn
Oo
Pp
Qq
Rr
Ss
Tt
Uu
Vv
Ww
Xx
Yy
Zz

lifeless ADJECTIVE

1 *her lifeless body*
dead
◆ FORMAL WORDS **deceased**
⊯ OPPOSITES **alive**
2 *a lifeless desert*
barren, bare, empty, desolate
⊯ OPPOSITES **fertile**

lift VERB

He lifted the child on to his shoulders.
raise, elevate, pick up, hoist
⊯ OPPOSITES **drop**

light¹ ADJECTIVE

1 *a light corner*
bright, well-lit, illuminated, sunny
⊯ OPPOSITES **dark, gloomy**
2 *light hair*
pale, fair, blond, blonde
3 *light colours*
pale, soft, faint, faded
⊯ OPPOSITES **dark, deep**

light² NOUN

1 *the light from the window*
illumination, brightness, glow,
brilliance, radiance
⊯ OPPOSITES **darkness**
2 *a light in the distance*
flash, gleam, glint, glow, glare

light³ VERB

1 *We lit the candles on the cake.*
set alight, set fire to
⊯ OPPOSITES **extinguish**
2 *The fireworks lit the sky.*
light up, illuminate, lighten, brighten
⊯ OPPOSITES **darken**

light⁴ ADJECTIVE

1 *She was as light as a feather.*
lightweight, weightless, slight, delicate
2 *He got off with a light punishment.*
trivial, trifling
⊯ OPPOSITES **important, serious**
3 *light wind and rain*
slight, soft, mild, gentle, faint
4 *We were all in a light mood.*
cheerful, cheery, carefree, lively, merry
⊯ OPPOSITES **solemn, serious**

like¹ PREPOSITION

*The creatures had eyes like green
jewels.*
similar to, resembling, the same
as, identical to, equivalent to,
corresponding to
⊯ OPPOSITES **unlike, dissimilar to**

like² VERB

⇒ For even more about this word, see
the next page
1 *I like her very much.*
love, be fond of, care for, admire, adore
2 *I like football a lot.*
enjoy, appreciate, be keen on
⊯ OPPOSITES **dislike**
3 *Would you like milk or juice?*
want, prefer, choose, select, desire,
wish
◇ INFORMAL WORDS **go for**
⊯ OPPOSITES **reject**

likely ADJECTIVE

It's likely that Zoe will be late.
probable, possible, predictable,
expected
◇ INFORMAL WORDS **odds-on**
⊯ OPPOSITES **unlikely**

likeness NOUN

1 *That bracelet bears a remarkable
likeness to the one I lost.*
similarity, resemblance
⊯ OPPOSITES **dissimilarity**
2 *a good likeness of the king*
image, representation, picture, portrait,
photograph

limit¹ NOUN

1 *the outer limits of the galaxy*
end, boundary, bound, border, frontier,
verge, edge, threshold
2 *a time limit*
restriction, limitation, cut-off point,
maximum

limit² VERB

*Spending money for the trip should be
limited to £3.*
restrict, confine, ration

like

Be specific in your writing and do not use the word **like** all the time. If you can, use words that describe more clearly how you are feeling.

These words show how much you really like a person, or something such as a pet:

admire
care for
be fond of

If you want to show that you like them very much indeed, you could use the words

adore
cherish
hold dear

These words show how much you really like something or like doing something:

appreciate
enjoy
be keen on
delight in

Over to you

In this piece of writing, could you use some better words instead of **like**?

I like my dad, and he likes to cook us food that we like for dinner. After dinner I like taking my dog out for a walk. She is called Breeze, and I like her very much.

Aa
Bb
Cc
Dd
Ee
Ff
Gg
Hh
Ii
Jj
Kk
Ll
Mm
Nn
Oo
Pp
Qq
Rr
Ss
Tt
Uu
Vv
Ww
Xx
Yy
Zz

limited ADJECTIVE

*We have a **limited** supply of money.*
restricted, fixed, rationed, controlled, confined, narrow
≠ OPPOSITES limitless

limp¹ VERB

*He was **limping** badly after his fall.*
hobble, falter

limp² ADJECTIVE

1 *a **limp** cabbage leaf*
floppy, flabby, soft, drooping
≠ OPPOSITES stiff
2 *a **limp** grip*
loose, slack, relaxed
≠ OPPOSITES firm
3 *I felt weak and **limp** in the heat.*
tired, weary, exhausted, weak, worn out
≠ OPPOSITES vigorous

line NOUN

1 *Draw a straight line.*
stroke, mark, rule, dash, underline, score
2 *She had lines of colour in her hair.*
stripe, bar, strip, band, strand, streak
3 *a line of cars*
row, rank, queue, file, column, procession, trail
4 *They crossed the state line.*
limit, boundary, border, borderline, edge, frontier
5 *the lines on his face*
crease, wrinkle, furrow
6 *He's in a different line of work now.*
field, area, occupation, business, trade, profession, job, employment

linger VERB

1 *We lingered for one last look before we left.*
stay, wait, remain, hang on, loiter, stop
✘ OPPOSITES leave, rush
2 *The smell of fish lingered in the kitchen for hours.*
last, remain, stay, persist, endure

link¹ NOUN

We have links with several schools overseas.
connection, association, tie, bond, relationship, union, attachment

link² VERB

1 *The two girls linked arms.*
join, connect, fasten, attach, hook up
✘ OPPOSITES separate, unfasten
2 *The police did not link her with the crime.*
connect, tie, associate, identify, relate
✘ OPPOSITES separate

liquid¹ NOUN

You must drink plenty of liquid in hot weather.
fluid, drink, juice

liquid² ADJECTIVE

liquid soap
fluid, runny, watery, wet
✘ OPPOSITES solid

list¹ NOUN

a list of names
record, roll, listing, register, file, catalogue, index, menu, directory, table

list² VERB

Please list all your hobbies.
note, write down, enter, record, register, catalogue, index
◆ FORMAL WORDS itemize

listen VERB

Listen carefully to what I am about to say.
pay attention, take notice, hear
◆ FORMAL WORDS heed, attend to

literature NOUN

1 *English literature*
writings, books
2 *He gave me some literature about the sports centre.*
information, leaflets, pamphlets, brochures, hand-outs
◇ INFORMAL WORDS bumf

litter¹ NOUN

Put your litter in the bin.
rubbish, refuse, trash, waste
◇ INFORMAL WORDS junk

litter² VERB

The street was littered with confetti.
scatter, strew, mess up, clutter
✘ OPPOSITES tidy

little ADJECTIVE

1 *a little puppy*
small, tiny, short, miniature, mini
◇ INFORMAL WORDS teeny
✘ OPPOSITES big
2 *a little pause*
brief, short, fleeting, passing
✘ OPPOSITES lengthy
3 *It's a lot of work for little money.*
meagre, insufficient, paltry
✘ OPPOSITES ample

live¹ VERB

1 *My great-grandmother lived till she was 90.*
exist, survive, stay alive

≠ OPPOSITES die

2 *We **live** in a top-floor flat.*
inhabit, lodge
♦ FORMAL WORDS dwell, reside

live² ADJECTIVE
*a **live** lobster*
alive, living, breathing
≠ OPPOSITES dead

lively ADJECTIVE
1 *The old lady is very **lively** for her age.*
alert, energetic, vigorous, active, agile, nimble, spirited, perky, vivacious
◇ INFORMAL WORDS chirpy
2 *a **lively** city*
busy, bustling, crowded, exciting, buzzing
≠ OPPOSITES inactive

living¹ ADJECTIVE
*our greatest **living** author*
alive, live, existing

living² NOUN
*What does your father do for a **living**?*
work, job, occupation, profession, income, livelihood

load¹ NOUN
1 *I was carrying a heavy **load**.*
burden, weight
2 *A lorry has shed its **load** on the motorway.*
cargo, goods, freight

load² VERB
1 *She arrived **loaded** with packages.*
burden, weigh down, weight
2 *They **loaded** the crates into the van.*
pack, pile, heap, fill, stack

loan NOUN
*a bank **loan***
advance, credit, mortgage

loathe VERB
*I absolutely **loathe** cricket.*
hate, detest, despise, dislike
≠ OPPOSITES adore, love

lobby NOUN
*the hotel **lobby***
foyer, hall, hallway, entrance hall, porch

local ADJECTIVE
1 *the **local** library*
regional, district, community, neighbourhood, provincial
≠ OPPOSITES national
2 *a **local** shop*
nearby, neighbourhood

locate VERB
1 *We can't **locate** the problem.*
find, discover, track down, detect, lay your hands on, identify
2 *The museum is **located** near the station.*
situate, position, place, set

location NOUN
*The school is in a central **location**.*
position, place, spot, situation, whereabouts

lock¹ NOUN
*Always use a good **lock** on your bike.*
fastening, bolt, clasp, padlock

lock² VERB
***Lock** all the doors and windows before you go to bed.*
fasten, secure, seal, bolt, latch
• **lock up**
*He was **locked up** in prison for ten years.*
imprison, jail, confine, shut in, shut up, cage
≠ OPPOSITES free

lodge VERB
1 *He **lodges** with an elderly couple.*
live, stay
♦ FORMAL WORDS dwell, reside
2 *The villa can **lodge** two whole families.*
house, accommodate, board, put up
3 *There is a coin **lodged** in the slot.*
get stuck, fix, embed

logical ADJECTIVE
*a **logical** argument*

Aa
Bb
Cc
Dd
Ee
Ff
Gg
Hh
Ii
Jj
Kk
Ll
Mm
Nn
Oo
Pp
Qq
Rr
Ss
Tt
Uu
Vv
Ww
Xx
Yy
Zz

reasonable, rational, sensible, consistent, valid, sound, clear, methodical, well-organized
≠ OPPOSITES **illogical, irrational**

loiter VERB

kids loitering around the school gates
hang about, linger, idle

lone ADJECTIVE

a lone eagle flying overhead
single, sole, solitary, unaccompanied, separate
≠ OPPOSITES **accompanied**

lonely ADJECTIVE

1 *a lonely old woman*
alone, friendless, lonesome, solitary
≠ OPPOSITES **popular**
2 *a lonely farmhouse*
isolated, remote, out-of-the-way, secluded, desolate
≠ OPPOSITES **easily reached**

long ADJECTIVE

1 *a long line*
lengthy, extensive
≠ OPPOSITES **short**
2 *a long wait*
lengthy, prolonged, long-drawn-out, extended, slow
≠ OPPOSITES **brief, short**

long for VERB

She longed for a pony.
want, wish, yearn for, crave, hanker after, desire, dream of, pine for

look¹ NOUN

1 *Have a look at this.*
glance, glimpse, peek, view, inspection, examination
2 *She has a very innocent look.*
appearance, manner, expression, face

look² VERB

1 *He looked at me from across the room.*
watch, observe, view, gaze, stare, glance, peep
2 *You look tired.*
seem, appear

• look after

Our gran looks after us while our parents are out at work.
take care of, mind, care for, keep an eye on, watch over, guard, protect, supervise
≠ OPPOSITES **neglect**

• look out

Look out for traffic when you cross the road.
watch out, beware, be careful, pay attention, keep an eye out

• look up

If you don't know the meaning, look up a dictionary.
search in, research in, refer to, consult

• look up to

He looks up to his older brother.
admire, respect, have a high opinion of
◆ FORMAL WORDS **esteem**

loom VERB

1 *A figure loomed out of the mist.*
appear, emerge, take shape
2 *The castle looms over the village.*
hang over, tower, overhang, rise, dominate

loop¹ NOUN

a loop of rope
curve, circle, ring, coil, curl, hoop

loop² VERB

Loop the string round the parcel.
coil, encircle, circle, curve round, turn, roll, knot

loose ADJECTIVE

1 *a loose tooth*
free, unfastened, untied, movable, unattached, insecure, wobbly
≠ OPPOSITES **firm, secure**
2 *loose clothing*
slack, baggy, hanging
≠ OPPOSITES **tight**
3 *a loose description*
vague, inexact, imprecise, indefinite, indistinct
≠ OPPOSITES **precise**

loosen VERB

1 *I loosened my grip on the rope.*

ease, relax, loose, slacken
2 *He loosened his shirt collar.*
undo, untie, unfasten

loot¹ NOUN
the pirates' loot
plunder, haul, booty, spoils
◇ INFORMAL WORDS swag

loot² VERB
The burglars looted the shop.
rob, raid, plunder, pillage, ransack

lose VERB
1 *I've lost my pencil.*
mislay, misplace
⊯ OPPOSITES find
2 *Roger lost the race.*
be beaten, be defeated, suffer defeat
⊯ OPPOSITES win

lot NOUN
1 *a lot of people*
great number, good deal, great deal
2 *a lot of food*
large amount, great amount, good deal, great deal
3 *another lot of visitors*
group, set, crowd, collection
4 *She baked a fresh lot of cookies.*
batch, quantity, assortment

lots NOUN
⇒ For even more about this word, see the next page
lots of things
plenty, a quantity, a great number, a great amount, a large number, a large amount, a good deal, a great deal
◇ INFORMAL WORDS tons, loads, masses, heaps, piles

loud ADJECTIVE
1 *a loud voice*
noisy, deafening, blaring, booming, ear-splitting
⊯ OPPOSITES quiet
2 *a loud tie*
garish, gaudy, flashy, showy
⊯ OPPOSITES subdued

lounge VERB
lounging around on the sofa
relax, laze, lie about, sprawl, lie back
◆ FORMAL WORDS recline

lovable ADJECTIVE
She's such a lovable little girl.
sweet, adorable, charming, lovely, delightful
⊯ OPPOSITES detestable

love¹ NOUN
a great love of animals
fondness, affection, liking, attachment, devotion, adoration, passion, tenderness, weakness
◇ INFORMAL WORDS soft spot
⊯ OPPOSITES hate, loathing

love² VERB
1 *He loves his children.*
adore, dote on, treasure, idolize, worship, hold dear
⊯ OPPOSITES detest, hate
2 *I love dancing.*
like, enjoy, take pleasure in, appreciate
⊯ OPPOSITES detest, hate

lovely ADJECTIVE
1 *We had a lovely time.*
delightful, pleasant, agreeable, enjoyable
⊯ OPPOSITES horrible
2 *What a lovely house!*
beautiful, charming, delightful, attractive, enchanting, pretty, adorable, sweet, exquisite
⊯ OPPOSITES ugly, hideous

loving ADJECTIVE
loving parents
affectionate, devoted, doting, fond, warm, tender

low ADJECTIVE
1 *a low wall*
short, small, little
⊯ OPPOSITES high
2 *Food supplies are low.*
poor, meagre, sparse
⊯ OPPOSITES plentiful

Aa
Bb
Cc
Dd
Ee
Ff
Gg
Hh
Ii
Jj
Kk
Ll
Mm
Nn
Oo
Pp
Qq
Rr
Ss
Tt
Uu
Vv
Ww
Xx
Yy
Zz

lots

If you use **a lot** or **lots** too much in your writing, it is boring. Try using other words instead.

> **a large amount**
> **a great number**
> **many**
> **a great deal**
> **plenty**
> **countless**
> **numerous**

Informal words are words you might use with your friends, but not in your school work. Here are some informal words for **lots**:

> **oodles**
> **tons**
> **masses**
> **heaps**
> **stacks**
> **loads**
> **piles**
> **hundreds**
> **thousands**
> **millions**
> **trillions**

You can have fun with these words:

> **There were oodles of noodles**
>
> **tons of suns**
>
> **heaps of sheets**
>
> **stacks of shacks**
>
> **piles of stiles**
>
> **hundreds of drums!**

3 *She was feeling a bit low.*
unhappy, depressed, gloomy
⊘ OPPOSITES cheerful
4 *That was a low trick to play on him.*
mean, base, contemptible
⊘ OPPOSITES honourable
5 *low prices*
cheap, inexpensive, reasonable
⊘ OPPOSITES exorbitant, high
6 *low lighting*
soft, subdued, muted
⊘ OPPOSITES harsh

lower VERB

1 *They lowered the flag after the ceremony.*
let down, drop, sink
⊘ OPPOSITES raise
2 *Shops need to lower their prices.*
cut, reduce, decrease, lessen
⊘ OPPOSITES increase, raise

loyal ADJECTIVE

She is a very loyal friend.
true, faithful, devoted, trustworthy
⊘ OPPOSITES disloyal

luck NOUN

1 *With some luck I might pass my exams.*
fortune, good fortune
⊘ OPPOSITES misfortune
2 *As luck would have it, I just missed the last bus.*
fate, chance, fortune, destiny
⊘ OPPOSITES design

lucky ADJECTIVE

I was lucky enough to win the raffle.
fortunate
⊘ OPPOSITES unlucky

ludicrous ADJECTIVE

a ludicrous sight
absurd, ridiculous, laughable, silly, crazy, nonsensical

lull[1] NOUN

a lull in the conversation
break, gap, pause, hush, silence, quiet, calm
◇ INFORMAL WORDS let-up

lull[2] VERB

The woman lulled her baby to sleep.
soothe, calm, hush, quieten down, quiet

luminous ADJECTIVE

luminous paint
glowing, bright, shining, radiant, brilliant

lump[1] NOUN

1 *a lump of sugar*
piece, mass, chunk, ball, cake, wedge, hunk
2 *She's got a small lump on her head.*
swelling, bulge, bump

lump[2] VERB

All the children were lumped together in one class.

group, combine, gather, collect, mass, merge, unite

lurch VERB

*He **lurched** from side to side as the bus went round a corner.*
rock, sway, stagger, reel, roll

lure VERB

*The robbers **lured** their victims into a trap.*
draw, lead on, entice, tempt, attract

lurk VERB

*There was someone **lurking** in the shadows.*
lie in wait, lie low, hide, skulk, prowl, sneak

luxurious ADJECTIVE

*a **luxurious** home*
magnificent, splendid, expensive, costly, lavish, deluxe
◇ INFORMAL WORDS plush

luxury NOUN

*They were living in **luxury** in the south of France.*
comfort, splendour, richness, magnificence, extravagance
◆ FORMAL WORDS opulence

Aa
Bb
Cc
Dd
Ee
Ff
Gg
Hh
Ii
Jj
Kk
Ll
Mm
Nn
Oo
Pp
Qq
Rr
Ss
Tt
Uu
Vv
Ww
Xx
Yy
Zz

Mm

machine NOUN
a washing machine
instrument, device, tool, mechanism, engine, apparatus, appliance

machinery NOUN
farm machinery
instruments, mechanism, tools, apparatus, equipment, tackle, gear

mad ADJECTIVE
1 *You have to be mad to run across the road.*
insane, lunatic, unbalanced, demented, out of your mind, crazy
◇ INFORMAL WORDS nuts, barmy, bonkers
⊘ OPPOSITES sane
2 *My dad was mad with me when I broke the window.*
angry, furious, enraged, infuriated, annoyed
⊘ OPPOSITES calm
3 *a mad idea*
illogical, unreasonable, absurd, foolish
⊘ OPPOSITES sensible
4 *She is mad about pop music.*
fanatical, enthusiastic, infatuated

madden VERB
Traffic jams really madden me.
anger, enrage, infuriate, incense, annoy, irritate
⊘ OPPOSITES calm

magazine NOUN
a fashion magazine
journal, paper, weekly, monthly, quarterly

magic NOUN
1 *black magic*
sorcery, enchantment, black art, witchcraft, wizardry

2 *He performs magic at children's parties.*
conjuring, illusion, tricks, trickery

magical ADJECTIVE
a magical fairy story
charming, enchanting, bewitching, fascinating, spellbinding

magnificent ADJECTIVE
a magnificent feast
splendid, grand, impressive, glorious, gorgeous, brilliant, excellent, majestic, superb
⊘ OPPOSITES modest, humble, poor

magnify VERB
1 *A telescope magnifies the objects viewed through it.*
enlarge, amplify, increase, expand
◇ INFORMAL WORDS blow up
2 *My annoyance was magnified because I was tired.*
intensify, boost, heighten, deepen, build up, overemphasize, overstate, overdo
⊘ OPPOSITES belittle, play down

mail¹ NOUN
The mail was delivered late this morning.
post, letters, correspondence, packages, parcels

mail² VERB
I mailed a parcel to my cousin.
post, send, forward

main ADJECTIVE
the main road
principal, chief, leading, first, prime, supreme, central
⊘ OPPOSITES minor, unimportant, insignificant

mainly ADVERB
My relatives are mainly American.
primarily, principally, chiefly, in the

main, mostly, on the whole, for the most part, above all, largely

maintain VERB

1 *Try to maintain the same rate of work.*
carry on, continue, keep up, retain
2 *She works to maintain her family.*
care for, look after, take care of, support, finance
(≠) OPPOSITES neglect
3 *He maintains that he never received the letter.*
claim, declare, state, insist, believe
(≠) OPPOSITES deny

maintenance NOUN

The house requires constant maintenance.
care, conservation, preservation, support, repairs, protection, upkeep, running
(≠) OPPOSITES neglect

major ADJECTIVE

1 *a major supermarket chain*
leading, large, important, big
(≠) OPPOSITES minor, unimportant
2 *the major difference between them*
main, most important, biggest, greatest
3 *The major part of the work is now done.*
greater, larger, bigger

majority NOUN

The majority of people are decent.
bulk, mass, most, greater part
(≠) OPPOSITES minority

make¹ VERB

1 *The company makes bicycles.*
create, manufacture, construct, build, produce, put together, originate, compose, form, shape
2 *You've made a mistake.*
cause, bring about, accomplish, give rise to, perform
3 *My mum made me wear a dress.*
force, oblige, compel, pressurize, press, require

4 *She was made class captain.*
appoint, elect, nominate
5 *The company made a huge profit last year.*
earn, gain, obtain
◆ FORMAL WORDS acquire
6 *Two and two makes four.*
compose, comprise, add up to, amount to
• **make out**
I couldn't quite make him out.
understand, work out, grasp, follow, fathom
• **make up**
She made up a story about her father being a millionaire.
create, invent, devise, dream up

make² NOUN

This sweatshirt is a good make.
brand, sort, type, style, variety, manufacture, model, mark

make-believe NOUN

a game of make-believe
pretence, imagination, fantasy, unreality, play-acting, role-play
(≠) OPPOSITES reality

male ADJECTIVE

a male model
masculine, manly, virile, boyish
(≠) OPPOSITES female

man NOUN

I don't know that man.
male, gentleman, fellow
◇ INFORMAL WORDS bloke, chap, guy

manage VERB

1 *The children managed the task quite easily.*
accomplish, succeed, bring about
(≠) OPPOSITES fail
2 *managing a small company*
administer, direct, run, command, supervise
(≠) OPPOSITES mismanage
3 *I can't manage on so little money.*
cope, survive, get by, get along, get on, make do

Aa Bb Cc Dd Ee Ff Gg Hh Ii Jj Kk Ll **Mm** Nn Oo Pp Qq Rr Ss Tt Uu Vv Ww Xx Yy Zz

manager NOUN
the manager of the store
director, administrator, controller, supervisor, governor, head, boss

mangle VERB
The car was mangled in a crash.
spoil, destroy, deform, wreck, twist, maul, distort, crush

mania NOUN
He has a mania for computer games.
passion, craze, obsession, enthusiasm, fad, infatuation, craving

manner NOUN
1 *You are expected to speak in the correct manner.*
way, method, means, fashion, style, form
2 *Her manner is a little unfriendly.*
behaviour, conduct, air, appearance

manners NOUN
Mind your manners.
behaviour, conduct, politeness

manoeuvre¹ NOUN
1 *Reversing can be a tricky manoeuvre.*
move, movement, operation
2 *a political manoeuvre*
action, exercise, plan, plot, ruse, tactic, trick, scheme, dodge

manoeuvre² VERB
trying to manoeuvre into a tight space
steer, navigate, move, handle, guide, pilot, direct, drive

manufacture VERB
The factory manufactures cars.
make, produce, construct, build, create, assemble, mass-produce, turn out

many ADJECTIVE
many years ago
numerous, countless, lots of, various, varied, sundry, diverse, umpteen
⊭ OPPOSITES few

mar VERB
Radio towers mar the countryside.
spoil, harm, hurt, damage, mutilate, injure, maim, scar, ruin, wreck
⊭ OPPOSITES enhance

march VERB
1 *The soldiers marched through the town.*
walk, stride, parade, pace, file
2 *She marched out, slamming the door.*
stalk, stride, stomp, flounce

margin NOUN
the margin of the lake
border, edge, boundary, rim, brink, limit, verge, side

marginal ADJECTIVE
a marginal improvement
borderline, minimal, insignificant, minor, slight, doubtful, low, small
⊭ OPPOSITES central, core

mark¹ NOUN
The hot cup left a mark on the table.
spot, stain, blemish, blot, blotch, smudge

mark² VERB
1 *He bumped a wall and marked the car's paintwork.*
scratch, scrape, stain, blemish, blot, smudge, scar
2 *The teacher is marking the exam papers.*
evaluate, assess, correct, grade

marry VERB
They married young.
get married, wed
♦ FORMAL WORDS join in matrimony
◇ INFORMAL WORDS tie the knot
⊭ OPPOSITES divorce

marsh NOUN
Many birds inhabit marshes.
marshland, bog, swamp

Aa
Bb
Cc
Dd
Ee
Ff
Gg
Hh
Ii
Jj
Kk
Ll
Mm
Nn
Oo
Pp
Qq
Rr
Ss
Tt
Uu
Vv
Ww
Xx
Yy
Zz

Aa
Bb
Cc
Dd
Ee
Ff
Gg
Hh
Ii
Jj
Kk
Ll
Mm
Nn
Oo
Pp
Qq
Rr
Ss
Tt
Uu
Vv
Ww
Xx
Yy
Zz

martial arts NOUN

Here are some types of martial arts:

aikido, capoeira, judo, jujitsu, karate, kick boxing, kung fu, tae kwon do, t'ai chi

marvel¹ NOUN
1 *a marvel of modern medicine*
wonder, miracle, phenomenon, spectacle, sensation
2 *a marvel at chess*
genius, prodigy
◇ INFORMAL WORDS whizz, ace

marvel² VERB
We all marvelled at his achievements.
wonder, gape, gaze, be amazed at

marvellous ADJECTIVE
We had a marvellous holiday.
wonderful, excellent, splendid, superb, magnificent, terrific, super, fantastic
≠ OPPOSITES terrible, awful

masculine ADJECTIVE
a masculine voice
male, manlike, manly, mannish, virile, macho
≠ OPPOSITES feminine

mash VERB
Mash the potatoes.
crush, pulp, beat, pound, grind, smash

mass NOUN
1 *a mass of papers*
heap, pile, load, collection, lot, group, batch, bunch
2 *The people surged forward in a mass.*
troop, crowd, band, horde, mob
3 *forming a solid mass*
lump, piece, chunk, block, hunk

massacre NOUN
the massacre of innocent people
slaughter, murder, blood bath, killing

massive ADJECTIVE
a massive building
huge, immense, enormous, vast, gigantic, big, bulky, solid, large-scale
≠ OPPOSITES tiny, small

master¹ NOUN
A servant had to obey his master.
ruler, chief, governor, head, boss, employer, commander, controller
≠ OPPOSITES servant

master² VERB
1 *She has mastered her fear of flying.*
conquer, defeat, triumph over, overcome, control
2 *I have mastered the basics of sign language.*
learn, grasp
◆ FORMAL WORDS acquire
◇ INFORMAL WORDS get the hang of

match¹ NOUN
1 *a football match*
game, contest, competition, bout, test, trial
2 *This lipstick is a perfect match for the nail varnish.*
partner, counterpart, mate, twin, fellow
3 *She's no match for the younger player.*
equal, rival, peer, competitor
4 *The lamp is an exact match for the one we broke.*
copy, duplicate, replica, double, look-alike

match² VERB
1 *I could never match Liam's talent for painting.*
equal, compare, measure up to, rival, compete, oppose
2 *Your shirt matches your eyes.*
fit, go with, agree, suit, harmonize, co-ordinate, go together, tone with
≠ OPPOSITES clash
• **match up**
The children were matched up with partners for the game.
pair, couple, team, unite, join, marry, mate, link, combine
≠ OPPOSITES separate

mate NOUN
1 *my best mate*
friend, companion, comrade, pal, partner
2 *a carpenter and his mate*
assistant, helper

material NOUN
1 *building materials*
stuff, substance, body, matter
2 *a material similar to velvet*
fabric, textile, cloth
3 *Her life would make good material for a novel.*
information, facts, data, evidence

matter[1] NOUN
1 *a very serious matter*
subject, issue, topic, question, affair, business, concern, event, episode, incident
2 *It's of no matter whether they like me or not.*
importance, significance, note
3 *What's the matter?*
trouble, problem, difficulty, worry
4 *organic matter*
substance, stuff, material, content

matter[2] VERB
It doesn't matter if you are a few minutes late.
count, be important, make a difference, mean something

mature ADJECTIVE
a mature attitude
adult, grown-up, grown, full-grown, fully fledged
(≠) OPPOSITES childish

maximum[1] ADJECTIVE
for maximum effect
greatest, highest, largest, biggest, most, utmost, supreme
(≠) OPPOSITES minimum

maximum[2] NOUN
Spend £20 at the maximum.
most, top, top point, utmost, upper limit, peak, summit, height
(≠) OPPOSITES minimum

maybe ADVERB
Maybe we'll go away for a few days.
perhaps, possibly
(≠) OPPOSITES definitely

meal NOUN

Here are some types of meal:
afternoon tea, banquet, barbeque, breakfast, brunch, buffet, dinner, elevenses, feast, lunch, picnic, snack, supper, takeaway, tea

mean[1] ADJECTIVE
1 *He is too mean to spend the money.*
miserly, selfish, tight-fisted
◇ INFORMAL WORDS tight, stingy, penny-pinching
(≠) OPPOSITES generous
2 *That was a mean thing to say.*
unkind, unpleasant, nasty, cruel
(≠) OPPOSITES kind

mean[2] VERB
1 *What does this word mean?*
represent, stand for, suggest, indicate, imply
2 *What do you mean to do with your old toys?*
intend, aim, plan

meaning NOUN
the meaning of the phrase
significance, sense, implication, explanation, interpretation

means NOUN
I will get there by whatever means I can.
method, way, medium, course, process

measure[1] NOUN
We will take measures to improve behaviour.
step, course, action, procedure, method

measure[2] VERB
The nurse will weigh and measure all the children.

Aa Bb Cc Dd Ee Ff Gg Hh Ii Jj Kk Ll **Mm** Nn Oo Pp Qq Rr Ss Tt Uu Vv Ww Xx Yy Zz

assess, weigh, value, gauge, judge, determine, calculate, estimate

measurement NOUN
The dressmaker will take your measurements.
dimension, size, extent, amount, area, height, depth, length, width, weight

meat NOUN

Here are some types of meat:

bacon, beef, chicken, duck, game, gammon, ham, kidney, lamb, liver, mutton, pheasant, pork, turkey, veal, venison

meddle VERB
She's always meddling in other people's business.
interfere, pry, intrude, butt in, tamper
◇ INFORMAL WORDS snoop

medicine NOUN
Take your medicine if you want to get better.
medication, drug, remedy, prescription

Here are some types of medicine:

ear drops, eye drops, gargle, inhaler, lozenge, nasal spray, ointment, painkiller, pill, syrup, tablet

medium¹ ADJECTIVE
of medium height
average, middle, middling, midway, standard, fair

medium² NOUN
a medium for telling people about local events
means, way, mode, channel, vehicle, instrument, agency

meek ADJECTIVE
She was too meek to argue.
modest, humble, patient, gentle, peaceful, tame, timid
⧧ OPPOSITES arrogant, rebellious

meet VERB
1 *I met Leroy in the street.*
come across, run across, run into, chance on, bump into
2 *Let's all meet at the station at four o'clock.*
gather, collect, assemble
⧧ OPPOSITES scatter
3 *The candidate for the job met all the requirements.*
fulfil, satisfy, match, answer, measure up to, equal
4 *Make a cross where the two lines meet.*
join, come together, connect, cross, touch

meeting NOUN
1 *their first meeting*
encounter, introduction, assignation
2 *A meeting of the school council will be held on Tuesday.*
assembly, gathering, conference, convention, rally, get-together, session

melancholy ADJECTIVE
in a melancholy mood
depressed, down, down-hearted, gloomy, low, sad, unhappy, miserable, mournful, dismal
⧧ OPPOSITES cheerful, joyful

mellow ADJECTIVE
1 *a warm mellow taste*
mature, smooth, ripe, juicy, full-flavoured, sweet, tender, mild
2 *He became more mellow as he got older.*
pleasant, relaxed, easy-going, placid, cheerful
◇ INFORMAL WORDS laid-back
⧧ OPPOSITES cold

melody NOUN
a beautiful melody
tune, air, theme

Aa Bb Cc Dd Ee Ff Gg Hh Ii Jj Kk Ll **Mm** Nn Oo Pp Qq Rr Ss Tt Uu Vv Ww Xx Yy Zz

melt VERB

*My ice cream **melted** in the hot sun.*
dissolve, thaw, liquefy
≠ OPPOSITES **freeze, solidify**

member NOUN

*a **member** of the youth club*
associate, representative, comrade,
fellow

memorable ADJECTIVE

*a **memorable** occasion*
unforgettable, remarkable, significant,
impressive, extraordinary, important,
outstanding, momentous
≠ OPPOSITES **forgettable, trivial,
unimportant**

memorize VERB

*I have **memorized** her telephone
number.*
learn, learn by heart, remember
≠ OPPOSITES **forget**

memory NOUN

1 *I have happy **memories** of my time in
Glasgow.*
recollection, remembrance,
reminiscence
2 *in **memory** of the dead*
commemoration, remembrance,
celebration

menace NOUN

1 *the **menace** of careless driving*
danger, peril, hazard, risk, threat
2 *Foxes are becoming a **menace** in our
gardens.*
nuisance, annoyance, pest

mend VERB

1 *I must have my shoes **mended**.*
repair, renovate, restore, fix, patch
≠ OPPOSITES **break**
2 *He's **mending** slowly after his illness.*
recover, get better, improve
≠ OPPOSITES **deteriorate**

mention VERB

*Did Michael **mention** my name?*
refer to, speak of, name, bring up,
report, communicate, reveal, state, hint
at, quote

merciful ADJECTIVE

*a **merciful** leader*
compassionate, forgiving, humane,
tender-hearted, pitying, gracious,
humanitarian, kind, mild
≠ OPPOSITES **hard-hearted, merciless**

merciless ADJECTIVE

*a **merciless** opponent*
pitiless, hard-hearted, hard, heartless,
inhumane, unforgiving, remorseless,
unpitying, cruel, callous
≠ OPPOSITES **compassionate, merciful**

mercy NOUN

*The guards showed **mercy** to the
prisoner.*
compassion, forgiveness, leniency, pity,
kindness
≠ OPPOSITES **cruelty, harshness**

mere ADJECTIVE

1 *It cost a **mere** two dollars.*
bare, no more than, just
2 *That is **mere** nonsense.*
sheer, plain, utter, pure, absolute,
complete

merge VERB

*The two companies have **merged**.*
join, unite, combine, blend, mix, mingle

merit[1] NOUN

*a certificate of **merit***
worth, excellence, value, quality, good,
goodness
≠ OPPOSITES **worthlessness**

merit[2] VERB

*The job **merits** your full attention.*
deserve, be worthy of, earn, justify,
warrant

merry ADJECTIVE

*They're a **merry** crowd.*
jolly, light-hearted, joyful, happy,
cheerful, glad
≠ OPPOSITES **gloomy, melancholy**

Aa
Bb
Cc
Dd
Ee
Ff
Gg
Hh
Ii
Jj
Kk
Ll
Mm
Nn
Oo
Pp
Qq
Rr
Ss
Tt
Uu
Vv
Ww
Xx
Yy
Zz

Aa
Bb
Cc
Dd
Ee
Ff
Gg
Hh
Ii
Jj
Kk
Ll
Mm
Nn
Oo
Pp
Qq
Rr
Ss
Tt
Uu
Vv
Ww
Xx
Yy
Zz

mess¹ NOUN

1 *I helped to clear up the mess after the party.*
chaos, untidiness, disorder, confusion, muddle, jumble, clutter, disorganization, shambles
≠ OPPOSITES order, tidiness
2 *He's got himself into a mess with his money.*
difficulty, trouble, fix, jam

mess² VERB

• **mess about**
Stop messing about and get on with your homework.
mess around, fool around, play, play around, play about
◇ INFORMAL WORDS muck about

• **mess up**
1 *Don't mess up my hair.*
disarrange, jumble, muddle, tangle, dishevel
2 *I think I've messed up my audition.*
botch, bungle, spoil
◇ INFORMAL WORDS muck up

message NOUN

an urgent message
communication, report, letter, memo, note, notice, fax, email, text message

messy ADJECTIVE

What a messy room!
untidy, muddled, cluttered, disorganized, chaotic, sloppy, dirty, grubby, confused
≠ OPPOSITES neat, ordered, tidy

metal NOUN

Here are some types of metal:

aluminium, brass, bronze, chrome, copper, gold, iron, lead, nickel, platinum, silver, stainless steel, steel, tin, titanium, zinc

method NOUN

1 *teaching methods*
way, approach, means, manner, fashion, process, procedure, technique
2 *You need to apply some method to your work.*
organization, order, structure, system, pattern, form, planning

middle¹ ADJECTIVE

the middle section
central, halfway, inner, inside

middle² NOUN

in the middle of the room
centre, halfway point, midpoint, inside
≠ OPPOSITES extreme, end, edge, beginning, border

mild ADJECTIVE

1 *mild manners*
gentle, calm, placid, soft, good-natured, kind, lenient, compassionate
≠ OPPOSITES harsh, fierce
2 *mild weather*
calm, warm, fair, pleasant
≠ OPPOSITES stormy
3 *a mild curry*
bland, mellow, smooth, soothing
≠ OPPOSITES strong

milky ADJECTIVE

a milky liquid
white, chalky, clouded, cloudy

mimic VERB

She mimics all her friends.
imitate, ape, parrot, impersonate, copy
◇ INFORMAL WORDS take off

mind¹ NOUN

1 *She has a very sharp mind.*
intelligence, brains, reason, sense, understanding, wits
2 *We're of the same mind.*
opinion, view, point of view, belief, attitude, judgement, feeling

mind² VERB

1 *I didn't really mind the noise.*
care, object, take offence, resent, disapprove, dislike
2 *Mind the step.*

pay attention, beware, heed, note, observe, be careful, watch

3 *The owner's daughter is **minding** the shop.*

look after, take care of, watch over, guard, have charge of

◇ INFORMAL WORDS keep an eye on

mine NOUN

1 *a coal **mine***

pit, colliery, coalfield, excavation

2 *a **mine** of information*

supply, source, stock, store, reserve, fund, hoard, wealth

mingle VERB

*I must **mingle** with the guests.*

mix, associate, socialize, circulate

miniature ADJECTIVE

*a **miniature** railway*

tiny, small, scaled-down, baby, pocket-sized, little, mini

◇ INFORMAL WORDS pint-sized

≠ OPPOSITES giant

minimum¹ ADJECTIVE

*the **minimum** wage*

minimal, least, lowest, slightest, smallest, tiniest

≠ OPPOSITES maximum

minimum² NOUN

*a **minimum** of 30 days*

least, lowest point, slightest

≠ OPPOSITES maximum

minor ADJECTIVE

*a **minor** problem*

lesser, secondary, smaller, inferior, insignificant, petty, trivial, trifling, slight

≠ OPPOSITES major, significant, important

minute ADJECTIVE

***minute** particles of dust*

tiny, microscopic, miniature, small

≠ OPPOSITES gigantic, huge

miraculous ADJECTIVE

*a **miraculous** cure*

wonderful, marvellous, extraordinary,

amazing, astounding, astonishing, unbelievable, incredible

≠ OPPOSITES natural, normal

misbehave VERB

*I hope you have not been **misbehaving** while I've been away.*

get up to mischief, mess about, play up, offend

◇ INFORMAL WORDS muck about, act up

mischievous ADJECTIVE

*a **mischievous** child*

naughty, impish, roguish, playful, teasing

≠ OPPOSITES well-behaved, good

miserable ADJECTIVE

1 *She was so **miserable** at boarding school.*

unhappy, sad, dejected, despondent, downcast, heartbroken, wretched, distressed, crushed

≠ OPPOSITES cheerful, happy

2 *a **miserable** wet day*

depressing, dreary, gloomy, dismal, joyless

≠ OPPOSITES pleasant

misery NOUN

1 *I could see the **misery** in her face.*

unhappiness, sadness, suffering, distress, depression, despair, gloom, grief

≠ OPPOSITES contentment

2 *They lived a life of **misery** in terrible conditions.*

hardship, deprivation, poverty, want, destitution

≠ OPPOSITES comfort

misfortune NOUN

*She enjoys other people's **misfortunes**.*

bad luck, setback, calamity, catastrophe, disaster, accident, trouble, hardship

≠ OPPOSITES luck, success

miss VERB

1 *You have **missed** the point of what I was saying.*

fail, lose, omit, overlook, pass over, slip, leave out, mistake, misunderstand

Aa
Bb
Cc
Dd
Ee
Ff
Gg
Hh
Ii
Jj
Kk
Ll
Mm
Nn
Oo
Pp
Qq
Rr
Ss
Tt
Uu
Vv
Ww
Xx
Yy
Zz

Aa
Bb
Cc
Dd
Ee
Ff
Gg
Hh
Ii
Jj
Kk
Ll
Mm
Nn
Oo
Pp
Qq
Rr
Ss
Tt
Uu
Vv
Ww
Xx
Yy
Zz

2 *The car just missed a pedestrian.*
avoid, escape, dodge, skip
3 *The girl missed her parents when she was away at camp.*
pine for, long for, yearn for, regret, grieve for, mourn, sorrow for

• **miss out**
You missed out bits of the story.
leave out, overlook, ignore, skip, omit

missing ADJECTIVE
a missing cat
absent, lost, gone, disappeared, unaccounted-for
⧸ OPPOSITES found, present

mission NOUN
1 *a peace mission*
operation, errand, task, undertaking, assignment, campaign, business
2 *His mission in life is to help people in need.*
duty, purpose, aim, goal, job, work

mist NOUN
mist swirling round the castle
haze, fog, smog, cloud, condensation, film, spray, drizzle, steam

mistake¹ NOUN
There's a mistake in your work.
error, inaccuracy, slip, slip-up, blunder, misjudgement, miscalculation, misunderstanding, misprint, misspelling

mistake² VERB
I mistook him for his brother.
mix up, confuse, muddle

misty ADJECTIVE
a misty morning
hazy, foggy, cloudy, blurred, fuzzy, smoky
⧸ OPPOSITES clear

mix VERB
1 *Mix the ingredients in a bowl.*
combine, blend, mingle, merge, join, unite, fold in
⧸ OPPOSITES divide, separate
2 *He doesn't mix with the neighbours much.*
associate, socialize, mingle, join

• **mix up**
1 *Mix up all the letters and then pick seven.*
mix, jumble
2 *Try not to mix up the two things.*
confuse, muddle, jumble
3 *She mixes me up when she keeps changing the subject.*
confuse, bewilder, muddle, perplex

mixed ADJECTIVE
a mixed salad
assorted, varied, miscellaneous

mixture NOUN
1 *Spoon the mixture into paper cake cases.*
mix, blend, combination, compound, union
2 *a mixture of singing, dancing and comedy*
assortment, variety

moan VERB
1 *The little boy was moaning in his sleep.*
sob, weep, whine, groan, whimper
2 *He's always moaning about something.*
complain, grumble, whine

mob¹ NOUN
an angry mob
crowd, mass, swarm, group, collection, flock, herd, pack

mob² VERB
The fans mobbed the band.
crowd, crowd round, surround, swarm round, jostle, besiege, pester

mobile ADJECTIVE
1 *a mobile home*
moving, movable, portable, travelling, roaming, roving, wandering
⧸ OPPOSITES immobile
2 *exercises to keep the joints mobile*
flexible, agile, active, energetic, nimble

mock VERB
She was mocked because she looked different.

ridicule, jeer, make fun of, laugh at, scoff, sneer, taunt, tease

model¹ NOUN

1 *a cardboard model of a ship*
copy, replica, representation, imitation, mock-up
2 *He's the model of what a student ought to be.*
example, pattern, standard, ideal
3 *the latest model of mini-scooter*
design, style, type, version

model² ADJECTIVE

a model patient
exemplary, perfect, typical, ideal

model³ VERB

He modelled a figure from clay.
make, form, mould, sculpt, carve, cast, shape, create, design

moderate ADJECTIVE

1 *I'm only a moderate skier.*
medium, ordinary, fair, indifferent, average, middle-of-the-road
⊉ OPPOSITES exceptional
2 *a more moderate view*
reasonable, restrained, sensible, calm, controlled, cool, mild
⊉ OPPOSITES immoderate

modern ADJECTIVE

1 *modern art*
current, contemporary, up-to-date, new, latest, present-day, recent, up-to-the-minute, state-of-the-art
⊉ OPPOSITES old
2 *My mum is very modern in her appearance.*
fashionable, stylish, in vogue, in style, modish, trendy
◇ INFORMAL WORDS cool
⊉ OPPOSITES old-fashioned, out-of-date

modernize VERB

The kitchen needs to be modernized.
renovate, refurbish, revamp, renew, update, improve, do up, redesign, remodel

modest ADJECTIVE

1 *He's very modest about his achievements.*
humble, quiet, reserved, retiring, shy
⊉ OPPOSITES conceited
2 *She makes a modest living out of her paintings.*
moderate, ordinary, fair, reasonable, limited, small
⊉ OPPOSITES exceptional, excessive

modify VERB

They had to modify their holiday plans when the weather changed.
change, alter, revise, vary, adapt, adjust, transform, reorganize

moist ADJECTIVE

a moist cloth
damp, clammy, humid, wet, dewy, watery, soggy
⊉ OPPOSITES dry

moisture NOUN

There was moisture in the air.
water, liquid, wetness, damp, dampness, humidity, vapour
⊉ OPPOSITES dryness

moment NOUN

I'll be with you in a moment.
second, instant, minute, split second, trice
◇ INFORMAL WORDS jiffy, tick

money NOUN

1 *I've forgotten my lunch money.*
cash, banknotes, change, funds, currency
◇ INFORMAL WORDS dough, dosh
2 *Only people with money can afford luxury holidays.*
wealth, riches, capital

monotonous ADJECTIVE

a monotonous existence
boring, dull, tedious, uninteresting, unchanging, uneventful, unvaried, uniform, repetitive
⊉ OPPOSITES lively, varied

Aa
Bb
Cc
Dd
Ee
Ff
Gg
Hh
Ii
Jj
Kk
Ll
Mm
Nn
Oo
Pp
Qq
Rr
Ss
Tt
Uu
Vv
Ww
Xx
Yy
Zz

Aa
Bb
Cc
Dd
Ee
Ff
Gg
Hh
Ii
Jj
Kk
Ll
Mm
Nn
Oo
Pp
Qq
Rr
Ss
Tt
Uu
Vv
Ww
Xx
Yy
Zz

monster NOUN
a film about a scary monster
beast, fiend, brute, barbarian, savage, villain, giant, ogre, freak

monstrous ADJECTIVE
1 *That was a monstrous thing to do.*
wicked, evil, cruel, outrageous, disgraceful, atrocious, dreadful, horrible, horrifying, terrible
2 *a monstrous mansion*
huge, enormous, gigantic, vast, immense, massive

mood NOUN
Kieran is in a grumpy mood today.
temper, frame of mind, state of mind

Here are some types of mood:

afraid, angry, anxious, ashamed, bored, carefree, depressed, disgusted, downcast, ecstatic, elated, embarrassed, excited, fed up, frightened, glum, grumpy, happy, hopeful, horrified, irritable, jolly, livid, lonely, melancholy, miserable, nervous, proud, sad, scared, stressed, surprised, sympathetic, terrified, worried

moody ADJECTIVE
He is hard to live with because he is so moody.
changeable, temperamental, unpredictable, irritable, short-tempered, sulky, sullen, gloomy, glum
(≠) OPPOSITES cheerful

mope VERB
She's been moping about since school finished.
brood, fret, sulk, pine, despair

moral[1] ADJECTIVE
She tries hard to live a moral life.
good, honourable, decent, upright, honest, proper, blameless, pure, noble
(≠) OPPOSITES immoral

moral[2] NOUN
The moral of the story is that crime doesn't pay.
lesson, message, teaching, meaning

morals NOUN
They must have no morals to behave so badly.
morality, principles, standards, ideals

more ADJECTIVE
I need more paper.
further, extra, additional, added, new, increased, other, repeated, spare
(≠) OPPOSITES less

mostly ADVERB
I mostly take the bus to school.
mainly, on the whole, chiefly, generally, usually, largely, for the most part, as a rule

motion NOUN
The motion of the car lulled the baby to sleep.
movement, action, moving, activity

motivate VERB
1 *Part of the coach's job is to motivate the team to win.*
encourage, inspire, urge, persuade, move
◇ INFORMAL WORDS egg on
(≠) OPPOSITES discourage
2 *He was motivated by greed.*
drive, push, propel, cause, prompt
(≠) OPPOSITES deter

motive NOUN
What was the motive for the crime?
cause, reason, purpose, grounds, motivation, intention, inspiration

motto NOUN
the school motto
saying, slogan, catchword, proverb, formula, rule, golden rule

mould VERB
She moulded the clay into animal shapes.
cast, shape, make, form, create, sculpt, model, work

mouldy ADJECTIVE
mouldy bread
musty, decaying, rotten, bad, spoiled, stale
⊉ OPPOSITES **fresh**

mound NOUN
a mound of clothes on the floor
heap, pile, stack

mount VERB
1 *The tension is mounting.*
increase, grow, rise, intensify
⊉ OPPOSITES **decrease**
2 *The jockey mounted his horse.*
climb, get up, get on, clamber up
⊉ OPPOSITES **dismount**

mourn VERB
People mourn when someone dies.
grieve, sorrow, regret, weep

mouth NOUN
the mouth of the cave
opening, cavity, entrance

move¹ VERB
1 *The traffic started moving again.*
stir, go, advance, budge, proceed, progress
2 *They're moving to London.*
relocate, move house, depart, go away, leave
3 *I was moved to write a letter of complaint.*
prompt, urge, drive, propel, inspire
4 *The sad film moved her to tears.*
affect, touch, stir

move² NOUN
1 *I'm trying to work out my next move.*
movement, motion, step, action
2 *a move to the city*
removal, relocation, transfer

movement NOUN
1 *jerky movements*
move, activity, act, action, moving
2 *the Green movement*
group, association, organization, party

moving ADJECTIVE
a moving story
touching, affecting, stirring
⊉ OPPOSITES **unemotional**

muck NOUN
Muck covered the windows.
dirt, grime, filth, mud, scum, sludge
◇ INFORMAL WORDS **gunge**

muddle¹ VERB
You're trying to muddle me.
confuse, bewilder, perplex
• **muddle up**
I muddled up clean and dirty clothes.
disorganize, disorder, mix up, mess up, jumble

muddle² NOUN
It will take me ages to sort out this muddle.
chaos, confusion, disorder, mess, mix-up, jumble, tangle

muffle VERB
1 *a device that muffles the noise of the engine*
deaden, dull, quieten, silence, stifle, suppress
2 *The children were muffled in scarves and woolly hats.*
wrap, cloak, cover

mug VERB
He was mugged by a group of youths.
attack, assault, steal from, rob, beat up, jump on

muggy ADJECTIVE
The weather is muggy and uncomfortable.
humid, sticky, stuffy, close, clammy, sweltering
⊉ OPPOSITES **dry**

multiply VERB
Sales of mobile phones have multiplied.
increase, expand, accumulate, intensify, build up
⊉ OPPOSITES **decrease, lessen**

munch VERB

*She was **munching** an apple.*
eat, chew, crunch

murder[1] NOUN

*a gruesome **murder***
killing, manslaughter, homicide, assassination, massacre

murder[2] VERB

*She **murdered** her husband.*
kill, slaughter, assassinate, massacre
◆ FORMAL WORDS slay

murky ADJECTIVE

*a **murky** November day*
dark, dingy, dismal, gloomy, dreary, dull, dim, cloudy, grey
(≠) OPPOSITES bright, clear

murmur NOUN

*We heard the **murmur** of voices.*
mumble, muttering, whisper, undertone, humming, rumble, drone, buzz, hum

muscular ADJECTIVE

*a **muscular** sportsman*
brawny, beefy, sinewy, athletic, powerfully built, strapping, powerful, strong
(≠) OPPOSITES puny, flabby, weak

music NOUN

Here are some types of music:
ambient, ballet, bhangra, blues, boogie-woogie, Cajun, chamber, choral, classical, country-and-western, dance, disco, drum and bass, electronic, emo, folk, funk, garage, gospel, heavy metal, hip-hop, house, indie, instrumental, jazz, jive, operatic, orchestral, pop, punk, ragtime, rap, reggae, rhythm and blues (R & B), rock, rock and roll, sacred, salsa, samba, ska, soul, swing, techno, world music

musical ADJECTIVE

*a **musical** voice*
tuneful, melodic, harmonious, sweet-sounding

musical instrument NOUN

Here are some musical instruments:
Stringed instruments:
banjo, cello, double bass, guitar, harp, mandolin, sitar, ukulele, viola, violin, zither
Instruments with keyboards:
accordion, concertina, harpsichord, organ, piano, synthesizer
Wind instruments:
bagpipes, bassoon, bugle, clarinet, cornet, didgeridoo, flute, French horn, harmonica, horn, kazoo, mouth organ, oboe, Pan-pipes, piccolo, recorder, saxophone, trombone, trumpet, tuba
Percussion instruments:
castanets, cymbal, glockenspiel, maracas, tambourine, triangle, tubular bells, xylophone
Drums:
bass drum, bodhran, bongo, kettledrum, snare drum, steel drum, tabla, timpani, tom-tom

musician NOUN

Here are some types of musician:
accordionist, backing singer, bass player, bugler, cellist, drummer, fiddler, flautist, guitarist, harpist, keyboard player, oboist, percussionist, pianist, piper, saxophonist, singer, soprano, tenor, trombonist, trumpeter, violinist

musty ADJECTIVE

*a **musty** smell*
mouldy, stale, stuffy, airless

Aa Bb Cc Dd Ee Ff Gg Hh Ii Jj Kk Ll **Mm** Nn Oo Pp Qq Rr Ss Tt Uu Vv Ww Xx Yy Zz

mute ADJECTIVE
He was mute with fear.
silent, dumb, wordless, speechless
⧣ OPPOSITES talkative

mutiny NOUN
the sailors' mutiny against the captain
rebellion, revolution, uprising, defiance, resistance, riot

mutter VERB
She was muttering under her breath.
mumble, murmur, rumble

mysterious ADJECTIVE
a mysterious stranger
mystifying, puzzling, perplexing, strange, baffling, curious, weird
⧣ OPPOSITES straightforward

mystery NOUN
the mystery of the missing diamonds
puzzle, secret, riddle, question

mystify VERB
Her reluctance to join in mystifies me.
puzzle, bewilder, baffle, perplex, confuse

mythical ADJECTIVE
mythical beasts
mythological, legendary, fabled, fairy-tale
⧣ OPPOSITES historical

Here are some mythical creatures:

abominable snowman, centaur, dragon, elf, fairy, giant, gnome, goblin, gorgon, griffin, hobgoblin, imp, leprechaun, Loch Ness monster, mermaid, minotaur, nymph, ogre, Pegasus, phoenix, pixie, satyr, sphinx, troll, unicorn, vampire

Aa
Bb
Cc
Dd
Ee
Ff
Gg
Hh
Ii
Jj
Kk
Mm
Nn
Oo
Pp
Qq
Rr
Ss
Tt
Uu
Vv
Ww
Xx
Yy
Zz

Nn

Aa
Bb
Cc
Dd
Ee
Ff
Gg
Hh
Ii
Jj
Kk
Ll
Mm
Nn
Oo
Pp
Qq
Rr
Ss
Tt
Uu
Vv
Ww
Xx
Yy
Zz

nag VERB
He nagged me into joining the club.
pester, plague, torment, harass, vex,
scold, irritate, annoy
◇ INFORMAL WORDS hassle

naked ADJECTIVE
naked bodies
nude, bare, undressed, unclothed,
uncovered, stripped, stark naked
⧧ OPPOSITES clothed, covered

name[1] NOUN
What's the name of her new book?
title, label, term

name[2] VERB
They named their cat Cleo.
call, christen, baptize, term, title,
entitle

nap NOUN
an afternoon nap
rest, sleep, siesta, snooze
◇ INFORMAL WORDS forty winks, kip

narrate VERB
Kirsty will narrate the story.
tell, relate, report, describe, recite

narrative NOUN
an exciting narrative
story, tale, account, report

narrow ADJECTIVE
a narrow passageway
tight, confined, constricted, cramped,
thin
⧧ OPPOSITES wide

nasty ADJECTIVE
1 *a nasty smell*
unpleasant, offensive, disgusting,
sickening, horrible, foul
⧧ OPPOSITES agreeable, pleasant
2 *a nasty remark*

malicious, mean, spiteful, vicious, cruel,
unkind
⧧ OPPOSITES kind

nation NOUN
the Arab nations
country, people, race, state, population,
community, society

native NOUN
a native of Switzerland
inhabitant, resident, national, citizen
⧧ OPPOSITES foreigner, outsider, stranger

natural ADJECTIVE
1 *It's only natural to defend members
of your family.*
ordinary, normal, common, regular,
standard, usual, typical
⧧ OPPOSITES unnatural
2 *a natural ability to sing in key*
inborn, instinctive, native

nature NOUN
1 *He has a very pleasant nature.*
character, personality, temperament
2 *problems of a different nature*
kind, sort, type, description, category,
variety, style, species

naughty ADJECTIVE
a naughty child
bad, badly behaved, mischievous,
disobedient
⧧ OPPOSITES good, well-behaved

navigate VERB
*The ship was safely navigated into the
port.*
steer, drive, direct, pilot, guide, handle,
manoeuvre

near ADJECTIVE
1 *our near neighbours*
nearby, close, bordering, alongside,
neighbouring

OPPOSITES **far**
2 *The exams are* ***near****.*
coming, forthcoming, approaching
OPPOSITES **distant**
3 *a* ***near*** *relation*
close, familiar, related
OPPOSITES **remote**

nearly ADVERB
I am ***nearly*** *twelve years old.*
almost, practically, virtually, approximately, more or less, as good as, just about, roughly

neat ADJECTIVE
a ***neat*** *appearance*
tidy, orderly, smart, trim, clean
OPPOSITES **untidy**

necessary ADJECTIVE
the ***necessary*** *equipment*
needed, required, essential, compulsory, vital, obligatory
OPPOSITES **unnecessary, unimportant**

need¹ VERB
1 *I* ***need*** *one more card to complete the set.*
miss, lack, want, require, demand, call for, have need of, crave
2 *You* ***need*** *to get your hair cut.*
have to, must, should, ought

need² NOUN
There's no ***need*** *to shout.*
call, demand, obligation, requirement

needless ADJECTIVE
needless *panic*
unnecessary, uncalled-for, unwanted
OPPOSITES **necessary, essential**

needy ADJECTIVE
aid parcels for ***needy*** *people*
poor, penniless, deprived, poverty-stricken, underprivileged
OPPOSITES **wealthy, well-off**

negative ADJECTIVE
a ***negative*** *attitude*

pessimistic, unenthusiastic, uninterested, unwilling
OPPOSITES **positive**

neglect VERB
He has been ***neglecting*** *his duty.*
forget, fail in, omit, overlook, let slide, shirk
OPPOSITES **remember**

neighbouring ADJECTIVE
neighbouring *countries*
bordering, near, nearby, connecting, next, surrounding
OPPOSITES **distant**

nerve NOUN
1 *He lost his* ***nerve*** *before his bungee jump.*
courage, bravery, spirit, vigour, daring, fearlessness, firmness, determination
◇ INFORMAL WORDS **guts**
OPPOSITES **weakness**
2 *What a* ***nerve*** *he's got!*
impudence, cheek, boldness, impertinence, insolence
OPPOSITES **timidity**

nervous ADJECTIVE
I was ***nervous*** *about the exams.*
excitable, anxious, nervy, on edge, edgy, jumpy, jittery, tense, fidgety, worried
OPPOSITES **calm, relaxed**

nestle VERB
The baby ***nestled*** *against his mother.*
snuggle, huddle, cuddle, curl up

neutral ADJECTIVE
1 *a* ***neutral*** *country*
impartial, uncommitted, unbiased, disinterested, undecided, non-committal, objective, indifferent
OPPOSITES **biased**
2 *a* ***neutral*** *colour*
dull, colourless, drab
OPPOSITES **colourful**

new ADJECTIVE
1 *a* ***new*** *car*
brand-new, unused, fresh
OPPOSITES **old**

Aa
Bb
Cc
Dd
Ee
Ff
Gg
Hh
Ii
Jj
Kk
Ll
Mm
Nn
Oo
Pp
Qq
Rr
Ss
Tt
Uu
Vv
Ww
Xx
Yy
Zz

2 *new technology*
modern, current, latest, recent, up-to-date, up-to-the-minute, trendy, advanced
OPPOSITES outdated, out-of-date
3 *new neighbours*
different, unfamiliar, unknown, strange

news NOUN
*Is there any **news** about the baby?*
report, account, information, word, latest

next ADJECTIVE
1 *the **next** street*
neighbouring, nearest, closest
2 *the **next** day*
following, subsequent, later
OPPOSITES previous, preceding

nice ADJECTIVE
⇒ For even more about this word, see the next page
*It was **nice** of you to bring me flowers.*
pleasant, agreeable, delightful, charming, likable, attractive, good, kind, friendly
OPPOSITES nasty, disagreeable, unpleasant

nimble ADJECTIVE
*She is very **nimble** for an old lady.*
agile, active, lively, smart, quick, sprightly
OPPOSITES clumsy, slow

nip VERB
*The dog **nipped** my finger.*
bite, pinch, squeeze, snip, clip, tweak, catch, grip

noble ADJECTIVE
1 *a **noble** family*
aristocratic, titled, high-ranking, upper-class
◇ INFORMAL WORDS blue-blooded
OPPOSITES low-born
2 *a **noble** deed*
honourable, virtuous, impressive, worthy, dignified, fine
OPPOSITES contemptible
3 *The horse is a **noble** animal.*
magnificent, splendid, dignified,

distinguished, grand, great, impressive, fine

noise NOUN
*We heard a loud **noise** from outside.*
sound, din, racket, row, clash, clatter, uproar, cry, blare
OPPOSITES quiet, silence

noisy ADJECTIVE
*a **noisy** party*
loud, deafening, ear-splitting, piercing, boisterous
OPPOSITES quiet, silent, peaceful

nonsense NOUN
*You're talking **nonsense**.*
rubbish, trash, gibberish, drivel, blather
◇ INFORMAL WORDS rot, twaddle
OPPOSITES sense

non-stop ADJECTIVE
non-stop action
never-ending, uninterrupted, continuous, constant, endless
OPPOSITES intermittent, occasional

normal ADJECTIVE
1 *in a **normal** day*
usual, standard, common, ordinary, conventional, average, regular, routine, typical, accustomed
OPPOSITES irregular
2 *He is very **normal** considering he is so famous.*
rational, reasonable, down-to-earth
OPPOSITES peculiar

normally ADVERB
***Normally** I walk to school if it isn't raining.*
ordinarily, usually, as a rule, generally, typically
OPPOSITES exceptionally

nosey ADJECTIVE
*a **nosey** neighbour*
inquisitive, prying, interfering, snooping, curious, eavesdropping

notch NOUN
*The joiner cut a **notch** in the wood.*

nice

Nice is one of the words which is used too often in English, because it can mean so many things.

You can use other words instead to create a picture of:

someone nice to know
friendly
kind
generous
polite
sweet
pleasant
good-natured
thoughtful
helpful
considerate
likeable
charming

a nice-looking person or thing
good-looking
beautiful
lovely
exquisite
smart
stylish
elegant
glamorous
fashionable

nice weather
fine
pleasant
wonderful
sunny

a nice event or day out
enjoyable
interesting
lovely

Aa
Bb
Cc
Dd
Ee
Ff
Gg
Hh
Ii
Jj
Kk
Ll
Mm
Nn
Oo
Pp
Qq
Rr
Ss
Tt
Uu
Vv
Ww
Xx
Yy
Zz

nice food
> **delicious**
> **tasty**
> **mouth-watering**

There are lots of informal words to describe nice food:
> **scrumptious**
> **scrummy**
> **yummy**

Over to you

Which advert would sell more biscuits?

- This is a nice biscuit with a nice filling.
- This is a yummy biscuit with a scrumptious filling.

This description of Count Dracula (before he turns into a vampire!) is improved by choosing some of the words from the lists above.

He was a nice (polite) man who was nice (charming) in every respect. The nice (sweet) lady whose party he was attending loved his nice (elegant) clothes and his nice (fashionable) hairstyle. She was disappointed when he said that he was unable to attend the opening of the nice (lovely) swimming pool at lunchtime the next day – he said that he had other things to do.

cut, nick, indentation, incision, score, groove, cleft, mark, snip

note¹ NOUN

1 *I've written a thank-you note to my aunt.*
letter, message, line, communication, reminder, memo, record
2 *There was an angry note in his voice.*
indication, token, mark, edge, hint

note² VERB

I note that you are not wearing your school uniform.
notice, observe, perceive, detect, mark, remark, mention, see, witness
- **note down**

He **noted down** her phone number.
record, register, write down, make a note of

noted ADJECTIVE

a noted violinist
famous, well-known, celebrated, eminent, prominent, great, distinguished, respected, recognized
(≠) OPPOSITES obscure, unknown

notice¹ VERB

I noticed that he wasn't paying attention.
note, remark, perceive, observe, see, mark, detect, spot
(≠) OPPOSITES ignore, overlook

notice² NOUN

1 *He gave notice he was resigning.*
notification, announcement, information, declaration, communication, warning
2 *a notice in the paper*
advertisement, poster, sign, bill
3 *She took no notice of what I said.*
attention, awareness, note, consideration, heed

noticeable ADJECTIVE

There was no noticeable difference.
evident, clear, distinct, plain, obvious, significant, unmistakable, conspicuous
≠ OPPOSITES inconspicuous, unnoticeable

notify VERB

You must notify the school if you are going to be absent.
inform, tell, advise, warn

notion NOUN

He had a strange notion that someone was spying on him.
idea, thought, belief, view, opinion

notorious ADJECTIVE

a notorious bank-robber
scandalous, dishonourable, disgraceful, well-known

nourish VERB

Rain will nourish the dry land.
feed, care for, provide for, sustain, support, tend

novel¹ ADJECTIVE

a novel idea
new, original, fresh, unfamiliar, unusual, uncommon, different, imaginative, unconventional, strange
≠ OPPOSITES familiar, ordinary

novel² NOUN

a novel about wizards
book, story, tale

now ADVERB

1 *Come here right now!*
immediately, at once, directly, instantly, straight away, promptly, next
2 *She is at university now.*
at present, nowadays, these days

nude ADJECTIVE

He was completely nude.
naked, bare, undressed, unclothed, stripped, stark naked, uncovered
≠ OPPOSITES clothed, dressed

nudge VERB

He nudged me in the ribs.
poke, prod, shove, dig, jog, push, elbow, bump

nuisance NOUN

It's a nuisance having to walk all the way home.
annoyance, inconvenience, bother, irritation, problem, trouble, drawback
◇ INFORMAL WORDS pain, drag

numb ADJECTIVE

My fingers were numb with the cold.
unfeeling, deadened, insensitive, frozen, immobilized
≠ OPPOSITES sensitive

number NOUN

1 *Add these numbers together.*
figure, numeral, digit, unit
2 *a large number of complaints*
total, sum, collection, amount, quantity

numerous ADJECTIVE

I've asked you to help numerous times.
many, abundant, several, plentiful
≠ OPPOSITES few

nurse VERB

She is nursing her sick child.
tend, care for, look after, treat

nutritious ADJECTIVE

a nutritious breakfast
nourishing, wholesome, healthful, health-giving, good
≠ OPPOSITES bad, unwholesome

Aa
Bb
Cc
Dd
Ee
Ff
Gg
Hh
Ii
Jj
Kk
Ll
Mm
Nn
Oo
Pp
Qq
Rr
Ss
Tt
Uu
Vv
Ww
Xx
Yy
Zz

Oo

oath NOUN

1 *He swore an **oath** of loyalty to the Queen.*
vow, pledge, promise, word, word of honour
2 *Hitting his finger with the hammer, he let out an **oath**.*
swear-word, curse, blasphemy

obedient ADJECTIVE

*an **obedient** child*
well-behaved, docile, dutiful, law-abiding, respectful
≠ OPPOSITES disobedient, rebellious

obey VERB

1 *It is important to **obey** the law.*
follow, keep, observe, heed, mind, be ruled by
≠ OPPOSITES disobey
2 *You should **obey** your parents.*
be ruled by, take orders from, heed, mind, submit to, yield to
≠ OPPOSITES disobey
3 *They refused to **obey** his order.*
carry out, follow, discharge, act upon, perform

object¹ NOUN

1 *a valuable **object***
thing, article, item
2 *the **object** of the exercise*
aim, objective, purpose, goal, target, intention, reason, point

object² VERB

*I **object** to that suggestion.*
disagree, protest, oppose, disapprove, complain
≠ OPPOSITES agree

objection NOUN

*There have been many **objections** to the proposal to close the school.*
protest, opposition, disapproval, complaint, challenge
≠ OPPOSITES agreement

objective¹ ADJECTIVE

*Try to take an **objective** view of the situation.*
fair, just, neutral, impartial, unbiased, detached, unprejudiced, open-minded
≠ OPPOSITES subjective

objective² NOUN

*Our **objective** is to raise £1000.*
aim, object, goal, end, purpose, ambition, target, intention

obligation NOUN

1 *You can try it out with no **obligation** to buy.*
commitment, requirement, bond
2 *I feel an **obligation** to look after her.*
duty, responsibility, commitment

obligatory ADJECTIVE

*The wearing of school uniform is not **obligatory**.*
compulsory, required, essential, necessary, enforced
≠ OPPOSITES optional

oblige VERB

1 *You are not **obliged** to join the swimming club.*
make, force, compel, require
2 *Would you **oblige** me by looking after the children for an hour?*
help, assist, do a favour

obnoxious ADJECTIVE

1 *He was particularly **obnoxious** to me today.*
unpleasant, disagreeable, nasty, horrid
≠ OPPOSITES pleasant
2 *an **obnoxious** smell*
disgusting, unpleasant, disagreeable,

nasty, horrid, repulsive, revolting, sickening
≠ OPPOSITES pleasant

obscene ADJECTIVE
obscene language
indecent, improper, immoral, shocking, offensive
≠ OPPOSITES decent, wholesome

obscure ADJECTIVE
1 *an obscure poet*
unknown, unimportant, little-known, unheard-of, minor
≠ OPPOSITES famous, renowned
2 *an obscure remark*
unclear, mysterious, deep, confusing
≠ OPPOSITES straightforward

observant ADJECTIVE
An observant witness took the car's number.
watchful, attentive, alert, eagle-eyed
≠ OPPOSITES unobservant

observation NOUN
1 *The doctors are keeping him under careful observation.*
watching, study, examination, attention
2 *He made an interesting observation about what was happening.*
remark, comment, statement

observe VERB
1 *Observe what happens next.*
watch, see, study, notice, keep an eye on
≠ OPPOSITES miss
2 *'That's odd,' she observed.*
say, remark, comment, mention
3 *We have to observe the rules.*
keep, carry out, follow, perform
≠ OPPOSITES break

obsession NOUN
an obsession with football
preoccupation, compulsion, mania, enthusiasm
◇ INFORMAL WORDS thing

obsolete ADJECTIVE
an obsolete machine
out-of-date, old-fashioned, dated, old, outmoded
≠ OPPOSITES modern, current, up-to-date

obstacle NOUN
1 *negotiating his way round the obstacles in the road*
obstruction, barrier, bar, hurdle
2 *She overcame all the obstacles to becoming an athlete.*
barrier, bar, obstruction, hurdle, hindrance, difficulty
≠ OPPOSITES advantage, help

obstinate ADJECTIVE
her obstinate refusal to join in
stubborn, pig-headed, persistent, headstrong, firm, determined

obstruction NOUN
1 *parked cars causing an obstruction*
block, obstacle, barrier, blockage, bar
2 *We must overcome all the obstructions to our plan's progress.*
hindrance, block, obstacle, barrier, difficulty
≠ OPPOSITES help

obvious ADJECTIVE
1 *It was obvious that he was lying.*
clear, evident, plain, undeniable, unmistakable, apparent
≠ OPPOSITES unclear
2 *The rash on your face is not very obvious.*
visible, noticeable, evident, conspicuous, apparent, prominent
≠ OPPOSITES unclear, indistinct

occasion NOUN
1 *The bus arrived late on three separate occasions.*
time, event, occurrence, incident, instance, case
2 *I have so far had no occasion to speak to him.*
chance, time, opportunity
3 *The wedding was a grand occasion.*
event, celebration, function, affair, party
◇ INFORMAL WORDS do

Aa
Bb
Cc
Dd
Ee
Ff
Gg
Hh
Ii
Jj
Kk
Ll
Mm
Nn
Oo
Pp
Qq
Rr
Ss
Tt
Uu
Vv
Ww
Xx
Yy
Zz

occasionally ADVERB

I occasionally play badminton after school.
sometimes, from time to time, at times, now and then, now and again, every so often, once in a while
≠ OPPOSITES frequently, often, always

occupation NOUN

What's his occupation?
job, profession, work, employment, trade, business

occupy VERB

1 *the people occupying the house next door*
live in, inhabit, stay in, own, possess
2 *He was completely occupied by his task.*
absorb, engross, engage, involve, preoccupy, busy, interest
3 *foreign troops occupying the country*
invade, seize, capture, take over, take possession of

occur VERB

The accident occurred at 9pm.
happen, come about, take place, turn out, develop

odd ADJECTIVE

1 *Our neighbour's always been a little bit odd.*
strange, unusual, peculiar, different, bizarre, eccentric, unconventional, weird
≠ OPPOSITES normal, usual
2 *I think something odd is going on.*
strange, unusual, uncommon, peculiar, abnormal, curious, bizarre, weird, extraordinary
≠ OPPOSITES normal, usual
3 *He likes the odd game of table tennis.*
occasional, irregular, random, casual
≠ OPPOSITES regular
4 *He was wearing odd socks.*
unmatched, unpaired, various, miscellaneous
5 *I found one odd shoe in the cupboard.*
single, spare, left-over

off ADJECTIVE

1 *This milk is off.*
bad, rotten, sour, turned, mouldy
2 *The match is off.*
cancelled, postponed

offence NOUN

1 *It is an offence to park here.*
crime, wrong, wrongdoing, misdeed, sin
2 *I did not mean to cause any offence.*
upset, hurt, resentment, indignation, outrage, hard feelings

offend VERB

1 *She offended him by laughing.*
upset, hurt, insult, injure, annoy, outrage
≠ OPPOSITES please
2 *The criminal has offended repeatedly.*
commit a crime, break the law, do wrong, sin, err

offensive ADJECTIVE

1 *an offensive smell*
unpleasant, disagreeable, disgusting, revolting, vile, nasty, obnoxious, repellent
≠ OPPOSITES pleasant
2 *offensive remarks*
rude, insolent, abusive, insulting, impertinent
≠ OPPOSITES polite

offer¹ NOUN

1 *an offer of a loan*
suggestion, proposal, proposition
2 *We have made an offer to buy a house.*
bid, tender

offer² VERB

1 *She offered him a drink.*
present, make available, hold out, provide
2 *Can you offer any suggestions on what to do next?*
put forward, suggest, provide, propose
3 *We offered to help.*
volunteer, come forward

official[1] ADJECTIVE
official documents
authorized, legitimate, formal, approved, proper
≠ OPPOSITES unofficial

official[2] NOUN
a government official
officer, executive

often ADVERB
1 *I don't go swimming very often.*
frequently, regularly, generally, much
≠ OPPOSITES rarely, seldom, never
2 *He's often asked me to lend him money.*
frequently, repeatedly, again and again, time after time, time and again, much
≠ OPPOSITES rarely, seldom, never

oily ADJECTIVE
oily food
greasy, fatty

OK[1] ADJECTIVE
1 *The party was OK but not great.*
all right, acceptable, fine, fair, satisfactory, reasonable, not bad, good, adequate
2 *Is it OK if I go round to Jaspal's house after school?*
all right, acceptable, permitted, satisfactory, in order
3 *Can you pop upstairs and check the baby's OK?*
all right, safe, well, fine, healthy

OK[2] INTERJECTION
OK, I'll do what you want.
all right, fine, very well, agreed, right, yes

old ADJECTIVE
1 *an old man*
aged, elderly
≠ OPPOSITES young
2 *an old manuscript*
ancient, antiquated
≠ OPPOSITES new
3 *a new computer to replace my old one*
out-of-date, obsolete, old-fashioned, worn-out
≠ OPPOSITES modern
4 *his old girlfriend*
former, previous, earlier, one-time, ex-
≠ OPPOSITES current

old-fashioned ADJECTIVE
an old-fashioned hairstyle
out-of-date, outdated, dated, unfashionable, obsolete, behind the times
≠ OPPOSITES modern, up-to-date

omit VERB
1 *I omitted question 3 because I didn't know the answer.*
leave out, exclude, miss out, pass over, overlook, skip
≠ OPPOSITES include
2 *He omitted to mention that it was his fault.*
forget, neglect, fail

ooze VERB
Blood oozed out of his cut finger.
seep, leak, escape, dribble

opaque ADJECTIVE
opaque glass
cloudy, clouded, murky, dull, dim, hazy
≠ OPPOSITES transparent, see-through

open[1] ADJECTIVE
1 *an open door*
unclosed, ajar, unlocked
≠ OPPOSITES shut
2 *an open jar*
unclosed, uncovered, unsealed
≠ OPPOSITES shut
3 *an open shirt*
unfastened, unclosed, gaping
4 *an open meeting*
public, general, unrestricted, free, accessible
≠ OPPOSITES closed, private, restricted
5 *He is open to attack.*
exposed, unprotected, unsheltered
6 *The roads are open again.*
clear, free, unobstructed
7 *open dislike*

Aa
Bb
Cc
Dd
Ee
Ff
Gg
Hh
Ii
Jj
Kk
Ll
Mm
Nn
Oo
Pp
Qq
Rr
Ss
Tt
Uu
Vv
Ww
Xx
Yy
Zz

obvious, plain, evident, noticeable, conspicuous
≠ OPPOSITES hidden
8 an **open** question
undecided, unresolved, unsettled, debatable
≠ OPPOSITES decided
9 an **open** manner
frank, candid, honest, natural
≠ OPPOSITES reserved

open² VERB

1 *Open the window.*
unfasten, unlock
≠ OPPOSITES close, shut
2 *Open the bottle.*
unseal, uncork
3 *Open your jacket.*
undo, unfasten
4 *She opened her heart to me.*
reveal, disclose, lay bare
≠ OPPOSITES hide
5 *She opened her arms wide.*
unfold, spread out, extend
6 *We'll open the show with a song.*
begin, start, commence, set in motion, launch
≠ OPPOSITES end, finish

opening NOUN

1 *an opening in the hedge*
gap, break, chink, crack, cleft, hole, split
2 *the opening of discussions*
start, beginning, launch
≠ OPPOSITES close, end

operate VERB

1 *This torch operates on batteries.*
work, function, act, perform, run, go
2 *people who operate machinery*
control, handle, manage, use, manoeuvre

operation NOUN

1 *the operation of the machine*
working, functioning, action, running, performance
2 *He runs a small catering operation.*
business, enterprise, concern, firm
3 *a rescue operation*
procedure, undertaking, proceeding, process, transaction, effort
4 *a military operation*
manoeuvre, campaign, action, task, exercise

opinion NOUN

What's your opinion of his behaviour?
belief, judgement, view, point of view, idea, feeling, assessment, notion

opponent NOUN

1 *Ravi is my opponent in the chess game.*
rival, enemy, foe, competitor, contestant, challenger
≠ OPPOSITES ally
2 *The scheme has many opponents.*
opposer, challenger, objector

opportunity NOUN

an opportunity to show what you can do
chance, opening, break, occasion, possibility

oppose VERB

He said he would crush anyone who opposed him.
be against, object to, resist, stand up to, take a stand against, defy, fight
≠ OPPOSITES defend, support

opposed ADJECTIVE

1 *I am opposed to religious bigotry.*
against, in opposition, hostile, anti
≠ OPPOSITES in favour
2 *He refuses to listen to anyone whose views are opposed to his.*
conflicting, in opposition, opposing, opposite, clashing, incompatible

opposite ADJECTIVE

1 *on the opposite bank*
facing, corresponding
2 *opposite views*
opposed, conflicting, hostile, inconsistent, different, contrasted, differing
≠ OPPOSITES same

Aa
Bb
Cc
Dd
Ee
Ff
Gg
Hh
Ii
Jj
Kk
Ll
Mm
Nn
Oo
Pp
Qq
Rr
Ss
Tt
Uu
Vv
Ww
Xx
Yy
Zz

opposition NOUN

Their plan met with a great deal of opposition.
hostility, resistance, disapproval
≠ OPPOSITES co-operation, support

optimistic ADJECTIVE

She has a very optimistic outlook on life.
hopeful, confident, positive, cheerful, bright
≠ OPPOSITES pessimistic

option NOUN

There are several options open to us.
choice, alternative, preference, possibility

optional ADJECTIVE

Attendance at the meetings is optional.
voluntary, unforced, non-compulsory
≠ OPPOSITES compulsory

orbit NOUN

the orbit of the moon
circuit, cycle, circle, course, path, revolution, rotation

ordeal NOUN

The hostages' ordeal was finally over.
suffering, troubles, anguish, agony, pain, torture, nightmare

order¹ NOUN

1 *I'm just obeying orders.*
command, instruction, direction
2 *We'll deal with your order immediately.*
request, booking, reservation, application, demand
3 *in alphabetical order*
arrangement, organization, grouping, sequence, classification, system
≠ OPPOSITES confusion, disorder
4 *The teacher tried to restore order in the class.*
peace, quiet, calm, law and order, discipline

order² VERB

1 *He ordered them to go.*
command, instruct, direct, require
2 *I've ordered a taxi.*
request, reserve, book, apply for
3 *The books are ordered by the author's name.*
arrange, organize, classify, group, sort out, lay out

ordinary ADJECTIVE

1 *It started off like any ordinary day.*
usual, common, regular, routine, everyday, typical, normal, customary
≠ OPPOSITES extraordinary, unusual
2 *You can use an ordinary kitchen bowl for this.*
average, commonplace, run-of-the-mill, plain, conventional, regular, standard

organization NOUN

1 *a religious organization*
group, association, institution, society, company, firm, club
2 *an efficient organization of data*
arrangement, system, classification, order, grouping, method, plan, structure

organize VERB

1 *I've organized all my CDs in alphabetical order.*
order, arrange, structure, group, classify, catalogue
≠ OPPOSITES disorganize
2 *We're going to organize a class committee.*
arrange, establish, found, set up, develop, run

origin NOUN

1 *the origin of the story*
source, foundation, base, cause, roots
2 *the origins of man*
beginning, start, launch, dawning, creation
≠ OPPOSITES end
3 *of Welsh origin*
ancestry, descent, family, parentage, pedigree, stock

original ADJECTIVE

1 *the original version*

Aa
Bb
Cc
Dd
Ee
Ff
Gg
Hh
Ii
Jj
Kk
Ll
Mm
Nn
Oo
Pp
Qq
Rr
Ss
Tt
Uu
Vv
Ww
Xx
Yy
Zz

first, early, earliest, starting, opening
≠ OPPOSITES **latest**
2 *a very original idea*
new, creative, fresh, imaginative,
inventive, unconventional, unusual,
unique
≠ OPPOSITES **unoriginal**

originate VERB
Karaoke originated in Japan.
begin, start, rise, arise, derive, come
from, evolve, emerge
≠ OPPOSITES **end**

ornament NOUN
china ornaments on the mantelpiece
decoration, adornment, trimming,
accessory, trinket, bauble

orthodox ADJECTIVE
using orthodox methods
conventional, accepted, traditional,
usual, well-established, established,
customary, recognized
≠ OPPOSITES **unorthodox**

outbreak NOUN
an outbreak of violence
outburst, flare-up, burst

outcome NOUN
a successful outcome
result, consequence, upshot, conclusion,
effect, end result

outcry NOUN
*There was an outcry when the cinema
was closed down.*
protest, complaint, objection, uproar,
cry, row, commotion

outfit NOUN
a wedding outfit
clothes, costume
◇ INFORMAL WORDS gear, get-up, togs

outlaw NOUN
a band of outlaws
bandit, robber, highwayman, criminal

outline NOUN
1 *an outline of the story*

summary, bare facts, sketch
2 *the outline of the hills*
shape, profile, form, contour, silhouette

outlook NOUN
1 *He has a cheerful outlook on life.*
attitude, view, viewpoint, point of view
2 *The outlook for small businesses is
good.*
future, expectations, forecast, prospect

outrage NOUN
1 *People wrote letters expressing their
outrage.*
anger, fury, rage, indignation, shock,
horror
2 *What has been done to these people
is an outrage.*
crime, atrocity, offence, injury, evil,
scandal

outrageous ADJECTIVE
outrageous behaviour
shocking, scandalous, offensive,
disgraceful

outside NOUN
*The house is painted pink on the
outside.*
exterior, front, surface, cover
≠ OPPOSITES **inside**

outsider NOUN
*He's always been treated like an
outsider.*
stranger, intruder, alien, non-member,
foreigner, misfit, odd man out

outskirts NOUN
on the outskirts of Dublin
edge, suburbs, fringes, borders,
boundary, margin
≠ OPPOSITES **centre**

outspoken ADJECTIVE
an outspoken critic of the government
frank, candid, blunt, unreserved, plain-
spoken, direct
≠ OPPOSITES **reserved**

outstanding ADJECTIVE
1 *an outstanding pianist*

Aa
Bb
Cc
Dd
Ee
Ff
Gg
Hh
Ii
Jj
Kk
Ll
Mm
Nn
Oo
Pp
Qq
Rr
Ss
Tt
Uu
Vv
Ww
Xx
Yy
Zz

excellent, distinguished, celebrated, exceptional, remarkable, superb, great, notable, extraordinary
≠ OPPOSITES ordinary
2 the **outstanding** beauty of the Alps
exceptional, remarkable, superb, great, impressive, striking, memorable, extraordinary
≠ OPPOSITES ordinary
3 an **outstanding** debt
owing, unpaid, due, unsettled, remaining, payable
≠ OPPOSITES paid, settled

overcast ADJECTIVE
The sky is **overcast**.
cloudy, grey, dull, dark, hazy
≠ OPPOSITES bright, clear

overcome VERB
1 We are determined to **overcome** our enemies.
conquer, defeat, beat, triumph over, overpower, overthrow, subdue
2 Vivien is trying to **overcome** her fear of flying.
conquer, defeat, beat, master, get the better of, triumph over, subdue

overflow VERB
1 If you don't turn off the taps, the bath water will **overflow**.
spill, run over, pour over, brim over, bubble over
2 The river is about to **overflow** its banks.
flood, submerge, soak, swamp, overrun, run over, pour over

overhead ADVERB
A plane flew **overhead**.
above, up above, on high
≠ OPPOSITES below

overlook VERB
1 a house **overlooking** the sea
look over, front on to, face, look on to, command a view of
2 We **overlooked** all the signs that he was ill.
miss, ignore, neglect, pass over, let pass

≠ OPPOSITES notice
3 I will **overlook** your lateness this once.
excuse, forgive, pardon, turn a blind eye to

overpowering ADJECTIVE
1 an **overpowering** urge to laugh
irresistible, overwhelming, powerful, strong, forceful, uncontrollable, extreme
2 an **overpowering** smell
strong, powerful, suffocating, unbearable, sickening

overrun VERB
1 The enemy troops have **overrun** the country.
invade, occupy, overwhelm, run riot over, swamp
2 The weeds have completely **overrun** the garden.
spread over, run riot over, swamp, swarm over, surge over, overwhelm

overtake VERB
She **overtook** a slow-moving vehicle.
pass, outdistance, outstrip, pull ahead of

overthrow VERB
The rebels have vowed to **overthrow** the government.
defeat, bring down, topple, conquer, beat, overcome, overpower, overturn, oust
≠ OPPOSITES install, protect, restore

overturn VERB
1 The boat **overturned**.
tip over, capsize, topple, overbalance, keel over
2 I knocked against the table and **overturned** my glass.
knock over, capsize, upset, tip over, spill

overwhelm VERB
1 Their problems **overwhelmed** them.
overcome, overpower, destroy, defeat, devastate
2 A tidal wave **overwhelmed** the village.
swamp, engulf, flood, devastate

Aa
Bb
Cc
Dd
Ee
Ff
Gg
Hh
Ii
Jj
Kk
Ll
Mm
Nn
Oo
Pp
Qq
Rr
Ss
Tt
Uu
Vv
Ww
Xx
Yy
Zz

3 *Your generosity **overwhelms** me.*
stagger, confuse
◇ INFORMAL WORDS bowl over, floor

owing to PREPOSITION
Owing to weather conditions, the trains are running late.
because of, as a result of, on account of, thanks to

own VERB
*I don't **own** a mobile phone.*
possess, have, hold, keep

• own up
*He **owned up** to stealing a chocolate bar.*
admit, confess, come clean, tell the truth

owner NOUN
*The **owner** of the shop was watching us.*
possessor, holder, proprietor

Pp

pace NOUN
1 *Take two paces to the right.*
step, stride, tread
2 *the pace of change*
progress, rate, speed, quickness,
rapidity, tempo

pack¹ NOUN
a pack of cigarettes
packet, box, carton, package, bundle

pack² VERB
1 *We packed all our books into boxes.*
wrap, parcel, package, bundle, stow,
store
2 *They were packed into the theatre.*
cram, stuff, crowd, press, ram, wedge

package NOUN
The postman delivered a package.
parcel, pack, packet, box, carton

pact NOUN
*They made a pact to support each
other.*
deal, agreement, bargain, arrangement,
treaty, bond, contract, understanding
⊘ OPPOSITES disagreement, quarrel

pad VERB
*The cushions are padded with
feathers.*
fill, stuff, pack, line, cushion, protect

page NOUN
The book has 160 pages.
leaf, sheet, side

pain NOUN
1 *a pain in my stomach*
hurt, ache, spasm, twinge, pang, stab,
sting, smart, soreness, discomfort
2 *the pain of losing her son*
anguish, agony, torment, torture,
distress, suffering
3 *My little sister is a bit of a pain.*

nuisance, bother, bore, annoyance,
burden
◇ INFORMAL WORDS headache

painful ADJECTIVE
1 *a painful wound*
sore, tender, aching, throbbing,
smarting, stabbing, agonizing,
excruciating
⊘ OPPOSITES painless, soothing
2 *a painful experience*
unpleasant, disagreeable, distressing,
upsetting, saddening, harrowing,
traumatic
⊘ OPPOSITES pleasant, agreeable

pains NOUN
*He was at pains to point out that he did
not agree.*
trouble, bother, effort, labour, care

paint VERB
painting the ceiling
colour, dye, tint, stain, lacquer, varnish,
glaze, coat, cover, decorate

pair NOUN
a pair of lovebirds
couple, duo, twins, two of a kind

pale ADJECTIVE
1 *You look a bit pale today.*
white, chalky, pasty, pasty-faced, sallow,
anaemic
⊘ OPPOSITES ruddy
2 *pale blue*
light, pastel, faded, washed-out,
colourless, weak, faint, dim
⊘ OPPOSITES dark

pamper VERB
His mother really pampers him.
cosset, mollycoddle, humour, indulge,
overindulge, spoil
⊘ OPPOSITES neglect, ill-treat

panel NOUN

a panel of judges
board, committee, jury, team

panic NOUN

There was panic in the streets.
agitation, alarm, dismay, fear, horror, terror, frenzy, hysteria
◇ INFORMAL WORDS flap
(≠) OPPOSITES calmness, confidence

pant VERB

He was panting after jogging round the block.
puff, blow, gasp, wheeze

pants NOUN

wearing only a vest and pants
underpants, drawers, panties, briefs, knickers, Y-fronts, boxer shorts, trunks, shorts

paper NOUN

1 *the Sunday papers*
newspaper, daily, broadsheet, tabloid, journal
◇ INFORMAL WORDS rag
2 *legal papers*
document, authorization, identification, certificate

parade NOUN

marching in the parade
procession, march, column, spectacle, pageant, display

paralyse VERB

He had been paralysed by his illness.
cripple, lame, disable, numb, deaden, incapacitate, immobilize

parcel NOUN

I posted a parcel to my cousin.
package, packet, pack, box, carton

parched ADJECTIVE

1 *a parched landscape*
arid, waterless, dry, dried up, dehydrated, scorched
2 *I'm absolutely parched.*
thirsty, dry
◇ INFORMAL WORDS gasping

pardon¹ VERB

1 *Pardon my ignorance.*
excuse, forgive, overlook
2 *The prisoner was pardoned.*
forgive, let off, release, free
(≠) OPPOSITES punish, condemn

pardon² NOUN

a pardon for your crimes
forgiveness, mercy, release, discharge
(≠) OPPOSITES punishment, condemnation

park NOUN

Here are some things you might see in a park:

bandstand, bench, bowling green, climbing frame, duck, flowerbed, gardener, lake, lawn, picnic table, playground, pond, putting green, roundabout, see-saw, slide, swan, swing, tree

part¹ NOUN

1 *a spare part*
piece, bit, component, element, fragment, segment, fraction, portion
(≠) OPPOSITES whole
2 *a different part of the company*
section, division, department, branch
3 *a remote part of the country*
district, region, area, territory

part² VERB

We parted at the railway station.
separate, part company, split up, break up
• **part with**
She wouldn't part with her teddy bear for anything.
let go of, give up, surrender, abandon, discard

partial ADJECTIVE

a partial victory
incomplete, limited, restricted, imperfect, unfinished
(≠) OPPOSITES complete, total

Aa
Bb
Cc
Dd
Ee
Ff
Gg
Hh
Ii
Jj
Kk
Ll
Mm
Nn
Oo
Pp
Qq
Rr
Ss
Tt
Uu
Vv
Ww
Xx
Yy
Zz

• partial to

*I'm very **partial to** chocolate ice cream.*
fond of, keen on, crazy about, mad about

participate VERB

*He refused to **participate** in the party preparations.*
take part, join in, contribute, be involved, share, co-operate, help, assist

particle NOUN

***particles** of food*
bit, piece, fragment, scrap, shred, speck, morsel, crumb, grain

particular ADJECTIVE

1 *on that **particular** day*
specific, precise, exact, distinct, special
≠ OPPOSITES general
2 *She is not very **particular** about keeping clean.*
fussy, choosy, fastidious

particulars NOUN

*The police took a note of his **particulars**.*
detail, specific, point, fact, circumstance

partly ADVERB

*You are both **partly** to blame.*
somewhat, to some extent, to a certain extent, up to a point, slightly, in part, partially, incompletely
≠ OPPOSITES completely, totally

partner NOUN

*dancing **partners***
associate, colleague, team-mate, accomplice, mate, companion

party NOUN

1 *a birthday **party***
celebration, get-together, gathering, reunion, function, reception
◇ INFORMAL WORDS do, knees-up
2 *a search **party***
team, squad, crew, gang, band, group
3 *a political **party***
side, league, alliance, association, faction

Here are some kinds of party:

birthday party, Christmas party, cocktail party, dinner party, fancy dress party, flatwarming, garden party, Hallowe'en party, hen party, housewarming, pyjama party, sleepover, slumber party, stag party, tea party

pass¹ VERB

1 *Leo **passed** the other runners and won the race.*
go beyond, outdo, outstrip, overtake, leave behind
2 *I read a magazine to **pass** the time.*
spend, while away, fill, occupy
3 *Time **passed** slowly till the holidays.*
go past, go by, elapse, lapse, roll, flow, run, move, go
4 *Would you **pass** the milk, please?*
give, hand, transfer
5 *I **passed** the exam.*
succeed, get through, qualify
• pass out
*He **passed out** when he saw the blood.*
faint, lose consciousness, black out, collapse, keel over, drop
◇ INFORMAL WORDS flake out

pass² NOUN

*a mountain **pass***
gorge, ravine, canyon, gap, passage

pass³ NOUN

*a backstage **pass***
permit, identification, ticket, licence, authorization, permission

passable ADJECTIVE

*He gave a **passable** performance.*
satisfactory, acceptable, average, moderate, fair, adequate, all right, OK, mediocre
≠ OPPOSITES unacceptable, excellent

passage NOUN

1 *a long dark **passage***
passageway, aisle, corridor, hall, hallway

Aa
Bb
Cc
Dd
Ee
Ff
Gg
Hh
Ii
Jj
Kk
Ll
Mm
Nn
Oo
Pp
Qq
Rr
Ss
Tt
Uu
Vv
Ww
Xx
Yy
Zz

2 *Tim read a short* **passage** *from the 'The Hobbit'.*
extract, excerpt, quotation, text, paragraph, section, piece, verse

passionate ADJECTIVE

1 *She feels* **passionate** *about animal rights.*
eager, keen, enthusiastic, fanatical, intense, strong, fierce
2 *He has a* **passionate** *nature.*
emotional, excitable, hot-headed, quick-tempered, impetuous, impulsive

passive ADJECTIVE

The little girl was strangely **passive**.
docile, unresisting, non-violent, patient, indifferent, lifeless
≢ OPPOSITES active, lively

past[1] ADJECTIVE

past experiences
former, previous, preceding, late

past[2] NOUN

in the **past**
history, former times, olden days
≢ OPPOSITES future

paste NOUN

wallpaper **paste**
adhesive, glue, gum, cement

pastime NOUN

My favourite **pastime** *is reading.*
hobby, activity, recreation, amusement, entertainment, relaxation
≢ OPPOSITES work

pat VERB

I **patted** *the dog.*
tap, dab, slap, touch, stroke, pet

patch VERB

His mother **patched** *his trousers.*
mend, repair, fix, cover, reinforce

path NOUN

1 *a* **path** *through the woods*
track, trail, walk, footpath, route, way, passage

2 *the* **path** *of the moon around the Earth*
route, course, direction

pathetic ADJECTIVE

1 *a* **pathetic** *sight*
sorry, miserable, sad, distressing, moving, touching, heart-rending, heartbreaking, pitiable
≢ OPPOSITES cheerful
2 *a* **pathetic** *attempt to be funny*
contemptible, useless, worthless, inadequate, feeble, laughable
◇ INFORMAL WORDS sad
≢ OPPOSITES admirable, excellent, valuable

patience NOUN

You need **patience** *to look after children.*
calmness, self-control, restraint, tolerance, endurance, persistence, perseverance
≢ OPPOSITES impatience, intolerance, exasperation

patient ADJECTIVE

You will have to be **patient** *till it's your turn.*
calm, self-controlled, restrained, indulgent, understanding, tolerant, uncomplaining, resigned
≢ OPPOSITES impatient, restless, intolerant, exasperated

patrol VERB

Soldiers **patrol** *the area.*
guard, protect, defend, go the rounds, tour, inspect

pattern NOUN

1 *a striped* **pattern**
decoration, ornamentation, design, style
2 *His idea was the* **pattern** *for many other schemes.*
model, template, guide, original

pause[1] VERB

She **paused** *for a moment before answering.*

halt, stop, break off, interrupt, take a break, rest, wait, delay, hesitate

pause² NOUN

a pause in the proceedings
halt, stoppage, interruption, break, lull, interval, delay
◇ INFORMAL WORDS breather, let-up

pay¹ VERB

1 *I'll pay the bill.*
settle, discharge, repay, refund
2 *He paid £80 for a pair of trainers.*
spend, pay out
◇ INFORMAL WORDS shell out
3 *The business didn't pay.*
benefit, profit, pay off, bring in
4 *I have paid for my mistakes.*
make amends, compensate, answer, suffer

pay² NOUN

an increase in pay
wages, salary, earnings, income, fee, payment, reward, compensation
◆ FORMAL WORDS recompense

peace NOUN

1 *a bit of peace and quiet*
silence, quiet, hush, stillness, tranquillity, calm, calmness
⌦ OPPOSITES noise, disturbance
2 *The two countries discussed peace.*
truce, ceasefire, harmony, agreement
⌦ OPPOSITES war, disagreement

peaceful ADJECTIVE

a peaceful atmosphere
quiet, still, restful, relaxing, calm, placid, undisturbed, untroubled
⌦ OPPOSITES noisy, disturbed, troubled, violent

peak NOUN

1 *the mountain peaks*
top, summit, crest, crown, height, tip, point
2 *at the peak of her career*
top, height, maximum, climax, tip, point

peculiar ADJECTIVE

1 *a peculiar person*
strange, odd, curious, funny, weird, bizarre, extraordinary, unusual
⌦ OPPOSITES ordinary
2 *an accent peculiar to the area*
characteristic, distinctive, specific, particular, special, individual, unique, singular
⌦ OPPOSITES general

peel NOUN

grated lemon peel
skin, rind, zest, peeling

peep VERB

She peeped through the keyhole.
look, peek, glimpse, spy, squint, peer

peer VERB

peering through the dirty window
look, gaze, examine, inspect, spy, snoop, peep, squint

pelt VERB

1 *The crowd pelted them with rotten fruit.*
bombard, shower, attack
2 *It's pelting outside.*
pour, teem, lash
◇ INFORMAL WORDS bucket down, rain cats and dogs
3 *Donna came pelting down the street.*
rush, hurry, charge, tear, dash, speed
◇ INFORMAL WORDS belt

penalty NOUN

the penalty for a crime
punishment, fine
⌦ OPPOSITES reward

penetrate VERB

The icy-cold wind penetrated all our clothing.
pierce, stab, prick, puncture, bore, enter, seep

people NOUN

1 *There were ten people in the queue.*
persons, individuals, humans, human beings, folk, public, general public
2 *the people of France*
population, inhabitants, citizens, community, society, nation

Aa
Bb
Cc
Dd
Ee
Ff
Gg
Hh
Ii
Jj
Kk
Ll
Mm
Nn
Oo
Pp
Qq
Rr
Ss
Tt
Uu
Vv
Ww
Xx
Yy
Zz

perceptive ADJECTIVE
*She made some **perceptive** comments.*
observant, sensitive, responsive, aware, alert, quick, sharp, shrewd
(≠) OPPOSITES unobservant

perfect ADJECTIVE
1 *a **perfect** performance*
faultless, impeccable, flawless, immaculate, spotless, blameless, pure, superb, excellent
(≠) OPPOSITES imperfect, flawed, blemished
2 *a **perfect** circle*
exact, precise, accurate, right, correct, true
(≠) OPPOSITES inaccurate, wrong
3 *He would make a **perfect** teacher.*
ideal, model, ultimate
(≠) OPPOSITES worst possible
4 *I felt a **perfect** fool.*
utter, absolute, sheer, complete, entire, total

perform VERB
1 *I'm only **performing** my duties.*
do, carry out, discharge, satisfy, complete, achieve, accomplish, bring off, pull off, bring about
2 *We are **performing** 'Hamlet'.*
stage, put on, present, represent, act, play, appear as

performance NOUN
1 *a **performance** of 'Macbeth'*
show, act, play, appearance, presentation, production, representation, portrayal, acting
2 *in the **performance** of his duty*
doing, carrying out, discharge, fulfilment, completion, achievement, accomplishment

performer NOUN
*a talented **performer***
actor, actress, player, artiste, entertainer

perfume NOUN
*the **perfume** of roses*
scent, fragrance, smell, odour, aroma, bouquet, sweetness

perhaps ADVERB
***Perhaps** you are right.*
maybe, possibly, conceivably

period NOUN
1 *I went through a very unhappy **period**.*
time, stretch, session, interval, space, span, spell, cycle
2 *the Jurassic **Period***
era, age, generation, date, years, time, stage, phase

perish VERB
1 *The fabric of my swimsuit has **perished**.*
rot, decay, decompose, disintegrate, crumble, collapse
2 *Thousands of soldiers **perished** in the war.*
fall, die, pass away

permanent ADJECTIVE
1 ***permanent** damage*
unchanging, eternal, everlasting, lifelong, long-lasting, lasting, enduring
(≠) OPPOSITES temporary
2 *a **permanent** job*
fixed, stable, lifelong, constant, long-lasting, lasting, enduring
(≠) OPPOSITES temporary

permissible ADJECTIVE
***permissible** behaviour*
permitted, allowable, allowed, all right, acceptable, proper, authorized, lawful, legal, legitimate
(≠) OPPOSITES prohibited, banned, forbidden

permission NOUN
*You must get **permission** to use the Internet.*
consent, agreement, approval, go-ahead, green light, authorization
(≠) OPPOSITES prohibition

permit[1] VERB
*Smoking is not **permitted** in public places.*
allow, let, consent, agree, admit, grant, authorize, license
(≠) OPPOSITES prohibit, forbid

permit² NOUN

*a fishing **permit***
pass, licence, authorization,
permission
⊜ OPPOSITES prohibition

persecute VERB

*They were **persecuted** for their religious views.*
hound, abuse, mistreat, oppress,
victimize, distress, torment, torture,
discriminate against
⊜ OPPOSITES pamper, spoil

persevere VERB

If you don't succeed right away,
persevere.
continue, carry on, keep going, soldier
on, persist, stand firm, stand fast
◇ INFORMAL WORDS stick at it, plug away
⊜ OPPOSITES give up, stop, discontinue

persist VERB

1 *He **persists** in calling me names.*
continue, carry on, keep at it, persevere,
insist
⊜ OPPOSITES stop
2 *If the problem **persists**, call a doctor.*
remain, linger, last, endure, continue,
carry on
⊜ OPPOSITES stop

persistent ADJECTIVE

1 *a **persistent** knocking sound*
constant, steady, continual, continuous,
relentless, repeated, enduring, endless,
never-ending
2 *She is very **persistent**.*
persevering, determined, resolute,
stubborn, obstinate, steadfast,
tenacious

person NOUN

*He is a very considerate **person**.*
individual, being, human being, human,
man, woman, body, soul, character

personal ADJECTIVE

1 *He has a **personal** trainer.*
own, private, special, particular,
individual

⊜ OPPOSITES public, general, universal
2 *That's a rather **personal** question.*
private, confidential, intimate
⊜ OPPOSITES public, general

personality NOUN

1 *She has an attractive **personality**.*
character, nature, temperament,
individuality, traits
2 *a TV **personality***
celebrity, public figure, VIP, star

persuade VERB

*I **persuaded** Kerry to come to the party.*
coax, lean on, talk into, bring round,
win over, convince, influence, prompt,
urge
⊜ OPPOSITES discourage

persuasive ADJECTIVE

1 *She has a very **persuasive** manner.*
forceful, influential, moving, touching
2 ***persuasive** arguments*
sound, valid, convincing, compelling,
effective, telling
⊜ OPPOSITES unconvincing

pest NOUN

*My little brother is such a **pest**.*
nuisance, bother, annoyance, irritation,
vexation, trial

pester VERB

*Natalie **pestered** her parents to buy her
a bicycle.*
nag, badger, hound, torment, worry,
bother, disturb, annoy, irritate
◇ INFORMAL WORDS hassle

pet¹ VERB

*She **petted** the puppy.*
stroke, cuddle, kiss

pet² NOUN

Here are some animals we keep as pets:

bird, budgerigar, canary, cat,
chinchilla, cockatoo, dog, ferret,
fish, gerbil, goldfish, guinea pig,

hamster, mouse, parrot, rabbit, rat, sea-monkey, snail, snake, spider, stick insect, terrapin, tortoise, turtle

petrified ADJECTIVE
*He was **petrified** at having to make a speech.*
terrified, frightened, horrified, appalled, paralysed, numb

petty ADJECTIVE
*a **petty** offence*
minor, unimportant, insignificant, trivial, secondary, small, little, trifling, paltry
⊯ OPPOSITES important, significant

phase NOUN
*the first **phase** of the plan*
stage, step, time, period, spell, season, chapter

phenomenon NOUN
1 *a natural **phenomenon***
occurrence, happening, event, incident, fact
2 *a child **phenomenon***
wonder, marvel, miracle, prodigy, curiosity, sensation

phone VERB
Phone for an ambulance.
telephone, ring, ring up, call, call up, dial, contact, get in touch
◇ INFORMAL WORDS give a buzz, give a tinkle

phoney ADJECTIVE
*a **phoney** name*
fake, forged, trick, false, assumed, affected, put-on, sham, pseudo, imitation
⊯ OPPOSITES real, genuine

photograph NOUN
*a framed **photograph** of her boyfriend*
photo, snap, snapshot, print, shot, picture, likeness

phrase NOUN
*a well-known **phrase** or saying*
expression, saying, idiom, slogan

physical ADJECTIVE
1 *a **physical** examination*
bodily, fleshly, mortal, earthly
⊯ OPPOSITES mental, spiritual
2 *physical objects*
material, concrete, solid, substantial, tangible, visible, real, actual
⊯ OPPOSITES insubstantial, abstract

pick VERB
1 *Pick a number.*
select, choose, opt for, decide on, settle on, single out
2 *picking strawberries*
gather, collect, harvest

picture[1] NOUN
1 *There was a **picture** of a horse on the wall.*
painting, portrait, drawing, sketch, illustration, photograph, print, representation, likeness, image
2 *Your story gives a good **picture** of what happened.*
portrayal, description, account, report, impression
3 *He is the **picture** of health.*
embodiment, personification, essence
4 *a cowboy **picture***
film, movie, motion picture

picture[2] VERB
1 *Picture the scene.*
imagine, conceive, visualize, see
2 *She was **pictured** sitting on a wall.*
describe, represent, show, portray, depict, draw, sketch, paint, photograph, illustrate

picturesque ADJECTIVE
*a **picturesque** village*
attractive, beautiful, pretty, charming, quaint, scenic
⊯ OPPOSITES unattractive

piece NOUN
1 *a **piece** of chocolate*

bit, scrap, lump, chunk, slice, part, segment, fragment, section, portion
2 *a piece in the paper*
article, item, report, study, work, composition, creation

pierce VERB
She's had her ears pierced.
penetrate, stick into, puncture, drill, bore, prick, stab, spear, skewer, spike

piercing ADJECTIVE
1 *a piercing cry*
shrill, high-pitched, loud, ear-splitting, sharp
2 *a piercing wind*
cold, bitter, raw, biting, fierce, severe, wintry, frosty, freezing

pile¹ NOUN
a pile of clothes on the floor
stack, heap, mound, mountain, mass, collection, assortment, hoard

pile² VERB
1 *magazines piled on the desk*
stack, heap, mass, build up, assemble, collect, hoard, store
2 *We all piled into the lift.*
pack, jam, crush, crowd, load

pillar NOUN
marble pillars
column, shaft, post, mast, support, prop

pin VERB
I pinned up a calendar.
tack, nail, fix, attach, join, staple, clip, fasten, secure

pinch VERB
1 *He pinched her cheek.*
squeeze, crush, press, tweak, nip, hurt, grip, grasp
2 *Her bike was pinched.*
steal, snatch
◇ INFORMAL WORDS nick

pine VERB
She is still pining for her lost dog.
long, yearn, ache, sigh, grieve, mourn, wish

pioneer NOUN
1 *the early pioneers in America*
colonist, settler, frontiersman, frontierswoman, explorer
2 *a pioneer in the field of medicine*
developer, leader, inventor, discoverer, innovator

pious ADJECTIVE
a good and pious man
devout, godly, saintly, holy, spiritual, religious, virtuous, moral

pipe NOUN
a gas pipe
tube, hose, piping, tubing, pipeline, line, main, channel, duct

pirate NOUN

Here are some words connected with pirates:
booty, buccaneer, buried treasure, corsair, cutlass, dragoon, eyepatch, hook, Jolly Roger, landlubber, mast, parrot, pieces of eight, pirate ship, rum, sails, sea shanty, skull and crossbones, treasure chest, walk the plank

pit NOUN
1 *the pit where my father worked*
mine, coalmine, colliery
2 *a gravel pit*
trench, ditch, hollow, dent, hole, cavity, crater, pothole

pitch¹ NOUN
1 *a football pitch*
ground, field, playing-field, arena, stadium
2 *a tune played at the correct pitch*
sound, tone, frequency, level

pitch² VERB
1 *He pitched the ball across the park.*
throw, fling, toss, lob, bowl, hurl, heave, sling, launch
◇ INFORMAL WORDS chuck
2 *The ship pitched and rolled.*

Aa
Bb
Cc
Dd
Ee
Ff
Gg
Hh
Ii
Jj
Kk
Ll
Mm
Nn
Oo
Pp
Qq
Rr
Ss
Tt
Uu
Vv
Ww
Xx
Yy
Zz

plunge, dive, drop, tumble, lurch, roll
3 *They **pitched** camp in a field.*
erect, put up, set up, place, station, settle

pitiful ADJECTIVE

1 *a **pitiful** example*
contemptible, despicable, inadequate, hopeless, sorry, insignificant, worthless
◇ INFORMAL WORDS pathetic, sad
2 *a **pitiful** wail*
mournful, distressing, heart-rending, pathetic, sad, miserable, poor, sorry

pity¹ NOUN

1 *We all felt **pity** for the flood victims.*
sympathy, regret, understanding, fellow feeling, compassion, mercy
✖ OPPOSITES cruelty, anger, scorn
2 *What a **pity** you missed the show!*
shame, misfortune, bad luck

pity² VERB

*I **pity** anyone who doesn't like good music.*
feel sorry for, feel for, sympathize with, grieve for, weep for

place¹ NOUN

1 *a good **place** for a music festival*
site, venue, location, situation, spot, point, position, locale
2 *Take your **place** at the top table.*
seat, space, room
3 *a **place** on the map*
city, town, village, locality, neighbourhood, district, area, region
4 *They're moving to a new **place** in town.*
building, property, residence, house, flat, apartment, home
◆ FORMAL WORDS dwelling

place² VERB

***Place** the book on the desk.*
put, set, position, locate, situate, lay, stand, deposit

plague¹ NOUN

1 *Thousands died from the **plague**.*
pestilence, epidemic, disease, infection, contagion

2 *a **plague** of wasps*
infestation, invasion

plague² VERB

*He's been **plaguing** me with questions all day.*
annoy, bother, disturb, trouble, pester, harass, torment, persecute

plain ADJECTIVE

1 *good **plain** cooking*
ordinary, basic, simple, modest
✖ OPPOSITES fancy, elaborate
2 *Her embarrassment was **plain** to see.*
obvious, evident, clear, apparent, visible, unmistakable
✖ OPPOSITES unclear, obscure
3 *plain speaking*
frank, blunt, outspoken, direct, straightforward, open, honest, truthful
✖ OPPOSITES devious, deceitful
4 *a **plain**, old-fashioned girl*
unattractive, unprepossessing, unlovely
✖ OPPOSITES attractive, good-looking
5 *plain fabric*
unpatterned, uncoloured, self-coloured
✖ OPPOSITES patterned

plan¹ NOUN

1 *I have a cunning **plan**.*
idea, suggestion, proposal, proposition, project, scheme, plot, strategy, programme
2 *the **plans** for the building*
layout, diagram, chart, map, drawing, sketch, design

plan² VERB

1 *The attack was carefully **planned**.*
plot, scheme, design, devise, frame, prepare, organize, arrange
2 *She **plans** to be a lawyer.*
aim, intend, propose

planet NOUN

Here are the planets in our solar system:

Earth, Jupiter, Mars, Mercury, Neptune, Saturn, Uranus, Venus

Aa Bb Cc Dd Ee Ff Gg Hh Ii Jj Kk Ll Mm Nn Oo Pp Qq Rr Ss Tt Uu Vv Ww Xx Yy Zz

plant¹ NOUN

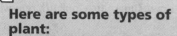

Here are some types of plant:

algae, bush, cactus, cereal, evergreen, fern, flower, fungus, grass, herb, herbaceous plant, house plant, lichen, moss, pot plant, shrub, tree, vegetable, vine, weed, wild flower
⇒ Also look up **flower**

plant² VERB

*We **planted** sunflower seeds in the garden.*
sow, seed, bury, transplant

plate NOUN

1 *a **plate** of biscuits*
dish, platter
2 *a colour **plate***
illustration, picture, print

platform NOUN

*The speaker took the **platform**.*
stage, podium, dais, stand

play¹ VERB

1 *The children are **playing** in the playground.*
amuse yourself, have fun, enjoy yourself
⧧ OPPOSITES work
2 *We all **play** a part in the running of the school.*
participate, take part, join in, compete
3 *France **played** Italy.*
oppose, vie with, challenge, take on
4 *Mel Gibson **played** Hamlet.*
act, perform, portray, represent, impersonate

play² NOUN

1 *Children must have time for **play**.*
fun, amusement, entertainment, recreation, sport, game, hobby, pastime
⧧ OPPOSITES work
2 *Alan has landed the main part in the **play**.*
drama, tragedy, comedy, farce, show, performance

player NOUN

1 *a football **player***
contestant, competitor, participant, sportsman, sportswoman
2 *The **players** took a bow.*
performer, entertainer, artiste, actor, actress, musician, instrumentalist

playful ADJECTIVE

***playful** teasing*
lively, spirited, mischievous, roguish, impish, good-natured, teasing, humorous
⧧ OPPOSITES serious

plea NOUN

*a **plea** for mercy*
appeal, petition, request, entreaty

plead VERB

*The hostages **pleaded** with him to let them go.*
beg, appeal, petition, ask, request

pleasant ADJECTIVE

1 *That makes a **pleasant** change.*
agreeable, nice, fine, lovely, delightful, enjoyable, amusing, pleasing, welcome, refreshing
⧧ OPPOSITES unpleasant, nasty
2 *a **pleasant** woman*
charming, likable, friendly, good-humoured, cheerful
⧧ OPPOSITES unpleasant, unfriendly

please VERB

*I took the job to **please** my parents.*
delight, charm, entertain, amuse, gladden, humour, indulge, satisfy, content, suit
⧧ OPPOSITES displease, annoy, anger, sadden

pleased ADJECTIVE

*The teacher was **pleased** with my work.*
contented, satisfied, glad, happy, delighted, thrilled
⧧ OPPOSITES displeased, annoyed

pleasure NOUN

*Parents get **pleasure** from seeing their children happy.*

Aa
Bb
Cc
Dd
Ee
Ff
Gg
Hh
Ii
Jj
Kk
Ll
Mm
Nn
Oo
Pp
Qq
Rr
Ss
Tt
Uu
Vv
Ww
Xx
Yy
Zz

satisfaction, contentment, happiness, joy, delight, amusement, entertainment, recreation, fun, enjoyment
≠ OPPOSITES sorrow, pain, trouble, displeasure

pledge[1] NOUN
He made a pledge of loyalty.
promise, vow, word of honour, oath, guarantee, assurance

pledge[2] VERB
We pledged £20 to the appeal.
promise, vow, swear, contract, guarantee, secure

plentiful ADJECTIVE
Food was plentiful in the camp.
ample, abundant, overflowing, generous, liberal
≠ OPPOSITES scarce, rare

plenty NOUN
We had plenty to eat.
abundance, enough, sufficiency
◇ INFORMAL WORDS lots, loads, masses, heaps, piles, stacks
≠ OPPOSITES scarcity, lack, want, need

plight NOUN
the plight of the refugees
predicament, dilemma, trouble, difficulty, state, situation, circumstances

plod VERB
The soldiers plodded through the mud.
trudge, tramp, stomp, plough
• plod on
We kept plodding on regardless.
drudge, labour, toil, grind, slog, persevere, soldier on

plot[1] NOUN
1 *the Gunpowder Plot*
conspiracy, intrigue, scheme, plan
2 *I couldn't follow the plot of the film.*
story, subject, theme, storyline

plot[2] VERB
He thinks everyone is plotting against him.
conspire, scheme, cook up, plan

pluck VERB
1 *She plucked her eyebrows.*
pull, draw, tug, snatch, pull off, remove, pick
2 *They plucked the berries from the bushes.*
pick, collect, gather, harvest
3 *He plucked at his guitar.*
pick, twang, strum

plug[1] NOUN
a bath plug
stopper, bung, cork

plug[2] VERB
1 *plugging a hole*
stop, stop up, bung, cork, block, close, seal, fill, pack, stuff
2 *The band have been plugging their new album.*
advertise, publicize, promote, push, mention

plump ADJECTIVE
She had been plump as a child.
fat, dumpy, tubby, stout, round, chubby, podgy, fleshy
≠ OPPOSITES thin, skinny

plunge VERB
1 *The aircraft plunged to earth.*
dive, jump, nosedive, dive-bomb, plummet, descend, go down, drop, fall
2 *Plunge your hand into cold water.*
dip, immerse, submerge

poem NOUN

Here are some types of poem:
ballad, epic, haiku, limerick, lyric, nursery rhyme, ode, saga, sonnet, tanka

point[1] NOUN
1 *Kindness is one of his good points.*
feature, attribute, aspect, detail, particular
2 *I don't see the point of going out in the rain.*

Aa Bb Cc Dd Ee Ff Gg Hh Ii Jj Kk Ll Mm Nn Oo Pp Qq Rr Ss Tt Uu Vv Ww Xx Yy Zz

use, purpose, motive, reason, object, intention, aim, end, goal, objective
3 the **point** of the story
meaning, essence, thrust, drift
4 a **point** on the route
place, position, situation, location, site, spot
5 at this **point** in time
moment, instant, stage, time, period

point² VERB

1 He **pointed** a gun at the bank clerk.
aim, direct, train, level
2 All the evidence **points** to the likely culprit.
indicate, signal, show
• **point out**
He **pointed out** the house where he was born.
show, indicate, draw attention to, point to, reveal, identify

pointless ADJECTIVE

a **pointless** argument
useless, vain, worthless, senseless, absurd, meaningless, aimless
⊜ OPPOSITES useful, meaningful

point of view NOUN

Try to see the other person's **point of view**.
opinion, view, belief, attitude, position, standpoint, viewpoint, outlook, approach, slant

poisonous ADJECTIVE

poisonous substances
toxic, venomous, lethal, deadly, fatal, mortal

poke VERB

He **poked** me in the back.
prod, stab, jab, thrust, push, shove, nudge, elbow, dig

policy NOUN

the school's **policy** on bullying
course of action, line, course, plan, programme, scheme, stance, position

polish¹ NOUN

a high **polish**

shine, gloss, sheen, lustre, brightness, brilliance, smoothness, finish, glaze
⊜ OPPOSITES dullness

polish² VERB

1 **Polish** your shoes.
shine, brighten, smooth, rub, buff, clean, wax
⊜ OPPOSITES tarnish, dull
2 They've been **polishing** their act.
improve, enhance, brush up, touch up, finish, perfect, refine

polite ADJECTIVE

making **polite** conversation
courteous, mannerly, respectful, civil, refined, cultured
⊜ OPPOSITES impolite, discourteous, rude

politics NOUN

Here are some words and phrases used in politics:

alliance, ballot, bill, by-election, cabinet, campaign, civil service, constitution, council, devolution, election, electoral register, general election, government, left wing, lobby, local government, majority, manifesto, parliament, party, referendum, right wing, shadow cabinet, state, vote, whip

poll NOUN

an opinion **poll**
ballot, vote, voting, referendum, canvass, opinion poll, survey, census, count, tally

pollution NOUN

air **pollution**
impurity, contamination, infection, corruption, dirtiness
⊜ OPPOSITES purification, purity, cleanness

pomp NOUN

an occasion full of **pomp** and ceremony
ceremony, ceremonial, ritual, solemnity,

Aa
Bb
Cc
Dd
Ee
Ff
Gg
Hh
Ii
Jj
Kk
Ll
Mm
Nn
Oo
Pp
Qq
Rr
Ss
Tt
Uu
Vv
Ww
Xx
Yy
Zz

grandeur, splendour, magnificence, pageantry, show, display
⊘ OPPOSITES simplicity

pony
⇒ see **horse**

pool NOUN
We put our money into a pool for sweets.
fund, bank, kitty, purse

poor ADJECTIVE
1 *a poor family*
needy, poverty-stricken, badly off, hard-up, bankrupt, penniless
◇ INFORMAL WORDS broke, stony-broke, skint
⊘ OPPOSITES rich, wealthy
2 *a poor mark*
bad, substandard, unsatisfactory, inferior, mediocre, second-rate, third-rate, shoddy, weak
◇ INFORMAL WORDS pathetic
⊘ OPPOSITES superior, impressive
3 *the poor souls*
unfortunate, unlucky, unhappy, miserable, pathetic
⊘ OPPOSITES fortunate, lucky

poorly ADJECTIVE
I've been feeling poorly all morning.
ill, sick, sickly, off-colour
◇ INFORMAL WORDS out of sorts, under the weather
⊘ OPPOSITES well, healthy

pop VERB
The cork popped when we opened the bottle of champagne.
burst, explode, go off, bang, crack, snap

popular ADJECTIVE
1 *the most popular girl in the class*
well-liked, favourite, liked, in demand, sought-after
2 *a popular hobby these days*
fashionable, trendy, common, widespread
⊘ OPPOSITES unpopular

population NOUN
the population of Liverpool
inhabitants, natives, residents, citizens, occupants, community, society, people, folk

portable ADJECTIVE
a portable DVD player
movable, transportable, compact, lightweight, handy, convenient
⊘ OPPOSITES fixed

portion NOUN
1 *This restaurant serves children's portions.*
helping, serving, slice, allotment, ration, quota, measure
2 *a portion of the prize money*
fraction, percentage, bit, piece, part, section, division, segment, share

portrait NOUN
portraits of my family
picture, painting, drawing, sketch, photograph, profile

portray VERB
Brad Pitt portrays a family man turned spy.
represent, depict, describe, play

pose VERB
The robber was posing as a salesman.
pretend, put on an act, pass yourself off, impersonate

posh ADJECTIVE
a posh hotel
fashionable, high-class, upper-class, luxury, deluxe, up-market
◇ INFORMAL WORDS la-di-da, swanky, classy, swish
⊘ OPPOSITES inferior, cheap

position NOUN
1 *What's the ship's position?*
place, situation, location, site, spot, point
2 *sitting in an awkward position*
posture, stance, pose, arrangement
3 *Pamela was offered the position of nanny.*

Aa Bb Cc Dd Ee Ff Gg Hh Ii Jj Kk Ll Mm Nn Oo **Pp** Qq Rr Ss Tt Uu Vv Ww Xx Yy Zz job, post, occupation, employment, office, duty, function, role

positive ADJECTIVE

1 *I am positive that he is the thief.*
sure, certain, convinced, confident
OPPOSITES uncertain
2 *positive criticism*
helpful, constructive, practical, useful, optimistic, hopeful, promising
OPPOSITES negative
3 *It is a positive disgrace!*
absolute, utter, sheer, complete, perfect

possess VERB

1 *I don't possess a mobile phone.*
have, own
2 *I was possessed by fear.*
grip, take over, overcome

possessions NOUN

He had all his possessions in one bag.
belongings, property, things, goods

possible ADJECTIVE

1 *It's possible that you are right.*
likely, probable, imaginable, conceivable
OPPOSITES impossible, unthinkable
2 *It's perfectly possible to swim across the river.*
achievable, feasible, attainable, conceivable, practicable, workable
OPPOSITES impossible, impracticable

possibly ADVERB

He is possibly the tallest man I have ever seen.
perhaps, maybe, conceivably, by any means, by any chance

post¹ NOUN

a wooden post
pole, stake, pillar, column, shaft, support

post² NOUN

She has applied for the post of manager.
job, employment, position, situation, place, office, vacancy

post³ NOUN

My parcel arrived by the first post.
mail, letters, collection, delivery

post⁴ VERB

I posted the letter yesterday.
send, mail, dispatch, forward

poster NOUN

a film poster
notice, placard, bill, announcement, sign, advertisement

postpone VERB

The wedding has been postponed for two months.
put off, put back, delay, suspend
OPPOSITES advance, bring forward

posture NOUN

Poor posture can cause backache.
position, stance, pose, attitude, bearing
◆ FORMAL WORDS carriage

potent ADJECTIVE

1 *a potent drug*
powerful, strong, intoxicating, effective
OPPOSITES weak
2 *a potent argument*
persuasive, convincing, forceful, influential, powerful, strong, effective
OPPOSITES weak

potential ADJECTIVE

a potential Olympic champion
possible, likely, probable, prospective, future, promising, budding

potion NOUN

a magic potion
mixture, concoction, brew, beverage, drink, medicine, tonic

pounce VERB

The tiger suddenly pounced on its prey.
spring, jump, leap, fall on, dive on, swoop, attack, strike, ambush

pound VERB

1 *Someone was pounding at the door.*
strike, thump, beat, drum, hammer, batter, bang, bash, smash

Aa
Bb
Cc
Dd
Ee
Ff
Gg
Hh
Ii
Jj
Kk
Ll
Mm
Nn
Oo
Pp
Qq
Rr
Ss
Tt
Uu
Vv
Ww
Xx
Yy
Zz

Aa

2 *pounding* the rock into dust
pulverize, powder, grind, mash, crush

pour VERB

1 *Shall I pour the tea?*
serve, decant, tip, empty
2 *It was pouring all day.*
rain, teem, lash
◇ INFORMAL WORDS bucket down, rain cats and dogs, chuck it down, tip it down

Bb

Cc

Dd

Ee

poverty NOUN

living in poverty
insolvency, bankruptcy, pennilessness, hardship, need, want
⊜ OPPOSITES wealth, richness, plenty

Ff

Gg

Hh

power NOUN

1 *political power*
command, authority, rule, control, influence
⊜ OPPOSITES subjection
2 *powers of arrest*
right, privilege, authorization, warrant
3 *The engine is losing power.*
strength, intensity, force, vigour, energy
⊜ OPPOSITES weakness
4 *He lost the power of speech.*
ability, capability, capacity, potential, faculty, competence
⊜ OPPOSITES inability

Ii

Jj

Kk

Ll

Mm

Nn

Oo

Pp

powerful ADJECTIVE

1 *a man of powerful build*
strong, mighty, robust, muscular
⊜ OPPOSITES weak
2 *a film with a powerful message*
effective, strong, impressive, convincing, persuasive, compelling, winning
⊜ OPPOSITES ineffective
3 *powerful world leaders*
leading, influential, high-powered, authoritative, commanding
⊜ OPPOSITES powerless

Qq

Rr

Ss

Tt

Uu

Vv

Ww

practical ADJECTIVE

1 *a practical plan*
useful, realistic, sensible, commonsense, practicable, workable
⊜ OPPOSITES impractical

Xx

Yy

Zz

2 *a practical person*
realistic, sensible, down-to-earth, matter-of-fact, hard-headed
⊜ OPPOSITES impractical, unrealistic

practically ADVERB

She is practically grown up.
almost, nearly, virtually, all but, just about, essentially, fundamentally, to all intents and purposes

practice NOUN

1 *our normal practice*
custom, tradition, convention, usage, habit, routine, way, method, system
2 *choir practice*
rehearsal, run-through, training, drill, exercise
3 *The plan will not work in practice.*
effect, reality, use, application
◆ FORMAL WORDS actuality
⊜ OPPOSITES theory, principle

practise VERB

1 *She is practising the violin.*
rehearse, run through, repeat, drill, exercise, train, study
2 *He wants to practise medicine.*
do, perform, carry out, put into practice, follow, pursue, undertake

praise VERB

The teacher praised John for making an effort.
admire, compliment, flatter, promote, cheer, congratulate, pay tribute to, honour
◇ INFORMAL WORDS rave over
⊜ OPPOSITES criticize

precaution NOUN

safety precautions
safeguard, security, protection, insurance, caution, preparation, provision

precede VERB

Spring precedes summer.
come before, lead, come first, go before
⊜ OPPOSITES follow, succeed

precious ADJECTIVE
1 *Val's cat is very **precious** to her.*
valued, treasured, prized, beloved, dearest, darling, favourite, loved, adored
2 *a **precious** stone*
valuable, expensive, costly, dear, priceless, rare

precise ADJECTIVE
1 *a **precise** answer*
exact, accurate, right, correct, factual
⊞ OPPOSITES imprecise, inexact
2 *He is very **precise** in his work.*
careful, meticulous, scrupulous, fastidious
⊞ OPPOSITES careless

predict VERB
*She claims she can **predict** the future.*
foretell, foresee, forecast, prophesy

predictable ADJECTIVE
*His answer was **predictable**.*
foreseeable, expected, anticipated, likely, probable, imaginable, foreseen, reliable, dependable
⊞ OPPOSITES unpredictable, uncertain

prefer VERB
*I **prefer** sweet to savoury foods.*
favour, like better, would rather, would sooner, desire, choose, select, opt for, go for, fancy
⊞ OPPOSITES reject

preferable ADJECTIVE
*I find basketball **preferable** to football.*
better, superior, nicer
⊞ OPPOSITES inferior

preference NOUN
1 *The black bag would be my **preference**.*
favourite, first choice, choice, pick, selection, wish, desire
2 *I have a **preference** for spicy foods.*
liking, fancy, inclination

pregnant ADJECTIVE
*a **pregnant** woman*
expectant, expecting
◆ FORMAL WORDS with child

prejudice NOUN
*racial **prejudice***
bias, discrimination, unfairness, injustice, intolerance, narrow-mindedness, bigotry, chauvinism
⊞ OPPOSITES fairness, tolerance

prejudiced ADJECTIVE
*He is **prejudiced** against anyone who is different from him.*
biased, discriminatory, unfair, unjust, intolerant, narrow-minded, bigoted, chauvinist
⊞ OPPOSITES impartial, fair, tolerant

premises NOUN
*his business **premises***
building, property, establishment, office, grounds, site, place

prepare VERB
1 *preparing to take over as president*
make ready, adapt, adjust, plan, organize, arrange, pave the way
2 *preparing for the match*
get ready, warm up, train, coach
3 *She is preparing for a piano exam.*
train, study, get ready

prepared ADJECTIVE
1 *prepared for action*
ready, waiting, set, fit, planned, organized, arranged
⊞ OPPOSITES unprepared, unready
2 *I'm not prepared to move house for my job.*
willing, ready, inclined, able
⊞ OPPOSITES unwilling

prescribe VERB
*medicine **prescribed** by a doctor*
direct, specify, require, recommend, propose, advise

presence NOUN
*Your **presence** at school is expected.*

Aa
Bb
Cc
Dd
Ee
Ff
Gg
Hh
Ii
Jj
Kk
Ll
Mm
Nn
Oo
Pp
Qq
Rr
Ss
Tt
Uu
Vv
Ww
Xx
Yy
Zz

attendance, company, occupancy, residence, existence
⊕ OPPOSITES absence

present¹ ADJECTIVE

1 *present at the meeting*
attending, here, there, near, at hand, to hand, available, ready
⊕ OPPOSITES absent
2 *at the present time*
current, contemporary, present-day, immediate, instant, existing
⊕ OPPOSITES past, out-of-date

present² VERB

1 *The mayor presented him with the award.*
award, grant, give, donate, hand over, hold out, offer
2 *The new car will be presented to the public.*
show, display, exhibit, demonstrate
3 *The school is presenting a concert.*
mount, stage, put on
4 *I would like to present Mr and Mrs MacLean.*
introduce, announce

present³ NOUN

a birthday present
gift, offering, donation
◇ INFORMAL WORDS prezzie

presently ADVERB

I will be there presently.
soon, shortly, in a minute, before long, by and by

preserve VERB

We like to preserve our customs.
maintain, sustain, continue, keep, retain, conserve, save, store
⊕ OPPOSITES destroy, ruin

press VERB

1 *Press the key marked 'Esc'.*
push, depress, squeeze, compress, squash, stuff, crush
2 *I pressed my trousers.*
iron, smooth, flatten
3 *She pressed him for an answer.*
urge, force, pressure, pressurize, demand, insist on, harass
4 *The crowd pressed around him.*
crowd, cram, swarm, surge, mill

pressure NOUN

1 *Apply pressure to the wound.*
force, weight, compression, squeezing
2 *the pressures of modern living*
stress, strain, difficulty, problem, demand

prestige NOUN

This name carries a lot of prestige.
status, reputation, standing, stature, distinction, esteem, regard
⊕ OPPOSITES unimportance

presume VERB

I presume this is correct.
assume, take it, think, believe, suppose, take for granted

presumptuous ADJECTIVE

It was presumptuous of him to expect to come with us.
bold, impertinent, impudent, insolent, overfamiliar, forward, pushy, arrogant, over-confident, conceited
⊕ OPPOSITES humble, modest

pretend VERB

1 *She pretended to like her birthday present.*
profess, put on, fake, simulate, act, play-act, go through the motions
2 *Let's pretend our house is a castle.*
imagine, make believe, suppose

pretty¹ ADJECTIVE

a pretty girl
attractive, good-looking, beautiful, lovely, cute, gorgeous, appealing, charming, dainty
⊕ OPPOSITES plain, unattractive, ugly

pretty² ADVERB

That was pretty funny.
fairly, somewhat, rather, quite, reasonably, moderately

prevent VERB

He stood in the doorway to prevent her from leaving.

Aa
Bb
Cc
Dd
Ee
Ff
Gg
Hh
Ii
Jj
Kk
Ll
Mm
Nn
Oo
Pp
Qq
Rr
Ss
Tt
Uu
Vv
Ww
Xx
Yy
Zz

stop, avoid, head off, ward off, stave off, thwart, inhibit, hinder, hamper, impede
⊘ OPPOSITES cause, help, foster, encourage, allow

previous ADJECTIVE
*my **previous** teacher*
preceding, earlier, prior, past, former, ex-, one-time, sometime
⊘ OPPOSITES following, subsequent, later

previously ADVERB
*He was **previously** a firefighter.*
formerly, once, earlier, before, beforehand
⊘ OPPOSITES later

prey NOUN
*The lion leapt on its **prey**.*
quarry, victim, game, kill

prey on VERB
1 *Large animals often **prey on** small animals.*
hunt, kill, devour, feed on, live off
2 *The problem was **preying on** my mind.*
worry, bother, haunt
◇ INFORMAL WORDS bug

price NOUN
*people moaning about the **price** of petrol*
value, worth, cost, expense, fee, charge, toll, rate, bill

priceless ADJECTIVE
*a **priceless** painting*
invaluable, expensive, costly, dear, precious, valuable, irreplaceable
⊘ OPPOSITES cheap

prick VERB
*I felt the needle **prick** my arm.*
pierce, puncture, jab, stab, sting, bite, prickle, itch, tingle

prickly ADJECTIVE
*a **prickly** bush*
thorny, brambly, spiny, spiky, bristly, rough, scratchy
⊘ OPPOSITES smooth

pride NOUN
1 *He has too much **pride** in his own achievements.*
conceit, vanity, bigheadedness, boastfulness, smugness, arrogance, self-importance, snobbery
⊘ OPPOSITES humility, modesty
2 *She was anxious to save her **pride**.*
dignity, self-respect, self-esteem, honour
⊘ OPPOSITES shame
3 *She takes great **pride** in her appearance.*
satisfaction, pleasure, delight

priest NOUN
*The **priest** conducted the service.*
minister, vicar, padre, father, man of God, man of the cloth, clergyman, member of the clergy

prim ADJECTIVE
*She is very **prim** and proper.*
prudish, strait-laced, formal, demure, proper, priggish, prissy, fussy, particular, precise
⊘ OPPOSITES informal, relaxed, easy-going

primary ADJECTIVE
*The girl's father is her **primary** carer.*
chief, principal, main, dominant, leading, foremost, greatest, highest, ultimate
⊘ OPPOSITES secondary, minor

prime ADJECTIVE
1 *prime beef*
best, choice, select, quality, first-class, first-rate, excellent, top, supreme, superior
⊘ OPPOSITES second-rate
2 *my **prime** concern*
chief, principal, main, predominant, primary
⊘ OPPOSITES secondary

primitive ADJECTIVE
1 *primitive cave paintings*
crude, rough, unsophisticated, uncivilized

Aa
Bb
Cc
Dd
Ee
Ff
Gg
Hh
Ii
Jj
Kk
Ll
Mm
Nn
Oo
Pp
Qq
Rr
Ss
Tt
Uu
Vv
Ww
Xx
Yy
Zz

Aa
Bb
Cc
Dd
Ee
Ff
Gg
Hh
Ii
Jj
Kk
Ll
Mm
Nn
Oo
Pp
Qq
Rr
Ss
Tt
Uu
Vv
Ww
Xx
Yy
Zz

⊯ OPPOSITES advanced, sophisticated, civilized
2 *primitive man*
early, elementary, primary, first, original, earliest

principal ADJECTIVE

*the **principal** reason for this decision*
main, chief, essential, primary, first, foremost, leading, dominant, prime
⊯ OPPOSITES minor, lesser, least

principle NOUN

1 *It goes against my **principles** to tell a lie.*
rule, formula, law, truth, code, standard, proposition
2 *a man of **principle***
honour, virtue, decency, morality, morals, ethics, standards, conscience

print NOUN

*The hunter found the lion's **prints**.*
mark, impression, fingerprint, footprint

prior ADJECTIVE

*I have a **prior** engagement.*
earlier, preceding, previous, former
⊯ OPPOSITES later

prison NOUN

*She was sent to **prison** for six months.*
jail, imprisonment, confinement, detention, custody

prisoner NOUN

*the **prisoners** in the jail*
captive, hostage, convict, inmate
◇ INFORMAL WORDS jailbird

private ADJECTIVE

1 *private papers*
secret, classified, confidential, intimate, personal
⊯ OPPOSITES public, open
2 *Let's go somewhere more **private**.*
isolated, secluded, hidden, concealed, secret, intimate
⊯ OPPOSITES public, open

privilege NOUN

*Members get special **privileges**.*
advantage, benefit, entitlement
⊯ OPPOSITES disadvantage

privileged ADJECTIVE

*She comes from a **privileged** background.*
advantaged, favoured, special, honoured, powerful
⊯ OPPOSITES disadvantaged, under-privileged

prize[1] NOUN

*Abbie won first **prize** in the dancing competition.*
reward, trophy, medal, award, winnings, jackpot, honour

prize[2] VERB

*I really **prize** my reading time.*
treasure, value, appreciate, cherish, hold dear
⊯ OPPOSITES despise

probable ADJECTIVE

*the **probable** cause of the accident*
likely, expected, possible
⊯ OPPOSITES improbable, unlikely

probe VERB

*The journalist **probed** the mystery.*
explore, examine, investigate, go into, look into

problem NOUN

1 *a medical problem*
trouble, worry, dilemma, difficulty, complication, snag
2 *a mathematical problem*
question, poser, puzzle, brainteaser, riddle

procedure NOUN

*the correct **procedure** for treating a wound*
routine, process, method, system, technique, practice

proceed VERB

***Proceed** along the corridor to the classroom.*

advance, go ahead, move on, progress, continue, carry on, press on
≠ OPPOSITES stop, retreat

proceeds NOUN
the proceeds from the sale of the house
income, takings, earnings, gain, profit
≠ OPPOSITES expenditure

process[1] NOUN
the printing process
procedure, operation, practice, method, system, technique

process[2] VERB
a factory where food is processed
deal with, handle, treat, prepare, refine, transform, convert, change, alter

procession NOUN
a procession of protesters
march, parade, line

proclaim VERB
Denzel was proclaimed the winner.
announce, declare, pronounce, make known

prod VERB
The child prodded his father in the stomach.
poke, jab, dig, elbow, nudge, push, shove

produce VERB
1 *The company produces electrical goods.*
create, make, manufacture, construct
2 *His speech produced howls of laughter.*
cause, give rise to, provoke, bring about, result in, create
3 *Caitlin has produced a very good story.*
create, invent, construct, compose
4 *He produced a letter from his pocket.*
bring out, show, exhibit, demonstrate, put forward, present, offer, give, supply, provide

production NOUN
1 *the production of oil and gas*
making, manufacture, construction, creation, preparation
2 *an amateur production*
staging, presentation, direction, management

profession NOUN
the medical profession
career, job, occupation, employment, business, line, line of work, trade

professional ADJECTIVE
1 *a professional pilot*
qualified, licensed, trained, experienced, practised, skilled, expert
≠ OPPOSITES amateur
2 *You've done a very professional job.*
skilled, expert, competent, businesslike, efficient
≠ OPPOSITES amateurish, unprofessional

proficient ADJECTIVE
a proficient swimmer
able, capable, skilled, expert, gifted, talented, skilful, competent
≠ OPPOSITES unskilled, incompetent

profit NOUN
The company made a huge profit last year.
gain, return, yield, proceeds, takings, earnings, winnings
≠ OPPOSITES loss

programme NOUN
1 *an exercise programme*
schedule, timetable, plan, scheme, project
2 *a television programme*
broadcast, show, performance, production, presentation

progress[1] NOUN
The school is pleased with the boy's progress.
development, evolution, growth, improvement, advance, headway, step forward
≠ OPPOSITES deterioration

Aa
Bb
Cc
Dd
Ee
Ff
Gg
Hh
Ii
Jj
Kk
Ll
Mm
Nn
Oo
Pp
Qq
Rr
Ss
Tt
Uu
Vv
Ww
Xx
Yy
Zz

Aa
Bb
Cc
Dd
Ee
Ff
Gg
Hh
Ii
Jj
Kk
Ll
Mm
Nn
Oo
Pp
Qq
Rr
Ss
Tt
Uu
Vv
Ww
Xx
Yy
Zz

progress² VERB

*The class has **progressed** from printing to joined-up writing.*
proceed, advance, make progress, make headway, come on, develop, improve
≠ OPPOSITES deteriorate

prohibit VERB

*Smoking is **prohibited** on buses.*
forbid, ban, bar, outlaw, rule out, prevent, stop, restrict
≠ OPPOSITES permit, allow, authorize

project¹ NOUN

*The class is doing a **project** on nature.*
assignment, task, job, work, occupation, activity, plan, scheme, programme

project² VERB

1 *Missiles were **projected** at the cities.*
throw, fling, hurl, launch, propel
2 *Shelves of books **project** from the walls.*
protrude, stick out, bulge, jut out, overhang

prolong VERB

*We do not want to **prolong** their suffering.*
lengthen, extend, stretch, draw out, spin out, drag out
≠ OPPOSITES shorten

prominent ADJECTIVE

1 *Put the poster in a **prominent** place.*
noticeable, conspicuous, obvious, unmistakable, striking, eye-catching
≠ OPPOSITES inconspicuous
2 *a **prominent** writer*
famous, well-known, celebrated, noted, distinguished, respected, leading, important
≠ OPPOSITES unknown, insignificant

promise¹ NOUN

*He made a **promise** to come back next month.*
vow, oath, word of honour, guarantee, assurance, commitment

promise² VERB

*I **promise** to pay you back on Friday.*
vow, swear, take an oath, give your word, guarantee, assure

promising ADJECTIVE

1 *a **promising** future*
bright, favourable, encouraging, hopeful, rosy
≠ OPPOSITES unpromising, discouraging
2 *a **promising** young actor*
bright, talented, gifted, budding, up-and-coming

promote VERB

1 *She was **promoted** to head teacher.*
upgrade, advance, move up, raise
≠ OPPOSITES demote
2 *He is **promoting** his new book.*
advertise, publicize, popularize, market, sell, push
◇ INFORMAL WORDS plug, hype
3 *a fitness instructor who is **promoting** a healthy lifestyle*
push, recommend, advocate, support, back, encourage

prompt¹ ADJECTIVE

1 *a **prompt** reply*
quick, swift, rapid, immediate, instant, instantaneous, speedy, unhesitating
≠ OPPOSITES slow, hesitant
2 *Be **prompt** as we haven't much time.*
punctual, on time, timely, early
≠ OPPOSITES late

prompt² VERB

*His words **prompted** an angry response.*
cause, give rise to, result in, produce, provoke, incite, encourage, inspire, stimulate, motivate
≠ OPPOSITES deter, dissuade

prone ADJECTIVE

*She is **prone** to jealousy.*
likely, given, inclined, apt, liable
≠ OPPOSITES unlikely, immune

pronounce VERB

1 *He **pronounces** his words clearly.*
say, utter, speak, express, voice, sound

2 *The teacher **pronounced** she was satisfied with Muhammad's work.*
declare, announce, proclaim, judge

pronounced ADJECTIVE
*a **pronounced** Liverpudlian accent*
clear, distinct, definite, marked, noticeable, conspicuous, evident, obvious, striking, unmistakable
⊘ OPPOSITES faint, vague

proof NOUN
*There was not enough **proof** to convict the suspect.*
evidence, documentation, demonstration, confirmation

prop¹ NOUN
*a clothes **prop** holding up the washing line*
support, stay, strut

prop² VERB
1 *propping up the wall*
support, sustain, uphold, maintain
2 *She **propped** her bike against the wall.*
lean, rest, stand

propel VERB
*The rocket was **propelled** into the air.*
move, drive, force, thrust, push, shove, launch, shoot, send
⊘ OPPOSITES stop

proper ADJECTIVE
1 *the **proper** way to make tea*
right, correct, accurate, exact, precise, true, genuine, real, actual
⊘ OPPOSITES wrong
2 *proper behaviour*
accepted, correct, suitable, appropriate, fitting, decent, respectable, polite, formal
⊘ OPPOSITES improper, indecent

property NOUN
1 *Look after your **property**.*
belongings, possessions, goods
2 *The rich woman owned a lot of property.*
land, acres, premises, buildings, houses

3 *a **property** of the medicine*
feature, trait, quality, characteristic, peculiarity

prophecy NOUN
*a **prophecy** of good luck*
prediction, forecast

proportion NOUN
1 *A large **proportion** of my diet is vegetarian.*
percentage, fraction, part, division, share, quota, amount
2 *The garage is in **proportion** to the rest of the house.*
balance, relationship, correspondence, ratio

proportions NOUN
*the **proportions** of the room*
dimensions, measurements, size, volume, capacity

propose VERB
1 *I **propose** that we arrange another meeting.*
suggest, recommend, move, advance, introduce, bring up, present, offer
⊘ OPPOSITES withdraw
2 *When do you **propose** to leave?*
intend, mean, aim, plan
3 *I **propose** Jamie as class representative.*
nominate, put up, put forward

prosecute VERB
*Shoplifters will be **prosecuted**.*
accuse, sue, take to court, summon, put on trial, try
⊘ OPPOSITES defend

prospect NOUN
*The **prospects** of winning are small.*
chance, odds, probability, likelihood, possibility, hope, expectation, outlook

prosper VERB
*The family business is **prospering**.*
boom, thrive, flourish, succeed, get on, advance, progress, grow rich
⊘ OPPOSITES fail

Aa
Bb
Cc
Dd
Ee
Ff
Gg
Hh
Ii
Jj
Kk
Ll
Mm
Nn
Oo
Pp
Qq
Rr
Ss
Tt
Uu
Vv
Ww
Xx
Yy
Zz

prosperous ADJECTIVE

*a **prosperous** businessman*
booming, thriving, flourishing, successful, rich, wealthy, well-off, well-to-do
(≠) OPPOSITES poor

protect VERB

*I wear sunglasses to **protect** my eyes.*
safeguard, defend, guard, screen, shield, look after, care for, shelter, preserve, save
(≠) OPPOSITES attack, neglect

protest¹ NOUN

1 *I am writing in **protest** against the planned cuts.*
objection, disapproval, opposition, complaint
(≠) OPPOSITES acceptance
2 *a **protest** against nuclear weapons*
demonstration, march, rally, strike

protest² VERB

*Local people are **protesting** against the new road.*
object, take exception, complain, appeal, demonstrate, oppose, disapprove
(≠) OPPOSITES accept

protrude VERB

*Her teeth **protrude**.*
stick out, poke out, come through, bulge, jut out, project, extend, stand out

proud ADJECTIVE

1 *He is too **proud** to speak to the neighbours.*
conceited, vain, bigheaded, boastful, arrogant, self-important, snobbish
◇ INFORMAL WORDS snooty, toffee-nosed, stuck-up
(≠) OPPOSITES humble, modest
2 *They are very **proud** of their children's achievements.*
satisfied, contented, pleased, delighted, honoured
(≠) OPPOSITES ashamed

prove VERB

*He was determined to **prove** his innocence.*
show, demonstrate, confirm, certify, establish, determine, try, test, examine, analyse
(≠) OPPOSITES disprove, falsify

provide VERB

*The villagers **provided** us with a place to stay.*
supply, stock, equip, prepare for, present, give, contribute, bring

provoke VERB

1 *Sometimes he deliberately **provokes** his father.*
annoy, irritate, offend, insult, anger, enrage, infuriate, madden, tease, taunt
(≠) OPPOSITES please
2 *The good idea **provoked** discussion.*
cause, give rise to, produce, inspire, prompt

prudent ADJECTIVE

*It would be **prudent** to save your money.*
wise, sensible, judicious, shrewd, careful, cautious
(≠) OPPOSITES unwise, careless, rash

pry VERB

*You should not **pry** into other people's business.*
meddle, interfere, poke your nose in, intrude, peer, snoop
(≠) OPPOSITES mind your own business

psychological ADJECTIVE

psychological problems
mental, intellectual, emotional, subconscious, unconscious
(≠) OPPOSITES physical

public¹ NOUN

*open to the **public***
people, population, masses, citizens, society, community, nation, country

public² ADJECTIVE

1 *public buildings*

state, national, civil, community, social, communal, collective, common, general, universal
⊯ OPPOSITES private, personal
2 *public knowledge*
known, well-known, recognized, acknowledged, open, published
⊯ OPPOSITES secret

publication NOUN
1 *a weekly publication*
magazine, newspaper, book, booklet, pamphlet, leaflet
2 *the publication of my next book*
release, printing

publicity NOUN
The band's new album has had lots of publicity.
advertising, promotion, build-up, limelight, splash
◇ INFORMAL WORDS plug, hype

publish VERB
I have written a novel that might be published.
produce, print, issue, bring out, distribute, circulate

puff[1] NOUN
not a puff of wind
breath, waft, whiff, draught, flurry, gust, blast

puff[2] VERB
puffing and blowing
breathe, pant, gasp, gulp, wheeze, blow, waft

pull VERB
1 *The car was pulling a caravan.*
tow, drag, haul, draw, tug, jerk
⊯ OPPOSITES push
2 *He pulled my hair.*
tug, jerk
◇ INFORMAL WORDS yank
3 *The dentist pulled one of my teeth.*
remove, take out, extract, pull out
4 *The circus always pulls the crowds.*
attract, draw, lure
⊯ OPPOSITES discourage
5 *I pulled a muscle in my leg.*

sprain, wrench, strain, injure
• **pull out**
He pulled out of the competition.
retreat, withdraw, leave, depart, quit, move out, desert, abandon
⊯ OPPOSITES join
• **pull through**
She pulled through against all the odds.
recover, rally, survive
• **pull up**
He pulled up by the side of the road.
stop, halt, park, draw up, pull in, pull over, brake

pulse NOUN
The nurse took his pulse.
beat, stroke, rhythm, throb, beating, pounding, drumming

punch VERB
He punched him in the face.
thump, hit, strike, jab, bash, cuff, box
◇ INFORMAL WORDS sock, wallop

punctual ADJECTIVE
Please be punctual as the bus leaves at nine o'clock.
prompt, on time, on the dot, exact, precise, early, in good time
⊯ OPPOSITES unpunctual, late

puncture VERB
A nail punctured my bike's front tyre.
prick, pierce, penetrate, perforate, cut, burst, flatten, deflate

punish VERB
If you break the school rules, you will be punished.
penalize, discipline, correct, scold
⊯ OPPOSITES reward

puny ADJECTIVE
a puny little man
weak, feeble, frail, underdeveloped
⊯ OPPOSITES strong, sturdy

pupil NOUN
Daniel is a model pupil.
student, scholar, schoolboy, schoolgirl, learner, apprentice, beginner
⊯ OPPOSITES teacher

Aa
Bb
Cc
Dd
Ee
Ff
Gg
Hh
Ii
Jj
Kk
Ll
Mm
Nn
Oo
Pp
Qq
Rr
Ss
Tt
Uu
Vv
Ww
Xx
Yy
Zz

purchase VERB

I would like to purchase a bicycle.
buy, pay for, obtain, get
OPPOSITES sell

pure ADJECTIVE

1 *pure gold*
unmixed, solid, natural, real, authentic, genuine, true
OPPOSITES impure
2 *pure water*
clean, clear, sterile, uncontaminated, unpolluted, hygienic, sanitary
OPPOSITES contaminated, polluted, impure
3 *pure nonsense*
sheer, utter, complete, total, thorough, absolute, perfect

purify VERB

Make sure the water you drink has been purified.
refine, filter, clean, cleanse, disinfect, sterilize
OPPOSITES contaminate, pollute

purple NOUN

Here are some shades of purple:

aubergine, lavender, lilac, mauve, mulberry, plum, violet

purpose NOUN

1 *My purpose was to earn enough money to buy a scooter.*
intention, aim, objective, goal, target, plan, vision
2 *What purpose will this gadget serve?*
use, function, application, good, advantage, benefit, value
• on purpose
He bumped into me on purpose.
purposely, deliberately, intentionally, consciously, knowingly
OPPOSITES accidentally

purse NOUN

I've lost my purse.

money-bag, wallet, pouch

pursue VERB

1 *He hopes to pursue a career in medicine.*
perform, engage in, practise, conduct, carry on, continue, keep on, keep up
2 *They were pursued by bears.*
chase, go after, follow, track, trail, shadow, tail, harass, hunt

pursuit NOUN

1 *The police officer was in pursuit of a thief.*
chase, tracking, stalking, trail, hunt
2 *leisure pursuits*
activity, interest, hobby, pastime, occupation

push VERB

1 *I was pushed to the front of the crowd.*
propel, thrust, ram, shove, jostle, elbow
OPPOSITES pull
2 *Push the button for help.*
prod, poke, press, squeeze
OPPOSITES pull
3 *He went on tour to push his new album.*
promote, advertise, publicize, boost
◇ INFORMAL WORDS plug

put VERB

1 *Put your bags over there.*
place, lay, set, stand, position
2 *Don't put all the blame on me.*
apply, inflict, assign
3 *You don't have to put it so bluntly.*
word, phrase, express, state
• put off
1 *The party has been put off till next week.*
delay, postpone, reschedule
2 *I won't be put off by the bad weather.*
deter, discourage, dishearten, dismay, disconcert
OPPOSITES encourage
• put out
Remember to put out the lights.
extinguish, switch off, turn off
OPPOSITES put on

• **put up**

1 *The children have **put up** a tent in the garden.*

erect, build, construct, assemble

2 *We can **put** you **up** for a couple of nights.*

accommodate, house, lodge, shelter

3 *The airlines have **put up** their prices.*

raise, increase

• **put up with**

*I won't **put up with** your insolence.*

stand, bear, stomach, suffer, tolerate, allow, accept, stand for

⊞ OPPOSITES object to, reject

puzzle NOUN

*The identity of the thief was a **puzzle**.*

question, poser, brainteaser, mindbender, riddle, mystery

puzzled ADJECTIVE

*I am **puzzled** as to why they left.*

baffled, mystified, perplexed, at a loss, confused, bewildered

Aa Bb Cc Dd Ee Ff Gg Hh Ii Jj Kk Ll Mm Nn Oo **Pp** Qq Rr Ss Tt Uu Vv Ww Xx Yy Zz

Qq

Aa
Bb
Cc
Dd
Ee
Ff
Gg
Hh
Ii
Jj
Kk
Ll
Mm
Nn
Oo
Pp
Qq
Rr
Ss
Tt
Uu
Vv
Ww
Xx
Yy
Zz

quaint ADJECTIVE
*a village with **quaint** cobbled streets*
picturesque, charming, old-fashioned,
old-world, unusual, curious
[≠] OPPOSITES modern

quake VERB
*The earth **quaked** as the volcano
erupted.*
shake, tremble, shudder, quiver, shiver,
vibrate, wobble, rock, sway

qualifications NOUN
*I didn't have the **qualifications** for the
job.*
certificate, diploma, training, skill,
competence, ability, capability,
aptitude, suitability

qualified ADJECTIVE
*a **qualified** librarian*
certified, chartered, licensed,
professional, trained, experienced,
skilled, expert, knowledgeable
[≠] OPPOSITES unqualified

quality NOUN
1 *She has many good **qualities**.*
property, characteristic, peculiarity,
feature
2 *This material is of poor **quality**.*
standard, grade, class, value, worth,
merit, condition
3 *Your work shows real **quality**.*
excellence, superiority

quantity NOUN
*We ate a large **quantity** of food.*
amount, total, mass, lot, share, portion

quarrel¹ NOUN
*She's had a **quarrel** with her sister.*
row, argument, squabble, tiff,
misunderstanding, disagreement,
dispute, difference, conflict, clash
[≠] OPPOSITES agreement

quarrel² VERB
***quarrelling** over which TV programme
to watch*
row, argue, bicker, squabble, fall out,
disagree, dispute, differ, clash, feud
[≠] OPPOSITES agree

quarters NOUN
*the servants' **quarters***
accommodation, lodgings, residence,
rooms, barracks
◆ FORMAL WORDS dwelling
◇ INFORMAL WORDS digs

queasy ADJECTIVE
*I felt a bit **queasy** in the stuffy room.*
sick, ill, unwell, groggy, sickened,
squeamish, faint, dizzy, giddy

queer ADJECTIVE
*A **queer** thing happened today.*
odd, mysterious, strange, unusual,
uncommon, weird, peculiar, funny,
puzzling, curious
[≠] OPPOSITES ordinary, usual, common

query NOUN
*I had a **query** about what might
happen.*
inquiry, question

quest NOUN
1 *a **quest** for knowledge*
search, hunt, pursuit
2 *the **quests** of explorers in the past*
mission, venture, journey, voyage,
expedition, exploration, adventure

question¹ NOUN
1 *I have a couple of **questions**.*
query, inquiry, poser, problem, difficulty
2 *the **question** of capital punishment*
issue, matter, subject, topic, point,
debate, dispute, controversy

question² VERB
1 *I questioned her about what happened.*
quiz, grill, interrogate, interview, examine, cross-examine, ask
2 *I question his ideas.*
query, challenge, dispute, doubt, disbelieve

queue NOUN
a queue of people waiting
line, file, string, procession, tailback

quick ADJECTIVE
1 *I've had a quick look through the book.*
fast, swift, rapid, speedy, hurried, hasty, brief
⊘ OPPOSITES slow
2 *a quick answer to the question*
prompt, ready, immediate, instant, instantaneous
3 *She's very quick at picking up new skills.*
clever, intelligent, quick-witted, smart, sharp, shrewd
⊘ OPPOSITES unintelligent, dull

quicken VERB
Her pace quickened.
accelerate, speed up, hurry, hasten
⊘ OPPOSITES slow

quiet ADJECTIVE
1 *in a quiet voice*
hushed, soft, low
⊘ OPPOSITES noisy, loud
2 *quiet surroundings*
peaceful, still, calm, undisturbed
3 *a quiet person*
shy, reserved, withdrawn, thoughtful, meek
⊘ OPPOSITES talkative, extrovert

quieten VERB
I tried to quieten the children.
silence, hush, calm

quit VERB
1 *He quit his job.*
leave, depart from, exit, surrender, give up, resign from, retire from, withdraw from
2 *She has quit smoking.*
stop, end, drop, give up
◆ FORMAL WORDS cease
◇ INFORMAL WORDS pack in

quite ADVERB
1 *She is quite clever but not brilliant.*
moderately, rather, somewhat, fairly, relatively
2 *That was quite the worst film I have ever seen.*
utterly, absolutely, totally, completely, entirely, wholly, fully, perfectly, exactly, precisely

quiver VERB
quivering like jelly
shake, tremble, shudder, shiver, quake, quaver, vibrate, wobble

quiz NOUN
a sports quiz
questionnaire, test, examination, competition

quotation NOUN
a quotation from Shakespeare
extract, excerpt, passage, piece
◇ INFORMAL WORDS quote

quote VERB
He can quote dialogue from films.
reproduce, echo, repeat, recite

Aa
Bb
Cc
Dd
Ee
Ff
Gg
Hh
Ii
Jj
Kk
Ll
Mm
Nn
Oo
Pp
Qq
Rr
Ss
Tt
Uu
Vv
Ww
Xx
Yy
Zz

Rr

race¹ VERB

She **raced** to answer the phone.
run, sprint, dash, tear, fly, speed, zoom,
rush, hurry

race² NOUN

a long-distance **race**
competition, contest, scramble

race³ NOUN

men and women of all **races** and
religions
people, nation, tribe, ancestry, line,
blood, stock

racket NOUN

1 Stop that terrible **racket**!
noise, din, uproar, row, fuss,
commotion, disturbance
2 a gambling **racket**
swindle, fraud, deception, scheme,
business, game
◇ INFORMAL WORDS con, fiddle

radiate VERB

1 heat **radiating** from the sun
shine, gleam, glow, beam, spread out,
pour
2 The sun **radiates** light to the earth.
give off, emit, send out, shine, beam,
shed, pour

rage NOUN

He was in a **rage**.
fury, anger, tantrum, temper

ragged ADJECTIVE

ragged clothes
shabby, tatty, frayed, torn, ripped,
tattered, worn-out, threadbare, scruffy

raid¹ NOUN

an air **raid**
attack, invasion, strike, blitz

raid² VERB

1 Bombers **raided** the city.
attack, descend on, invade, storm
2 The rioters **raided** the shops.
loot, pillage, plunder, ransack, rifle

rain¹ NOUN

I was caught in the **rain**.
rainfall, raindrops, drizzle, shower,
cloudburst, downpour, torrent, storm

rain² VERB

It's **raining** heavily.
pour, spit, drizzle, shower, teem, pelt
◇ INFORMAL WORDS bucket

rainbow NOUN

Here are the colours of the rainbow:

red, orange, yellow, green, blue,
indigo, violet

raise VERB

1 He **raised** the blind and looked out of
the window.
lift, elevate, hoist, jack up
⊭ OPPOSITES lower
2 Security levels were **raised** after the
attack.
increase, heighten, strengthen,
intensify, boost
⊭ OPPOSITES decrease, reduce
3 We are trying to **raise** money for
charity.
collect, get, obtain, gather
4 She has **raised** three children on her
own.
bring up, rear, provide for, care for
5 He **raised** the subject of pocket
money.
bring up, introduce, present, put
forward, suggest

Aa
Bb
Cc
Dd
Ee
Ff
Gg
Hh
Ii
Jj
Kk
Ll
Mm
Nn
Oo
Pp
Qq
Rr
Ss
Tt
Uu
Vv
Ww
Xx
Yy
Zz

rally NOUN
an anti-war rally
gathering, assembly, convention, conference, meeting, march, demonstration

ram VERB
1 *He rammed the car in front.*
hit, strike, crash into, smash into, slam into
2 *The boy rammed his hands into his pockets.*
stuff, force, drive, thrust, cram, pack, jam

ramble VERB
1 *We ramble in the hills most weekends.*
walk, hike, trek, tramp, stroll, wander, roam, rove
2 *He rambles on for hours about himself.*
chatter, babble, go on, gabble
◇ INFORMAL WORDS rabbit on, witter on

rampage VERB
A group of teenagers was rampaging about the town centre.
run wild, run amok, run riot, rush, tear

ramshackle ADJECTIVE
a ramshackle old house
rickety, dilapidated, tumbledown, broken-down, crumbling, ruined, derelict
≠ OPPOSITES solid, stable

random ADJECTIVE
1 *a random accident of fate*
chance, casual, incidental, unplanned, accidental, aimless, purposeless
≠ OPPOSITES deliberate
2 *random tests*
unsystematic, irregular, haphazard, unplanned, indiscriminate
≠ OPPOSITES systematic

range[1] NOUN
This sweater comes in a wide range of colours.
variety, assortment, selection, collection, lot, series

range[2] VERB
Swimming classes range from beginners' to advanced.
vary, run, extend, reach

rank NOUN
1 *an army officer of high rank*
level, grade, degree, class, status, standing, position, station
2 *ranks of shelves*
row, line, range, column, file, series

ransack VERB
1 *I ransacked my bag trying to find my keys.*
search, go through, scour, comb, rummage through, rifle
2 *Burglars ransacked the house.*
raid, sack, strip, loot, plunder, pillage

rap VERB
She rapped on the window.
knock, hit, strike, tap, thump

rapid ADJECTIVE
a rapid pace
fast, swift, speedy, quick, prompt, brisk, hurried, hasty
≠ OPPOSITES slow

rare ADJECTIVE
1 *Foxes are rare around these parts.*
uncommon, unusual, scarce, sparse, infrequent
≠ OPPOSITES common, abundant, frequent
2 *She shows rare skill in painting.*
excellent, exquisite, superb, exceptional, remarkable

rarely ADVERB
I very rarely have headaches.
seldom, hardly ever, infrequently, little
≠ OPPOSITES often, frequently

rash ADJECTIVE
Don't make any rash decisions.
reckless, hot-headed, headstrong, impulsive, impetuous, hasty, careless, unthinking
≠ OPPOSITES cautious, wary, careful

Aa
Bb
Cc
Dd
Ee
Ff
Gg
Hh
Ii
Jj
Kk
Ll
Mm
Nn
Oo
Pp
Qq
Rr
Ss
Tt
Uu
Vv
Ww
Xx
Yy
Zz

Aa
Bb
Cc
Dd
Ee
Ff
Gg
Hh
Ii
Jj
Kk
Ll
Mm
Nn
Oo
Pp
Qq
Rr
Ss
Tt
Uu
Vv
Ww
Xx
Yy
Zz

rate¹ NOUN

1 *instruments which measure your heart* **rate**
speed, time, tempo
2 *interest* **rates**
charge, fee, hire, toll, tariff, price, cost, amount, figure

rate² VERB

He is highly **rated** *as a goalkeeper.*
respect, admire, value
◆ FORMAL WORDS esteem

rather ADVERB

1 *It was* **rather** *funny.*
quite, moderately, slightly, a bit, somewhat, fairly, pretty
2 *I would* **rather** *go to the cinema than watch a video.*
preferably, sooner, instead

ration¹ NOUN

our **ration** *of sweets for this week*
allowance, allocation, allotment, share, portion, helping

ration² VERB

During the war, food was scarce and had to be **rationed.**
control, restrict, limit

rattle VERB

1 *There's something* **rattling** *inside the tin.*
clatter, jingle, jangle, clank
2 *The old car* **rattled** *as it went along.*
shake, vibrate, jolt, jar, bounce, bump

rave VERB

He was ranting and **raving** *about the phone bill.*
rage, storm, thunder, roar, rant, babble

raw ADJECTIVE

1 *raw vegetables*
uncooked, fresh
≠ OPPOSITES cooked, done
2 *raw cotton*
unprocessed, unrefined, untreated, crude, natural
≠ OPPOSITES processed, refined

3 *My hands were* **raw** *and bleeding.*
sore, scratched, grazed, scraped, bloody, tender
4 *a* **raw** *December wind*
cold, chilly, bitter, biting, piercing, freezing
≠ OPPOSITES warm

ray NOUN

A **ray** *of light shone through the darkness.*
beam, shaft, flash, gleam, glint, spark

reach¹ VERB

1 *We* **reached** *our destination at midnight.*
arrive at, get to, achieve, make
2 *I couldn't* **reach** *his hand.*
get to, touch, contact, grasp
3 *I* **reached** *for my pen.*
stretch, extend, grasp

reach² NOUN

The book I wanted was just out of my **reach.**
range, scope, extent, stretch, grasp

reaction NOUN

Her **reaction** *to the news was to burst into tears.*
response, reply, answer

read VERB

1 *Read all the questions before you begin.*
study, pore over, scan, skim
2 *The petrol gauge* **read** *zero.*
show, indicate, display, register, record

readily ADVERB

I would **readily** *give a donation to the fund.*
willingly, unhesitatingly, gladly, eagerly, promptly
≠ OPPOSITES unwillingly, reluctantly

ready ADJECTIVE

1 *I'm* **ready** *to go.*
prepared, waiting, set, organized
≠ OPPOSITES unprepared
2 *I'm* **ready** *to help in any way.*
willing, inclined, happy, eager, keen
≠ OPPOSITES unwilling, reluctant

real ADJECTIVE
 1 *real diamonds*
 genuine, authentic, bona fide
 ≠ OPPOSITES imitation, artificial
 2 *Her gratitude was real.*
 sincere, genuine, authentic, true,
 honest, heartfelt
 ≠ OPPOSITES false

realistic ADJECTIVE
 1 *This is not a realistic idea.*
 practical, down-to-earth, commonsense,
 sensible, rational, logical
 ≠ OPPOSITES unrealistic, impractical,
 irrational, idealistic
 2 *a realistic statue*
 lifelike, authentic, natural
 3 *a realistic account of events*
 true, truthful, faithful, genuine, real

reality NOUN
 *She seems unable to separate reality
 from fantasy.*
 truth, fact, realism, existence,
 genuineness

realize VERB
 1 *I realize that this will be difficult.*
 understand, recognize, accept,
 appreciate
 2 *When we realized what was
 happening, we rushed to help.*
 understand, grasp, catch on, recognize

really ADVERB
 1 *I'm really sorry.*
 very, indeed, extremely
 2 *I really think you should apologize.*
 truly, actually, honestly, sincerely,
 genuinely, positively, certainly

realm NOUN
 a peer of the realm
 kingdom, monarchy, principality,
 empire, country, state, land

rear¹ ADJECTIVE
 the rear rows of seats in the hall
 back, hind, hindmost, rearmost, last
 ≠ OPPOSITES front

rear² NOUN
 the rear of the ship
 back, stern, end, tail
 ≠ OPPOSITES front

rear³ VERB
 They have reared three children.
 bring up, raise, foster

reason¹ NOUN
 1 *the reason for his behaviour*
 cause, explanation, excuse, justification,
 defence, motive, grounds, basis
 2 *He has lost his reason.*
 sense, logic, reasoning, sanity, mind,
 intellect, understanding, wisdom,
 judgement

reason² VERB
 1 *I reasoned that I would have to work
 really hard.*
 work out, conclude, deduce, think,
 figure out
 2 *Don't try to reason with her while
 she's in a temper.*
 urge, persuade, move, debate with,
 discuss with

reasonable ADJECTIVE
 1 *That seems like a reasonable idea.*
 sensible, wise, intelligent, rational,
 logical, practical, sound, well-thought-out
 ≠ OPPOSITES irrational
 2 *a reasonable price*
 inexpensive, acceptable, satisfactory,
 moderate, fair, modest
 3 *I'm reasonable at maths but bad at
 French.*
 average, satisfactory, moderate, fair

reassure VERB
 *She is nervous and needs to be
 reassured.*
 encourage, comfort, cheer
 ≠ OPPOSITES alarm

rebel VERB
 1 *The starving peasants rebelled.*
 revolt, mutiny, rise up, run riot
 2 *She rebelled against her parents.*
 disobey, defy, resist

Aa
Bb
Cc
Dd
Ee
Ff
Gg
Hh
Ii
Jj
Kk
Ll
Mm
Nn
Oo
Pp
Qq
Rr
Ss
Tt
Uu
Vv
Ww
Xx
Yy
Zz

Aa
Bb
Cc
Dd
Ee
Ff
Gg
Hh
Ii
Jj
Kk
Ll
Mm
Nn
Oo
Pp
Qq
Rr
Ss
Tt
Uu
Vv
Ww
Xx
Yy
Zz

rebellion NOUN
1 the **rebellion** against the government
revolt, revolution, rising, uprising, mutiny
2 his **rebellion** against his strict upbringing
defiance, resistance, opposition, disobedience

rebound VERB
The ball **rebounded** off the goalpost.
bounce, recoil, return, ricochet

rebuke VERB
He was **rebuked** for biting his nails.
scold, tell off, reprimand, reproach
⊯ OPPOSITES praise, compliment

recede VERB
1 He **receded** into the darkness.
go back, return, retire, withdraw, retreat, sink
⊯ OPPOSITES advance
2 In time, the painful memory **receded**.
lessen, dwindle, decrease, shrink, slacken, subside

receive VERB
1 I **received** your letter today.
get, be sent, obtain, take, pick up, collect
⊯ OPPOSITES send
2 The director **received** the best-film award.
get, be given, accept, obtain, take, pick up, collect
⊯ OPPOSITES give, donate

recent ADJECTIVE
recent developments in medicine
new, latest, current, present-day, contemporary, modern, up-to-date, novel, fresh
⊯ OPPOSITES old, out-of-date

recently ADVERB
I **recently** had my hair cut short.
lately, newly, freshly, not long ago

reception NOUN
The band got a great **reception** from the audience.
response, welcome, treatment, acceptance, greeting, reaction, acknowledgement

recite VERB
He **recited** stories he had been told as a child.
repeat, tell, narrate, relate, speak, perform

reckless ADJECTIVE
reckless driving
careless, heedless, thoughtless, negligent, irresponsible, rash, wild
⊯ OPPOSITES cautious, wary, careful

reckon VERB
1 He is **reckoned** to be a great actor.
consider, regard, rate, judge
2 The house is **reckoned** to be worth half a million pounds.
value, rate, judge, evaluate, assess, estimate, gauge
3 I **reckon** that it will rain.
think, believe, imagine, fancy, suppose, assume, guess
4 I have **reckoned** the cost at £300.
calculate, figure out, work out, add up, total, tally, count, number

recognize VERB
1 I **recognize** you from your photograph.
know, identify, remember, recollect, recall
2 I **recognize** that I may have been wrong.
admit, confess, acknowledge, accept, grant, appreciate, understand, realize

recommend VERB
1 My doctor **recommended** a change in my diet.
advise, urge, suggest, propose, put forward, advance
⊯ OPPOSITES disapprove
2 I strongly **recommend** this film.
put forward, praise, approve, vouch for
◇ INFORMAL WORDS plug
⊯ OPPOSITES disapprove

record[1] NOUN

a record of events
note, register, log, report, account, minutes, entry, document, file

record[2] VERB

Record the dates and times of each visit.
note, enter, write down, register, log, put down, document

recording NOUN

1 *a recording of film themes*
record, disc, CD, cassette, tape
2 *a recording of the interview*
tape, video, DVD

recover VERB

1 *She had pneumonia, but she is recovering now.*
get better, improve, pick up, mend, heal, pull through
◆ FORMAL WORDS convalesce, recuperate
⊞ OPPOSITES worsen
2 *We will try to recover your stolen goods.*
get back, regain, retrieve, repossess, reclaim, restore
⊞ OPPOSITES lose

recovery NOUN

He has made a rapid recovery.
improvement, mending, healing
◆ FORMAL WORDS recuperation, convalescence
⊞ OPPOSITES worsening

recreation NOUN

1 *I like to read for recreation.*
fun, enjoyment, pleasure, amusement, entertainment, leisure, relaxation, play
2 *Among his many recreations, he lists skateboarding and windsurfing.*
hobby, pastime, interest, entertainment, amusement, sport

rectify VERB

1 *She has rectified the mistake.*
correct, put right, right, remedy, fix, amend, adjust
2 *He refuses to rectify his behaviour.*
improve, remedy, correct, mend, amend, adjust, reform

recuperate VERB

She needs time to recuperate after her operation.
recover, get better, improve, pick up, mend
⊞ OPPOSITES worsen

recur VERB

If the problem recurs, go back to the doctor.
return, repeat, persist, reappear, keep happening

recycle VERB

I always recycle carrier bags.
reuse, reprocess, reclaim, salvage, save

red NOUN

Here are some shades of red:

burgundy, cerise, cherry, crimson, maroon, ruby, russet, scarlet, vermilion

reduce VERB

Shops will need to reduce their prices.
lessen, decrease, cut, slash, lower
⊞ OPPOSITES increase, raise

reel VERB

1 *He was reeling about all over the pavement.*
stagger, totter, wobble, sway, stumble, lurch
2 *Her head was reeling after she heard the news.*
spin, wheel, whirl, swirl

refer to VERB

1 *Refer to the dictionary for the meaning of a word.*
look up, consult, turn to, resort to
2 *She referred to him by name.*
mention, touch on, speak of, bring up
◆ FORMAL WORDS allude to
3 *What does this letter refer to?*
concern, apply to, relate to, belong to

Aa
Bb
Cc
Dd
Ee
Ff
Gg
Hh
Ii
Jj
Kk
Ll
Mm
Nn
Oo
Pp
Qq
Rr
Ss
Tt
Uu
Vv
Ww
Xx
Yy
Zz

Aa
Bb
Cc
Dd
Ee
Ff
Gg
Hh
Ii
Jj
Kk
Ll
Mm
Nn
Oo
Pp
Qq
Rr
Ss
Tt
Uu
Vv
Ww
Xx
Yy
Zz

refined ADJECTIVE
*a very **refined** lady*
cultured, civilized, cultivated, polished, sophisticated, gentlemanly, ladylike, well-bred, well-mannered, polite
(≠) OPPOSITES coarse, vulgar, rude

reflect VERB
*She **reflected** on what she had done.*
think, ponder, consider, mull over, deliberate, contemplate, meditate

reform VERB
*He has promised to **reform** his character.*
change, amend, improve, correct, mend

refreshing ADJECTIVE
*a **refreshing** drink*
reviving, cool, invigorating, energizing, stimulating

refuge NOUN
1 *a **refuge** for stray dogs*
shelter, sanctuary
2 *an expedition to a **refuge** on the island*
retreat, hideout, hide-away, resort
3 *There was no **refuge** from the storm.*
shelter, sanctuary, asylum, protection

refund VERB
*Your money will be **refunded** if you have a receipt.*
repay, return, restore
◆ FORMAL WORDS reimburse

refuse VERB
1 *She **refused** his invitation.*
turn down, reject, decline
(≠) OPPOSITES accept
2 *They **refused** him access to the building.*
deny, disallow, withhold
(≠) OPPOSITES allow, permit

regain VERB
1 *He **regained** consciousness after a short time.*
recover, get back, return to
2 *The troops **regained** control of the town.*

get back, recover, reclaim, retake, recapture, retrieve

regard VERB
*I **regard** him to be a musical genius.*
consider, judge, rate, value, think, believe, look upon, view

regarding PREPOSITION
*I am writing to your parents **regarding** your truancy.*
about, with regard to, as regards, concerning, with reference to, as to

region NOUN
*a hilly **region***
area, land, territory, country, province, district, zone, sector, place

register¹ NOUN
*the **register** of births, marriages and deaths*
record, roll, list, index, directory, log, file

register² VERB
*The thermometer **registered** 22 degrees.*
show, display, read, indicate

regret VERB
*I **regret** the chances I have thrown away.*
be sorry about, lament, mourn, grieve for

regular ADJECTIVE
1 *a change from her **regular** routine*
usual, routine, typical, habitual, customary, ordinary, everyday
2 *It's a bit different from a **regular** DVD.*
usual, typical, conventional, standard, ordinary, common, everyday
(≠) OPPOSITES unusual, unconventional
3 *a **regular** pulse*
steady, rhythmic, constant, unvarying, uniform, even
(≠) OPPOSITES irregular

regulate VERB
1 *the group that **regulates** energy prices*

control, direct, guide, govern, manage, run, monitor, organize
2 *Turn this knob to regulate the volume.*
control, set, adjust, tune, moderate, balance

regulation NOUN
You must abide by the regulations.
rule, law, decree, order, commandment, requirement

rehearsal NOUN
a rehearsal for the concert
practice, drill, exercise, preparation

rehearse VERB
rehearsing her part for the school play
practise, drill, train, go over, prepare, try out, repeat

reign VERB
Queen Elizabeth reigns over the United Kingdom.
rule, govern, command

reinforce VERB
The wall has been reinforced with wooden props.
strengthen, fortify, toughen, harden, stiffen, support, prop
⊞ OPPOSITES weaken, undermine

reject VERB
1 *She rejected all offers of help.*
refuse, decline, turn down
⊞ OPPOSITES accept, choose, select
2 *We rejected his idea as being too impractical.*
discard, condemn, exclude, eliminate, scrap
⊞ OPPOSITES accept, choose, select

rejoice VERB
The players are rejoicing after their victory.
celebrate, glory, triumph

relate VERB
1 *Police say the two incidents are not related.*
link, connect, join, associate

2 *a letter relating to the school trip*
concern, refer, apply
3 *a book relating their adventures*
tell, narrate, report, describe

relation NOUN
This event has no relation to what happened yesterday.
link, connection, relationship

relations NOUN
1 *all our friends and relations*
relatives, family
2 *We would like to establish friendly relations with our new neighbours.*
connections, relationship, terms, dealings, communications, contact, associations

relationship NOUN
1 *the relationship between the friends*
connection, bond, link, association
2 *the relationship between increasing pollution and the rise in asthma*
connection, link, association, parallel

relative NOUN
a close relative
relation, family member

relax VERB
1 *I like to relax at the weekend by going bowling.*
rest, unwind, calm down
2 *A massage will help to relax your shoulder muscles.*
loosen, slacken, soften, ease, rest
⊞ OPPOSITES tighten

relaxed ADJECTIVE
1 *a relaxed atmosphere*
informal, casual, comfortable, easy-going, unhurried, leisurely
◇ INFORMAL WORDS laid-back
⊞ OPPOSITES tense
2 *a relaxed attitude*
easy-going, informal, casual, cool, calm
◇ INFORMAL WORDS laid-back
⊞ OPPOSITES tense

release VERB
1 *He is due to be released from prison.*

Aa Bb Cc Dd Ee Ff Gg Hh Ii Jj Kk Ll Mm Nn Oo Pp Qq Rr Ss Tt Uu Vv Ww Xx Yy Zz

free, set free, liberate, deliver, discharge
≠ OPPOSITES imprison
2 *She released the dog from its lead.*
loose, unloose, unleash, unfasten, free
3 *The band's new album will be released next week.*
launch, issue, publish, circulate, distribute

relent VERB
My parents relented and said I could go to the concert.
give in, give way, yield, soften, weaken

relevant ADJECTIVE
all the relevant documents
significant, related, applicable, apt, appropriate, suitable, fitting, proper
≠ OPPOSITES irrelevant, inapplicable, inappropriate, unsuitable

reliable ADJECTIVE
1 *She's always been a reliable friend.*
dependable, responsible, trustworthy, honest, faithful, true
≠ OPPOSITES unreliable, untrustworthy
2 *reliable information*
certain, sure, dependable, true
≠ OPPOSITES unreliable, doubtful

relief NOUN
1 *It was such a relief to know he was there.*
comfort, reassurance, consolation
2 *bringing relief to the victims of the earthquake*
help, aid, assistance, support

relieve VERB
1 *She took a painkiller to relieve her headache.*
ease, soothe, cure, lighten, soften
≠ OPPOSITES intensify
2 *He was relieved of his duties.*
free, release

religion NOUN
people of different religions
faith, belief, creed, denomination

🖐

Here are the names of some religions:
Baha'i, Buddhism, Christianity, Hinduism, Islam, Jainism, Judaism, paganism, Rastafari, Sikhism, Taoism, Zoroastrianism

religious ADJECTIVE
1 *religious writings*
spiritual, sacred, holy, divine, devotional, scriptural, theological
≠ OPPOSITES secular
2 *a religious person*
devout, godly, God-fearing, church-going
≠ OPPOSITES ungodly

relish VERB
I relished every mouthful of the curry.
enjoy, like, appreciate

reluctant ADJECTIVE
He was reluctant to help with the washing up.
unwilling, hesitant, slow, unenthusiastic, grudging
≠ OPPOSITES willing, ready, eager

rely on VERB
1 *I can always rely on you to tell me the truth.*
depend, count, bank, reckon, trust
2 *I rely on him for good advice.*
depend, lean

remain VERB
1 *Sunita and Megan remained after school.*
stay, linger, wait
≠ OPPOSITES go, leave, depart
2 *The problem of lack of funds remains.*
continue, stay, persist

remainder NOUN
the remainder of the holidays
rest, balance, remains

remains NOUN
the remains of the picnic

remnants, rest, remainder, leavings, leftovers, scraps, crumbs, debris

remark¹ NOUN

Do you have any remarks to add before we finish?
comment, opinion, reflection, statement, declaration

remark² VERB

I remarked that we had met before.
comment, observe, note, mention, say, state, declare

remarkable ADJECTIVE

1 *She showed remarkable courage.*
extraordinary, striking, impressive, noteworthy, amazing, exceptional, outstanding, notable
⊯ OPPOSITES average, ordinary, commonplace, usual
2 *Something remarkable has just happened.*
extraordinary, surprising, amazing, strange, odd, unusual, uncommon
⊯ OPPOSITES average, ordinary, commonplace, usual

remedy NOUN

a remedy for stomachache
cure, antidote, medicine, treatment, therapy, relief

remember VERB

1 *I can't remember his name.*
recall, recollect, recognize, place
⊯ OPPOSITES forget
2 *We spent the evening remembering our school days.*
recall, recollect, summon up, think back to
⊯ OPPOSITES forget
3 *She is trying to remember her lines for the play.*
memorize, learn, retain

remind VERB

1 *If I forget to post this letter, remind me.*
prompt, nudge, jog your memory, refresh your memory
2 *This reminds me of my childhood.*
bring to mind, call to mind

reminder NOUN

a reminder to phone Joel
prompt, prompting, nudge

remnant NOUN

the remnants of the meal
remainder, scrap, piece, bit, fragment, leftover, residue, trace

remorse NOUN

He showed no remorse for his crimes.
regret, shame, guilt, guilty conscience, sorrow

remote ADJECTIVE

a remote island
distant, far, faraway, far-off, out-of-the-way, isolated, lonely
⊯ OPPOSITES close, nearby

remove VERB

1 *She is having a tooth removed.*
pull out, extract, take away
2 *Remove the label from the package.*
take off, detach, cut off
3 *He removed his hat.*
take off, strip, shed
4 *His name was removed from the list.*
delete, erase, strike out, get rid of, eliminate
5 *revolutionaries trying to remove the dictator*
dismiss, discharge, throw out, oust, depose, get rid of

render VERB

The bomb squad rendered the device harmless.
make, cause to be, leave

renovate VERB

The old hall has been renovated.
restore, renew, repair, overhaul, modernize, refurbish, refit
◇ INFORMAL WORDS do up

renowned ADJECTIVE

a renowned scientist
famous, well-known, celebrated, famed, noted, distinguished, notable
⊯ OPPOSITES unknown, obscure

Aa
Bb
Cc
Dd
Ee
Ff
Gg
Hh
Ii
Jj
Kk
Ll
Mm
Nn
Oo
Pp
Qq
Rr
Ss
Tt
Uu
Vv
Ww
Xx
Yy
Zz

Aa
Bb
Cc
Dd
Ee
Ff
Gg
Hh
Ii
Jj
Kk
Ll
Mm
Nn
Oo
Pp
Qq
Rr
Ss
Tt
Uu
Vv
Ww
Xx
Yy
Zz

rent VERB

*We **rented** a car when we were on holiday.*
hire, lease, charter

repair VERB

*We need to **repair** the roof.*
mend, fix, patch up, restore, renovate, renew

repay VERB

1 *We still have to **repay** our loan from the bank.*
pay back, refund, settle, square
2 *I can never **repay** you for all your help.*
pay back, compensate, reward

repeat VERB

1 *I will **repeat** what I said, but more slowly this time.*
say again, restate, echo
◆ FORMAL WORDS reiterate
2 *She **repeated** the poem in front of the class.*
recite, quote, relate
3 *I would not like to **repeat** that experience.*
reproduce, duplicate, redo

repeatedly ADVERB

*I have asked you **repeatedly** not to use my pen.*
again and again, time after time, time and time again, over and over, frequently, often

repel VERB

1 *The boys managed to **repel** their attackers.*
drive back, hold off, ward off, resist, fight off
2 *That smell **repels** me.*
disgust, revolt, nauseate, sicken, offend
⊘ OPPOSITES attract, delight

replace VERB

1 ***Replace** the lid when you have used the jam.*
put back, return
2 *A new head teacher will **replace** Mrs Jones when she retires.*
take the place of, succeed, follow
3 *A supply teacher will **replace** your usual one for a few days.*
take the place of, deputize for, substitute for

replica NOUN

*a **replica** of the Mona Lisa*
copy, model, imitation, reproduction, duplicate, clone

reply[1] NOUN

*His only **reply** was a laugh.*
answer, response, retort, reaction, comeback

reply[2] VERB

*He **replied** angrily to my question.*
answer, respond, retort, react

report[1] NOUN

1 *a **report** on the party conference*
article, piece, write-up, record, account, description, story
2 *He issued a brief **report** to the press.*
statement, declaration, announcement, communication, message
3 *There has been no further **report** on the accident.*
news, announcement, communication, information, word, message

report[2] VERB

1 *journalists who **reported** the story*
communicate, publish, circulate, recount, relate, cover, document, record
2 *You must **report** the incident to the police.*
announce, declare, communicate, notify, tell, state

reporter NOUN

*a sports **reporter***
journalist, correspondent, columnist, newspaperman, newspaperwoman, hack, commentator

represent VERB

1 *This sign **represents** a school crossing.*

stand for, symbolize, denote, mean, express
◆ FORMAL WORDS **designate**
2 *Time is represented as an old man with a beard.*
symbolize, depict, portray, picture, draw, illustrate, personify, show
3 *the lawyer who represented me in court*
appear for, act for, speak for
4 *This represents a serious threat to our plans.*
be, amount to
◇ INFORMAL WORDS **constitute**

reprimand NOUN
a severe reprimand
reproach, lecture
◇ INFORMAL WORDS **telling-off, ticking-off, talking-to, dressing-down**

reproduce VERB
He is always trying to reproduce his brother's achievements.
copy, duplicate, repeat, imitate, match, recreate

reproduction NOUN
a reproduction of the painting
copy, print, duplicate, replica, imitation
⇥ OPPOSITES **original**

reptile NOUN

Here are some types of reptile:
Snakes:
adder, anaconda, asp, boa constrictor, cobra, grass snake, king cobra, mamba, puff adder, python, rattlesnake, sidewinder, tree snake, viper
Lizards:
chameleon, frilled lizard, gecko, iguana, lizard, monitor lizard, skink, slow-worm
Turtles:
giant tortoise, green turtle, snapping turtle, terrapin, tortoise

Other reptiles:
alligator, crocodile

reputation NOUN
1 *He has a reputation for being ruthless.*
name, fame, celebrity, distinction
2 *The scandal ruined his reputation.*
good name, honour, character, name

request¹ NOUN
1 *a request for help*
appeal, call, demand, plea, application
2 *Do you have any special requests?*
wish, want, requirement, demand, desire

request² VERB
They requested our assistance.
ask for, demand, require, seek, desire, beg, appeal for

rescue VERB
1 *She was rescued from captivity.*
save, deliver, free, liberate, release
2 *I managed to rescue the file I deleted.*
save, recover, salvage

resemblance NOUN
a strong resemblance between the two brothers
likeness, similarity, sameness, closeness, parallel, correspondence

resemble VERB
Philip closely resembles his father.
be like, look like, take after, mirror, echo, duplicate, parallel
⇥ OPPOSITES **differ from**

resent VERB
I resent having to bring him along with us.
grudge, begrudge, take offence at, take amiss, object to, take exception to, dislike
⇥ OPPOSITES **accept, like**

Aa
Bb
Cc
Dd
Ee
Ff
Gg
Hh
Ii
Jj
Kk
Ll
Mm
Nn
Oo
Pp
Qq
Rr
Ss
Tt
Uu
Vv
Ww
Xx
Yy
Zz

Aa
Bb
Cc
Dd
Ee
Ff
Gg
Hh
Ii
Jj
Kk
Ll
Mm
Nn
Oo
Pp
Qq
Rr
Ss
Tt
Uu
Vv
Ww
Xx
Yy
Zz

resentful ADJECTIVE
He was resentful about being left out of the team.
bitter, grudging, embittered, hurt, wounded, offended, aggrieved, put out, angry
◇ INFORMAL WORDS miffed, peeved
≠ OPPOSITES satisfied, contented

reservation NOUN
1 *I have some reservations about this plan.*
doubt, misgiving, qualm, hesitation, second thought
2 *Native Americans living on a reservation*
reserve, preserve, park, sanctuary, homeland

reserve¹ VERB
We have reserved a table in the restaurant.
book, order, secure

reserve² NOUN
1 *a nature reserve*
park, reservation, preserve, sanctuary
2 *He's the second reserve for the match today.*
substitute, replacement, stand-in

reserved ADJECTIVE
She's very quiet and reserved.
shy, retiring, silent, standoffish, unapproachable, restrained, uncommunicative
≠ OPPOSITES friendly, open

residence NOUN
the Ashmores' residence
home, place, house, lodgings, quarters
◆ FORMAL WORDS dwelling

resident NOUN
1 *residents of the city*
inhabitant, citizen, local, householder, occupier
≠ OPPOSITES non-resident
2 *hotel residents*
tenant, lodger, guest
≠ OPPOSITES non-resident

resign VERB
He resigned as captain of the cricket club.
quit, stand down, leave, abdicate
≠ OPPOSITES join
• resign yourself
I had resigned myself to waiting in a queue for tickets.
accept, reconcile yourself, bow, submit, yield
≠ OPPOSITES resist

resist VERB
1 *I can't resist chocolate.*
refuse, avoid, say no to
≠ OPPOSITES accept
2 *They resisted all the changes the government tried to introduce.*
oppose, defy, fight, combat

resolve VERB
1 *I resolved to work harder this term.*
decide, make up your mind, determine
2 *This is a problem that can easily be resolved.*
sort out, fix, settle, conclude, work out, solve

resources NOUN
1 *The school doesn't have the resources to buy a minibus.*
funds, money, wealth, riches, capital, assets, property, means
2 *the country's natural resources*
materials, supplies, reserves

respect¹ NOUN
1 *We should treat elderly people with respect.*
honour, politeness, courtesy
≠ OPPOSITES disrespect
2 *She had earned the respect of everyone who knew her.*
admiration, esteem, appreciation
≠ OPPOSITES disrespect
3 *Your drawing is better than Richard's in every respect.*
way, point, aspect, feature, characteristic, particular, detail, sense

respect[2] VERB

1 *I really respect her as a person.*
admire, appreciate, value
≠ OPPOSITES despise, scorn
2 *You must respect the school rules.*
obey, observe, heed, follow, honour
≠ OPPOSITES ignore, disobey

respectable ADJECTIVE

1 *She comes from a respectable family.*
honourable, worthy, respected, upright,
honest, decent
≠ OPPOSITES dishonourable,
disreputable
2 *I got a respectable score in the quiz.*
acceptable, passable, adequate, fair,
reasonable, considerable
≠ OPPOSITES inadequate

respond VERB

He didn't respond when I spoke to him.
answer, reply, retort, react

response NOUN

*Her response to my question was to
shrug her shoulders.*
answer, reply, retort, comeback,
reaction
≠ OPPOSITES query

responsibility NOUN

*Looking after the hamster is your
responsibility.*
duty, obligation, task

responsible ADJECTIVE

1 *Are you responsible for this mess?*
to blame, guilty, at fault, accountable
2 *Children must be accompanied by a
responsible adult.*
dependable, reliable, trustworthy,
steady, sensible
≠ OPPOSITES irresponsible, unreliable,
untrustworthy

rest[1] VERB

1 *Rest for a moment before you
continue.*
stop, pause, halt
♦ FORMAL WORDS cease
≠ OPPOSITES continue

2 *She was resting on the sofa.*
relax, sit, lounge, laze, lie down
≠ OPPOSITES work
3 *He rested his guitar against the wall.*
put, place, lean, prop, support, stand

rest[2] NOUN

1 *Try to get some rest.*
leisure, relaxation, lie-down
≠ OPPOSITES action, activity
2 *I need a rest from tidying my room.*
break, pause, interval
◇ INFORMAL WORDS breather
≠ OPPOSITES work
3 *an arm rest*
support, prop, stand, base

rest[3] NOUN

Take what you want and leave the rest.
remainder, others, leftovers, remnants

restless ADJECTIVE

1 *You've been restless all day – what's
the matter?*
jumpy, unsettled, fidgety, agitated,
nervous, anxious, fretful, edgy
≠ OPPOSITES calm, relaxed, comfortable
2 *She had a very restless night.*
unsettled, disturbed, troubled, sleepless
≠ OPPOSITES comfortable

restore VERB

1 *Order has been restored after last
night's riots.*
return, reinstate, re-establish, reintroduce
≠ OPPOSITES remove
2 *The old church has been restored.*
repair, renovate, rebuild, reconstruct,
refurbish, mend, fix
≠ OPPOSITES damage

restrain VERB

1 *You should restrain that dog on a
leash.*
hold back, keep back, check, curb,
control
≠ OPPOSITES release
2 *I tried to restrain my anger.*
control, suppress, subdue, check, curb,
stop, prevent
≠ OPPOSITES release

Aa
Bb
Cc
Dd
Ee
Ff
Gg
Hh
Ii
Jj
Kk
Ll
Mm
Nn
Oo
Pp
Qq
Rr
Ss
Tt
Uu
Vv
Ww
Xx
Yy
Zz

Aa
Bb
Cc
Dd
Ee
Ff
Gg
Hh
Ii
Jj
Kk
Ll
Mm
Nn
Oo
Pp
Qq
Rr
Ss
Tt
Uu
Vv
Ww
Xx
Yy
Zz

restrict VERB

We have had to restrict the number of guests.
limit, bound, control, regulate
≠ OPPOSITES broaden

result[1] NOUN

He walks with a limp as a result of a road accident.
consequence, effect, reaction, outcome, product
≠ OPPOSITES cause

result[2] VERB

1 *Blood poisoning resulted from an infected cut.*
follow, happen, occur, arise, spring, derive, stem, develop
≠ OPPOSITES cause
2 *Michael's hard work resulted in success.*
end, finish, terminate, culminate

resume VERB

We will resume classes after lunch.
continue, restart, reopen, carry on with, go on with, proceed with

retain VERB

Retain a copy of the form for your files.
keep, hold, reserve, hold back, save
≠ OPPOSITES release

retire VERB

My father is not old enough to retire.
give up work, stop working
≠ OPPOSITES start working

retreat VERB

1 *He retreated from the room before anyone noticed him.*
withdraw, draw back, retire, leave, depart, quit
≠ OPPOSITES advance
2 *Most animals retreat from fire.*
withdraw, draw back, recoil, shrink
≠ OPPOSITES advance

retrieve VERB

1 *I retrieved my book from where I had left it.*
fetch, bring back, get back, recover
≠ OPPOSITES lose
2 *an attempt to retrieve all he had lost*
regain, get back, recapture, recoup, recover, salvage, redeem, restore
≠ OPPOSITES lose

return VERB

1 *We return home on Friday.*
come back, go back
≠ OPPOSITES leave, depart
2 *We had to return the way we had come.*
go back, backtrack
3 *She refuses to return his letters.*
give back, hand back, send back, deliver, put back, replace, restore
≠ OPPOSITES take

reveal VERB

1 *She took off her hat to reveal her red hair.*
show, expose, uncover, display, exhibit
≠ OPPOSITES hide, conceal, mask
2 *He was revealed as a fraud.*
expose, uncover, unveil, unmask
3 *Nina refused to reveal the whereabouts of her father.*
tell, disclose, give away, betray, leak, communicate, announce, proclaim

revenge NOUN

I want revenge for the trick he played on me.
retaliation, vengeance, satisfaction, reprisal, retribution

revere VERB

a leader who is revered by his people
respect, honour, pay homage to, worship, adore
≠ OPPOSITES despise, scorn

reverse[1] VERB

1 *She reversed into the parking space.*
go backwards, back, drive backwards
≠ OPPOSITES advance
2 *A mirror reverses the image.*
transpose, turn round, invert
3 *They have refused to reverse their decision.*
change, overturn, alter

reverse² NOUN

He says one thing and does the reverse.
opposite, contrary

review¹ VERB

Let's review the situation after the holidays.
reconsider, re-evaluate, re-examine, rethink, reassess

review² NOUN

1 *a review of the safety regulations*
examination, analysis, study, survey, reassessment, re-evaluation, re-examination
2 *The film has had excellent reviews.*
report, criticism, assessment, evaluation
◇ INFORMAL WORDS write-up

revise VERB

1 *You will have to revise your work to improve it.*
change, alter, modify, amend, correct
2 *I soon began to revise my first impression of her.*
change, alter, reconsider, re-examine, review

revive VERB

1 *The woman who fainted revived quickly.*
come round, recover, awaken, reawaken
2 *A cold drink will revive you after your long walk.*
refresh, revitalize, restore, invigorate
⊘ OPPOSITES weary

revolt VERB

1 *a group revolting against the government*
rebel, mutiny, rise, riot, resist
⊘ OPPOSITES submit
2 *The violence of the film revolted me.*
disgust, sicken, nauseate, repel, offend, shock
⊘ OPPOSITES please, delight

revolting ADJECTIVE

1 *a revolting smell*
disgusting, sickening, nauseating,

repulsive, obnoxious, horrible, distasteful, offensive
⊘ OPPOSITES pleasant, delightful, attractive
2 *a revolting little boy*
disgusting, repulsive, obnoxious, nasty, horrible, appalling, offensive
⊘ OPPOSITES pleasant, delightful, attractive

revolution NOUN

1 *the French Revolution*
revolt, rebellion, mutiny, rising, uprising
2 *Allow the engine to go through several revolutions.*
rotation, turn, spin, cycle, circuit, round, circle

revolutionary ADJECTIVE

revolutionary ideas
new, innovative, different, drastic, radical

revolve VERB

The Earth revolves round the sun.
rotate, turn, pivot, swivel, spin, wheel, whirl, circle

reward¹ NOUN

1 *We are offering a reward for finding our missing cat.*
payment, bonus
⊘ OPPOSITES punishment
2 *his well-earned reward for valour in battle*
decoration, prize, honour, medal
⊘ OPPOSITES punishment

reward² VERB

1 *She was rewarded for handing in the purse she had found.*
pay, repay
◆ FORMAL WORDS recompense
⊘ OPPOSITES punish
2 *The policeman was rewarded for his bravery in saving the child.*
decorate, honour

rewarding ADJECTIVE

a long and rewarding career
satisfying, profitable, worthwhile,

Aa
Bb
Cc
Dd
Ee
Ff
Gg
Hh
Ii
Jj
Kk
Ll
Mm
Nn
Oo
Pp
Qq
Rr
Ss
Tt
Uu
Vv
Ww
Xx
Yy
Zz

valuable, advantageous, beneficial, fulfilling
⊘ OPPOSITES unrewarding, unsatisfying

rhyme NOUN
He recited a short rhyme.
verse, poem, ode, limerick

rhythm NOUN
dancing to the rhythm of the music
beat, pulse, time, tempo, lilt, swing

rich ADJECTIVE
1 *a rich family*
wealthy, moneyed, well-to-do, well-off
◇ INFORMAL WORDS loaded, minted
⊘ OPPOSITES poor
2 *rich decorations*
splendid, lavish, sumptuous, luxurious, gorgeous, fine, ornate
⊘ OPPOSITES plain

riches NOUN
All her riches couldn't buy her happiness.
wealth, money, fortune, assets, property, resources
⊘ OPPOSITES poverty

rickety ADJECTIVE
a rickety old bridge
shaky, unsteady, wobbly, unstable, insecure, ramshackle
⊘ OPPOSITES stable, strong

rid VERB
We want to rid the school of bullies.
free, clear, purge, relieve
• **get rid of**
I finally got rid of all my baby toys.
dispose of, remove, do away with, dispense with
◇ INFORMAL WORDS dump

riddle NOUN
Can you solve this riddle?
puzzle, poser, problem, brain-teaser

ridicule VERB
The other children ridiculed her for her accent.
make fun of, mock, jeer, tease, rib, taunt
◇ INFORMAL WORDS send up
⊘ OPPOSITES praise

ridiculous ADJECTIVE
1 *That's a ridiculous idea.*
absurd, nonsensical, silly, foolish, stupid, laughable, outrageous, preposterous
⊘ OPPOSITES sensible
2 *the ridiculous antics of the clowns*
comical, absurd, funny, hilarious

right[1] ADJECTIVE
1 *the right answer*
correct, accurate, exact, precise, true, actual, real
⊘ OPPOSITES wrong, incorrect
2 *the right way to behave*
proper, becoming, appropriate, suitable, fit, desirable
⊘ OPPOSITES improper, unsuitable
3 *We must do what is right.*
fair, just, lawful, good, virtuous, moral, ethical, honourable
⊘ OPPOSITES unfair, wrong

right[2] NOUN
I know my rights as a human being.
privilege, due, claim, power, entitlement

rightful ADJECTIVE
1 *The stolen car has now been returned to its rightful owner.*
lawful, legal, legitimate, true, real, valid, proper, authorized
⊘ OPPOSITES wrongful, unlawful
2 *a rightful judgement*
just, lawful, correct, proper, suitable, due
⊘ OPPOSITES wrongful

rigid ADJECTIVE
1 *a rigid board*
stiff, inflexible, unbending, hard, firm, fixed
⊘ OPPOSITES flexible, elastic
2 *a rigid rule*
strict, fixed, set, firm, invariable, unalterable, inflexible
⊘ OPPOSITES changeable, variable, flexible

Aa
Bb
Cc
Dd
Ee
Ff
Gg
Hh
Ii
Jj
Kk
Ll
Mm
Nn
Oo
Pp
Qq
Rr
Ss
Tt
Uu
Vv
Ww
Xx
Yy
Zz

3 *My father was **rigid** when it came to religion.*
inflexible, unbending, harsh, severe, unrelenting, strict, stern, uncompromising
⊘ OPPOSITES flexible

rim NOUN
*the **rim** of the glass*
edge, lip, brim, brink
⊘ OPPOSITES centre, middle

ring¹ NOUN
1 *The glass left a **ring** on the table.*
circle, round, loop, hoop
2 *a gold **ring***
band, hoop, circle

ring² VERB
*The building was **ringed** by armed police officers.*
surround, encircle, enclose

ring³ VERB
1 *The cathedral bells **rang**.*
chime, peal, toll, clang, sound
2 *I'll **ring** you tomorrow.*
telephone, phone, call, ring up

rinse VERB
*I **rinsed** my mug under the tap.*
wash, swill, bathe, clean, cleanse, dip

riot¹ NOUN
*There have been **riots** in the streets.*
disturbance, rising, uprising, disorder, confusion, commotion, revolt, rebellion
⊘ OPPOSITES order, calm

riot² VERB
*People have been **rioting** in protest.*
run wild, rise up, run riot, rampage, revolt, rebel

rip VERB
*I **ripped** the box open with a pair of scissors.*
tear, split, cut, slit, slash, hack

ripe ADJECTIVE
*a **ripe** banana*
ripened, mature, grown, developed

ripen VERB
*Don't eat the plums before they have **ripened**.*
mature, develop, age

rise VERB
1 *The sun had **risen** above the horizon.*
go up, ascend, climb, mount, soar
⊘ OPPOSITES descend
2 *The temperature is **rising** again.*
increase, go up, soar, escalate, intensify, grow
⊘ OPPOSITES fall
3 *We were told to **rise** when the head teacher came into the room.*
stand up, get up, arise, jump up, spring up
⊘ OPPOSITES sit down

risk NOUN
1 *putting your children at **risk***
danger, peril, jeopardy, hazard
⊘ OPPOSITES safety
2 *There's a **risk** of rain in the afternoon.*
chance, possibility, likelihood

risky ADJECTIVE
*It's a **risky** business.*
dangerous, unsafe, hazardous, chancy, uncertain, touch-and-go, tricky
◇ INFORMAL WORDS dicey
⊘ OPPOSITES safe

ritual NOUN
1 *a religious **ritual***
ceremony, practice, formality, solemnity, rite, service
2 *the family **ritual** of Sunday lunch*
custom, practice, habit, routine, tradition, procedure, convention

rival¹ NOUN
*a sporting **rival***
opponent, competitor, contender, challenger, adversary
⊘ OPPOSITES colleague, associate

rival² VERB
*Her singing voice cannot **rival** yours.*
compete with, contend with, match, equal

Aa
Bb
Cc
Dd
Ee
Ff
Gg
Hh
Ii
Jj
Kk
Ll
Mm
Nn
Oo
Pp
Qq
Rr
Ss
Tt
Uu
Vv
Ww
Xx
Yy
Zz

rivalry NOUN

*There is a friendly **rivalry** between the two musicians.*
competition, competitiveness, contest, conflict, struggle, opposition
⊯ OPPOSITES co-operation

river NOUN

*fishing in the **river***
waterway, watercourse, tributary, stream

roam VERB

roaming around the countryside
wander, rove, range, walk, ramble, stroll, stray
⊯ OPPOSITES stay

roar VERB

*He was **roaring** at the children.*
shout, bellow, yell, bawl, howl, thunder
⊯ OPPOSITES whisper

rob VERB

*They **robbed** a bank.*
steal from, hold up, raid, burgle, loot, pillage, plunder, ransack

robust ADJECTIVE

robust mountaineers
strong, sturdy, tough, hardy
⊯ OPPOSITES weak, feeble

rock¹ NOUN

*a sculpture carved out of a **rock***
stone, boulder, pebble

Here are some types of rock:

chalk, coal, flint, granite, limestone, marble, obsidian, pumice, quartz, sandstone, slate

rock² VERB

*The boat **rocked** from side to side.*
sway, swing, wobble, roll, pitch, toss, lurch

rod NOUN

*an iron **rod***
stick, bar, shaft, pole, baton, wand, cane

rogue NOUN

1 *He was a bit of a **rogue** when he was young.*
scamp, scoundrel, rascal
2 *heartless **rogues** who prey on pensioners*
villain, swindler, fraud, cheat
◇ INFORMAL WORDS crook, con man

role NOUN

1 *the lead **role** in a new film*
part, character, representation, portrayal
2 *I was landed with the **role** of peacemaker.*
job, part, function, task, duty, post, position

roll VERB

1 *The ball **rolled** down the hill.*
rotate, revolve, turn, spin, wheel, twirl, whirl
2 *I **rolled** the wool up into a ball.*
wind, coil, twist, curl, wrap
3 *The ship **rolled** in the choppy seas.*
toss, rock, sway, pitch, lurch

romance NOUN

1 *her latest **romance***
love affair, affair, relationship
2 *the **romance** of living on a tropical island*
excitement, adventure, mystery, charm, fascination, glamour

romantic ADJECTIVE

1 *some **romantic** idea about living in the Scottish Highlands*
fanciful, fairy-tale, idealistic, starry-eyed, dreamy, unrealistic, impractical, wild
⊯ OPPOSITES real, practical
2 *a **romantic** scene in the film*
sentimental, loving, passionate, tender
◇ INFORMAL WORDS lovey-dovey, soppy, sloppy, mushy
⊯ OPPOSITES unromantic, unsentimental

Aa Bb Cc Dd Ee Ff Gg Hh Ii Jj Kk Ll Mm Nn Oo Pp Qq Rr Ss Tt Uu Vv Ww Xx Yy Zz

Rome NOUN

Here are some words connected with ancient Rome:

basilica, baths, centurion, chariot, colosseum (or coliseum), emperor, fort, forum, gladiator, hypocaust, temple, toga, road

room NOUN

1 *We have no* **room** *for an exercise bike.*
space, volume, capacity, headroom, legroom, elbow-room
2 *There is a lot of* **room** *for improvement here.*
scope, range, extent

Here are some types of room:

Rooms in a house:
attic, basement, bathroom, bedroom, boxroom, cellar, cloakroom, conservatory, dining room, drawing room, dressing-room, front room, guest room, hall, kitchen, kitchenette, landing, larder, laundry, lavatory, library, living-room, loft, lounge, nursery, pantry, playroom, porch, reception room, salon, scullery, sitting room, spare room, study, toilet, utility room, WC
Rooms in schools and workplaces:
boardroom, changing room, classroom, common room, dormitory, foyer, games room, gymnasium, laboratory, lobby, music-room, office, reception, sickroom, staffroom, stockroom, storeroom, studio, waiting room, workroom, workshop

roomy ADJECTIVE

a very **roomy** *basement*
spacious, large, sizable, broad, wide, extensive, ample, generous
≠ OPPOSITES cramped, small, tiny

root NOUN

the **root** *of the problem*
source, origin, cause, starting point, heart, core, basis, foundation

rope NOUN

The hostage's hands were tied up with **rope**.
cord, line, cable, string

rot VERB

If you leave food out of the fridge, it will **rot**.
decay, decompose, fester, spoil, go bad, go off

rotate VERB

The telescope **rotates** *on a circular axis.*
turn, revolve, spin, pivot, swivel, roll

rotten ADJECTIVE

1 **rotten** *wood*
decayed, rotting, decaying, disintegrating
2 **rotten** *fruit*
decayed, decomposed, bad, off, mouldy, rotting
≠ OPPOSITES fresh
3 *We had a* **rotten** *holiday.*
inferior, bad, poor, inadequate
◇ INFORMAL WORDS lousy
≠ OPPOSITES good

rough ADJECTIVE

1 *a* **rough** *surface*
uneven, bumpy, lumpy, irregular, coarse
≠ OPPOSITES smooth
2 **rough** *treatment*
harsh, severe, tough, hard, cruel, brutal, drastic, extreme
≠ OPPOSITES mild
3 *His* **rough** *words hurt my feelings.*
harsh, hard, cruel, curt, sharp
≠ OPPOSITES mild
4 *a* **rough** *figure*
approximate, estimated, imprecise, inexact
≠ OPPOSITES accurate
5 *I have a* **rough** *idea of what she looks like.*

Aa
Bb
Cc
Dd
Ee
Ff
Gg
Hh
Ii
Jj
Kk
Ll
Mm
Nn
Oo
Pp
Qq
Rr
Ss
Tt
Uu
Vv
Ww
Xx
Yy
Zz

vague, approximate, general
≠ OPPOSITES accurate
6 *a rough sea*
stormy, choppy, violent, wild
≠ OPPOSITES calm

round¹ ADJECTIVE
1 *a round coin*
spherical, circular, ring-shaped, disc-shaped, rounded, curved
2 *She's rather small and round.*
rotund, plump, stout

round² NOUN
1 *a round of golf*
cycle, series, sequence, period, bout, session, game, match
2 *The security guard was doing his rounds.*
beat, circuit, lap, course, routine

round³ VERB
As we rounded the corner, we could see the sea.
go round, circle, turn
• round off
We rounded off the holiday with a day at a theme park.
finish, finish off, complete, end, close, conclude
≠ OPPOSITES begin
• round up
The teacher rounded up all the children.
gather, herd, assemble, rally, collect, group
≠ OPPOSITES scatter

roundabout ADJECTIVE
That's a roundabout way to get to the park.
indirect, twisting, winding
≠ OPPOSITES straight, direct

rouse VERB
1 *It's difficult to rouse Natalie on school mornings.*
wake, wake up, awaken, arouse
2 *His shifty behaviour roused my suspicions.*
awaken, arouse, stir, start, stimulate
3 *Her speech roused the crowd to a frenzy.*

excite, move, arouse, stir, stimulate, whip up

route NOUN
We took the scenic route round the coast.
way, course, run, path, road

routine NOUN
1 *part of their daily routine*
practice, custom, habit, pattern
2 *a fitness routine*
system, procedure, way, method, formula

row¹ NOUN
rows of seats
line, tier, bank, column, file, string, series

row² NOUN
1 *Hannah has had a row with her boyfriend.*
quarrel, argument, dispute, squabble, tiff, fight
2 *Stop that row immediately!*
noise, racket, din, uproar, commotion, disturbance
≠ OPPOSITES calm

rowdy ADJECTIVE
rowdy behaviour
disorderly, noisy, loud, rough, boisterous, unruly, riotous, wild
≠ OPPOSITES quiet, peaceful

royal ADJECTIVE
1 *the royal family*
regal, majestic, noble
2 *a hotel which offers royal hospitality*
splendid, grand, stately, magnificent, superb

Here are some members of a royal family:

duchess, duke, emperor, empress, king, monarch, prince, prince consort, princess, queen

Aa Bb Cc Dd Ee Ff Gg Hh Ii Jj Kk Ll Mm Nn Oo Pp Qq **Rr** Ss Tt Uu Vv Ww Xx Yy Zz

rub VERB
1 *I rubbed my aching feet.*
stroke, caress, massage, knead
2 *My sandal is rubbing against my toe.*
chafe, grate, scrape
3 *I rubbed the silver tray until it gleamed.*
polish, scour, scrub, clean, wipe, shine
• **rub out**
If you make a mistake, rub it out.
erase, obliterate, delete, cancel

rubbish NOUN
1 *rubbish scattered on the beach*
waste, refuse, garbage, trash, junk, litter
2 *You're talking rubbish.*
nonsense, drivel, gibberish, balderdash
◇ INFORMAL WORDS gobbledegook, rot
⊯ OPPOSITES sense

rude ADJECTIVE
1 *Tony was rude to the teacher.*
impolite, disrespectful, impertinent, impudent, cheeky, insolent, insulting, bad-mannered
⊯ OPPOSITES polite, courteous
2 *I don't like rude jokes.*
vulgar, obscene, coarse, offensive, dirty, naughty

ruin¹ VERB
1 *I've ruined my chances of winning now.*
spoil, botch, damage, wreck
◇ INFORMAL WORDS mess up
2 *Ashley jumped on my sandcastle and ruined it.*
destroy, break, smash, shatter, wreck, demolish

ruin² NOUN
financial ruin
insolvency, bankruptcy, failure

rule¹ NOUN
1 *That's against the rules.*
regulation, law, order, principle, guideline
2 *He had complete rule over his lands.*
power, mastery, authority, command, control, influence

3 *The king's rule has ended.*
reign, government, regime
• **as a rule**
As a rule, I go into town on a Saturday.
usually, normally, ordinarily, generally

rule² VERB
1 *Queen Victoria ruled the country for many years.*
reign, govern
2 *The general ruled his men by fear.*
manage, command, lead, direct, control
3 *The court ruled in our favour.*
judge, decide, find, pronounce

rumour NOUN
There's a rumour that Mr Lamont is leaving.
story, hearsay, gossip, talk, whisper, word, news

run VERB
⇒ For even more about this word, see the next page
1 *I had to run for the bus.*
race, sprint, jog, tear, dash, hurry, rush
2 *The bus route runs through the village.*
go, pass, move, proceed
3 *The engine runs on diesel.*
work, function, operate, perform
4 *She runs a design company.*
manage, head, lead, direct, superintend, supervise, oversee, control
5 *He is running for president.*
compete, stand
6 *The series ran for ten years.*
continue, last, go on, carry on
7 *The path runs all the way down to the river.*
continue, go, extend, reach, stretch, spread, range
8 *I can hear water running.*
flow, stream, pour, gush
• **run away**
The boys ran away when the police arrived.
flee, escape, bolt, run off, make off
◇ INFORMAL WORDS scarper, beat it, clear off
⊯ OPPOSITES stay

run

There are many words you can use instead of **run**. All of the words below describe how someone is moving. They can help you to create a much clearer picture of what is happening.

These words describe someone moving in a hurry:

charge
career
tear
dash
hurry
rush
race
speed
dart
fly

These words describe someone moving nervously, or with short steps, like a small animal:

scuttle
scamper
scurry

These words describe how you might run in a race or competition:

sprint
jog

These words are for running away:

escape
flee
run off
bolt

There are many informal words which mean run away:

scoot
scarper
beat it
clear off
make off
take off

Aa
Bb
Cc
Dd
Ee
Ff
Gg
Hh
Ii
Jj
Kk
Ll
Mm
Nn
Oo
Pp
Qq
Rr
Ss
Tt
Uu
Vv
Ww
Xx
Yy
Zz

Over to you

Can you put some of these words to use? Which words could you use instead of **run** in these sentences?

1 As soon as the bell rang, the excited children **ran** down the school corridor and into the playground.

2 The sudden thunderstorm sent the shoppers **running** into shops for shelter.

3 When he heard the starting pistol the athlete **ran** down the track.

4 The robbers **ran away** from the bank with a hoard of gold and jewels.

5 '**Run away**' shouted the angry woman to the stray cat in her garden.

runner NOUN
a long-distance **runner**
athlete, jogger, sprinter

runny ADJECTIVE
runny honey
flowing, fluid, liquid
(≠) OPPOSITES solid

rural ADJECTIVE
rural areas
country, rustic, agricultural
(≠) OPPOSITES urban

rush¹ NOUN
1 *There was a sudden* **rush** *toward the door.*
dash, race, scramble, stampede
2 *There's no* **rush** *– we've got plenty of time.*
hurry, haste, urgency

rush² VERB
1 *The children* **rushed** *out of the classroom.*
hurry, bolt, tear, dash, race, run, scramble, stampede, charge
2 *We* **rushed** *the job to finish it on time.*
hurry, accelerate, speed up, press, push

rusty ADJECTIVE
The metal was **rusty** *with age.*
corroded, rusted, rust-covered, tarnished, discoloured, dull

ruthless ADJECTIVE
a **ruthless** *tyrant*
merciless, pitiless, hard-hearted, hard, heartless, callous, cruel, harsh, severe
(≠) OPPOSITES merciful, compassionate

Ss

sack VERB

*He was **sacked** for poor timekeeping.*
fire, dismiss, discharge
◇ INFORMAL WORDS axe

sacred ADJECTIVE

sacred music
holy, divine, religious

sacrifice VERB

*The PE teacher **sacrificed** his lunch break to referee the football match.*
give up, abandon, surrender, let go

sad ADJECTIVE

⇒ For even more about this word, see the next page
1 *I felt **sad** when my dog died.*
unhappy, sorrowful, grief-stricken, miserable, dejected, down, despondent, depressed, low
⊯ OPPOSITES happy, cheerful
2 *sad news*
upsetting, distressing, painful, depressing, heart-rending, tragic, unfortunate
⊯ OPPOSITES fortunate, lucky

safe ADJECTIVE

1 *Is the water **safe** to drink?*
harmless, non-toxic, non-poisonous, uncontaminated
⊯ OPPOSITES dangerous, harmful, unsafe
2 *Make your property **safe** from burglars.*
protected, secure, guarded
⊯ OPPOSITES vulnerable, exposed
3 *The missing children were found **safe** and well.*
unharmed, undamaged, uninjured, unhurt, all right
4 *He likes to take the **safe** course of action.*
cautious, unadventurous
⊯ OPPOSITES risky

safety NOUN

1 *Airlines need to improve **safety** on flights.*
security, protection, safeguard
⊯ OPPOSITES danger, jeopardy, risk
2 *She reached the **safety** of the house.*
shelter, protection, cover, refuge
⊯ OPPOSITES danger, jeopardy, risk

sag VERB

1 *The chair **sagged** in the middle.*
sink, bend, bag, droop, hang, dip
⊯ OPPOSITES bulge, rise
2 *She **sagged** into an armchair.*
sink, drop, slump, flop
⊯ OPPOSITES rise

sail VERB

1 *They **sailed** for France yesterday.*
set sail, embark, put to sea
2 *She **sailed** round the world single-handed.*
voyage, cruise

sailor NOUN

*My uncle is a **sailor** in the Royal Navy.*
seafarer, mariner, seaman, marine, yachtsman, yachtswoman

sake NOUN

*Don't stay in for my **sake**.*
benefit, advantage, good, welfare, behalf, interest, account

salary NOUN

*a monthly **salary***
pay, payment, wages, earnings, income

sale NOUN

1 *the **sale** of property*
selling, marketing, dealing, trade
2 *We've made three **sales** so far.*
deal, transaction

sad

If someone is a little sad, you could use these words:

- unhappy
- heavy-hearted
- downcast
- dejected
- blue
- doleful
- downhearted
- despondent
- tearful
- glum
- gloomy
- low

If someone is very sad, you could use these words:

- sorrowful
- upset
- distressed
- depressed
- grief-stricken
- miserable
- crestfallen
- woebegone

words to use for a sad book or a sad film

- poigant
- touching
- heart-rending
- depressing

words to use to about sad news

- painful
- upsetting
- distressing
- grievous
- unfortunate
- lamentable
- serious
- grave
- tragic

sorry
regrettable
disastrous

Over to you

Make your reader feel sorry for the character in this story by using some of these words instead of **sad**:

She turned her **sad** face to me and spoke in a **sad** way about what had happened. I became **sad** too on hearing her **sad** account. **Sad**, we both left the scene.

salvage VERB
I managed to salvage most of my papers from the fire.
save, preserve, rescue, recover, retrieve, reclaim
≠ OPPOSITES waste, abandon

same ADJECTIVE
1 *We turned up wearing the same outfit.*
identical, twin, duplicate
≠ OPPOSITES different
2 *These two words have much the same meaning.*
similar, alike, like, comparable, equivalent, corresponding, interchangeable
≠ OPPOSITES different, opposite

sample¹ NOUN
a sample of fabric
specimen, example, model, piece

sample² VERB
Would you like to sample this new drink?
try, test, taste, experience
◇ INFORMAL WORDS check out

sane ADJECTIVE
No sane person would attempt such a feat.
rational, balanced, stable, sound-minded, sensible, reasonable
≠ OPPOSITES insane, mad, crazy, foolish

sap VERB
The flu has sapped her strength.
drain, exhaust, weaken, reduce
≠ OPPOSITES strengthen, build up, increase

sarcastic ADJECTIVE
He makes sarcastic comments at my expense.
ironical, mocking, sneering, scathing, cynical, cutting

satisfaction NOUN
I felt a sense of satisfaction when I finished my homework.
fulfilment, contentment, happiness, pleasure, wellbeing, self-satisfaction, pride
≠ OPPOSITES dissatisfaction, displeasure

satisfactory ADJECTIVE
The quality of your work is not satisfactory.
acceptable, passable, up to the mark, fair, average, adequate, sufficient, good enough
◇ INFORMAL WORDS all right, OK
≠ OPPOSITES unsatisfactory, unacceptable, inadequate

satisfy VERB
1 *Nothing seems to satisfy him.*
content, please
≠ OPPOSITES dissatisfy

2 *This applicant seems to **satisfy** all our requirements.*
meet, fulfil, answer, fill, qualify
⊉ OPPOSITES fail

saunter VERB

*He **sauntered** along the road as if he had plenty of time.*
stroll, amble, wander

savage ADJECTIVE

1 *a **savage** and unprovoked attack*
cruel, fierce, ferocious, vicious, inhuman, brutal, barbaric, bloodthirsty
2 *a **savage** tiger*
wild, untamed, undomesticated, fierce, ferocious
⊉ OPPOSITES tame

save VERB

1 *I'm **saving** to buy a CD player.*
economize, cut back, budget
2 *Try to **save** some money every month in case of emergencies.*
put by, preserve, keep, set aside, hoard
⊉ OPPOSITES spend, squander, waste
3 *He **saved** the animals from captivity.*
rescue, deliver, free
4 *They built a wall to **save** the village from being flooded.*
protect, guard, screen, shield, safeguard, spare, prevent

savings NOUN

*I have some **savings** in the building society.*
fund, capital, store, reserves, resources

say VERB

⇒ For even more about this word, see the next page
1 *I couldn't bring myself to **say** the words out loud.*
speak, express, utter, voice, pronounce, mention
2 *He **said** his full name.*
state, speak
3 *Try to **say** your lines without looking at the script.*
speak, recite, repeat

4 *She **said**, 'Hi, I haven't seen you for ages!'*
remark, exclaim, comment, observe

saying NOUN

*a well-known **saying***
expression, proverb, slogan, phrase, quotation

scale VERB

*They **scaled** the wall with difficulty.*
climb, ascend, mount, clamber up, scramble up, shin up

scamper VERB

*The squirrel **scampered** off when it heard me.*
run, scuttle, scurry, scoot, dart, dash, rush, hurry

scan VERB

1 *I **scanned** the horizon for any sign of a ship.*
survey, examine, scrutinize, study, search, check
2 *He quickly **scanned** the book.*
glance over, skim, flick through, thumb through

scandal NOUN

1 *a political **scandal***
disgrace, outrage, offence
2 *She couldn't face the **scandal** when the story got out.*
disgrace, discredit, dishonour, shame, embarrassment
3 *spreading all the latest **scandal***
gossip, rumours, dirt

scandalous ADJECTIVE

scandalous behaviour
shocking, appalling, atrocious, outrageous, disgraceful, shameful

scanty ADJECTIVE

scanty evidence
meagre, little, limited, restricted, inadequate, insufficient, insubstantial
⊉ OPPOSITES ample, plentiful, adequate, sufficient, substantial

Aa
Bb
Cc
Dd
Ee
Ff
Gg
Hh
Ii
Jj
Kk
Ll
Mm
Nn
Oo
Pp
Qq
Rr
Ss
Tt
Uu
Vv
Ww
Xx
Yy
Zz

say

This is another word which means to **say**:
>**remark**

If someone is asking a question, you could say that they
>**ask**
>**inquire**
>**question**

If they are asking in an angry way, they might
>**demand**

If someone is answering a question, you could say that they
>**reply**
>**respond**

If they are answering in an angry way, they might
>**retort**

If someone is giving information, they might
>**state**
>**tell**
>**inform**
>**communicate**
>**mention**

Using words other than **said** in your stories give clues about people's feelings.

These words are for saying something with a laugh. They might suggest a happy character:
>**laughed**
>**chuckled**
>**giggled**

These words are for saying something while crying or complaining. They would suggest an unhappy character:
>**complained**
>**whimpered**
>**sobbed**
>**moaned**
>**whined**

These words are for saying something quietly:
whispered

These words are for saying something loudly. They might suggest an angry character:
shouted
shrieked
yelled

Over to you

Can you put some of these words to use? Which words could you use instead of **said** in these sentences?

1 'Come here!' she **said**.

2 'Help me,' she **said**.

3 'Get out of here!' she **said**.

4 'Don't speak to me ever again!' he **said**.

5 'Come here!' she **said**.

6 'Hey!' she **said**.

Aa
Bb
Cc
Dd
Ee
Ff
Gg
Hh
Ii
Jj
Kk
Ll
Mm
Nn
Oo
Pp
Qq
Rr
Ss
Tt
Uu
Vv
Ww
Xx
Yy
Zz

scar¹ NOUN
This wound will leave a permanent scar.
mark, wound, injury, blemish

scar² VERB
He is scarred for life.
mark, disfigure, mutilate, damage

scarce ADJECTIVE
1 *Food is scarce in the refugee camps.*
lacking, sparse, scanty, insufficient
(≠) OPPOSITES plentiful, abundant
2 *Jobs are scarce on the island.*
few, rare, infrequent, uncommon, unusual
(≠) OPPOSITES plentiful, common

scarcely ADVERB
I have scarcely enough money for my fare.
hardly, barely, only just

scare¹ VERB
1 *The way he drives really scares me.*
frighten, startle, alarm, panic, terrify
(≠) OPPOSITES reassure, calm
2 *He was punished for scaring the younger children.*
frighten, intimidate, threaten, terrorize
(≠) OPPOSITES reassure, calm

scare² NOUN
1 *You gave me a scare when you jumped out.*
fright, start, shock
(≠) OPPOSITES reassurance, comfort
2 *The building was evacuated after a bomb scare.*
alarm, panic, terror
(≠) OPPOSITES reassurance, comfort

scary ADJECTIVE
a scary film

frightening, alarming, disturbing, terrifying, spine-chilling, chilling, eerie
◇ INFORMAL WORDS creepy, spooky

scatter VERB

1 *Scatter the seeds lightly over the soil.*
spread, strew, sprinkle, sow, fling, shower
≢ OPPOSITES gather, collect
2 *The boys scattered when the head teacher appeared.*
separate, divide, break up, disperse
≢ OPPOSITES gather

scene NOUN

1 *the scene of the crime*
site, place, area, spot, whereabouts, location, environment, setting
2 *The scene on stage is that of a courtroom.*
setting, backdrop, set
3 *We looked out on a beautiful scene.*
view, landscape, prospect, sight, spectacle, picture
4 *Don't make a scene in public.*
fuss, commotion, to-do, performance, drama, exhibition

scenic ADJECTIVE

We took the scenic road home.
picturesque, beautiful, striking, impressive, spectacular, breathtaking
≢ OPPOSITES dull, dreary

scent NOUN

the scent of roses
smell, perfume, fragrance, aroma, odour
≢ OPPOSITES stink

schedule NOUN

1 *Can you fit me into your busy schedule?*
timetable, programme, agenda, diary, calendar, plan, scheme
2 *a detailed schedule of events*
programme, plan, scheme, list, catalogue

scheme[1] NOUN

1 *a traffic-calming scheme*
plan, programme, project, idea, proposal, proposition, suggestion
2 *a detailed scheme of the building*
plan, outline, design, arrangement, draft

scheme[2] VERB

1 *What new trick are you both scheming now?*
plot, plan, devise, work out
2 *He schemed to have his rival removed.*
plot, conspire, manoeuvre, pull strings, plan, contrive

scholar NOUN

1 *Try to be a better scholar from now on.*
pupil, student
2 *a mathematics scholar*
academic, intellectual
◇ INFORMAL WORDS egghead

school NOUN

Here are some types of school:

Schools for young children:
infant school, kindergarten, nursery school
Schools for older children:
combined school, high school, middle school, primary school, secondary school
Schools for older students:
sixth-form college, upper school
Other schools:
academy, boarding school, city academy, college, faith school, finishing school, foundation school, grammar school, preparatory school, private school, public school, secondary modern, specialist school, special school, summer school, Sunday school

science NOUN

Here are the names of some sciences:

aeronautics, anatomy, archaeology,

Aa
Bb
Cc
Dd
Ee
Ff
Gg
Hh
Ii
Jj
Kk
Ll
Mm
Nn
Oo
Pp
Qq
Rr
Ss
Tt
Uu
Vv
Ww
Xx
Yy
Zz

astronomy, biology, botany, chemistry, climatology, computer science, earth science, ecology, electronics, engineering, environmental science, genetics, geography, geology, information technology, mechanics, medicine, metallurgy, meteorology, nanotechnology, physics, physiology, psychology, zoology

scientific ADJECTIVE
a scientific study
systematic, exact, precise, accurate, methodical, controlled, analytical, thorough

scoff VERB
He scoffed at their efforts.
mock, ridicule, poke fun, sneer, scorn, belittle
◆ FORMAL WORDS disparage
◇ INFORMAL WORDS knock
⊘ OPPOSITES praise, compliment, flatter

scold VERB
She scolded the children for staying out too late.
tell off, reprimand, take to task, reproach, blame, lecture
◇ INFORMAL WORDS nag
⊘ OPPOSITES praise, commend

scoop VERB
1 *I scooped a hole in the ground with my bare hands.*
dig, gouge, scrape, hollow, excavate, shovel
2 *Scoop the sauce over the fish.*
ladle, spoon, dip

scope NOUN
1 *the scope of our project*
range, area, reach, extent, span, breadth, coverage
2 *You have the scope to do whatever you want.*
opportunity, room, space, capacity, freedom, liberty

scorch VERB
The sun had scorched the grass.
burn, singe, char, blacken

score¹ NOUN
What's the latest score?
result, total, sum, tally, points, marks

score² VERB
1 *He scored ten points in the last minute.*
gain, make, earn, achieve, attain, win
◇ INFORMAL WORDS chalk up, notch up
2 *the person in charge of scoring the game*
count, register, record, total
3 *Her shoes scored the floorboards.*
scratch, scrape, graze, mark, gouge, cut, slash

scorn NOUN
They treated my suggestion with scorn.
contempt, scornfulness, disdain, sneering, mockery, ridicule
⊘ OPPOSITES admiration, respect

scour¹ VERB
You will have to scour the pots and pans.
scrub, rub, polish, clean

scour² VERB
The police are scouring the countryside for clues.
search, hunt, comb

scowl VERB
The girl scowled when I spoke to her.
glower, frown, glare
⊘ OPPOSITES smile, grin, beam

scramble VERB
1 *scrambling up the rocks*
climb, scale, clamber, scrabble, crawl
2 *The children scrambled to get on the bus.*
rush, hurry, run, push, jostle, struggle

scrap¹ VERB
1 *You should scrap that old car and get a new one.*
throw away, discard

Aa
Bb
Cc
Dd
Ee
Ff
Gg
Hh
Ii
Jj
Kk
Ll
Mm
Nn
Oo
Pp
Qq
Rr
Ss
Tt
Uu
Vv
Ww
Xx
Yy
Zz

◇ INFORMAL WORDS dump, ditch
2 *I've scrapped my plan to go to the cinema.*
drop, abandon, cancel

scrap² NOUN
1 *scraps of food*
bit, piece, fragment, part, crumb, morsel, shred
2 *a heap of scrap*
waste, junk, rubbish, refuse

scrap³ NOUN
The two boys had a scrap in the playground.
fight, scuffle, brawl, squabble, wrangle
⊯ OPPOSITES peace, agreement

scrape VERB
1 *I fell down and scraped my hands.*
scratch, graze, skin, scuff
2 *Scrape the mud off your boots.*
clean, rub, scour, remove
3 *the sound of fingernails scraping on a chalkboard*
grate, grind, rasp

scratch VERB
1 *Try not to scratch the itchy spots.*
claw, scrape, rub
2 *I have scratched the table.*
mark, score, cut, scrape, scuff

scream VERB
children screaming on the roller-coaster
shriek, screech, cry, shout, yell, bawl, roar

screen¹ NOUN
a screen separating the two areas
partition, shield, guard

screen² VERB
1 *a hedge screening the garden*
hide, conceal
⊯ OPPOSITES expose
2 *A garden umbrella screened me from the sun.*
protect, shield, shelter
⊯ OPPOSITES expose

scribble VERB
She scribbled her phone number on a scrap of paper.
scrawl, write, pen, jot, dash off

script NOUN
a film script
text, lines, words, dialogue, screenplay

scrub VERB
scrubbing the floor
rub, brush, clean, wash, cleanse, scour

scruffy ADJECTIVE
1 *a scruffy old coat*
shabby, tattered, worn-out, ragged
2 *a scruffy old tramp*
shabby, untidy, messy, unkempt, dishevelled, bedraggled, ragged
⊯ OPPOSITES tidy, well-dressed

scuffle NOUN
A scuffle broke out in the street.
fight, scrap, tussle, brawl, commotion, disturbance

seal¹ VERB
a machine for sealing jars
close, shut, stop, plug, cork, fasten, secure
⊯ OPPOSITES unseal

seal² NOUN
the royal seal
stamp, signet

search¹ NOUN
1 *the search for the missing child*
hunt, quest, pursuit
2 *a search of all the houses in the area*
examination, exploration, scrutiny, inspection, investigation
3 *a search into the causes of the problem*
investigation, inquiry, research, survey, probe

search² VERB
1 *I'm searching for my black socks.*
seek, look, hunt
2 *The police searched the area.*
examine, scour, comb, scrutinize,

inspect, check, investigate
3 *I searched all the drawers for the key.*
rummage through, rifle, ransack
4 *The suspects were searched for weapons.*
check, frisk, examine, scrutinize, inspect

seaside NOUN

Here are some things you might see at the seaside:

amusements, bay, boat, bucket and spade, candy floss, caravan park, cliff, crab, deck chair, donkey, driftwood, dune, hammock, ice cream, jellyfish, kiosk, lifeguard, lighthouse, ocean, palm tree, parasol, pebble, pier, rock pool, sand, sandcastle, sea, seagull, seashell, seaweed, starfish, sunlounger, surfer, waves, windbreak, yacht

season NOUN
the fishing season
period, spell, term, time

seat NOUN
a garden seat
chair, bench, pew, stool

second NOUN
I'll be with you in a second.
moment, minute, instant, flash
◇ INFORMAL WORDS tick, jiffy

secret ADJECTIVE
1 *the secret lives of the rich and famous*
private, personal, hidden, concealed, unseen
≠ OPPOSITES public, open
2 *a secret passageway*
hidden, private, concealed, disguised, camouflaged
≠ OPPOSITES public, open
3 *a secret mission*
classified, confidential, undercover, undisclosed, unrevealed, unknown
◇ INFORMAL WORDS hush-hush
≠ OPPOSITES well-known

secretary NOUN
a medical secretary
personal assistant, PA, typist, clerk

secretive ADJECTIVE
He's very secretive about his past.
uncommunicative, unforthcoming, tight-lipped, reserved
◇ INFORMAL WORDS cagey
≠ OPPOSITES open, communicative

section NOUN
1 *The bookcase arrived in sections to be assembled.*
part, component, bit, piece, segment
≠ OPPOSITES whole
2 *A section of the rock was taken for examination.*
part, fraction, fragment, bit, piece, portion, segment
≠ OPPOSITES whole

secure ADJECTIVE
1 *Keep your valuables in a secure place.*
safe, protected, sheltered
≠ OPPOSITES insecure, vulnerable
2 *Make sure all the doors and windows are secure.*
fastened, locked
≠ OPPOSITES insecure
3 *The house is built on secure foundations.*
firm, stable, steady, solid
≠ OPPOSITES unstable
4 *a secure job*
reliable, steady, dependable
≠ OPPOSITES unreliable
5 *secure in the knowledge that I had done all I could*
confident, certain, sure, assured, reassured
≠ OPPOSITES uneasy, ill at ease

sedate ADJECTIVE
She was very sedate and ladylike.
dignified, sober, proper, demure, composed, unruffled, calm, quiet
≠ OPPOSITES undignified, lively, agitated

Aa
Bb
Cc
Dd
Ee
Ff
Gg
Hh
Ii
Jj
Kk
Ll
Mm
Nn
Oo
Pp
Qq
Rr
Ss
Tt
Uu
Vv
Ww
Xx
Yy
Zz

see VERB

1 *I could see the island in the distance.*
make out, perceive, glimpse, spot, distinguish, identify, sight, notice
2 *I can't see Clint going to ballet classes.*
imagine, picture, visualize
3 *I see your point.*
understand, grasp, follow, realize, recognize, appreciate
4 *Could you go and see if the baby's all right?*
discover, find out, learn
5 *Can I see you home?*
accompany, lead, usher, escort
6 *She is going to see her aunt.*
visit, meet, spend time with
7 *He's been seeing a nice girl.*
go out with, date

seek VERB

1 *Police are still seeking the men who carried out the robbery.*
look for, search for, hunt, pursue
2 *I think you should seek help with your problem.*
look for, ask for, invite, request

seem VERB

You seem worried.
appear, look, sound

seeming ADJECTIVE

his seeming kindness
apparent, outward, superficial
≠ OPPOSITES real

seep VERB

Blood seeped out of the wound.
ooze, leak, well, trickle, dribble, soak

segment NOUN

1 *grapefruit segments*
section, bit, piece, slice, portion, wedge
≠ OPPOSITES whole
2 *The box is divided into four segments.*
section, division, compartment, part
≠ OPPOSITES whole

seize VERB

1 *He seized my hand.*
grab, snatch, grasp, clutch, grip, hold, take, catch
≠ OPPOSITES let go, release, hand back
2 *The kidnappers were seized by the police.*
capture, arrest, apprehend
◇ INFORMAL WORDS nab, collar
≠ OPPOSITES let go, release

seldom ADVERB

I am seldom sick.
hardly ever, rarely, infrequently, occasionally
≠ OPPOSITES often, usually

select VERB

He was selected as class representative.
choose, pick, single out, decide on, appoint, elect, opt for

selfish ADJECTIVE

She is too selfish to help you out.
self-centred, egocentric, egotistic, self-interested
≠ OPPOSITES unselfish, selfless, generous, considerate

sell VERB

The corner shop sells newspapers.
deal in, trade in, stock, handle, hawk
≠ OPPOSITES buy

send VERB

1 *I sent you a birthday card.*
post, mail, forward
2 *He suddenly pushed me and sent me flying across the room.*
propel, drive, move, throw, fling, hurl
• **send for**
1 *The head teacher sent for Toby.*
summon, call for
≠ OPPOSITES dismiss
2 *Let's send for a catalogue.*
order, request

senior ADJECTIVE

1 *a senior police officer*
high-ranking, higher, superior, major, chief
≠ OPPOSITES junior
2 *showing respect to those senior in age*
older, elder
≠ OPPOSITES junior

Aa Bb Cc Dd Ee Ff Gg Hh Ii Jj Kk Ll Mm Nn Oo Pp Qq Rr Ss Tt Uu Vv Ww Xx Yy Zz

sensation NOUN
1 *I felt a **sensation** of movement.*
feeling, sense, impression, perception, awareness, consciousness
2 *The report caused a **sensation**.*
excitement, commotion, stir, thrill

sense¹ NOUN
1 *a **sense** of longing*
feeling, sensation, impression, perception
2 *Luckily, she had the **sense** to realize what was happening.*
understanding, brains, wit, wisdom, intelligence, cleverness, judgement, intuition
◇ OPPOSITES **foolishness**

sense² VERB
*I **sensed** his disapproval.*
feel, suspect, detect, notice, realize, understand, grasp

sensible ADJECTIVE
1 *a **sensible** plan*
wise, shrewd, commonsense, logical, reasonable, realistic, practical, sound
◇ OPPOSITES **senseless, foolish, unwise**
2 *a **sensible** woman*
wise, shrewd, intelligent, level-headed, down-to-earth, sane, rational, practical
◇ OPPOSITES **senseless, foolish, unwise**

sensitive ADJECTIVE
1 *My skin is very **sensitive** to the sun.*
susceptible, vulnerable, responsive
2 *He is **sensitive** about his height.*
touchy, vulnerable, thin-skinned, easily upset
◇ OPPOSITES **insensitive, thick-skinned**

sentence VERB
1 *He was **sentenced** for his part in the robbery.*
punish, penalize
2 *The court **sentenced** him to death.*
condemn, doom

sentimental ADJECTIVE
1 *He's very **sentimental** about his home town.*
emotional, tender, soft-hearted, nostalgic
◇ INFORMAL WORDS soppy
◇ OPPOSITES **unsentimental, realistic, cynical**
2 *sentimental love songs*
romantic, touching, tear-jerking
◇ INFORMAL WORDS weepy, lovey-dovey, corny, soppy, slushy, mushy, sloppy

separate¹ ADJECTIVE
1 *Keep raw meats **separate** from cooked meats.*
apart, isolated, divided, disconnected, detached
◇ OPPOSITES **together**
2 *These are two **separate** issues.*
different, unrelated, individual, unconnected, distinct
◇ OPPOSITES **attached, linked**

separate² VERB
1 ***Separate** the yolk of the egg from the white.*
divide, disconnect, disentangle, cut off, remove, detach
◇ OPPOSITES **combine**
2 *She was **separated** from the rest of the community.*
isolate, segregate, cut off, detach
3 *The road **separated** into two paths.*
divide, split, branch, fork, diverge
◇ OPPOSITES **unite, combine**
4 *My parents have **separated**.*
split up, part, divorce, part company

sequence NOUN
1 *a **sequence** of events*
series, succession, run, progression, chain, train, course, set
2 *The story is told in chronological **sequence**.*
order, arrangement, progression

serene ADJECTIVE
*She looked so **serene** and peaceful.*
calm, composed, placid, untroubled, undisturbed, still, quiet, peaceful
◇ OPPOSITES **troubled, disturbed**

Aa
Bb
Cc
Dd
Ee
Ff
Gg
Hh
Ii
Jj
Kk
Ll
Mm
Nn
Oo
Pp
Qq
Rr
Ss
Tt
Uu
Vv
Ww
Xx
Yy
Zz

Aa
Bb
Cc
Dd
Ee
Ff
Gg
Hh
Ii
Jj
Kk
Ll
Mm
Nn
Oo
Pp
Qq
Rr
Ss
Tt
Uu
Vv
Ww
Xx
Yy
Zz

series NOUN
*a **series** of incidents*
sequence, set, succession, run, progression, chain, train, course

serious ADJECTIVE
1 *a **serious** error*
important, significant, crucial
(≠) OPPOSITES trivial, slight
2 *a **serious** accident*
grave, severe, dangerous
(≠) OPPOSITES minor, slight, trivial
3 *She wore a **serious** expression.*
solemn, unsmiling, humourless, grim, sober, stern
(≠) OPPOSITES smiling
4 *Are you **serious** about wanting to help?*
sincere, in earnest

serve VERB
1 *Dinner is **served** at seven o'clock.*
present, distribute, dish up, provide, supply
2 *Are you being **served**?*
wait on, attend, help, aid, assist
3 *She has **served** our family for many years.*
work for, help, aid, assist
4 *It won't **serve** our purpose if you lose your temper.*
benefit, further, help, aid, assist

service¹ NOUN
1 *calls to bring back national **service***
employment, work, labour, business, duty, function
2 *I am glad to be of **service** to you.*
use, usefulness, advantage, benefit, help, assistance

service² VERB
*The car is due to be **serviced**.*
check, maintain, overhaul, repair, recondition, tune

session NOUN
1 *a court **session***
meeting, sitting, hearing, assembly, conference, discussion
2 *The new school **session** begins next week.*
period, time, term, year

set¹ NOUN
1 *a **set** of place mats*
collection, series, batch, assortment
2 *an unexpected **set** of events*
series, sequence
3 *He was always in the top **set** at school.*
class, category
4 *She longs to be part of the fashionable **set**.*
group, band, gang, crowd, circle

set² VERB
1 *I have **set** the alarm for seven o'clock.*
adjust, regulate, co-ordinate
2 *Let's **set** a date for our next meeting.*
arrange, schedule, specify, fix, establish, decide, settle, resolve
◆ FORMAL WORDS designate
3 *People gathered to watch the sun **set**.*
go down, sink, dip, subside, disappear, vanish
(≠) OPPOSITES rise
4 *The jelly has **set**.*
solidify, congeal, thicken, gel, stiffen, harden, crystallize
5 ***Set** your bags down on the floor.*
put, place, arrange, stick, park, deposit
6 *The hotel is **set** in magnificent grounds.*
locate, situate, position
7 *The pole is **set** in a concrete block.*
fix, lodge, stick
• **set off**
1 *We **set off** for home just after lunch.*
leave, depart, set out, start out, begin
2 *Somebody **set off** a firework.*
detonate, light, ignite, explode
3 *The decision **set off** a storm of protest.*
trigger off, spark off, start
• **set up**
1 *They have **set up** a business together.*
start, establish, begin, introduce
2 *I'll **set up** a meeting for next week.*
arrange, organize

setback NOUN

*He's suffered a few **setbacks** in his career.*
delay, hold-up, problem, snag, hitch, hiccup
⊘ OPPOSITES boost, advance, help, advantage

setting NOUN

*The hotel is in a very picturesque **setting**.*
surroundings, environment, background, position, location, locale, site

settle VERB

1 *The matter is **settled**, so let's talk about something else.*
decide, resolve, complete, conclude, arrange
2 *A robin **settled** on the branch.*
land, descend, alight
3 *The Pilgrim Fathers **settled** in America.*
colonize, occupy, populate, people, inhabit
4 *We **settled** our hotel bill before we left.*
pay, clear, discharge

severe ADJECTIVE

1 *a **severe** expression*
stern, disapproving, sober, strait-laced, grim
⊘ OPPOSITES kind, compassionate, sympathetic
2 *a **severe** teacher*
strict, stern, rigid, unbending, harsh, tough, hard, demanding
⊘ OPPOSITES kind, compassionate, sympathetic, lenient, mild
3 *severe pain*
acute, intense, extreme, fierce
⊘ OPPOSITES mild
4 *severe shortages*
serious, extreme, distressing
⊘ OPPOSITES slight

sew VERB

*My mother taught me how to **sew** and knit.*

stitch, tack, baste, hem, darn, embroider

shabby ADJECTIVE

1 *shabby clothes*
ragged, tattered, frayed, worn, worn-out, moth-eaten, scruffy, tatty
⊘ OPPOSITES smart
2 *a **shabby** room in a cheap hotel*
seedy, scruffy, dingy, run-down
⊘ OPPOSITES smart
3 *a **shabby** trick*
mean, contemptible, despicable, rotten, low, shameful, dishonourable
⊘ OPPOSITES honourable, fair

shade¹ NOUN

1 *I prefer to sit in the **shade**.*
shadow, shadiness, darkness, semi-darkness, dimness, gloom, gloominess
2 *a bright **shade** of pink*
hue, colour, tint, tone, tinge

shade² VERB

1 *I had to **shade** my eyes from the sudden light.*
shield, screen, protect, cover, veil, conceal
2 *The clouds **shaded** the sun.*
obscure, cloud, dim, darken, shadow, overshadow

shadow¹ NOUN

*The room was in **shadow**.*
shade, darkness, semi-darkness, dimness, gloom

shadow² VERB

*The detective **shadowed** the man through the town.*
follow, tail, stalk, trail, watch

shady ADJECTIVE

1 *a **shady** corner of the garden*
shaded, shadowy, dim, dark, cool
⊘ OPPOSITES sunny, sunlit, bright
2 *a **shady** character*
suspicious, dubious, suspect, dishonest, crooked, untrustworthy, disreputable, unscrupulous
◇ INFORMAL WORDS fishy
⊘ OPPOSITES honest, trustworthy, honourable

Aa
Bb
Cc
Dd
Ee
Ff
Gg
Hh
Ii
Jj
Kk
Ll
Mm
Nn
Oo
Pp
Qq
Rr
Ss
Tt
Uu
Vv
Ww
Xx
Yy
Zz

Aa
Bb
Cc
Dd
Ee
Ff
Gg
Hh
Ii
Jj
Kk
Ll
Mm
Nn
Oo
Pp
Qq
Rr
Ss
Tt
Uu
Vv
Ww
Xx
Yy
Zz

shake VERB

1 *He **shook** his fist at us.*
wave, flourish, brandish, wag, waggle
2 *The wind **shook** the branches.*
rattle, joggle, jolt, jerk, twitch
3 *The ladder **shook** under me.*
wobble, totter, sway, rock
4 *He was **shaking** with fear.*
tremble, quiver, quake, shiver, shudder
5 *The news **shook** her.*
upset, distress, shock, disturb, unsettle

shaky ADJECTIVE

*a **shaky** bridge*
unstable, unsteady, precarious, wobbly, rocky, tottering, rickety, insecure
(≠) OPPOSITES firm, strong

shallow ADJECTIVE

1 *a **shallow** cut*
surface, skin-deep, superficial, slight
(≠) OPPOSITES deep
2 *the **shallow** lifestyle of these celebrities*
frivolous, meaningless, trivial, foolish
(≠) OPPOSITES profound, deep

shame NOUN

1 *To my **shame**, I was caught stealing.*
embarrassment, humiliation, remorse, guilt
(≠) OPPOSITES honour, credit, distinction, pride
2 *You have brought **shame** on your parents.*
disgrace, dishonour, scandal, humiliation
(≠) OPPOSITES honour, credit, distinction, pride

shameful ADJECTIVE

*their **shameful** treatment of the prisoners*
disgraceful, outrageous, scandalous, abominable, wicked, contemptible, unworthy, dishonourable
(≠) OPPOSITES honourable, worthy

shape¹ NOUN

1 *a square **shape***
form, outline, silhouette, profile, lines, figure
2 *a bath sponge in the **shape** of a boat*
form, outline, model, mould, pattern, format
3 *Wear clothes that flatter your **shape**.*
figure, outline, silhouette, physique, build, frame

Here are some different shapes:

Curved shapes:
circle, semicircle, quadrant, oval, ellipse, crescent
Triangles:
equilateral triangle, isosceles triangle, right-angled triangle, scalene triangle
Quadrilaterals:
diamond, kite, oblong, parallelogram, rectangle, rhombus, square, trapezium
Polygons:
pentagon, hexagon, heptagon, octagon, nonagon, decagon
Polyhedrons:
cube, cuboid, prism, pyramid, tetrahedron, pentahedron, octahedron, cone, cylinder, sphere, hemisphere

shape² VERB

1 *He **shaped** the clay into a ball.*
form, fashion, model, mould, cast, sculpt, carve, whittle
2 *We began to **shape** our plans.*
make, produce, construct, create, devise, frame, plan, prepare

share¹ NOUN

*You will get your **share** of the money.*
part, portion, ration, quota, allowance, allocation, proportion, percentage

share² VERB

1 *We **shared** the expenses.*
split, divide, go halves on
2 *The group leader **shared** the tasks.*

divide, distribute, give out, deal out, allot, allocate, assign

sharp ADJECTIVE

1 *a sharp needle*
pointed, razor-sharp, cutting, jagged, barbed, spiky
(≠) OPPOSITES blunt
2 *a sharp outline*
clear, clear-cut, well-defined, distinct, marked, crisp
(≠) OPPOSITES blurred
3 *He may be 80, but he is still very sharp.*
quick-witted, alert, shrewd, astute, perceptive, observant, clever
(≠) OPPOSITES slow, stupid
4 *a sharp stabbing pain*
acute, sudden, violent, fierce, intense, severe, piercing, stabbing
(≠) OPPOSITES gentle
5 *a sharp taste*
sour, tart, vinegary, bitter, acid
(≠) OPPOSITES bland
6 *a sharp reply*
cutting, biting, sarcastic, scathing
(≠) OPPOSITES mild

shatter VERB

1 *The windscreen shattered when a small stone hit it.*
smash, break, splinter, crack, split, burst, explode
2 *Her life was shattered by the accident.*
destroy, wreck, ruin, overturn, upset

shed¹ VERB

1 *The snake shed its skin.*
cast off, cast, moult, discard
2 *A lorry has shed its load.*
spill, drop, pour, shower, scatter

shed² NOUN

a garden shed
hut, outhouse, shack

sheen NOUN

the sheen of her hair
gloss, shine, brightness, brilliance, shininess, polish
(≠) OPPOSITES dullness

sheer ADJECTIVE

1 *sheer stupidity*
total, utter, complete, absolute, thorough, pure, downright, out-and-out
2 *a sheer drop*
steep, vertical, abrupt
(≠) OPPOSITES gentle, gradual
3 *sheer fabric*
fine, thin, flimsy, gauzy, transparent, see-through
(≠) OPPOSITES thick, heavy

sheet NOUN

1 *a clean sheet of paper*
page, leaf, piece
2 *a sheet of glass*
pane, piece, panel, slab
3 *a sheet of ice on the canal*
layer, covering, coating, film

shelf NOUN

a set of wooden shelves
ledge, mantelpiece, sill

shell NOUN

monkey nuts in their shells
covering, case, hull, husk, crust, casing

shelter¹ NOUN

1 *a shelter for the homeless*
refuge, sanctuary, haven, accommodation, lodging
2 *We ran for shelter from the storm.*
protection, cover, shade, defence, safety, refuge
(≠) OPPOSITES exposure

shelter² VERB

1 *This umbrella will shelter you from the rain.*
cover, screen, shade, protect, safeguard, guard, shield
(≠) OPPOSITES expose
2 *The villagers sheltered the refugees.*
protect, shield, harbour, hide, accommodate, put up

shield VERB

Wear a big hat to shield your face from the sun.

Aa
Bb
Cc
Dd
Ee
Ff
Gg
Hh
Ii
Jj
Kk
Ll
Mm
Nn
Oo
Pp
Qq
Rr
Ss
Tt
Uu
Vv
Ww
Xx
Yy
Zz

protect, guard, safeguard, screen, shade, cover
≠ OPPOSITES expose

Aa

shift VERB
1 *Ali helped me to* **shift** *the furniture.*
move, relocate, reposition, rearrange, transpose, transfer, switch
2 *Could you* **shift** *out of the way, please?*
move, budge, change position

Bb

Cc

Dd

shine VERB
1 *The sun was* **shining** *on the sea.*
beam, glow, flash, glare
2 *The diamonds* **shone** *in the light.*
glitter, gleam, glint, sparkle, twinkle, shimmer, glisten, glimmer

Ee

Ff

Gg

Hh

shiny ADJECTIVE
a **shiny** *gold buckle*
bright, polished, glossy, gleaming, glistening
≠ OPPOSITES dull, matt

Ii

Jj

Kk

ship
⇒ see **boat**

Ll

shiver VERB
I **shivered** *in the cold.*
shake, shudder, tremble, quiver, quake

Mm

Nn

Oo

shock¹ NOUN
1 *They have not got over the* **shock** *of being burgled.*
upset, fright, bombshell, thunderbolt, blow, distress
≠ OPPOSITES delight, pleasure, reassurance
2 *You gave me a* **shock** *jumping out like that.*
fright, start, surprise

Pp

Qq

Rr

Ss

Tt

Uu

shock² VERB
1 *His bad language* **shocked** *my grandmother.*
offend, appal, disgust, outrage, scandalize, horrify, stun
≠ OPPOSITES delight, please, reassure
2 *We were* **shocked** *at the violence we witnessed.*

Vv

Ww

Xx

Yy

Zz

horrify, disgust, revolt, sicken, appal, shake, unsettle
≠ OPPOSITES delight, please, reassure

shocking ADJECTIVE
1 **shocking** *cruelty*
appalling, horrifying, atrocious, abominable, dreadful, ghastly, hideous, sickening, distressing
≠ OPPOSITES acceptable, satisfactory
2 **shocking** *language*
disgraceful, appalling, outrageous, scandalous, abominable, detestable, dreadful, disgusting, offensive
≠ OPPOSITES acceptable, satisfactory
3 *a* **shocking** *smell*
horrible, disgusting, revolting, repulsive, sickening, nauseating, offensive
≠ OPPOSITES pleasant, delightful
4 *Your clothes are in a* **shocking** *state.*
terrible, appalling, dreadful, awful, frightful, disgraceful
≠ OPPOSITES acceptable, satisfactory, pleasant, delightful

shoddy ADJECTIVE
1 **shoddy** *goods*
inferior, second-rate, cheap, tatty, trashy, rubbishy
≠ OPPOSITES superior, well-made
2 *I won't accept* **shoddy** *work.*
inferior, second-rate, poor, careless, slipshod, slapdash
≠ OPPOSITES superior

shoe NOUN

Here are some types of shoe:
boots, clogs, espadrilles, flip-flops, moccasins, platforms, plimsolls, pumps, sandals, shoes, slippers, stilettos, trainers, walking boots, wellington boots

shoot VERB
1 *We were* **shooting** *arrows at a target.*
fire, discharge, launch, propel, hurl, fling, project

2 *He suddenly **shot** forward into the road.*
speed, dart, bolt, dash, tear, rush, race, charge
3 *He was **shot** in the street.*
hit, kill, gun down
◇ INFORMAL WORDS blast

shop NOUN

Here are some types of shop:

Large shops:
department store, hypermarket, supermarket, superstore
Food shops:
baker, butcher, confectioner, dairy, delicatessen, fish-and-chip shop, fishmonger, greengrocer, grocer, health-food shop, sweet shop, takeaway, tuck shop
Clothes shops:
boutique, dress shop, milliner, outfitter, shoe shop, tailor
Other types of shop:
bookshop, charity shop, chemist, computer shop, electrical shop, florist, hardware shop, ironmonger, jeweller, newsagent, pharmacy, stationer, tobacconist, toy shop

shore NOUN
*a sandy **shore***
beach, seashore, sands, front, coast, lakeside, bank

short ADJECTIVE
1 *a **short** visit*
brief, fleeting, momentary
≠ OPPOSITES long
2 *a **short** story*
brief, concise, compact, shortened, abbreviated, summarized
≠ OPPOSITES long
3 *This is the **short** version of a longer article.*
shortened, abbreviated, summarized
≠ OPPOSITES long
4 *She was rather **short** with me.*

snappy, gruff, sharp, abrupt, rude, impolite, discourteous
≠ OPPOSITES polite
5 *a **short** person*
small, little, low, petite, squat, dumpy
≠ OPPOSITES tall
6 *Money is **short** this month so we can't afford luxuries.*
scarce, inadequate, insufficient, lacking, low, sparse
≠ OPPOSITES adequate, ample

shortage NOUN
*a **shortage** of food*
scarcity, inadequacy, insufficiency, lack, want
≠ OPPOSITES sufficiency

shorten VERB
*She **shortened** her name from Stephanie to Steph.*
cut, abbreviate, abridge, reduce
≠ OPPOSITES lengthen

shortly ADVERB
*We'll be home **shortly**.*
soon, before long, presently, by and by

shot NOUN
1 *a **shot** from a gun*
blast, discharge, bang
2 *I had a **shot** at skiing.*
attempt, try, turn
◇ INFORMAL WORDS go, bash, crack, stab

shout VERB
*There's no need to **shout**.*
yell, call, cry, scream, shriek, roar, bellow, bawl

shove VERB
*I was **shoved** to the back of the crowd.*
push, thrust, drive, propel, force, jostle, elbow, shoulder

show[1] NOUN
1 *She is singing in a West End **show**.*
entertainment, spectacle, performance, production
2 *The gallery is putting on a **show** of his paintings.*

Aa
Bb
Cc
Dd
Ee
Ff
Gg
Hh
Ii
Jj
Kk
Ll
Mm
Nn
Oo
Pp
Qq
Rr
Ss
Tt
Uu
Vv
Ww
Xx
Yy
Zz

exhibition, demonstration, presentation, display, showing

show² VERB

1 *Can you show me how to use the dishwasher?*
demonstrate, explain, instruct, teach
2 *He shows great promise as a guitarist.*
exhibit, display
3 *Will you show him out, please?*
lead, guide, conduct, usher, escort, accompany

• **show off**
1 *He's just showing off in front of his friends.*
boast, strut, swagger, brag
2 *She showed off her new dress.*
exhibit, parade, flaunt

shower VERB

He showered her with presents.
overwhelm, load, heap, lavish

showy ADJECTIVE

a showy outfit
flashy, gaudy, garish, loud, fancy
◇ INFORMAL WORDS swanky, flash
(≠) OPPOSITES quiet, restrained

shred NOUN

1 *There were shreds of carrot left in the bottom of the pan.*
scrap, bit, piece, fragment
2 *not a shred of evidence*
scrap, jot, iota, atom, grain, trace

shrewd ADJECTIVE

a shrewd businessman
smart, clever, sharp, perceptive, knowing, cunning, crafty
(≠) OPPOSITES unwise, naïve, unsophisticated

shriek VERB

She shrieked with surprise.
scream, screech, squawk, squeal, cry, shout, yell

shrill ADJECTIVE

Her shrill voice carried right across the playground.
piercing, high, high-pitched, sharp,

penetrating, screeching, ear-splitting
(≠) OPPOSITES deep, low, soft, gentle

shrink VERB

1 *My T-shirt has shrunk in the wash.*
get smaller, contract, decrease, lessen, dwindle, shorten, narrow
(≠) OPPOSITES expand, stretch
2 *She doesn't shrink from her duties.*
recoil, back away, shy away, withdraw, shun
(≠) OPPOSITES accept

shrivel VERB

The plant started to shrivel in the heat.
dry up, wither, wilt, shrink, dwindle, dehydrate

shudder VERB

I shuddered going into that dark creepy house.
shiver, shake, tremble, quiver, quake

shuffle VERB

1 *Shuffle the cards before you deal.*
mix up, jumble, rearrange, reorganize, shift around, switch
2 *She shuffled across the room in her slippers.*
shamble, scuffle, scrape, drag

shut VERB

Shut the window.
close, slam, seal, fasten, secure, lock, latch, bolt, bar
(≠) OPPOSITES open

• **shut up**
1 *Oh, do shut up!*
be quiet, be silent, hush up, hold your tongue
◇ INFORMAL WORDS pipe down, clam up
2 *He is shut up in prison.*
confine, coop up, imprison, jail

shy ADJECTIVE

She is too shy to approach a stranger.
timid, bashful, reserved, retiring, self-conscious, modest, nervous
(≠) OPPOSITES bold, confident

sick ADJECTIVE

1 *I hear you've been sick all this week.*

ill, unwell, poorly, sickly, under the weather
◇ INFORMAL WORDS laid up
≢ OPPOSITES well, healthy
2 I'm **sick** of being kept waiting.
tired, bored, fed up, weary

sickly ADJECTIVE
a **sickly** child
unhealthy, delicate, weak, feeble, frail
≢ OPPOSITES healthy, robust, sturdy, strong

side NOUN
1 the **side** of the lake
edge, margin, border, boundary, limit, brink, bank, shore
2 The shape has four **sides**.
face, facet, surface
3 There are two **sides** to every argument.
viewpoint, standpoint, view
4 Both **sides** played well in the final.
team, crew
5 Which **side** do you support in this dispute?
party, camp, cause

side with VERB
You don't have to **side with** anyone in the argument.
support, back, agree with, stand up for, take the side of

sift VERB
Sift the flour into the mixing bowl.
sieve, strain, filter

sigh VERB
1 He **sighed** in exasperation.
breathe out, exhale
2 'I have to do everything around here,' she **sighed**.
complain, moan

sight¹ NOUN
1 He lost his **sight** as he got older.
vision, eyesight, seeing
2 We watched the ship till it was out of **sight**.
view, range, field of vision, visibility
3 She faints at the **sight** of spiders.

view, glance, glimpse
4 You look a **sight** dressed like that.
eyesore, monstrosity
◇ INFORMAL WORDS fright

sight² VERB
I **sighted** the comet just above the horizon.
spot, see, observe, glimpse, distinguish, make out

sign NOUN
1 a division **sign**
symbol, token, figure, representation
2 The company's **sign** appears on all their products.
emblem, badge, logo
3 There was no **sign** of her anywhere.
indication, mark, clue, hint, suggestion, trace
4 He gave no **sign** that he had heard me.
indication, signal, gesture
5 The **sign** said, 'Keep off the grass'.
notice, poster, board, placard
6 a **sign** of things to come
omen, forewarning, foreboding

signal¹ NOUN
Give me a **signal** when you want to leave.
sign, indication, gesture, cue

signal² VERB
The police **signalled** to us to stop.
gesture, wave, beckon, motion, nod, sign, indicate

significant ADJECTIVE
This will make a **significant** difference to our lives.
important, serious, noteworthy, critical, vital, marked, considerable
≢ OPPOSITES insignificant, unimportant, trivial

signify VERB
A sign with an 'i' on it **signifies** tourist information.
mean, denote, symbolize, represent, stand for, indicate, show

Aa
Bb
Cc
Dd
Ee
Ff
Gg
Hh
Ii
Jj
Kk
Ll
Mm
Nn
Oo
Pp
Qq
Rr
Ss
Tt
Uu
Vv
Ww
Xx
Yy
Zz

silence¹ NOUN

There was complete silence when she walked in.

quiet, quietness, hush, peace, stillness, calm, soundlessness

≠ OPPOSITES noise, sound

silence² VERB

The thick carpet silenced the sound of his footsteps.

quieten, quiet, hush, mute, muffle

silent ADJECTIVE

1 *The garden was completely silent in the darkness.*

quiet, noiseless, soundless, peaceful, still, hushed

≠ OPPOSITES noisy, loud

2 *We fell silent as we gazed out over the valley.*

quiet, mute, dumb, speechless, tongue-tied

≠ OPPOSITES noisy, talkative

3 *a silent man who rarely smiled*

quiet, taciturn, reserved

≠ OPPOSITES noisy, talkative

silly ADJECTIVE

1 *You've been a very silly young man.*

foolish, stupid, idiotic, daft, childish, immature, irresponsible, scatterbrained

≠ OPPOSITES wise, sensible, mature, clever, intelligent

2 *It was just a silly prank.*

foolish, stupid, senseless, pointless, idiotic, daft, ridiculous, absurd, meaningless

≠ OPPOSITES wise, sensible, clever, intelligent

similar ADJECTIVE

Our backgrounds were very similar.

alike, like, close, related, corresponding, equivalent, comparable

≠ OPPOSITES dissimilar, different

similarity NOUN

There is no similarity between the two cases.

resemblance, likeness, closeness, relation, correspondence, equivalence, comparability

≠ OPPOSITES dissimilarity, difference

simple ADJECTIVE

1 *a simple question*

easy, straightforward, uncomplicated, clear, plain, understandable

≠ OPPOSITES difficult, hard, complicated

2 *a simple person*

unsophisticated, natural, innocent, naïve

≠ OPPOSITES sophisticated

simply ADVERB

1 *The dish consists simply of pasta, tomatoes and basil.*

just, merely, only, solely, purely

2 *That's a simply ridiculous idea.*

totally, utterly, completely, wholly, absolutely, quite, really

3 *Explain it to me very simply.*

clearly, plainly, obviously

sin NOUN

Most people believe it is a sin to kill.

crime, offence, wrongdoing, evil, wrong

sincere ADJECTIVE

1 *a sincere and dependable man*

honest, truthful, frank, open, direct, straightforward

≠ OPPOSITES insincere, hypocritical

2 *a sincere apology*

honest, serious, earnest, heartfelt, wholehearted, real, true, genuine

≠ OPPOSITES insincere, hypocritical

sing VERB

She sings with a band.

chant, croon, serenade, yodel, warble, chirp, hum

singe VERB

I singed my hair on a lit candle.

burn, scorch, char, blacken, sear

single ADJECTIVE

1 *I haven't had a single reply to my invitations.*

one, singular, sole, only, lone, solitary

Aa Bb Cc Dd Ee Ff Gg Hh Ii Jj Kk Ll Mm Nn Oo Pp Qq Rr Ss Tt Uu Vv Ww Xx Yy Zz

≠ OPPOSITES multiple

2 *Every single child received a present.*
individual, unique, particular, exclusive

3 *Are you married or single?*
unmarried, free, unattached

≠ OPPOSITES married, attached

single-handed ADVERB

He has brought up the children single-handed.

alone, solo, unaccompanied, unaided, unassisted, independently

single out VERB

1 *She was singled out for the lead part in the school play.*

choose, select, pick, hand-pick

2 *He felt singled out by the other children.*

set apart, separate, isolate

3 *I'd like to single out one entry in particular.*

identify, distinguish, highlight, pinpoint

sinister ADJECTIVE

a sinister plot

threatening, menacing, disturbing, evil

≠ OPPOSITES harmless, innocent

sink VERB

1 *The sun sank behind the hills.*

descend, dip, set, disappear, vanish

≠ OPPOSITES rise

2 *She sank to her knees with exhaustion.*

drop, slip, fall, slump, droop

≠ OPPOSITES rise

3 *The model ship sank in the pond.*

plunge, dive, plummet, submerge

≠ OPPOSITES float

sit VERB

Come and sit on the sofa beside me.
settle, rest, perch

site NOUN

the site where the accident happened
place, location, spot, position, situation, setting, scene, area

situation NOUN

1 *an attractive situation for a picnic*

place, site, location, position, spot, setting

2 *a tricky situation*

state of affairs, case, circumstances, predicament, state, condition

size NOUN

The boxes come in various sizes.
measurement, dimensions, proportions, volume, bulk, mass, extent

sketch¹ NOUN

He did a quick sketch of the garden's layout.

drawing, design, plan, diagram, outline

sketch² VERB

I sketched the view from the garden.

draw, pencil, outline, draft, rough out, block out

skilful ADJECTIVE

a skilful footballer

capable, able, competent, expert, masterly, accomplished, skilled, practised

≠ OPPOSITES clumsy, awkward

skill NOUN

artistic skill

ability, skilfulness, talent, knack, training, experience, expertise, competence

skilled ADJECTIVE

a skilled carpenter

skilful, trained, experienced, practised, accomplished, expert, able

≠ OPPOSITES unskilled, inexperienced

skim VERB

A stone skimmed over the surface of the water.

glide, brush, skate, plane, sail, fly

• **skim through**

I quickly skimmed through the questions.

scan, look through, skip through

skin NOUN

1 *There was a skin on the custard.*

film, coating, surface

Aa
Bb
Cc
Dd
Ee
Ff
Gg
Hh
Ii
Jj
Kk
Ll
Mm
Nn
Oo
Pp
Qq
Rr
Ss
Tt
Uu
Vv
Ww
Xx
Yy
Zz

2 *I peeled the **skin** off the banana.*
peel, rind, husk, casing, crust

skinny ADJECTIVE
*a **skinny** fashion model*
thin, lean, scrawny, scraggy, skin-and-bone, underfed, undernourished
≠ OPPOSITES fat, plump

skip VERB
1 *The girl **skipped** down the street.*
hop, jump, leap, dance, prance
2 *I **skipped** a page of my book.*
miss out, miss, omit, leave out

sky NOUN
*There was not a cloud in the **sky**.*
heavens, space, atmosphere, air

slab NOUN
*a **slab** of toffee*
piece, block, lump, chunk, hunk, wedge, slice, portion

slack ADJECTIVE
1 *My trousers are too **slack**.*
loose, sagging, baggy
≠ OPPOSITES tight
2 *a **slack** period*
quiet, idle, inactive, slow
≠ OPPOSITES busy
3 *a **slack** attitude to his work*
careless, inattentive, lax, negligent

slacken VERB
*He **slackened** his grip.*
loosen, release, relax, ease
≠ OPPOSITES tighten

• slacken off
*Custom in the café **slackens off** after lunch time.*
lessen, ease, reduce, decrease, diminish, slow, slow down
≠ OPPOSITES increase, intensify, quicken

slam VERB
*She stormed out, **slamming** the door.*
bang, crash, smash

slant VERB
*Your writing **slants** to the right.*
tilt, slope, incline, lean, angle

slap VERB
*She **slapped** his face in anger.*
smack, spank, hit, strike, cuff, bang
◇ INFORMAL WORDS clout

slash VERB
*His jacket was **slashed** to ribbons.*
cut, slit, gash, rip, tear

slaughter VERB
*the young men who were **slaughtered** in the war*
kill, murder, massacre
◆ FORMAL WORDS slay

slave VERB
*She **slaved** away at her homework.*
toil, labour, drudge, sweat, grind
◇ INFORMAL WORDS slog

sleek ADJECTIVE
***sleek** shiny hair*
shiny, glossy, smooth, silky
≠ OPPOSITES rough, unkempt

sleep VERB
*I can't **sleep** with all that noise going on.*
doze, slumber, drop off, nod off
◇ INFORMAL WORDS kip, doss down, snooze

sleepy ADJECTIVE
*In the evening I began to feel **sleepy**.*
drowsy, tired, weary, slow, sluggish, inactive
≠ OPPOSITES awake, alert, restless

slender ADJECTIVE
*a tall **slender** girl*
slim, thin, slight, graceful
≠ OPPOSITES fat

slice¹ NOUN
*a **slice** of melon*
piece, slab, wedge, segment, section, portion

slice² VERB
*She **sliced** the cake.*
cut, carve, chop, divide

Aa Bb Cc Dd Ee Ff Gg Hh Ii Jj Kk Ll Mm Nn Oo Pp Qq Rr **Ss** Tt Uu Vv Ww Xx Yy Zz

slick ADJECTIVE
a slick performance
skilful, professional

slide VERB
We slid down the hill on our sledge.
slip, slither, skid, glide, plane, coast, skim

slight ADJECTIVE
a slight mistake
small, minor, unimportant, insignificant, trivial, paltry, little
⊘ OPPOSITES major, significant, noticeable

slim ADJECTIVE
a slim figure
slender, thin, trim
⊘ OPPOSITES fat, chubby

sling VERB
He slung the apple core in the bin.
throw, hurl, fling, heave, pitch, toss
◇ INFORMAL WORDS chuck, lob

slink VERB
Why were you slinking around outside the house?
sneak, steal, creep, sidle, slip, prowl, skulk

slip VERB
1 *I slipped on the ice.*
slide, glide, skate, skid, stumble, trip, fall
2 *She slipped into the room unseen.*
sneak, slink, steal, creep

slippery ADJECTIVE
a slippery surface
slippy, icy, greasy, glassy, smooth
⊘ OPPOSITES rough

slit¹ NOUN
a skirt with a slit at the side
opening, cut, gash, slash, split, tear

slit² VERB
He slit his hand on the broken glass.
cut, gash, slash, slice, split, rip, tear

slither VERB
The python slithered across the grass.
slide, slip, glide, creep, snake, worm

slogan NOUN
an advertising slogan
catch-phrase, jingle, motto, catchword, battle-cry

slope¹ NOUN
The house is built on a slope.
hill, ramp, slant, tilt

slope² VERB
The golf course fairway slopes to the left.
slant, lean, tilt, incline, rise, fall

sloppy ADJECTIVE
1 *a sloppy mixture*
runny, watery, wet, liquid, mushy, slushy
⊘ OPPOSITES solid
2 *sloppy work*
careless, slapdash, slipshod, untidy, messy, clumsy
◇ INFORMAL WORDS hit-or-miss
⊘ OPPOSITES careful, exact, precise
3 *a sloppy song*
sentimental, schmaltzy
◇ INFORMAL WORDS soppy, mushy, slushy

slot NOUN
Put a coin in the slot.
hole, opening, slit, groove, channel, gap, space

slouch VERB
1 *She was slouching over her desk.*
slump, hunch, droop, lounge, loll
2 *He slouched across the room.*
shuffle, shamble

slow ADJECTIVE
⇒ For even more about this word, see the next page
1 *a slow pace*
leisurely, unhurried, loitering, dawdling, lazy, creeping, plodding
⊘ OPPOSITES quick, fast, swift, rapid, speedy

Aa
Bb
Cc
Dd
Ee
Ff
Gg
Hh
Ii
Jj
Kk
Ll
Mm
Nn
Oo
Pp
Qq
Rr
Ss
Tt
Uu
Vv
Ww
Xx
Yy
Zz

slow

The words below also tell you something about a person or creature and how they are moving. Although they are all words you can use instead of **slow**, they paint pictures of very different characters!

These words describe a slow pace. They help us to picture a relaxed person or creature:

leisurely
gradual
steady
unhurried
relaxed

These words also describe a slow pace, but this time they suggest someone is finding things hard going:

ponderous
plodding
sluggish

These words show that you do not approve of the way a person acts:

lazy
idle
tardy

These words show that someone is taking their time with a task to do it properly:

careful
cautious
deliberate
painstaking

Over to you

Can you change the word **slow** in the sentences below to improve them?

The climber was determined to reach the snowy peak ahead of him; he made slow progress but this paid off. Carefully he took the last slow steps to the top of the peak and unfurled his country's flag ...

2 *He's too **slow** to understand.*
stupid, slow-witted, dim
◇ INFORMAL WORDS thick
≠ OPPOSITES clever, intelligent
3 *I found the film very **slow** and much too long.*
prolonged, long-drawn-out, boring, dull, uninteresting, uneventful
≠ OPPOSITES brisk, lively, exciting

slow down VERB
Slow down in case you have an accident.
brake, decelerate
≠ OPPOSITES speed up, accelerate

slump[1] NOUN
1 *a **slump** in sales*
fall, drop, downturn, collapse, failure
≠ OPPOSITES boom
2 *the stock market **slump** of the late 1980s*
recession, depression, crash, failure
≠ OPPOSITES boom

slump[2] VERB
1 *Trade **slumped** in the winter.*
drop, collapse, fall, plunge, plummet, sink, fail
2 *He **slumped** against the wall in exhaustion.*
sag, droop, slouch, lounge, flop

sly ADJECTIVE
1 *He's up to his **sly** tricks again.*
crafty, cunning, clever, shrewd, devious, tricky, underhand, scheming
≠ OPPOSITES honest, frank, open
2 *a **sly** grin*
mischievous, knowing, roguish
3 *They kept giving each other **sly** little looks.*
stealthy, shifty, furtive, secretive
≠ OPPOSITES honest, frank, open

smack VERB
*The woman **smacked** her child because he was naughty.*
hit, strike, slap, spank, cuff
◇ INFORMAL WORDS whack

small ADJECTIVE
➡ For even more about this word, see the next page

1 *a **small** child*
little, tiny, petite, miniature, mini, pocket-sized
≠ OPPOSITES large, big, huge
2 *a **small** detail*
unimportant, petty, trivial, insignificant, minor, inconsiderable
≠ OPPOSITES great

smart[1] ADJECTIVE
1 *You look very **smart** in that outfit.*
stylish, elegant, chic, fashionable, neat, tidy, trim, well-groomed
≠ OPPOSITES dowdy, unfashionable, untidy, scruffy
2 *That was a **smart** move.*
clever, intelligent, bright, sharp, shrewd
≠ OPPOSITES stupid, slow

smart[2] VERB
*My arm **smarts** where I burned it.*
sting, hurt, prickle, burn, tingle

smash VERB
1 *The burglars **smashed** a window.*
break, shatter, demolish, destroy
2 *He **smashed** his fist angrily on the table.*
crash, strike, bang, bash, thump

smear VERB
*His face was **smeared** with mud.*
daub, plaster, spread, cover, coat, smudge, streak

smell NOUN
*a **smell** coming from the kitchen*
odour, scent, perfume, fragrance, aroma, stench, stink

smile VERB
*She **smiled** when she opened her birthday present.*
beam, grin, simper, smirk

smoke NOUN
Smoke rose from the chimney.
fumes, exhaust, smog

smooth[1] ADJECTIVE
1 *a nice **smooth** surface*
level, plane, even, flat, horizontal, flush

Aa
Bb
Cc
Dd
Ee
Ff
Gg
Hh
Ii
Jj
Kk
Ll
Mm
Nn
Oo
Pp
Qq
Rr
Ss
Tt
Uu
Vv
Ww
Xx
Yy
Zz

small

Instead of using the word **small**, choose a word that tells your reader exactly what you mean.

To describe a small human, creature, or house, you could use the words
little
short
petite
mini
pocket-sized

To describe something very small, you could use the words
tiny
minute
miniature

These words suggest that something is small and not strong:
puny
slight

You could use these words to describe a small amount that is not enough:
scanty
meagre
paltry
limited
inadequate
insufficient
trifling

You could use these words to describe a small problem that is not important:
unimportant
petty
insignificant
minor
negligible

Over to you

Could you use some of these words in the sentences that follow?

1 The _____ creature walked across the table.

2 Tinkerbell's _____ figure appeared at the window.

3 Tom Thumb was a _____ boy.

4 She was _____ and _____ but her voice was powerful and filled the hall!

5 She thought that £5 was a _____ amount to pay for chocolates.

6 Children used to work in coalmines for a _____ amount of money.

Aa
Bb
Cc
Dd
Ee
Ff
Gg
Hh
Ii
Jj
Kk
Ll
Mm
Nn
Oo
Pp
Qq
Rr
Ss
Tt
Uu
Vv
Ww
Xx
Yy
Zz

≠ OPPOSITES rough, lumpy
2 *The plane made a **smooth** landing.*
steady, easy, effortless
≠ OPPOSITES bumpy, irregular, unsteady
3 *smooth shiny hair*
silky, shiny, glossy
≠ OPPOSITES rough
4 *smooth water*
calm, undisturbed, peaceful, glassy
≠ OPPOSITES rough, choppy
5 *a smooth talker*
persuasive, slick, glib, smooth-talking, suave
◇ INFORMAL WORDS smarmy

smooth² VERB

*She **smoothed** out the creases in her dress.*
flatten, iron, press
≠ OPPOSITES wrinkle, crease

smother VERB

*He tried to **smother** her with a pillow.*
suffocate, choke, stifle

smudge¹ NOUN

*There was a **smudge** of ink on the printout.*
smear, blot, stain, spot, streak

smudge² VERB

*He had **smudged** the glass with his sticky fingers.*
smear, daub, mark, spot, stain, dirty

smug ADJECTIVE

*He looked **smug** because he knew the answer.*
self-satisfied, complacent, superior, self-righteous, conceited
≠ OPPOSITES humble, modest

snack NOUN

*A light **snack** will keep us going.*
refreshment, bite, nibble

snag NOUN

*We've hit a **snag**.*
problem, drawback, catch, difficulty, complication, setback, hitch, obstacle

snake NOUN

Here are some types of snake:

adder, anaconda, asp, boa constrictor, cobra, grass snake, king cobra, mamba, puff adder, python, rattlesnake, sidewinder, tree snake, viper

Aa
Bb
Cc
Dd
Ee
Ff
Gg
Hh
Ii
Jj
Kk
Ll
Mm
Nn
Oo
Pp
Qq
Rr
Ss
Tt
Uu
Vv
Ww
Xx
Yy
Zz

snap VERB
The twig snapped.
break, crack, split, separate

snatch VERB
1 *He snatched my bag from my shoulder and ran off.*
grab, seize, take, pluck, pull, wrench
2 *He snatched my hand and held it tight.*
grab, seize, take, clutch, grasp, grip

sneak VERB
We'll sneak away when nobody is looking.
slip, creep, steal, slink, skulk

sneer VERB
They sneered at his attempt to tell a joke.
laugh, scorn, look down on, scoff, jeer, mock, ridicule

snide ADJECTIVE
a snide remark
nasty, hurtful, unkind, mean, spiteful, malicious, sneering
◆ FORMAL WORDS disparaging
⊭ OPPOSITES complimentary

snobbish ADJECTIVE
They are too snobbish to be friends with the rest of us.
superior, arrogant
◇ INFORMAL WORDS snooty, stuck-up, toffee-nosed, high and mighty

snoop VERB
Don't snoop about in my room.
spy, sneak, pry

snooze VERB
snoozing in front of the TV
nap, doze, sleep
◇ INFORMAL WORDS kip

snub VERB
She snubbed her ex-boyfriend at the party.
insult, cut, cold-shoulder, slight, put down, shame, humiliate
◇ INFORMAL WORDS brush off

snug ADJECTIVE
a snug little cottage
cosy, warm, comfortable, homely, intimate

soak VERB
1 *I got soaked in the rain.*
wet, drench, bathe
2 *Soak the kidney beans overnight in cold water.*
steep, submerge, immerse
• **soak up**
The cloth will soak up the spilt milk.
absorb

soar VERB
1 *The bird soared up into the sky.*
fly, wing, glide, rise, ascend, climb
⊭ OPPOSITES fall, plummet
2 *House prices are soaring.*
rise, increase, climb, mount, spiral, rocket
⊭ OPPOSITES fall, plummet

sob VERB
The woman sobbed with relief when her child was found.
cry, weep, bawl, howl, blubber, snivel

sober ADJECTIVE
1 *a sober attitude to life*
solemn, serious, staid, steady, sedate, calm, composed, unruffled, unexcited
⊭ OPPOSITES excited
2 *Let's take a sober look at the situation.*
realistic, rational, level-headed, practical, reasonable, clear-headed
⊭ OPPOSITES unrealistic, irrational

so-called ADJECTIVE
a so-called psychic who turned out to be a fraud
supposed, alleged, self-styled, would-be, pretended

society NOUN

the photographic society
club, association, circle, group, guild

soft ADJECTIVE

1 *a soft mattress*
yielding, flexible
≠ OPPOSITES hard
2 *a soft dough*
squashy, yielding, spongy, pulpy
≠ OPPOSITES hard
3 *soft colours*
pale, light, pastel, delicate, subdued, muted
≠ OPPOSITES harsh
4 *soft lighting*
subdued, muted, dim, faint
≠ OPPOSITES harsh
5 *soft music*
quiet, subdued, muted, faint, pleasant
≠ OPPOSITES harsh
6 *a soft texture*
velvety, furry, downy, silky, smooth
≠ OPPOSITES rough
7 *You're too soft with that boy.*
easy-going, lenient, lax, permissive, indulgent, tolerant, soft-hearted
≠ OPPOSITES strict, severe
8 *Under that gruff exterior, he is really quite soft.*
kind, generous, gentle, soft-hearted
≠ OPPOSITES strict, severe
9 *Don't go soft on us now!*
weak, sensitive, spineless
◇ INFORMAL WORDS wimpy, wet
≠ OPPOSITES tough

soggy ADJECTIVE

The ground was soggy after the rain.
soaked, sodden, drenched, waterlogged, saturated, sopping, dripping

soil¹ NOUN

digging in the soil
earth, clay, dirt, dust, ground, land

soil² VERB

His overalls were soiled with grease.
dirty, stain, spot, smudge, smear

soldier NOUN

My friend's dad is a soldier.
warrior, fighter

Here are some types of soldier:

cadet, cavalryman, commando, guardsman, gunner, infantryman, lancer, marine, officer, paratrooper, private, sentry, trooper
Words connected with soldiers:
armoured car, artillery, barracks, bayonet, bedroll, body armour, boots, bullet, camouflage, cannon, cartridge belt, cavalry, grenade, gun, helmet, Jeep, kit, kitbag, parade, pistol, rifle, sandbag, tank, uniform

sole ADJECTIVE

1 *My sole desire is to be happy.*
only, single, singular, one, lone, solitary, alone
≠ OPPOSITES multiple
2 *He has sole possession of the property.*
exclusive, unique, individual
≠ OPPOSITES shared

solemn ADJECTIVE

1 *a solemn expression*
serious, grave, sober, sombre
≠ OPPOSITES light-hearted
2 *a solemn occasion*
grand, stately, majestic, formal, dignified, awe-inspiring, impressive, imposing

solid ADJECTIVE

1 *solid rock*
firm, hard, dense, compact
≠ OPPOSITES hollow
2 *a solid foundation*
strong, sturdy, substantial, sound, unshakable
3 *a solid dependable person*
reliable, dependable, trustworthy, sensible, level-headed
≠ OPPOSITES unreliable, unstable

Aa
Bb
Cc
Dd
Ee
Ff
Gg
Hh
Ii
Jj
Kk
Ll
Mm
Nn
Oo
Pp
Qq
Rr
Ss
Tt
Uu
Vv
Ww
Xx
Yy
Zz

solution NOUN

the solution to the problem
answer, result, explanation, resolution, key, remedy

solve VERB

I can't solve all your problems for you.
work out, figure out, puzzle out, decipher, crack, answer, settle, clear up, explain

sometimes ADVERB

Sometimes I walk home and other times I take the bus.
occasionally, now and again, now and then, once in a while, from time to time
OPPOSITES always, never

song NOUN

He wrote a song for his mother.
tune, ditty, air

Here are some types of song:

anthem, ballad, blues, calypso, carol, chant, dirge, folk song, gospel song, hymn, jingle, love song, lullaby, nursery rhyme, pop song, psalm, serenade, shanty, spiritual, yodel
⇒ Also look up **poem**

soon ADVERB

It will soon be winter.
shortly, presently, in a minute, before long, in the near future

soothe VERB

1 *This ointment will soothe the pain.*
relieve, ease, lessen, reduce
OPPOSITES aggravate
2 *It took a long time to soothe the baby.*
calm, comfort, settle, compose, hush, lull, pacify, quiet, still
OPPOSITES irritate

sophisticated ADJECTIVE

1 *a sophisticated woman of the world*
worldly, worldly-wise, cultured, cultivated, refined, polished
OPPOSITES unsophisticated, naïve
2 *sophisticated equipment*
advanced, high-tech, state-of-the-art, cutting-edge, complicated, complex, intricate, elaborate
OPPOSITES primitive, simple

sore ADJECTIVE

a sore leg
painful, hurting, aching, smarting, stinging, tender, sensitive, inflamed, red, raw

sorrow NOUN

They could not hide their sorrow at their loss.
sadness, unhappiness, grief, mourning, misery, distress, anguish
OPPOSITES happiness, joy

sorry ADJECTIVE

1 *He said he was sorry for upsetting me.*
apologetic, regretful, remorseful, repentant, conscience-stricken, guilt-ridden, shamefaced
OPPOSITES unashamed
2 *I was sorry to hear your sad news.*
sympathetic, compassionate, understanding, pitying, concerned, moved
OPPOSITES uncaring

sort[1] VERB

I sorted my CDs alphabetically.
class, group, categorize, order, classify, catalogue, arrange, organize
• **sort out**
1 *Can you sort out your washing for me?*
separate, divide, choose, select
2 *There's a lot to sort out before we move.*
arrange, tidy up, neaten, organize
3 *We managed to sort out the misunderstanding.*
resolve, clear up, deal with, clarify

sort[2] NOUN

A piano is a sort of musical instrument.

kind, type, breed, species, variety, order, class, category, group

sound¹ NOUN

*the **sound** of hammering*
noise, din, resonance, reverberation, tone, report

sound² ADJECTIVE

1 *He's 80 but his heart is still **sound**.*
fit, well, healthy, vigorous, sturdy, firm, unhurt, uninjured
OPPOSITES unfit, ill, shaky
2 *The walls of the castle were **sound**.*
solid, whole, complete, intact, perfect, unbroken, undamaged
OPPOSITES damaged
3 *a **sound** argument*
valid, well-founded, reasonable, rational, logical, water-tight, reliable, trustworthy
OPPOSITES unsound, unreliable, poor

sour ADJECTIVE

1 *a **sour** grapefruit*
tart, sharp, acid, vinegary, bitter
OPPOSITES sweet, sugary
2 *a **sour** expression*
bad-tempered, disagreeable, peevish, snappy, embittered
OPPOSITES good-natured, generous

source NOUN

*the **source** of the problem*
origin, beginning, start, commencement, cause, root

sow VERB

sowing seeds
plant, seed, scatter, spread

space NOUN

1 *There wasn't enough **space** for all my books.*
room, place, accommodation, capacity, elbow-room
2 *an empty **space***
blank, gap, opening, omission
3 *creatures from **space***
outer space, deep space

Here are some words connected with space:

asteroid, astronaut, black hole, capsule, comet, constellation, cosmos, galaxy, meteor, milky way, moon, nebula, planet, probe, rocket, satellite, shooting star, solar system, space shuttle, space station, star, sun, universe
⇒ Also look up **planet**

spacious ADJECTIVE

*a nice **spacious** room*
roomy, big, large, sizable, broad, wide, extensive, open, uncrowded
OPPOSITES small, cramped, confined

span¹ NOUN

*the **span** of an eagle's wings*
spread, stretch, reach, range, scope, extent, length, distance

span² VERB

*The story **spans** three generations of a family.*
bridge, link, cross, extend, cover

spare¹ ADJECTIVE

*a **spare** pair of trousers*
reserve, emergency, extra, additional, leftover, remaining, unused, over, free
OPPOSITES necessary, vital, used

spare² VERB

1 *No one was **spared** in the attack.*
pardon, let off, reprieve, release, free
2 *Can you **spare** £5?*
afford, part with, give, provide

spark NOUN

*A **spark** from the fire burned a hole in the rug.*
flash, flare, gleam, glint, flicker

sparkle VERB

*The diamonds in her ring **sparkled**.*
twinkle, glitter, flash, gleam, glint, glisten, shimmer, shine, beam

Aa
Bb
Cc
Dd
Ee
Ff
Gg
Hh
Ii
Jj
Kk
Ll
Mm
Nn
Oo
Pp
Qq
Rr
Ss
Tt
Uu
Vv
Ww
Xx
Yy
Zz

Aa
Bb
Cc
Dd
Ee
Ff
Gg
Hh
Ii
Jj
Kk
Ll
Mm
Nn
Oo
Pp
Qq
Rr
Ss
Tt
Uu
Vv
Ww
Xx
Yy
Zz

sparse ADJECTIVE
Vegetation is sparse in this area.
scarce, scanty, meagre, scattered, infrequent
(≠) OPPOSITES plentiful, thick, dense

speak VERB
They speak to each other on the phone every day.
talk, say, declare, express, tell, chat, communicate, discuss

special ADJECTIVE
1 *a special occasion*
important, significant, momentous, major, memorable, remarkable, extraordinary, exceptional
(≠) OPPOSITES normal, ordinary, usual
2 *her own special way of doing things*
different, distinctive, characteristic, peculiar, singular, individual, unique, exclusive
(≠) OPPOSITES general, common

speciality NOUN
Mum's speciality is spaghetti bolognese.
talent, strength, field

specific ADJECTIVE
I don't know the specific address of the shop but it's next to the station.
precise, exact, particular, special, definite, clear-cut, explicit, unambiguous
(≠) OPPOSITES vague, approximate

specify VERB
Please specify which colour you would prefer.
state, identify, spell out, define, list, name, indicate, describe

specimen NOUN
a specimen of your work
sample, example, instance, illustration, model

spectacle NOUN
the spectacle of the Edinburgh Tattoo
show, performance, display, scene, sight, wonder, marvel, phenomenon

spectacular ADJECTIVE
a spectacular fireworks display
grand, splendid, magnificent, sensational, impressive, stunning, dramatic, breathtaking, dazzling, eye-catching
(≠) OPPOSITES unimpressive, ordinary

spectator NOUN
There were very few spectators at the athletics meeting.
watcher, viewer, onlooker, bystander, witness, eye witness, observer
(≠) OPPOSITES player, participant

speech NOUN
The best man made a speech at the wedding.
talk, address, lecture, monologue, soliloquy
◇ INFORMAL WORDS spiel

speed¹ NOUN
He drove off at top speed.
rate, pace, tempo, quickness, swiftness, rapidity
(≠) OPPOSITES slowness, delay

speed² VERB
The car sped down the road.
race, tear, zoom, bowl along, sprint, gallop, hurry, rush
◇ INFORMAL WORDS belt
(≠) OPPOSITES dawdle, crawl
• **speed up**
We will have to speed up to get there on time.
accelerate, hurry up
◇ INFORMAL WORDS get a move on, put your foot down, step on it
(≠) OPPOSITES slow down

spell NOUN
a spell in the army
period, time, bout, session, term, season, interval, stretch, turn, stint

spend VERB
1 *I've spent all my pocket money.*
pay out, invest, lay out, waste, squander, fritter, use up

◇ INFORMAL WORDS fork out, shell out, splash out
≠ OPPOSITES save, hoard
2 We **spent** the day at the zoo.
pass, fill, occupy, use, employ, apply, devote

sphere NOUN
a golden **sphere**
ball, globe, orb

spice NOUN

Here are some types of spice:
cardamom, chilli, cinnamon, cloves, coriander, cumin, curry, ginger, nutmeg, turmeric
⇒ Also look up **herb**

spike NOUN
an umbrella with a **spike** on the end
point, prong, spine, nail, stake

spill VERB
1 I **spilt** my drink.
overturn, upset, slop, overflow, tip
2 The contents of my bag **spilt** all over the ground.
tip, discharge, shed, scatter

spin VERB
spinning a coin
turn, revolve, rotate, twist, twirl, wheel, whirl, swirl, reel

spine NOUN
curvature of the **spine**
backbone, spinal column, vertebrae

spirit NOUN
1 haunted by **spirits**
ghost, spectre, phantom, apparition, angel, demon
2 She showed great **spirit** in standing up to the bullies.
courage, willpower, backbone, strength, liveliness, vivacity, sparkle, vigour, energy, zest

spite NOUN
He broke my favourite toys out of **spite**.
spitefulness, malice, venom, bitterness, bad feeling
≠ OPPOSITES goodwill, compassion, affection

spiteful ADJECTIVE
spiteful remarks
malicious, catty, snide, cruel, vindictive, vengeful, nasty
≠ OPPOSITES charitable, affectionate

splash VERB
1 The children were **splashing** in the water.
bathe, paddle, wade, dabble
2 Water **splashed** over the edge of the bucket.
spatter, splatter, slop, slosh, plop
◇ INFORMAL WORDS splodge

splendid ADJECTIVE
a **splendid** feast
brilliant, glorious, magnificent, luxurious, impressive, outstanding, superb, excellent, wonderful, marvellous
≠ OPPOSITES drab, ordinary, run-of-the-mill

splendour NOUN
the **splendour** of the palace
glory, magnificence, majesty, richness, pomp, ceremony, display, show, spectacle
≠ OPPOSITES drabness

splinter NOUN
I got a **splinter** of wood in my finger.
sliver, chip, fragment, flake, shaving, paring

split¹ NOUN
1 a **split** in the rock
division, break, gap, cleft, crevice, crack, tear, rip, slit, slash
2 a **split** in the family
discord, division, difference, break-up, rift

Aa
Bb
Cc
Dd
Ee
Ff
Gg
Hh
Ii
Jj
Kk
Ll
Mm
Nn
Oo
Pp
Qq
Rr
Ss
Tt
Uu
Vv
Ww
Xx
Yy
Zz

Aa
Bb
Cc
Dd
Ee
Ff
Gg
Hh
Ii
Jj
Kk
Ll
Mm
Nn
Oo
Pp
Qq
Rr
Ss
Tt
Uu
Vv
Ww
Xx
Yy
Zz

split² VERB

1 *We split the cost four ways.*
divide, halve, slice up, share, distribute, parcel out
2 *You've split your trousers.*
burst, tear, rip, slit, slash
• **split up**
The band has split up.
break up, separate, part, disband

spoil VERB

1 *A silly haircut spoiled his good looks.*
upset, ruin, destroy, damage, harm
2 *Grandparents often spoil their grandchildren.*
indulge, pamper, baby

sport NOUN

My favourite sport is athletics.
exercise, activity, pastime, amusement, entertainment, play

Here are some different sports:

Racket sports:
badminton, squash, table-tennis, tennis
Ball games:
American football, Australian Rules football, baseball, basketball, billiards, bowls, cricket, croquet, football, golf, handball, hockey, hurling, kabaddi, lacrosse, netball, pitch and putt, polo, pool, putting, rounders, rugby, shinty, snooker, soccer, tenpin bowling, volleyball
Athletics:
cross-country, discus, high jump, hurdling, javelin, long jump, marathon, pole vault, running, shotput, triple jump
Water sports:
angling, canoeing, diving, fishing, rowing, sailing, skin-diving, surfing, swimming, synchronized swimming, water polo, water-skiing, windsurfing, yachting
Winter sports:
bobsleigh, curling, ice hockey, ice-skating, skiing, snowboarding, speed skating, tobogganing
Target sports:
archery, darts, quoits
Martial arts:
judo, jujitsu, karate, tae kwon do
Other fighting sports:
boxing, fencing, wrestling
Outdoor pursuits:
climbing, mountaineering, orienteering, potholing, rock climbing, walking
Racing:
cycle racing, drag-racing, go-karting, greyhound-racing, horse-racing, motor racing, speedway racing, stock-car racing
Equestrian sports:
dressage, horse racing, hunting, show-jumping, steeple chase, three-day eventing, trotting
Hunting:
clay-pigeon shooting, shooting
Sports in the air:
gliding, sky-diving
Other sports:
gymnastics, weightlifting

sporting ADJECTIVE

He was very sporting in his defeat.
sportsmanlike, gentlemanly, decent, considerate, fair
(≠) OPPOSITES unsporting, ungentlemanly, unfair

sports day NOUN

Here are some sports day events:

egg and spoon race, high jump, hurdles, long jump, mums' and dads' race, obstacle course, relay, running race, sack race, three-legged race, tug of war, wheelbarrow race

spot¹ NOUN

1 *spots of blood*

dot, speckle, fleck, mark, speck, blotch, blot, smudge, splash
2 *We found a quiet **spot** for our picnic.*
place, point, position, situation, location, site, scene

spot[2] VERB
*I **spotted** a heron by the water's edge.*
see, notice, observe, detect, identify, recognize

spotless ADJECTIVE
*a **spotless** white shirt*
immaculate, clean, white, gleaming, spick and span, unmarked, unstained, unblemished
⊯ OPPOSITES dirty

spout VERB
*Water was **spouting** out of the broken pipe.*
jet, spurt, squirt, spray, shoot, gush, stream

sprawl VERB
*He was **sprawling** in an armchair, watching television.*
flop, slump, slouch, loll, lounge

spray NOUN
*a fine **spray** of sea water*
moisture, drizzle, mist, foam, froth

spread VERB
1 *She **spread** her arms wide.*
stretch, extend, sprawl, broaden, widen, expand, swell
2 *He **spread** the map out on the table.*
open, unroll, unfurl, unfold, fan out, cover, lay out, arrange
⊯ OPPOSITES fold, furl
3 *Don't go **spreading** gossip.*
broadcast, transmit, communicate, publicize, advertise, publish, circulate
⊯ OPPOSITES suppress

sprightly ADJECTIVE
*a **sprightly** woman of 74*
agile, nimble, active, energetic, lively, spirited
⊯ OPPOSITES doddering, inactive, lifeless

spring VERB
1 *The lion **sprang** out of the bushes.*
jump, leap, vault, bound, hop, bounce, recoil
2 *His confidence **springs** from self-belief.*
originate, derive, come, stem, arise, start, sprout, grow, develop

sprinkle VERB
***Sprinkle** icing sugar over the cake.*
shower, spray, spatter, scatter, dust, powder

sprout VERB
*Buds had begun to **sprout** on the trees.*
shoot, bud, grow, develop, come up, spring up

spruce ADJECTIVE
*Dad looked very **spruce** in his dinner jacket.*
smart, elegant, neat, trim, well-dressed, well-turned-out, well-groomed
⊯ OPPOSITES scruffy, untidy

spur VERB
*We were **spurred** on by the thought of the end of our journey.*
goad, prod, stimulate, prompt, drive, urge, encourage, motivate
⊯ OPPOSITES curb, discourage

spurt VERB
*Oil **spurted** from a hole in the ground.*
gush, squirt, jet, shoot, burst

spy[1] NOUN
*He was a government **spy** during the war.*
secret agent, undercover agent, double agent

spy[2] VERB
*I **spied** a ring in the long grass.*
spot, glimpse, notice, observe, discover

squabble VERB
*The children have been **squabbling** all morning.*
bicker, wrangle, quarrel, row, argue, clash, brawl, scrap, fight

Aa
Bb
Cc
Dd
Ee
Ff
Gg
Hh
Ii
Jj
Kk
Ll
Mm
Nn
Oo
Pp
Qq
Rr
Ss
Tt
Uu
Vv
Ww
Xx
Yy
Zz

Aa
Bb
Cc
Dd
Ee
Ff
Gg
Hh
Ii
Jj
Kk
Ll
Mm
Nn
Oo
Pp
Qq
Rr
Ss
Tt
Uu
Vv
Ww
Xx
Yy
Zz

squander VERB
He has squandered all the money he won.
waste, misuse, fritter away, throw away, spend
◇ INFORMAL WORDS blow

square VERB
Your answers don't square with mine.
tally, agree, correspond, match

squash VERB
1 *He sat on the cakes and squashed them.*
crush, flatten, press, squeeze, compress, pound, pulp, smash
≠ OPPOSITES stretch, expand
2 *We all squashed into the car.*
crowd, squeeze, jam, pack, cram

squat¹ ADJECTIVE
He's too short and squat to be a model.
short, stocky, dumpy, chunky, stubby
≠ OPPOSITES slim, lanky

squat² VERB
The man squatted on the floor to talk to the child.
crouch, stoop, bend, sit

squeeze VERB
1 *Squeeze a lemon into some hot water.*
press, squash, crush
2 *He squeezed her tight.*
press, squash, crush, grip, clasp, clutch, hug, embrace, cuddle
3 *There were six of us squeezed into the car.*
cram, stuff, pack, crowd, wedge, jam, force, ram, push

squirt VERB
He squirted us with his water pistol.
spray, spurt, jet, shoot, spout, gush

stab¹ NOUN
I felt a stab of pain.
ache, pang, twinge, prick

stab² VERB
He was stabbed in the chest.

pierce, puncture, cut, wound, injure, knife, spear, stick, jab, thrust

stable ADJECTIVE
1 *Make the bookcase stable before you start filling it.*
steady, firm, secure, fixed, balanced
≠ OPPOSITES unstable, wobbly, shaky
2 *He is in a stable relationship with his girlfriend.*
steady, secure, established, strong, lasting, enduring, permanent
≠ OPPOSITES unstable, shaky

stack¹ NOUN
a stack of magazines
heap, pile, mound, mass, load, hoard, stockpile

stack² VERB
Stack the dishes beside the sink.
heap, pile, load, gather, save, hoard, stockpile

staff NOUN
a new member of staff
workforce, employees, workers, crew, team, personnel

stage NOUN
The final stage of the journey was made by bus.
step, phase, period, division, point

stagger VERB
1 *The foal staggered to its feet.*
lurch, totter, teeter, wobble, sway, rock, reel, falter, hesitate
2 *The price of the boots staggered me.*
surprise, amaze, astound, astonish, stun, stupefy, dumbfound, shake, shock

stain¹ NOUN
a gravy stain on the tablecloth
mark, spot, blemish, blot, smudge, discoloration

stain² VERB
You have stained your shirt with coffee.
mark, spot, blemish, blot, smudge, discolour, dirty, soil

stale ADJECTIVE
stale cakes
dry, hard, old, musty, fusty
⊭ OPPOSITES fresh

stalk VERB
The tiger was stalking its prey.
track, trail, hunt, follow, pursue,
shadow, tail

stall VERB
*He's stalling for time because he doesn't
want to make a decision.*
play for time, delay, hedge

stammer VERB
*He stammered over his speech because
he was nervous.*
stutter, stumble, falter, hesitate, splutter

stamp VERB
1 *A horse stamped on my foot.*
trample, crush, beat, pound
2 *I had my passport stamped at the
airport.*
imprint, impress, print, inscribe,
engrave, mark

stand VERB
1 *The whole audience stood and
cheered.*
rise, get up, stand up
2 *Stand the ladder against the wall.*
put, place, set, position, station, rest
3 *I can't stand gardening programmes.*
bear, tolerate, suffer
• **stand for**
'MP' stands for 'Member of Parliament'.
represent, symbolize, mean, signify,
denote, indicate
• **stand out**
*The colour stands out against the
background.*
stick out, show up
• **stand up for**
I always stood up for my little brother.
defend, stick up for, side with, fight for,
support, protect
⊭ OPPOSITES attack
• **stand up to**
You must stand up to the bullies.

defy, oppose, resist, withstand, face,
confront, brave
⊭ OPPOSITES give in to

standard¹ ADJECTIVE
standard equipment
normal, average, typical, stock, basic,
usual, customary, regular, official,
established
⊭ OPPOSITES abnormal, unusual,
irregular

standard² NOUN
1 *The band's new album is not up to
their usual standard.*
level, specification, grade, quality
2 *the new safety standards for schools*
norm, average, pattern, example,
sample, guideline

staple ADJECTIVE
*Rice is the staple food in many
countries.*
basic, fundamental, primary, key,
main, chief, major, principal, essential,
standard
⊭ OPPOSITES minor

star NOUN
the star of the show
celebrity, idol, lead, leading man,
leading lady, superstar, megastar

stare VERB
Stop staring out of the window.
gaze, look, watch, gape, goggle, glare
◇ INFORMAL WORDS gawp, gawk

start¹ NOUN
the start of the day
beginning, commencement, outset,
opening
◇ INFORMAL WORDS kick-off
⊭ OPPOSITES close, stop, finish, end

start² VERB
1 *I started running.*
begin, commence, open, instigate, set
out
◇ INFORMAL WORDS kick off
⊭ OPPOSITES stop, finish, end
2 *He started a business with his brother.*

Aa
Bb
Cc
Dd
Ee
Ff
Gg
Hh
Ii
Jj
Kk
Ll
Mm
Nn
Oo
Pp
Qq
Rr
Ss
Tt
Uu
Vv
Ww
Xx
Yy
Zz

begin, commence, originate, create, found, establish, set up, launch, open

⊘ OPPOSITES close

3 *The horse started at the sudden noise.*
jump, jerk, twitch, flinch

startle VERB
You startled me, jumping out like that.
surprise, amaze, astonish, astound, shock, scare, frighten, alarm, upset

⊘ OPPOSITES calm

starving ADJECTIVE
aid for the starving millions in Africa
hungry, underfed, undernourished, ravenous, famished

state¹ NOUN
1 *I inquired after his state of health.*
condition, shape, situation, position, circumstances

2 *good relations between states*
nation, country, land, territory, kingdom, republic, government

state² VERB
Please state your name and number after the tone.
say, declare, announce, report, communicate, specify, express, voice

statement NOUN
a statement of the facts
account, report, bulletin, announcement, declaration, communication, testimony

static ADJECTIVE
a static caravan
stationary, motionless, immobile, still, resting, fixed

⊘ OPPOSITES mobile

station VERB
a soldier stationed in Cyprus
locate, set, install, post, send, appoint, assign

stationary ADJECTIVE
He bumped into a stationary car.
motionless, immobile, still, static,

standing, resting, parked, moored

⊘ OPPOSITES mobile, moving, active

statue NOUN
a marble statue of the president
figure, head, bust, statuette, carving

status NOUN
Doctors and lawyers have high status.
rank, level, class, station, standing, position, prestige, distinction, importance

⊘ OPPOSITES unimportance, insignificance

stay VERB
1 *They stayed friends throughout their lives.*
continue, remain, endure, linger, persist

2 *We stayed with friends in London.*
live, lodge, be accommodated

◆ FORMAL WORDS reside

steady ADJECTIVE
1 *Put a book under the table leg to make it steady.*
stable, balanced, fixed, immovable, firm, even

⊘ OPPOSITES unsteady, unstable

2 *The father is a steady influence in that family.*
stable, balanced, calm, consistent, constant

⊘ OPPOSITES unsteady, unstable

steal VERB
1 *The boys stole a car.*
thieve, take, snatch, swipe, shoplift

◇ INFORMAL WORDS lift, pinch, nick

⊘ OPPOSITES return, give back

2 *I stole out of the room.*
creep, tiptoe, slip, slink, sneak

stealthy ADJECTIVE
a stealthy military operation
secret, secretive, quiet, sly, cunning, sneaky, underhand

⊘ OPPOSITES open

steam NOUN
Steam was coming out of the kettle.

Aa Bb Cc Dd Ee Ff Gg Hh Ii Jj Kk Ll Mm Nn Oo Pp Qq Rr **Ss** Tt Uu Vv Ww Xx Yy Zz vapour, mist, haze, condensation, moisture, dampness

steep ADJECTIVE
a steep slope
sheer, abrupt, sudden, sharp
⧸ OPPOSITES gentle, gradual

steer VERB
I was allowed to steer my uncle's boat.
pilot, guide, direct, control

stem¹ NOUN
Trim the stems of the flowers.
stalk, shoot, branch, trunk

stem² VERB
Apply pressure to the wound to stem the bleeding.
stop, halt, block, check, curb, restrain, contain, resist

step¹ NOUN
1 *Take a step forward.*
pace, stride, footstep, tread
2 *What's the next step?*
move, act, action, movement, stage, phase
3 *the next step up*
rung, stair, level

step² VERB
stepping out in the rain
pace, stride, tread, stamp, walk, move
• **step up**
The school has stepped up security.
increase, raise, build up, intensify, speed up
⧸ OPPOSITES decrease

sterile ADJECTIVE
It is essential to use sterile equipment in operations.
germ-free, sterilized, disinfected, antiseptic, uncontaminated
⧸ OPPOSITES septic, contaminated

stern ADJECTIVE
wearing a stern expression
strict, severe, hard, tough, harsh, cruel, grim
⧸ OPPOSITES kind, gentle, mild

stick¹ VERB
1 *He stuck his head out of the window.*
thrust, poke, stab
2 *The nurse stuck a needle in my arm.*
stab, jab, pierce, penetrate, puncture, spear
3 *Stick the two edges together.*
glue, gum, paste, cement, bond
4 *The mud was sticking to his clothes.*
attach, fasten, adhere
• **stick out**
My ears stick out.
protrude, jut out, project
• **stick up for**
You should stick up for your friends.
stand up for, speak up for, defend, support, uphold
⧸ OPPOSITES attack

stick² NOUN
1 *We gathered sticks for a fire.*
branch, twig
2 *He walks with a stick.*
cane, birch, rod, pole, stake

sticky ADJECTIVE
1 *a sticky substance*
adhesive, gummed, tacky, gluey, gummy
◇ INFORMAL WORDS gooey
⧸ OPPOSITES dry
2 *The weather was hot and sticky.*
humid, clammy, muggy, close, sultry
⧸ OPPOSITES fresh, cool

stiff ADJECTIVE
1 *stiff joints*
rigid, inflexible, unbending, unyielding, hard, solid
⧸ OPPOSITES flexible
2 *His manner was very stiff.*
formal, pompous, standoffish, cold, prim, strict, severe, harsh
⧸ OPPOSITES informal
3 *a stiff test*
difficult, hard, tough, awkward
⧸ OPPOSITES easy

stifle VERB
1 *The smoke was stifling us.*
smother, suffocate, strangle, choke
2 *I had to stifle a laugh.*

Aa
Bb
Cc
Dd
Ee
Ff
Gg
Hh
Ii
Jj
Kk
Ll
Mm
Nn
Oo
Pp
Qq
Rr
Ss
Tt
Uu
Vv
Ww
Xx
Yy
Zz

muffle, silence, suppress, check, restrain, repress

still ADJECTIVE

1 *Be **still** while I fix your hair.*
stationary, motionless, lifeless
≠ OPPOSITES active
2 *a **still** night*
calm, tranquil, undisturbed, unruffled, peaceful, hushed, quiet, silent, noiseless
≠ OPPOSITES noisy

stimulate VERB

*Children need to be **stimulated** to learn.*
inspire, motivate, encourage, urge, fire, spur, prompt
≠ OPPOSITES discourage, hinder

sting VERB

*My eyes were **stinging** with the smoke.*
smart, tingle, burn

stink[1] NOUN

*a **stink** of rotten eggs*
smell, odour, stench
◇ INFORMAL WORDS pong, niff, whiff

stink[2] VERB

*His clothes **stink** of cigarette smoke.*
smell, reek
◇ INFORMAL WORDS pong, hum

stir VERB

***Stir** the mixture until it is smooth.*
mix, blend, beat

• **stir up**
*He was trying to **stir up** his classmates to misbehave.*
rouse, arouse, inflame, stimulate, spur, prompt, provoke, incite, instigate, agitate
≠ OPPOSITES calm, discourage

stock[1] NOUN

1 *The supermarket keeps moving its **stock** around.*
goods, merchandise, wares, range
2 *We have a good **stock** of food at home.*
store, supply, reserve, fund, stockpile, hoard

stock[2] VERB

*The corner shop **stocks** newspapers.*
keep, carry, sell, trade in, deal in, handle, supply, provide

stocky ADJECTIVE

*a short **stocky** man who looked like a boxer*
sturdy, solid, chunky, short, squat, dumpy, stubby
≠ OPPOSITES tall, skinny

stomach NOUN

*I had pains in my **stomach** and felt sick.*
gut, insides, belly, abdomen, paunch
◇ INFORMAL WORDS tummy

stony ADJECTIVE

*a **stony** beach*
pebbly, shingly, rocky

stoop VERB

*The tall man **stooped** to get under the low fence.*
hunch, bow, bend, lean, duck, crouch

stop[1] NOUN

*The bus came to a **stop** at the terminal.*
halt, standstill, stoppage, end, finish
≠ OPPOSITES start, beginning

stop[2] VERB

1 *Please **stop** shouting.*
halt, end, finish, quit
◆ FORMAL WORDS cease
◇ INFORMAL WORDS pack in
≠ OPPOSITES start, continue
2 *A security guard **stopped** him entering.*
prevent, bar, hinder, check, restrain

store[1] NOUN

1 *a good **store** of food for the winter*
stock, supply, provision, fund, reserve, hoard, stockpile, quantity
≠ OPPOSITES scarcity
2 *a clothes **store***
shop, outlet, showroom
3 *All the old files are kept in the **store**.*
storeroom, storehouse, warehouse

store² VERB

Store your bread in a breadbin.
save, keep, put away, lay by, reserve, stock, lay in, hoard, stockpile
◇ INFORMAL WORDS stash
(≠) OPPOSITES use

storey NOUN

a flat on the top storey
floor, level, stage, deck

storm NOUN

Here are some kinds of storm:

blizzard, cyclone, dust storm, electrical storm, hailstorm, hurricane, ice storm, monsoon, rainstorm, sand storm, snow storm, thunderstorm, tornado, typhoon, whirlwind

story NOUN

Tell us a story.
tale, fiction, yarn

Here are some types of story:

adventure story, bedtime story, children's story, comedy, crime story, detective story, fable, fairy tale, fantasy, folk tale, ghost story, historical tale, horror story, legend, love story, mystery, myth, parable, romance, saga, science fiction, short story, spine-chiller, spy story, supernatural tale, thriller

stout ADJECTIVE

1 *He is getting rather stout since he gave up jogging.*
fat, plump, fleshy, overweight, heavy, bulky, big, brawny, beefy, burly
(≠) OPPOSITES thin, lean, slim
2 *stout packaging*
strong, tough, thick, sturdy
(≠) OPPOSITES flimsy
3 *a stout defence*
brave, courageous, fearless, bold
(≠) OPPOSITES cowardly, timid

stow VERB

Stow your hand luggage under the seat in front.
put away, store, load, pack, cram, stuff
◇ INFORMAL WORDS stash
(≠) OPPOSITES unload

straight ADJECTIVE

1 *a straight line*
level, even, flat, horizontal, upright, vertical, direct, true
(≠) OPPOSITES bent, crooked
2 *a straight answer*
frank, honest, blunt, direct

straightforward ADJECTIVE

The exam was quite straightforward.
easy, simple, uncomplicated
(≠) OPPOSITES complicated

strain¹ NOUN

She is feeling the strain of working too hard.
stress, anxiety, pressure, tension, exertion, effort
(≠) OPPOSITES relaxation

strain² VERB

1 *I've strained a muscle in my leg.*
pull, twist, sprain, tear, stretch, tighten
2 *The children won't eat soup unless it is strained.*
sieve, sift, screen, separate, filter, purify, drain
3 *If you don't rest, you may strain yourself.*
weaken, tire, tax, overwork

strand NOUN

a strand of hair
fibre, wire, thread, string, piece, length

stranded ADJECTIVE

We missed the last bus and were left stranded in the city.
marooned, high and dry, abandoned, in the lurch

strange ADJECTIVE

1 *That was a very strange way to behave.*
odd, peculiar, funny, curious, queer, weird, bizarre, eccentric, abnormal, extraordinary
≠ OPPOSITES ordinary, common
2 *We found ourselves in a strange land.*
new, novel, untried, unknown, unheard-of, unfamiliar, foreign
≠ OPPOSITES well-known, familiar

stranger NOUN

Don't talk to strangers.
newcomer, visitor, non-member, outsider, foreigner
≠ OPPOSITES local, native

strangle VERB

She was strangled with a scarf.
throttle, choke, suffocate, stifle, smother

strap NOUN

Fasten the straps of your shoes.
thong, tie, band, belt, leash

stray VERB

When you go on a school trip, don't stray from your group.
wander off, get lost, ramble, roam, straggle

streak¹ NOUN

She has blonde streaks in her hair.
line, stroke, smear, band, stripe, strip, trace

streak² VERB

1 *His black hair is streaked with grey.*
band, stripe, fleck
2 *The boy streaked past us.*
speed, tear, hurtle, sprint, gallop, fly, dart, flash, zoom, whizz

stream¹ NOUN

1 *fishing in the stream*
river, creek, brook, beck, burn, tributary
2 *a steady stream of letters*
flow, run, flood, torrent

stream² VERB

Tears streamed down her face.
run, flow, pour, spout, gush, flood, cascade

strength NOUN

She proved her strength in the athletics events.
toughness, robustness, sturdiness, muscle, power, vigour, stamina, fitness
≠ OPPOSITES weakness, feebleness

strengthen VERB

1 *Her confidence strengthened over time.*
increase, heighten, intensify
≠ OPPOSITES weaken
2 *Exercise will strengthen your muscles.*
reinforce, toughen, harden, stiffen, invigorate
≠ OPPOSITES weaken

strenuous ADJECTIVE

1 *strenuous work*
hard, tough, demanding, gruelling, tiring, exhausting
≠ OPPOSITES easy, effortless
2 *James made a strenuous effort to improve his handwriting.*
active, energetic, vigorous, earnest, determined, spirited

stress¹ NOUN

She is off work, suffering from stress.
pressure, strain, tension, worry, anxiety
◇ INFORMAL WORDS hassle
≠ OPPOSITES relaxation

stress² VERB

She stressed the need to be on time.
emphasize, highlight, underline, repeat
≠ OPPOSITES understate, downplay

stretch¹ NOUN

1 *a stretch of water*
expanse, spread, space, area
2 *a short stretch in prison*
period, time, term, spell, stint, run

stretch² VERB

1 *We stretched the tent over the poles.*

pull, tighten, strain, extend, lengthen, expand
⊞ OPPOSITES compress
2 *A long night of studying stretched ahead of me.*
extend, spread, unfold, unroll, reach

strict ADJECTIVE

1 *a strict teacher*
stern, no-nonsense, firm, harsh, severe
⊞ OPPOSITES easy-going, flexible
2 *strict instructions*
exact, precise, accurate, literal, true, meticulous, particular
⊞ OPPOSITES loose

strike VERB

striking the gong
hit, knock, collide with, slap, smack, thump, beat, pound
◇ INFORMAL WORDS wallop, hammer

striking ADJECTIVE

a striking resemblance between mother and daughter
noticeable, conspicuous, outstanding, remarkable, extraordinary, memorable, impressive, dazzling, astonishing, stunning
⊞ OPPOSITES unimpressive

string NOUN

1 *a piece of string*
twine, cord, rope, cable, fibre
2 *a string of disasters*
series, succession, sequence, chain, line, row

strip¹ VERB

1 *He was stripped naked.*
undress, unclothe, uncover, expose, lay bare, bare
⊞ OPPOSITES dress, clothe, cover
2 *They stripped the bark off the tree.*
peel, skin

strip² NOUN

a strip of leather
ribbon, thong, strap, belt, sash, band, piece, bit

stripe NOUN

black and white stripes
band, line, bar, flash, streak, strip, belt

strive VERB

striving to lose weight
try, attempt, endeavour, struggle, strain, work, fight, compete

stroke¹ NOUN

a single stroke of the axe
blow, hit, knock, swipe

stroke² VERB

The woman stroked her child's hair.
pet, touch, pat, rub, massage

stroll VERB

strolling along the lane
saunter, dawdle, ramble, wander

strong ADJECTIVE

1 *strong shoes*
tough, hard-wearing, heavy-duty, sturdy, stout
⊞ OPPOSITES flimsy
2 *a big strong man*
robust, sturdy, strapping, stout, burly, well-built, beefy, brawny, muscular, powerful
⊞ OPPOSITES weak, feeble
3 *strong feelings*
intense, deep, vivid, fierce, violent, vehement, keen, eager
⊞ OPPOSITES indecisive
4 *a strong curry*
highly-flavoured, hot, spicy, highly-seasoned, sharp
⊞ OPPOSITES mild, bland
5 *a strong argument*
convincing, persuasive, effective, telling, forceful, compelling
⊞ OPPOSITES unconvincing

structure NOUN

1 *a concrete-and-steel structure*
construction, erection, building
2 *the structure of the company*
arrangement, organization, set-up, form, shape, design, make-up, formation

Aa
Bb
Cc
Dd
Ee
Ff
Gg
Hh
Ii
Jj
Kk
Ll
Mm
Nn
Oo
Pp
Qq
Rr
Ss
Tt
Uu
Vv
Ww
Xx
Yy
Zz

Aa
Bb
Cc
Dd
Ee
Ff
Gg
Hh
Ii
Jj
Kk
Ll
Mm
Nn
Oo
Pp
Qq
Rr
Ss
Tt
Uu
Vv
Ww
Xx
Yy
Zz

struggle¹ NOUN

1 *It's a struggle to bring up a family.*
difficulty, problem, effort, exertion, work
≠ OPPOSITES ease
2 *There was a struggle and one of the men was hurt.*
clash, conflict, fight, battle, contest

struggle² VERB

struggling to survive with little money
strive, work, strain, fight, battle, wrestle, grapple, contend, compete
≠ OPPOSITES yield, give in

stubborn ADJECTIVE

She was stubborn and refused to join in the game.
obstinate, pig-headed, inflexible, headstrong, self-willed, difficult, unmanageable
≠ OPPOSITES flexible, yielding

stuck-up ADJECTIVE

We thought she was stuck-up but she was just shy.
snobbish, haughty, high and mighty, condescending, proud, arrogant, conceited
◇ INFORMAL WORDS snooty, bigheaded
≠ OPPOSITES humble, modest

student NOUN

a medical student
undergraduate, postgraduate, scholar, schoolboy, schoolgirl, pupil, learner, trainee, apprentice

studious ADJECTIVE

She is a very studious child.
scholarly, academic, intellectual, serious, thoughtful, hard-working, industrious, careful, attentive
≠ OPPOSITES lazy, idle

study VERB

1 *I'm studying for my history test.*
read, learn, revise, cram, read up
◇ INFORMAL WORDS swot
2 *She is studying biology at university.*
read, learn, research, investigate, analyse, examine

3 *I studied the map carefully.*
survey, scan, examine, scrutinize, pore over

stuff¹ NOUN

1 *sticky stuff*
material, fabric, matter, substance
2 *You can leave your stuff in a locker.*
belongings, possessions, things, articles, kit, tackle, equipment
◇ INFORMAL WORDS gear

stuff² VERB

He stuffed some clothes into a bag.
pack, load, fill, cram, force, push, shove, ram, wedge, jam
≠ OPPOSITES unload, empty

stuffy ADJECTIVE

It was so stuffy in the waiting room.
musty, stale, airless, unventilated, stifling, close, muggy
≠ OPPOSITES airy, well-ventilated

stumble VERB

He stumbled on the uneven ground.
trip, slip, fall, lurch, stagger, flounder, blunder

stump VERB

I was stumped by his question.
defeat, outwit, perplex, puzzle, baffle, mystify, confuse, bewilder
◇ INFORMAL WORDS flummox, bamboozle
≠ OPPOSITES assist

stun VERB

1 *I was stunned by his stupidity.*
amaze, astonish, astound, stagger, shock, dumbfound
2 *The blow to her head stunned her.*
daze, knock out, stupefy

stunt NOUN

a dangerous stunt
feat, exploit, act, deed, trick, turn

stupid ADJECTIVE

1 *He was too stupid to know any better.*
silly, foolish, brainless, idiotic, simple-minded, slow, dim

◇ INFORMAL WORDS dense, thick, dumb
≠ OPPOSITES sensible, wise, clever, intelligent
2 *That was a really **stupid** thing to say.*
silly, foolish, irresponsible, indiscreet, foolhardy, rash, senseless, absurd, daft, ridiculous, laughable
≠ OPPOSITES sensible, wise, clever, intelligent

sturdy ADJECTIVE
*The captain of the hockey team was a **sturdy** girl.*
strong, robust, stout, well-built, powerful, muscular, athletic, hardy, vigorous
≠ OPPOSITES weak, flimsy, puny

stutter VERB
*When Ryan met his football hero, he could only **stutter**.*
stammer, hesitate, falter, stumble, mumble

style NOUN
1 *a different **style** of teaching*
technique, approach, method, manner, way
2 *dressed in the latest **style***
fashion, vogue, trend
3 *He has lots of **style**.*
elegance, smartness, chic, flair, stylishness, taste, polish, refinement, sophistication
≠ OPPOSITES tastelessness
4 *a new **style** of jacket*
appearance, cut, design, pattern, shape, form, sort, type, variety

stylish ADJECTIVE
*a **stylish** haircut*
fashionable, in vogue, voguish, trendy, polished, refined, sophisticated, chic
◇ INFORMAL WORDS cool, classy
≠ OPPOSITES old-fashioned

subdue VERB
1 *The police managed to **subdue** the protesters.*
control, check, quieten, overpower, crush, defeat, suppress

≠ OPPOSITES arouse
2 *I tried to **subdue** my fear of flying.*
overcome, suppress, conquer, master, control, check, moderate, reduce
≠ OPPOSITES arouse, awaken

subdued ADJECTIVE
*Maria seemed **subdued** after hearing the news.*
sad, downcast, dejected, quiet, serious, grave, solemn
≠ OPPOSITES lively, excited

subject¹ NOUN
*a discussion on the **subject** of medicine*
topic, theme, matter, issue, question, point, case, affair, business

subject² VERB
*We were **subjected** to a stream of insults.*
expose, lay open, put through, submit

submit VERB
1 *He finally **submitted** to pressure to join in.*
yield, give in, surrender, knuckle under, bow, bend, stoop, agree, comply
≠ OPPOSITES resist
2 *I **submitted** an application form for the job.*
present, offer, put forward
≠ OPPOSITES withdraw

subsequent ADJECTIVE
*next week and the **subsequent** three weeks*
following, later, future, next, succeeding
≠ OPPOSITES previous, earlier

subside VERB
1 *After a while, the pain **subsided**.*
decrease, lessen, dwindle, decline, die down, ease
≠ OPPOSITES increase
2 *The whole building is **subsiding**.*
sink, collapse, settle, descend, fall, drop, lower
≠ OPPOSITES rise

Aa
Bb
Cc
Dd
Ee
Ff
Gg
Hh
Ii
Jj
Kk
Ll
Mm
Nn
Oo
Pp
Qq
Rr
Ss
Tt
Uu
Vv
Ww
Xx
Yy
Zz

substance NOUN
a poisonous substance
matter, material, stuff, fabric

substantial ADJECTIVE
1 *There has been no substantial change.*
great, considerable, significant, important, worthwhile
≠ OPPOSITES insubstantial, insignificant, small
2 *a substantial stone house*
large, big, sizable, massive, bulky, hefty, well-built, stout, sturdy, strong
≠ OPPOSITES small

substitute[1] NOUN
The soccer team has eleven players plus two substitutes.
reserve, stand-by, understudy, stand-in, replacement, surrogate, deputy

substitute[2] VERB
Substitute skimmed milk for full-cream milk.
change, exchange, swap, switch, interchange, replace

subtle ADJECTIVE
1 *subtle colours*
delicate, understated, faint, mild, fine, refined, sophisticated
≠ OPPOSITES overpowering, blatant, obvious
2 *a subtle argument*
artful, cunning, crafty, sly, devious, shrewd
≠ OPPOSITES open

subtract VERB
Subtract two from four to make two.
deduct, take away, remove, withdraw, debit
≠ OPPOSITES add

succeed VERB
1 *He succeeded in his attempt to climb Mount Everest.*
triumph, make it, get on, thrive, prosper, make good
≠ OPPOSITES fail

2 *Winter succeeds autumn.*
follow, replace
≠ OPPOSITES precede

success NOUN
1 *She owes her success to hard work.*
triumph, victory, achievement, fame
2 *His last film was a great success.*
winner, bestseller, hit, sensation
≠ OPPOSITES failure, disaster

successful ADJECTIVE
1 *the successful team*
victorious, winning, lucky, fortunate
≠ OPPOSITES unsuccessful, unprofitable
2 *a successful writer*
famous, well-known, popular, leading, bestselling, top
≠ OPPOSITES unknown

suck VERB
sucking a lollipop
draw in, absorb, soak up, drain

suddenly ADVERB
A dog suddenly jumped at me.
unexpectedly, without warning, from out of nowhere, out of the blue

sudden ADJECTIVE
a sudden urge to burst out laughing
unexpected, unforeseen, abrupt, quick, swift, rapid, hurried, rash, impetuous, impulsive
≠ OPPOSITES expected, predictable, gradual, slow

suffer VERB
1 *She has been suffering in silence.*
hurt, ache, agonize, grieve, sorrow
2 *The police have suffered a setback in their investigation.*
experience, undergo, go through, bear, tolerate, endure, feel

suffering NOUN
The nurses ease the suffering of the patients.
pain, discomfort, agony, anguish, distress, misery, hardship, ordeal, torment, torture
≠ OPPOSITES ease, comfort

Aa
Bb
Cc
Dd
Ee
Ff
Gg
Hh
Ii
Jj
Kk
Ll
Mm
Nn
Oo
Pp
Qq
Rr
Ss
Tt
Uu
Vv
Ww
Xx
Yy
Zz

suffocate VERB
*They **suffocated** in the smoke from the fire.*
smother, stifle, choke, strangle, throttle

suggest VERB
1 *I would like to **suggest** a solution.*
propose, put forward, recommend, advise
2 *Are you **suggesting** that I am lying?*
hint, indicate, imply, insinuate

suggestion NOUN
*That was a helpful **suggestion**.*
proposal, proposition, recommendation, idea, plan

suit VERB
*It doesn't **suit** me to go to the cinema on Friday.*
satisfy, please, be convenient for, be acceptable to
⚡ OPPOSITES displease, inconvenience

suitable ADJECTIVE
*Black nail varnish is not **suitable** for school.*
appropriate, fitting, suited, due, apt, acceptable, proper, right
⚡ OPPOSITES unsuitable, inappropriate

sulk VERB
*Gemma is **sulking** because she was not allowed to go out.*
mope, brood, pout
◇ INFORMAL WORDS be in a huff

sulky ADJECTIVE
*He changed from a happy child into a **sulky** teenager.*
brooding, moody, morose, resentful, grudging, disgruntled, put out, bad-tempered, sullen
◇ INFORMAL WORDS in a huff
⚡ OPPOSITES cheerful, good-tempered

sullen ADJECTIVE
*a **sullen** expression*
sulky, moody, morose, glum, gloomy, silent, surly
⚡ OPPOSITES cheerful, happy

sum NOUN
1 *a small **sum** of money*
amount, number, quantity
2 *The **sum** of two and three is five.*
total, sum total, whole, tally, reckoning, score, result

summit NOUN
*They reached the **summit** of the mountain.*
top, peak, pinnacle, point, crown, height
⚡ OPPOSITES bottom, foot

summon VERB
*We were **summoned** to the head teacher's room.*
call, send for, invite, beckon, gather, assemble
⚡ OPPOSITES dismiss

sunny ADJECTIVE
*a **sunny** day*
fine, cloudless, clear, summery, sunlit, bright, brilliant
⚡ OPPOSITES sunless, dull

sunrise NOUN
*We got up at **sunrise** to make an early start.*
dawn, crack of dawn, daybreak, daylight

sunset NOUN
*We all gathered to watch the beautiful **sunset**.*
sundown, dusk, twilight, evening, nightfall

superb ADJECTIVE
*They did a **superb** live version of their single.*
excellent, first-rate, first-class, magnificent, splendid, wonderful, marvellous, admirable, impressive, breathtaking
⚡ OPPOSITES bad, poor, inferior

superior ADJECTIVE
1 *superior accommodation*
excellent, first-class, first-rate, exclusive,

Aa
Bb
Cc
Dd
Ee
Ff
Gg
Hh
Ii
Jj
Kk
Ll
Mm
Nn
Oo
Pp
Qq
Rr
Ss
Tt
Uu
Vv
Ww
Xx
Yy
Zz

Aa
Bb
Cc
Dd
Ee
Ff
Gg
Hh
Ii
Jj
Kk
Ll
Mm
Nn
Oo
Pp
Qq
Rr
Ss
Tt
Uu
Vv
Ww
Xx
Yy
Zz

select, fine, deluxe, unrivalled
◇ INFORMAL WORDS top-notch, top-flight
≠ OPPOSITES inferior, average
2 *His painting is* **superior** *to mine.*
better, preferred, greater, higher
≠ OPPOSITES worse, lower
3 *She has a very* **superior** *manner.*
haughty, pretentious, snobbish, condescending, patronizing
◇ INFORMAL WORDS snooty
≠ OPPOSITES humble

supervise VERB
1 *Children must be* **supervised** *by an adult.*
oversee, watch over, look after, control, handle
2 *His job is to* **supervise** *the factory.*
manage, run, direct, control, conduct

supervision NOUN
1 *the* **supervision** *of the department*
management, running, administration, direction, control, superintendence, charge
2 *Keep the children under* **supervision**.
care, guidance, instruction, control

supervisor NOUN
the office **supervisor**
inspector, leader, boss, chief, director, administrator, manager, foreman, forewoman

supple ADJECTIVE
It is important to keep **supple** *as you get older.*
flexible, bending, pliant, agile
≠ OPPOSITES stiff, rigid, inflexible

supplies NOUN
Our **supplies** *of food have almost run out.*
stores, provisions, food, equipment, materials

supply¹ NOUN
a **supply** *of clean water*
source, amount, quantity, stock, fund, store, reserve, stockpile, hoard
≠ OPPOSITES lack

supply² VERB
You will be **supplied** *with pencils and paper.*
provide, equip, stock, give, donate, contribute, yield, produce, sell
≠ OPPOSITES take, receive

support¹ NOUN
1 *The prime minister has the* **support** *of the public.*
backing, loyalty, defence, protection, approval, encouragement, comfort, help, aid, assistance
≠ OPPOSITES opposition, hostility
2 *a roof* **support**
prop, post, pillar, crutch, foundation

support² VERB
1 *I* **support** *the local cricket team.*
back, follow, stand up for, second, defend, promote, aid, assist, rally round
≠ OPPOSITES oppose
2 *posts* **supporting** *the ceiling*
hold up, bear, carry, reinforce, strengthen
3 *I have a family to* **support**.
maintain, keep, provide for, feed, nourish
≠ OPPOSITES live off

supporter NOUN
football **supporters**
fan, follower, defender, seconder, helper, ally, friend
≠ OPPOSITES opponent

suppose VERB
I **suppose** *I could come over later.*
assume, presume, expect, guess, believe, think, consider, judge, imagine
≠ OPPOSITES know
• **be supposed to**
You are **supposed to** *reply in writing.*
meant to, intended to, expected to, required to, obliged to

suppress VERB
1 *The government* **suppressed** *the protests.*
crush, stamp out, quash, quell, subdue, stop, silence, censor, stifle

OPPOSITES encourage, incite
2 *I had to **suppress** my laughter.*
silence, stifle, smother, conceal,
withhold, hold back, contain, restrain,
check

supreme ADJECTIVE
*of **supreme** importance*
best, greatest, highest, top, first,
foremost, chief, principal, unsurpassed,
incomparable

sure ADJECTIVE
1 *I am **sure** you will do well in the
exam.*
certain, convinced, assured, confident,
positive, definite
OPPOSITES unsure, uncertain,
doubtful
2 *The band's new single is **sure** to be a
big hit.*
certain, bound, guaranteed
OPPOSITES unsure, uncertain,
doubtful

surface NOUN
*a mark on the **surface** of the wood*
top, outside, exterior, façade, veneer,
covering, skin
OPPOSITES inside, interior

surly ADJECTIVE
*She has been **surly** and short-tempered
recently.*
gruff, ungracious, bad-tempered, cross,
grouchy, crusty, sullen, sulky, morose
OPPOSITES friendly, polite

surpass VERB
*You have **surpassed** all my expectations.*
beat, outdo, exceed, outstrip, better,
outshine

surplus NOUN
*We have produced a **surplus** of butter.*
excess, remainder, balance, glut, surfeit
OPPOSITES lack, shortage

surprise¹ NOUN
1 *You can imagine her **surprise** when
she saw him.*
amazement, astonishment, wonder,

bewilderment, shock
OPPOSITES composure
2 *Her announcement was a complete
surprise.*
shock, revelation, bombshell, bolt from
the blue

surprise² VERB
*Her wonderful singing voice **surprised**
me.*
startle, amaze, astonish, astound,
stagger

surprising ADJECTIVE
*He moved with **surprising** speed for an
elderly man.*
amazing, astonishing, astounding,
staggering, stunning, extraordinary,
remarkable, startling, unexpected,
unforeseen
OPPOSITES unsurprising, expected

surrender VERB
*The enemy eventually **surrendered**.*
give in, give up, quit, capitulate, submit,
concede, yield

surround VERB
*The star was **surrounded** by
photographers.*
encircle, ring, encase, enclose, hem in,
besiege

surrounding ADJECTIVE
*the **surrounding** countryside*
encircling, bordering, neighbouring,
nearby

surroundings NOUN
*The hotel was in beautiful
surroundings.*
neighbourhood, locality, setting,
environment, background

survey¹ NOUN
*a **survey** of people's views*
review, overview, scrutiny, examination,
inspection, study, appraisal, assessment,
measurement

survey² VERB
surveying the view

Aa
Bb
Cc
Dd
Ee
Ff
Gg
Hh
Ii
Jj
Kk
Ll
Mm
Nn
Oo
Pp
Qq
Rr
Ss
Tt
Uu
Vv
Ww
Xx
Yy
Zz

look at, contemplate, observe, supervise, scan, scrutinize, examine, inspect, study, consider

survive VERB

1 *He has **survived** three heart attacks.*
withstand, weather, beat
2 *a tradition that still **survives***
endure, last, stay, remain, exist
3 *She **survived** her husband by ten years.*
outlive, outlast

suspect VERB

1 *The police **suspected** him of murdering his wife.*
doubt, distrust, mistrust, call into question
2 *I **suspect** he is unhappy.*
believe, fancy, feel, guess, suppose, consider

suspend VERB

1 *A chandelier was **suspended** from the ceiling.*
hang, dangle, swing
2 *The court case was **suspended** for a month.*
delay, postpone, put off, discontinue, interrupt, adjourn
⊯ OPPOSITES continue
3 *He's been **suspended** from the team.*
ban, bar, remove, expel

suspense NOUN

*They kept us in **suspense** until the last minute.*
uncertainty, anxiety, tension, apprehension, anticipation, expectation, excitement
⊯ OPPOSITES certainty, knowledge

suspicion NOUN

*I was filled with **suspicion**.*
doubt, distrust, mistrust, wariness, caution, misgiving, apprehension
⊯ OPPOSITES trust

suspicious ADJECTIVE

1 *He gave me a **suspicious** look.*
doubtful, unbelieving, suspecting, distrustful, mistrustful, wary, apprehensive, uneasy
⊯ OPPOSITES trustful, confident
2 *a **suspicious** character*
dubious, questionable, suspect, irregular, shifty, shady
◇ INFORMAL WORDS dodgy, fishy
⊯ OPPOSITES trustworthy, innocent

sustain VERB

*You cannot **sustain** that pace for long.*
maintain, keep going, keep up, continue, prolong, hold

swallow up VERB

*The boat was **swallowed up** by the waves.*
engulf, envelop, overwhelm

swamp[1] NOUN

*plants that grow in **swamps***
bog, marsh, fen, quagmire, quicksand, mire, mud

swamp[2] VERB

*The flood water **swamped** the valley.*
flood, submerge, drench, saturate, waterlog, sink

swap VERB

*We **swapped** telephone numbers.*
exchange, switch, interchange, trade

swarm VERB

*The city is **swarming** with tourists.*
teem, crawl, bristle

sway VERB

*The bushes **swayed** from side to side in the wind.*
rock, roll, lurch, swing, wave, bend, lean

swear VERB

*He **swore** he would get revenge on the bully.*
vow, promise, pledge, testify, declare, insist

sweat VERB

*I was **sweating** after my exercise class.*
perspire, swelter, drip

sweep VERB

***sweeping** the floor*

Aa
Bb
Cc
Dd
Ee
Ff
Gg
Hh
Ii
Jj
Kk
Ll
Mm
Nn
Oo
Pp
Qq
Rr
Ss
Tt
Uu
Vv
Ww
Xx
Yy
Zz

brush, dust, clean

sweet¹ ADJECTIVE

1 *This pineapple is very **sweet**.*
sugary, syrupy, sweetened, delicious
⊭ OPPOSITES savoury, salty, sour, bitter
2 *She has a very **sweet** nature.*
pleasant, lovely, attractive, appealing, lovable, charming, affectionate, kind, dear, darling
⊭ OPPOSITES unpleasant, nasty
3 *smelling **sweet***
fresh, clean, wholesome, pure, clear, perfumed, fragrant, aromatic

sweet² NOUN

*Jake brought some **sweets** to school.*
candy, confectionery

Here are some types of sweet:

aniseed ball, barley sugar, bonbon, bubble gum, butterscotch, chewing gum, chocolate, coconut ice, cola cube, dolly mixture, fudge, gobstopper, jelly baby, jelly bean, liquorice, lollipop, marshmallow, marzipan, nougat, pastilles, pear drop, rock, toffee, toffee apple, truffle, Turkish delight, wine gum

swell VERB

*When you boil rice, it **swells**.*
expand, inflate, blow up, puff up, bloat, fatten, bulge, balloon, grow, intensify
⊭ OPPOSITES shrink, contract, decrease, dwindle

swerve VERB

*The driver **swerved** to avoid hitting a dog.*
turn, bend, veer, swing

swift ADJECTIVE

*a **swift** drink*
fast, quick, rapid, speedy, flying, hurried, hasty, short
◇ INFORMAL WORDS nippy

⊭ OPPOSITES slow, sluggish, unhurried

swim NOUN

Here are some styles of swimming:

backstroke, breaststroke, butterfly, crawl, doggy paddle, sidestroke
Here are some things you might see at a swimming pool:
armbands, changing room, deep end, diving board, diving platform, float, goggles, lifebelt, lifeguard, rubber ring, shallow end, shower, swimming costume, swimming hat, towel, trunks

swindle VERB

*He was charged with **swindling** pensioners out of their savings.*
cheat, defraud, diddle, fleece, trick, deceive, dupe
◇ INFORMAL WORDS do, rip off, con

swing VERB

1 *The girl's ponytail **swung** as she walked.*
hang, suspend, dangle, wave, sway
2 *She **swung** round when she heard her name.*
veer, swerve, turn, whirl, twirl, spin, rotate

swirl VERB

*The water **swirled** round in the whirlpool.*
churn, spin, twirl, whirl, wheel, twist, curl

switch VERB

*The twins **switched** position as a joke.*
change, exchange, swap, trade, interchange, substitute, replace, rearrange

swivel VERB

*He **swivelled** round on his computer chair.*
pivot, spin, rotate, revolve, turn, twirl, wheel

Aa Bb Cc Dd Ee Ff Gg Hh Ii Jj Kk Ll Mm Nn Oo Pp Qq Rr Ss Tt Uu Vv Ww Xx Yy Zz

Aa
Bb
Cc
Dd
Ee
Ff
Gg
Hh
Ii
Jj
Kk
Ll
Mm
Nn
Oo
Pp
Qq
Rr
Ss
Tt
Uu
Vv
Ww
Xx
Yy
Zz

swoop VERB

The cat swooped on the mouse.
pounce, dive, plunge, lunge, drop, fall, descend, rush

swop
⇒ see **swap**

symbol NOUN

A white dove is a symbol of peace.
sign, token, representation, mark, emblem, badge, logo, character, figure, image

sympathetic ADJECTIVE

Your teacher will be sympathetic to your problems.
understanding, supportive, comforting, consoling, concerned, caring, compassionate, kind
≠ OPPOSITES unsympathetic, indifferent, callous

sympathize VERB

I can sympathize with your point of view.
understand, pity, feel for, identify with, respond to
≠ OPPOSITES ignore, disregard

sympathy NOUN

I have nothing but sympathy for these people.
understanding, comfort, consolation, condolences, pity, compassion, tenderness, warmth, fellow-feeling
≠ OPPOSITES indifference, insensitivity, callousness

synthetic ADJECTIVE

synthetic cream
manufactured, man-made, simulated, artificial, imitation, fake, bogus, mock, sham, pseudo
≠ OPPOSITES genuine, real, natural

system NOUN

a good system of government
method, mode, technique, procedure, process, routine, practice

table NOUN
*a **table** of contents*
list, diagram, chart, graph, index,
register, record

tack VERB
1 *He **tacked** a poster to the notice
board.*
fasten, add, attach, fix, nail, pin
2 *She **tacked** the two pieces of cloth
together.*
stitch, sew

tackle¹ NOUN
*fishing **tackle***
equipment, tools, implements,
apparatus, rig, trappings
◇ INFORMAL WORDS gear

tackle² VERB
1 *We must **tackle** this work
immediately.*
deal with, begin, embark on, set about,
undertake, take on, attend to, grapple
with, handle
≠ OPPOSITES avoid, sidestep
2 *I decided to **tackle** him about his
behaviour.*
confront, challenge, encounter, face up
to
≠ OPPOSITES avoid
3 *The policeman **tackled** the thief and
brought him down.*
grab, seize, grasp

tactful ADJECTIVE
*It wasn't very **tactful** of you to ask her
age.*
diplomatic, discreet, careful, subtle,
sensitive, thoughtful, considerate, polite
≠ OPPOSITES tactless, indiscreet,
thoughtless, rude

tactics NOUN
*They are using delaying **tactics**.*

policy, campaign, plan, approach,
strategy, moves, manoeuvres

tactless ADJECTIVE
*a **tactless** thing to say*
undiplomatic, indiscreet, careless,
insensitive, thoughtless, inconsiderate,
rude, impolite
≠ OPPOSITES tactful, diplomatic,
discreet

tag¹ NOUN
*Put name **tags** on your school uniform.*
label, sticker, tab, ticket, marker,
identification, slip

tag² VERB
***Tag** all the boxes to be moved.*
label, mark, identify
• **tag along**
*Do you mind if I **tag along** with you?*
join, accompany

tail¹ NOUN
*the **tail** of the aircraft*
rear, end, extremity, rear end

tail² VERB
*The private detective **tailed** him for
three weeks.*
follow, pursue, shadow, dog, stalk,
track, trail
• **tail off**
1 *Ticket sales have **tailed off**.*
decrease, decline, drop, fall away,
dwindle, taper off
≠ OPPOSITES increase, grow
2 *Her voice **tailed off** as she saw his
expression.*
fade, taper off, peter out, die out

take VERB
1 *She **took** his hand.*
seize, grab, snatch, grasp, hold, catch
2 *He **took** a new job in London.*
get, obtain

◆ FORMAL WORDS acquire
3 *Take any book you like.*
pick, choose, select
4 *He took his mother's surname.*
adopt, assume
5 *Take five from ten.*
subtract, remove, take away, deduct
⊯ OPPOSITES add, put back
6 *You shouldn't take anything that doesn't belong to you.*
steal, carry off
◇ INFORMAL WORDS nick, pinch
7 *It takes courage to admit you were wrong.*
need, require, demand, call for
8 *Will you take me to my seat, please?*
accompany, escort, lead, guide, conduct, usher
9 *He took me home in a taxi.*
bring, convey, carry, transport, ferry
10 *He cannot take pain.*
bear, tolerate, stand, stomach, suffer
• **take in**
She was completely taken in by his lies.
deceive, fool, dupe, mislead, trick, hoodwink, cheat, swindle
◇ INFORMAL WORDS con, bamboozle
• **take part**
Would you like to take part in the quiz?
join, participate, compete

takeover NOUN
a takeover of the company by a bigger one
merger, combination

tale NOUN
1 *He told me the whole tale of his journey.*
story, yarn, narrative, account, report
2 *an unlikely tale about a monster in the lake*
tall story, old wives' tale, superstition, fable, myth, legend

talent NOUN
artistic talent
gift, genius, flair, knack, skill, ability, capacity, aptitude
⊯ OPPOSITES inability, weakness

talented ADJECTIVE
a talented musician
gifted, brilliant, accomplished, able, capable, skilful
⊯ OPPOSITES inept

talk¹ VERB
1 *We talked about music and films.*
speak, chat, gossip, chatter, discuss
◇ INFORMAL WORDS natter
2 *She's just talking nonsense.*
speak, utter, say

talk² NOUN
1 *We had a long talk about the future.*
conversation, discussion, chat, chatter
◇ INFORMAL WORDS natter
2 *That's not true – it's just talk.*
gossip, hearsay, rumour
3 *I had to give a talk on global warming.*
speech, lecture, address

talkative ADJECTIVE
He was in a talkative mood tonight.
chatty, communicative, vocal, unreserved, gossipy
⊯ OPPOSITES taciturn, quiet, reserved

tall ADJECTIVE
1 *a tall building*
high, lofty, towering
⊯ OPPOSITES low
2 *I've never seen anyone so tall.*
big, great, giant, gigantic
⊯ OPPOSITES short, small

tame ADJECTIVE
1 *a tame owl*
domesticated, trained, broken in, manageable
⊯ OPPOSITES wild, unmanageable
2 *a tame little woman*
meek, manageable, gentle, unresisting, obedient
⊯ OPPOSITES wild, unmanageable, rebellious
3 *The party was pretty tame.*
boring, dull, tedious, uninteresting, bland, insipid, unadventurous, lifeless
⊯ OPPOSITES exciting

Aa
Bb
Cc
Dd
Ee
Ff
Gg
Hh
Ii
Jj
Kk
Ll
Mm
Nn
Oo
Pp
Qq
Rr
Ss
Tt
Uu
Vv
Ww
Xx
Yy
Zz

tamper VERB

1 *Don't **tamper** with my computer.*
interfere, meddle, tinker, fiddle
◇ INFORMAL WORDS mess
2 *tampering with the evidence*
alter, fix, rig

tang NOUN

*the **tang** of lime juice*
taste, sharpness, bite, flavour, savour, smack

tangle VERB

1 *Someone had **tangled** all the wires.*
entangle, knot, snarl, twist, interweave, interlace, intertwine
⊯ OPPOSITES disentangle
2 *Dolphins get **tangled** in the fishing nets.*
catch, entangle, snarl, ensnare, entrap
⊯ OPPOSITES disentangle
• **tangle up**
*He had got **tangled up** in a dangerous situation.*
involve, implicate

tap VERB

tapping on the door
knock, hit, strike, rap, beat, drum

tape NOUN

1 *a bunch of letters tied up with **tape***
binding, band, strip, ribbon
2 *I have a **tape** of the band's concert.*
recording, video, cassette

target NOUN

*We are close to our **target** of raising £1000.*
aim, purpose, intention, ambition, goal, objective

tarnish VERB

1 *The brass fender is **tarnished**.*
discolour, rust, dull, dim, darken, stain, spot
⊯ OPPOSITES polish, brighten
2 *a scandal which had **tarnished** his reputation*
stain, blacken, spoil, blot

tart ADJECTIVE

*If the lemonade is too **tart**, add some sugar.*
sour, sharp, acid, bitter, vinegary, tangy

task NOUN

*The teacher gave each child a **task** to do.*
job, chore, duty, assignment, exercise, errand, undertaking, mission

taste¹ NOUN

1 *a **taste** of garlic*
flavour, savour, relish, smack, tang
⊯ OPPOSITES blandness
2 *Rebecca has good **taste** in clothes.*
judgement, discrimination, discernment, appreciation, tastefulness
⊯ OPPOSITES tastelessness

taste² VERB

*He **tasted** the soup and said it was delicious.*
try, sample, nibble, sip, test

Here are some ways of describing taste:

acid, appetizing, bitter, bittersweet, citrus, creamy, delicious, fruity, hot, meaty, mouthwatering, peppery, salty, savoury, sharp, sour, spicy, sugary, sweet, tangy, tart, tasty, vinegary

tasteful ADJECTIVE

tasteful decoration
refined, elegant, smart, stylish, artistic, beautiful, exquisite, graceful
⊯ OPPOSITES tasteless, garish

tasteless ADJECTIVE

1 *This melon is **tasteless**.*
flavourless, insipid, bland, mild, weak, watery, flat
⊯ OPPOSITES tasty
2 *a **tasteless** outfit*
flashy, inelegant, vulgar, cheap, gaudy, garish, loud
◇ INFORMAL WORDS naff

Aa
Bb
Cc
Dd
Ee
Ff
Gg
Hh
Ii
Jj
Kk
Ll
Mm
Nn
Oo
Pp
Qq
Rr
Ss
Tt
Uu
Vv
Ww
Xx
Yy
Zz

Aa
Bb
Cc
Dd
Ee
Ff
Gg
Hh
Ii
Jj
Kk
Ll
Mm
Nn
Oo
Pp
Qq
Rr
Ss
Tt
Uu
Vv
Ww
Xx
Yy
Zz

≠ OPPOSITES tasteful, elegant
3 *a tasteless remark*
vulgar, unseemly, improper, indiscreet, rude, crude
◇ INFORMAL WORDS naff

tasty ADJECTIVE
a tasty snack
delicious, luscious, appetizing, mouthwatering, tangy, savoury, sweet
◇ INFORMAL WORDS scrumptious, yummy
≠ OPPOSITES tasteless, insipid

tattered ADJECTIVE
tattered old clothes
ragged, frayed, threadbare, ripped, torn, tatty, shabby, scruffy
≠ OPPOSITES smart, neat

taunt VERB
The other girls taunted her because of her accent.
tease, torment, jeer, mock, ridicule, sneer at, insult
◇ INFORMAL WORDS rib

taut ADJECTIVE
1 *a taut rope*
tight, stretched, rigid, tense
≠ OPPOSITES slack, loose
2 *massaging my taut shoulder muscles*
tense, tight, strained, unrelaxed, stiff, rigid
≠ OPPOSITES slack, loose, relaxed

teach VERB
1 *My dad is teaching me how to drive.*
instruct, train, coach, direct, show, demonstrate, advise, inform
≠ OPPOSITES learn
2 *She teaches at the local college.*
instruct, coach, tutor, lecture, educate
≠ OPPOSITES learn

teacher NOUN
a music teacher
instructor, schoolteacher, schoolmaster, master, schoolmistress, mistress, tutor, lecturer, trainer, coach
≠ OPPOSITES pupil

team NOUN
1 *the school hockey team*
side, line-up, squad, crew
2 *a team of workmen*
crew, squad, shift, gang, band, group

tear¹ VERB
1 *He tore his sleeve on a nail.*
rip, rend, divide, shred
2 *The sharp claws tore his hand.*
scratch, mangle
3 *She tore the book out of his hand.*
pull, snatch, grab, seize, wrest
4 *The pickpocket tore down the street.*
rush, dash, hurry, speed, race, run, sprint, bolt
◇ INFORMAL WORDS belt

tear² NOUN
There's a tear in your shirt.
rip, rent, slit, hole, split, rupture, gash

tease VERB
1 *I was teased about my new hairstyle.*
taunt, bait, plague, torment, mock, ridicule, gibe
◇ INFORMAL WORDS needle, rag, rib
2 *She kept teasing me to tell her what had happened.*
pester, annoy, badger, worry, plague, torment

technical ADJECTIVE
a technical expert
scientific, mechanical, technological, electronic

tedious ADJECTIVE
a tedious lesson
boring, uninteresting, unexciting, dull, dreary, monotonous, tiresome, wearisome
≠ OPPOSITES lively, interesting, exciting

telephone VERB
Write or telephone for further details.
phone, ring, call, call up, dial
◇ INFORMAL WORDS buzz

television NOUN

Here are some types of television show:

cartoon, chat show, children's programme, comedy, current affairs, crime, detective drama, documentary, drama, film, game show, music show, news, quiz show, reality show, soap opera, wildlife programme

tell VERB

1 *Tell him what you have done.*
inform, notify, let know, acquaint with, communicate to, disclose, reveal
2 *I cannot tell a lie.*
speak, utter, say, state
3 *Tell me a story.*
narrate, relate, report, describe
4 *The receptionist told me to wait in the waiting room.*
order, command, direct, instruct
5 *I can't tell one twin from the other.*
distinguish, differentiate, discriminate, recognize, identify

• **tell off**
Gita was told off for chatting in class.
scold, reprimand, reprove, lecture, reproach
◇ INFORMAL WORDS tick off

temper NOUN

1 *He lost his temper and stormed out.*
self-control, calm, composure
◇ INFORMAL WORDS cool
⊐ OPPOSITES anger, rage
2 *I hope you are in a better temper today.*
mood, humour
3 *She is known for her sweet temper.*
nature, character, temperament, disposition
4 *She's in a temper because her brother broke her CD player.*
rage, bad mood, fury, passion, tantrum
⊐ OPPOSITES calmness, self-control

temporary ADJECTIVE

1 *a temporary power cut*
brief, impermanent, passing, fleeting, short-lived, momentary
⊐ OPPOSITES permanent, everlasting
2 *a temporary solution*
short-term, provisional, makeshift, stopgap
⊐ OPPOSITES permanent

tempt VERB

1 *She tempted me to have another cake.*
entice, coax, persuade, lure, invite
⊐ OPPOSITES discourage, dissuade
2 *I was tempted by the low prices.*
attract, entice, lure, draw, woo, seduce
⊐ OPPOSITES discourage, dissuade, repel

tend¹ VERB

I tend to go out on a Friday.
be inclined, be likely, be liable, prefer

tend² VERB

1 *nurses tending the sick*
care for, look after, nurse, minister to, serve, attend
⊐ OPPOSITES neglect, ignore
2 *A neighbour tended the children while I was in hospital.*
look after, care for, protect, watch, mind, minister to
⊐ OPPOSITES neglect, ignore

tendency NOUN

1 *He has a tendency to drive too fast.*
inclination, partiality, predisposition, liability, proneness
2 *the growing tendency to marry later in life*
trend, bias, inclination

tender ADJECTIVE

1 *She was a tender mother and a faithful wife.*
loving, kind, gentle, caring, warm, fond, affectionate, tender-hearted, soft-hearted
⊐ OPPOSITES hard-hearted, callous
2 *a tender story about young love*

Aa
Bb
Cc
Dd
Ee
Ff
Gg
Hh
Ii
Jj
Kk
Ll
Mm
Nn
Oo
Pp
Qq
Rr
Ss
Tt
Uu
Vv
Ww
Xx
Yy
Zz

tennis → test

romantic, sentimental, emotional, sensitive, sympathetic, compassionate
3 *at the* **tender** *age of nine*
youthful, immature, impressionable, vulnerable
(≠) OPPOSITES mature
4 **tender** *meat*
soft, succulent
(≠) OPPOSITES tough, hard
5 *The skin around my wound is still a bit* **tender***.*
sore, painful, aching, smarting, bruised, inflamed, raw

tennis NOUN

Here are some words used in tennis:

ace, advantage, backhand, ball, ball boy, ball girl, baseline, court, deuce, doubles, forehand, game, grand slam, line, love, match, net, racquet, serve, set, singles, smash, tournament, umpire, volley

tense ADJECTIVE

1 *My shoulder muscles were* **tense***.*
stiff, tight, taut, stretched, strained, rigid
(≠) OPPOSITES loose, slack
2 *She felt* **tense** *before the interview.*
nervous, anxious, worried, uneasy, apprehensive, edgy, jumpy, keyed up
◇ INFORMAL WORDS jittery
(≠) OPPOSITES calm, relaxed

tension NOUN

The **tension** *of the last few days has made her ill.*
nervousness, anxiety, worry, uneasiness, apprehension, edginess, suspense
(≠) OPPOSITES calmness, relaxation

term NOUN

1 *'Wireless' is an old-fashioned* **term** *for 'radio'.*
word, name, title, phrase, expression
2 *in her second* **term** *at school*
session, course, season
3 *He is now facing a long* **term** *in prison.*

period, time, spell, span, stretch, interval

terrible ADJECTIVE

1 *a* **terrible** *crime*
dreadful, shocking, appalling, outrageous, horrible, hideous, gruesome, horrific, distressing
2 *a* **terrible** *actor*
bad, awful, frightful, dreadful, shocking, appalling
(≠) OPPOSITES excellent, wonderful, superb
3 *a* **terrible** *thing to do to anyone*
horrible, disgusting, revolting, repulsive, offensive, hateful, horrid, obnoxious, foul, vile
(≠) OPPOSITES excellent, wonderful, superb
4 *in* **terrible** *trouble*
serious, severe, extreme, desperate, grave

terrific ADJECTIVE

1 *They put on a* **terrific** *show.*
excellent, wonderful, marvellous, outstanding, brilliant, magnificent, superb, fantastic, sensational, amazing
(≠) OPPOSITES awful, terrible, appalling
2 *a* **terrific** *thunderclap*
huge, enormous, gigantic, tremendous, great, intense

terrify VERB

Flying **terrifies** *me.*
frighten, terrorize, intimidate, scare, alarm

territory NOUN

foreign **territory**
land, country, sector, region, area, district, zone, terrain

terror NOUN

The children screamed in **terror***.*
fear, panic, shock, fright, alarm

test¹ NOUN

1 **tests** *on a new model of car*
trial, try-out, experiment, check, investigation, analysis, examination
2 *a maths* **test**

examination, assessment, evaluation

test[2] VERB

1 *They need to **test** the drug for possible side effects.*
check, examine, investigate, analyse, try, experiment
2 *The teacher **tested** the class in spelling.*
examine, assess, evaluate

thank VERB

*I would like to **thank** everyone who helped me.*
say thank you to, be grateful to, acknowledge, recognize, credit

thankful ADJECTIVE

1 *We were just **thankful** to have got home safely.*
grateful, contented, relieved, pleased, appreciative
≠ OPPOSITES ungrateful, unappreciative
2 *I am **thankful** to you for all your help.*
grateful, appreciative
◆ FORMAL WORDS obliged, indebted
≠ OPPOSITES ungrateful, unappreciative

thanks NOUN

*I would like to show my **thanks** for all your help.*
gratitude, gratefulness, appreciation, acknowledgement, recognition, credit, thanksgiving

thaw VERB

*The sun will **thaw** the ice and snow.*
melt, defrost, de-ice, soften, liquefy, dissolve
≠ OPPOSITES freeze

theft NOUN

*the **theft** of money from the till*
stealing, robbery, thieving, pilfering

theme NOUN

*The **theme** of the speech was global warming.*
subject, topic, idea, gist, essence

theory NOUN

1 *There are many **theories** as to why*

dinosaurs died out.
idea, assumption, presumption, guess, speculation, notion
◆ FORMAL WORDS conjecture
≠ OPPOSITES certainty
2 *a political **theory** for successful government*
plan, proposal, scheme, system
≠ OPPOSITES practice

therapy NOUN

*a course of **therapy** for skin problems*
treatment, remedy, cure, healing

therefore ADVERB

*I have spent all my pocket money; **therefore**, I can't go to the cinema.*
so, consequently, as a result, thus

thick ADJECTIVE

1 *a **thick** waist*
wide, broad, fat, heavy, solid
≠ OPPOSITES thin, slim, slender, slight
2 *a **thick** forest*
dense, close, compact
3 *a **thick** sauce*
concentrated, condensed
4 *The city centre was **thick** with shoppers.*
full, packed, crowded, chock-a-block, swarming, teeming, bursting

thief NOUN

*the **thief** who took all our money*
robber, bandit, mugger, pickpocket, burglar, house-breaker, stealer, pilferer

thin ADJECTIVE

⇒ For even more about this word, see the next page
1 *I was quite **thin** when I was a teenager.*
slim, slender, slight, lean
≠ OPPOSITES fat, broad
2 *She became very **thin** when she was ill.*
skinny, bony, scraggy, scrawny, gaunt, underweight, undernourished
≠ OPPOSITES fat, broad
3 *a **thin** fabric*
fine, delicate, light, flimsy, filmy, sheer,

Aa
Bb
Cc
Dd
Ee
Ff
Gg
Hh
Ii
Jj
Kk
Ll
Mm
Nn
Oo
Pp
Qq
Rr
Ss
Tt
Uu
Vv
Ww
Xx
Yy
Zz

thin

The words below can all be used to describe someone who is **thin**. As well as painting a more detailed picture, they can also tell your reader how you feel about someone.

A person who is thin or dainty in a healthy or attractive way can be described as
lean
slim
slender
slight

These words can describe someone who is tall and thin:
lanky
spindly

These words describe someone who is probably a bit too thin. They are not very polite ways of describing someone:
skinny
bony
gaunt
skeletal
scraggy
scrawny

Someone who is unhealthily or dangerously thin could be described as
emaciated
underweight
undernourished

Over to you

Choose a word carefully to replace **thin** in the following sentences.

1 The dancers warmed up for the big show. They had been practising for months and were **thin** and supple.

2 My brother is tall and **thin**. He's much taller than me.

3 Alison has been on a diet for ages. I think she should stop soon as she's looking too **thin**.

> **4** She discovered the brown and white mongrel wandering the streets. Although he was filthy and **thin**, he licked her hand and wagged his tail.

see-through, transparent
≠ OPPOSITES **thick**
4 *thin soup*
watery, runny, weak
≠ OPPOSITES **thick**

thing NOUN
⇒ For even more about this word, see the next page
1 *He makes things out of matchsticks.*
object, article, item
2 *one of the things we need to discuss*
item, detail, particular, feature, factor, element, point
3 *A strange thing happened.*
happening, occurrence, event, incident, affair, circumstance

think VERB
1 *I think he's telling the truth.*
believe, consider, regard, judge, conclude, reason
2 *How many people do you think will come?*
estimate, reckon, calculate
3 *I can't think what will happen next.*
imagine, conceive, suppose, presume, expect, foresee, anticipate
4 *We were trying to think of the actor's name.*
remember, recollect, recall
• **think over**
Think over my suggestion.
consider, ponder, mull over, meditate on, contemplate, muse on, reflect on, weigh up
◇ INFORMAL WORDS **chew over**

thorn NOUN
Roses have thorns on their stems.
spike, point, barb, prickle, spine, needle

thorough ADJECTIVE
1 *She is always very thorough in her*

work.
careful, conscientious, efficient, painstaking, scrupulous, meticulous
≠ OPPOSITES **partial, superficial, careless**
2 *You made a thorough mess of that.*
complete, total, utter, absolute, sheer, out-and-out, downright
≠ OPPOSITES **partial**

thought NOUN
1 *I will give your idea some thought.*
consideration, thinking, attention, study, scrutiny
2 *The thought of growing old horrified her.*
idea, notion, concept, conception
3 *What are your thoughts on the subject?*
opinion, idea, belief, conviction, view, judgement, conclusion
4 *You must have some thought for others.*
consideration, thoughtfulness, kindness, care, concern, compassion, sympathy

thoughtful ADJECTIVE
1 *She had a thoughtful look on her face.*
pensive, wistful, dreamy, thinking, absorbed
2 *a kind and thoughtful person*
considerate, kind, unselfish, helpful, caring, sensitive
≠ OPPOSITES **thoughtless, insensitive, selfish**

thoughtless ADJECTIVE
That was a thoughtless thing to say.
inconsiderate, unthinking, insensitive, selfish, uncaring, tactless, undiplomatic
≠ OPPOSITES **thoughtful, considerate**

Aa
Bb
Cc
Dd
Ee
Ff
Gg
Hh
Ii
Jj
Kk
Ll
Mm
Nn
Oo
Pp
Qq
Rr
Ss
Tt
Uu
Vv
Ww
Xx
Yy
Zz

thing

'Throw me my things!' screamed the diver, but the boy was confused and didn't know that he meant the breathing apparatus.

Instead of using the word **thing**, choose a word that tells your reader exactly what you mean.

something you can use
> **gadget**
> **tool**
> **implement**
> **instrument**
> **machine**
> **apparatus**

something of interest in a place or a book
> **feature**
> **detail**
> **fact**
> **idea**
> **thought**
> **factor**

something that happens
> **incident**
> **event**
> **occurrence**
> **affair**
> **happening**
> **phenomenon**

Over to you

Can you use some of these words in the following sentences?

1 He was an excellent handyman because he always had the right _____ for the job.

2 The _____ was designed by Stevenson and it still works today.

3 The best _____ of the house is the huge garden.

4 I know a lot of _____ about what happened.

thrash VERB

1 *The boy was **thrashed** severely.*
beat, whip, lash, flog, spank
◇ INFORMAL WORDS clobber, lay into, wallop, belt
2 *The school netball team **thrashed** the opposition.*
defeat, beat
◇ INFORMAL WORDS hammer
3 ***thrashing** her arms about in the water*
thresh, flail, toss, jerk

threadbare ADJECTIVE

threadbare clothes
worn, frayed, ragged, moth-eaten, scruffy, shabby
≠ OPPOSITES new

threat NOUN

1 *The **threat** of punishment made him behave.*
menace, warning
2 *the ever-present **threat** of war*
danger, menace, risk, hazard, peril

threaten VERB

1 *They **threatened** us to make us hand over the money.*
menace, intimidate, browbeat, bully, terrorize
2 *the climate change which **threatens** the planet*
endanger, jeopardize, menace

thrill VERB

*Meeting my hero **thrilled** me.*
excite, electrify, exhilarate, move, stir, stimulate
≠ OPPOSITES bore

thrive VERB

1 *This plant is **thriving** now that it has been moved indoors.*
flourish, grow, develop, bloom, blossom
≠ OPPOSITES fail, die
2 *The business **thrived** under the new management.*
succeed, prosper, flourish, boom, grow, increase, profit

≠ OPPOSITES fail

throb VERB

1 *My heart **throbbed** with excitement.*
pound, beat, thump, palpitate, pulsate
2 *The motorcycle's engine **throbbed**.*
vibrate, pulse, pulsate, beat, palpitate

throttle VERB

*The attacker tried to **throttle** him.*
strangle, choke

throw VERB

*He **threw** the ball into the air.*
hurl, pitch, sling, cast, toss, launch, propel, send
◇ INFORMAL WORDS chuck, lob
• **throw away**
*I **threw away** all his letters.*
dispose of, scrap, discard, throw out
◇ INFORMAL WORDS ditch, dump
≠ OPPOSITES keep, preserve, rescue

thrust VERB

1 *He **thrust** his way to the front of the crowd.*
push, shove, butt, ram, force
2 *He **thrust** me out of the room.*
push, shove, force, drive, propel
3 *He **thrust** the knife in.*
stick, plunge, jab, stab, press, force

thump VERB

1 *He **thumped** his fist on the table.*
bang, crash, thud, batter, pound, hammer, beat, knock
2 *I'll **thump** you if you do that again.*
hit, strike, punch, cuff, smack, thrash
◇ INFORMAL WORDS whack, wallop, clout

tick VERB

Tick the appropriate box.
mark, indicate, choose, select
• **tick off**
*Todd was **ticked off** for not doing his homework.*
scold, reprimand
◇ INFORMAL WORDS tell off
≠ OPPOSITES praise, compliment

ticket NOUN

1 *a bus **ticket***

Aa
Bb
Cc
Dd
Ee
Ff
Gg
Hh
Ii
Jj
Kk
Ll
Mm
Nn
Oo
Pp
Qq
Rr
Ss
Tt
Uu
Vv
Ww
Xx
Yy
Zz

Aa
Bb
Cc
Dd
Ee
Ff
Gg
Hh
Ii
Jj
Kk
Ll
Mm
Nn
Oo
Pp
Qq
Rr
Ss
Tt
Uu
Vv
Ww
Xx
Yy
Zz

pass, card, certificate, token, voucher, coupon, slip
2 *the price on the* **ticket**
label, card, slip, tag, sticker

tickle VERB
1 *It* **tickles** *me to hear my grandmother's stories.*
amuse, delight, please, entertain
2 *stories which will* **tickle** *your imagination*
excite, thrill, stimulate

tidy ADJECTIVE
1 *a* **tidy** *room*
neat, orderly, organized, spick-and-span, shipshape, well-kept, ordered, uncluttered
≠ OPPOSITES untidy, messy, disorganized
2 *She always looks so* **tidy** *when she leaves for work.*
neat, smart, spruce, trim
≠ OPPOSITES untidy, messy
3 *a* **tidy** *sum of money*
large, substantial, sizable, considerable, generous, ample
≠ OPPOSITES small, insignificant

tie VERB
1 **Tie** *the two pieces together with string.*
fasten, attach, join, connect, link, unite, bind
2 *The dog was* **tied** *to the post by its lead.*
secure, rope, lash, strap, bind
• **tie up**
We **tied up** *the boat at the jetty.*
secure, moor, tether, attach, rope, lash, bind

tight ADJECTIVE
1 *Keep the fishing line* **tight**.
taut, stretched, tense, rigid, stiff
≠ OPPOSITES loose, slack
2 **tight** *trousers*
close-fitting, taut, stretched, snug
≠ OPPOSITES loose, slack
3 *a* **tight** *space*
cramped, constricted, restricted, limited

tilt VERB
1 *The boat* **tilted** *as everyone rushed to the side.*
slant, slope, incline, pitch, list, tip, lean
2 **Tilt** *your soup plate away from you.*
tip, lean, incline

time NOUN
1 *I can only stay for a short* **time**.
period, spell, stretch, term, span, duration, interval, space, while
2 *dancing in* **time** *to the music*
rhythm, tempo, beat
3 *at that* **time** *in his life*
point, moment, stage, instance, occasion
4 *I see her at the same* **time** *every week.*
date, day, hour
5 *in Roman* **times**
age, era

Here are some names of periods of time:

Long periods:
age, century, eon, epoch, era, eternity, generation, lifetime, millennium
Periods during a year:
day, fortnight, month, quarter, season, week, weekend
Periods during a day:
half-hour, hour, minute, quarter-hour, second
Very short periods:
instant, microsecond, millisecond, moment
Times of the day:
afternoon, bedtime, dawn, daytime, dusk, evening, midday, morn, morning, night, nightfall, night-time, noon, sunrise, sunset, sun-up, tea-time, the early hours, twilight

timetable NOUN
1 *a railway* **timetable**
schedule, programme, agenda, calendar, listing
2 *the school* **timetable**
curriculum, programme, syllabus

timid ADJECTIVE

*She was too **timid** to argue.*
nervous, shy, shrinking, retiring, apprehensive, afraid, fearful, cowardly, faint-hearted
≢ OPPOSITES brave, bold

tingle VERB

*My fingers were **tingling** with the cold.*
prickle, sting, tickle, itch

tinker VERB

*Who has been **tinkering** with the video?*
fiddle, play, toy, meddle, tamper

tint NOUN

1 *walls painted in a delicate **tint** of blue*
shade, colour, hue, tinge, tone
2 *She bought a red **tint** for her hair.*
dye, stain, rinse, wash, colour

tiny ADJECTIVE

1 *a **tiny** woman*
small, minute, little, petite, dwarfish, miniature
◇ INFORMAL WORDS teeny, pint-sized, mini
≢ OPPOSITES huge, enormous, immense
2 *only a **tiny** amount*
small, minute, slight, insignificant
◇ INFORMAL WORDS teeny
≢ OPPOSITES huge, enormous, immense

tip¹ NOUN

1 *the **tip** of the pencil*
end, point, top, head
2 *the **tip** of the iceberg*
peak, point, summit, top, cap, crown, head

tip² VERB

1 ***Tip** your head forward a little.*
lean, incline, slant, tilt
2 *The ladder **tipped** and crashed to the ground.*
tilt, topple over, capsize, upset, overturn

tip³ NOUN

1 *He gave us a few useful **tips**.*
hint, pointer, suggestion, advice, information, inside information

2 *We gave the waiter a **tip**.*
gratuity, gift

tired ADJECTIVE

*You must be **tired** after your long journey.*
exhausted, weary, drowsy, sleepy, worn out, drained, fatigued
◇ INFORMAL WORDS bushed, whacked, shattered, beat, dead beat, dog-tired, all in
≢ OPPOSITES lively, energetic, rested, refreshed

tire out VERB

*The children **tired** their grandparents **out**.*
exhaust, weary, fatigue, wear out, drain
≢ OPPOSITES invigorate, refresh

tiresome ADJECTIVE

1 *a **tiresome** chore*
boring, dull, tedious, monotonous, uninteresting, tiring
≢ OPPOSITES interesting, stimulating
2 *my **tiresome** next-door neighbour*
annoying, troublesome, trying, irritating, exasperating

title NOUN

1 *the **title** on the cover of the book*
heading, headline, caption, inscription, name
2 *the **title** 'Prince of Wales'*
rank, status, office, position

toast VERB

*We **toasted** marshmallows at the bonfire.*
brown, grill, roast, heat, warm

together ADVERB

1 *We'll solve this problem **together**.*
with each other, jointly, side by side, shoulder to shoulder
≢ OPPOSITES separately, individually, alone
2 *We all sang 'Happy Birthday' **together**.*
at the same time, all at once, as one, simultaneously, collectively
≢ OPPOSITES separately, individually, alone

Aa
Bb
Cc
Dd
Ee
Ff
Gg
Hh
Ii
Jj
Kk
Ll
Mm
Nn
Oo
Pp
Qq
Rr
Ss
Tt
Uu
Vv
Ww
Xx
Yy
Zz

toil VERB

*Dad **toiled** in the garden all day.*
work, labour, slave, drudge, slog
◇ INFORMAL WORDS graft, plug away, sweat, grind

token NOUN

1 *This gift is a **token** of my gratitude.*
symbol, representation, mark, sign, indication, demonstration, expression, evidence, proof
2 *a gift **token***
voucher, coupon
3 *a telephone **token***
counter, disc

tolerant ADJECTIVE

1 *You should be **tolerant** towards people with different opinions from yours.*
open-minded, fair, unprejudiced, broad-minded, liberal
(≠) OPPOSITES intolerant, biased, prejudiced, bigoted
2 *Luckily I had a very **tolerant** teacher.*
sympathetic, charitable, kind-hearted, understanding, forgiving
(≠) OPPOSITES intolerant, unsympathetic
3 *She's far too **tolerant** with those children.*
easy-going, forgiving, lenient, indulgent, permissive, lax
(≠) OPPOSITES intolerant, unsympathetic

tolerate VERB

1 *The teacher does not **tolerate** rudeness.*
allow, put up with, stand, take, accept, permit
2 *I couldn't **tolerate** the pain any longer.*
bear, put up with, endure, suffer, stand, take

toll NOUN

*You have to pay a **toll** to drive across the bridge.*
charge, fee, payment, tax

tone NOUN

1 *an angry **tone** of voice*
pitch, note, inflection, accent, stress, emphasis
2 *dressed completely in brown **tones***
shade, tint, tinge, colour, hue
3 *the relaxed **tone** of the office*
manner, mood, air, attitude, spirit, quality, feel, style

tone down VERB

*He was ordered to **tone down** his outrageous behaviour.*
moderate, subdue, restrain, play down, reduce

tool NOUN

*gardening **tools***
implement, instrument, utensil, gadget, device, apparatus, appliance

Here are some types of tool:

axe, chisel, drill, fork, hammer, hoe, mallet, pickaxe, pliers, sander, saw, screwdriver, spade, spirit level, trowel, wrench

top¹ NOUN

1 *the **top** of the hill*
peak, head, crest, crown, summit, height
(≠) OPPOSITES bottom, base, nadir
2 *Put the **top** back on the toothpaste.*
lid, cap, cover, cork, stopper

top² VERB

*We hope to **top** last year's achievement.*
beat, exceed, outstrip, better, excel, surpass, outshine, outdo

topic NOUN

*Someone suggest a **topic** for our discussion.*
subject, theme, issue, question, matter, point

topical ADJECTIVE

*a radio programme which discusses **topical** issues*

current, contemporary, up-to-date, up-to-the-minute, recent, newsworthy, popular

topple VERB
1 *A display **toppled** over in the supermarket.*
fall over, overbalance, tumble, collapse, overturn, capsize
2 *The winds **toppled** dozens of trees.*
knock over, knock down, upset, overturn

torment VERB
1 *My little brothers used to **torment** me when they were younger.*
annoy, tease, provoke, harass, pester, bother, plague
2 *I was **tormented** with feelings of guilt.*
torture, trouble, worry, harass, plague, distress, pain

torrent NOUN
1 *The rain was coming down in **torrents**.*
downpour, deluge, cascade, shower
2 *A **torrent** of water was rushing down the hill.*
stream, gush, rush, flood, spate, cascade
⊘ OPPOSITES trickle

torture[1] NOUN
1 *The prisoners had been subjected to **torture**.*
torment, pain, abuse, ill-treatment, agony, suffering, martyrdom
2 *the **torture** of waiting for news of her missing child*
agony, pain, suffering, distress, misery, anguish, torment

torture[2] VERB
1 *The victim had been **tortured** and then killed.*
torment, abuse, ill-treat, martyr
2 *He **tortured** us by making us wait for the result.*
distress, torment, pain

toss VERB
1 *He **tossed** the wrapper in the bin.*
throw, flip, fling, sling, hurl
◇ INFORMAL WORDS chuck, lob
2 *The boat **tossed** from side to side in the stormy sea.*
roll, heave, pitch, lurch, jolt, rock
3 *The girl **tossed** and turned all night.*
thrash, squirm, wriggle

total[1] ADJECTIVE
1 *The **total** amount raised was £750.*
full, complete, entire, whole
2 *It's **total** chaos in there.*
complete, utter, absolute, outright, sheer, downright, thorough, all-out

total[2] NOUN
*We have had a **total** of 25 replies.*
sum, whole, entirety, totality, all, lot, amount

total[3] VERB
*The cost of the repairs **totals** £250.*
come to, amount to, add up to, reach
• total up
*I have **totalled up** the bill.*
add up, tot up, count up, reckon

touch VERB
1 *He **touched** her hand.*
feel, handle, finger, brush, graze, stroke
2 *The houses are so close they are almost **touching**.*
meet, come into contact, come together
3 *The little girl's letter **touched** me.*
move, stir, upset, disturb, impress, affect
• touch on
*He **touched on** the subject of discipline.*
mention, refer to, raise, bring up

touchy ADJECTIVE
*Why are you so **touchy** today?*
irritable, quick-tempered, bad-tempered, grumpy, grouchy, cross, edgy
⊘ OPPOSITES calm

tough ADJECTIVE
1 *a **tough** material*
strong, resistant, sturdy, solid, rigid, stiff, inflexible, hard

Aa
Bb
Cc
Dd
Ee
Ff
Gg
Hh
Ii
Jj
Kk
Ll
Mm
Nn
Oo
Pp
Qq
Rr
Ss
Tt
Uu
Vv
Ww
Xx
Yy
Zz

OPPOSITES fragile, delicate, weak
2 *He's a tough character.*
rough, violent, vicious, hardened
≠ OPPOSITES gentle, soft
3 *She is tough on her children.*
harsh, severe, strict, stern
≠ OPPOSITES gentle
4 *a tough problem*
difficult, hard, puzzling, perplexing, baffling, troublesome
≠ OPPOSITES easy, simple

tour NOUN
a tour to the Lake District
journey, visit, expedition, trip, outing, excursion

tourist NOUN
catering for foreign tourists
traveller, holidaymaker, visitor, sightseer, tripper, voyager, globetrotter

tournament NOUN
an annual golf tournament
championship, series, competition, contest, match, event, meeting

tow VERB
The car had to be towed to the garage.
pull, tug, draw, trail, drag, lug, haul

towards PREPOSITION
1 *towards the end of the holidays*
just before, approaching, nearing, close to, nearly at, almost at, coming up to
2 *His feelings towards her have changed.*
about, regarding, with regard to, with respect to, concerning, for

tower NOUN
the towers of the castle
turret, steeple, spire, belfry

toxic ADJECTIVE
toxic chemicals
poisonous, harmful, unhealthy, dangerous, deadly, lethal
≠ OPPOSITES harmless, safe

toy NOUN

Here are some types of toy:

Outdoor toys:
ball, bicycle, climbing-frame, football, Frisbee®, go-kart, hobby-horse, hula-hoop, kite, paddling pool, pedal-car, pogo stick, roller skates, sandpit, scooter, see-saw, skateboard, skipping rope, slide, spacehopper, swing, Swingball®, trampoline, walkie-talkie, water pistol

Indoor toys:
Action Man®, balloon, Barbie doll®, blackboard and easel, building bricks, computer game, crayons, doll, doll's house, farm, fivestones, fort, garage, glove puppet, gyroscope, jack-in-the-box, jigsaw puzzle, kaleidoscope, Lego®, marbles, Meccano®, model car, modelling clay, paints, Plasticene®, PlayStation®, rattle, rocking-horse, Scalextric®, soft toy, spinning top, tea set, teddy bear, toy soldier, train set, video game, Wendy house, yo-yo

trace¹ NOUN
She has a trace of an Irish accent.
hint, suggestion, spot, bit, jot, touch

trace² VERB
1 *The man is trying to trace his family.*
find, discover, detect, unearth, seek, track, track down
2 *Police have traced the two suspects to a house in London.*
track, track down, trail, stalk, hunt, follow, pursue, shadow

track¹ NOUN
1 *deer tracks in the woods*
trail, footstep, footprint, footmark, mark, trace
2 *a dirt track leading to a cottage*
path, trail, way, route

Aa Bb Cc Dd Ee Ff Gg Hh Ii Jj Kk Ll Mm Nn Oo Pp Qq Rr Ss **Tt** Uu Vv Ww Xx Yy Zz

track² VERB

The hunters tracked a bear.
follow, stalk, trail, hunt, pursue, chase
• **track down**
1 *I managed to track down most of the people on the list.*
find, discover, trace, dig up, unearth
2 *The police have pledged to track down these terrorists.*
find, hunt down, run to earth, catch, capture

trade¹ NOUN

1 *China's trade with the West*
commerce, business, dealing, buying and selling, exchange
2 *Trade has been brisk today.*
business, dealing, custom, transactions
3 *learning his trade as a joiner*
occupation, job, business, profession, calling, craft, skill

trade² VERB

the merchants who trade in the marketplace
deal, do business, transact, buy and sell

traditional ADJECTIVE

a traditional way of life
conventional, customary, accustomed, established, fixed, long-established, old, historic
⊨ OPPOSITES unconventional, new, modern, contemporary

traffic NOUN

1 *road traffic*
vehicles, transport
2 *the traffic in endangered animal species*
trade, commerce, business, dealing, trafficking, exchange

traffic jam NOUN

a traffic jam on the motorway
jam, bottleneck, gridlock, obstruction

tragedy NOUN

Any accidental death is a real tragedy.
misfortune, blow, calamity, disaster, catastrophe

tragic ADJECTIVE

1 *the tragic loss of a young life*
heartbreaking, dreadful, shocking, appalling, awful, calamitous, disastrous, catastrophic
2 *a tragic figure standing all alone*
sad, sorrowful, heartbreaking, miserable, unhappy, unfortunate, unlucky, pathetic
⊨ OPPOSITES happy, comic

trail¹ NOUN

1 *a trail through the forest*
path, track, footpath, road, route, way
2 *A snail had left a slimy trail on the ground.*
track, footprints, footmarks, trace

trail² VERB

1 *The child trailed a blanket behind her.*
drag, pull, tow
2 *Kelly trailed behind the rest of the group.*
lag, straggle, dawdle, loiter, linger
3 *trailing the thieves to their hideout*
follow, track, stalk, hunt, pursue, chase, shadow
◇ INFORMAL WORDS tail

train¹ VERB

1 *Lindsay has trained her dog to do tricks.*
teach, instruct, coach, tutor, educate, drill
2 *Ahmed is training for the marathon.*
prepare, exercise, work out, practise, rehearse

train² NOUN

Here are some words connected with trains:

boiler, bridge, carriage, departures board, diesel, driver, engine, fenders, first class, footplate, freight train, guard, junction, platform, refreshment trolley, restaurant car, signals, sleeper, standard class, station, steam engine, ticket, ticket inspector, timetable, tracks, tunnel, whistle

Aa
Bb
Cc
Dd
Ee
Ff
Gg
Hh
Ii
Jj
Kk
Ll
Mm
Nn
Oo
Pp
Qq
Rr
Ss
Tt
Uu
Vv
Ww
Xx
Yy
Zz

Aa
Bb
Cc
Dd
Ee
Ff
Gg
Hh
Ii
Jj
Kk
Ll
Mm
Nn
Oo
Pp
Qq
Rr
Ss
Tt
Uu
Vv
Ww
Xx
Yy
Zz

tramp¹ NOUN

*A **tramp** came to the door asking for food.*
vagrant, vagabond, down-and-out
◇ INFORMAL WORDS dosser

tramp² VERB

1 *tramping through the snow*
trudge, walk, march, tread, plod, traipse, trail
2 *tramping all over the countryside*
hike, walk, trek, ramble, roam, rove

trample VERB

*A boy was **trampled** in the stampede.*
crush, tread on, stamp on, squash, flatten

tranquil ADJECTIVE

1 *a **tranquil** scene*
peaceful, calm, restful, still, undisturbed, quiet, hushed, silent
≠ OPPOSITES noisy, disturbed
2 *I felt **tranquil** as I watched the sun set.*
calm, composed, peaceful, placid, relaxed, serene, untroubled, undisturbed
◇ INFORMAL WORDS laid-back
≠ OPPOSITES agitated, disturbed, troubled

transfer VERB

1 *He has been **transferred** to another school.*
move, change, shift, remove, relocate
2 *We were **transferred** to the airport by bus.*
transport, carry, convey

transform VERB

*We're going to **transform** the boxroom into an office.*
change, alter, adapt, convert, remodel, reconstruct
≠ OPPOSITES preserve, maintain

translate VERB

*This book has been **translated** from French.*
interpret, change, alter, convert, transform

transmit VERB

1 *The concert will be **transmitted** on Sunday evening.*
broadcast, show, televise, radio, relay, network
≠ OPPOSITES receive
2 *Malaria is **transmitted** to humans by mosquitoes.*
spread, communicate, convey, carry, bear, relay, transfer

transparent ADJECTIVE

transparent plastic
clear, see-through, sheer
≠ OPPOSITES opaque

transport VERB

*Slaves were **transported** from Africa to America.*
convey, carry, bear, take, fetch, bring, move, shift, transfer

trap¹ NOUN

*He set a **trap** to catch rabbits.*
snare, net, noose, booby-trap, pitfall

trap² VERB

*people who **trap** animals for their fur*
catch, snare, net, ensnare

trash NOUN

1 *Will you take out the **trash**, please?*
rubbish, garbage, refuse, junk, waste, litter
2 *That programme is a lot of **trash**.*
rubbish, garbage, dross

travel VERB

*They have **travelled** all round Europe.*
journey, voyage, go, move, proceed, progress, tour
≠ OPPOSITES stay, remain

Here are some ways to travel:

By aeroplane:
fly, pilot
By bicycle:
cycle, freewheel, ride

By boat:
cruise, paddle, punt, row, sail
By car:
drive, motor
On foot:
hike, hitch-hike, jog, march, ramble, run, stroll, trek, walk

traveller NOUN

weary travellers
tourist, voyager, globetrotter, tripper, holidaymaker

treacherous ADJECTIVE

1 *He was betrayed by a treacherous friend.*
disloyal, traitorous, unfaithful, untrustworthy, false, deceitful, double-crossing
(≠) OPPOSITES loyal, faithful, dependable
2 *treacherous roads*
dangerous, hazardous, risky, precarious, icy, slippery
(≠) OPPOSITES safe

tread VERB

1 *We trod carefully through the woods.*
step, walk, tramp
2 *You're treading on my toes.*
step, stamp, trample, press, crush, squash

treasure[1] NOUN

They discovered some hidden treasure.
riches, fortune, wealth, money, cash, gold, jewels

treasure[2] VERB

I treasured the memories of our time together.
cherish, value, prize, hold dear, love
(≠) OPPOSITES belittle

treat VERB

1 *They have always treated us with kindness.*
behave towards, deal with, manage, handle
2 *She still treats me like a child.*
regard, consider

3 *She is being treated for shingles.*
attend to, nurse, tend, care for
4 *an old remedy for treating rheumatism*
heal, cure

treatment NOUN

1 *taken into hospital for treatment*
care, nursing, therapy, surgery, healing
2 *a new treatment for asthma*
cure, remedy, medication
3 *I couldn't complain about his treatment of me.*
behaviour, handling, management, usage, conduct

treaty NOUN

an arms treaty
agreement, pact, convention, contract, bond, alliance

tree NOUN

Here are some types of tree:

alder, apple, ash, bay, beech, birch, blackthorn, cedar, cherry, chestnut, cypress, ebony, elder, elm, eucalyptus, fig, fir, gum, hawthorn, hazel, holly, horse chestnut, larch, laurel, lime, linden, magnolia, mahogany, maple, monkey puzzle, mulberry, oak, olive, palm, pear, pine, poplar, redwood, rowan, spruce, sycamore, walnut, willow, witch hazel, yew

tremble VERB

1 *He was trembling with excitement.*
shake, quake, shiver, shudder, quiver
2 *The ground beneath our feet began to tremble.*
shake, vibrate, quake, wobble, rock

tremendous ADJECTIVE

1 *It's a tremendous film.*
wonderful, marvellous, sensational, extraordinary, amazing, incredible, terrific
(≠) OPPOSITES ordinary
2 *a tremendous amount of work*

Aa
Bb
Cc
Dd
Ee
Ff
Gg
Hh
Ii
Jj
Kk
Ll
Mm
Nn
Oo
Pp
Qq
Rr
Ss
Tt
Uu
Vv
Ww
Xx
Yy
Zz

huge, immense, vast, colossal, gigantic

trend NOUN

1 *the growing **trend** towards organic food*
tendency, inclination, leaning, swing
2 *the latest **trends** in footwear*
fashion, craze, vogue, mode, style, look
◇ INFORMAL WORDS rage

trial NOUN

*conducting **trials** of the new software*
test, experiment, examination, check, dry run, dummy run

tribe NOUN

*a Native American **tribe***
race, nation, people, clan, family, house, dynasty, branch

tribute NOUN

*They paid **tribute** to all the people who had helped them.*
praise, compliment, homage, respect, honour, acknowledgement, gratitude

trick¹ NOUN

1 *Stephen played a **trick** on his sister.*
joke, hoax, practical joke, prank, stunt
◇ INFORMAL WORDS leg-pull
2 *a **trick** to get hold of the old woman's money*
deception, fraud, swindle, deceit, hoax, dodge
3 *He entertained the children with magic **tricks**.*
illusion, artifice, feat, stunt

trick² VERB

*They **tricked** us into giving them money.*
deceive, dupe, fool, hoodwink, mislead, cheat, swindle
◇ INFORMAL WORDS pull someone's leg, con, diddle

trickle VERB

*The water **trickled** from the tap.*
dribble, run, leak, seep, ooze, drip, drop
◆ FORMAL WORDS exude
⊘ OPPOSITES stream, gush

tricky ADJECTIVE

*a **tricky** problem*
difficult, awkward, problematic, complicated, knotty, thorny, delicate
⊘ OPPOSITES easy, simple

trim¹ ADJECTIVE

1 *The garden is looking nice and **trim**.*
neat, tidy, orderly, shipshape, spick-and-span
⊘ OPPOSITES scruffy
2 *He looked very **trim** in his suit and tie.*
neat, tidy, spick-and-span, spruce, smart, dapper
⊘ OPPOSITES untidy, scruffy

trim² VERB

*He was **trimming** the hedge.*
cut, clip, crop, dock, prune, pare, neaten, tidy

trip¹ VERB

*I **tripped** over a shoe left on the stair.*
stumble, slip, fall, tumble, stagger

trip² NOUN

1 *a **trip** to the seaside*
outing, excursion, jaunt, ride, drive, spin
2 *a **trip** to the Continent*
journey, voyage, tour

triumph NOUN

*fresh from her **triumph** at the Olympics*
success, win, victory, achievement, accomplishment, feat
⊘ OPPOSITES failure

trivial ADJECTIVE

*a **trivial** matter*
unimportant, insignificant, minor, petty, small, little, meaningless
⊘ OPPOSITES important, significant, profound

troop¹ NOUN

*a **troop** of cavalry*
unit, squadron, division, company, squad

troop² VERB

*We all **trooped** along to the assembly hall.*

Aa
Bb
Cc
Dd
Ee
Ff
Gg
Hh
Ii
Jj
Kk
Ll
Mm
Nn
Oo
Pp
Qq
Rr
Ss
Tt
Uu
Vv
Ww
Xx
Yy
Zz

go, march, parade, flock, crowd

troops NOUN
the troops fighting overseas
soldiers, army, military, servicemen, servicewomen

trophy NOUN
He keeps his fishing trophies in a cabinet.
prize, cup, award

trouble¹ NOUN
1 *I had trouble booking a flight.*
difficulty, bother, inconvenience
2 *He told me his troubles.*
problem, difficulty, misfortune, pain, heartache, concern, worry, anxiety
3 *There was trouble in the streets.*
disorder, unrest, commotion, disturbance, tumult
≠ OPPOSITES order

trouble² VERB
It troubles me that I can do nothing to help him.
bother, disturb, upset, distress, sadden, pain, worry
≠ OPPOSITES reassure, help

troublesome ADJECTIVE
1 *He knew how to deal with troublesome pupils.*
annoying, irritating, bothersome, difficult, demanding, tiresome
2 *a troublesome problem*
difficult, hard, tricky, thorny, demanding
≠ OPPOSITES easy, simple

truce NOUN
The two sides called a truce.
ceasefire, peace
◇ INFORMAL WORDS let-up
≠ OPPOSITES war, hostilities

trudge VERB
trudging up the hill
plod, tramp, clump, stump, traipse, slog, trek, march

true ADJECTIVE
1 *All of this information is true.*
correct, exact, precise, accurate, right, factual, truthful, valid
≠ OPPOSITES false, wrong, incorrect, inaccurate
2 *He always hid his true feelings.*
real, genuine, actual, authentic
3 *a true friend*
loyal, faithful, constant, firm, trustworthy, trusty, devoted
≠ OPPOSITES unfaithful, disloyal

trunk NOUN
1 *a trunk full of old clothes*
chest, case, suitcase, box, crate
2 *the trunk of a tree*
shaft, stem, stock, stalk

trust¹ NOUN
You have betrayed my trust.
faith, belief, expectation, reliance, confidence, assurance, conviction, certainty
≠ OPPOSITES distrust, mistrust, doubt

trust² VERB
1 *You can trust me to keep a secret.*
rely on, depend on, count on, bank on, expect
≠ OPPOSITES distrust, mistrust
2 *I trust what he says.*
believe, rely on, depend on, count on, bank on, swear by
≠ OPPOSITES distrust, mistrust, doubt, disbelieve

trustworthy ADJECTIVE
1 *I need someone trustworthy to look after my cat.*
dependable, reliable, responsible, sensible
≠ OPPOSITES untrustworthy, unreliable, irresponsible
2 *We need someone trustworthy to act as our club treasurer.*
honest, honourable, principled
≠ OPPOSITES untrustworthy, dishonest

truth NOUN
I am determined to find out the truth.
facts, reality
◆ FORMAL WORDS actuality
≠ OPPOSITES lie, falsehood

Aa
Bb
Cc
Dd
Ee
Ff
Gg
Hh
Ii
Jj
Kk
Ll
Mm
Nn
Oo
Pp
Qq
Rr
Ss
Tt
Uu
Vv
Ww
Xx
Yy
Zz

truthful ADJECTIVE

1 *a truthful answer*
honest, frank, candid, straight, sincere, true
≢ OPPOSITES untruthful, deceitful, false, untrue
2 *a truthful account of the incident*
true, exact, precise, accurate, correct, realistic, faithful
≢ OPPOSITES untruthful, false, untrue
3 *He's always been a truthful child.*
honest, trustworthy, reliable
≢ OPPOSITES untruthful, deceitful

try¹ VERB

1 *Try to get here on time.*
attempt, endeavour, undertake, seek, strive
2 *Would you like to try one of my scones?*
sample, test, taste
3 *I'd love to try windsurfing.*
attempt
◇ INFORMAL WORDS have a go at, have a shot at

try² NOUN

If you fail first time, have another try.
attempt, endeavour, effort
◇ INFORMAL WORDS go, bash, crack, shot, stab

trying ADJECTIVE

1 *He's a very trying person to live with.*
annoying, irritating, exasperating, troublesome, tiresome
≢ OPPOSITES easy
2 *She's been through a very trying time.*
difficult, hard, tough, demanding, testing
≢ OPPOSITES easy

tuck VERB

She tucked her handkerchief into her pocket.
push, insert, thrust, stuff, cram

tug VERB

1 *Ben tugged Meena's pigtail.*
pull, wrench, jerk, pluck

2 *She tugged the child along by his hand.*
pull, draw, tow, haul, drag, lug, heave

tumble VERB

The old lady tumbled down the stairs.
fall, topple, plummet, pitch

tune NOUN

a catchy tune
melody, theme, song

tunnel NOUN

a secret tunnel under the building
passage, passageway, subway, underpass, burrow, shaft

turmoil NOUN

There was turmoil in the streets after the election.
disorder, confusion, commotion, disturbance, trouble, chaos, uproar
≢ OPPOSITES calm, peace, quiet

turn¹ VERB

1 *The wheel was turning round and round.*
revolve, circle, spin, twirl, whirl, rotate, roll
2 *The telescope turns on its axis.*
revolve, twist, pivot, swivel, rotate, roll, move, shift
3 *The caterpillar turned into a butterfly.*
change, transform
4 *We are going to turn this room into a nursery.*
change, transform, alter, modify, convert, adapt, adjust
5 *It's turned cold now.*
go, become, grow
• turn down
I turned down the chance to go to Rome.
decline, reject, refuse
≢ OPPOSITES accept
• turn out
1 *Things didn't turn out the way I had hoped.*
happen, come about, result, end up, develop
2 *Turn out the lights before you go to bed.*

Aa
Bb
Cc
Dd
Ee
Ff
Gg
Hh
Ii
Jj
Kk
Ll
Mm
Nn
Oo
Pp
Qq
Rr
Ss
Tt
Uu
Vv
Ww
Xx
Yy
Zz

switch off, turn off, unplug, disconnect
⊘ OPPOSITES turn on
- **turn up**

*Lots of people **turned up** at the party.*
arrive, show up, appear, attend

turn² NOUN

1 *Give the wheel a couple of **turns**.*
rotation, revolution, cycle, spin, twirl,
twist
2 *a **turn** in the road*
bend, twist, curve, loop
3 *It's your **turn** to use the computer.*
go, chance, opportunity, occasion, stint,
period, spell
4 *The patient has taken a **turn** for the
worse.*
change, alteration, shift

twinge NOUN

*I felt a **twinge** in my shoulder.*
pain, pang, throb, stab, stitch, prick

twinkle VERB

*His eyes **twinkled**.*
sparkle, glitter, shimmer, glisten,
glimmer, glint, shine

twirl VERB

*We **twirled** round and round on the
dance floor.*
spin, whirl, wheel, rotate, revolve, turn,
twist

twist VERB

1 *She **twisted** her hair round her fingers.*
wind, turn, coil, curl, twine
2 *The fibres are **twisted** together to
form string.*
wind, twine, entwine, weave, entangle
3 *I **twisted** round to see what was
happening behind me.*
turn, spin, swivel, pivot
4 *He **twisted** his ankle.*
sprain, wrench, rick, strain
5 *You're **twisting** my words.*
change, alter, misquote, misrepresent

twitch VERB

*A muscle in my left eye began to **twitch**.*
jerk, jump, blink, tremble, shake

type NOUN

*a **type** of pasta*
sort, kind, form, variety, class,
category

typical ADJECTIVE

1 *He's just a **typical** teenager.*
standard, normal, usual, average,
conventional
⊘ OPPOSITES unusual
2 *a **typical** example*
standard, representative, characteristic,
model, stock
⊘ OPPOSITES unusual

tyrant NOUN

*The country was ruled by a **tyrant**.*
dictator, authoritarian, bully,
oppressor

Aa
Bb
Cc
Dd
Ee
Ff
Gg
Hh
Ii
Jj
Kk
Ll
Mm
Nn
Oo
Pp
Qq
Rr
Ss
Tt
Uu
Vv
Ww
Xx
Yy
Zz

Uu

ugly ADJECTIVE

1 *an **ugly** face*
unattractive, unsightly, plain, hideous
(≠) OPPOSITES attractive, beautiful, handsome, pretty
2 *She made an **ugly** scene in public.*
unpleasant, disagreeable, nasty, horrid, offensive, disgusting, revolting, frightful, terrible
(≠) OPPOSITES pleasant

ultimate ADJECTIVE

1 *the **ultimate** round in the competition*
final, last, closing, concluding, eventual
2 *the **ultimate** end of the universe*
furthest, extreme
3 *the **ultimate** adventure*
greatest, supreme, utmost, highest, perfect
4 *our **ultimate** aim*
fundamental, radical, primary, basic

unable ADJECTIVE

1 *She was **unable** to hide her anger.*
incapable, powerless
(≠) OPPOSITES able, capable
2 *He is **unable** to cope with this job.*
incapable, unfit, unequipped, unqualified, incompetent, inadequate
(≠) OPPOSITES able, capable

unbeatable ADJECTIVE

1 ***unbeatable** value*
excellent, matchless, supreme
2 *an **unbeatable** team*
unstoppable, excellent, invincible

unbelievable ADJECTIVE

*The concert was just **unbelievable**.*
incredible, astonishing, staggering, extraordinary

uncertain ADJECTIVE

1 *We were **uncertain** whether to believe him.*
unsure, unconvinced, doubtful, dubious, undecided, hesitant, wavering
(≠) OPPOSITES certain, sure
2 *The weather is **uncertain**.*
changeable, variable, inconstant, erratic

uncomfortable ADJECTIVE

1 *an **uncomfortable** bed*
irritating, disagreeable, painful, awkward, hard, cramped
(≠) OPPOSITES comfortable
2 *I feel **uncomfortable** asking him for money.*
awkward, embarrassed, self-conscious, uneasy, troubled, worried
(≠) OPPOSITES relaxed

unconscious ADJECTIVE

1 *Chloe was **unconscious** for several minutes.*
knocked out, stunned, out, senseless
◇ INFORMAL WORDS out cold, out for the count
(≠) OPPOSITES conscious
2 ***unconscious** of his surroundings*
unaware, oblivious, blind, deaf, ignorant
(≠) OPPOSITES aware
3 *the **unconscious** cruelty of her actions*
unintentional, unwitting, inadvertent, accidental
(≠) OPPOSITES deliberate
4 *an **unconscious** reaction*
involuntary, automatic, reflex, instinctive, subconscious
(≠) OPPOSITES conscious

uncover VERB

1 *a detective who is determined to **uncover** the facts*
discover, detect, unearth, expose, reveal
(≠) OPPOSITES conceal, suppress
2 *Do not **uncover** your head in the hot sun.*

expose, strip, bare, unwrap, open, reveal, show
≠ OPPOSITES cover, conceal

undergo VERB
*She **underwent** major surgery.*
experience, go through, suffer, bear, stand, endure, withstand

underhand ADJECTIVE
__underhand__ ways to hurt people
sly, crafty, sneaky, furtive, devious, dishonest, deceitful, fraudulent, crooked
◇ INFORMAL WORDS shady
≠ OPPOSITES honest, open, above board

understand VERB
1 *I **understand** what you're saying.*
see, grasp, take in, follow, perceive, realize, recognize, appreciate
◆ FORMAL WORDS comprehend
◇ INFORMAL WORDS get, cotton on
≠ OPPOSITES misunderstand
2 *I **understand** that everyone is invited.*
believe, think, hear, learn, gather, assume, presume, suppose

understanding NOUN
1 *He shows little **understanding** of mathematics.*
knowledge, grasp, sense, judgement, insight, appreciation, awareness, perception
◆ FORMAL WORDS comprehension
2 *We have come to an **understanding** about paying back the loan.*
agreement, arrangement
3 *They treated me with **understanding**.*
sympathy, empathy, patience

undo VERB
1 *He **undid** the top two buttons of his shirt.*
open, untie, unbuckle, unbutton, unzip, unlock, unwrap
≠ OPPOSITES fasten, do up
2 *His hopes of victory were **undone** by an accident in the first round.*
ruin, destroy, wreck, overturn, upset

uneasy ADJECTIVE
1 *I feel **uneasy** about letting you go on your own.*
anxious, uncomfortable, worried, nervous, agitated, edgy, troubled, unsure
◇ INFORMAL WORDS jittery
≠ OPPOSITES calm, composed
2 *There was an **uneasy** peace after the fighting.*
strained, tense, shaky, unsettled, insecure

unemployed ADJECTIVE
*Dave has been **unemployed** since the factory closed down.*
out of work, jobless, laid off, redundant
◇ INFORMAL WORDS on the dole
≠ OPPOSITES employed, in work

uneven ADJECTIVE
1 *__uneven__ ground*
rough, bumpy
≠ OPPOSITES flat, level
2 *an **uneven** number*
odd, unequal
≠ OPPOSITES even
3 *__uneven__ teeth*
crooked, lopsided, squint
≠ OPPOSITES even

unexpected ADJECTIVE
*His visit was **unexpected**.*
unforeseen, surprising, startling, amazing, astonishing, unanticipated, unpredictable
≠ OPPOSITES expected, predictable

unfair ADJECTIVE
1 *__unfair__ treatment of the poor*
biased, unjust, prejudiced, bigoted, discriminatory, unbalanced, one-sided
≠ OPPOSITES fair, just, unbiased
2 *He sued the company for **unfair** dismissal.*
unjust, undeserved, unmerited, unwarranted, uncalled-for
≠ OPPOSITES fair, just, deserved
3 *charged with **unfair** business practices*
dishonest, unethical, unscrupulous, unprincipled, wrongful
≠ OPPOSITES fair

Aa Bb Cc Dd Ee Ff Gg Hh Ii Jj Kk Ll Mm Nn Oo Pp Qq Rr Ss Tt **Uu** Vv Ww Xx Yy Zz

unfamiliar ADJECTIVE

1 an *unfamiliar* land
foreign, strange, alien, unexplored, unknown
≠ OPPOSITES familiar
2 He brought many *unfamiliar* plants back from his travels.
strange, unusual, uncommon, curious, unknown, different, new, novel
≠ OPPOSITES familiar, customary
3 I am *unfamiliar* with this kind of computer.
unaccustomed, unacquainted, inexperienced, unpractised
≠ OPPOSITES familiar

unfortunate ADJECTIVE

1 the *unfortunate* family whose house burned down
unlucky, luckless, poor, wretched, unhappy, doomed, ill-fated
≠ OPPOSITES fortunate, happy
2 an *unfortunate* mistake
disastrous, adverse, unfavourable, calamitous
3 He made an *unfortunate* remark.
regrettable, unsuitable, inappropriate, inopportune, untimely
≠ OPPOSITES fitting, appropriate

unfriendly ADJECTIVE

The locals were very *unfriendly* towards me.
hostile, distant, standoffish, unapproachable, inhospitable, unneighbourly, unwelcoming, cold, chilly
≠ OPPOSITES friendly, amiable

unhappy ADJECTIVE

I could tell by her face that she was *unhappy*.
sad, sorrowful, miserable, melancholy, depressed, despondent, dejected, downcast, gloomy
≠ OPPOSITES happy

unhealthy ADJECTIVE

1 She was still *unhealthy* for weeks after she had measles.
unwell, sick, ill, poorly, sickly, weak, feeble, frail

≠ OPPOSITES healthy, fit
2 *unhealthy* food
unwholesome, unhygienic, harmful, unnatural
≠ OPPOSITES wholesome, hygienic, natural

unidentified ADJECTIVE

an *unidentified* caller
unknown, unrecognized, unnamed, nameless, anonymous, incognito, mysterious
≠ OPPOSITES identified, known, named

unimportant ADJECTIVE

unimportant details
insignificant, irrelevant, minor, trivial, trifling, petty, slight, small, worthless
≠ OPPOSITES important, significant, relevant, vital

uninteresting ADJECTIVE

an *uninteresting* day at school
boring, tedious, monotonous, humdrum, dull, dreary, uneventful, unexciting
≠ OPPOSITES interesting, exciting

unique ADJECTIVE

a *unique* feature of this species of animal
single, one-off, sole, only, lone, solitary
≠ OPPOSITES common

unkind ADJECTIVE

It was *unkind* of you to point out her mistake.
cruel, callous, hard-hearted, uncharitable, nasty, malicious, spiteful, mean
≠ OPPOSITES kind

unlikely ADJECTIVE

an *unlikely* story
improbable, far-fetched, unconvincing, unbelievable, incredible, doubtful, dubious, questionable, implausible
≠ OPPOSITES likely

unlucky ADJECTIVE

1 the *unlucky* people who lost all their money when the company failed

Aa
Bb
Cc
Dd
Ee
Ff
Gg
Hh
Ii
Jj
Kk
Ll
Mm
Nn
Oo
Pp
Qq
Rr
Ss
Tt
Uu
Vv
Ww
Xx
Yy
Zz

unfortunate, luckless, unhappy, miserable, wretched, unsuccessful
≠ OPPOSITES lucky
2 *Many people believe that Friday the 13th is an* **unlucky** *date.*
ill-fated, jinxed, doomed, cursed, unfavourable, disastrous
≠ OPPOSITES lucky

unnecessary ADJECTIVE
It was **unnecessary** *to be so rude.*
needless, unneeded, uncalled-for, unwanted, non-essential
≠ OPPOSITES necessary, essential

unpleasant ADJECTIVE
1 *He was very* **unpleasant** *to me today.*
nasty, disagreeable, offensive
≠ OPPOSITES pleasant, agreeable, nice
2 *an* **unpleasant** *smell*
disagreeable, nasty, offensive, repulsive, bad
≠ OPPOSITES pleasant, agreeable, nice

unpopular ADJECTIVE
the most **unpopular** *girl in the class*
disliked, hated, detested, unloved, unwanted, rejected, shunned
≠ OPPOSITES popular

unusual ADJECTIVE
1 *Did you notice anything* **unusual** *about him?*
odd, uncommon, rare, unfamiliar, strange, curious, queer, unconventional, different
≠ OPPOSITES usual, ordinary
2 *an* **unusual** *talent for singing*
extraordinary, remarkable, exceptional, uncommon, rare
≠ OPPOSITES usual, ordinary

unwanted ADJECTIVE
unwanted *attention*
undesired, uninvited, unwelcome, rejected, unrequired, unneeded, unnecessary
≠ OPPOSITES wanted, needed, necessary

unwilling ADJECTIVE
1 *I was* **unwilling** *to give up hope just yet.*
reluctant, resistant, opposed, averse, loath
◆ FORMAL WORDS indisposed
≠ OPPOSITES willing
2 *an* **unwilling** *accomplice in the crime*
reluctant, resistant, unenthusiastic, grudging
≠ OPPOSITES willing, enthusiastic

update VERB
I will give you my new address to **update** *your address book.*
bring up to date, revise, amend, correct, renew, modernize

upheaval NOUN
Moving house caused a great deal of **upheaval.**
disruption, disturbance, upset, chaos, confusion, disorder, turmoil

uphill ADJECTIVE
It's an **uphill** *struggle to pay our bills.*
hard, difficult, tough, taxing, strenuous, gruelling, punishing
≠ OPPOSITES easy

upkeep NOUN
We could not afford the **upkeep** *of such a big house.*
running, maintenance, preservation, conservation, care, support, keep
≠ OPPOSITES neglect

upper ADJECTIVE
1 *the* **upper** *flat in the building*
top, higher, high, topmost, uppermost
≠ OPPOSITES lower
2 *the* **upper** *ranks of the army*
higher, superior, senior, top, uppermost
≠ OPPOSITES lower, inferior

upright ADJECTIVE
1 *an* **upright** *position*
vertical, erect, straight
≠ OPPOSITES horizontal, flat
2 *an* **upright** *citizen*
honest, good, virtuous, righteous,

Aa
Bb
Cc
Dd
Ee
Ff
Gg
Hh
Ii
Jj
Kk
Ll
Mm
Nn
Oo
Pp
Qq
Rr
Ss
Tt
Uu
Vv
Ww
Xx
Yy
Zz

upstanding, noble, honourable, principled
≠ OPPOSITES dishonest

uproar NOUN
*There was an **uproar** in the school hall.*
commotion, noise, din, racket, tumult, turmoil, confusion, disorder

upset VERB
1 *The boy's behaviour has **upset** his parents.*
distress, grieve, dismay, trouble, worry, disturb, bother, shake, disconcert
2 *This will **upset** all my plans.*
spoil, mess up, disturb, confuse, disorganize
3 *The child **upset** the milk jug.*
overturn, tip, spill, capsize, topple

upside down ADJECTIVE
*There was an **upside down** flag on the wall.*
upturned, inverted, wrong way up, upset, overturned

up-to-date ADJECTIVE
*an **up-to-date** computer*
modern, fashionable, latest, recent, new, current, contemporary
◇ INFORMAL WORDS trendy
≠ OPPOSITES out-of-date, old-fashioned

urge¹ NOUN
*I had a sudden **urge** to laugh out loud.*
desire, wish, inclination, longing, impulse, compulsion
≠ OPPOSITES disinclination

urge² VERB
1 *I **urged** him to go back to school.*
encourage, advise, recommend
≠ OPPOSITES discourage
2 *He **urged** his horse on through the storm.*
drive, push, goad, spur, press, compel, force
≠ OPPOSITES deter, hinder

urgent ADJECTIVE
*an **urgent** need for medical equipment*
immediate, important, top-priority,

critical, crucial, pressing, compelling
≠ OPPOSITES unimportant

use¹ VERB
1 *Use your imagination.*
employ, exercise, utilize, practise
2 *I don't know how to **use** a microwave.*
operate, work, apply, handle

use² NOUN
1 *I have no **use** for a lawnmower since I have no garden.*
need, cause, necessity, call
2 *the increasing **use** of computer graphics in films*
usage, application
3 *What is the **use** of a car if you can't afford petrol?*
point, object, end, purpose

useful ADJECTIVE
1 *useful advice*
helpful, practical, effective, profitable, valuable, worthwhile, advantageous, beneficial
≠ OPPOSITES useless, ineffective, worthless
2 *a useful tool*
handy, convenient, all-purpose, practical, effective
≠ OPPOSITES useless, worthless

useless ADJECTIVE
1 *a useless gadget*
worthless, unusable, ineffective, impractical
◇ INFORMAL WORDS no good
≠ OPPOSITES useful, helpful, effective
2 *It's **useless** to try to help.*
pointless, futile, hopeless, worthless
≠ OPPOSITES useful, helpful

usual ADJECTIVE
1 *It looks very different from a **usual** mobile phone.*
normal, ordinary, typical, conventional, accepted, recognized, standard, familiar, common
≠ OPPOSITES unusual, strange, rare
2 *a change from his **usual** routine*
regular, routine, habitual, customary,

Aa
Bb
Cc
Dd
Ee
Ff
Gg
Hh
Ii
Jj
Kk
Ll
Mm
Nn
Oo
Pp
Qq
Rr
Ss
Tt
Uu
Vv
Ww
Xx
Yy
Zz

accustomed, everyday, general, ordinary
≠ OPPOSITES unusual

usually ADVERB

I usually walk to school.
normally, generally, as a rule, ordinarily, by and large, on the whole, mainly, chiefly, mostly
≠ OPPOSITES exceptionally

utensil NOUN

ladles and other kitchen utensils
tool, implement, instrument, device, gadget, apparatus, appliance

utter[1] ADJECTIVE

There was a look of utter fury on his face.
absolute, complete, total, out-and-out, downright, sheer, perfect

utter[2] VERB

She didn't utter another word.
say, speak, voice, express, pronounce, deliver

utterly ADVERB

I was utterly disgusted by his behaviour.
absolutely, completely, totally, wholly, thoroughly, downright, perfectly

Aa
Bb
Cc
Dd
Ee
Ff
Gg
Hh
Ii
Jj
Kk
Ll
Mm
Nn
Oo
Pp
Qq
Rr
Ss
Tt
Uu
Vv
Ww
Xx
Yy
Zz

Vv

vacant ADJECTIVE

1 *Is this seat **vacant**?*
unoccupied, empty, unfilled, free, available, not in use
≠ OPPOSITES occupied, engaged
2 *She had a **vacant** expression on her face.*
blank, expressionless, vague, absent-minded, unthinking, dreamy
≠ OPPOSITES animated, lively

vague ADJECTIVE

1 *a **vague** outline of a person*
indistinct, ill-defined, blurred, hazy, dim, shadowy, fuzzy
≠ OPPOSITES clear
2 *a **vague** description*
unclear, indefinite, imprecise, unspecific, inexact, hazy, uncertain
≠ OPPOSITES specific, definite
3 *a **vague** feeling of worry*
indefinite, undefined, undetermined, unspecific, generalized
≠ OPPOSITES specific, definite

vain ADJECTIVE

1 *I made a **vain** attempt to persuade Tom to join us.*
useless, futile, pointless, unproductive, unprofitable
≠ OPPOSITES fruitful, successful
2 *He won the argument, but it was a **vain** victory.*
hollow, empty, trivial, unimportant
3 *He is very **vain** about his achievements.*
conceited, proud, self-satisfied, arrogant, self-important, swaggering
◇ INFORMAL WORDS bigheaded, stuck-up
≠ OPPOSITES modest

valid ADJECTIVE

*a **valid** passport*
legal, official, lawful, legitimate,
authentic, genuine, binding
≠ OPPOSITES unofficial, invalid

valuable ADJECTIVE

1 *This necklace is very **valuable**.*
precious, costly, expensive, dear, high-priced
≠ OPPOSITES worthless
2 *the most **valuable** friend I have*
valued, precious, prized, treasured
≠ OPPOSITES worthless
3 *The advice you gave me was very **valuable**.*
helpful, worthwhile, useful, beneficial, invaluable, constructive, profitable
≠ OPPOSITES useless

value[1] NOUN

1 *What is the **value** of the painting?*
cost, price, rate, worth
2 *Do these alternative therapies have any **value**?*
worth, use, usefulness, merit, benefit, advantage, good
3 *I place a great deal of **value** on honesty.*
worth, importance, significance

value[2] VERB

1 *I **value** his opinion highly.*
prize, appreciate, treasure, hold dear, respect, cherish
◆ FORMAL WORDS esteem
≠ OPPOSITES scorn
2 *We are having the house **valued**.*
evaluate, assess, estimate, price, rate, appraise

vanish VERB

1 *The ghost **vanished** before our eyes.*
disappear, fade, dissolve, depart, exit
≠ OPPOSITES appear, materialize
2 *This species is **vanishing** from the planet.*
disappear, die out, cease to exist

vanity NOUN

She refused to wear her glasses out of vanity.
conceit, conceitedness, pride, arrogance, self-love
◇ INFORMAL WORDS bigheadedness
⧧ OPPOSITES modesty

variable ADJECTIVE

The standard of his school work is variable.
changeable, varying, shifting, unpredictable, unstable, unsteady
⧧ OPPOSITES fixed, stable

variety NOUN

1 *The shop sells a variety of sweets.*
range, assortment, mixture, collection, medley
2 *There is a great deal of variety in the band's music.*
variation, difference, dissimilarity, diversity
3 *a new variety of rose*
type, kind, sort, class, category, species, breed

various ADJECTIVE

1 *Various people have admired my new trainers.*
several, many, numerous
2 *He enjoys various hobbies.*
different, diverse, varied, varying, assorted, miscellaneous

vary VERB

1 *Our opinions about books we like vary.*
differ, diverge, disagree
2 *I like to vary my packed lunches.*
diversify, reorder, alternate
3 *You can vary the pitch by turning this knob.*
change, alter, modify, transform

vast ADJECTIVE

1 *a vast building*
huge, immense, massive, gigantic, enormous, colossal, tremendous, monstrous
2 *plans to explore the vast reaches of outer space*
unlimited, immeasurable, never-ending

vault¹ VERB

He tried to vault over the gate.
jump, leap, spring, bound, leap-frog

vault² NOUN

The gold was kept in a sealed vault.
cellar, crypt, strongroom, cavern

veer VERB

When you come to a fork in the road, veer left.
turn, swerve, swing, change direction, shift, wheel

vegetable NOUN

Here are some types of vegetable:

Green vegetables:
asparagus, broccoli, Brussels sprout, cabbage, celery, chard, chicory, cress, kale, lettuce, rocket, spinach, watercress
Root vegetables:
beetroot, carrot, cassava, celeriac, garlic, leek, onion, parsnip, potato, radish, spring onion, swede, sweet potato, turnip, yam
Fruits and flowers used as vegetables:
artichoke, aubergine, cauliflower, courgette, cucumber, mangetout, marrow, okra, pepper, pumpkin, squash, tomato
Beans and seeds:
broad bean, butter bean, chickpea, French bean, green bean, kidney bean, lentil, mangetout, pea, runner bean, sweetcorn

vehicle NOUN

Here are some types of vehicle:

Motor vehicles:
bus, car, coach, lorry, minibus, taxi, truck, van

Aa Bb Cc Dd Ee Ff Gg Hh Ii Jj Kk Ll Mm Nn Oo Pp Qq Rr Ss Tt Uu **Vv** Ww Xx Yy Zz

Cycles:
bicycle, moped, motorcycle, penny-farthing, scooter, tandem, tricycle
Rail vehicles:
monorail, train, tram, tube, underground train
Snow vehicles:
bobsleigh, ski-doo, sled, sledge, sleigh, snowmobile, toboggan
Water vehicles:
boat, hovercraft, jet-ski, ship
Aircraft:
aeroplane, airship, helicopter, hot-air balloon
Horse-drawn vehicles:
cart, gig, trap, wagon
Working vehicles:
ambulance, bulldozer, combine harvester, digger, fire engine, fork-lift, snowplough, steamroller, tanker, tractor
Holiday vehicles:
camper, caravan

vein NOUN
He rambled in the same vein for half an hour.
style, manner, way, mode, tendency, strain, tone

vengeance NOUN
He swore vengeance on his enemies.
revenge, retaliation, retribution
◇ INFORMAL WORDS **tit for tat**
⊯ OPPOSITES **forgiveness**

verdict NOUN
The jury gave a verdict of 'not guilty'.
judgement, decision, conclusion, finding, assessment, opinion

verge NOUN
1 *a car parked on the grass verge*
border, edge, margin, limit, rim, boundary, threshold
2 *She was on the verge of tears.*
brink, edge, point, threshold

versatile ADJECTIVE
1 *a very versatile actor*

adaptable, flexible, all-round, many-sided, resourceful
⊯ OPPOSITES **inflexible**
2 *a very versatile tool*
adaptable, multipurpose, adjustable, general-purpose
⊯ OPPOSITES **inflexible**

version NOUN
a modern version of a Greek play
adaptation, portrayal, reading, interpretation, translation, rendering

vertical ADJECTIVE
vertical stripes
upright, perpendicular, upstanding, erect, on end
⊯ OPPOSITES **horizontal**

very¹ ADVERB
⇒ For even more about this word, see the next page
a very loud noise
extremely, greatly, highly, truly, remarkably, particularly, really, absolutely
⊯ OPPOSITES **slightly, scarcely**

very² ADJECTIVE
1 *standing on the very spot where the photograph was taken*
actual, real, same, selfsame, identical, exact
2 *I am annoyed by the very mention of his name.*
mere, simple, sheer, plain

veto VERB
The head teacher vetoed our plans for a school trip.
forbid, reject, turn down, disallow, ban, prohibit, block
⊯ OPPOSITES **approve**

vibrate VERB
1 *The washing machine made the floor vibrate.*
shake, quiver, shudder, shiver, tremble
2 *The music vibrated through the walls.*
pulsate, reverberate, throb

very

There are many words you can use instead of **very**:

extremely
incredibly
remarkably
highly
unbelievably
particularly
exceptionally
exceedingly
absolutely
noticeably
unusually

Try using these words when you want to say that someone is very good at something:

- Ronaldo is an **unbelievably** talented footballer.

- Picasso was an **exceptionally** skilled painter.

- Mozart was an **extremely** able musician from the age of six.

- Queen Elizabeth I was an **exceedingly** clever queen.

Over to you

This story is boring because the person telling it keeps using the word **very**. Use the list of words above to make it more interesting.

I was **very** annoyed that my mum had given my brother a **very** large sum of money. Then I was **very** angry when, after he had spent it all, he stole my purse. I was **very** shocked to see my brother stealing. He is a **very** wicked boy!

Aa
Bb
Cc
Dd
Ee
Ff
Gg
Hh
Ii
Jj
Kk
Ll
Mm
Nn
Oo
Pp
Qq
Rr
Ss
Tt
Uu
Vv
Ww
Xx
Yy
Zz

vicious ADJECTIVE
1 a *vicious* criminal
wicked, immoral, depraved, unprincipled, corrupt
≠ OPPOSITES virtuous
2 a *vicious* dog
savage, wild, dangerous

3 a *vicious* attack
savage, violent, barbarous, brutal

victim NOUN
a *murder* **victim**
sufferer, casualty
≠ OPPOSITES offender, attacker

victimize VERB

He felt he was being victimized by the bullies.
pick on, persecute, discriminate against, prey on, bully

victorious ADJECTIVE

the victorious boxer
winning, champion, triumphant, conquering, unbeaten, successful, prize-winning
(≠) OPPOSITES defeated, unsuccessful

victory NOUN

the school team's victory in the tournament
win, conquest, triumph, success, superiority, mastery
(≠) OPPOSITES defeat, loss

view¹ NOUN

1 *She holds strong political views.*
opinion, attitude, belief, feeling, sentiment, notion
2 *Our hotel room had a view of the sea.*
scene, sight, outlook, prospect
3 *He disappeared from view.*
sight, vision, visibility

view² VERB

1 *Krishnan's suggestion was viewed favourably.*
regard, consider, contemplate, judge, think about
2 *Curious people came to view the scene.*
look at, observe, watch, see, examine, inspect, scan, survey

viewer NOUN

viewers of the television show
watcher, spectator, observer, onlooker

vigilant ADJECTIVE

Be vigilant for pickpockets.
watchful, alert, attentive, observant, on your guard, on the lookout
(≠) OPPOSITES inattentive

vigorous ADJECTIVE

1 *vigorous exercise*
strenuous, energetic, active, lively, brisk, dynamic, intense
(≠) OPPOSITES mild
2 *a vigorous and athletic young man*
strong, energetic, active, lively, healthy, robust, vital, dynamic
(≠) OPPOSITES weak, feeble
3 *a vigorous performance*
spirited, energetic, lively, brisk, dynamic, forceful, powerful, full-blooded, intense
(≠) OPPOSITES weak, feeble

vigour NOUN

1 *The illness had robbed him of his usual vigour.*
energy, vitality, liveliness, health, robustness, stamina, strength, soundness
(≠) OPPOSITES weakness
2 *She cleaned the house with vigour.*
energy, spirit, gusto, activity, power, force, forcefulness, dynamism
(≠) OPPOSITES weakness

vile ADJECTIVE

1 *He is a vile criminal.*
contemptible, depraved, wicked, sinful, evil, impure, corrupt, despicable, vicious
(≠) OPPOSITES pure, worthy
2 *a vile smell*
disgusting, nasty, horrid, foul, repulsive, repugnant, revolting, offensive
(≠) OPPOSITES pleasant, lovely

villain NOUN

a gang of villains who were responsible for the crime
evil-doer, scoundrel, rogue, criminal, rascal

violent ADJECTIVE

1 *a violent crime*
cruel, brutal, aggressive, bloodthirsty, murderous, savage, vicious
2 *a violent outburst*
wild, unrestrained, uncontrollable, passionate, furious
(≠) OPPOSITES peaceful, gentle
3 *a violent thunderstorm*
powerful, severe, destructive, devastating, forceful, rough, turbulent

Aa
Bb
Cc
Dd
Ee
Ff
Gg
Hh
Ii
Jj
Kk
Ll
Mm
Nn
Oo
Pp
Qq
Rr
Ss
Tt
Uu
Vv
Ww
Xx
Yy
Zz

≠ OPPOSITES calm, moderate

4 a *violent pain*
intense, strong, severe, sharp, acute, extreme, painful, agonizing
≠ OPPOSITES moderate

virtually ADVERB
The party was virtually over when Lee arrived.
practically, in effect, almost, nearly, as good as

virtue NOUN
Mother Teresa was known for her charity and virtue.
goodness, morality, uprightness, worthiness, righteousness, integrity, honour, incorruptibility
≠ OPPOSITES vice

virtuous ADJECTIVE
They are virtuous people.
good, moral, righteous, upright, worthy, honourable, incorruptible, high-principled
≠ OPPOSITES immoral, corrupt

visible ADJECTIVE
1 *The house was visible between the trees.*
noticeable, discernible, observable, conspicuous, clear, distinguishable, detectable
≠ OPPOSITES invisible, hidden
2 *his visible dislike of my friends*
obvious, apparent, noticeable, evident, unconcealed, undisguised, unmistakable, clear, open
≠ OPPOSITES hidden

vision NOUN
1 *She claims she saw a vision of her dead grandmother.*
apparition, hallucination, illusion, phantom, ghost, spectre
2 *You need good vision to be an airline pilot.*
eyesight, sight, seeing, perception

visit¹ NOUN
a visit to my uncle's house
call, stay, stop, excursion

visit² VERB
I'm going to visit my grandparents.
call on, call in on, stay with, look in on, look up, see
◇ INFORMAL WORDS drop in on, pop in on

visitor NOUN
1 *We have visitors from America staying with us.*
caller, guest
2 *Hundreds of visitors come to the castle every month.*
tourist, holidaymaker

visualize VERB
Try to visualize a beautiful scene.
imagine, picture, envisage, conceive

vital ADJECTIVE
1 *It is vital to make sure you have enough food and water.*
essential, critical, crucial, necessary, indispensable, urgent, life-or-death
≠ OPPOSITES inessential
2 *a vital part of the plan*
important, significant, basic, fundamental, essential, necessary, indispensable, decisive
≠ OPPOSITES inessential

vivid ADJECTIVE
1 *a vivid shade of orange*
bright, colourful, intense, strong, rich, vibrant, brilliant, glowing
≠ OPPOSITES colourless, dull
2 *vivid memories of her childhood in Dublin*
clear, memorable, powerful, distinct, sharp, realistic
≠ OPPOSITES vague

vocal ADJECTIVE
He was very vocal in his disagreement with the plan.
outspoken, frank, forthright, plain-spoken
≠ OPPOSITES silent

Aa
Bb
Cc
Dd
Ee
Ff
Gg
Hh
Ii
Jj
Kk
Ll
Mm
Nn
Oo
Pp
Qq
Rr
Ss
Tt
Uu
Vv
Ww
Xx
Yy
Zz

voice[1] NOUN
a deep voice
tone of voice, way of speaking

voice[2] VERB
He voiced his disappointment with their behaviour.
express, say, utter, air, speak of, convey, declare

volume NOUN
1 *Measure the volume of the tank.*
size, bulk, capacity, dimensions
2 *the volume of complaints the programme received*
number, amount, mass, quantity
3 *a story published in two volumes*
book, tome, publication

voluntary ADJECTIVE
a voluntary contribution
optional, spontaneous, unforced
(≠) OPPOSITES compulsory

volunteer VERB
Finn volunteered to hand out leaflets.
offer, propose, step forward

vomit VERB
Julia has been vomiting all night.
be sick, heave, retch
◇ INFORMAL WORDS throw up

vote[1] VERB
We voted Rabia the most popular girl in the class.
elect, choose, opt for, declare
◇ INFORMAL WORDS plump for

vote[2] NOUN
We're having a vote for class representative.
election, ballot, poll, referendum

vow[1] NOUN
When they married, they made vows.
promise, oath, pledge

vow[2] VERB
She vowed to return home some day.
swear, promise, pledge

voyage NOUN
They made a voyage to the Caribbean.
journey, trip, passage, expedition, crossing

vulgar ADJECTIVE
1 *a vulgar man*
unrefined, uncouth, coarse, common, crude, ill-bred
(≠) OPPOSITES refined
2 *vulgar language*
rude, indecent, indelicate
(≠) OPPOSITES decent

vulnerable ADJECTIVE
1 *We have to protect the elderly and other vulnerable people.*
defenceless, helpless, unprotected, weak
(≠) OPPOSITES protected, strong
2 *The castle is vulnerable to attack.*
exposed, defenceless, open, unprotected, wide open
(≠) OPPOSITES protected, strong

Aa
Bb
Cc
Dd
Ee
Ff
Gg
Hh
Ii
Jj
Kk
Ll
Mm
Nn
Oo
Pp
Qq
Rr
Ss
Tt
Uu
Vv
Ww
Xx
Yy
Zz

Ww

waddle VERB
*The ducks **waddled** back to the pond.*
toddle, wobble, sway, shuffle

wag VERB
*The dog **wagged** its tail when it saw me.*
wave, shake, waggle, swing, wiggle

wage NOUN
*a decent **wage** for the work*
payment, pay, fee, earnings, salary,
wage-packet, recompense

wail VERB
*The woman was **wailing** in pain.*
cry, moan, howl, bawl, weep

wait¹ VERB
1 *Wait here while I go to post a letter.*
stay, remain, rest, linger
(≠) OPPOSITES proceed, go ahead
2 *Let's **wait** and see what happens first.*
delay, hold back, pause
(≠) OPPOSITES proceed, go ahead

wait² NOUN
*We had a long **wait** before the bus
came.*
delay, hold-up, interval, pause, halt

wake VERB
1 *I **woke** when the alarm went off.*
rise, get up, arise, come to, come round,
wake up
(≠) OPPOSITES sleep
2 *Wake me at seven o'clock.*
awaken, arouse, get up, bring to, bring
round

walk¹ VERB
⇒ For even more about this word, see
the next page
*We **walked** to school in the rain.*
stroll, march, tramp, trek, trudge,
saunter, amble, hike
◇ INFORMAL WORDS traipse

walk² NOUN
*We went for a **walk** in the country.*
stroll, amble, ramble, saunter, march,
hike, tramp, trek

wallow VERB
1 *The hippos were **wallowing** in the
mud.*
loll, lie, roll, wade, splash
2 *We **wallowed** in our success.*
revel, indulge, luxuriate, relish, bask,
enjoy, glory, delight

wander VERB
1 *We've been **wandering** about the old
town.*
roam, rove, ramble, saunter, stroll,
range, drift
2 *Don't **wander** away from your group
on the outing.*
stray, drift, roam, straggle, deviate,
depart, go astray

wane VERB
*My enthusiasm had begun to **wane**.*
lessen, fade, diminish, decrease, decline,
subside, dwindle, ebb
(≠) OPPOSITES increase

want¹ VERB
⇒ For even more about this word, see
the next page
1 *I really **want** a puppy for my birthday.*
wish, desire, crave, fancy, long for, pine
for, yearn for
2 *This room **wants** a lick of paint.*
need, require, demand, lack, call for

want² NOUN
*There is a **want** of good shops in this
area.*
lack, need, dearth, insufficiency,
deficiency, shortage, inadequacy

war NOUN
*Many people were killed in the **war**.*

walk

If you want to describe someone when they are walking, there are lots of interesting words you can use. Make sure you choose your words carefully to give an accurate description of what is happening.

If someone is walking slowly, you could say that they
amble
saunter
wander
stroll

If someone is walking quietly and they don't want to be heard or seen, they might
tiptoe
creep
shuffle

Someone walking with big steps could
stride
lope
strut
swagger

Someone walking with heavy steps might
plod
stomp
tramp
trample
trudge

If you go for a brisk walk, especially in the countryside, you might
hike
ramble
trek
march

If someone walks with difficulty, you could say they
hobble
limp
stumble
stagger
lurch

Someone who is nervous or who is impatient might
pace

Over to you

Can you replace the word **walk** in these sentences with one of the words from the list above?

1 Isabel and Sam **walked** slowly down the lane with their mum.

2 Mum **walked** past the baby's room – she didn't want to wake him up.

3 On Sundays I love to go for a long **walk** in the mountains.

4 'Ouch!' screamed James as he stubbed his toe. He **walked** over to a chair and sat down, nursing his foot.

conflict, warfare, fighting, battle, combat, hostilities
≠ OPPOSITES peace, ceasefire

ward off VERB
The young man managed to ward off his attackers.
fend off, deflect, parry, repel, stave off, thwart, beat off, turn away, block

wares NOUN
The shop displays its wares in the window.
goods, merchandise, stock, products, produce
◇ INFORMAL WORDS stuff

warlike ADJECTIVE
a warlike nation
aggressive, combative, bloodthirsty, war-mongering, hostile, antagonistic, belligerent, unfriendly
◆ FORMAL WORDS militaristic
≠ OPPOSITES friendly, peaceable

warm ADJECTIVE
1 *warm water*
tepid, heated, lukewarm
≠ OPPOSITES cool
2 *a warm personality*
friendly, kindly, sympathetic, affectionate, tender
≠ OPPOSITES unfriendly
3 *They gave us a warm welcome.*
friendly, hearty, hospitable
≠ OPPOSITES unfriendly
4 *a warm day*
sunny, fine, hot
≠ OPPOSITES cool

warn VERB
1 *The boys were warned about the dangers of playing near the railway.*
tell, alert, notify, inform, put on your guard
◇ INFORMAL WORDS tip off
2 *He warned me not to get involved in the argument.*
advise, caution, counsel

warning NOUN
1 *a warning that the water was going to be turned off*
notification, alert, notice, advance notice, hint, alarm, threat
◇ INFORMAL WORDS tip-off
2 *a government health warning*

want

You can use these words instead of **want**:

    feel like
    fancy
    wish for

These words mean you want something very much indeed:

    desire
    crave
    hanker after
    pine for
    long for
    yearn for
    hunger for
    thirst for

This meaning of want means you need something:

    need
    require
    demand
    lack

Over to you

Some of these words and phrases could be used to sell things. Can you pick them out?

1 Have you ever longed for the perfect holiday – a long sandy beach, palm trees, blue seas?

  Well, whatever you yearn for can be yours – you are just one phone call away from paradise!

2 One taste of our chocolate ice cream and you will hunger for more.

advice, counsel, caution

warp VERB
The door frame has become warped over the years.
distort, twist, bend, deform, misshape

(≠) OPPOSITES **straighten**

wary ADJECTIVE
1 *The little girl is very wary of dogs.*
suspicious, guarded, on your guard, distrustful

OPPOSITES careless

2 *Keep a wary eye on the traffic as you cross the road.*
watchful, cautious, careful, on the lookout, heedful, attentive, alert, wide-awake
OPPOSITES careless, heedless

wash VERB

1 *washing the floors*
clean, cleanse, scrub, swab down, rinse, swill
2 *I would like to wash before dinner.*
bathe, bath, shower

waste¹ VERB

Don't waste your money on that rubbish.
squander, misspend, misuse, fritter away, spend, throw away
◇ INFORMAL WORDS blow
OPPOSITES economize

waste² NOUN

the disposal of waste
rubbish, refuse, trash, garbage, leftovers, dregs, litter, scrap, dross

waste³ ADJECTIVE

1 *waste materials*
unwanted, useless, worthless, unused, left-over
2 *waste land*
uncultivated, empty, uninhabited, bare, barren, desolate, wild

wasteful ADJECTIVE

It is very wasteful to throw away uneaten food.
extravagant, spendthrift, uneconomical, ruinous
OPPOSITES economical, thrifty

watch VERB

1 *The children are watching cartoons.*
look at, observe, see, stare at, peer at, gaze at, view
2 *Will you please watch my bag for a moment?*
look after, guard, keep an eye on, mind, protect, take care of

• **watch out**
Watch out for those holes in the road.
look out, pay attention, be careful, take heed

watchful ADJECTIVE

You need to be watchful for pickpockets.
alert, attentive, heedful, observant, on your guard, wide-awake, wary, cautious
OPPOSITES unobservant, inattentive

water VERB

Remember to water the plants.
wet, moisten, dampen, soak, spray, sprinkle, hose
OPPOSITES dry out, parch

watery ADJECTIVE

1 *watery eyes*
moist, wet, damp
OPPOSITES dry
2 *a rather watery soup*
weak, watered-down, diluted, tasteless, thin, runny, flavourless
◇ INFORMAL WORDS wishy-washy

wave¹ NOUN

waves crashing on the shore
ripple, breaker, roller, billow

wave² VERB

1 *The boy waved to me to come over.*
signal, beckon, gesture, indicate, sign
2 *waving a flag*
shake, flap, swing, brandish, flourish
3 *reeds waving in the wind*
flap, flutter, quiver, ripple, sway

waver VERB

1 *I am wavering between France and Spain for my holidays.*
hesitate, dither, falter
OPPOSITES decide
2 *The temperature wavered between 70 and 80 degrees all week.*
vary, seesaw
3 *wavering on the edge of the cliff*
wobble, shake, sway, tremble, totter

way NOUN

1 *the best way to make pastry*

Aa Bb Cc Dd Ee Ff Gg Hh Ii Jj Kk Ll Mm Nn Oo Pp Qq Rr Ss Tt Uu Vv **Ww** Xx Yy Zz

Aa
Bb
Cc
Dd
Ee
Ff
Gg
Hh
Ii
Jj
Kk
Ll
Mm
Nn
Oo
Pp
Qq
Rr
Ss
Tt
Uu
Vv
Ww
Xx
Yy
Zz

method, approach, manner, technique, procedure, means, mode
2 *the **ways** of the South American Indians*
custom, practice, habit, usage, characteristic, trait, nature
3 *Is this the **way** to the station?*
route, direction, course, path
4 *Let's take the back **way** to avoid the traffic.*
road, access, avenue, track, passage, highway, street, lane

weak ADJECTIVE

1 *She was **weak** for months after her illness.*
feeble, frail, unhealthy, sickly, delicate, fragile
⊨ OPPOSITES strong
2 *a **weak** excuse*
feeble, flimsy, unconvincing, lame
⊨ OPPOSITES sound
3 *a **weak** spot*
vulnerable, unprotected, unguarded, defenceless, exposed
⊨ OPPOSITES secure
4 *a **weak** government*
ineffectual, powerless, indecisive, irresolute, inadequate
⊨ OPPOSITES powerful
5 *He's too **weak** to stand up to his wife.*
cowardly, spineless, ineffectual
6 *weak tea*
watery, tasteless, thin, diluted
⊨ OPPOSITES strong

weaken VERB

*After a while, the storm **weakened**.*
lessen, wane, fade, ease up, dwindle, flag, fail

weakness NOUN

*Impatience is one of his **weaknesses**.*
fault, failing, flaw, shortcoming, blemish, defect, deficiency
⊨ OPPOSITES strength

wealth NOUN

1 *a man of great **wealth***
riches, money, cash, fortune, means, substance

⊨ OPPOSITES poverty
2 *Her personal **wealth** has been estimated at over thirty million pounds.*
assets, funds, fortune, capital, possessions, property, estate
⊨ OPPOSITES poverty
3 *The area offers a **wealth** of leisure activities.*
abundance, plenty, fullness, store

wealthy ADJECTIVE

*He comes from a **wealthy** family.*
rich, well-off, moneyed, comfortable, well-to-do
◇ INFORMAL WORDS flush, loaded, rolling in it, well-heeled,
⊨ OPPOSITES poor, impoverished

wear VERB

1 *I'll **wear** my green jacket.*
dress in, have on, put on, don, sport
2 *Her face **wore** a huge grin.*
show, carry, bear, display
• **wear down**
*a rock formation which has been **worn down** by the weather over the centuries*
erode, deteriorate, corrode, fray, rub, grind
• **wear off**
*After a while, the excitement began to **wear off**.*
decrease, dwindle, diminish, weaken, fade, lessen, peter out, disappear
⊨ OPPOSITES increase
• **wear out**
*The long journey **wore** him **out**.*
exhaust, fatigue, tire out, sap

weary ADJECTIVE

*I felt **weary** after going round the shops all day.*
tired, exhausted, fatigued, sleepy, worn out, drained, drowsy
◇ INFORMAL WORDS all in, done in, dead beat, dog-tired, whacked
⊨ OPPOSITES refreshed

weather NOUN

*What is the **weather** like today?*
climate, conditions, temperature

Here are some types of weather:

Wind:
breeze, cyclone, gale, hurricane, monsoon, squall, tornado, typhoon, whirlwind
Moisture:
cloud, dew, fog, mist, smog
Rain:
deluge, downpour, drizzle, shower
Sun:
haze, heatwave, sunshine
Storm:
electric storm, lightning, thunder
Ice and snow:
black ice, blizzard, frost, hail, ice storm, sleet, slush, snowstorm, thaw
⇒ Also look up **storm**

weave VERB
*The car was **weaving** about on the road.*
zigzag, wind, twist, criss-cross

wedding NOUN
*I was invited to a **wedding**.*
marriage, wedlock
♦ FORMAL WORDS matrimony
⊅ OPPOSITES divorce

wedge VERB
*I was **wedged** between two people on the seat.*
squeeze, jam, cram, pack, ram, stuff, push, thrust, force

weep VERB
*She **wept** with joy when her son returned home.*
cry, sob, wail, bawl, snivel, whimper
◇ INFORMAL WORDS blub, blubber
⊅ OPPOSITES rejoice

weight NOUN
1 *The **weight** of the lorry was too much for the bridge to bear.*
heaviness, gravity, pressure, mass, force
⊅ OPPOSITES lightness

2 *He hurt his back carrying a heavy **weight**.*
load, burden

weird ADJECTIVE
1 *Her behaviour became more and more **weird**.*
strange, bizarre, freakish, mysterious, queer, grotesque
◇ INFORMAL WORDS far-out, way-out
⊅ OPPOSITES usual
2 *There have been several **weird** happenings in this house.*
strange, uncanny, eerie, creepy, supernatural, ghostly, mysterious
◇ INFORMAL WORDS spooky
⊅ OPPOSITES usual

welcome¹ VERB
1 *They **welcomed** me with open arms.*
greet, hail, receive, meet, embrace
⊅ OPPOSITES reject, snub
2 *I would **welcome** some help with my homework.*
accept, appreciate, approve of
⊅ OPPOSITES reject, snub

welcome² NOUN
*We were given a very warm **welcome**.*
reception, greeting, acceptance, hospitality
♦ FORMAL WORDS salutation
◇ INFORMAL WORDS red carpet

welcome³ ADJECTIVE
*This is **welcome** news.*
pleasing, acceptable, desirable, pleasant, agreeable, appreciated, delightful
⊅ OPPOSITES unwelcome

welfare NOUN
*I am concerned about the children's **welfare**.*
well-being, health, happiness, benefit, good, advantage, interest

well ADJECTIVE
1 *I hope you're **well** and happy.*
healthy, in good health, fit, sound, robust, strong, thriving, flourishing
⊅ OPPOSITES ill

Aa
Bb
Cc
Dd
Ee
Ff
Gg
Hh
Ii
Jj
Kk
Ll
Mm
Nn
Oo
Pp
Qq
Rr
Ss
Tt
Uu
Vv
Ww
Xx
Yy
Zz

Aa
Bb
Cc
Dd
Ee
Ff
Gg
Hh
Ii
Jj
Kk
Ll
Mm
Nn
Oo
Pp
Qq
Rr
Ss
Tt
Uu
Vv
Ww
Xx
Yy
Zz

2 *I trust that all is **well**.*
satisfactory, right, all right, good, pleasing, proper, agreeable, fine
(≠) OPPOSITES **bad**

wet ADJECTIVE
1 *wet ground*
damp, moist, soaked, sodden, saturated, soggy, sopping, waterlogged, spongy
(≠) OPPOSITES **dry**
2 *wet clothes*
damp, moist, soaked, soaking, sodden, saturated, sopping, dripping
(≠) OPPOSITES **dry**
3 *It's been wet all afternoon.*
rainy, raining, showery, teeming, pouring, drizzling
(≠) OPPOSITES **dry**

wheel VERB
1 *I tapped him on the shoulder and he wheeled round.*
turn, spin, twirl, whirl, swing
2 *The telescope can wheel round on its axis.*
rotate, turn, roll, revolve, swivel
3 *The vultures were beginning to wheel in the sky overhead.*
circle, orbit, twirl

whiff NOUN
a whiff of garlic
smell, puff, hint, trace, odour, aroma, sniff, scent

whip VERB
whipping the horses
beat, flog, lash, scourge, birch, cane, strap, thrash

whirl VERB
The dancers whirled round and round.
spin, turn, twirl, pivot, wheel, rotate, revolve

whisk VERB
Whisk the eggs to a creamy consistency.
whip, beat

whisper VERB
1 *He whispered her name.*

murmur, mutter, mumble, breathe, hiss, sigh
(≠) OPPOSITES **shout**
2 *The branches whispered in the wind.*
rustle, sigh, murmur, hiss

whole ADJECTIVE
He spent the whole day in bed.
entire, complete, full, total, undivided
(≠) OPPOSITES **partial**

wholesome ADJECTIVE
good wholesome food
healthy, nutritious, nourishing, beneficial, invigorating
(≠) OPPOSITES **unhealthy**

wholly ADVERB
1 *She was wholly responsible for the accident.*
completely, entirely, fully, absolutely, totally, utterly, altogether, thoroughly
(≠) OPPOSITES **partly**
2 *He relies wholly on his parents for support.*
exclusively, only, solely
(≠) OPPOSITES **partly**

wicked ADJECTIVE
a wicked criminal
evil, sinful, immoral, depraved, corrupt, vicious
(≠) OPPOSITES **good, upright**

wide ADJECTIVE
1 *a wide street*
broad, roomy, spacious, vast, immense
(≠) OPPOSITES **narrow**
2 *wide influence*
extensive, wide-ranging, comprehensive, far-reaching, general
(≠) OPPOSITES **restricted**

widespread ADJECTIVE
Starvation is widespread throughout the country.
extensive, prevalent, rife, general, universal, wholesale, far-reaching, common
(≠) OPPOSITES **limited**

wield VERB

wielding a weapon
brandish, flourish, swing, wave, handle

wild ADJECTIVE

1 *a wild animal*
untamed, undomesticated, savage, ferocious, fierce
⌦ OPPOSITES tame
2 *the wild tribes who live in the mountains*
uncivilized, primitive, barbarous
⌦ OPPOSITES civilized
3 *a wild landscape*
uncultivated, desolate, uninhabited
⌦ OPPOSITES cultivated
4 *a wild gang of youths*
rowdy, lawless, disorderly, riotous, unrestrained, unruly, unmanageable
⌦ OPPOSITES restrained
5 *wild weather*
stormy, tempestuous, rough, blustery, turbulent
⌦ OPPOSITES calm

wilful ADJECTIVE

1 *wilful neglect of your duty*
deliberate, conscious, intentional, voluntary, premeditated
⌦ OPPOSITES unintentional
2 *a wilful child who was determined to get her own way*
stubborn, self-willed, obstinate, pig-headed, inflexible
⌦ OPPOSITES good-natured

will NOUN

1 *He has lost the will to live.*
wish, desire, inclination, fancy, mind
2 *Marianne has a very strong will.*
determination, purpose, resolve, resolution, will-power, aim, intention

willing ADJECTIVE

1 *I'm willing to answer any questions you may have.*
prepared, disposed, inclined, content, pleased, favourable, agreeable, happy
⌦ OPPOSITES unwilling, disinclined, reluctant
2 *a willing volunteer*

eager, enthusiastic, ready
⌦ OPPOSITES unwilling, disinclined, reluctant

wilt VERB

1 *The flowers are wilting now.*
droop, sag, wither, shrivel, flop, go limp
⌦ OPPOSITES perk up
2 *Our initial enthusiasm began to wilt.*
wane, flag, dwindle, weaken, diminish, fail, fade
⌦ OPPOSITES perk up

wily ADJECTIVE

defeated by a wily opponent
cunning, shrewd, scheming, crafty, foxy, tricky, sly
◇ INFORMAL WORDS fly

win VERB

1 *We had a race and Mike won easily.*
be victorious, triumph, succeed, come first, finish first
⌦ OPPOSITES fail, lose
2 *Dad won a holiday in a competition.*
gain, achieve, attain, receive, obtain, get
◆ FORMAL WORDS acquire

wind¹ NOUN

The strong wind blew tiles off the roof.
breeze, draught, gust, gale, hurricane, tornado, cyclone

wind² VERB

1 *She wound the wool into a ball.*
coil, twist, curl, loop, furl, roll
2 *The serpent wound around his ankle.*
coil, curl, spiral, twine, encircle
3 *The road winds through the valley.*
turn, curve, bend, zigzag

windy ADJECTIVE

It's cold and windy outside.
breezy, blowy, gusty, blustery, squally
⌦ OPPOSITES calm

wink VERB

The car headlights winked in the distance.
twinkle, glimmer, glint, gleam, sparkle, flicker, flash

Aa
Bb
Cc
Dd
Ee
Ff
Gg
Hh
Ii
Jj
Kk
Ll
Mm
Nn
Oo
Pp
Qq
Rr
Ss
Tt
Uu
Vv
Ww
Xx
Yy
Zz

Aa
Bb
Cc
Dd
Ee
Ff
Gg
Hh
Ii
Jj
Kk
Ll
Mm
Nn
Oo
Pp
Qq
Rr
Ss
Tt
Uu
Vv
Ww
Xx
Yy
Zz

winner NOUN
*The **winners** of the heats will go on into the finals.*
victor, champion, prizewinner, medallist, title-holder
⚐ OPPOSITES loser

winning ADJECTIVE
*the **winning** contestant*
victorious, successful, triumphant, unbeaten, undefeated
⚐ OPPOSITES losing

wipe VERB
*Please **wipe** the basin after washing your hands.*
clean, rub, dry, dust, brush, mop, swab, sponge
• **wipe out**
*Many were **wiped out** in the attack.*
destroy, massacre, slaughter, exterminate, annihilate, obliterate

wisdom NOUN
***Wisdom** comes with age and experience.*
understanding, knowledge, learning, intelligence, sense, comprehension, judgement, discernment
⚐ OPPOSITES folly, stupidity

wise ADJECTIVE
1 *My grandmother is a very **wise** woman.*
understanding, knowing, intelligent, clever, aware, discerning, perceptive
⚐ OPPOSITES foolish, stupid
2 *a **wise** decision*
sensible, reasonable, sound, shrewd, well-advised
⚐ OPPOSITES ill-advised

wish NOUN
*My dearest **wish** is to go to India.*
desire, hankering, inclination, preference, yearning, urge, whim, hope

wish for VERB
*They have all the toys that they could **wish for**.*
want, desire, yearn for, long for, hanker after, crave, hope for

wit NOUN
1 *She speaks with a lot of **wit**.*
humour, comedy
◆ FORMAL WORDS jocularity
⚐ OPPOSITES seriousness
2 *He didn't have the **wit** to realize what was happening.*
intelligence, sense, cleverness, brains, common sense, wisdom, understanding, intellect
⚐ OPPOSITES stupidity

withdraw VERB
1 *He **withdrew** in horror at the sight.*
recoil, shrink back, draw back, pull back
2 *She **withdrew** her hand quickly.*
pull back, draw back
3 *I would like to **withdraw** my complaint.*
take back, retract, cancel, recall

wither VERB
*Your plants will **wither** if you don't water them.*
wilt, droop, shrink, shrivel, dry, decay, perish, fade
⚐ OPPOSITES flourish, thrive

withhold VERB
1 *She gave her name but **withheld** her address.*
keep back, retain, hold back, reserve, hide, conceal
⚐ OPPOSITES give
2 *He was asked to **withhold** his comments until after the meeting.*
hold back, suppress, restrain, repress, control, check

withstand VERB
1 *The castle can **withstand** an enemy attack.*
resist, oppose, defy, take on, hold out against, hold off, survive, weather
⚐ OPPOSITES give in to, yield to
2 *She could not **withstand** criticism from her mother.*
stand, stand up to, face, cope with,

endure, bear, tolerate, put up with, hold out against
≢ OPPOSITES give in to, yield to

witness¹ NOUN

*a **witness** to the crime*
onlooker, eye-witness, looker-on, observer, spectator, viewer, watcher, bystander

witness² VERB

*I **witnessed** the accident.*
see, observe, notice, note, view, watch, look on

witty ADJECTIVE

witty talk
humorous, amusing, comic, sparkling, funny
◆ FORMAL WORDS jocular
≢ OPPOSITES dull, unamusing

wobble VERB

*The dishes **wobbled** and then crashed to the floor.*
shake, tremble, quake, sway, teeter, totter, rock, waver

wobbly ADJECTIVE

*a **wobbly** table*
unstable, shaky, rickety, unsteady, teetering, tottering, unbalanced, unsafe
◇ INFORMAL WORDS wonky
≢ OPPOSITES stable, steady

woman NOUN

*The **woman** with the red hair is my mother.*
lady, female, girl

wonder¹ VERB

1 *I **wonder** what Steve is doing tonight.*
ask yourself, speculate, ponder, puzzle, enquire, query, think, meditate
2 *We all **wondered** at Katherine's beautiful singing.*
be amazed, marvel, gape, be surprised

wonder² NOUN

*The girls watched the ballet in **wonder**.*
amazement, awe, astonishment, admiration, wonderment, fascination

wonderful ADJECTIVE

*We had a **wonderful** time on holiday.*
excellent, marvellous, magnificent, outstanding, superb, delightful, sensational, tremendous
◇ INFORMAL WORDS super, terrific, brilliant, great, fabulous, fantastic
≢ OPPOSITES appalling, dreadful

wood NOUN

1 *The builders left piles of **wood** behind.*
timber, lumber, planks
2 *We went for a walk in the **wood**.*
forest, woods, woodland, trees, plantation, thicket, grove

Here are some types of wood:

ash, balsa, bamboo, cedar, chestnut, chipboard, ebony, hardboard, mahogany, oak, pine, plywood, redwood, sandalwood, teak, walnut, whitewood, willow
⇒ Also look up **tree**

wooden ADJECTIVE

1 *wooden beams*
timber, woody
2 *He was a very **wooden** actor.*
emotionless, lifeless, expressionless, unemotional, stiff, rigid, deadpan
≢ OPPOSITES lively

woolly ADJECTIVE

1 *a **woolly** material*
woollen, fleecy, downy, shaggy, fuzzy
2 *My memory of yesterday's events is a bit **woolly**.*
unclear, hazy, blurred, confused, muddled, vague, indefinite
≢ OPPOSITES clear, distinct

word NOUN

1 *What does this **word** mean?*
term, expression, name
2 *I'll have a **word** with him later.*
talk, conversation, chat, discussion, consultation

Aa
Bb
Cc
Dd
Ee
Ff
Gg
Hh
Ii
Jj
Kk
Ll
Mm
Nn
Oo
Pp
Qq
Rr
Ss
Tt
Uu
Vv
Ww
Xx
Yy
Zz

3 *I'd like to say a **word** to you all about road safety.*
comment, statement, remark, advice, warning
4 *Has there been any **word** on Michael's whereabouts?*
news, information, report, communication, notice, message, bulletin, statement
5 *I give you my **word** that I will call you tomorrow.*
promise, pledge, oath, assurance, vow, guarantee

work¹ NOUN
1 *What sort of **work** are you in?*
job, occupation, employment, profession, trade, business, line of business
2 *He is doing important **work** for the government.*
task, assignment, job, chore, duty, commission
3 *We put in a lot of **work** on the garden.*
toil, labour, effort, exertion, industry
◇ INFORMAL WORDS slog, graft, elbow grease

work² VERB
1 *I am not **working** at the moment.*
be employed, have a job, earn your living
≠ OPPOSITES be unemployed
2 *I've been **working** hard in the kitchen.*
toil, labour, drudge, slave
≠ OPPOSITES play, rest
3 *The coffee machine is not **working**.*
function, go, operate, perform, run
≠ OPPOSITES break down
4 *I know how to **work** this computer.*
use, operate, handle, manage, control
• **work out**
1 *I **worked out** the sum in my head.*
solve, resolve, calculate, figure out, puzzle out
2 *Our new arrangements are really **working out**.*
go well, succeed, prosper
3 *Things didn't **work out** the way I had hoped.*

turn out, develop, evolve
◇ INFORMAL WORDS pan out

world NOUN
*every country in the **world***
Earth, globe, planet

worn ADJECTIVE
*The cuffs of your shirt are **worn**.*
shabby, threadbare, worn-out, tatty, tattered, frayed, ragged
≠ OPPOSITES new, unused

worried ADJECTIVE
*She always wears a **worried** expression.*
anxious, troubled, uneasy, apprehensive, concerned, bothered, tense, nervous
≠ OPPOSITES calm, unworried, unconcerned

worry¹ VERB
1 *She is **worrying** about her exams.*
be anxious, be troubled, fret, brood
≠ OPPOSITES be unconcerned
2 *Stop **worrying** me when I'm busy!*
bother, irritate, plague, pester, torment, annoy, vex, harass
◇ INFORMAL WORDS hassle
≠ OPPOSITES comfort

worry² NOUN
*I have a lot of **worries** at the moment.*
problem, trouble, responsibility, burden, concern, care

worsen VERB
*The patient's condition **worsened** overnight.*
get worse, weaken, deteriorate, decline, sink
◇ INFORMAL WORDS go downhill
≠ OPPOSITES improve

worship VERB
1 *Many people **worship** God in church on Sundays.*
glorify, honour, praise, pray to
2 *She **worships** her parents.*
love, revere, adore, idolize, respect
≠ OPPOSITES despise, hate

worth NOUN

1 *She has proved her **worth** as a friend.*
worthiness, merit, value, quality
⊄ OPPOSITES worthlessness
2 *He feels as if his life has no **worth** without her.*
value, benefit, advantage, importance, significance, use, usefulness, utility
⊄ OPPOSITES worthlessness

worthless ADJECTIVE

1 *a **worthless** piece of junk*
valueless, useless, cheap, poor, trashy, trifling, paltry
⊄ OPPOSITES valuable
2 *All this talk is **worthless** unless it is accompanied by action.*
useless, pointless, meaningless, futile, unimportant, insignificant

worthwhile ADJECTIVE

*Nursing is a very **worthwhile** job.*
useful, valuable, worthy, good, helpful, beneficial, constructive
⊄ OPPOSITES worthless

worthy ADJECTIVE

1 *working for a **worthy** cause*
praiseworthy, creditable, commendable, valuable, worthwhile, admirable, fit, deserving
⊄ OPPOSITES unworthy
2 *a **worthy** citizen*
respectable, reputable, good, honest, honourable, decent, upright, righteous
⊄ OPPOSITES unworthy, disreputable

wound¹ NOUN

*a head **wound***
injury, hurt, cut, gash, scar

wound² VERB

*He was **wounded** in the war.*
injure, hurt, damage, harm, cut

wrap VERB

1 *She **wrapped** the baby in a shawl.*
cover, envelop, fold, enclose, cocoon, cloak, roll up, bundle up
⊄ OPPOSITES unwrap

2 *I have **wrapped** Mum's birthday present.*
pack up, package, parcel

wreck VERB

1 *The burglars had **wrecked** the house.*
destroy, ruin, demolish, devastate, shatter, smash, break, write off
⊄ OPPOSITES conserve, repair
2 *This has **wrecked** all my plans.*
spoil, destroy, ruin, play havoc with

wreckage NOUN

*the **wreckage** of the crashed aeroplane*
remains, debris, rubble, ruins, fragments, pieces

wrench VERB

1 *The vandals **wrenched** the door off its hinges.*
twist, yank, wrest, jerk, pull, tug, force, tear
2 *I **wrenched** my ankle as I fell.*
sprain, strain, twist

wriggle VERB

1 *She **wriggled** out of his grasp.*
squirm, writhe, twist, sidle, manoeuvre, dodge
2 *I **wriggled** along on my stomach.*
crawl, squirm, wiggle, worm, snake, slink, edge

wring VERB

*We **wrung** the water out of our soaking-wet clothes.*
squeeze, twist, extract, screw

wrinkle¹ NOUN

*The material was full of **wrinkles**.*
crease, furrow, line, fold, gather, pucker, crumple

wrinkle² VERB

*Try not to **wrinkle** your dress when you sit down.*
crease, furrow, fold, crinkle, crumple

write VERB

1 *I **wrote** my name on my jotter.*
pen, inscribe, set down, scribble, scrawl
2 *He is **writing** a book.*

Aa
Bb
Cc
Dd
Ee
Ff
Gg
Hh
Ii
Jj
Kk
Ll
Mm
Nn
Oo
Pp
Qq
Rr
Ss
Tt
Uu
Vv
Ww
Xx
Yy
Zz

compose, pen, draft, draw up, create
• **write down**
*A reporter **wrote down** everything she said.*
record, jot down, set down, take down, transcribe, copy

writer NOUN
*He is a **writer** of detective stories.*
author, scribe, wordsmith, novelist, dramatist, playwright, columnist
◇ INFORMAL WORDS hack, penpusher, scribbler

writhe VERB
*She was **writhing** in agony.*
squirm, wriggle, thresh, thrash, twist, toss, struggle

writing NOUN
*Your **writing** is very messy.*
handwriting, script, scrawl, scribble, hand

wrong ADJECTIVE
1 *The address on this letter is **wrong**.*
incorrect, inaccurate, mistaken, false, in error, imprecise
≠ OPPOSITES correct, right
2 *I didn't mean to say anything **wrong**.*
inappropriate, unsuitable, improper, unacceptable, unfitting, inapt
≠ OPPOSITES suitable, right
3 *It was very **wrong** of you all to gang up on one girl.*
unfair, unjust, blameworthy, bad, wicked, evil, immoral
≠ OPPOSITES good, moral
4 *This business practice is **wrong** and must be stopped at once.*
unethical, unlawful, illegal, dishonest, criminal, crooked
5 *Something is **wrong** with my computer.*
faulty, out of order, defective, amiss, awry, not right

wry ADJECTIVE
*Our teacher has a **wry** sense of humour.*
mocking, ironic, dry, sarcastic

Yy

ADJECTIVE

yearly visit to London

annual

yell VERB

There is no need to yell!

shout, scream, bellow, roar, bawl, cry

◇ INFORMAL WORDS holler

(≠) OPPOSITES whisper

yellow NOUN

Here are some shades of yellow:

buff, canary, gold, lemon, primrose, saffron

yield VERB

1 *She yielded to temptation and had a chocolate.*

give way, give in, submit, succumb, bow, cave in, knuckle under

(≠) OPPOSITES resist, withstand

2 *The orchard yielded a good crop of apples.*

produce, bear, supply, provide, generate, bring in

◆ FORMAL WORDS bring forth

young ADJECTIVE

Don't blame her, she's just young.

youthful, juvenile, infant, junior, adolescent

(≠) OPPOSITES adult, old

youth NOUN

1 *a gang of youths*

adolescent, youngster, juvenile, teenager, boy, young man

◇ INFORMAL WORDS kid

2 *the youth of today*

young people, the young, younger generation

3 *He was a bit wild in his youth.*

adolescence, teens, childhood, boyhood, girlhood, immaturity

(≠) OPPOSITES adulthood

Zz

Aa
Bb
Cc
Dd
Ee
Ff
Gg
Hh
Ii
Jj
Kk
Ll
Mm
Nn
Oo
Pp
Qq
Rr
Ss
Tt
Uu
Vv
Ww
Xx
Yy
Zz

zany ADJECTIVE

*a **zany** sense of humour*
comical, funny, amusing, crazy, clownish, eccentric
◇ INFORMAL WORDS loony, wacky
≠ OPPOSITES serious

zealous ADJECTIVE

*a **zealous** supporter of his local football club*
ardent, fervent, devoted, enthusiastic, intense, fanatical, keen, eager, earnest
≠ OPPOSITES apathetic, uninterested, indifferent

zero NOUN

*The temperature fell below **zero**.*
nothing, nought
◇ INFORMAL WORDS zilch

zodiac NOUN

Here are the signs of zodiac:

Aquarius (Water-bearer), Aries (Ra.) Cancer (Crab), Capricorn (Goat), Gemini (Twins), Leo (Lion), Libra (Balance), Pisces (Fishes), Sagittarius (Archer), Scorpio (Scorpion), Taurus (Bull), Virgo (Virgin)

zone NOUN

*different **zones** of the city*
region, area, district, territory, section, sector, belt

zoom VERB

*A motorcycle **zoomed** past.*
race, rush, tear, dash, speed, fly, hurtle, shoot, whirl